GERMAN PANZERS

OF WORLD WAR II

THE WORLD'S GREAT WEAPONS

GERMAN PANZERS

OF WORLD WAR II

THE WORLD'S GREAT WEAPONS

Jorge Rosado & Chris Bishop

amber
BOOKS

This edition published in 2013 by
Amber Books Ltd
74–77 White Lion Street
London
N1 9PF
United Kingdom
www.amberbooks.co.uk
Appstore: itunes.com/apps/amberbooksltd
Facebook: www.facebook.com/amberbooks
Twitter: @amberbooks
Email: enquiries@amberbooks.co.uk

The material in this book has previously appeared in the books
The Essential Tank Identification Guide: Wehrmacht Panzer Divisions 1939–45
and *The Essential Tank Identification Guide: Waffen-SS Divisions 1939–45*

ISBN: 978-1-782740-65-0

Printed in China

PICTURE CREDITS

Photographs
Art-Tech/MARS: 8, 90, 108, 117, 171, 196, 258, 286
Cody Images: 6, 12, 14, 15, 25, 62, 64, 75, 83, 99, 120, 130, 139, 144, 176, 184, 186, 190,
   192, 194, 195, 199, 214, 223, 225, 230, 242, 245, 256, 263, 269, 278, 285, 291, 292,
   294, 303, 306, 310, 312, 320, 324, 329, 335, 347, 348, 356, 362
Will Fowler: 151
Ukrainian State Archive: 125

Artworks
Alcaniz Fresno's S.A.: 199–370 all except for those listed below
Art-Tech/Aerospace: 201t, 234t&b, 245b, 246, 247, 251, 258, 258c, 275t&c, 276 both,
   281tr&br, 286, 292t, 293t, 294r, 306b, 309t, 312, 315b, 323 both, 325tl&b, 327t, 333,
   335t, 339b, 345l, 346, 351r, 353b, 364b, 368r, 371
Art-Tech/Jorge Rosado: 14–189 all, 199b, 200, 205t, 206t, 208b, 209, 210 all, 212 all, 215t,
   217t&tc, 218, 221, 222b, 223b, 225t, 226, 227t, 228–229 all, 231, 232t, 234c, 235,
   236b, 237–238 all, 240–241 all, 242b, 243 both, 248b, 254, 259b, 261, 262c&b, 263b,
   264–266 all, 267b, 268 all, 279b, 271 all, 273t, 274t, 275b, 287c&b, 290 both, 295 both,
   297, 299c&b, 303b, 305b, 334, 335c, 337, 340 top two rows, 376t

Contents

Volume One:
Werhmacht
Panzer Divisions

Introduction

Although they existed for less than a decade from the foundation of the first units in 1935, the Panzer Divisions of the *Wehrmacht* changed the face of modern warfare.

THROUGH A SERIES OF RAPID and sharp campaigns the German army was able to demonstrate to the whole world that it was master of a new form of warfare. *Blitzkrieg* enabled the *Wehrmacht* to overcome the bloody attritional strategies of World War I, and to humble enemy after enemy at minimum cost to the German nation and at maximum cost to its opponents.

The roots of *Blitzkrieg* lay in the German infiltration tactics of 1918. Special assault divisions with heavily-armed 'storm troopers' broke through weak points in the Allied lines. The troops carried heavy loads of grenades, machine guns and trench mortars, giving them superior firepower at the point of contact. They were supported by precision artillery fire and ground attack aircraft. Isolated pockets of defenders were dealt with by follow-up units: the storm troopers raged on through the Allied rear areas.

After the war, a few military theorists realized that armoured vehicles would add an extra dimension to the new German tactics. Most armies in the 1920s saw tanks purely as a means of supporting the infantry, but men like Liddell Hart, Fuller and Martel advocated the establishment of a much more mobile armoured force for use in future wars.

Balanced force

British theories regarding a balanced armoured force were examined in great detail by the *Truppenamt*, the clandestine General Staff of the *Reichswehr*. One of the most important of the officers involved was Colonel Heinz Guderian. Guderian took the ideas of Liddell Hart, Martel and Fuller and expanded them, proposing that any future armoured force had to be a balance of all arms, with the main striking force being provided by a mobile spearhead of tanks, mechanised infantry and artillery.

Guderian had to fight some opposition within the German army, but much of the General Staff looked on his ideas with favour. When the Nazis came to power, he found an even greater supporter in Hitler, who encouraged the efforts of the panzer troops at every stage. As a result, he was able to put some of his ideas into practice as the first experimental tank formations appeared in 1934, and the first true panzer divisions were formed a year later.

◀ **Czech-built Tank**

A Panzer 38(t) from General Erwin Rommel's 7th Panzer Division moves along a road in northern France as part of the *Fall Gelb* campaign of May 1940.

Panzer Division Organization

The organization of the standard panzer division changed greatly during World War II. The rapid evolution of armoured formations was inspired by combat experience, and by the massive increase in the capabilities of tanks and other armoured vehicles.

IN A MANUAL WRITTEN soon after the establishment of the *Panzerwaffe*, the function of the new German panzer arm was defined as 'the creation of rapid concentrations of considerable fighting power, obtaining quick decisions by breakthroughs, deep penetration on wide fronts and the destruction of the enemy'. This policy was being advocated at a time when other armies were still slowing their armour to move at the pace of the marching soldier. The Germans preferred to increase the speed of their infantry, initially by carrying them on trucks and later by mounting them in specialized half-tracks.

Although the tanks were to be the spearhead, the first panzers were primarily training machines. They were small, lightly armed and armoured, and had definite tactical limitations; production of better designs was slow and expensive. But they were highly mobile, which was vital since speed was the essence of the newly emerging concept of *Blitzkrieg*.

The spearhead of the early panzer divisions was provided by a panzer brigade of two panzer regiments. The regiment in turn was divided into two light companies operating Panzer Is and IIs, and a medium company with Panzer IIs and IVs. This was matched by a motorized infantry or *Schützen* brigade. Typically, a panzer division would have a strength of some 300 armoured fighting vehicles.

Organization of 1st Panzer Division
1939
   1. *Schützen-Brigade*
    Schützen-Regiment 1 (two battalions)
    Kradschützen-Bataillon 1 (motorcyle battalion)
   1. *Panzer-Brigade*
    Panzer-Regiment 1 (two abteilungen)
    Panzer-Regiment 2 (two abteilungen)
   73. *Artillerie-Regiment* (two abteilungen)
   Aufklärungs-Abteilung 4
   Panzerjäger-Abteilung 37
   Pionier-Bataillon 37
   Nachrichten-Abteilung 37
   37th Divisional Support Unit

1940
Experience in Poland had shown that the panzer brigade formation was too large and unwieldy for tactical use, so after the invasion of France most divisions were reduced to a single panzer regiment, and the armoured and infantry brigade headquarters were dissolved. Total tank strength was typically 150.
   Schützen-Regiment 1 (two battalions)
   Schützen-Regiment 113 (two battalions)
   Panzer-Regiment 1 (two abteilungen)
   Artillerie-Regiment 73 (three abteilungen)
   Kradschützen-Abteilung 1
   Aufklärungs-Abteilung 4
   Panzerjäger-Abteilung 37
   Pionier-Bataillon 37
   Nachrichten-Abteilung 37
   37th Divisional Support Unit

1943
The organisation of panzer divisions was continually changing as new weapons became available. By the time of the battle of Kursk, nearly all of the early, light armoured vehicles had been withdrawn from service apart from a few Panzer IIs used for reconnaissance and security, and the 1st Panzer Division was almost exclusively equipped with around 160 long-barrelled Panzer IVs.
   Panzergrenadier-Regiment 1 (two battalions)
   Panzergrenadier-Regiment 113 (two battalions)
   Panzer-Regiment 1 (two abteilungen)
   Panzer-Artillerie-Regiment 73 (four abteilungen)
   Panzer-Aufklärungs-Abteilung 1
   Panzerjäger-Abteilung 37
   Panzer-Pionier-Bataillon 37
   Panzer-Nachrichten-Bataillon 37
   Heeres-Flak-Abteilung 299
   37th Divisional Support Unit

1944
In August 1944 a new divisional structure (see opposite) was created as the entire *Panzerwaffe* was reorganized after the loss of Normandy to the Allies.

Type 44 Panzer Division (Nominal strength 14,691)

Divisional Headquarters (520 men)

Panzer Regiment (2006 men)
    Regimental Staff Company (5 x Pz.IV, 3 x PzBfWg.V)
        Flak Platoon (8 x 37-mm Flak 43 on Pz IV)
    1st Panzer Battalion (76-94 Pz.V Panther)
        Staff Company (5 x Pz.V, 3 x PzBfWg.V,
            3 x Flakvierling 20mm SP Guns)
        Four tank companies (each with 17 or 22 Pz.V Panther)
        Armoured maintenance company
        Armoured Supply Company
    2nd Panzer Battalion (76-94 Pz.IV)
        Staff Company (5 x Pz.IV, 3 x PzBfWg.IV,
            3 x Flakvierling 20mm SP Guns)
        Four tank companies (each with 17 or 22 Pz.IV)
        Armoured Maintenance Company
        Armoured Supply Company

1st Armoured Panzergrenadier Regiment (2287 men)
    Regimental Staff Company
    1st Panzergrenadier Battalion
        Battalion Staff
        Three Panzergrenadier Companies (half track)
        Heavy Company (half track)
            Infantry Gun Platoon
            Mortar Platoon
        Panzergrenadier Supply Company
    2nd Panzergrenadier Battalion
        Battalion Staff
        Three Panzergrenadier Companies (motorized)
        Heavy Company (motorised)
            Engineer Platoon
            Panzerjäger Platoon
            Infantry Gun Platoon
            SP Gun Battery
        Pioneer Company (motorized)

1st Motorised Panzergrenadier Regiment (2219 men)
    Regimental Staff Company
    Two Motorised Panzer Grenadier Battalions, each with
        Battalion Staff
        Three Panzergrenadier companies (Motorised)
        Motorised Heavy Company
        Supply Company
    Heavy Infantry Gun Company
    Pioneer Company

Self-propelled Panzerjäger battalion (475 men)
    Staff Company (3 PzJg IV)
    Motorised PanzerJäger Company (12 x 7.5cm PaK 40)
    Two self-propelled PanzerJäger Companies (14 PzJg IV)
    Supply Company

Armoured Reconnaissance Battalion (945 men)
    Staff Company (10 x Sd Kfz 251, 16 x Armoured cars)
    Armoured Reconnaissance Company (16 x Luchs Light
        Tanks) or Armoured Car Company (25 Armoured cars
        and Sd Kfz 250)
    Light Armoured Reconnaissance Company
        (30 Sd Kfz 250)
    Panzer Grenadier Company Company (23 Sd Kfz 251))
    Armoured Heavy Company

    Heavy Gun Platoon (6 x Sd Kfz 251/9)
    Mortar Platoon (6 x Sd Kfz 251/2)
    Pioneer Platoon
  Supply Company

Panzer Artillery Regiment (1315 men)
    Regimental Staff Battery
    1st self-propelled battalion
        2 light batteries (12 x leFH Sd Kfz 124 Wespe)
        1 heavy battery (6 x sFH Sd Kfz 165 Hummel)
    2nd Battalion (motorized)
        Staff Battery
        2 light batteries (12 x 10.5cm leFH 18)
    3rd Battalion (motorized)
        Staff Battery
        2 heavy batteries (8 x 15cm sFH 18)
        Gun Battery (4 x 10cm K 18)

Army Flak Battalion (635 men)
Armoured Pioneer Battalion (874 men)
Armoured Signals Battalion (463 men)
Field Replacement Battalion (973 men)
    Including 800 replacement troops
Panzer Supply Troop (781 men)
Vehicle Maintenance Troop (417 men)
Medical and Ambulance Companies (530 men)
Administration, Military Police and Other units (251 men)

KEY TO TACTICAL SYMBOLS USED IN ORGANIZATION CHARTS

Tactische Fernzeiche or Map Symbol for Regiment or larger-sized formation

Map Symbol for Battalion or *Abteilung*

St — *Stab* or Staff companies of Panzer Regiments

m — *Mittlerer* or Medium as applied to a Panzer Company

l — *Leichte* or light as applied to a Panzer Company

Sturmgeschütz or Assault Gun Company

Flammpanzer or Flamethrower Troop

Heavy self-propelled artillery battalion

Panzer *Abteilung* in *Leichte* motorised division 1938-1939

Self-propelled 2cm (0.8in) Flak detachment

Chapter 1

Pre-War Panzer Divisions

In the years after World War I, tank enthusiasts
in the German Army faced considerable resistance from the
conservative cavalry and artillery officers who dominated
the senior ranks of the *Reichswehr*. Nevertheless, new
theories of armoured warfare were developed, and with
Hitler's accession to power in 1933, the Panzer men gained
the support of the one man who could see their ideas into
practice. With the *Führer's* support, the *Wehrmacht*
established its first Panzer units in 1934, and in 1935
the first true Panzer divisions were created.

◀ **Early triumphs**
Panzerkampfwagen IIs of the 3rd Panzer Division parade in triumph through Wenceslas Square in Prague
just days after Germany occupied Czechoslovakia in March 1939.

1st Panzer Division

At its foundation in 1935, the 1st Panzer Division was a shadow of the mighty fighting machine that it was to become, but with the 2nd and 3rd Divisions it allowed the *Wehrmacht* to work out the new rules of armoured warfare.

THE FIRST PANZER DIVISIONS were established in 1935, after Hitler repudiated the Treaty of Versailles and brought into the open the massive expansion of the *Wehrmacht*, which he had secretly begun soon after coming to power. The 1st Panzer Division was formed in Weimar from elements of the 3rd *Kavallerie-Division*, and was placed under the command of *General der Kavallerie* Maximilian von Weichs. 1st Panzer Division, known initially as the 1st Panzer Brigade, included the 1st Panzer Regiment which was stationed at Erfurt, and the 2nd Panzer Regiment located in Eisenach. Other units attached to the division included the 1st *Schützen* Brigade (a motorized infantry unit with two battalions together with a motor-cycle battalion), 4th Reconnaissance Company, 37th Artillery Regiment and 37th Communications Company.

▼ **Battle Tank**
The Panzerkampfwagen III was intended to be the mainstay of Germany's Panzer forces, but few were in service at the start of World War II.

INSIGNIA

The original tactical symbol for the 1st Panzer Division was introduced on its formation in 1935. It was used until 1940.

Several variants of the original oak leaf design were used in the pre-war period and into the first campaigns of World War II.

During the second half of 1940, a simpler system of divisional identification was introduced. They were usually very simple outlines in white or yellow and were designed to be instantly recognizable.

Late in 1940 an even simpler system was introduced, using straight lines that were easy to apply, remember and recognize.

Each Panzer *Abteilung* included four light companies. Each company had a commander's platoon (with five tanks – one Pz.Kpfw II and four Pz.Kpfw I, which later became three Pz.Kpfw II and two Pz.Kpfw I). Each company had three more platoons with a similar structure. The tiny machine-gun armed Pz.Kpfw I was never intended to be more than a stopgap until the more battleworthy PzKpfw III and Pz.Kpfw IV medium tanks could be introduced.

Early in 1938, new commanders took over existing divisions, and the 1st Panzer Division was now commanded by *General* Rudolf Schmidt. Soon afterwards, the German army occupied Austria as that country was incorporated into the Reich. Only the 2nd Panzer Division was involved. In March 1939, German troops occupied the remaining part of Czechoslovakia, after the earlier takeover of the Sudetenland, but the only Panzer unit involved was the 3rd Panzer Division.

The 1st Panzer Division had to wait until the invasion of Poland to see its operational debut. By that time, each Panzer Regiment had 150–156 tanks, including 12 command tanks.

▲ **Training tank in combat**
The tiny Panzerkampfwagen I, armed only with machine guns, served in frontline units during the campaigns in Poland and France.

Commanders

Generaloberst R. Schmidt *(1 Sept 1939 – 2 Nov 1939)*	Generalleutnant R. Koll *(1 Jan 1944 – 19 Feb 1944)*
General der Panzertruppen F. Kirchner *(2 Nov 1939 – 17 July 1941)*	Generalleutnant W. Marcks *(19 Feb 1944 – 25 Sept 1944)*
General der Panzertruppen W. Kruger *(17 July 1941 – 1 Jan 1944)*	Generalleutnant E. Thunert *(25 Sept 1944 – 8 May 1945)*

Fall Weiss: the invasion of Poland
1 SEPTEMBER 1939

The invasion of Poland saw five German armies, a total of 42 divisions, cross the border. Most were infantry on foot, but the *Wehrmacht* fielded six Panzer and four *Leichte* Divisions.

FOR THE INVASION OF POLAND, the 1st Panzer Division served with Army Group South, where it formed part of Hoeppner's XVI *Panzerkorps* in von Reichenau's 10th Army. The Panzers were the spearhead of the German drive on Warsaw, reaching the outskirts of the city within a week. A counterattack by the Polish Pomoroze and Poznan Armies, bypassed in the earlier fighting, forced the Germans to detach motorized units, including 1st Panzer, from Warsaw to deal with the threat. The

German tanks closed a ring of steel around the Poles, and in the Battle of Bzura 19 Polish divisions were destroyed or captured, and over 52,000 prisoners were taken by the *Wehrmacht*. In December 1939, the division returned to Germany.

Panzer Unit	Pz. I	Pz. II	Pz. III	Pz. IV	Pz. Bef.
1st Pz. Rgt.	39	60	20	28	6
2nd Pz. Rgt.	54	62	6	28	6

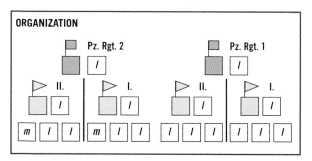

ORGANIZATION

▶ Panzerkampfwagen I Ausf B (Sd Kfz 101)

Pz. Rgt 1 / II Battalion / 5th Company / 2nd Zug / tank number 4

This vehicle was destroyed in combat in an action that took place south of Petrikau during the Polish campaign.

Specifications

Crew: 2	Engine: Maybach NL38TR
Weight: 6.4 tonnes (5.8 tons)	Speed: 40km/hr (24.9mph)
Length: 4.42m (14.5ft)	Range: 170km (105.6 miles)
Width: 2.06m (6.8ft)	Radio: FuG2
Height: 1.72m (5.6ft)	

The Germans used the white cross as their national insignia for the 1939 Poland campaign, but it was later changed because it provided an excellent target for enemy antitank gunners.

▶ Panzerkampfwagen IV Ausf B (Sd Kfz 161)

Pz. Rgt 1 / II Battalion / 8th Company / Company HQ tank of Hptm Von Kockeritz

This vehicle participated in the battle of Bzura, 16 September 1939. Two stripes on the turret rear were the unit's marks of recognition.

Specifications

Crew: 5	Engine: Maybach HL120TR
Weight: 20.7 tonnes (18.8 tons)	Speed: 40km/hr (24.9mph)
Length: 2.92m (9.6ft)	Range: 200km (124.3 miles)
Width: 2.83m (9.3ft)	Radio: FuG5
Height: 2.68m (8.8ft)	

⊠ *Fall Gelb*: the French campaign
10 MAY 1940

In February 1940, the 1st Panzer Division under its new commander, *General der Panzertruppen* Friedrich Kirchner, was deployed to the *Westwall* to prepare for the campaign in the West.

THE 1ST PANZER DIVISION came under the command of Guderian's XIX *Panzerkorps*, which also included the 7th and 10th Divisions, for the surprise German attack through the Ardennes on 10 May. Breaking through at Sedan, Guderian's corps raced for the Channel, cutting off the bulk of the Allied field army in Belgium. After the British evacuation from Dunkirk, the Germans reorganized to strike southwards.

The 1st Panzer Division took part in the initial attack on the Aisne, on 5 June. After some hard fighting, the French defensive lines were breached, and the Panzers fanned out through France. The final French capitulation came on 22 June.

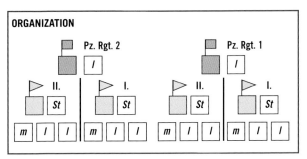

Panzer Unit	Pz. I	Pz. II	Pz. III	Pz. IV	Pz. Bef.
1st Pz. Rgt.	26	49	28	20	4
2nd Pz. Rgt.	26	49	30	20	4

▶ Panzerbefehlswagen III Ausf E (Sd Kfz 266-267-268)

Pz. Rgt 2 / II Battalion / Stabskompanie / Signal Platoon / Commander's command tank

Although it looks like a standard tank, the turret was fixed and a dummy gun was fitted in an attempt to avoid drawing enemy attention to the command tank.

Specifications

Radio:

FuG6 + FuG2 (Sd Kfz 266)

FuG6 + FuG8 (Sd Kfz 267)

FuG6 + FuG7 (Sd Kfz 268)

▶ Panzerkampfwagen II Ausf C (Sd Kfz 121)

Pz. Rgt 1 / II Battalion / 5th Company / 1st Zug / tank number 4

The PzKpfw II formed the backbone of the Panzer divisions during the Polish and French campaigns. Although its armour and armament were inferior to other

tanks of the day, its speed of 40km/h (24.9mph) allowed it to outmanoeuvre most Allied tanks. The white dot after the number 514 was used to indicate that this tank belonged to the 1st Regiment of the Division.

Specifications

Crew: 3	Engine: Maybach HL62TR
Weight: 9.8 tonnes (8.9 tons)	Speed: 40km/hr (24.9mph)
Length: 4.81m (15.8ft)	Range: 200km (124.3 miles)
Width: 2.22m (7.3ft)	Radio: FuG5
Height: 1.99m (6.5ft)	

▶ Panzerkampfwagen II Ausf C (Sd Kfz 121)

Pz. Rgt 2 / II Battalion / 5th Company / 2nd Zug / tank number 2

The 2nd Regiment differentiated its tanks from those of the 1st Regiment by underlining the turret numbers with a white band. This PzKpfw II C is armed with

a 20mm (0.78in) KwK30 L/55 cannon and a 7.92 MG34. The tank carries 18 ten-round magazines for the cannon, and 1425 rounds for the belt-fed machine gun.

Specifications

Crew: 3	Engine: Maybach HL62TR
Weight: 9.8 tonnes (8.9 tons)	Speed: 40km/hr (24.9mph)
Length: 4.81m (15.8ft)	Range: 200km (124.3 miles)
Width: 2.22m (7.3ft)	Radio: FuG5
Height: 1.99m (6.5ft)	

▶ Panzerfunkwagen (Sd Kfz 263) 8-Rad

37th Nachtrichten Abteilung (Signal Battalion)

The Heavy Armoured Radio Vehicle was not intended as a fighting machine, and was armed with a single MG34 for self-defence. Its main function was to serve as a mobile communications station for Panzer unit commanders. The vertical antenna behind the fighting compartment was extendable to 9m (29.5ft) height.

Specifications

Crew: 5	Engine: Büssing-NAG L8V
Weight: 8.9 tonnes (8.1 tons)	Speed: 100km/hr (62.1mph)
Length: 5.85m (19.2ft)	Range: 300km (186.4 miles)
Width: 2.2m (7.3ft)	Radio: 1 Satz Funkgerat für Pz
Height: 2.9m (9.5ft)	Funktrupp

▶ Mittlerer Schützenpanzerwagen Ausf A (Sd Kfz 251/1)

1st Schützen Brigade / II Battalion / 10th Company

Lessons learned in Spain taught the *Wehrmacht* that tanks needed infantry protection when operating in restricted terrain. Armoured half-tracks allowed infantry to accompany tanks in the advance, where they would be used to 'mop up' pockets of enemy resistance.

Specifications

Crew: 2 plus 10 troops	Engine: Maybach HL42TUKRM
Weight: 8.8 tonnes (8 tons)	Speed: 53km/hr (32.9mph)
Length: 5.98m (19.6ft)	Range: 300km (186.4 miles)
Width: 2.1m (6.9ft)	Radio: FuG Spr Ger 1
Height: 1.75m (5.7ft)	

▶ Panzerkampfwagen III Ausf E (Sd Kfz 141)

Pz. Rgt 2 / II Battalion / 7th Company / 2nd Zug / tank number 3

96 Ausf E model Panzer IIIs were built for the German Army between December 1938 and October 1939. Later models were built in much greater numbers.

Specifications

Crew: 5	Engine: Maybach HL120TR
Weight: 21.5 tonnes (19.5 tons)	Speed: 40km/hr (24.9mph)
Length: 5.38m (17.7ft)	Range: 165km (102.5 miles)
Width: 2.91m (9.5ft)	Radio: FuG5
Height: 2.44m (8ft)	

Barbarossa: the attack on Russia
22 JUNE 1941

The 1st Panzer Division saw extensive combat in the invasion of the Soviet Union, on both the Northern and Central sectors of the Eastern Front.

AFTER THE FRENCH CAMPAIGN, the 1st Panzer Division was transferred to XVI *Panzerkorps*, attached to the 18th Army in East Prussia. In March 1941, it became a reserve unit for 4th *Panzergruppe*, where it was brought up to strength for the impending invasion of the USSR.

Operation *Barbarossa* saw Germany amass seven armies and four *Panzergruppe* – which were armoured armies in all but name – into three main Army Groups. The 1st Panzer

Panzer Unit	Pz. I	Pz. II	Pz. III	Pz. IV	Pz. Bef.
1st Pz. Rgt.	15	43	75	28	8

Division, as part of General Hoeppner's 4th *Panzergruppe*, was attached to von Leeb's Army Group North. Striking through the Baltic States out of East Prussia on 22 June 1941, Army Group North was targeted on Leningrad, and in the next months 1st Panzer saw intensive action at Dunaberg and on the approaches to Leningrad.

On the Central Front

In October 1941, the Division was transferred to Hoth's 3rd *Panzergruppe*, part of Army Group Centre.

ORGANIZATION

Pz. Rgt. 1

I

II.

I.

St

St

m l l

m l l

▶ Panzerkampfwagen III Ausf F (Sd Kfz 141)

Pz. Rgt 1 / I Battalion / Stabskompanie / Signal Platoon / tank number 3

The Pz.Kpfw III Ausf F differed from the Ausf E model in having an additional 30mm (1.2in) of armour plate bolted to the turret and hull front. Other minor changes were made to the turret, the commander's cupola and the engine.

Specifications

Crew: 5	Engine: Maybach HL120TRM
Weight: 21.8 tonnes (19.8 tons)	Speed: 40km/hr (24.9mph)
Length: 5.38m (17.7ft)	Range: 165km (102.5 miles)
Width: 2.91m (9.5ft)	Radio: FuG5
Height: 2.44m (8ft)	

▶ Panzerkampfwagen IV Ausf D (Sd Kfz 161)

Pz. Rgt 1 / I Battalion / 4th Company / 2nd Zug / tank number 3

The fundamental mission of the *Mittlerer Panzer Kompanie*, or Medium Panzer Company, was to support the attack of the *Leichte Panzer Kompanien*. These would attack while the heavier tanks like this Panzer IV provided close support, engaging enemy tanks, field fortifications and antitank weapons.

Specifications

Crew: 5	Engine: Maybach HL120TRM
Weight: 22 tonnes (20 tons)	Speed: 40km/hr (24.9mph)
Length: 5.92m (19.4ft)	Range: 200km (124.3 miles)
Width: 2.84m (9.3ft)	Radio: FuG5
Height: 2.68m (8.8ft)	

Stabskompanie einer Panzer-Abteilung K.St.N.1150

The *Stabs* – 'Staff', or headquarters – Company of a Panzer Battalion early in the war was equipped in much the same as one of the light companies, with the addition of extra command and communication capacity in the shape of two or three Panzerbefehlswagen, or command tanks.

Signal Platoon: 2 Bef.Pz. III, Pz.Kpfw III

Light Platoon: 5 Pz.Kpfw II

Engineer Platoon: 3 Pz.Kpfw II

Specifications

Crew: 5	Engine: Maybach HL120TRM
Weight: 24 tonnes (21.8 tons)	Speed: 40km/hr (24.9mph)
Length: 5.41m (17.7ft)	Range: 165km (102.5 miles)
Width: 2.95m (9.7ft)	Radio: FuG5
Height: 2.44m (8ft)	

◀ **Panzerkampfwagen III Ausf H (Sd Kfz 141)**

Pz. Rgt 1 / II Battalion / 7th Company / 1st Zug / Zug Commander Leutnant Fromme

On 7 July 1941, Lt. Fromme destroyed nine Soviet tanks in this vehicle. The Ausf H had new sprocket and idler wheels and extra armour to protect against antitank guns like the British 2-pdr (37mm), the American 37mm (1.5in) M5 and the Soviet 45mm (1.8in) model 1937.

▼ **Ladungsleger auf Panzerkampfwagen I Ausf B**

37th Pioneer Battalion / 3rd Armoured Engineers Company

Demolition charge-laying tank. This version used a cable-operated arm, which pivoted over the tank to place a 50kg (110lb) explosive charge.

Specifications

Crew: 2	Engine: Maybach NL38TR
Weight: c. 6.6 tonnes (6 tons)	Speed: 40km/hr (24.9mph)
Length: 4.42m (14.5ft)	Range: 170km (105.6 miles)
Width: 2.06m (6.8ft)	Radio: FuG2
Height: 1.72m (5.6ft)	

▶ **15cm sIG33 (Sf) auf Panzerkampfwagen I Ausf B**

702th schwere Infanteriegeschutz abteilung

This vehicle mounts the well proven 15cm (6in) sIG33 L/11 howitzer, which was carried on an early Pz.Kpfw I chassis. The howitzer could provide both direct and indirect artillery fire support.

Specifications

Crew: 4	Engine: Maybach NL38TR
Weight: 9.4 tonnes (8.5 tons)	Speed: 40km/hr (24.9mph)
Length: 4.67m (15.3ft)	Range: 140km (87 miles)
Width: 2.06m (6.8ft)	Armament: One 15cm (6in) sIG33 L/11
Height: 2.8m (9.2ft)	

▶ **Leichter Gepanzerter Beobachtungswagen (Sd Kfz 253)**

73rd Artillery Regiment

Semi-tracked light armoured artillery observation post.

Specifications

Crew: 4	Engine: Maybach HL42TRKM
Weight: 6.3 tonnes (5.73 tons)	Speed: 65km/hr (40.4mph)
Length: 4.7m (15.4ft)	Range: 320km (198.8 miles)
Width: 1.95m (6.4ft)	Radio: FuG15 and/or FuG16
Height: 1.8m (6.2ft)	

Fall Blau: the Eastern Front
28 JUNE 1942

With the failure to capture Moscow in the winter of 1941, the German Army had to implement major organizational changes to respond to the arrival at the front of 90 new Russian tank brigades in the spring of 1942.

AFTER A YEAR OF COMBAT around Rshev, the 1st Panzer Division was pulled out of the front and sent to France for refitting. It had suffered a considerable reduction in strength aside from combat losses: *Panzer-Abteilung* I of Panzer Regiment 1 was detached from the division, being sent to the newly formed 16th *Panzergrenadier* Division, where it was renamed *Panzer-Abteilung* 116.

With the loss of *Panzer-Abteilung* I, the Division had only one battalion of Panzers on strength, that being *Panzer-Abteilung* II/Panzer-Regiment 1. For six months, the tank strength of the Division was limited to seven Panzer IVs, 26 Panzer IIIs, and 12 light Panzer IIs and Czech-built Panzer 38(t)s.

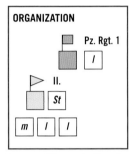

ORGANIZATION

Panzer Unit	Pz. II	Pz. 38t	Pz. III	Pz. IV	Pz. Bef.
1st Pz. Rgt.	2	10	26	10	4

▶ **Panzerkampfwagen IV Ausf E (Sd Kfz 161)**
Pz. Rgt 1 / II Battalion / 4th Company / 2nd Zug / tank number 4
The Ausf E was a major improvement over the Ausf D. It had additional armour plate, with a thickness ranging from 20mm (0.8in) to 50mm (2in). All Pz.Kpfw IVs at this time were still armed with the short-barrelled 75mm (3in) L24 gun.

Specifications
Crew: 5	Engine: Maybach HL120TRM
Weight: 23.2 tonnes (21 tons)	Speed: 42km/hr (26mph)
Length: 5.92m (19.4ft)	Range: 200km (124.3 miles)
Width: 2.84m (9.3ft)	Radio: FuG5
Height: 2.68m (8.8ft)	

▶ **Panzerjäger 38(t) fur 7.62cm PaK36(r) (Sd Kfz 139)**
37th Panzerjäger Battalion / 1st Company / tank number 1
The Sd Kfz139 was an interim tank-destroyer design. It mounted the powerful Russian 76.2mm (3in) FK296 antitank gun, great numbers of which had been captured during the 1941 summer offensive.

Specifications
Crew: 4	Engine: Praga EPA or EPA/2
Weight: 11.76 tonnes (10.67 tons)	Speed: 42km/hr (26mph)
Length: 5.85m (19.2ft)	Range: 185km (115 miles)
Width: 2.16m (7ft)	Radio: FuG Spr d
Height: 2.5m (8.2ft)	

▶ Panzerkampfwagen KV Ia 753(r)

Pz. Rgt 1 / Captured Russian tank

The Model 1939 was the first standard production version of the Soviet KV-1 heavy tank. Much more heavily armoured than any German tank, it mounted a powerful 76mm (3in) L-11 cannon in a low-slung gun mantlet. The Germans often added a commander's cupola to captured tanks pressed into *Wehrmacht* service.

Specifications

Crew: 5
Weight: 46.6 tonnes (42.3 tons)
Length: 6.68m (21.9ft)
Width: 3.32m (10.9ft)
Height: 2.71m (8.9ft)
Engine: V-2K
Speed: 35km/hr (21.7mph)
Range: 180km (111.8 miles)
Radio: 10R

▶ Panzerkampfwagen KV Ia 753(r)

Pz. Rgt 1 / Captured Russian tank

The KVs were impervious to the fire of German 37mm (1.5in) antitank guns, which prompted Russian tank commanders to roll over such guns instead of wasting ammo on them. This is a KV-1 model 1940, which is armed with the new longer-barrelled F-32 76mm (3in) cannon.

Specifications

Crew: 5
Weight: 46.6 tonnes (42.3 tons)
Length: 6.68m (21.9ft)
Width: 3.32m (10.9ft)
Height: 2.71m (8.9ft)
Engine: V-2K
Speed: 35km/hr (21.7mph)
Range: 180km (111.8 miles)
Radio: 10R

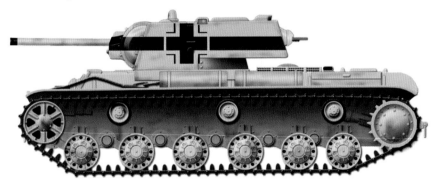

▶ Panzerkampfwagen KV Ia 753(r)

Pz. Rgt 1 / Captured Russian tank

The heavy fighting around Rshev saw the 1st Panzer Division losing tanks faster than they could be replaced. To maintain its fighting strength, the division was forced to press into service any available tank. This is a KV-1 model 1942, which has a cast-metal turret that was stronger than those used on earlier variants.

Specifications

Crew: 5
Weight: 45.7 tonnes (41.5 tons)
Length: 6.68m (21.9ft)
Width: 3.32m (10.9ft)
Height: 2.71m (8.9ft)
Engine: V-2K
Speed: 35km/hr (21.7mph)
Range: 160km (99.4 miles)
Radio: 10R

▶ **Panzerkampfwagen IV Ausf F2 (Sd Kfz 161/1)**

Pz. Rgt 1 / II Battalion / 4th Company / 1st Zug / tank number 2

With the arrival of the long-barrelled Ausf F2 in the summer of 1942, the Germans now had a tank that could match the heavy Soviet tanks, and which was superior to all other Allied tanks then in service.

Specifications

Crew: 5	Engine: Maybach HL120TRM
Weight: 25.4 tonnes (23 tons)	Speed: 40km/hr (24.9mph)
Length: 5.62m (18.4ft)	Range: 200km (124.3 miles)
Width: 2.84m (9.3ft)	Radio: FuG5
Height: 2.68m (8.8ft)	

 # Year of retreat

NOVEMBER 1943

The 1st Panzer Division was transferred to Germany and then to France in January 1943 for refitting. In June, it was sent to the Balkans, moving on to Greece for coastal defence duty.

I T REMAINED IN GREECE until November, when the Division returned to the Eastern Front, to the Ukraine. In December 1943, it was attached to XLVII *Panzerkorps* at Zhitomir. It took part in the counteroffensive at Kiev attached to 4th *Panzer-Armee* and later took part in defensive actions near Berdichev. Following the massive Soviet summer offensive in June 1944, which saw the destruction of Army Group Centre, 1st Panzer played its part in the German counteroffensive, attached to XLVIII *Panzerkorps*. However, following the failure to hold the southern flank, it was forced to retreat back across the Vistula.

In October, it was sent to Hungary. In May 1945, it was in Austria, where the 1st Panzer Division surrendered to the US Army.

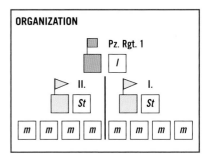

ORGANIZATION

Panzer Unit	VK 1801	Pz. IV	Pz. V	Flammpz	Pz. Bef.
1st Pz. Rgt.	8	95	76	7	8

▶ **Panzerkampfwagen I Ausf F**

Pz. Rgt 1 / Special Regiment Platoon

The VK 1801 was an experimental heavily armoured small infantry assault tank. In 1942, eight were issued to the 1st Panzer Division for combat evaluation. The tank was armed with two 7.92mm (0.3in) MG34 machine guns.

Specifications

Crew: 2	Engine: Maybach HL45p
Weight: 23.2 tonnes (21 tons)	Speed: 25km/hr (15.5mph)
Length: 4.38m (14.4ft)	Range: 150km (93.2 miles)
Width: 2.64m (8.7ft)	Radio: FuG5
Height: 2.05m (8.2ft)	

▶ Mittlerer Flammpanzerwagen Gerat 916 Ausf C (Sd Kfz 251/16)

Unknown formation

Based on the versatile Sd Kfz 251 half-track, this flamethrowing vehicle carried 700 litres (739.7 quarts) of inflammable fuel, which was enough for 80 bursts of up to two seconds.

Specifications

Crew: 5	MG42,
Weight: 9.5 tonnes (8.62 tons)	earlier models also carried a
Armament: two 1.4cm (0.6in)	single 0.7cm (0.3in) man-
Flammenwerfer,	portable Flammenwerfer 42
two 7.62mm (0.3in) MG34 or	

▶ Panzerjäger 38(t) mit 7.5cm PaK40/3 Ausf M (Sd Kfz 138)

37th Panzerjäger Battalion

With 975 units produced between April 1943 and May 1944, the Marder III was readily available to Panzerjäger battalions of both Panzer and infantry divisions on all fronts. This example was used in the heavy fighting that took place in the unsuccessful defence of Budapest, Hungary, during the winter of 1944 and into 1945, when the city fell to the Soviets.

Specifications

Crew: 4	Engine: Praga AC
Weight: 11.6 tonnes (10.5 tons)	Speed: 42km/hr (26mph)
Length: 4.95m (16.2ft)	Range: 190km (118 miles)
Width: 2.15m (7ft)	Radio: FuG Spr d
Height: 2.48m (8.1ft)	

Specifications

Crew: 5	Engine: Maybach HL230P30
Weight: 50.2 tonnes (45.5 tons)	Speed: 46km/hr (28.6mph)
Length: 8.86m (29ft)	Range: 200km (124.3 miles)
Width: 3.4m (11.2ft)	Radio: FuG5
Height: 2.98m (9.8ft)	

▲ Panzerkampfwagen V Ausf G (Sd Kfz 171)

Pz. Rgt 1 / I Battalion / 4th Company / 3rd Zug / tank number 3

The Panther entered service in large numbers in 1944, but by 15 March 1945 the Division had only 10 operational Pz.Kpfw V tanks. The 1st Panzer Division surrendered to US forces in May 1945.

2nd Panzer Division

The 2nd Panzer Division fought from the beginning of World War II to the end, seeing action on both Eastern and Western Fronts as well as in the Balkans.

▲ **Preparing for War**
The German army mounted large-scale armoured exercises from 1936, using the light Panzer I to develop many of the techniques of *Blitzkrieg,* or 'Lightning War'.

ESTABLISHED IN OCTOBER 1935, the 2nd Panzer Division differed from the 1st and 3rd Divisions in that it was commanded by an *Oberst,* or Colonel, rather than a General. However, that *Oberst* was Heinz Guderian, the inspiration behind Germany's *Panzerwaffe.*

Headquartered at Wurzburg, the tank component of the 2nd Panzer Division was provided by the 3rd Panzer Regiment, located at Kamenz, and the 4th Panzer Regiment at Ohrdruf. Other units in the table of organization included the 2nd *Schützen* Brigade with two battalions, the 2nd Motorcycle Battalion, the 5th Reconnaissance Company, the two battalions of the 74th Artillery Regiment and various signals, antitank and pioneer battalions.

Commanders

General der Panzertruppen R. Veiel
(1 Sep 1939 – 17 Feb 1942)

General der Panzertruppen H. Esebeck
(17 Feb 1942 – 1 June 1942)

Generalleutnant A. Lenski
(1 June 1942 – 5 Sept 1942)

Generalleutnant V. Lubbe
(5 Sept 1942 – 1 Feb 1944)

General der Panzertruppen H. Luttwitz
(1 Feb 1944 – 5 May 1944)

Generalleutnant F. Westhoven
(5 May 1944 – 27 May 1944)

General der Panzertruppen H. Luttwitz
(27 May 1944 – 31 Aug 1944)

Generalmajor H. Schonfeld
(31 Aug 1944 – 15 Dec 1944)

Generalmajor M. Lauchert
(14 Dec 1944 – 20 Mar 1945)

Generalmajor O. Munzel
(20 Mar 1945 – 1 Apr 1945)

Oberst C. Stollbrock
(1 Apr 1945 – 8 May 1945)

In February and March of 1936, the three Panzer Divisions deployed in an extensive series of training exercises on proving grounds at Staumuhlen. In fact, they were being used as a reserve force for the German operation to take control of the Rhineland. Following the reoccupation on 7 March 1936, all units, including the Panzer Divisions, returned to their home bases.

Austrian Anschluss

On 12 March 1938, German forces occupied Austria. 2nd Panzer Division, together with the SS Regiment *Leibstandarte Adolf Hitler* (selected because it was fully motorized) were placed under Guderian's overall command. In the bloodless occupation, the 2nd Panzer Division covered 700 km (435 miles) in 48 hours. Valuable lessons were learned about rapid, long-distance movement in the process, since the division lost about a third of its tanks en route because of mechanical failure. The division remained in Austria, which was to be its new home base.

Fall Weiss: the invasion of Poland
1 SEPTEMBER 1939

The 2nd Panzer Division was a key part of the fast-moving German mechanized spearhead force that outmanoeuvred and destroyed the Polish Army in September 1939.

IN SEPTEMBER 1939, the 2nd Panzer Division was assigned to Army Group South, being part of XVIII *Panzerkorps* in General List's 14th Army. This force was the southernmost of Germany's armies, tasked with smashing through the Polish Krakow Army before racing deep into Poland as the outer arm of a vast pincer movement. It was then to destroy Polish reserves massing to the south of Warsaw, before linking up with Guderian's *Panzerkorps,* which

had attacked out of East Prussia. The 2nd Panzer Division suffered relatively heavy losses in Poland when compared with the other Panzer divisions, and in January 1940 it was sent to the Eifel region to refit.

ORGANIZATION

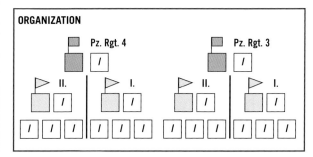

Panzer Unit	Pz. I	Pz. II	Pz. III	Pz. IV	Pz. Bef.
3rd Pz. Rgt.	62	78	3	8	9
4th Pz. Rgt.	62	77	3	9	11

Specifications

Crew: 2
Weight: 6.4 tonnes (5.8 tons)
Length: 4.42m (14.5ft)
Width: 2.06m (6.8ft)
Height: 1.72m (5.6ft)

Engine: Maybach NL38TR
Speed: 40km/hr (24.9mph)
Range: 170km (105.6 miles)
Radio: FuG2

▲ **Panzerkampfwagen I Ausf B (Sd Kfz 101)**

Pz. Rgt 4 / II Battalion / 3rd Company

The vehicle depicted was a survivor of the Polish campaign. The crew had toned down the side turret crosses but left the one in the rear to aid recognition from the air. The divisional rhomboid symbol was painted onto the hull rear and on the lower left front armour plate.

▶ **Panzerkampfwagen III Ausf A (Sd Kfz 141)**

Unknown formation

Early Panzer IIIs were armed with a 3.7cm (1.5in) KwK L46.5 gun, and carried 150 rounds of explosive and armour-piercing ammunition. The suspension proved unsatisfactory and all Ausf As had been withdrawn by February 1940.

Specifications

Crew: 5
Weight: 17 tonnes (15.4 tons)
Length: 5.69m (18.7ft)
Width: 2.81m (9.2ft)
Height: 2.34m (7.7ft)

Engine: Maybach HL108TR
Speed: 35km/hr (21.7mph)
Range: 165km (102.5 miles)
Radio: FuG5

∘∘ *Fall Gelb*: the French campaign
10 MAY 1940

The German offensive in the Low Countries tempted the Allies northwards out of their defensive positions into Belgium. This left them vulnerable to a Panzer attack through the Ardennes.

BURSTING THROUGH the supposedly impassible Ardennes on 10 May, von Rundstedt's Army Group A caught the Allies totally by surprise. The attack was spearheaded by Guderian's XIX *Panzerkorps*, comprising the 1st, 2nd and 10th Panzer Divisions. Guderian's corps was across the Meuse at Sedan by 14 May. It reached Abbeville by the 20th, and a battalion of the 2nd Panzer Division was the first German unit to reach the sea. However, after taking Calais, Hitler ordered the Panzers to halt, allowing the British to escape from Dunkirk.

After the Allied defeat at Dunkirk, Guderian's newly renamed *Panzergruppe* raced with equal speed through France, with the 2nd Panzer Division reaching the Swiss border on 17 June.

ORGANIZATION

Panzer Unit	Pz. I	Pz. II	Pz. III	Pz. IV	Pz. Bef.
3rd Pz. Rgt.	22	55	29	16	8
4th Pz. Rgt.	23	60	29	16	8

▶ **Panzerkampfwagen II Ausf C (Sd Kfz 121)**

Pz. Rgt 3 / II Battalion / 5th Company / 2nd Zug / tank number 4

Although the Pz.Kpfw II was used in combat with enemy tanks early in the war, its 2cm (0.8in) gun was really too small for the role. With the entry into service of larger, more heavily gunned tanks after 1940, the light Panzer IIs were used for reconnaissance until phased out of service with the *Panzerwaffe* late in 1943.

Specifications

Crew: 3	Engine: Maybach HL62TR
Weight: 9.8 tonnes (8.9 tons)	Speed: 40km/hr (24.9mph)
Length: 4.81m (15.8ft)	Range: 200km (124.3 miles)
Width: 2.22m (7.3ft)	Radio: FuG5
Height: 1.99m (6.5ft)	

▶ **Schwerer Panzerspahwagen (Sd Kfz 231) 6-Rad**

5th Reconnaissance Battalion

This heavy armoured car bears the name of 'Salzburg' next to the divisional symbol, reflecting the 2nd Panzer Division's Austrian connections.

Specifications

Crew: 4	Speed: 70km/hr (43.5mph)
Weight: 5.9 tonnes (5.35 tons)	Range: 300km (186.4 miles)
Length: 5.57m (18.3ft)	Radio: FuG Spr Ger 'a'
Width: 1.82m (6ft)	
Height: 2.25m (7.4ft)	

War in the Balkans
6 APRIL 1941

In the spring of 1941, Germany was forced to come to the assistance of Italy in the Balkans.

FOLLOWING THE FALL OF FRANCE, the 2nd Panzer Division transferred to Poland, where it was used for occupation duties. At the same time, it lost the 4th Panzer Regiment, which was used as the Panzer nucleus of the newly formed 13th Panzer Division.

Balkan campaign

The Italian fiasco in Greece forced Hitler to send troops to save his fellow dictator, Benito Mussolini. An invasion of Greece was planned, together with the conquest of Yugoslavia, where a military coup had overturned the pro-German Government. 2nd Panzer Division was assigned to Field Marshal List's 12th Army, tasked with attacking Greece through Macedonia. The Division made one of the key manoeuvres of the whole campaign, outflanking the Greek positions along the Metaxas Line.

Panzer Unit	Pz. II	Pz. III(37)	Pz. III(50)	Pz. IV	Pz. Bef.
3rd Pz. Rgt.	45	27	44	20	6

The 2nd helped take Athens in Greece, along with the 6th *Gebirgs* Division. After the campaign, the wheeled units entrained in Croatia for Germany. The tracked elements of the division returned by sea from the Greek port of Patras, but most were lost when two transports were sunk by British mines.

ORGANIZATION

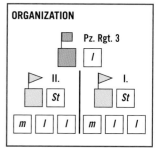

◀ **Kleiner Panzerbefehlswagen (Sd Kfz 265)**

Pz. Rgt 3 / Regiment Staff Signal Platoon

The Sd Kfz 265 was a variant of the Pz.Kpfw I with a built-up fixed superstructure, making room for a map board and a powerful radio. As a command tank, it had two radios, a FuG2 listening receiver and a FuG6 ultra shortwave transmitter/receiver with 3–6km (1.9–3.7 miles) voice or 4–8km (2.5–5 miles) range.

Specifications

Crew: 3

Weight: 6.5 tonnes (5.9 tons)

Length: 4.42m (14.5ft)

Width: 2.06m (6.8ft)

Height: 1.99m (6.5ft)

Engine: Maybach NL38TR

Speed: 40km/hr (24.9mph)

Range: 170km (105.6 miles)

Radio: FuG2 and FuG6

▶ **15cm sIG33 (Sf) auf Panzerkampfwagen I Ausf B**

703rd Schwere Infanteriegeschütz Abteilung

As a horse-drawn howitzer, the 15cm (6in) sIG33 L/11 was too slow to follow the Panzers, so it was mounted onto a Pz.Kpfw I chassis, wheels and trail included. It could be dismounted and used as a conventional towed gun. This example carried the name 'Alte Fritz' on the front shield beneath the gun.

Specifications

Crew: 4

Weight: 9.4 tonnes (8.5 tons)

Length: 4.67m (15.3ft)

Width: 2.06m (6.8ft)

Height: 2.8m (9.2ft)

Engine: Maybach NL38TR

Speed: 40km/hr (24.9mph)

Range: 140km (87 miles)

Armament: One 15cm (6in) sIG33 L/11

Fall Blau: the Eastern Front
28 JUNE 1942

The 3rd Regiment, 1st Battalion was detached to the 33rd Panzer Regiment, 9th Panzer Division.

THE LOSS OF MUCH of its armour returning from Greece meant that the 2nd Panzer Division could play no part in the early stages of Operation *Barbarossa*. It was building up its manpower in Germany when the invasion of the Soviet Union began, but soon afterwards, in July of 1941, it was transferred to Poland. In August 1941, it was sent to the south of France to re-equip before entraining for Russia, arriving at the front in October 1941.

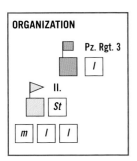

ORGANIZATION
Pz. Rgt. 3

Drive on Moscow

The 2nd Panzer Division was assigned to XXXX *Korps*, 4th *Panzergruppe*, Army Group Centre, arriving at the front to play its part on the drive on Moscow. After fighting through Roslavl and Vyazma, it reached the outskirts of Moscow at the onset of the bitter Russian winter. Along with the rest of Germany's forces in the region, 2nd Panzer Division was pushed back from the gates of Moscow by the massive Soviet winter counteroffensive.

Panzer Unit	Pz. II	Pz. 38t	Pz. III	Pz. IV	Pz. Bef.
3rd Pz. Rgt.	22	33	20	5	2

▶ **Panzerkampfwagen III Ausf J (Sd Kfz 141)**

Pz. Rgt 3 / II Battalion / 6th Company / Company HQ

The German flag was often used as an air recognition aid, but only during those times that the *Luftwaffe* was able to maintain air superiority. This Headquarters Panzer III displays a winged serpent in a shield, one of a series of non-standard markings used by the 6th Company to identify its tank platoons.

Specifications

Crew: 5	Engine: Maybach HL120TRM
Weight: 24 tonnes (21.5 tons)	Speed: 40km/hr (24.9mph)
Length: 6.28m (20.6ft)	Range: 155km (96.3 miles)
Width: 2.95m (9.7ft)	Radio: FuG5
Height: 2.5m (8.2ft)	

▶ **Panzerkampfwagen III Ausf J (Sd Kfz 141)**

Pz. Rgt 3 / II Battalion / 6th Company / 2nd Zug / tank number 4

The entire production run of 1549 J model Pz.Kpfw IIIs was taken up in replacing the 1400 examples of Panzer IIIs lost during the first years of the war – almost the entire inventory of earlier Ausf E, F, G and H models. Note the diamond outline used by the 2nd Platoon contrasting with the shield used by Company Headquarters above.

Weapons Specifications

Main Gun: 5cm (2in) KwK39 L/60	Co-axial MG: 7.92mm (0.3in) MG 34
Ammunition: 92 rounds	Hull MG: 7.92mm (0.3in) MG34
Traverse: 360° (manual)	Ammunition: 4950 rounds Patr
Elevation: -10° to +20°	SmK
Sight: TZF5e	MG sight: KgZF2

▶ **Panzerkampfwagen III Ausf J (Sd Kfz 141)**

Pz. Rgt 3 / II Battalion / 6th Company / 3rd Zug / tank number 1

The Pz.Kpfw III Ausf J was armed with a 5cm (2in) KwK L/42 with 84 rounds and two 7.92mm (0.3in) MG34 machine guns with 4950 rounds. This example is from the 3rd Platoon of the same company as the previous examples, and uses a triangle outline around the winged serpent. A Panzer rhomboid and the '6' are painted on the vision slit.

Specifications

Crew: 5	Engine: Maybach HL120TRM
Weight: 24 tonnes (21.5 tons)	Speed: 40km/hr (24.9mph)
Length: 6.28m (20.6ft)	Range: 155km (96.3 miles)
Width: 2.95m (9.7ft)	Radio: FuG5
Height: 2.5m (8.2ft)	

Stabskompanie einer Panzer-Abteilung K.St.N.1150

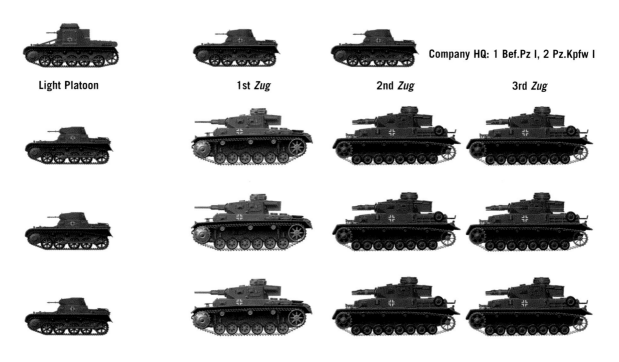

Company HQ: 1 Bef.Pz I, 2 Pz.Kpfw I

Light Platoon   **1st *Zug***   **2nd *Zug***   **3rd *Zug***

Organization of a Light Company type 'a' effective March 1939

Until 1939, the standard light Panzer companies in Panzer battalions were exclusively equipped with Panzer Is and IIs in four platoons – 1st, 2nd and 3rd *Zugen*, or platoons, with two Panzer Is and three Panzer IIs, the 4th *Zug* being equipped with five Panzer IIs. However, the new Medium Panzer IIIs and IVs were now entering service. Until enough had been delivered to form medium companies, they were deployed in 'Light Panzer Company Type A' formations, with the command troop operating seven Panzer Is and IIIs while the 1st, 2nd and 3rd platoons, three tanks strong, were equipped with Panzer IIIs and Panzer IVs.

✠ The last summer offensive
1 JULY 1943

The Division had authorized the formation of a *Flammpanzer* platoon early in 1943, but none of the flame-throwing tanks were in service at the time of the Kursk offensive.

FOLLOWING THE RETREAT from Moscow, the 2nd Panzer Division was heavily engaged in the actions to blunt the Soviet counteroffensive on the central front. For most of 1942, it was attached to XXXXI *Panzerkorps*, initially with 3rd *Panzerarmee* at Karmanovo, but from February under the control of the 9th Army. After months of heavy fighting around Rzhev and Byeloye, the Division was withdrawn in August, forming part of 9th Army's reserve while being brought back up to strength. In 1942, *Panzer-Abteilung* I of Panzer Regiment 3 was transferred to the 33rd Panzer Regiment, leaving the division with only a single *Abteilung* of Panzers. *Aufklärungs-Abteilung* 5 was converted into a motorcycle battalion, and as *Kradschützen-Abteilung* 24 was transferred to the 24th Panzer Division.

Divisional Organization

In 1943, the main fighting units in the divisional organization included the 2/3rd Panzer Regiment, the 2nd *Panzergrenadier* Regiment, the 304th *Panzergrenadier* Regiment, the 2nd Reconnaissance Battalion, the 74th Panzer Artillery Regiment, the 18th *Panzerjäger* Battalion and the 273rd Army Flak Battalion. During the year, the 276th *Sturmgeschütz*, or Assault Gun Battalion, was assigned to the Division.

In 1942, the division still had a dozen Panzer IIs and more than 40 Panzer IIIs in its vehicle park, but by the summer of 1943 these had all been replaced. At the time of the Battle of Kursk, 2/3rd Panzer Regiment had four companies, each with 22 Panzer IVs. It also received seven Panzer III flamethrower tanks, but these were not yet operational at Kursk.

Some of the Division's artillery units still used towed guns, but the 1st Battalion of the 74th Panzer Artillery Regiment had by now re-equipped with two batteries each of six Wespe 10.5cm (4.1in) self-propelled guns, and a battery of six Hummel 15cm (6in) self-propelled guns. The division's tank hunter regiment began to re-equip with self-propelled

Panzer Unit	Pz. II	Pz.III(50)	Pz.III(75)	Pz. IV	Pz. Bef.
3rd Pz. Rgt.	12	20	20	60	6

systems at the same time. The divisional Flak battalion included two batteries of four towed 8.8cm (3.5in) weapons, which could be used against both aircraft and tanks.

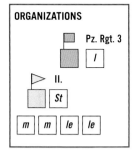

Kursk and After

In May 1943, 2nd Panzer Division was pulled back from the frontline, going into 2nd Panzer Army's reserve at Smolensk as the *Wehrmacht* High Command built up strength for the offensive against the Kursk Salient. For this, launched in July 1943, it was attached to XXXXVII *Panzerkorps* in Model's 9th Army. This was the main strike force of the northern prong of the giant pincer movement designed to destroy the Soviet forces located in the bulge in the frontlines around Kursk.

The attack was launched on 5 July 1943. Several delays had given the Soviets time to reinforce the salient, and progress was slow. As resistance stiffened, the German advance was stopped. In 10 days of fighting, 4th Panzer Army in the south had advanced just 32km (19.9 miles), and in the north Model's 9th Army, including 2nd Panzer, had penetrated just 19km (11.8 miles) into Soviet-held territory.

The end came when the Soviets launched a major counteroffensive in the north, forcing 9th Army to withdraw. In all, the Kursk battle had cost the *Wehrmacht* 50,000 dead, and had seen the loss of more than 1000 tanks.

Over the next months, 2nd Panzer Division was all but used up in the series of costly defensive battles around Kiev and along the Dnieper River. By the end of 1943, the division was in reserve, supporting the 2nd Army around Gomel.

▶ **Panzerkampfwagen III Ausf M (Sd Kfz 141/1)**

Pz. Rgt 3 / II Battalion

For much of the war, the 2nd Panzer Division continued to recruit most of its personnel from Austria. As a result, the Viennese coat of arms was used to adorn many of the formation's vehicles.

Specifications	
Crew: 5	Engine: Maybach HL120TRM
Weight: 25 tonnes (22.7 tons)	Speed: 40km/hr (24.9mph)
Length: 6.41m (21ft)	Range: 155km (96.3 miles)
Width: 2.95m (9.7ft)	Radio: FuG5
Height: 2.5m (8.2ft)	

▶ **Panzerkampfwagen III Ausf N (Sd Kfz 141/2)**

Pz. Rgt 3 / II Battalion

20 Ausf N were operational with the Division in time for the summer offensive of 1943. Armed with a short-barrelled 7.5cm (3in) gun, the type was used for close support against infantry positions and enemy strongpoints.

Specifications	
Crew: 5	Height: 2.5m (8.2ft)
Weight: 25.4 tonnes (23 tons)	Engine: Maybach HL120TRM
Length: 5.52m (18.1ft) Ausf L or	Speed: 40km/hr (24.9mph)
5.65m (18.5ft) Ausf M conversion	Range: 155km (96.3 miles)
Width: 2.95m (9.7ft)	Radio: FuG5

▶ **Panzerkampfwagen IV Ausf H (Sd Kfz 161/2)**

Pz. Rgt 3 / II Battalion

The Ausf H model was armed with a long-barelled 7.5cm (3in) KwK40 L/48 cannon, and provided much of the strike power of the Panzer divisions in 1943 and 1944. The tank could carry 87 rounds of ammunition, divided between high explosive, armour-piercing and smoke shells. This Panzer Regiment 3 vehicle does not display the unit tactical number on the turret.

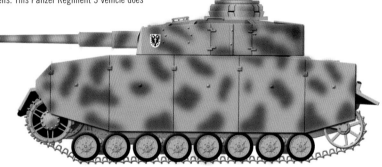

Specifications	
Crew: 5	Engine: Maybach HL120TRM
Weight: 27.6 tonnes (25 tons)	Speed: 38km/hr (23.6mph)
Length: 7.02m (23ft)	Range: 210km (130.5 miles)
Width: 2.88m (9.4ft)	Radio: FuG5
Height: 2.68m (8.8ft)	

The Western Front
JUNE 1944

On 15 January 1944, the remains of the 2nd Panzer Division were withdrawn from combat on the Eastern Front, and the formation was sent to France to be rebuilt.

FROM FEBRUARY 1944, *Panzer-Abteilung* I of Panzer Regiment 3 was rebuilt with Pz.Kpfw V Panther tanks, providing the division with two *Abteilungen* of Panzers for the first time in two years. On 7 May 1944, *Panzer-Abteilung* I/*Panzer-Regiment* 3 became *Panzer-Abteilung* 507, an independent unit equipped with Tiger tanks. Later, on 30 June 1944, the unit was returned to the 2nd Panzer Division, again becoming *Panzer-Abteilung* I/*Panzer-Regiment* 3, exchanging its Tigers for Panthers in the process.

Normandy Battles
After a period of rest in France, the Division was deployed to Amiens as part of the reserve force for Army Group B. It was ordered to the Normandy Front after the invasion, but destroyed bridges and constant air attack meant that it took more than a week to reach the battle zone. Attached to XXXXVII Corps of *Panzergruppe* West, it saw heavy fighting against the British before being detached for the abortive Mortain offensive designed to split the American forces threatening to break through the

German defences. As the Americans broke out from the bridgehead, the German Panzers were pushed back to their starting points and beyond. The 2nd Panzer Division was caught and nearly destroyed in the Falaise pocket. It managed to break out through the Falaise Gap, suffering staggering losses in men and materiel while doing so.

Panzer Unit	Pz. IV	Pz. V	FlkPz	StuG	B IV
3rd Pz. Rgt.	98	79	12	10	36

ORGANIZATION

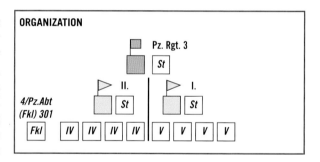

Specifications
Crew: 5

Weight: 49.4 tonnes (44.8 tons)

Length: 8.86m (29ft)

Width: 3.42m (11.2ft)

Height: 2.98m (9.8ft)

Engine: Maybach HL230P30

Speed: 46km/hr (28.6mph)

Range: 200km (124.3 miles)

Radio: FuG5

▼ Panzerkampfwagen V Ausf A (Sd Kfz 171)
Pz. Rgt 3 / I Battalion / 3rd Company / 1st Zug / tank number 1

After heavy losses on the Eastern Front, the division was sent to Amiens, France at the beginning of 1944 to be refitted. While there, the I *Abteilung* of Panzer Regiment 3 was reformed and equipped with the Pz.Kpfw V Panther.

▶ **Panzerkampfwagen IV Ausf H (Sd Kfz 161/2)**
Pz. Rgt 3 / II Battalion / 8th Company / 2nd Zug / tank number 1

By 1944, the Division had consolidated all Pz.Kpfw IV tanks into the II *Abteilung*. German commanders usually assigned their best crews to older model tanks; the reasoning was that their experience would compensate for any mechanical inferiority.

Specifications

Crew: 5	Engine: Maybach HL120TRM
Weight: 27.6 tonnes (25 tons)	Speed: 38km/hr (23.6mph)
Length: 7.02m (23ft)	Range: 210km (130.5 miles)
Width: 2.88m (9.4ft)	Radio: FuG5
Height: 2.68m (8.8ft)	

▶ **Panzerkampfwagen IV Ausf H (Sd Kfz 161/2)**
Pz. Rgt 3 / II Battalion / 8th Company / 2nd Zug / tank number 5

After heavy losses fighting in the area of Villers-Bocage, the 2nd Panzer Division was ordered to take part in the counterattack at Mortain, designed to drive a wedge between the Allied armies. The offensive failed, and the division was later trapped in the Falaise pocket.

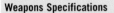

Weapons Specifications

Main Gun: 7.5cm (3in) KwK40 L/48	Co-axial MG: 7.92mm (0.3in) MG 34
Ammunition: 87 rounds	Hull MG: 7.92mm (0.3in) MG34
Traverse: 360° (electric)	Ammunition: 3150 rounds
Elevation: -8° to +20°	Patr SmK
Sight: TZF5f/1	MG sight: KgZF2

▶ **15cm Schweres Infanteriegeschütz 33 (Sf)**
auf Panzerkampfwagen 38(t) Ausf H (Sd Kfz 138/1)
2nd Panzergrenadier Regiment / II Battalion / Self-propelled Infantry Gun Company

Ninety examples of this heavy infantry gun, based in the chassis of the Czech-built Panzer 38(t), were produced between February and April 1943, and the equipment was still in service with the 2nd Panzer Division in Normandy in June 1944.

Specifications

Crew: 5	Engine: Praga EPA/2
Weight: 12.7 tonnes (11.5 tons)	Speed: 35km/hr (21.7mph)
Length: 4.61m (15.1ft)	Range: 185km (115 miles)
Width: 2.16m (7ft)	Radio: FuG16
Height: 2.4m (7.9ft)	

▼ Leichter Schützenpanzerwagen (Sd Kfz 250/9)

2nd Reconnaissance Battalion / 2nd Reconnaissance Company

With the urgent need for a better reconnaissance vehicle to replace ineffective armoured cars and vulnerable motorcycles, the Sd Kfz250 was selected as a replacement. Mounting the turret of the Sd Kfz 222 light armoured car, it was so successful that production of the Sd Kfz 222 was terminated in favour of the half-track.

Specifications

Crew: 3	Engine: Maybach HL42TUKRM
Weight: 6.6 tonnes (6.02 tons)	Speed: 60km/hr (37.3mph)
Length: 4.61m (15.1ft)	Range: 300km (186.4 miles)
Width: 1.95m (6.4ft)	Radio: FuG 12
Height: 2.16m (7ft)	

▶ Schwerer Panzerspähwagen (5cm) (Sd Kfz 234/2)

2nd Reconnaissance Battalion / 4th Reconnaissance Company 'Puma'

This was one of the most capable armoured cars built during World War II, and 25 Pumas were issued to one of the companies in the 2nd Panzer Division's reconnaissance battalion. Its main armament consisted of one 5cm (2in) KwK 39/1 L60 cannon, for which it carried 55 rounds of ammunition.

Specifications

Crew: 4	Engine: Tatra 103
Weight: 12.9 tonnes (11.74 tons)	Speed: 80km/hr (49.7mph)
Length: 6.8m (22.3ft)	Range: 900km (559.2 miles)
Width: 2.4m (7.9ft)	Radio: Fu Spr Ger 'a'
Height: 2.28m (7.5ft)	

▼ Mittlerer Schützenpanzerwagen I Ausf D (Sd Kfz 251/9)

2nd Reconnaissance Battalion / 5th Heavy Reconnaissance Company

The mission of the Sd Kfz 251/9 was to provide fire support to the other companies of the 2nd Reconnaissance Battalion. This vehicle was also known by the unofficial designation of 'Stummel', in reference to the short 7.5cm (3in) KwK L/24 mounted in the superstructure. The gun became available when the Panzer IVs that had originally carried it were upgunned, and when mounted on the half-track, it was redesignated as the K51(Sf). The vehicle could carry 52 rounds for the gun.

Specifications

Crew: 3	Engine: Maybach HL42TUKRM
Weight: 9.4 tonnes (8.53 tons)	Speed: 53km/hr (32.9mph)
Length: 5.98m (19.6ft)	Range: 300km (186.4 miles)
Width: 2.1m (6.9ft)	Radio: FuG Spr Ger f
Height: 2.07m (6.8ft)	

▶ Mittlerer Pionierpanzerwagen Ausf D (Sd Kfz 251/7)

38th Panzer Pioneer Battalion

This vehicle was built to carry a *Sturmpionier* squad of combat engineers into
battle, along with all of their equipment. It was fitted with racks for demolition
charges, flamethrowers and mines, and it carried a small assault bridge.

Specifications

Crew: 7/8	Engine: Maybach HL42TUKRM
Weight: 8.9 tonnes (8.07 tons)	Speed: 53km/hr (32.9mph)
Length: 0m (0ft)	Range: 300km (186.4 miles)
Width: 0m (0ft)	Radio: FuG5 when operating with
Height: 2.7m (8.9ft)	a Panzer HQ company

▶ 7.5cm Sturmgeschütz 40 Ausf G (Sd Kfz 142/1)

Panzer-Abteilung (Fkl) 301 / 4th Company / 2nd Zug / tank number 2 (Attached)

The Radio Control Armoured Unit, (Fkl) 301, detached its 4th Company for service with the 2nd Panzer Division, and it saw combat against the Allies in Normandy.
The box behind the armoured fighting compartment housed a powerful command radio transmitter used to detonate explosive charges remotely.

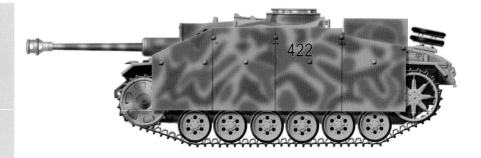

Specifications

Crew: 4
Weight: 26.3 tonnes (23.9 tons)
Length: 6.77m (22.2ft)
Width: 2.95m (9.7ft)
Height: 2.16m (7ft)
Engine: Maybach HL120TRM
Speed: 40km/hr (24.9mph)
Range: 155km (96.3 miles)
Radio: FuG 15 and FuG 16

▶ Schwerer Ladungstrager (Sd Kfz 301) Ausf A

Panzer-Abteilung (Fkl) 301 / 4th Company (Attached)

The remote control tracked demolition charge layer was desgned to carry a 500kg (1100lb) demolition charge to a target. The driver would drop the charge and
get clear before the explosives were detonated. Alternatively, the vehicle could be remotely controlled by radio. The unit's mission was to use the charges to clear
paths through minefields and to destroy enemy fortifications.

Specifications

Crew: 1	Engine: Borgward 6M RTBV
Weight: 4 tonnes (3.6 tons)	Speed: 38km/hr (23.6mph)
Length: 3.65m (12ft)	Range: 212km (131.7 miles)
Width: 1.8m (6.2ft)	Radio: EP3 with UKE6
Height: 1.19m (3.9ft)	

The Battle of the Bulge
14 DECEMBER 1944

The Division was wrecked in the Falaise Pocket, with only a small personnel cadre being able to escape. On rebuilding, the 1st Battalion was equipped with Panthers while the 2nd Battalion was a mixed unit with two companies of Pz.Kpfw IV and two *Sturmgeschütz* companies.

AFTER ITS DESTRUCTION in Normandy, the remaining cadre of the 2nd Panzer Division was withdrawn to Wittlich in the Eifel area of Germany, where the division was reformed and reequipped. To make up numbers, it absorbed the remains of the 352nd Infantry Division. At the end of 1944, it was attached to Hasso von Manteuffel's 5th *Panzerarmee*, for use in the surprise winter attack to be launched against the Allies in the Ardennes. It was a massive operation, and 2nd Panzer advanced further than any other formation. However, the offensive failed and the division suffered heavily.

At the end of March 1945, what remained of 2nd Panzer was absorbed by the scraped together Thuringen Panzer Brigade in the Mosel region and at Fulda. With little fuel or equipment left, the unit surrendered to US troops at Plauen in May, 1945.

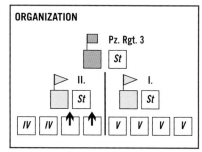

ORGANIZATION

Panzer Unit	Pz. IV	Pz. V	StuG	FlkPz(20)	FlkPz(37)
3rd Pz. Rgt.	28	64	24	7	4

Specifications
Crew: 4
Weight: up to 27.6 tonnes (25 tons)
Length: 6.85m (22.5ft)
Width: 6.7m (22ft)
Height: 1.85m (6ft)
Engine: Maybach HL120TRM
Speed: 38km/hr (23.6mph)
Range: 210km (130.5 miles)
Radio: FuG 15 and FuG 160

▼ **Sturmgeschütz neuer Art mit 7.5cm PaK l/48 auf Fahrgestell Panzerkampfwagen IV (Sd Kfz 162)**

38th Panzerjäger Battalion

The *Jagdpanzer* IV was also commonly known as 'Guderian's Duck', because the Inspector General of Panzer Troops had played a large part in its development.

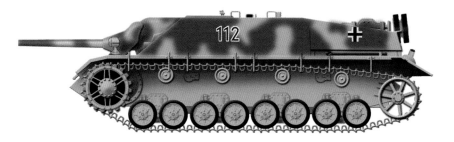

▶ **Flakpanzer IV / 2cm Vierling**

Pz. Rgt 3

Air defence assets became vital to the *Panzerwaffe* as Allied air superiority began to tell. The Flakpanzer IV, also known as *Wirbelwind* (or 'Whirlwind'), was armed with a quadruple 2cm (0.8in) *Flakvierling* mount.

Specifications
Crew: 5
Weight: 24.3 tonnes (22 tons)
Length: 5.92m (19.4ft)
Width: 2.9m (9.5ft)
Height: 2.76m (9ft)
Engine: Maybach HL120TRM
Speed: 38km/hr (23.6mph)
Range: 200km (124.3 miles)
Radio: FuG2 and FuG5

3rd Panzer Division

The third of the original Panzer divisions was established, like the 1st and 2nd Panzer Divisions, on 15 October 1935. It was commanded by *Generalmajor* Ernst Fessmann.

THE 3RD PANZER DIVISION was headquartered at Berlin. In September 1937, the Division, along with the 1st Panzer Brigade, took part in a series of manoeuvres around Neusterlitz. Soon afterwards, Fessman was succeeded as divisional commander by *Generalmajor* Geyr von Schweppenburg. In March 1939, Germany took over the remaining part of Czechoslovakia after the occupation of the Sudetenland. Elements of the 3rd Panzer Division reached Prague at 8.20am on 13 March 1939, followed by the 6th Panzer Regiment in the afternoon. Two days later, the tanks led the first German parade through the Czech capital.

Commanders

General der Panzertruppen L. Schweppenburg *(1 Sep 1939 – 7 Oct 1939)*	Generalleutnant F .Westhoven *(1 Oct 1942 – 25 Oct 1943)*
General der Panzertruppen H. Stumpff *(7 Oct 1939 – Sept 1940)*	Generalleutnant F. Bayerlein *(25 Oct 1943 – 5 Jan 1944)*
General der Panzertruppen F. Kuhn *(Sept 1940 – 4 Oct 1940)*	Oberst R. Lang *(5 Jan 1944 – 25 May 1944)*
General der Panzertruppen H. Stumpff *(4 Oct 1940 – 13 Nov 1940)*	Generalleutnant W. Philipps *(25 May 1944 – 1 Jan 1945)*
Generalfeldmarschall W. Model *(13 Nov 1940 – 1 Oct 1941)*	Generalmajor W. Soth *(1 Jan 1945 – 19 Apr 1945)*
General der Panzertruppen H. Breith *(1 Oct 1941 – 1 Oct 1942)*	Oberst V. Schone *(19 Apr 1945 – 8 May 1945)*

INSIGNIA

 3rd Panzer originated in Berlin, and its first tactical symbol represented the Brandenburg Gate. The symbol was later used by the 20th Panzer Division.

 In the system introduced in 1940, 3rd Panzer's symbol followed in sequence from the 1st and 2nd Divisions.

 Tactical symbol used by 6th Panzer Regiment of the 3rd Panzer Division.

 The symbol of the city of Berlin is the bear. Since the 3rd Division was established in Berlin, it used a bear as a *Zusatz*, or additional symbol.

 Variant of the Divisional bear insignia.

 Another bear variant used by the Division was a shield containing the heraldic bear of the city of Berlin.

Fall Weiss: the invasion of Poland

1 SEPTEMBER 1939

On 17 August 1939, Germany's Panzer units were given their war orders. On 25 August, they began moving towards the eastern borders of the Reich.

ON 1 SEPTEMBER 1939, World War II began as German Armies poured over the Polish border. The 3rd Panzer Division was attached to General Heinz Guderian's XIX *Panzerkorps*, based in Pomerania. As hostilities started, Guderian's corps seized the Polish Corridor, cutting Poland off from the Baltic. Racing through northern Poland, led by the tanks of the 3rd Panzer Division, Guderian's corps formed the outer ring of the massive pincer that would encircle and defeat the Polish army.

Panzer Unit	Pz. I	Pz. II	Pz. III	Pz. IV	Pz. Bef.
5th Pz. Rgt.	63	77	3	9	8
6th Pz. Rgt.	59	79	3	9	8
Pz.Lehr Abt	0	20	37	14	2

Victory in Poland

On 18 September, 3rd Panzer made contact south of Brest-Litovsk with the XXII *Panzerkorps* advancing from the south. With the closing of the pincers, the fate of Poland's field army was sealed. Warsaw fell on 27 September, and the last Polish troops still fighting surrendered on 6 October.

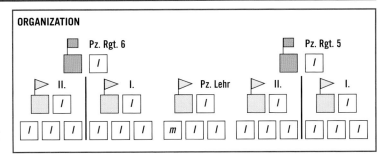

Company HQ: 1 Bef.Pz. I, 1 Pz.Kpfw II, 2 Pz.Kpfw I

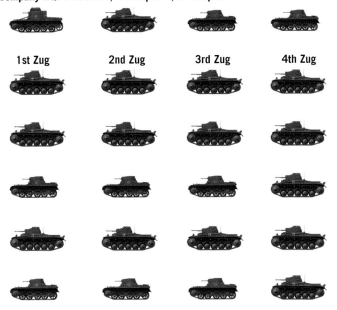

Leichte Panzerkompanie K.St.N.1171

Theoretical organization of a light company effective March 1939. When the Panzer divisions were created, the official table of organization of a light panzer company included one light *Zug*, or platoon, of five Panzer IIs, and the remaining three platoons were intended to be equipped with five Panzer IIIs each. However, production was slow. Early variants had too little armour protection and unsatisfactory suspension. Fewer than 150 Panzer IIIs had been manufactured by the outbreak of war, and only 98 tanks were actually operational.

Plans had been modified to reduce the number of Panzer IIIs to just three tanks to equip a single *Zug* in one of the regiment's 'a'-type light company, giving a division a total Panzer III strength of between six and 12 tanks.

However, supplies were so short that some of the panzer divisions in Poland were exclusively equipped with Panzer Is and Panzer IIs. These were deployed in five-tank platoons as illustrated, with three further gun tanks and a command tank assigned to company headquarters.

Fall Gelb: the French campaign
10 May 1940

The 3rd Panzer Division was attached to Army Group B during the Western campaign, and did not take part in the surprise attack through the Ardennes.

3RD PANZER DROVE into Holland and Belgium as part of the force intended to pull the Allies out of France and into the Low Countries. When the attack on France started, 3rd Panzer advanced west of Paris.

Panzer Unit	Pz. I	Pz. II	Pz. III	Pz. IV	Pz. Bef.
5th Pz. Rgt.	22	55	29	16	8
6th Pz. Rgt.	23	60	29	16	8

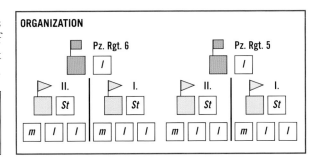

▶ Panzerkampfwagen IV Ausf D (Sd Kfz 161)

Unknown formation

The Pz.Kpfw IV's short-barrelled 7.5cm (3in) L/24 gun was not designed as an antitank weapon, but was powerful enough to deal with most Allied tanks in 1940.

Specifications

Crew: 5	Engine: Maybach HL120TRM
Weight: 22 tonnes (20 tons)	Speed: 40km/hr (24.9mph)
Length: 5.92m (19.4ft)	Range: 200km (124.3 miles)
Width: 2.84m (9.3ft)	Radio: FuG5
Height: 2.68m (8.8ft)	

▶ Panzerkampfwagen II Ausf C (Sd Kfz 121)

Unknown formation

The 3rd Panzer Division claimed 87 enemy tank kills in 1940. Actions in France included a major engagement with the French 3rd Mechanized Division.

Specifications

Crew: 3	Engine: Maybach HL62TR
Weight: 9.8 tonnes (8.9 tons)	Speed: 40km/hr (24.9mph)
Length: 4.81m (15.8ft)	Range: 200km (124.3 miles)
Width: 2.22m (7.3ft)	Radio: FuG5
Height: 1.99m (6.5ft)	

▶ Munitionsschlepper auf Panzerkampfwagen I Ausf A (Sd Kfz 111)

Unknown formation

A number of early Pz.Kpfw I Ausf As were converted into ammunition carriers. The Sd Kfz 111 was developed to supply ammunition to frontline units under fire and served during the invasion of Poland and France. This example carries a standard Panzer Death's Head insignia, which differed from that used by the SS.

▼ Infanterie Sturmsteg auf Fahrgestell Panzerkampfwagen IV

39th Panzer Pioneer Battalion

Four assault bridges were delivered to each full Panzer division in 1940.

Specifications

Crew: 2	Engine: Krupp M305
Weight: 5.5 tonnes (5 tons)	Speed: 37km/hr (23mph)
Length: 4.02m (13.2ft)	Range: 95km (59 miles)
Width: 2.06m (6.8ft)	Radio: None
Height: 1.4m (4.6ft)	

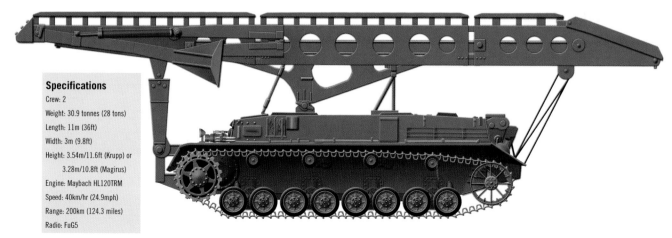

Specifications

Crew: 2
Weight: 30.9 tonnes (28 tons)
Length: 11m (36ft)
Width: 3m (9.8ft)
Height: 3.54m/11.6ft (Krupp) or
      3.28m/10.8ft (Magirus)
Engine: Maybach HL120TRM
Speed: 40km/hr (24.9mph)
Range: 200km (124.3 miles)
Radio: FuG5

▶ **Panzerkampfwagen I
Ausf B (Sd Kfz 101)**

Unknown formation

It has been suggested that 3rd
Panzer's Divisional symbol, a
lopsided 'E', was a stylized
representation of the famous
Brandenburg Gate in Berlin.

Specifications

Crew: 2	Engine: Maybach NL38TR
Weight: 6.4 tonnes	Speed: 40km/hr
(5.8 tons)	(24.9mph)
Length: 4.42m (14.5ft)	Range: 170km
Width: 2.06m (6.8ft)	(105.6 miles)
Height: 1.72m (5.6ft)	Radio: FuG2

 # *Barbarossa*: the attack on Russia
22 JUNE 1941

Panzer Regiment 5 was detached along with other divisional units in January 1941 to reinforce the 5th *Leichte* Panzer Division, which was to form part of the newly created *Afrika Korps*.

AFTER REFITTING IN GERMANY, the 3rd Panzer Division formed part of Guderian's 2nd *Panzergruppe* in Russia in July 1941. By September, hard use meant that its tank strength had fallen from nearly 200 to about 50, most of which were Panzer IIs.

ORGANIZATION

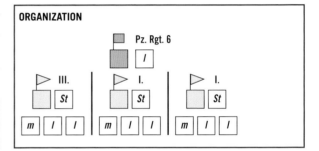

Panzer Unit	Pz. II	Pz.III(37)	Pz.III(50)	Pz. IV	Pz. Bef.
6th Pz. Rgt.	58	29	81	20	15

▶ **Panzerkampfwagen III Ausf J (Sd Kfz 141)**

Pz. Rgt 6 / I Battalion / 1st Company / 2nd Zug / tank number 2

The Pz.Kpfw III's three-man turret reduced crew workloads considerably.

Specifications

Crew: 5	Engine: Maybach HL120TRM
Weight: 24 tonnes (21.5 tons)	Speed: 40km/hr (24.9mph)
Length: 5.52m (18.1ft)	Range: 155km (96.3 miles)
Width: 2.95m (9.7ft)	Radio: FuG5
Height: 2.5m (8.2ft)	

▶ **Panzerkampfwagen III Ausf H (Sd Kfz 141)**

Pz. Rgt 6 / II Battalion / 5th Company / 3rd Zug / tank number 1

Two-colour tactical numbers improved poor-weather identification.

Specifications

Crew: 5	Engine: Maybach HL120TRM
Weight: 24 tonnes (21.8 tons)	Speed: 40km/hr (24.9mph)
Length: 5.41m (17.7ft)	Range: 165km (102.5 miles)
Width: 2.95m (9.7ft)	Radio: FuG5
Height: 2.44m (8ft)	

Fall Blau: the Eastern Front
28 JUNE 1942

The Soviet winter offensive petered out in March 1942, and the *Wehrmacht* began planning its summer offensive. The main German attack was to be switched from Moscow to the south.

IN MARCH 1943, the 3rd Panzer Division transferred from Army Group Centre to the 6th Army at Kharkhov. After taking part in von Manstein's masterly victory there, it was again transferred, to von Kleist's 1st *Panzerarmee*, part of

Army Group A. Kleist's Panzers raced southeast towards the Caucasus mountains and the vital oilfields beyond, while the German 6th Army was directed at the Volga.

The stalemate and eventual annihilation of the 6th Army at Stalingrad over the winter of 1942/43 threatened to cut off Army Group A in the Caucasus, but von Kleist managed a superb fighting retreat. The 3rd Panzer Division was again transferred at the beginning of 1943, being assigned to Army Group Don at Rostov.

ORGANIZATION

Pz. Rgt. 6
I

III.
St
m | l | l

II.
St
m | l | l

I.
St
m | l | l

Panzer Unit	Pz. II	Pz. III(kz)	Pz. III(lg)	Pz. IV(kz)	Pz. IV(lg)
6th Pz. Rgt.	25	66	40	21	12

▶ **Mittlerer Schützenpanzerwagen Ausf C (Sd Kfz 251/1)**

3rd Schutzen Regiment

This troop-carrying half-track is depicted as it was when the 3rd Panzer Division was serving with Army Group

South before the advance into the Caucasus that summer. It is armed with a captured Soviet

PTRD-41 antitank rifle, which could penetrate the side armour of a Pz.Kpfw III.

Specifications

Crew: 2 plus 12 troops	(7ft) with MG shield
Weight: 9.9 tonnes (9 tons)	Engine: Maybach HL42TUKRM
Length: 5.98m (19.6ft)	Speed: 53km/hr (32.9mph)
Width: 2.1m (6.9ft)	Range: 300km (186.4 miles)
Height : 1.75m (5.7ft) or 2.16m	Radio: FuG Spr Ger f

▶ **Mittlerer Kommandopanzerwagen Ausf B (Sd Kfz 251/6)**

Unknown formation

The 2.8cm (1.1in) *Panzerbuchse* 41 was not a standard weapon for the Sd Kfz 251/6 armoured command post. It fired a high-velocity round through a barrel which tapered from 28mm (1.1in) at the chamber to 20mm (0.8in) at the muzzle.

Specifications

Crew: 8	Engine: Maybach HL42TUKRM
Weight: 9.4 tonnes (8.5 tons)	Speed: 53km/hr (32.9mph)
Length: 5.98m (19.6ft)	Range: 300km (186.4 miles)
Width: 2.1m (6.9ft)	Radio: FuG11 plus FuG Tr
Height: 2.4m (7.9ft)	

The last summer offensive
1 JULY 1943

The 3rd Panzer Battalion was disbanded in May 1943. The 1st Battalion was refitted as a Pz.Kpfw V Panther *Abteilung* and was combat-ready by August 1943.

THE MASSIVE SOVIET offensives launched after the *Wehrmacht*'s failure at Kursk meant that Army Group South, which included 3rd Panzer Division, was forced to withdraw through the Ukraine.

3rd Panzer was commanded by Fritz Bayerlein, a veteran of the Desert War, and was at Kirovograd when the town was surrounded by a surprise Soviet offensive in December 1943. 3rd Panzer led the breakout from the pocket, finally meeting up with a relief force led by the elite *Grossdeutschland* Division.

The *Wehrmacht*'s retreats continued through 1944 and 1945 through the Ukraine. The 3rd Panzer Division fought its way back through Uman, across the Bug and into Poland.

Briefly transferred to the remnants of Army Group Centre as the *Wehrmacht* tried to stabilize the front following its destruction, the division was moved to Hungary in January 1945. 3rd Panzer fought in Hungary until April 1945, when it retreated to Austria where it later surrendered to the US Army.

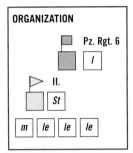

ORGANIZATION

Pz. Rgt. 6 / I / II. / St / m / le / le / le

Panzer Unit	Pz. II	Pz. III(50)	Pz. III(75)	Pz. IV	Pz. Bef.
6th Pz. Rgt.	7	42	17	23	1

Black and pink are the colours of the Panzer troops, black uniforms being worn with pink *Waffenfarbe*, or piping.

▶ **Mittlerer Funkpanzerwagen Ausf D (Sd Kfz 251/3)**

Pz. Rgt 6 / Regimental Staff Company

The Iron Cross in the corner of 6th Regiment's command standard shows the regimental commander was a Knight's Cross holder. Variants of this radio vehicle were used by several command levels, with radio fit depending on the role.

Specifications (Radio)

Crew: 7	Command post: FuG12, FuG11,
Divisional: FuG8, FuG5, FuG4	plus Kdo FuG Tr.
Division to Artillery: FuG8, FuG4	*The Kdo FuG Tr was deployed with*
Division to Panzer: FuG8, FuG5	*a variety of transmitters with*
Ground-to-air: FuG7, FuG1	*powers from 15 to 100 Watts*

▶ **Panzerkampfwagen IV Ausf H (Sd Kfz 161/2)**

Pz. Rgt 6 / II Battalion / 2nd Company / 2nd Zug / tank number 1

This vehicle took part in 3rd Panzer's long defensive retreat through 1944. The *Schürzen*, or side skirts, provided protection against shaped-charge antitank rounds or grenades.

Specifications

Crew: 5	Engine: Maybach HL120TRM
Weight: 27.6 tonnes (25 tons)	Speed: 38km/hr (23.6mph)
Length: 7.02m (23ft)	Range: 210km (130.5 miles)
Width: 2.88m (9.4ft)	Radio: FuG5
Height: 2.68m (8.8ft)	

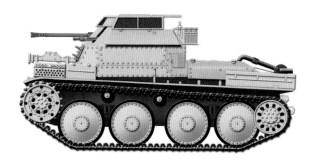

◀ **Aufklärungspanzerwagen 38 (2cm) (Sd Kfz 140/1)**

3rd Reconnaissance Battalion / 1st Company

The Sd Kfz 140/1 was one of the last variants of the Panzer 38(t) chassis. It is armed with a 2cm (0.8in) KwK38 L/55 cannon. In September 1944, the 1st Company received 25 vehicles, nine of which carried FuG12 long-range radios.

Specifications

Crew: 2	Engine: Praga EPA/2
Weight: 10.7 tonnes (9.75 tons)	Speed: 42km/hr (26mph)
Length: 4.51m (14.8ft)	Range: 210km (130.5 miles)
Width: 2.14m (7ft)	Radio: FuG12
Height: 2.17m (7.1ft)	

▶ **Panzerkampfwagen IV Ausf H (Sd Kfz 161/2)**

Pz. Rgt 6

By 1944, the Pz.Kpfw IV was showing its age. Even though the long-barrelled KwK40 L/48 could penetrate the armour of a T-34 from a distance of up to 1200m (3973ft) when using Pz.gr 39 ammunition, the tank could no longer match the capabilities of the latest T-34/85 and JS-122 tanks.

Specifications

Crew: 5	Engine: Maybach HL120TRM
Weight: 27.6 tonnes (25 tons)	Speed: 38km/hr (23.6mph)
Length: 7.02m (23ft)	Range: 210km (130.5 miles)
Width: 2.88m (9.4ft)	Radio: FuG5
Height: 2.68m (8.8ft)	

Specifications

Crew: 5	Engine: Maybach HL230P30
Weight: 49.4 tonnes (44.8 tons)	Speed: 46km/hr (28.6mph)
Length: 8.86 m (29ft)	Range: 200km (124.3 miles)
Width: 3.42m (11.2ft)	Radio: FuG5
Height: 2.98m (9.8ft)	

▼ **Panzerkampfwagen V Ausf A (Sd Kfz 171)**

Kampfgruppe / Pz. Rgt 6

By December 1944, the 3rd Panzer Division had been reorganized as a Panzer *Kampfgruppe* with a mixed tank company of Pz.Kpfw IVs and Pz.Kpfw Vs. It had a total of 20 operational tanks.

4th Panzer Division

Further expansion of the *Panzerwaffe* meant that by the autumn of 1938, six new Panzer brigades had been formed. The 7th Brigade was to be the nucleus of a new Panzer division.

THE 4TH PANZER DIVISION was raised at Wurzburg on 10 October 1938. The division's Panzer brigade included the 35th and 36th Panzer Regiments. In August 1939, the first three panzer divisions were identical in size and organization, but the 4th Panzer Division still lacked some of its motorized infantry and antitank units.

Commanders

Generaloberst G. Reinhardt
(1 Sept 1939 – 5 Feb 1940)

Generalleutnant L. von Radlmeier
(5 Feb 1940 – 8 June 1940)

Generalleutnant J. Stever
(8 June 1940 – 24 July 1940)

Generalleutnant H. Boineburg-Lengsfeld
(24 July 1940 – 8 Sept 1940)

General der Panzertruppen W. von Langermann
(8 Sept 1940 – 27 Dec 1941)

General der Panzertruppen D. Saucken
(27 Dec 1941 – 2 Jan 1942)

General der Panzertruppen W. von Langermann
(2 Jan 1942 – 6 Jan 1942)

General der Panzertruppen H. Eberbach
(6 Jan 1942 – 2 Mar 1942)

Generalleutnant O. Heidkamper
(2 Mar 1942 – 4 Apr 1942)

General der Panzertruppen H. Eberbach
(4 Apr 1942 – 14 Nov 1942)

Generalleutnant E. Schneider
(14 Nov 1942 – 31 May 1943)

General der Panzertruppen D. von Saucken
(31 May 1943 – Jan 1944)

Generalleutnant H. Junck
(Jan 1944 – Feb 1944)

General der Panzertruppen D. von Saucken
(Feb 1944 – 1 May 1944)

Generalleutnant C. Betzel
(1 May 1944 – 27 Mar 1945)

Oberst E. Hoffmann
(27 Mar 1945 – 8 May 1945)

INSIGNIA

Tactical insignia used on vehicles of the 4th Panzer Division on its formation in 1938 and 1939.

Alternative insignia based on a runic symbol used in the first half of 1940.

Standard wartime insignia used by 4th Panzer, following on from those used by the 1st, 2nd and 3rd Panzer Divisions.

Unit insignia used by the 35th Panzer Regiment, one of the constituent units of the 4th Panzer Division.

Fall Weiss: the invasion of Poland
1 SEPTEMBER 1939

For the Polish campaign, the 4th Panzer Division was attached to General Hoeppner's XVI *Panzerkorps*, serving alongside the 1st Panzer Division.

HOEPPNER'S CORPS PROVIDED the striking power for General von Reichenau's 10th Army, which was tasked with driving towards Warsaw. From the start of the invasion on 1 September, the Division advanced at breakneck pace. 4th Panzer units reached the outskirts of Warsaw on 8 September, and entered the city the next day. However, the *Wehrmacht* learned a valuable lesson about fighting in built-up areas: tanks are extremely vulnerable in such terrain, and the division lost 50 of its 120 tanks in the action before it was replaced by infantry units.

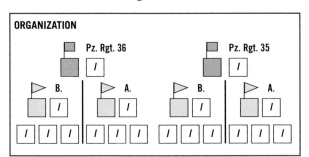

ORGANIZATION

Pz. Rgt. 36   Pz. Rgt. 35

B.   A.   B.   A.

Panzer Unit	Pz. I	Pz. II	Pz. III	Pz. IV	Pz. Bef.
35th Pz. Rgt.	99	64	0	6	8
36th Pz. Rgt.	84	66	0	6	8

During the Polish campaign, a low visibility cross was created by painting it completely yellow or painting the centre yellow and leaving a white border.

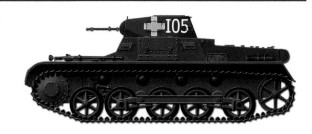

▲ **Panzerkampfwagen I Ausf B (Sd Kfz 101)**

Pz. Rgt 35 / A Battalion / Stabskompanie / Light Platoon / tank number 5

This vehicle participated in the battle of Bzura, 16 September 1939.

Specifications

Crew: 2	Engine: Maybach NL38TR
Weight: 6.4 tonnes (5.8 tons)	Speed: 40km/hr (24.9mph)
Length: 4.42m (14.5ft)	Range: 170km (105.6 miles)
Width: 2.06m (6.8ft)	Radio: FuG2
Height: 1.72m (5.6ft)	

▶ **Panzerbefehlswagen III Ausf D1 (Sd Kfz 267-268)**

Pz. Rgt 36 / B Battalion / Stabskompanie / Signal Platoon

Thirty Ausf D1 tanks were produced between June 1938 and March 1939. The turret was bolted into place, and a dummy gun was fitted to make this command tank look like a standard gun tank.

Specifications

Crew: 5	Engine: Maybach HL 108TR
Weight: 20 tonnes (18.2 tons)	Speed: 40km/hr (24.9mph)
Length: 5.98m (19.6ft)	Range: 165km (102.5 miles)
Width: 2.87m (9.4ft)	Radio: FuG6 plus FuG7 or FuG8
Height: 2.42m (7.9ft)	

▶ **Panzerkampfwagen II Ausf B (Sd Kfz 121)**

Pz. Rgt 35 / I Battalion / 1st Company / 4th Zug / tank number 5

This early Panzer II was one of 50 Panzers destroyed during the fight for Warsaw.

Specifications

Crew: 3	Engine: Maybach HL62TR
Weight: 8.7 tonnes (7.9 tons)	Speed: 40km/hr (24.9mph)
Length: 4.76m (15.6ft)	Range: 200km (124.3 miles)
Width: 2.14m (7ft)	Radio: FuG5
Height: 1.96m (6.4ft)	

⌀ *Fall Gelb*: the French campaign
10 MAY 1940

Following the conquest of Poland, 4th Panzer Division returned to Germany. Based in the Niederrhein, it formed part of 6th Army's reserve in Army Group B.

IN MAY 1940, 4TH PANZER remained with General Hoeppner's XVI *Panzerkorps*, which was taking up positions on the Belgian/Dutch border. Together with 3rd Panzer, the Division would provide the

Panzer Unit	Pz. I	Pz. II	Pz. III	Pz. IV	Pz. Bef.
35th Pz. Rgt.	69	50	20	12	5
36th Pz. Rgt.	66	55	20	12	5

armoured punch for von Bock's Army Group B attacking Holland and Belgium. Serving as a 'Matador's cape' to draw the attention of the Anglo-French High Command, the Panzers attacked towards Brussels and Liege. The plan worked perfectly. As the Allies rushed into Belgium, the main German attack erupted out of the Ardennes.

Following Dunkirk, 4th Panzer was redeployed with all the rest of Germany's armour along the line of the Somme. Launching the battle for France on 5 June, the Division advanced through the centre of the country, reaching as far south as Grenoble in the Alps by the time the Armistice was signed at Compiègne on 22 June.

Following the victory, 4th Panzer remained on occupation duties in France until March 1941.

ORGANIZATION

Specifications

Crew: 2	Engine: Maybach NL38TR
Weight: 6.4 tonnes (5.8 tons)	Speed: 40km/hr (24.9mph)
Length: 4.42m (14.5ft)	Range: 170km (105.6 miles)
Width: 2.06m (6.8ft)	Radio: FuG2
Height: 1.72m (5.6ft)	

▲ **Panzerkampfwagen I Ausf B (Sd Kfz 101)**

Pz. Rgt 36 / I Battalion / 1st Company / 3rd Zug / tank number 3

The Pz.Kpfw I Ausf B mounted two 7.92mm (0.3in) MG13 machine guns for which it carried 2250 rounds of ammunition. The small dot after the turret number was an identification mark carried by Panzer Regiment 36 vehicles.

▶ **Panzerbefehlswagen III Ausf E (Sd Kfz 266-267-268)**

Pz. Rgt 36 / Regimental Staff Company / HQ tank of Hptm Jesse

'RN1' stands for *Regiment Nachrichten-1* (Regimental Signal Platoon – 1). The German National Flag draped across the command radio antenna supplemented the white rectangular air recognition sign painted on the engine deck.

Specifications

Crew: 5	Engine: Maybach HL120TR
Weight: 21.5 tonnes (19.5 tons)	Speed: 40km/hr (24.9mph)
Length: 5.38m (17.7ft)	Range: 165km (102.5 miles)
Width: 2.91m (9.5ft)	Radio: FuG6 plus FuG2 or FuG7 or
Height: 2.44m (8ft)	FuG8

▶ **Panzerkampfwagen III Ausf F (Sd Kfz 141)**

Pz. Rgt 36 / I Battalion / 1st Company / 5th Zug / tank number 6

The Ausf F model of the Panzer III was armed with a 3.7cm (1.5in) KwK L/46.5 cannon. This was ineffective against tanks like the French Somua and the Char D2, since at combat ranges most of the shots just bounced off the enemy armour.

Specifications

Crew: 5	Engine: Maybach HL120TR
Weight: 21.8 tonnes (19.8 tons)	Speed: 40km/hr (24.9mph)
Length: 5.38m (17.7ft)	Range: 165km (102.5 miles)
Width: 2.91m (9.5ft)	Radio: FuG5
Height: 2.44m (8ft)	

▶ **Panzerkampfwagen III als Tauchpanzer**

Pz. Rgt 35 / I Battalion / 2nd Company / 2nd Zug / tank number 1

In preparation for the planned invasion of England, 168 tanks were
converted into 'diving tanks' to operate in up to 15m (49.2ft) of water.
This tank belonged to the 3rd Panzer Division before it was transferred.

Specifications

Crew: 5

Weight: 21.8 tonnes (19.8 tons)

Length: 5.38m (17.7ft)

Width: 2.91m (9.5ft)

Height: 2.44m (8ft)

Engine: Maybach HL120TR

Speed: 40km/hr (24.9mph)

Range: 165km (102.5 miles)

Radio: FuG5

▶ **Kleiner Panzerbefehlswagen (Sd Kfz 265)**

Unknown formation

Although not an official variant, the Sd Kfz 265 command tank was pressed into service as an armoured
ambulance, room for casualties being made by removing the command radios.

Specifications

Crew: 2/3

Weight: 6.5 tonnes (5.9 tons)

Length: 4.42m (14.5ft)

Width: 2.06m (6.8ft)

Height: 1.99m (6.5ft)

Engine: Maybach NL38TR

Speed: 40km/hr (24.9mph)

Range: 170km (105.6 miles)

Radio: None, or FuG2

Barbarossa: the attack on Russia
22 JUNE 1941

In this period, the 36th Regiment was detached to form the core of the 14th Panzer Division.

IN APRIL 1941, THE DIVISION was sent from
occupation duties in France to refit in reserve with
Army Group B in East Prussia. In June 1941, it was
returned to combat status with XXIV *Panzerkorps*.
This formed part of Guderian's *Panzergruppe* 2, the
tank army that was to lead Army Group Centre's
drive into the
Soviet Union.
After smashing
through the Red
Army at Gomel
and Smolensk,
Guderian's
panzers were
diverted to assist
Army Group

Panzer Unit	Pz. II	Pz. III(37)	Pz. III(50)	Pz. IV	Pz. Bef.
35th Pz. Rgt.	44	31	74	20	8

South at Kiev. In the largest battle of encirclement in
history, more than half a million Soviet soldiers were
taken prisoner.

When the advance towards Moscow resumed at
the end of September, 4th Panzer led Guderian's
Panzergruppe, reaching Orel on 3 October after
driving through 200 km (124.3 miles) of woodlands
in two days. However, as autumn set in, the road
towards Tula turned to a river of mud, which froze as
winter arrived. In December, in an assault on Tula,
4th Panzer reached the outskirts of the city, but was
forced to pull back by new Soviet counterattacks.

ORGANIZATION

Pz. Rgt. 35

I

II. | I.

St | St

m | l | l | l | m | l | l | l

Specifications

Crew: 3	Engine: Maybach HL62TR
Weight: 9.8 tonnes (8.9 tons)	Speed: 40km/hr (24.9mph)
Length: 4.81m (15.8ft)	Range: 200km (124.3 miles)
Width: 2.22m (7.3ft)	Radio: FuG5
Height: 1.99m (6.5ft)	

▲ **Panzerkampfwagen II Ausf B (Sd Kfz 121)**

Pz. Rgt 35 / I Battalion / Stabskompanie / Light Platoon / tank number 6

The Panzer II's 2cm (0.8in) *Panzergranate* (armour-piercing) round was ineffective against Russian armour. Crews usually loaded *Sprenggranate* (high-explosive fragmentation) shells, which were very effective against live targets and soft-skin vehicles. This particular tank had a memorial inscription in honour of Frank Lott, a crewman killed in action, painted in the turret.

Fall Blau: the Eastern front
28 JUNE 1942

A Panzer battalion from the Division was renamed 3/15th Panzer Regiment and was sent to re-inforce the 11th Panzer Division.

THE SOVIET COUNTEROFFENSIVES around Moscow were mounted by fresh troops from Siberia, with full winter equipment and training. Already suffering from the harsh conditions for which they were not prepared, 2nd *Panzerarmee* was forced back towards Orel. The Soviet offensives continued through the winter, but lost momentum by the end of March.

The German High Command decided that the *Wehrmacht*'s 1942 summer offensive would take place in the south, pushing towards the Volga and the Caucasus oil fields. The 4th Panzer Division was to play no part in it, remaining with 2nd *Panzerarmee* on the Orel Front for the next 18 months.

ORGANIZATION

Pz. Rgt. 35 | I

II. | St

m | I | I | I

Panzer Unit	Pz. II	Pz. III	Pz. IV	Pz. Bef.
35th Pz. Rgt.	13	28	5	2

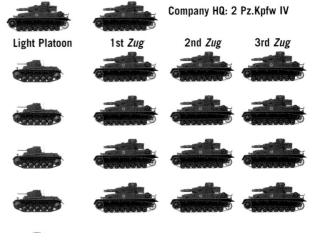

Company HQ: 2 Pz.Kpfw IV

Light Platoon   **1st *Zug***   **2nd *Zug***   **3rd *Zug***

Mittlerer Panzerkompanie K.St.N.1175

The standard organization of a Panzer division at the outbreak of war in 1939 included two Panzer regiments operating as a Panzer brigade. Combat operations showed the brigade to be slightly unwieldy, and by the end of 1941 most Panzer divisions had a single Panzer regiment. This was divided into two or three battalions, each consisting of a staff company, a medium company and two or three light companies. All Panzer companies had a light platoon with five Panzer IIs: the other platoons of the light companies operated with five Panzer IIIs, while the medium company had three platoons of four Panzer IVs, as illustrated here.

The last summer offensive
1 July 1943

The 35th Panzer Regiment was reinforced in February 1943, when the independent 700th *Panzer Verband* was disbanded and its remnants were absorbed into the 4th Panzer Division.

THE 4TH PANZER DIVISION played a supporting role in the great battle at Kursk in July 1943. The 2nd *Panzerarmee* was supposed to guard the flank of Model's 9th Army, but was attacked itself by Soviet forces bursting out from the Kursk salient.

After Kursk, the German armies in the East were on the defensive. 4th Panzer remained with Army Group Centre for the next year, being driven back through Desna, Gomel and the Pripjet Marshes. In May 1944, it was moved to Army Group North in the Ukraine for refitting – which meant that it avoided the annihilation of Army Group Centre in June 1944. In July 1944, the Division was sent northwards as the High Command tried to stabilize the line. From August 1944, it saw combat in the Baltic states, being forced out of Latvia and Lithuania in October. It fought in the Courland pocket until January 1945, eventually retreating to West Prussia, where it surrendered to the Red Army.

ORGANIZATION

Pz. Rgt. 35

I

I.

St

m m m m

Panzer Unit	Pz. III	Pz. IV(kz)	Pz. IV(lg)	Pz. Bef
35th Pz. Rgt.	15	1	79	6

▶ **Panzerfunkwagen (Sd Kfz 263) 8-Rad**

79th Nachrichten Abteilung (Signal Battalion)

The Sd Kfz 263 was an extremely capable communications vehicle issued to the signal battalions of both motorized and Panzer divisions, as well as being used to provide mobile signal capacity to corps and army headquarters.

Specifications

Crew: 5

Weight: 8.9 tonnes (8.1 tons)

Length: 5.85m (19.2ft)

Width: 2.2m (7.2ft)

Height: 2.9m (9.5ft)

Engine: Büssing-NAG L8V

Speed: 100km/hr (62.1mph)

Range: 300km (186.4 miles)

Radio: 1 Sätz Funkgerät für (m) Pz Funktruppe b

▶ **Panzerkampfwagen II Ausf L (Sd Kfz 123)**

4th Reconnaissance Battalion / 2nd Company (Luchs)

100 of the redesigned Pz.Kpfw II Ausf L Luchs, or 'Lynx', were built between September 1943 and January 1944. 4th Panzer was one of two units to receive a full company. In October 1943, the division reported 27 'Lynx' ready for combat.

Specifications

Crew: 4

Weight: 14.3 tonnes (13 tons)

Length: 4.63m (15.2ft)

Width: 2.48m (8.1ft)

Height: 2.21m (7.3ft)

Engine: Maybach HL66P

Speed: 60km/hr (37.3mph)

Range: 290km (180.2 miles)

Radio: FuG12 plus FuG Spr a

▶ Panzerkampfwagen IV Ausf G (Sd Kfz 161/1 und 161/2)
Pz. Rgt 35 / I Battalion

After the abortive German offensive at Kursk, the 4th
Panzer Division was involved in a series of very costly
defensive battles protecting the retreat of Army Group Centre.

Specifications
Crew: 5	Engine: Maybach HL120TRM
Weight: 25.9 tonnes (23.5 tons)	Speed: 40km/hr (24.9mph)
Length: 6.62m (21.7ft)	Range: 210km (130.5 miles)
Width: 2.88m (9.4ft)	Radio: FuG5
Height: 2.68m (8.8ft)	

▶ Panzerkampfwagen II Ausf L (Sd Kfz 123)
4th Reconnaissance Battalion / 2nd Company (Luchs)

Based on the Panzer II but with a completely new suspension and a new, larger
turret, the Luchs also had a wider hull and tracks.

Armament Specifications
Main gun: 2cm (0.8in) KwK38 L/55	Secondary armament: 7.92mm (0.3in) MG 34
Ammunition: 330 rounds	Ammunition: 2250 rounds
Turret traverse: 360° (manual)	Sights: KgZF2
Elevation: -9° to +18°	
Sights: TZF6/38	

▶ Schwerer Panzerspähwagen (7.5cm) (Sd Kfz 233)
4th Reconnaissance Battalion / 3rd Armoured Car Company

A late version of the Sd Kfz 233, this has 30mm (1.2in) frontal armour. A
six-sided armour shield protected the short-barrelled 7.5cm (3in) gun.

Specifications
Crew: 3	Engine: Büssing-NAG L8V
Weight: 9.6 tonnes (8.7 tons)	Speed: 80km/hr (49.7mph)
Length: 5.85m (19.2ft)	Range: 300km (186.4 miles)
Width: 2.2m (7.2ft)	Radio: FuG Spr Ger 'a'
Height: 2.25m (7.4ft)	

▶ Leichter Schützenpanzerwagen (3.7cm PaK) (Sd Kfz 250/10)
4th Reconnaissance Battalion

The Sd Kfz 250/10 provided heavy support fire for reconnaissance units. The
obsolete 3.7cm (1.5in) PaK36 was not highly regarded: it was nicknamed the 'door
knocker', because of its inability to penetrate the armour of Soviet tanks.

Specifications
Crew: 4	Engine: Maybach KL42TRKM
Weight: 6.3 tonnes (5.67 tons)	Speed: 60km/hr (37.3mph)
Length: 4.56m (15ft)	Range: 320km (198.8 miles)
Width: 1.95m (6.4ft)	Radio: FuG Spr Ger 1
Height: 1.97m (6.5ft)	

▶ 7.5cm PaK40/2 auf Fahrgestell Panzerkampfwagen II (Sf) (Sd Kfz 131)

49th Panzerjäger Battalion

The Marder II was a tank hunter that mounted a powerful antitank
gun on a modified Panzer II chassis. Six kill rings are painted on the barrel of this example.

Specifications

Crew: 3	Engine: Maybach HL62TRM
Weight: 11.9 tonnes (10.8 tons)	Speed: 40km/hr (24.9mph)
Length: 6.36m (20.9ft)	Range: 190km (118 miles)
Width: 2.28m (7.5ft)	Radio: FuG Spr 'd'
Height: 2.2m (7.2ft)	

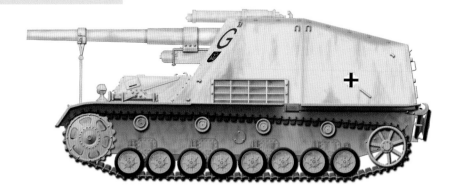

Specifications

Crew: 6
Weight: 26.5 tonnes (24 tons)
Length: 7.17m (23.5ft)
Width: 2.97m (9.7ft)
Height: 2.81m (9.2ft)
Engine: HL120TRM
Speed: 42km/hr (26mph)
Range: 215km (133.6 miles)
Radio: FuG Spr 1

▲ 15cm Schwere Panzerhaubitze auf Fahrgestell Panzerkampfwagen III/IV (Sf) (Sd Kfz 165)

103rd Panzer Artillery Regiment / 3rd (mot) Battalion

The SdKfz 165 first saw action at Kursk in 1943. This example belongs to one of the two heavy batteries assigned to the 4th Panzer Division's Artillery Regiment.

▶ Mittlerer Kommandopanzerwagen Ausf B (Sd Kfz 251/6)

4th Panzer Division / Division Staff / command vehicle of Gen Lt Deitrich von Saucken

The SdKfz 251/6 was a command and control vehicle for senior officers. It carried the same radios as
the similar 251/3, but its equipment fit also included the 'Enigma' cryptographic machine.

Specifications

Crew: 8	Engine: Maybach HL42TUKRM
Weight: 9.4 tonnes (8.5 tons)	Speed: 53km/hr (32.9mph)
Length: 5.98m (19.6ft)	Range: 300km (186.4 miles)
Width: 2.1m (6.9ft)	Radio: FuG11 plus FuG Tr 100W;
Height: 1.75m (5.7ft)	later FuG19 plus FuG12

▶ Mittlerer Schützenpanzerwagen Ausf C (Sd Kfz 251/1)

12th Panzergrenadier Regiment

Kurland, 1944. The Sd Kfz 251/1 crew consisted of a driver, co-driver and a 10-man grenadier squad.

Specifications

Crew: 2 plus 10 infrantrymen	Engine: Maybach HL42TUKRM
Weight: 8.8 tonnes (8 tons)	Speed: 53km/hr (32.9mph)
Length: 5.98m (19.6ft)	Range: 300km (186.4 miles)
Width: 2.1m (6.9ft)	Radio: FuG Spr Ger 1
Height: 1.75m (5.7ft)	

▶ Panzerkampfwagen V Ausf A (Sd Kfz 171)

Pz. Rgt 35 / I Battalion / 1st Company / 1st Zug / tank number 3

In June 1944, the Division was reinforced with a Panther *Abteilung* of 79 tanks. The old 1st Battalion, equipped with Pz.Kpfw IVs, was renamed the 2nd Battalion while the Panther unit became the 1st Battalion.

Specifications

Crew: 5	Height: 2.98m (9.8ft)
Weight: 49.4 tonnes	Engine: Maybach HL230P30
(44.8 tons)	Speed: 46km/hr (28.6mph)
Length: 8.86m (29ft)	Range: 200km (124.3 miles)
Width: 3.42m (11.2ft)	Radio: FuG5

▶ Panzerkampfwagen IV Ausf H (Sd Kfz 161/2)

Pz. Rgt 35 / II Battalion / 5th Company / Company HQ tank

In July 1944, 4th Panzer was sent to the Warsaw area where it clashed with the Soviet 2nd Tank Army.

Specifications

Crew: 5	Engine: Maybach HL120TRM
Weight: 27.6 tonnes (25 tons)	Speed: 38km/hr (23.6mph)
Length: 7.02m (23ft)	Range: 210km (130.5 miles)
Width: 2.88m (9.4ft)	Radio: FuG5
Height: 2.68m (8.8ft)	

▼ Schützenpanzerwagen I Ausf D (Sd Kfz 251/3)

33rd Panzergrenadier / Regimental Staff Company

By the end of 4 July, Panzer Division had been divided into two *kampfgruppen*.

Black and green are the colours of the *Panzergrenadiers.*

Specifications

Crew: 8	Engine: Maybach HL42TUKRM
Weight: 9.4 tonnes (8.5 tons)	Speed: 53km/hr (32.9mph)
Length: 5.98m (19.6ft)	Range: 300km (186.4 miles)
Width: 2.1m (6.9ft)	Radio: Various, depending upon
Height: 1.75m (5.7ft)	mission

◀ Leichter Panzerspähwagen (2cm) (Sd Kfz 222)

Kampfgruppe Christen / 4th Reconnaissance Battalion

The 4th Panzer Division fought back through the Baltic states in the last months of the war. The division surrendered to the Soviets in West Prussia in April 1945.

Specifications

Crew: 3

Weight: 5.3 tonnes (4.8 tons)

Length: 4.8m (15.7ft)

Width: 1.95m (6.4ft)

Height: 2m (6.6ft)

Engine: Horch 3.5 or 3.8

Speed: 85km/hr (52.8mph)

Range: 300km (186.4 miles)

Radio: FuG Spr Ger 'a'

5th Panzer Division

The 5th Panzer Division came into being on 24 November 1938, two weeks after 4th Panzer Division was set up. Its first commander was *Generalleutnant* Heinrich von Viettinghoff-Scheel.

THE MAIN COMPONENTS of the 5th Panzer Division, which was established at Oppeln (now Opole in Poland), included the 5th *Schützen* Brigade, which provided the motorized infantry strength, and the 8th Panzer Brigade, which included the 31st and 15th Panzer Regiments. Each regiment had two battalions, consisting of an armoured signals platoon, a staff platoon with light tanks, three light Panzer companies, one motorized infantry platoon, one supply unit and a maintenance company.

Commanders

Generaloberst H. Viettinghoff-Scheel
(1 Sept 1939 – 8 Oct 1939)

Generalleutnant M. Hartlieb-Walsporn
(8 Oct 1939 – 29 May 1940)

General der Panzertruppen J. Lemelsen
(29 May 1940 – 25 Nov 1940)

General der Panzertruppen G. Fehn
(25 Nov 1940 – 10 Aug 1942)

Generalleutnant E. Metz
(10 Aug 1942 – 1 Feb 1943)

Generalmajor J. Nedtwig
(1 Feb 1943 – 20 June 1943)

Generalleutnant E. Fackenstedt
(20 June 1943 – 7 Sept 1943)

General der Panzertruppen K. Decker
(7 Sept 1943 – 15 Oct 1944)

Generalmajor R. Lippert
(16 Oct 1944 – 5 Feb 1945)

Generalmajor G. Hoffmann-Schonborn
(5 Feb 1945 – Apr 1945)

Oberst der Reserve H. Herzog
(Apr 1945 – 8 May 1945)

INSIGNIA

 Standard tactical symbol used by the 5th Panzer Division in 1940, following on from the first four panzer divisions.

 From 1941, 5th Panzer Division changed its tactical symbol to a cross. It would continue to use the symbol until 1945.

 Variants of standard tactical symbols were often used. In this instance, the 5th Panzer cross is painted onto a black panel.

 Additional insignia painted onto vehicles of the 31st Panzer Regiment, 5th Panzer Division, in 1941 and 1942

⅄₀ *Fall Weiss*: the invasion of Poland
1 SEPTEMBER 1939

Although it had been in existence for less than a year, the 5th Panzer Division was ready for action when German forces invaded Poland on 1 September 1939.

ATTACKING OUT OF SILESIA, the 5th Panzer Division formed part of VIII *Panzerkorps* in General List's 14th Army. Controlled by von Rundstedt's Army Group South, the mission of the corps was to defeat the Polish armies on the Vistula, before driving towards Warsaw and Brest Litovsk.

The mobile forces of 14th Army, made up from two *Panzerkorps*, formed the southern prong of the massive, fast-moving pincer movement that was to meet Guderian's panzers at Brest-Litovsk and which sealed the fate of Poland.

ORGANIZATION

Pz. Rgt. 31 / I
II. / I   I. / I
I / I   I / I

Pz. Rgt. 15 / I
II. / I   I. / I
I / I   I / I

Panzer Unit	Pz. I	Pz. II	Pz. III	Pz. IV	Pz. Bef.
15th Pz. Rgt.	72	81	3	8	11
31st Pz. Rgt.	80	63	0	6	11

▲ **Panzerkampfwagen II Ausf C (Sd Kfz 121)**

Unknown formation

The 5th Panzer Division used a two-digit tactical number system (platoon and tank number) during the invasion of Poland. Their tanks were recognizable by the use of a yellow tank rhomboid painted on the turret sides.

Specifications

Crew: 3
Weight: 9.8 tonnes (8.9 tons)
Length: 4.81m (15.8ft)
Width: 2.22m (7.3ft)
Height: 1.99m (6.5ft)
Engine: Maybach HL62TR
Speed: 40km/hr (24.9mph)
Range: 200km (124.3 miles)
Radio: FuG5

▲ **Panzerkampfwagen I Ausf B (Sd Kfz 101)**

Unknown formation

In combat, the Pz.Kpfw I's task was to conduct reconnaissance. It was also used to protect the flanks of an advance from enemy infantry. This particular vehicle was knocked out at Pszczyna, fighting the 6th Polish Infantry Division.

Specifications

Crew: 2
Weight: 60.4 tonnes (5.8 tons)
Length: 4.42m (14.5ft)
Width: 2.06m (6.8ft)
Height: 1.72m (5.6ft)
Engine: Maybach NL38TR
Speed: 40km/hr (24.9mph)
Range: 170km (105.6 miles)
Radio: FuG2

▶ **Panzerkampfwagen IV Ausf B (Sd Kfz 161)**

Unknown formation

Small numbers of the Pz.Kpfw IV Ausf B reached service in time for the Polish campaign. They were issued to the 4th *Zugen* of *Leichte Panzerkompanies*.

Specifications

Crew: 5
Weight: 20.7 tonnes (18.8 tons)
Length: 5.92m (19.4ft)
Width: 2.83m (9.3ft)
Height: 2.68m (8.8ft)

Engine: Maybach HL120TR
Speed: 40km/hr (24.9mph)
Range: 200km (124.3 miles)
Radio: FuG5

Fall Gelb: the French campaign
10 MAY 1940

The 5th Panzer Division was withdrawn from Poland in December 1939.

Panzer Unit	Pz. I	Pz. II	Pz. III	Pz. IV	Pz. Bef.
15th Pz. Rgt.	51	61	24	16	15
31st Pz. Rgt.	46	59	28	16	11

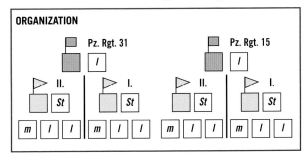

ORGANIZATION

Pz. Rgt. 31   I

Pz. Rgt. 15   I

II. St   I. St   II. St   I. St

m l l   m l l   m l l   m l l

THE DIVISION MOVED towards the Ardennes in April 1940, where it formed part of General Herman Hoth's XV *Panzerkorps*. Crossing the Meuse at Dinant with Rommel's 7th Panzer Division, it was part of the tank force that swept towards the coast, cutting off the Allied armies at Dunkirk.

▶ Panzerkampfwagen IV Ausf D (Sd Kfz 161)

4th Panzer Division, 1940

The Ausf D variant of the Pz.Kpfw IV was introduced in October 1939. The main improvements over earlier variants were the provision of thicker armour and the fitting of an external mantlet or gun shield for the 7.5cm (3in) KwK. Some 229 examples of this model were produced between October 1939 and May 1941.

Specifications

Crew: 5

Weight: 22 tonnes (20 tons)

Length: 5.92m (19.4ft)

Width: 2.84m (9.3ft)

Height: 2.68m (8.8ft)

Engine: Maybach HL120TRM

Speed: 40km/hr (24.9mph)

Range: 200km (124.3 miles)

Radio: FuG5

✕ War in the Balkans
6 APRIL 1941

Early in 1941, 5th Panzer Division was transferred to Field Marshal List's 12th Army in Romania and Bulgaria. The Division played a key part in Germany's conquest of the Balkans.

CROSSING THE YUGOSLAV BORDER on 6 April, the 5th Panzer Division drove towards Skopje as part of *Panzergruppe* Kleist before turning northwards to seize Nis in company with the 11th Panzer Division. By 17 April, the Germans had captured Belgrade, and the Yugoslav government was forced to surrender.

Turning southwards, 5th Panzer drove through the centre of Greece. After passing through Lamia, the Division encountered a stubborn British rearguard on the ancient battlefield of Thermopylae. Forced to

attack in single file, the division lost 20 Panzers in quick succession, and the delay allowed the British to withdraw safely.

Chasing the retreating British southwards, 5th Panzer crossed the Corinth canal on 28 April. The panzers headed for the beaches at Kalamata where an evacuation was taking place, and after a vicious fight captured the last 7000 British soldiers on the beach.

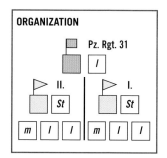

ORGANIZATION

Pz. Rgt. 31

Panzer Unit	Pz. I	Pz. II	Pz. III	Pz. IV	Pz. Bef.
31st Pz. Rgt.	9	40	51	16	5

▶ Panzerkampfwagen III Ausf E (Sd Kfz 141)

Pz. Rgt 31 / I Battalion / 1st Company / 2nd Zug / tank number 3

Nineteen Pz.Kpfw III armed with the 3.7cm (1.5in) cannon were listed operational at the time of 5th Panzer's attack through the centre of Greece.

Specifications

Crew: 5

Weight: 21.5 tonnes (19.5 tons)

Length: 5.38m (17.7ft)

Width: 2.91m (9.5ft)

Height: 2.44m (8ft)

Engine: Maybach HL120TR

Speed: 40km/hr (24.9mph)

Range: 165km (102.5 miles)

Radio: FuG5

▶ Panzerkampfwagen IV Ausf F (Sd Kfz 161)

Pz. Rgt 31 / I Battalion / 4th Company / 5th Zug / tank number 1

The rapid German attack in the Balkans eventually forced the Greeks to surrender, while the British fought a series of stubborn rearguard actions.

Specifications

Crew: 5	Engine: Maybach HL120TRM
Weight: 24.6 tonnes (22.3 tons)	Speed: 42km/hr (26mph)
Length: 5.92m (19.4ft)	Range: 200km (124.3 miles)
Width: 2.84m (9.3ft)	Radio: FuG5
Height: 2.68m (8.8ft)	

▶ Schwere Panzerspähwagen (Fu) 8-rad (Sd Kfz 232)

Unknown unit

The SdKfz 232 had driving controls at both front and rear, allowing for rapid manoeuvring of the vehicle in reverse.

Specifications

Crew: 4	Engine: Büssing-NAG L8V
Weight: 9.1 tonnes (8.3 tons)	Speed: 85km/hr (52.8mph)
Length: 5.85m (19.2ft)	Range: 300km (186.4 miles)
Width: 2.2m (7.2ft)	Radio: FuG12 plus
Height (no aerial): 2.35m (7.7ft)	fuG Spr Ger 'a'

The 704th was the last of the six *Infanteriegeschütz Abteilung* to still be listed in service in 1943.

Specifications

Crew: 4	Engine: Maybach NL38TR
Weight: 9.4 tonnes (8.5 tons)	Speed: 40km/hr (24.9mph)
Length: 4.67m (15.3ft)	Range: 140km (87 miles)
Width: 2.06m (6.8ft)	Armament: One 15cm (6in) sIG33 L/11
Height: 2.8m (9.2ft)	

▲ 15cm sIG33 (Sf) auf Panzerkampfwagen I Ausf B

704th Schwere Infanteriegeschütz Abteilung

The 15cm (6in) sIG howitzer could be dismounted and used as towed artillery.

▶ Mittlerer Schützenpanzerwagen I Ausf B (Sd Kfz 251/1)

5th Schützen Regiment / II Battalion / 9th Company

The Sd Kfz 251/1 Ausf B eliminated the vision ports in the side of the vehicle. Early vehicles like this had unprotected machine gun mounts; armoured shields would become standard in new models, and were retrofitted to earlier variants.

Specifications

Crew: 2 plus 12 troops	2.16m (7ft) with MG shield
Weight: 9.9 tonnes (9 tons)	Engine: Maybach HL42TUKRM
Length: 5.98m (19.6ft)	Speed: 53km/hr (32.9mph)
Width: 2.1m (6.9ft)	Range: 300km (186.4 miles)
Height : 1.75m (5.7ft) or	Radio: FuG Spr Ger f

▶ Panzerkampfwagen III Ausf J (Sd Kfz 141)

Pz. Rgt 31

The 5th Panzer Division was expecting to join the *Afrika Korps* in 1941. Its tanks had already been painted in desert colours when orders came to proceed immediately to Russia to compensate for the heavy losses in Panzers experienced by the *Wehrmacht*. The crew of this tank had added an improvised stowage rack on the tailplate.

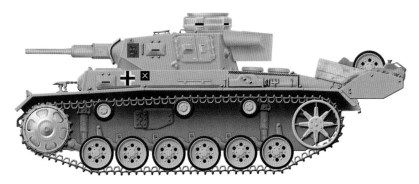

Specifications

Crew: 5

Weight: 24 tonnes (21.5 tons)

Length: 6.28m (20.6ft)

Width: 2.95m (9.7ft)

Height: 2.5m (8.2ft)

Engine: Maybach HL120TRM

Speed: 40km/hr (24.9mph)

Range: 155km (96.3 miles)

Radio: FuG5

▶ Panzerkampfwagen III Ausf J (Sd Kfz 141)

Pz. Rgt 31

By December 1941, 5th Panzer was with Army Group Centre advancing towards Moscow. Like the rest of the *Wehrmacht*, its tank crews were ill-prepared for freezing temperatures and atrocious weather.

Weapons Specifications

Main Gun: 5cm (2in) KwK39 L/60	Co-axial MG: 7.92mm (0.3in) MG 34
Ammunition: 92 rounds	Hull MG: 7.92mm (0.3in) MG34
Traverse: 360° (manual)	Ammunition: 4950 rounds Patr
Elevation: -10° to +20°	SmK
Sight: TZF5e	MG sight: KgZF2

▶ Panzerkampfwagen III Ausf J (Sd Kfz 141)

Pz. Rgt 31

The Germans were unprepared for the Russian winter. Tanks and weapons froze, while winter clothing was in short supply. Even white paint was lacking: this tank has an improvised disruptive camouflage scheme using broad stripes of lime whitewash.

Armour Thickness

Turret: 57mm (2.2in) front, 30mm
(1.2in) side, rear 30mm (1.2in),
top 10mm (0.4in)
Superstructure: 50–70mm (2–2.8in)
front, 30mm (1.2in) side; 50mm

(2in) rear
Hull: 50mm (2in) front, 30mm (1.2in)
side, 50mm (2in) rear, 16mm
(0.6in) bottom
Mantlet: 50–70mm (2–2.8in)

▶ **Panzerkampfwagen III Ausf F (Sd Kfz 141)**

Pz. Rgt 31 / I Battalion / 3rd Company / 2nd Zug / tank number 1

The last 100 Pz.Kpfw III Ausf F had the 50mm (2in) KwK L/42 cannon, in place of the 37mm (1.5in) KwK L/46.5 . The 'Rommel Kit' stowage box, standard from the Ausf G onwards, was a retro-fit to this vehicle.

Specifications

Crew: 5	Engine: Maybach HL120TRM
Weight: 21.8 tonnes (19.8 tons)	Speed: 40km/hr (24.9mph)
Length: 5.38m (17.7ft)	Range: 165km (102.5 miles)
Width: 2.91m (9.5ft)	Radio: FuG5
Height: 2.44m (8ft)	

 # *Fall Blau*: the Eastern Front

28 JUNE 1942

The 5th Panzer Division arrived on the Eastern Front just in time for Army Group Centre's unsuccessful drive on Moscow.

AFTER THE RETREAT from Moscow, 5th Panzer remained with 4th *Panzerarmee* around Gshatsk until May. In the summer of 1942, it was transferred to the control of 9th Army, taking part in the series of battles around Rshev. It remained in the region until the winter, when it was transferred to 3rd *Panzerarmee* at Vyasma.

In 1942, Army Group Centre, while far from being a sideshow, was no longer the main area of German operations. The High Command's attention was primarily on the Summer Offensive in the South, *Fall Blau*, and on the bid to seize Leningrad. Ordered to hold its positions, Army Group Centre spent most of 1942 trying to pinch off strips of Soviet-held territory which were interspersed with German fortified areas, or 'Hedgehogs'.

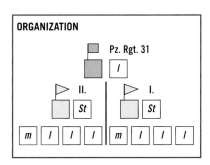

Panzer Unit	Pz. II	Pz. III(kz)	Pz. IV(kz)	Pz. Bef.
31st Pz. Rgt.	26	55	13	9

▶ **Panzerbefehlswagen III Ausf E (Sd Kfz 266-267-268)**

Pz. Rgt 31 / I Battalion / Stabskompanie / Signal Platoon / tank number 2

The Russians became adept in locating and knocking out command tanks, which were easy to recognize by their frame antennae. As a result, Panzer commanders were forced to travel in normal Panzers, with signal officers riding in a second tank close by.

Specifications

Crew: 5	Engine: Maybach HL120TRM
Weight: 21.5 tonnes (19.5 tons)	Speed: 40km/hr (24.9mph)
Length: 5.38m (17.7ft)	Range: 185km (115 miles)
Width: 2.91m (9.5ft)	Radio: FuG6 plus FuG 2 (266) or
Height: 2.44m (8ft)	FuG 8 (267) or FuG7 (268)

The last offensive
1 JULY 1943

In the six months prior to the Battle of Kursk, the 5th Panzer Division had been involved in heavy fighting as part of Army Group Centre in Vyasma and Demjansk.

IN MARCH 1943, THE DIVISION was transferred to the 2nd *Panzerarmee* in the Orel sector. For the Kursk Offensive, the army was tasked with providing flank security to the attack by 9th Army, but it came under heavy Soviet attack and was forced to withdraw as the offensive was called off by Hitler.

Over the next year, 5th Panzer Division retreated through Bryansk, Gomel and the Pripjet Marshes to Poland, where it had started three years before. After surviving the massive Soviet offensives of 1944, it ended the war fighting in Latvia, in the Courland pocket and in East Prussia, where it finally surrendered to the Red Army in April 1945 near Danzig.

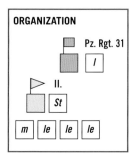

ORGANIZATION

Panzer Unit	Pz. II	Pz. III(75)	Pz. IV(lg)	Pz. Bef.
31st Pz. Rgt.	0	17	76	9

▶ **Leichter Panzerspähwagen (Fu) (Sd Kfz 261)**

77th Panzer Signal Battalion

The Sd Kfz 261 was identical to the Sd Kfz 223 light armoured car, except that it lacked a turret. The vehicle had an FuG10 radio capable of transmitting signals up to 40km (24.9 miles) using key or 10km (6.2 miles) using voice. A second set, the FuG Spr, was used for inter-vehicle communication.

Specifications

Crew: 4	Engine: Horch 3.5l or 3.8l
Weight: 4.7 tonnes (4.3 tons)	Speed: 85km/hr (52.8mph)
Length: 4.83m (15.8ft)	Range: 310km (192.6 miles)
Width: 1.99m (6.5ft)	Radio: FuG Spr Ger 'a' plus FuG7 or FuG12
Height: 1.78m (5.8ft)	

 The standard military map symbol for self-propelled artillery was used to identify Hummels of the 3rd Battalion, 103rd Panzer Artillery Regiment.

▼ **15cm (6in) Schwere Panzerhaubitze auf Fahrgestell Panzerkampfwagen III/IV (Sf) (Sd Kfz 165)**

116th Panzer Artillery Regiment / 1st (self-propelled) Battalion

The Hummel self-propelled howitzer was based on a modified Panzer IV hull.

Specifications

Crew: 6

Weight: 26.5 tonnes (24 tons)

Length: 7.17m (23.5ft)

Width: 2.97m (9.7ft)

Height: 2.81m (9.2ft)

Engine: HL120TRM

Speed: 42km/hr (26mph)

Range: 215km (133.6 miles)

Radio: FuG Spr 1

◀ Fiat-Ansaldo Carro Armato L 6/40

3rd Italian Armoured Battalion (Attached)

From November 1943 to September 1944, an Italian battalion was listed in the Division order of battle. The L6/40 was armed with one 2cm (0.8in) Breda cannon. Secondary armament consisted of one 8mm (0.3in) Breda machine gun.

Specifications

Crew: 2	Engine: SPA 18 D
Weight: 7.5 tonnes (6.8 tons)	Speed: 42km/hr (26mph)
Length: 3.78m (12.4ft)	Range: 200km (124.3 miles)
Width: 1.92m (6.3ft)	Radio: RF 1 CA
Height: 2.03m (6.7ft)	

This version of the National Insignia was standard between 1940 and 1945.

Specifications

Crew: 5

Weight: 50.2 tonnes (45.5 tons)

Length: 8.86 m (29ft)

Width: 3.4m (11.2ft)

Height: 2.98m (9.8ft)

Engine: Maybach HL230P30

Speed: 46km/hr (28.6mph)

Range: 200km (124.3 miles)

Radio: FuG5

▲ Panzerkampfwagen V Ausf G (Sd Kfz 171)

Pz. Rgt 31 / I Battalion / 1st Company / 3rd Zug / tank number 5

Although a superb tank, the complex and expensive Panther was built in much smaller numbers than the American M4 Sherman or the Soviet T-34, both of which were available in huge quantities.

▶ Panzerkampfwagen IV Ausf H (Sd Kfz 161/2)

Pz. Rgt 31 / II Battalion / 8th Company / 3rd Zug / tank number 1

This vehicle was in action in West Prussia in March 1945. A month later, the 5th Panzer Division surrendered to thc Soviets near Danzig.

Specifications

Crew: 5	Engine: Maybach HL120TRM
Weight: 27.6 tonnes (25 tons)	Speed: 38km/hr (23.6mph)
Length: 7.02m (23ft)	Range: 210km (130.5 miles)
Width: 2.88m (9.4ft)	Radio: FuG5
Height: 2.68m (8.8ft)	

Chapter 2

1939
Panzer Divisions

The initial growth of Germany's *Panzerwaffe*
came to a brief halt in the late 1930s. However, as war
loomed, even the most reactionary officers in the General
Staff realized that armoured formations were the way of the
future, and the expansion of the Panzer arm continued at an
even greater pace. The first new Panzer divisions were
formed in 1939 from the so-called '*Leichte*', or Light,
divisions, which had been created by the cavalry, and which
were now converted into fully-fledged armoured divisions.

◀ **Growth of the *Panzerwaffe***
Although powerful fighting vehicles like the Panzer IV were in service with the German Army by 1939, the
small tanks with which the *Panzerwaffe* had learned its trade served far longer than expected.

6th Panzer Division

The 6th Panzer Division was formed at Wuppertal in October 1939, by converting the 1st _Leichte Division,_ which had fought in the Polish campaign.

THE LIGHT DIVISIONS were a product of the internal politics of the _Wehrmacht._ For centuries, the cavalry had been the premier arm of the German Army, officered almost exclusively by aristocrats. Senior cavalrymen had been most vocal in their opposition to the Panzers, fearing that the new arm would detract from their own standing. That opposition had almost crippled the early _Panzerwaffe,_ since the cavalry insisted on controlling reconnaissance units. Similarly, the infantry controlled the _Schützen_ units, and the artillery controlled the guns of the early Panzer divisions.

In 1938, the _Wehrmacht_ underwent a major upheaval. Hitler dismissed the War Minister, General von Blomberg, and the Commander-in-Chief, General von Fritsch. The _Führer_ took direct control of the Armed Forces, and Hitler was a Panzer enthusiast.

Cavalry Panzers

Clearly, Panzers were the way of the future. The cavalrymen formed four _Leichte,_ or Light, Divisions. These were essentially motorized infantry units with four rifle battalions, to which was added a single tank battalion (which by the outbreak of war in 1939 had been increased to two battalions in a Panzer

▼ **Armoured Artillery**
As the war progressed, the Panzers were joined on the frontline by armoured and self-propelled artillery pieces and assault guns like the _Sturmgeschütz._

INSIGNIA

Standard tactical insignia used on vehicles of the 6th Panzer Division in 1940.

As more divisions formed, the similarity of the standard tactical symbols became confusing. 6th Panzer adopted this new insignia in 1941.

An additional tactical symbol applied to vehicles of the 6th Panzer Division during the advance on Moscow in 1941.

6th Panzer, June 1943. A completely new set of symbols were introduced for divisions taking part in the Battle of Kursk.

---

regiment). The rifle battalions were called _Kavallerieschützen,_ or Cavalry Rifle units. Finding tanks for these new units stretched Germany's limited tank-building capability. Some tanks were taken from those destined for new Panzer units, but more than half came from newly acquired Czech stocks.

As it crossed the Polish border on 1 September 1939, the 1st _Leichte_ Division, commanded by _Generalleutnant_ Friedrich-Wilhelm von Löper, had 65 Pz.Kpfw IIs, 41 Pz.KpfW IVs, 112 Czech-built Pz.Kpfw 35(t)s and eight Panzer 35 command tanks, for a total of 226 Panzers.

Commanders

General der Panzertruppen W. Kempf _(18 Oct 1939 – 6 Jan 1941)_	Generalleutnant R. Freiherr von Waldenfels _(21 Aug 1943 – 8 Feb 1944)_
Generalleutnant F. Landgraf _(6 Jan 1941 – June 1941)_	Generalleutnant W. Marcks _(8 Feb 1944 – 21 Feb 1944)_
General der Panzertruppen W. Ritter von Thoma _(June 1941 – 15 Sept 1941)_	Generalleutnant R. Freiherr von Waldenfels _(21 Feb 1944 – 13 Mar 1944)_
Generalleutnant F. Landgraf _(15 Sept 1941 – 1 Apr 1942)_	Generalleutnant W. Denkert _(13 Mar 1944 – 28 Mar 1944)_
Generaloberst E. Raus _(1 Apr 1942 – 7 Feb 1943)_	Generalleutnant R. Freiherr von Waldenfels _(28 Mar 1944 – 23 Nov 1944)_
Generalleutnant W. von Hunersdorff _(7 Feb 1943 – 16 July 1943)_	Oberst F. Jurgens _(23 Nov 1944 – 20 Jan 1945)_
Generalmajor W. Crisolli _(16 July 1943 – 21 Aug 1943)_	Generalleutnant R. Freiherr von Waldenfels _(20 Jan 1945 – 8 May 1945)_

☈ *Fall Weiss*: the invasion of Poland
1 SEPTEMBER 1939

Although relatively lightly equipped with tanks, 1st *Leichte Division* was used as a regular Panzer division during the Invasion of Poland.

THE 1ST *LEICHTE* DIVISION was assigned with the 3rd *Leichte* Division to General von Reichenau's 10th Army, part of General von Rundstedt's Army Group South. In the initial stages of the invasion, 1st *Leichte* was part of the 10th Army reserve as the Germans drove to encircle the Polish armies at Radom. By 5 September, they were already halfway to Warsaw. The Poles launched a counterattack out of the Pomorze pocket, but the Germans encircled the Poles on the Bzura, using 1st Panzer together with 1st, 2nd and 3rd *Leichte* Divisions.

After the fall of Poland, the *Leichte* divisions were reorganized as full Panzer divisions.

ORGANIZATION

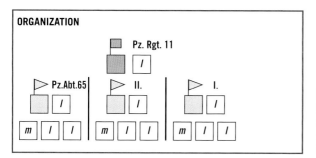

Panzer Unit	Pz. II	Pz. 35(t)	Pz. IV	Pz.Bef.35(t)
11st Pz. Rgt.	45	75	27	6
Pz.Abt.65	2	37	14	2

▶ **Panzerkampfwagen 35(t)**

1 Leichte Division Pz. Rgt 11 / I Battalion / 2nd Company / Company HQ tank of Hptm Mecke

When Germany occupied the Czech Republic, it immediately pressed into service all their war material, which included 219 Pz.Kpfw 35(t) light tanks. It was much more powerful than the PzKpfw I or II, with a 37mm (1.5in) gun renowned for its accuracy. In German service, the tank was modified to accept two radio sets and an extra crewman – a loader – was added.

Specifications

Crew: 4	Engine: Skoda T11
Weight: 11.6 tonnes (10.5 tons)	Speed: 35km/hr (21.7mph)
Length: 4.9m (16ft)	Range: 190km (118 miles)
Width: 2.1m (6.9ft)	Radio: FuG37(t)
Height: 2.35m (7.7ft)	

▼ **Panzerkampfwagen II Ausf C (Sd Kfz 121)**

1 Leichte Division

The cavalry branch of the German Army, which claimed descent from the Teutonic Knights of medieval times, fought tenaciously for its place in twentieth-century warfare. The creation of the *Leichte* Divisions was a political compromise to allow the aristocrat *Kavallerie* to play its part in mechanized warfare. The cavalrymen considered their mechanized infantry units to be dragoons or mounted infantry, who had simply replaced their horses with trucks and tanks.

Specifications

Crew: 3	Engine: Maybach HL62TR
Weight: 9.8 tonnes (8.9 tons)	Speed: 40km/hr (24.9mph)
Length: 4.81m (15.8ft)	Range: 200km (124.3 miles)
Width: 2.22m (7.3ft)	Radio: FuG5
Height: 1.99m (6.5ft)	

Fall Gelb: the French campaign
10 MAY 1939

Experience in Poland had shown the *Leichte* Divisions had not been a success. On 10 October, they were reorganized, and 1st *Leichte* Division became 6th Panzer Division.

AFTER REORGANIZING as a full Panzer Division (though still operating with a large number of Czech tanks), 6th Panzer Division was assigned to Reinhardt's XLI *Panzerkorps* for the assault on the west. Along with the corps commanded by Hoth and Guderian, XLI *Panzerkorps* formed the armoured spearhead of the German drive through the Ardennes. 6th Panzer met with some difficulties on the way to the Meuse, mainly caused by congestion. Finally crossing on 15 May, it raced through northern France, trying to catch up with Guderian's Panzers. In the process, it overran and largely destroyed the French 2nd *Division des Cuirassées Rapide*, which had been scattered by the German advance.

Panzer Unit	Pz. II	Pz. 35(t)	Pz. IV	Pz.Bef.35(t)
6th Pz. Div.	60	118	31	14

ORGANIZATION

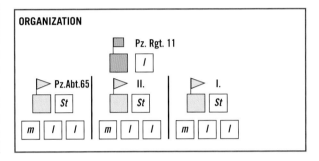

▶ Panzerkampfwagen IV Ausf D (Sd Kfz 161)

Unknown formation

In October 1939, the *Leichte* Division was reorganized as the 6th Panzer Division. In the early stages of the war, each tank's tactical number was painted onto a black metal plate shaped like the rhomboid used as the map symbol for armour.

Specifications

Crew: 5	Engine: Maybach HL120TRM
Weight: 22 tonnes (20 tons)	Speed: 40km/hr (24.9mph)
Length: 5.92m (19.4ft)	Range: 200km (124.3 miles)
Width: 2.84m (9.3ft)	Radio: FuG5
Height: 2.68m (8.8ft)	

▶ Panzerkampfwagen 35(t)

Pz. Rgt 11 / II Battalion / 5th Company / Company HQ

Between 1935 and 1938, 424 Panzer 35(t)s were produced and the *Wehrmacht* pressed 219 into service. The Pz.Kpfw 35(t) was armed with one 37mm (1.5in) KwK34(t) L/40 cannon and carried a mix of 72 high explosive and antitank rounds.

Weapons Specifications

Main armament: 3.7cm (1.4in) KwK34(t) L/34	Co-axial MG: 7.92mm (0.3in) MG37(t)
Ammunition: 72 rounds	Hull MG: 7.92mm (0.3in) MG37(t)
Traverse: 360° (manual)	Ammunition: 1800 rounds
Elevation: -10° to +25°	MG sight: MGZF(t)
Sight: TZF (t)	

▶ Panzerkampfwagen IV Ausf E (Sd Kfz 161)

Unknown formation

The invasion of the Low Countries caused the reaction planned for by the German High Command: it drew the French and British armies north into Belgium. The powerful German armoured thrust though the Ardennes, followed by a race for the coast, then came as a surprise, cutting through Allied lines of communication like a sickle cutting through long grass.

Specifications

Crew: 5	Engine: Maybach HL120TRM
Weight: 23.2 tonnes (21 tons)	Speed: 42km/hr (26mph)
Length: 5.92m (19.4ft)	Range: 200km (124.3 miles)
Width: 2.84m (9.3ft)	Radio: FuG5
Height: 2.68m (8.8ft)	

▶ Panzerkampfwagen 35(t)

65th Battalion / Stabskompanie / Signal Platoon / HQ tank of Oberstleutnant Schenk

The 65th Tank Battalion was an independent unit within the 6th Panzer Division, and had a different set of tactical numbers. A01 indicates the first tank of the command company. The crew consisted of a driver, machine gunner/radioman, loader and the tank commander, who also had to operate the main gun.

Armour Specifications

Turret: 25mm (1in) front, 15mm (0.6in) side,	Hull: 25mm (1in) front, 16mm (0.6in) side
15mm (0.6in) rear, 8mm (0.3in) top	16mm (0.6in) back, 8mm (0.3in)
Superstructure: 25mm (1in) front, 16mm	underside
(0.6in) side, 15mm (0.6in) rear, 8mm	Gun mantlet: 25mm (1in)
(0.3in) top	

▶ Panzerbefehlswagen 35(t)

65th Battalion / Stabskompanie / Signal Platoon / tank of Oberstleutnant Marquart

The *stabskompanie* of the 65th Battalion operated Panzer 35(t) command tanks. These were equipped with two-way radios in addition to the receive-only sets carried by all German tanks. The 10-watt FuG37(t) transmitter/receiver had a voice range of about 1 km (0.6 miles).

Specifications

Crew: 4	Engine: Skoda T11
Weight: 11.6 tonnes (10.5 tons)	Speed: 35km/hr (21.7mph)
Length: 4.9m (16ft)	Range: 190km (118 miles)
Width: 2.1m (6.9ft)	Radio: FuG37(t)
Height: 2.35m (7.7ft)	

✕✕ *Barbarossa*: the attack on Russia
22 JUNE 1941

Initially assigned to Army Group North's reserve during Operation *Barbarossa*, 6th Panzer Division went into action with XLI *Panzerkorps*, part of the 4th *Panzergruppe*.

FIGHTING WITH GREAT FEROCITY, the division was one of the first to pierce the Stalin Line and reach Leningrad, where it took part in the early stages of the siege of the city. In October 1941, the division was transferred to LVI *Panzerkorps*, part of the 3rd *Panzergruppe* with Army Group Centre. Suffering heavy losses in the drive on Moscow and in the Soviet counterattack that followed, the 6th Panzer Division was transferred to the 9th Army, where it took part in the fighting around Rzhev. As the Soviet winter offensive petered out, the division was transferred to France for rest and rebuilding.

ORGANIZATION

Pz. Rgt. 11

I

Pz.Abt.65 — St

II. — St

I. — St

m / l — m / l — m / l

Panzer Unit	Pz. II	Pz. 35(t)	Pz. IV	Pz.Bef35(t)	Pz. Bef.
6th Pz. Div.	47	155	30	5	8

▶ **Panzerbefehlswagen III Ausf E (Sd Kfz 266-267-268)**

Pz. Rgt 11 / I Battalion / Stabskompanie / Signal Platoon / signal officer tank

45 Pz. Bef Ausf E were produced between July 1939 and February 1940.

Specifications

Crew: 5	Engine: Maybach HL120TR
Weight: 21.5 tonnes (19.5 tons)	Speed: 40km/hr (24.9mph)
Length: 5.38m (17.7ft)	Range: 165km (102.5 miles)
Width: 2.91m (9.5ft)	Radio: FuG6 plus FuG2 or FuG7
Height: 2.44m (8ft)	or FuG8

▶ **Panzerkampfwagen 35(t)**

Pz. Rgt 11 / II Battalion / Stabskompanie / Signal Platoon / commander's command tank

The 6th Panzer Division served with Army Group North. By August 1941, the Division had lost 35 Panzers. Damaged tanks could be repaired only by cannibalizing others, as parts for older Czech tanks were no longer being made. By the end of the winter, most Pz.Kpfw 35(t) were lost or out of action.

Specifications

Crew: 4	Engine: Skoda T11
Weight: 11.6 tonnes (10.5 tons)	Speed: 35km/hr (21.7mph)
Length: 4.9m (16ft)	Range: 190km (118 miles)
Width: 2.1m (6.9ft)	Radio: FuG37(t)
Height: 2.35m (7.7ft)	

▶ 4.7cm PaK(t) (Sf) auf Panzerkampfwagen I Ausf B

41st Panzerjäger Battalion

The Czech 4.7cm (1.9in) antitank gun mounted on an obsolete Pz.Kpfw I chassis proved to be an effective weapon until confronted with the Russian T-34 and KV tanks, which started to appear in numbers at the end of 1941. The five-sided gun shield is characteristic of an early production model.

Specifications

Crew: 3	Engine: Maybach NL38TR
Weight: 7 tonnes (6.4 tons)	Speed: 40km/hr (24.9mph)
Length: 4.42m (14.5ft)	Range: 140km (87 miles)
Width: 2.06m (6.8ft)	Radio: FuG2
Height: 2.25m (7.4ft)	

▶ Panzerkampfwagen II Ausf F (Sd Kfz 121)

Unknown formation

The Ausf F was a version of the Panzer II with extra armour. This variant had 30mm (1.2in) of armour plate protecting all front areas of the tank, which was more than double the thickness of armour carried by the earlier Ausf C.

Specifications

Crew: 3	Engine: Maybach HL62TR
Weight: 10.5 tonnes (9.5 tons)	Speed: 40km/hr (24.9mph)
Length: 4.81m (15.8ft)	Range: 200km (124.3 miles)
Width: 2.28m (7.5ft)	Radio: FuG5
Height: 2.15m (7ft)	

▶ Panzerkampfwagen 35(t)

Pz. Rgt 11 / II Battalion / 7th Company / 2nd Zug / tank number 2

Designed to be manoeuvrable and able to travel great distances, the Pz.Kpfw 35(t) used a pneumatically-operated transmission. This should have been ideal for operations in Russia, but it proved to be a great weakness when confronted by the harsh conditions of the Russian winter.

Specifications

Crew: 4	Engine: Skoda T11
Weight: 11.6 tonnes (10.5 tons)	Speed: 35km/hr (21.7mph)
Length: 4.9m (16ft)	Range: 190km (118 miles)
Width: 2.1m (6.9ft)	Radio: FuG37(t)
Height: 2.35m (7.7ft)	

▶ Mittlerer Gepanzerter Beobachtungskraftwagen (Sd Kfz 254)

76th Panzer Artillery Regiment / 76th (mot) Observation Battery

Designed for the Austrian army, the SdKfz 254 was a wheel-cum-track medium armoured observation post. This example served at Leningrad in 1941.

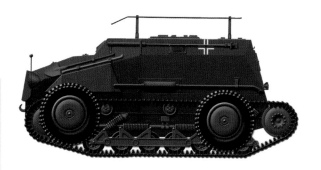

Specifications

Crew: 7	Engine: Saurer CRDv diesel
Weight: 7 tonnes (6.4 tons)	Speed: 60km/hr (37.3mph)
Length: 4.56m (15ft)	Range: 500km (310.7 miles)
Width: 2.02m (6.6ft)	Radio: FuG8, FuG4, FuG Spr Ger 1
Height: 1.88m (6.2ft)	

▶ Gepanzerter Selbstfahrlafette für Sturmgeschütz 7.5cm Kanone Ausf B (Sd Kfz 142)

Unknown formation

6th Panzer was transferred to 3.*Pz.Gruppe* , Army Group Centre, in October 1941, and was nearly wiped out during the winter of 1941–42. It was re-equipped in France in 1942, acquiring a battalion of assault guns in the process.

Specifications

Crew: 4	Engine: Maybach HL120TR
Weight: 21.6 tonnes (19.6 tons)	Speed: 40km/hr (24.9mph)
Length: 5.38m (17.7ft)	Range: 160km (99.4 miles)
Width: 2.92m (9.6ft)	Radio: FuG15 or FuG16
Height: 1.95m (6.4ft)	

During the assault on Moscow, September–October 1941, the Division used a yellow war hatchet as a temporary divisional insignia.

▼ Panzerbefehlswagen III Ausf H (Sd Kfz 266-267-268)

Pz. Rgt 11 / I Regimental Staff Company

By November 1942, the bulk of 6th Panzer's tanks were Pz.Kpfw IIIs.

Specifications

Crew: 5	Engine: Maybach HL120TRM
Weight: 24 tonnes (21.8 tons)	Speed: 40km/hr (24.9mph)
Length: 5.4m (17.7ft)	Range: 165km (102.5 miles)
Width: 2.95m (9.7ft)	Radio: FuG6 plus FuG2 or FuG7 or
Height: 2.44m (8ft)	FuG8

▶ **Schwerer Panzerfunkwagen (Sd Kfz 263) 6-Rad**

82nd Nachtrichen Abteillung (Signal Battalion)

Syscheva, March 1942. This armoured car bears the name of 'Peterle' next to the division symbol. Although similar to the Sd Kfz 231, the Sd Kfz 263 had a fixed turret and it was not intended as a scout car. It was primarily a command post, equipped with long-range radios, and it was issued to signals units within most armoured formations.

Specifications

Crew: 5	Engine: Büssing-NAG G or DB MO9 or
Weight: 6.6 tonnes (6 tons)	Magirus s88
Length: 5.57m (18.3ft)	Speed: 70km/hr (43.5mph)
Width: 1.82m (6ft)	Range: 300km (186.4 miles)
Height: 2.25m/7.4ft (no aerial)	Radio: FuG Spr Ger 'a'

 # The last summer offensive
1 JULY 1943

The Division returned from France after refitting at the end of 1942. It arrived on the Eastern Front to join Army Group South just in time for the attempt to rescue the 6th Army at Stalingrad.

WHILE REFITTING, THE DIVISION lost the 65th Battalion, which was merged with the 11th Panzer Regiment. Assigned to Hoth's 4th *Panzerarmee*, it led the attack on the Soviets encircling Stalingrad, penetrating to the Tschir river less than 21 km (13 miles) from the city before being stopped. During the Battle of Kursk, it served with Army Detachment *Kempf*, supporting 4th *Panzerarmee* in the southern sector. Afterwards, the Division was heavily engaged around Kharkov and in the retreat to the Dnieper, fighting back through the Southern Ukraine. In 1945, it saw action at Budapest, then retreated through Austria to Moravia, surrendering there to the Red Army.

ORGANIZATION

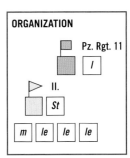

Panzer Unit	Pz. II	Pz. III	Pz. IV	Pz. Bef.	Flmmpz
11th Pz. Rgt.	13	52	32	6	14

▶ **Panzerkampfwagen III Ausf M (Sd Kfz 141/1)**

Pz. Rgt 11 / II Battalion / 6th Company / HQ tank

In 1943, 6th Panzer listed 34 Pz.Kpfw III armed with the long 5cm (2in) KwK39 L/60 as operational. The 6th participated in the retaking of the city of Kharkov that year and formed part of the southern pincer attack at Kursk during Operation *Zitadelle*.

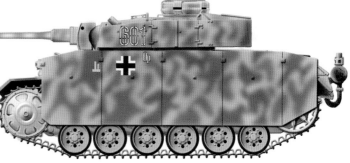

Specifications

Crew: 5	Engine: Maybach HL120TRM
Weight: 25 tonnes (22.7 tons)	Speed: 40km/hr (24.9mph)
Length: 6.41m (21ft)	Range: 155km (96.3 miles)
Width: 2.95m (9.7ft)	Radio: FuG5
Height: 2.5m (8.2ft)	

▶ Panzerkampfwagen III Ausf M (Sd Kfz 141/1)

Pz. Rgt 11 / II Battalion / 6th Company / Company HQ tank number 2

The second tank in the Company HQ section was usually assigned to the unit's adjutant. In the event that the company commander's tank was damaged, he could use this tank to continue in control of the battle.

Weapons Specifications

Main gun: 5cm (2in) KwK39 L/60	Co-axial MG: 7.92mm (0.3in) MG34
Ammunition: 92 rounds	Hull MG: 7.92mm (0.3in) MG34
Traverse: 360° (manual)	Ammunition: 3750 rounds of
Elevation: -10° to +20°	Patr SmK
Sight: TZF5e	MG sight: KgZF2

▶ Panzerkampfwagen III Ausf N (Sd Kfz 141/2)

Pz. Rgt 11 / II Battalion / 7th Company / 3rd Zug / tank number 1

The Ausf N was armed with a short 7.5cm (3in) KwK L/24, which fired a much more powerful high explosive round than the gun it replaced, the 5cm (2in) L/60. The letters 'OP' in the side of the tank may refer to the 11th Regiment commander, *Oberst* von Oppein-Bronikowski.

Specifications

Crew: 5	Engine: Maybach HL120TRM
Weight: 25.4 tonnes (23 tons)	Speed: 40km/hr (24.9mph)
Length: 5.65m (18.5ft)	Range: 155km (96.3 miles)
Width: 2.95m (9.7ft)	Radio: FuG5
Height: 2.5m (8.2ft)	

Panzer-Flamm-Zug K.St.N.1190

Infantry flamethrowers had been in use since World War I, and were horribly effective in close-range combat dealing with enemy fortifications and in built-up areas. Mounting a flamethrower in an armoured vehicle meant that larger weapons and much more incendiary fuel could be carried. In 1942, it was decided to equip each panzer division with a flamethrower platoon, and in 1943 the theoretical establishment of such platoons was to include seven Panzerkampfwagen III (Fl) tanks. One hundred tanks were produced between February and April 1943, and three divisions had operational *Flamm-Zugen* by the time of the Kursk battles.

▶ Panzerkampfwagen III (Fl) (Sd Kfz 141/3)

Pz. Rgt 11 / II Battalion / 8th Company / 5th Flamm Zug / tank number 1

The 8th Company at Kursk had a *Panzer-Flamm-Zug* attached as its 5th Platoon. Experience in Stalingrad suggested the need for a dedicated Panzer armed with a flamethrower for use in close-range urban combat.

Specifications

Crew: 3	Engine: Maybach HL120TRM
Weight: 25.4 tonnes (23 tons)	Speed: 40km/hr (24.9mph)
Length: 6.41m (21ft)	Range: 155km (96.3 miles)
Width: 2.95m (9.7ft)	Radio: FuG5 (plus FuG2 in platoon
Height: 2.5m (8.2ft)	commander's tank)

PanzerKompanie 'Panther'

The arrival of the Panzerkampfwagen V Panther in increasing numbers at the end of 1943 brought about a major reorganization of the armoured component of a Panzer division. It now consisted of a single panzer regiment of two battalions, the first equipped with Panthers and the second with Panzer IVs. The Panther battalion deployed one staff company with five Panthers and three command tanks, and four tank companies, each with a two-tank company HQ and three or four five-tank platoons, for a battalion total of between 72 and 91 tanks. In January 1944, the 1st Battalion of the 11th Panzer Regiment was converted to a Panther unit.

Company HQ: 2 Pz.Kpfw V

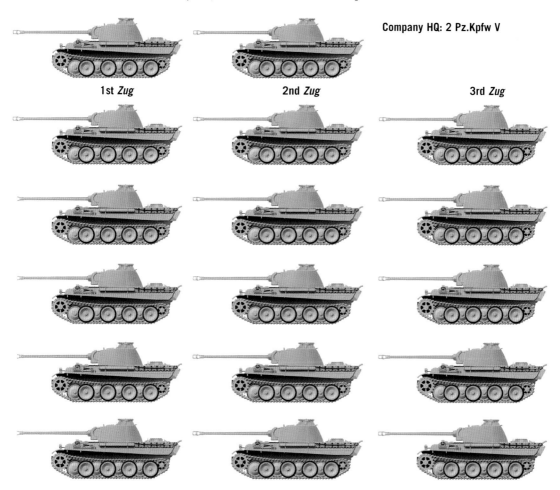

1st *Zug*   **2nd *Zug***   **3rd *Zug***

✕✕ Schwer Panzergruppe Bake
1943–1945

Early in 1944, *Oberstleutnant* Dr. Franz Bake of the 6th Panzer Division was assigned to command a special heavy Panzer unit bearing his own name.

FRANZ BAKE was one of the outstanding tank commanders of World War II. An infantry corporal during World War I, he qualified as a dentist in the 1920s, before joining the reserves in the 1930s. Called up for World War II, he served as an antitank platoon leader in France in 1940. He became a tank commander before the invasion of the Soviet Union, rising through the command ranks to lead Panzer Regiment 11 of 6th Panzer Division in November 1943.

Panzer Regiment Bake

Early in 1944, Bake was assigned to command a special armoured unit that would serve as a 'Fire Brigade'. Incorporating the 503rd Heavy Panzer *Abteilung*, Panzer Regiment Bake included 34 Tiger Is, 123 Panthers and a number of Hummel self-propelled guns from 1st Battalion, 88th Artillery Division. The Fire Brigade concept was intended to

encourage enemy armour to penetrate the German front and then to cut them off from their supporting infantry. The German infantry would seal the gap while the Panzer force would attack from the flank and rear, destroying the Soviet tanks.

Bake's personal heroism was rewarded when Swords were added to the Knight's Cross with Oakleaves he already held. He was also awarded four 'Individual Tank Destruction Badges', each given for the single-handed destruction of five enemy tanks. Bake left 6th Panzer later in 1944. In 1945, after transferring to the regular army from the reserves (as a reserve officer he could not be promoted beyond *Oberst*), he was appointed commander of 13th Panzer Division *Feldherrnhalle* 2.

▼ Panzerkampfwagen VI Ausf E (Sd Kfz 181)

Schwere Panzergruppe Bake / Pz. Abt. 503 / 1st Company / 3rd Zug / tank number 2

Early in 1944 at the Balabonowka Pocket, *Panzer-Regiment Bake* engaged the III Soviet Tank Corps in a five-day battle. Tigers formed the centre of Bake's formation while the faster Panthers in two wedge formations outflanked the enemy. By the end, 268 enemy tanks and 156 guns had been destroyed for the loss of one Tiger and four Panthers.

Specifications

Crew: 5	Engine: Maybach HL210P45
Weight: 62.8 tonnes (57 tons)	Speed: 38km/hr (23.6mph)
Length: 8.45m (27.7ft)	Range: 140km (87 miles)
Width: 3.7m (12.1ft)	Radio: FuG5
Height: 2.93m (9.6ft)	

7th Panzer Division

Like the 6th Panzer Division, 7th Panzer Division was formed in October 1939 by the conversion of one of the *Wehrmacht*'s *Leichte* Divisions to full Panzer Division status.

▲ **Battle of France**

Panzer IIs of Rommel's 7th Panzer Division cross a pontoon bridge in 1940. The 'R' on the turret indicates that it is from the regimental staff company.

T HE 2ND *LEICHTE* DIVISION was officially formed on 10 November 1938 at Gera, to the south of Leipzig. Despite the fact that Germany had very little cavalry strength, the cavalry arm was the most prestigious in the German armed forces, and the light divisions had been formed primarily as a sop to the few but highly influential cavalry officers who dominated the high command.

In 1939, the 2nd *Leichte* Division was under the command of *General de Kavallerie* Stumme. At full strength, the division comprised 457 officers and warrant officers leading 11,000 NCOs and men.

Panzer strength

The Division was organized and equipped into a tank-light, infantry-heavy unit. The 6th and 7th *Kavallerie Schützen* Regiments each consisted of two battalions of motorized infantry. Other divisional units included a reconnaissance regiment, an artillery regiment, an antitank battalion, a pioneer or combat engineer battalion, a signals battalion and other service and support units.

Divisional armoured strength was provided by a single Panzer unit, the 33rd Panzer Battalion. This included one motorized signals platoon, one staff platoon, three light panzer companies, one motorized

reserve platoon, one motorized maintenance platoon, and one light supply column. At the outbreak of war, the Panzer *Abteilung* had 62 tanks available, mostly Pz.Kpfw Is and IIs, with a few Pz.Kpfw IIIs and IVs becoming operational.

The support units included more supply, maintenance and fuel columns, a divisional administration unit, a field bakery, a butcher detachment, various medical and veterinary units, a military police troop and a field post office.

Commanders

General der Kavallerie G. Stumme *(18 Oct 1939 – 5 Feb 1940)*	Generalmajor G. Schmidhuber *(2 May 1944 – 9 Sept 1944)*
Generalmajor E. Rommel *(5 Feb 1940 – 14 Feb1941)*	General der Panzertruppen Dr. K. Mauss *(9 Sept 1944 – 31 Oct 1944)*
General der Panzertruppen H. Freiherr von Funck *(14 Feb1941 – 17 Aug 1943)*	Generalmajor H. Mader *(31 Oct 1944 – 30 Nov 1944)*
Oberst W. Glasemer *(17 Aug 1943 – 20 Aug 1943)*	General der Panzertruppen Dr. K. Mauss *(30 Nov 1944 – 5 Jan 1945)*
General der Panzertruppen H. von Manteuffel *(20 Aug 1943 – 1 Jan 1944)*	Generalmajor M. Lemke *(5 Jan 1945 – 23 Jan 1945)*
Generalmajor A. Schulz *(Jan 1944 – 28 Jan 1944)*	General der Panzertruppen Dr. K. Mauss *(23 Jan 1945 – 22 Mar 1945)*
Oberst W. Glasemer *(28 Jan 1944 – 30 Jan 1944)*	Oberst H. Christern *(23 Mar 1945 – 8 May 1945)*
General der Panzertruppen Dr. K. Mauss *(30 Jan 1944 – 2 May 1944)*	

INSIGNIA

Standard tactical symbol for the 7th Panzer Division, introduced in the second half of 1940.

New tactical symbol introduced in 1941, and generally carried by divisional vehicles to the end of the war.

Alternative tactical symbol carried by 7th Panzer Division vehicles.

Special tactical symbol adopted by 7th Panzer for the Battle of Kursk.

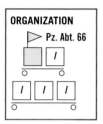 *Fall Weiss*: the invasion of Poland

1 SEPTEMBER 1939

Together with the 3rd *Leichte* Division, the 2nd *Leichte* Division formed the XV Motorized Corps in the 10th Army, attached to Army Group South for the Polish campaign.

THE BEGINNING OF THE INVASION of Poland saw the 2nd *Leichte* Division launching its attack from the area around Horneck in Silesia. As part of the armoured spearhead of von Reichenau's 10th Army, its mission was to take part in the elimination of Polish forces around the key cities of Kielce and Radom. The Division advanced without much in the way of fighting, reaching Radom by 9 September. However, fighting was harder elsewhere, and the Division was one of several diverted to deal with a Polish counterattack at Bzura, to the west of Warsaw.

After the battle, the Division advanced towards Modlin, continuing to encircle the south of the Polish capital. The Poles capitulated on 27 September 1939, and German units not needed for occupation duty were ordered home on 1 October.

Arriving in Thuringia in mid-October, the 2nd *Leichte* prepared for radical change. As a result of combat experience in Poland, the *Wehrmacht* had learned some lessons about what kind of units were needed in large-scale combat. As a result, the four *Leichte* divisions were to be reorganized as fully-fledged Panzer divisions, to be numbered from 6 to 9. The 2nd *Leichte* Division was renamed the 7th Panzer Division on 18 October 1939.

ORGANIZATION

▷ Pz. Abt. 66

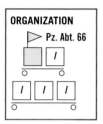 *Fall Gelb*: the French campaign

10 MAY 1940

A command change in February 1940 brought an unknown General to lead the 7th Panzer Division, but Erwin Rommel's abilities would soon make him a household name in Germany.

COMMANDED BY *GENERALMAJOR* (later Field Marshal) Erwin Rommel from February 1940 to February 1941, the 7th Panzer Division played a key role in the invasion of France in May and June of 1940. It was assigned to Hoth's XV *Panzerkorps*, part of Army Group A's powerful armoured force which struck through the Ardennes.

7th Panzer was one of the first armoured units across the Meuse at Dinant, and raced towards the Somme. The only check came when Rommel's division had to fight off a British counterattack at Arras, which had already rattled the 3rd SS Division *Totenkopf*.

Under Rommel's command, the 7th Panzer earned the sobriquet *Gespenster-Division,* or the 'Ghost Division' – the speed of its advance left the French uncertain when or where on the battlefield it would appear next. 7th Panzer was the first German unit to cross the Seine, and on 19 June Rommel's panzers took the key port of Cherbourg.

ORGANIZATION

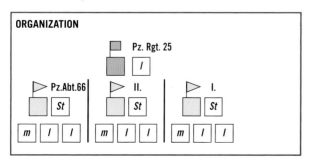

Panzer Unit	Pz. I	Pz. II	Pz. 38(t)	Pz. IV	Pz.Bef38(t)
7th Pz. Div.	34	68	91	24	8

▶ Panzerfunkwagen (Sd Kfz 263) 8-Rad

Division Staff / Signal Platoon / Command car of Major-General Erwin Rommel

The 7th Panzer was called the 'Ghost Division' because the Allies never knew its exact location during the battle for France. Neither did the German High Command for much of the time, though Rommel could have used his communications vehicle to keep in touch. Rommel's command car carried the license plate WH 143149 painted on the vehicle's bow.

Specifications

Crew: 5	Engine: Büssing-NAG L8V
Weight: 8.9 tonnes (8.1 tons)	Speed: 100km/hr (62.1mph)
Length: 5.85m (19.2ft)	Range: 300km (186.4 miles)
Width: 2.2m (7.2ft)	Radio: 1 Sätz Funkgerät für (m) Pz
Height: 2.9m (9.5ft)	Funktruppe b

▶ Panzerbefehlswagen 38(t) Ausf B

Pz. Rgt 25 / Regimental Staff Company / Signal Platoon / tank number 2

The British armoured attack near Arras caught the SS *Totenkopf* (mot) Division by surprise. The British force was composed of 74 vehicles, including thickly armoured Matilda infantry tanks. The British gave the Germans a major scare, until Rommel used the *Luftwaffe* 88mm (3.5in) anti-aircraft guns attached to his division to engage the otherwise invulnerable Matilda. Other *Luftwaffe* assistance came from Ju-87 Stuka attacks called in by Rommel's 7th Panzer.

Specifications

Crew: 4	Engine: Praga EPA
Weight: 10.5 tonnes (9.5 tons)	Speed: 42km/hr (26mph)
Length: 4.61m (15.1ft)	Range: 250km (155.3 miles)
Width: 2.14m (7ft)	Radio: FuG37(t)
Height: 2.4m (7.9ft)	

▶ Panzerkampfwagen 38(t) Ausf B

Pz. Rgt 25 / I Battalion / 1st Company / 2nd Zug / tank number 3

The Czech-built Pz.Kpfw 38(t) was used in place of the Pz.Kpfw III in the table of organization of the 7th Panzer Division. The large red tactical number was characteristic of 7th Panzer vehicles in the early years of the war.

Weapons Specifications

Main gun: 3.7cm (1.5in) KwK38(t) L/47.8	Co-axial MG: 7.92mm (0.3in) MG37(t)
Ammunition: 42 rounds	Hull MG: 7.92mm (0.3in) MG37(t)
Traverse: 360° (manual)	Ammunition: 2400 rounds
Elevation: -10° to +14°	MG sight: MGZF(t)
Sight: TZF(t)	

▶ Panzerkampfwagen I Ausf B (Sd Kfz 101)

Pz. Rgt 25 / I Battalion / 1st Company / 4th Zug / tank number 1

675 Ausf B variants of the Panzer I were manufactured from August 1935 to June 1937. The Ausf B is easily distinguishable from the Ausf A; it had five road wheels, four return rollers and a longer chassis. The armour was unchanged, being 13mm (0.5in) thick on the front and sides and only 6mm (0.2in) at the top.

Specifications
Crew: 2
Weight: 6.4 tonnes (5.8 tons)
Length: 4.42m (14.5ft)
Width: 2.06m (6.8ft)
Height: 1.72m (5.6ft)
Engine: Maybach NL38TR
Speed: 40km/hr (24.9mph)
Range: 170km (105.6 miles)
Radio: FuG2

▶ Schwerer Panzerspähwagen (Sd Kfz 231) 6-Rad

37th Reconnaissance Battalion

The Sd Kfz 231 was armed with one 20mm (0.8in) KwK30 L/55 cannon and carried 200 rounds of ammunition. Secondary armament consisted of one MG13 machine gun with 1500 rounds of ammunition.

Specifications

Crew: 4	Engine: Büssing-NAG G or Daimler-Benz
Weight: up to 6.6 tonnes (6 tons)	M09 or Magirus s88
Length: 5.57m (18.3ft)	Speed: 70km/hr (43.5mph)
Width: 1.82m (6ft)	Range: 300km (186.4 miles)
Height: 2.25m (7.4ft)	Radio: FuG Spr Ger 'a'

▶ 15cm sIG33 (Sf) auf Panzerkampfwagen I Ausf B

705th Schwere Infanteriegeschütz Abteilung

Mounting a standard 15cm (6in) field gun onto the chassis of a Panzer I allowed the German Army to provide Panzer and motorized divisions with heavyweight artillery support at all times. This particular vehicle had the name 'Berta' painted on the front shield under the gun barrel.

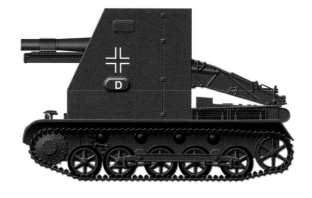

Specifications

Crew: 4	Engine: Maybach NL38TR
Weight: 9.4 tonnes (8.5 tons)	Speed: 40km/hr (24.9mph)
Length: 4.67m (15.3ft)	Range: 140km (87 miles)
Width: 2.06m (6.8ft)	Radio: Name
Height: 2.8m (9.2ft)	

▶ Ladungsleger auf Panzerkampfwagen I Ausf B

58th Pioneer Battalion / 3rd Armoured Engineers Company

Demolition charge-laying tank. Each Pioneer Panzer Battalion had ten *Ladungsleger* in its organization chart. This vehicle was equipped with a rear deck demolition charge mounted on a special sledge, and was used to clear obstacles in the path of the assault troops.

Specifications
Crew: 2
Weight: 6.6 tonnes (6 tons)
Length: 4.42m (14.5ft)
Width: 2.06m (6.8ft)
Height: 1.72m (5.6ft)
Engine: Maybach NL38TR
Speed: 40km/hr (24.9mph)
Range: 170km (105.6 miles)
Radio: FuG2

Barbarossa: the attack on Russia
22 JUNE 1941

After the victory in France, 7th Panzer remained there on occupation duties until early in 1941. Then Rommel left for Africa, and the Division returned to Germany to prepare for Russia.

A S PART OF *GENERALOBERST* Hermann Hoth's 3rd *Panzergruppe* on the northern flank of Army Group Centre, the 7th Panzer Division attacked across the Memel River in Lithuania and, after taking Vilnius, crossed into Russia proper. The division continued its advance through Minsk and Vitebsk before taking part in the capture of Smolensk in July 1941. In the battle for Moscow, a regiment of the Division captured the bridge across the Volga-Moscow Canal at Yakhroma on 28 November 1941.

However, with no German reserves available to exploit the bridgehead, its troops had reluctantly to withdraw back across the canal. In January, the retreat continued back to the defensive lines at Rzhev.

Panzer Unit	Pz. II	Pz. 38(t)	Pz. IV	Pz.Bef38(t)	Pz. Bef.
25th Pz. Rgt.	53	167	30	7	8

ORGANIZATION

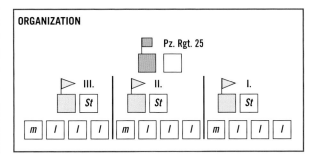

▶ **Panzerkampfwagen IV Ausf E (Sd Kfz 161)**

Pz. Rgt 25 / I Battalion / 4th Company / 2nd Zug / tank number 1

Although Germany deployed 5264 tanks during the invasion of the USSR, they faced 20,000 tanks and other AFVs of the Red Army. However, German tactics enabled them to defeat this far more numerous force.

Specifications

Crew: 5

Weight: 23.2 tonnes (21 tons)

Length: 5.92m (19.4ft)

Width: 2.84m (9.3ft)

Height: 2.68m (8.8ft)

Engine: Maybach HL120TRM

Speed: 42km/hr (26mph)

Range: 200km (124.3 miles)

Radio: FuG5

▶ **Panzerkampfwagen II Ausf C (Sd Kfz 121)**

Pz. Rgt 25 / II Battalion / Stabskompanie / Light Platoon / tank number 8

The Light Platoon was used by Panzer battalion commanders to perform reconnaissance missions ahead of their main combat units.

Specifications

Crew: 3

Weight: 9.8 tonnes (8.9 tons)

Length: 4.81m (15.8ft)

Width: 2.22m (7.3ft)

Height: 1.99m (6.5ft)

Engine: Maybach HL62TR

Speed: 40km/hr (24.9mph)

Range: 200km (124.3 miles)

Radio: FuG5

▶ **Panzerkampfwagen II Ausf C (Sd Kfz 121)**

Pz. Rgt 25 / III Battalion / Stabskompanie / Light Platoon / tank number 14

Although long replaced as a frontline battle tank, the Panzer II continued to serve as a reconnaissance vehicle as late as the Kursk battles in 1943.

Specifications

Crew: 3	Engine: Maybach HL62TR
Weight: 9.8 tonnes (8.9 tons)	Speed: 40km/hr (24.9mph)
Length: 4.81m (15.8ft)	Range: 200km (124.3 miles)
Width: 2.22m (7.3ft)	Radio: FuG5
Height: 1.99m (6.5ft)	

 The 7th Panzer Division continued to use simple tactical symbols until the end of the war: this was a variant symbol used from 1941 to 1945.

Specifications

Crew: 9	Engine: Maybach HL85TUKRM
Weight: 22 tonnes (20 tons)	Speed: 50km/hr (31mph)
Length: 7.35m (24.1ft)	Range: 260km (161.6 miles)
Width: 2.5m (8.2ft)	Radio: FuG Spr Ger 'a' or none.
Height: 2.8m (9.2ft)	

▼ **8.8cm FlaK 18 (Sf) auf Zugkraftwagen 12t (Sd Kfz 8)**

19th Heavy Panzerjäger Battalion (Attached)

Although specialized antitank variants of the famous 'acht-acht' existed, the 8.8cm (3.5in) FlaK 18 L/56 anti-aircraft gun was a dual-purpose weapon that could destroy any Soviet tank.

▶ **Panzerkampfwagen 38(t) Ausf E/F**

Pz. Rgt 25 / III Battalion / 10th Company / Company HQ

525 Ausf E/F variants of the Pz.Kpfw 38(t) were produced between November 1940 and October 1941. Although protection had been increased, it was too lightly armoured for the Eastern Front and its gun was too small. By September 1941, the last vehicles were being withdrawn from the frontline by the 7th Panzer Division.

Specifications

Crew: 4	Engine: Praga EPA
Weight: 10.9 tonnes (9.85 tons)	Speed: 42km/hr (26mph)
Length: 4.61m (15.1ft)	Range: 250km (155.3 miles)
Width: 2.14m (7ft)	Radio: FuG37(t)
Height: 2.4m (7.9ft)	

⊥ The last summer offensive
1 JULY 1943

1943 saw the turning point of World War II, as for the first time the Soviets stopped a German summer offensive in its tracks, and then took the initiative on the Eastern Front.

AFTER SERVING IN THE DEFENSIVE lines near Rzhev for the first months of 1942, the 7th Panzer Division transferred to France in May 1942 for a much-needed rest and refit. After a period in the South of France, the division returned to the Eastern Front in December, where it was assigned to the reserve of Army Group Don. Attached to III *Panzerkorps* of 1st *Panzerarmee*, the division took part in Operation *Zitadelle* at Kursk, fighting in the Biglerons sector with Army Detachment *Kempf*. After the retreat from Kursk, 7th Panzer Division fought at Kiev and Zhitomir, forming part of the XXXXVIII Corps with 4th *Panzerarmee* and Army Group South. Hard fighting in the autumn of 1943 saw the division once again suffering heavy losses.

ORGANIZATION

Pz. Rgt. 25
I
II. — St
I. — St
m · le · le
m · le · le

Panzer Unit	Pz. II	Pz. III(50)	Pz. III(75)	Pz. IV	Pz. Bef.
25th Pz. Rgt.	12	43	12	38	5

▶ **Panzerbefehlswagen mit 5cm KwK39 L/60**

Pz. Rgt 25 / I Battalion / Stabskompanie / Signal Platoon / tank number 2

The Ausf K command tank was based on the Ausf L or M chassis. Fifty were produced between December 1942 and February 1943. It was armed with one 5cm (2in) L/60.

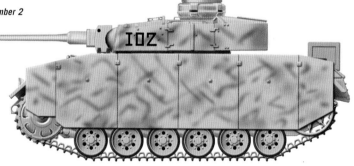

Specifications

Crew: 5
Weight: 25.4 tonnes (23 tons)
Length: 6.41m (21ft)
Width: 2.95m (9.7ft)
Height: 2.51m (8.2ft)

Engine: Maybach HL120TRM
Speed: 40km/hr (24.9mph)
Range: 155km (96.3 miles)
Radio: FuG5 plus FuG7 or FuG8

⊥ The last year on the Eastern front
1944

The Division had re-equipped the 1st Battalion with 79 Panthers by May 1944; the 2nd Battalion was still operating Pz.Kpfw IVs. In January 1945, near Deutsch-Eylau, the 7th Panzer Division, at that time reduced to 20 operational tanks, engaged a much larger Russian force. Facing odds of more than ten to one, the division was destroyed, but it was quickly re-built.

IN NOVEMBER 1943, 7th Panzer Division was one of the units assigned to the Zhitomir campaign. Under the command of General Hermann Balck, the XLVIII *Panzerkorps* advanced northwards to Zhitomir, smashing an armoured fist through the Soviet line on 15 November. The Russian Third

ORGANIZATION
▷ I. Pz. Rgt. 25
☐ St
V V V V

Guards Tank Army mounted counterattacks east of Zhitomir, and Balck promptly took the decision to entrap the enemy army within a pocket. By 24 November, the Soviet forces in the pocket had been eliminated.

Tarnopol break out

In March 1944, the 7th Panzer Division was encircled in a pocket around Kamenez-Podolsk, and the Germans were forced to attempt another break out towards Tarnopol. 7th Panzer played a major part in the break-out.

After 21 June, 7th Panzer was raced to the front in an attempt to stem the flood of Red Army tanks after the destruction of Army Group Centre. In July, 7th Panzer was transferred to Lithuania. Engaged on the Vistula over the winter, 7th Panzer Division was used to delay Soviet attacks on Danzig. Some elements of the Division fought at Berlin, before surrendering to the British in May 1945.

▶ **Mittlerer Schützenpanzerwagen Ausf D (Sd Kfz 251/3)**

Kampfgruppe / 78th Panzer Artillery Regiment

East Pomerania, March 1945. By this time, the 7th Panzer Division had been reduced to a *Kampfgruppe* with a mixed battalion (10 Pz.Kpfw V and 13 Pz.Kpfw IV) and an assortment of units attached as available.

Specifications

Crew: 2 plus 12 troops	Engine: Maybach HL42TUKRM
Weight: 9.9 tonnes (9 tons)	Speed: 53km/hr (32.9mph)
Length: 5.98m (19.6ft)	Range: 300km (186.4 miles)
Width: 2.1m (6.9ft)	Radio: FuG Spr Ger 'f'
Height: 2.16m (7ft)	

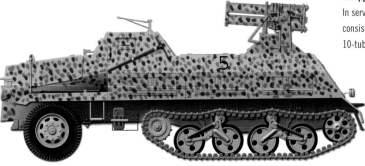

◀ **15cm Panzerwerfer 42 auf Sf (Sd Kfz 4/1)**

Kampgruppe / 78th Panzer Artillery Regiment

In service in East Pomerania in March 1945. A *Nebelwerfer* Battery consists of six launchers and each vehicle was armed with a 10-tube rocket launcher.

Specifications

Crew: 3	Engine: Opel 3.6l 6-cyl
Weight: 7.8 tonnes (7.1 tons)	Speed: 40km/hr (24.9mph)
Length: 6.0m (19.7ft)	Range: 130km (80.8 miles)
Width: 2.2m (7.2ft)	Radio: FuG Spr Ger 'f'
Height: 2.5m (8.2ft)	

Specifications

Crew: 4	Engine: Maybach HL42TUKRM
Weight: 9.9 tonnes (9 tons)	Speed: 53km/hr (32.9mph)
Length: 5.98m (19.6ft)	Range: 300km (186.4 miles)
Width: 2.1m (6.9ft)	Radio: FuG Spr Ger 'f'
Height: 2.16m (7ft)	

▲ **Mittlerer Schützenpanzerwagen Ausf D (Sd Kfz 251/22)**

Kampfgruppe / 7th Reconnaissance Battalion / 5th Heavy Company / Panzerjäger Platoon

As Soviet tanks approached the borders of the Reich, orders were issued to produce as many vehicles equipped with antitank weapons as possible. The PaK 40 antitank gun was mounted onto a half-track, using its standard field carriage but minus the wheels.

8th Panzer Division

The 8th Panzer Division came into existence in October 1939, when the 3rd *Leichte* Division was upgraded and renamed following service in the invasion of Poland.

THE 3RD *LEICHTE* DIVISION was originally formed on 10 November 1938 at Cottbus, a small garrison town northeast of Dresden. It was one of the four 'Light' Divisions formed by the cavalry in competition with the new armoured divisions being formed by the *Panzerwaffe*.

At the time of the invasion of Poland, the division was commanded by *Generalmajor* Kuntzen. Divisional strength was 438 officers and around 10,300 NCOs and men. The division was organized and equipped as follows:

8th *Kavallerie Schützen* Regiment with two motorized infantry battalions, one motorcycle platoon and one heavy company with machine guns, mortars and PAK antitank guns;

9th *Kavallerie Schützen* Regiment with one motorized infantry battalion and one motorcycle infantry battalion;

1st Battalion, 8th Reconnaissance Regiment with one motorcycle company, two armoured car companies and one heavy company with two 7.5cm (3in) infantry guns and three 3.7cm (1.5in) PAK 36 antitank guns;

67th Panzer Battalion, equipped with Panzer IIs, and Panzer 38(t)s in three light panzer companies;

80th Artillery Regiment of two motorized battalions, each three batteries of truck-towed 10.5cm (4.1in) leFH field howitzers;

43rd *Panzerabwehr* Battalion, made up from three companies each with 12 3.7-cm (1.5-in) PAK 36

antitank guns;

59th Pioneer Battalion with two Pioneer (combat engineer) companies, one motorized pioneer company, one bridging company and one engineering supply column;

4th Battalion, 3rd Signals Regiment;

58th Divisional Service units, operating supply, fuels and maintenance columns;

59th Divisional Administration unit;

59th Motorized Field Bakery;

59th Motorized Field Hospital;

1st and 2nd Motorized Medical companies;

59th Veterinary company;

59th Motorized Field Police Troop;

59th Motorized Field Post Office.

Commanders

General der Panzertruppen A. Kuntzen *(16 Oct 1939 – 20 Feb 1941)*	General der Panzertruppen E. Brandenberger *(10 Nov 1942 – 17 Jan 1943)*
General der Panzertruppen E. Brandenberger *(20 Feb 1941 – 21 Apr 1941)*	Generalleutnant S. Fichtner *(17 Jan 1943 – 20 Sept 1943)*
Generalleutnant W. Neumann-Silkow *(21 Apr 1941 – 26 May 1941)*	Generalmajor G. Frolich *(20 Sept 1943 – 1 Apr 1944)*
General der Panzertruppen E. Brandenberger *(26 May 1941 – 8 Dec 1941)*	Generalmajor W. Friebe *(1 Apr 1944 – 21 July 1944)*
Generalleutnant W. Huhner *(8 Dec 1941 – 20 Mar 1942)*	Generalmajor G. Frolich *(21 July 1944 – 5 Jan 1945)*
General der Panzertruppen E. Brandenberger *(20 Mar 1942 – 6 Aug 1942)*	Generalmajor H. Hax *(5 Jan 1945 – 8 May 1945)*
Generalleutnant J. Schrotter *(6 Aug 1942 – 10 Nov 1942)*	

▲ **Panzerkampfwagen 38(t)**

The growth of the *Panzerwaffe* coincided with the occupation of Czechoslovakia, and Czech factories provided much of the tank strength for the new divisions.

Fall Weiss: the invasion of Poland
1 SEPTEMBER 1939

At full strength, the 3rd *Leichte* Division had 332 officers, 105 warrant officers, 1616 NCOs and 8719 soldiers. The 67th Panzer Battalion had 45 Pz.Kpfw II, 59 Pz.Kpfw 38(t) and 2 Pz.Bef 38(t). In October 1939, the Division was reorganized as the 8th Panzer Division.

FROM ITS BASE AT GERA in Thuringia, where it had been formed under the supervision of *Wehrkreis* (Military Administrative District) IX, the 3rd Light Division was mobilized for the invasion of Poland on 28 August 1939. It was moved to Horneck in Silesia, where along with the 2nd Light Division it became part of *Generalleutnant* Stumme's XV Motorized Corps of von Reichenau's 10th Army assigned to Army Group South. XV Corps advanced rapidly towards Kielce on the outbreak of war, going on to reach the key city of Radom on 9 September. It was then diverted with other armoured and motorized formations by a serious Polish counterattack on the Bzura river, to the west of Warsaw. The Germans won the largest battle of encirclement up to that time, before pressing on to surround the Polish capital.

After the Polish capitulation, the Division was pulled back to Germany, where it was reorganized and strengthened to become the 8th Panzer Division. There it went into Army Group B's reserve until called on for the Western campaign.

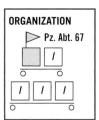

ORGANIZATION
▷ Pz. Abt. 67

◀ **Panzerkampfwagen 38(t) Ausf A**

3 Leichte Division / Pz.Abt. 67 / 3rd Company / 1st Zug / tank number 3

150 Ausf A were produced from May to November 1939. The original Czech LT Vz 38 was armed with a semi-automatic SKODA A7 gun and carried a crew of three. Its ammunition consisted of 5 spring-loaded magazines with 18 rounds each and 2400 rounds for both machine guns. The tank had no intercom, the commander communicating with the driver using a coloured lights system.

Specifications	
Crew: 4	Engine: Praga EPA
Weight: 10.5 tonnes (9.5 tons)	Speed: 42km/hr (26mph)
Length: 4.61m (15.1ft)	Range: 250km (155.3 miles)
Width: 2.14m (7ft)	Radio: FuG37(t)
Height: 2.4m (7.9ft)	

▶ **Panzerkampfwagen II Ausf D (Sd Kfz 121)**

3 Leichte Division / Pz.Abt. 67 / 3rd Company / 1st Zug / tank number 4

Forty-three Ausf D were produced between May 1938 and August 1939. They were issued only to the *Leichte* Divisions. The Pz.Kpfw II Ausf D was developed to replace horse-mounted German Cavalry units. With a speed of 55km/hr (34.2mph), it was well suited to the pursuit and reconnaissance missions for which it was designed.

Specifications	
Crew: 3	Engine: Maybach HL62TRM
Weight: 11 tonnes (10 tons)	Speed: 55km/hr (34.2mph)
Length: 4.65m (15.3ft)	Range: 200km (124.3 miles)
Width: 2.3m (7.5ft)	Radio: FuG5
Height: 2.06m (6.8ft)	

Fall Gelb: the French campaign
10 May 1940

8th Panzer Division was assigned to General Reinhardt's XLI *Panzerkorps*, in the centre of Army Group A's armoured thrust through the supposedly impassable Ardennes.

REINHARDT'S CORPS MADE SLOWER progress than those of Guderian and Hoth, being caught up in a monumental traffic jam as three *Panzerkorps* tried to funnel through the narrow, twisting roads passing through the heavily forested Ardennes.

Leichte PanzerKompanie

The light panzer companies of the former *Leichte* divisions began to re-equip after the Polish campaign, replacing many of their Panzer IIs with the Czech-built Panzer 38(t). The companies themselves operated mixed *Zugen*, or platoons, with four Panzer 38(ts) and a single Panzer II.

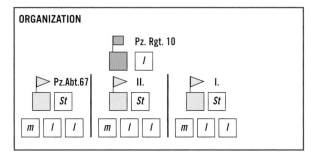

Panzer Unit	Pz. II	Pz. 38(t)	Pz. IV	Pz.Bef.38(t)
8th Pz. Div.	58	116	23	15

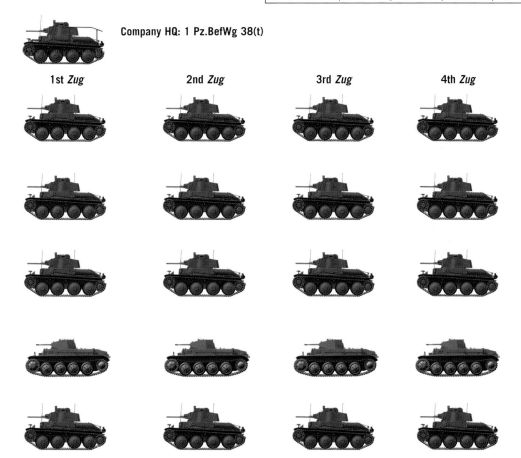

Company HQ: 1 Pz.BefWg 38(t)

1st *Zug*   2nd *Zug*   3rd *Zug*   4th *Zug*

War in the Balkans
6 APRIL 1941

The last thing Hitler wanted was a war in the Balkans, diverting forces from his planned strike on Russia. However, he had to help fellow fascist dictator Mussolini, who was in trouble.

THE 8TH PANZER DIVISION was attached to General Maximilian von Weichs' 2nd Army in Hungary, which was tasked with taking the northern half of Yugoslavia in a lightning assault. The 8th Panzer Division crossed the Hungarian border on 6 April 1941, outflanking Yugoslavian defensive positions and driving rapidly towards Belgrade. By 15 April, Belgrade, Zagreb and Sarajevo had been taken, and the Yugoslav government surrendered two days later.

The campaign was described by some German officers as a parade: less than 600 German casualties were recorded. However, much harder days were to follow as a bitter partisan war began.

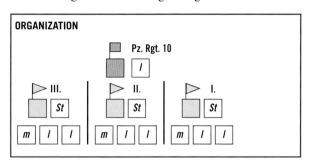

ORGANIZATION

Panzer Unit	Pz. II	Pz. 38(t)	Pz. IV	Pz.Bef.38(t)
10th Pz. Reg.	49	125	30	not known

 # *Barbarossa*: the attack on Russia
22 JUNE 1941

After the conquest of Yugoslavia, the 8th Panzer Division was sent by train to the Reich Protectorate of Bohemia for refitting, ready for the invasion of the USSR.

THE 8TH PANZER DIVISION was assigned to General Hoeppner's 4th *Panzergruppe* of Army Group North for Operation *Barbarossa*. Its main target was Leningrad. Driving rapidly through the Baltic states, the Panzers outpaced their supporting infantry. After fighting through Dvinsk, the Panzers were already approaching Pskov when their infantry units were

Panzer Unit	Pz. II	38(t)	Pz. IV	Pz.Bef38(t)	Pz.Bef
10th Pz. Rgt.	49	118	30	7	8

just clearing Daugavpils, more than 100 km (62 miles) back. In spite of the anguished pleas of the Panzer commanders, who wanted to continue the drive through the demoralized Soviet armies towards Leningrad, the Panzers were ordered to wait for their infantry. This gave the Soviets a little time to regroup, which meant that resistance was much stiffer by the time the offensive resumed.

By the time 8th Panzer reached Leningrad, the chances of taking the city had gone, and the Germans settled in for a siege. 8th Panzer continued to serve on the Leningrad Front for the next year, being moved to Army Group Centre in December 1942.

ORGANIZATION

▶ Panzerbefehlswagen 38(t) Ausf B

Pz. Rgt 10 / II Battalion / Stabskompanie / Signal Platoon

This command tank variant used rod antennae instead of the large frame antenna characteristic of other command tanks. To make space for extra radios in the cramped interior, the bow machine gun and its ammunition were removed. A rounded plate would usually be bolted over the empty MG position.

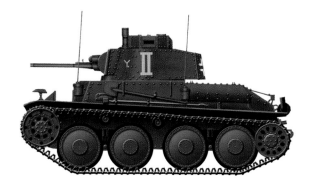

Specifications

Crew: 4	Engine: Praga EPA
Weight: 10.5 tonnes (9.5 tons)	Speed: 42km/hr (26mph)
Length: 4.61m (15.1ft)	Range: 250km (155.3 miles)
Width: 2.14m (7ft)	Radio: FuG37(t) plus FuG6
Height: 2.4m (7.9ft)	

▶ Panzerkampfwagen II Ausf C (Sd Kfz 121)

Pz. Rgt 10 / II Battalion / Stabskompanie / Light Platoon

8th Panzer was part of the 4th *Panzergruppe*, Army Group North. The Pz.Kpfw II Ausf D was withdrawn from service after the invasion of France was completed. Its chassis was used for conversion to Pz.Kpfw II (*Flamm*) flamethrowers, while it was replaced in frontline service by the earlier but more numerous Ausf C.

Specifications

Crew: 3	Engine: Maybach HL62TR
Weight: 9.8 tonnes (8.9 tons)	Speed: 40km/hr (24.9mph)
Length: 4.81m (15.8ft)	Range: 200km (124.3 miles)
Width: 2.22m (7.3ft)	Radio: FuG5
Height: 1.99m (6.5ft)	

▶ Panzerkampfwagen 38(t) Ausf C

Pz. Rgt 10 / II Battalion / 7th Company / 3rd Zug / tank number 1

110 Ausf C models were produced between May and August 1940. At the start of Operation *Barbarossa*, four Panzer divisions used the Pz.Kpfw 38(t) as their main battle tank. Six months later, losses of this model would reach 796 units. Too small to be upgraded further, the Germans started passing them to other Axis allies or assigning them to anti-partisan duties.

Specifications

Crew: 4	Engine: Praga EPA
Weight: 10.5 tonnes (9.5 tons)	Speed: 42km/hr (26mph)
Length: 4.61m (15.1ft)	Range: 250km (155.3 miles)
Width: 2.14m (7ft)	Radio: FuG37(t)
Height: 2.4m (7.9ft)	

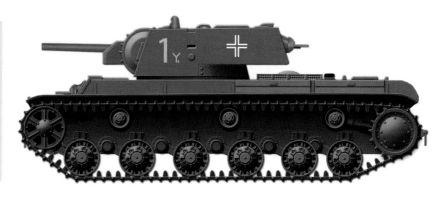

Specifications

Crew: 5

Weight: 46.6 tonnes (42.3 tons)

Length: 6.68m (21.9ft)

Width: 3.32m (10.9ft)

Height: 2.71m (8.9ft)

Engine: V-2K

Speed: 35km/hr (21.7mph)

Range: 180km (111.8 miles)

Radio: 10R

▲ **Panzerkampfwagen KV Ia 753(r)**

Pz. Rgt 10

A captured Russian KV-1 model 1940, armed with a 76mm (3in) F-32 cannon. The Panzer divisions encountered several of these heavy tanks in their drive towards Leningrad, and only the 8.8cm (3.5in) anti-aircraft gun was capable of knocking out the thickly armoured Soviet vehicle.

Ⓨ *Fall Blau*: the Eastern Front
28 JUNE 1942

In May 1942, the 2nd Panzer Battalion was detached to form part of a new Panzer division, becoming the 3rd Battalion, 2nd Regiment, 16th Panzer Division.

AFTER THE FAILURE to take Leningrad at the end of 1941, 8th Panzer Division fought around the small Russian town of Cholm, on the Lovat River in the Kalinin sector. German troops had entered the Leningrad suburbs of Slutsk and Pushkin, and had seized the Summer Palace of the Tsars at Krasnoye Selo. A Soviet counteroffensive in January aimed at relieving Leningrad failed, but the bitter fighting had isolated numerous pockets of the German invaders.

One of those pockets was at Cholm, where the Red Army had cut off some 6000 German troops in the town. For the next four months, they would conduct an epic defence, withstanding over 100 infantry assaults and more than 40 armoured attacks.

The German defenders were eventually relieved on 5 May, but the area around Cholm remained a major combat area, since it could serve as a springboard for a campaign to relieve the even larger German pocket at Demjansk, where the bulk of the German II Corps was trapped.

Although the German High Command continued in its desire to take Leningrad, Hitler's obsession with Stalingrad and the Caucasus oilfields meant that

Panzer Unit	Pz. II	38(t)	Pz. IV	Pz.Bef.38(t)
10th Pz. Rgt.	1	65	2	0

Army Group South carried the full weight of German power, and that Army Groups Centre and North were simply expected to hold the line while the summer offensive in the south went ahead.

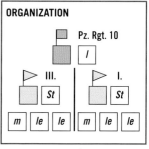

ORGANIZATION

The 8th Panzer Division continued to operate around Cholm through the summer and the autumn. From March through to July, it was attached to XXXIX Corps of the 15th Army. In August, 8th Panzer would have been involved in Operation *Lichtschlag*, a German plan to break the deadlock around Leningrad by mounting a major offensive north of Cholm to the Lovat River. However, the division was transferred to Army Group Centre in December of 1942.

⅋ The last summer offensive
1 July 1943

The 3rd Battalion was disbanded in October 1942 and its remnants were absorbed by the 1st Battalion. In the summer of 1943, the Division was assigned to Army Group Centre, where it formed part of the north pincer attack at Kursk.

IN DECEMBER 1942, 8th Panzer was attached to LIX Corps of Army Group Centre, and it took part in operations around Smolensk and Bryansk over the next two months. In April 1943, it was again moved to become part of the XXIII *Panzerkorps*, attached to 2nd *Panzerarmee* on the Orel sector.

2nd *Panzerarmee* was intended to play a supporting role during the Battle of Kursk, providing flank protection for the main Northern strike force,

Model's 9th Army. In the event, a Soviet counter-attack out of the Kursk Salient brought the army into more direct action than it had expected.

Following the rebuff at Kursk, the 8th Panzer Division played its part in the long retreat through the Ukraine, taking part in the fighting around Kiev and being used in the German tactical victory at Zhitomir. By January 1944, however, it was fighting to avoid encirclement and destruction in the Kamenez-Podolsk pocket near Tarnopol.

ORGANIZATIONS

Pz. Rgt. 10
I
I.
St
m | le | le | le

Panzer Unit	Pz. II	Pz. 38(t)	Pz. III	Pz. IV	Pz. Bef.
10th Pz. Rgt.	14	3	59	22	14

⅋ The last year on the Eastern Front
1944

By September 1944, 8th Panzer had been reorganized as a 'Type 44' division: the 2nd and 4th companies of the divisional Panzer battalion were re-equipped with the Pz.Kpfw V Panther.

DURING THE RETREAT THROUGH the Ukraine, the 8th Panzer Division had been in continuous action, taking part in major battles at Zhitomir and Tarnopol. In May 1944, it was placed into Army Group North Ukraine's reserve, before being called into action in the retreat through Brody and Lemberg and back into Poland.

The German Army Groups in the southern sectors of the Eastern Front avoided the fate of Army Group Centre, wiped out by the Soviet Operation *Bagration* in the summer of 1944, but they were placed under considerable pressure by the southern Soviet fronts, which launched their own series of offensives in August 1944.

The 8th Panzer Division fought back through the Carpathian mountains and into Slovakia as

Germany's allies Romania, Slovakia and Hungary either changed sides or were occupied by German troops to prevent their switch to the Allies.

In December 1944, the Division found itself under the control of Army Group South at Budapest. Hitler's determination to hold the Hungarian capital cost the *Wehrmacht* dearly. After failing to relieve the city with the last of its first line panzer forces, the German High Command transferred what was left of the 8th Panzer Division to Army Group Centre, where it was attached to the 17th Army in Moravia. The 8th Panzer Division eventually surrendered to the Red Army at Brno.

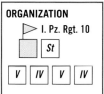

ORGANIZATION

I. Pz. Rgt. 10
St
V | IV | V | IV

9th Panzer Division

The last of the pre-war *Leichte* divisions to be brought up to full Panzer Division status, the 9th Panzer Division came into existence on 1 March 1940.

THE 4TH *LEICHTE* DIVISION was formed at Vienna on 1 April 1938, soon after the *Anschluss* between Austria and Germany. Manpower was provided by the former Austrian army. In March 1939, it took part in the occupation of Czechoslovakia. As with the other Light divisions, its fighting strength was provided by two motorized infantry regiments and a single understrength Panzer battalion, the 33rd.

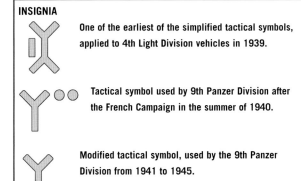

INSIGNIA

One of the earliest of the simplified tactical symbols, applied to 4th Light Division vehicles in 1939.

Tactical symbol used by 9th Panzer Division after the French Campaign in the summer of 1940.

Modified tactical symbol, used by the 9th Panzer Division from 1941 to 1945.

Commanders

General der Panzertruppen A. Ritter von Hubicki *(3 Jan 1940 – 15 Apr 1942)*	Generalleutnant E. Jolasse *(27 Nov 1943 – 10 Aug 1944)*
Generalleutnant J. Baßler *(15 Apr 1942 – 27 July 1942)*	Oberst M. Sperling *(10 Aug 1944 – 3 Sept 1944)*
Generalmajor H. von Hulsen *(27 July 1942 – 4 Aug 1942)*	Generalmajor G. Muller *(3 Sept 1944 – 16 Sept 1944)*
Generalleutnant W. Scheller *(4 Aug 1942 – 22 July 1943)*	Generalleutnant H. von Elverfeldt *(16 Sept 1944 – 6 Mar 1945)*
Generalleutnant E. Jolasse *(22 July 1943 – 1 Oct 1943)*	Oberst H. Zollenkopf *(6 Mar 1945 – 26 Apr 1945)*
Generalmajor Dr. J. Schulz *(1 Oct 1943 – 27 Nov 1943)*	

▶ **Balkans Interlude**
Motorized infantry pass in review in Athens after the victory in the Balkans in 1941. The 9th Panzer Division played a key part in the campaign.

⊠ *Fall Weiss*: the invasion of Poland
1 SEPTEMBER 1939

With just 57 fighting tanks, the 4th Light Division was the weakest armoured formation that took part in the German invasion of Poland in September 1939.

THE INVASION OF POLAND saw the 4th Light Division assigned to XVIII Army Corps of General List's 14th Army, part of Army Group South. On 19 August, the division received its war orders to move to forming up points in the Tatra Mountains.

Commanded by *General der Panzertruppen* Dr. Alfred Ritter von Hubicki, 4th Light was part of the drive to encircle and defeat the Polish Krakow Army, a mission that was completed in just over a week. At the end of the campaign the Division was located at Tomaszow, facing westward after outflanking the Poles.

The Division remained in Poland until 25 October, when it returned to Germany. On 3 January 1940, the Division was reorganized and upgraded to become the 9th Panzer Division.

ORGANIZATION

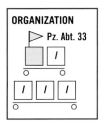

Pz. Abt. 33

Y°° *Fall Gelb*: the French campaign
10 MAY 1940

On January 1940, the 4th Light Division was reorganized as the 9th Panzer Division.

THE NEWLY FORMED 9th Panzer Division was one of the few armoured formations assigned to von Bock's Army Group B for the attack on the west in May 1940. After driving towards Rotterdam, the Division moved southward following the Belgian capitulation, and formed the northern flank of the German forces that surrounded Dunkirk. Transferring to *Panzergruppe Kleist* for the Battle of France, it drove through the centre of the country, reaching Lyon by the time of the Armistice at the end of June.

9th Panzer remained in France for two months, eventually being ordered back to Germany and then on to occupation duties in Poland in September 1940.

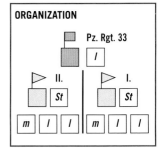

ORGANIZATION

Pz. Rgt. 33

Panzer Unit	Pz. I	Pz. II	Pz. III	Pz. IV	Pz. Bef.
33rd Pz. Rgt.	30	54	41	16	12

▶ **Panzerkampfwagen IV Ausf E (Sd Kfz 161)**

Pz. Rgt 33 / I Battalion / 4th Company / 2nd Zug / tank number 1

The 9th Panzer Division was the only armoured unit assigned to the invasion of the Low Countries. The defensive postures adopted by the Belgians and Dutch around their canal systems were inadequate to stop a three-dimensional attack composed of fast mechanized units and paratroops.

Specifications

Crew: 5	Engine: Maybach HL120TRM
Weight: 23.2 tonnes (21 tons)	Speed: 42km/hr (26mph)
Length: 5.92m (19.4ft)	Range: 200km (124.3 miles)
Width: 2.84m (9.3ft)	Radio: FuG5
Height: 2.68m (8.8ft)	

▶ **15cm sIG33 (Sf) auf Panzerkampfwagen I Ausf B**

701st Schwere Infanteriegeschütz Abteilung

The sIG33 was an awkward design, and its tall shape made the vehicle a good target. The high centre of gravity and overloaded chassis hindered its cross-country capability. However, vehicles armed with a 15cm (6in) howitzer provided effective close fire support to *Panzergrenadier* Regiments on all fronts. The 701st Abteilung was disbanded in June 1943.

Specifications

Crew: 4	Engine: Maybach NL38TR
Weight: 9.4 tonnes (8.5 tons)	Speed: 40km/hr (24.9mph)
Length: 4.67m (15.3ft)	Range: 140km (87 miles)
Width: 2.06m (6.8ft)	Radio: FuG5
Height: 2.8m (9.2ft)	

Barbarossa: the attack on Russia
22 June 1941

9th Panzer Division would have been with Army Group Centre for the invasion of Russia, had it not been diverted south to take part in the Balkans campaign.

ATTACHED TO XXXX CORPS of 12th Army, 9th Panzer along with the elite *Leibstandarte* SS brigade attacked Yugoslavia through Macedonia. Cutting the Yugoslavs off from any British or Greek assistance, the Division seized Skopje before Yugoslavia fell.

Withdrawn from the Balkans, the Division was rested and refitted for *Barbarossa*, the invasion of the Soviet Union. In July, 9th Panzer was attached to XIV *Panzerkorps* of the 1st *Panzergruppe*, fighting with Army Group South. It saw action at Uman, Kiev, where it played an important part in the encirclement and capture of more than 600,000 Soviet troops, and in the continuing German drive on to the Dnieper River.

On 9 October, Panzer was transferred to LXVIII *Panzerkorps* of Guderian's 2nd *Panzergruppe* in time for Operation *Typhoon*, Army Group Centre's delayed assault on Moscow. In November, it was fighting at Briansk, and at the end of the year it was involved in fighting off the Soviet winter offensive.

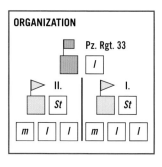

ORGANIZATION

Pz. Rgt. 33

I

II. St

I. St

m l m l l

Panzer Unit	Pz. I	Pz. II	Pz. III	Pz. IV	Pz. Bef.
33rd Pz. Rgt.	8	32	71	20	12

▼ **Panzerkampfwagen I Ausf B (Sd Kfz 101)**
Pz. Rgt 33 / I Battalion / 3rd Company / 2nd Zug / tank number 1
By 1941, the Pz.Kpfw I was obsolete. Orders were issued to convert all the models at hand into *Munitionsschlepper*, or ammunition carriers. This was originally to be accomplished by building a wooden box on the top of the chassis, but in most cases the removal of the turret provided sufficient space to carry cargo.

Specifications

Crew: 2	Engine: Maybach NL38TR
Weight: 6.4 tonnes (5.8 tons)	Speed: 40km/hr (24.9mph)
Length: 4.42m (14.5ft)	Range: 170km (105.6 miles)
Width: 2.06m (6.8ft)	Radio: FuG2
Height: 1.72m (5.6ft)	

▶ **Panzerkampfwagen III Ausf H (Sd Kfz 141)**
Pz. Rgt 33 / I Battalion / 3rd Company / 2nd Zug / tank number 3
A total of 308 Ausf H variants of the Panzer III were produced between October 1940 and April 1941. This model was armed with one 5cm (2in) KwK L/42 cannon and carried 99 *Panzergranate* and *Sprenggranaten*.

Specifications

Crew: 5	Engine: Maybach HL120TRM
Weight: 24 tonnes (21.8 tons)	Speed: 40km/hr (24.9mph)
Length: 5.41m (17.7ft)	Range: 165km (102.5 miles)
Width: 2.95m (9.7ft)	Radio: FuG5
Height: 2.44m (8ft)	

▶ **Panzerkampfwagen II Ausf C (Sd Kfz 121)**
Pz. Rgt 33 / I Battalion / 4th Company / 1st Zug / tank number 3
Medium Panzer companies usually had five Pz.Kpfw II assigned for reconnaissance. The tactical number on this example may indicate that the light platoon was designated 1st *Zug* and that the other Pz.Kpfw IV *Zug* were renumbered accordingly.

Specifications

Crew: 3	Engine: Maybach HL62TR
Weight: 9.8 tonnes (8.9 tons)	Speed: 40km/hr (24.9mph)
Length: 4.81m (15.8ft)	Range: 200km (124.3 miles)
Width: 2.22m (7.3ft)	Radio: FuG5
Height: 1.99m (6.5ft)	

▶ **Mittlerer Kommandopanzerwagen Ausf C (Sd Kfz 251/6)**
Unknown formation
This command vehicle had a FuG11 radio with a range of 50km (31 miles) using key and 10km (6.2 miles) transmitting voice. It used a frame antenna.

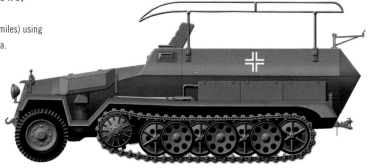

Specifications

Crew: 8	Engine: Maybach HL42TUKRM
Weight: 9.4 tonnes (8.5 tons)	Speed: 53km/hr (32.9mph)
Length: 5.98m (19.6ft)	Range: 300km (186.4 miles)
Width: 2.1m (6.9ft)	Radio: FuG11 plus FuG Tr 100W;
Height: 1.75m (5.7ft)	later FuG19 plus FuG12

Fall Blau: the Eastern Front
28 JUNE 1942

In 1942, Hitler abandoned plans to take Moscow as his eyes turned southward with plans to cross the Volga and to seize the Caucasus region and its oilfields.

THE EFFECT OF *FALL BLAU*, the plan for Germany's summer offensive in the south, was to leave Army Groups Centre and North in limbo. Denied the resources to mount any major offensives, Army Group Centre in particular was left to hold the line

against an increasingly strong Soviet army. At the beginning of 1942, 9th Panzer was on the line near Kursk. Along with the rest of XLVIII Corps, it was transferred to Army Group South, though it remained in the Kursk sector. When *Fall Blau* opened, forces on the northern flank of the offensive were used to attack past Kursk towards Voronezh, which was reached after a month of fighting across the steppes. In August, the Division was placed in reserve before being pulled back to Army Group Centre at Orel.

ORGANIZATION

Pz. Rgt. 33
I

III. | II. | I.
St | St | St

m / / | m / / | m / /

Panzer Unit	Pz. II	Pz. III	Pz. IV(kz)	Pz. IV(lg)	Pz. Bef.
33rd Pz. Rgt.	22	99	9	12	2

⛣ The last summer offensive
1 JULY 1943

The 9th Panzer Division's armoured strength was halved in 1943, when the 3rd Battalion was disbanded and the 2nd Battalion was detached to become the 51st Panzer Battalion.

AT THE BEGINNING OF 1943, the 9th Panzer Division had been returned from Army Group South to Army Group Centre, serving with XXVII Corps of the 9th Army at Rshev. In February, it was transferred to Army Corps *Burdach*, and in March it moved on to Army Corps *Scheele*, part of the 2nd *Panzerarmee* that was located in the Orel sector of the front.

In April 1943, the 9th Panzer Division was placed in the Army Group Reserve before being attached to 2nd *Panzerarmee* Reserve. Over the next two months, the Division was brought up to strength ready for Operation *Zitadelle*, the German offensive at Kursk.

In July 1943, the division was assigned to XLVII Corps of 9th Army. Commanded by General Model, 9th Army was the main strike force of the northern pincer that was intended to isolate and destroy the huge bulge in the frontline around the city of Kursk.

Kursk offensive

When the German offensive at Kursk opened in the early hours of 5 July, 9th Panzer Division could field a single battalion of 14 Panzer IIs, 59 Panzer IIIs and 20 Panzer IVs to cut the Soviet salient. The 2nd Battalion had been detached to become an independent Tiger battalion.

Panzer Unit	Pz. II	Pz. III	Pz. IV(kz)	Pz. IV(lg)	Pz. Bef.
33rd Pz. Rgt.	1	38	8	30	6

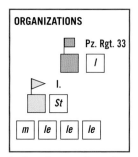

9th Army's assault could make little headway against the Soviet defences. In two days of fierce fighting in sweltering heat, Model's army lost 10,000 men and more than 200 armoured vehicles. Over the next eight days, the Germans advanced less than 20 km (12.4 miles), before being forced to retreat by a Soviet counteroffensive.

The operation at Kursk was the last major German offensive in the East as the *Wehrmacht* lost the initiative to the Red Army. For the rest of the year, 9th Panzer continued to retreat, taking heavy losses in the murderous fighting on the Dnieper River.

In August, 9th Panzer was again transferred, becoming part of XLI Corps of the 2nd *Panzerarmee* at Briansk. In September, it was moved south to join the reconstituted 6th Army at Mius and Stalino. In October, it was fighting with 1st Panzer Army at Zaparozhe, and at the end of the year it was in action at Krivoi Rog.

▶ **7.5cm PaK40/3 auf Panzerkampfwagen 38(t) Ausf H (Sd Kfz 138)**

50th Panzerjäger Battalion

Nine kills rings are painted on the barrel of this vehicle. After the failure of the Kursk offensive, the 9th Panzer was heavily involved in the defensive battles that drove the *Wehrmacht* back to the Dneipr River, and suffered serious losses in the winter of 1943–44.

Specifications

Crew: 4	Engine: Praga EPA/2
Weight: 11.9 tonnes (10.8 tons)	Speed: 35km/hr (21.7mph)
Length: 5.77m (18.9ft)	Range: 250km (155.3 miles)
Width: 2.16m (7ft)	Radio: FuG5
Height: 2.51m (8.2ft)	

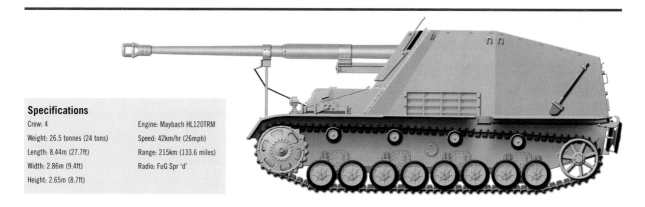

Specifications

Crew: 4	Engine: Maybach HL120TRM
Weight: 26.5 tonnes (24 tons)	Speed: 42km/hr (26mph)
Length: 8.44m (27.7ft)	Range: 215km (133.6 miles)
Width: 2.86m (9.4ft)	Radio: FuG Spr 'd'
Height: 2.65m (8.7ft)	

▲ **8.8cm PaK43/1 (L/71) auf Fahrgestell Panzerkampfwagen III/IV (Sf)**

50th Panzerjäger Battalion

A total of 30 'Nashorn' was listed as operational in 1943. When employed from defensive positions, the 'Nashorn' was a formidable weapon. It was able to defeat any armour with its 8.8cm (3.5in) cannon, and several instances were recorded of a single tank destroyer annihilating a whole company of Russian tanks.

Panzer-Jäger-Kompanie 'Nashorn' (8.8cm PaK43) K.St.N 1148b

Introduced in 1943, the Nashorn, or 'Rhinoceros', was a powerful self-propelled tank-hunter mounting the PaK variant of the 8.8cm (3.5in) FlaK gun onto a modified Panzer IV. This was lengthened, and the motor was moved forward from the rear to the centre of the vehicle. The Nashorns were issued to independent *schwere Panzerjäger abteilungen*, attached to formations at corps or army level. Typically, a heavy *Panzerjäger* battalion would include a staff battery with three Nashorns and three *Flakvierling* quad 2cm (0.8in) air defence guns, and three *Panzerjäger* companies arranged as seen here.

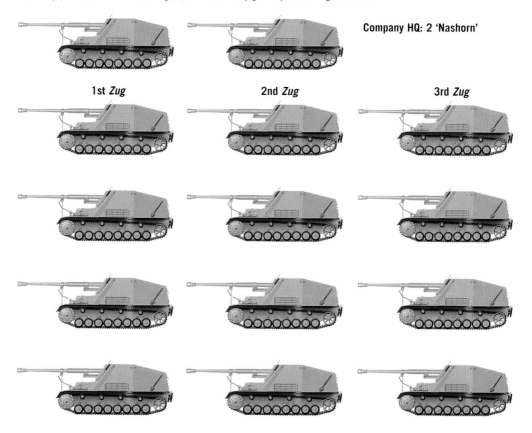

Company HQ: 2 'Nashorn'

1st *Zug*   **2nd *Zug***   **3rd *Zug***

The Western Front
JUNE 1944

Early in 1944, the 9th Panzer Division arrived in Carcassonne in southern France, where it was to be refitted. It absorbed the 155th Reserve Panzer Division in the process.

THE 51ST BATTALION had traded in its Tigers for Panthers, and rejoined the division as the 2nd Battalion, 33rd Panzer Regiment. The 1st Battalion was now equipped with long-barrelled Panzer IVs. Based in the South of France, it was in no position to intervene when the Allies landed in Normandy in June 1944. Ordered north in July, it took weeks to cover the distance. *Maquis* attacks and sabotaged bridges delayed matters, and as they got closer to Normandy, Allied air attacks meant that they were only able to travel during the short summer nights. By the time the unit arrived in Normandy, the Americans had already broken out of the beachhead, and the British were pressing southward from Caen. The Division arrived on the battle front just in time to be caught in the Falaise Pocket, escaping only after most of its men were killed or captured, and with only 12 tanks.

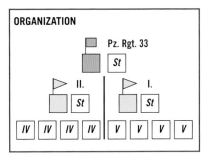

ORGANIZATION

Pz. Rgt. 33
St
II. *St*
I. *St*
IV IV IV IV | V V V V

Panzer Unit	Pz. IV	Pz. V	Flk.Pz
33rd Pz. Rgt.	79	79	8

▶ **Jagdpanzer 38(t) Hetzer (Panzerjäger 38(t)) fur 7.5cm PaK39**
50th Panzerjäger Battalion

Some 2584 Hetzers were produced from April 1944 to May 1945. The MG34 or MG42 machine gun was internally controlled. This effective tank-destroyer was armed with one 7.5cm (3in) PaK39 L/48 cannon, and carried 41 rounds of ammunition.

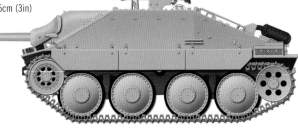

Specifications

Crew: 4	Engine: Praga AC/2
Weight: 17.4 tonnes (15.75 tons)	Speed: 42km/hr (26mph)
Length: 6.38m (20.9ft)	Range: 177km (110 miles)
Width: 2.63m (8.6ft)	Radio: FuG5 plus FuG Spr 1
Height: 2.17m (7.1ft)	

▶ **Panzerkampfwagen II Ausf L (Sd Kfz 123)**
9th Reconnaissance Battalion / 1st Company (Luchs)

With the invasion of Normandy, the Division was ordered north. Only able to travel at night because of Allied air superiority over the invasion front, it arrived after the American breakout, Operation *Cobra*, and was caught in the Falaise Pocket. A full company with 29 of these modernized Panzer IIs was in the divisional inventory in August 1943.

Specifications

Crew: 4	Engine: Maybach HL66P
Weight: 14.3 tonnes (13 tons)	Speed: 60km/hr (37.3mph)
Length: 4.63m (15.2ft)	Range: 290km (180.2 miles)
Width: 2.48m (8.1ft)	Radio: FuG12 plus FuG Spr 'a'
Height: 2.21m (7.3ft)	

▶ **Leichte Feldhaubitze 18/2 auf Fahrgestell Panzerkampfwagen II (Sf)**

102nd Panzer Artillery Regiment / 2nd Battalion

The need to provide artillery support to the fast-moving Panzer divisions led to the development of many new examples of self-propelled artillery. 676 Wespe, or 'Wasp', SP guns were produced between February 1943 and July 1944. The Wespe mounted the LeFH 18M L/28 10.5cm (4.1in) howitzer, and was built on the production lines of the now obsolete Pz.Kpfw II.

Specifications

Crew: 5	Engine: Maybach HL62TR
Weight: 12.1 tonnes (11 tons)	Speed: 40km/hr (24.9mph)
Length: 4.81m (15.8ft)	Range: 220km (136.7 miles)
Width: 2.28m (7.5ft)	Radio: FuG Spr 1
Height: 2.3m (7.5ft)	

The Battle of the Bulge
14 DECEMBER 1944

Only 2000 men and 12 tanks escaped from the Falaise Pocket, but a major refit brought the Division up to combat strength in time for the winter offensive in the Ardennes in 1944.

THE ARDENNES OFFENSIVE was Hitler's last gamble in the West. Manteuffel's 5th *Panzerarmee* achieved some success, but was fought to a standstill after penetrating more than 100 km (62 miles) into the Allied lines. Manteuffel called for reinforcements, and 9th Panzer was one of the Panzer divisions that were sent to his assistance, when it was attached to the XLVII Corps. However, even before it arrived, the American 1st and 3rd Armies had begun to roll the German spearheads back. When an Allied counteroffensive began on 3 January, the Germans had nothing left to fight it.

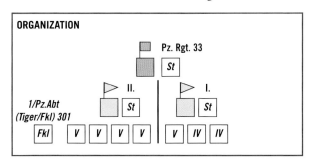

ORGANIZATION

Pz. Rgt. 33

St

II. I.

St St

1/Pz.Abt
(Tiger/Fkl) 301

Fkl V V V V V IV IV

Panzer Unit	Pz. IV	Pz. V	StuG	FlkPz(20)	FlkPz(37)
33rd Pz. Rgt.	28	57	14	4	4

▼ **Schwerer Ladungstrager (Sd Kfz 301) Ausf B**

I Battalion / Schwere Panzer Abteilung (Tiger-Fkl) 301 (Attached)

The *Ladungstrager* was a remote-controlled tracked demolition charge layer. Once the enemy realized that demolition charge layers were being used against them, their first action was to identify and knock out their control vehicle. By using the Tiger I heavy tank as a control vehicle, the 301st had a weapon with enough armour and firepower to keep the enemy at bay and to enable the unit to complete its mission.

Specifications

Crew: 1 (or 0 when remote-controlled)	Engine: Borgward 6M RTBV
Weight: 4 tonnes (3.6 tons)	Speed: 38km/hr (23.6mph)
Length: 3.65m (12ft)	Range: 212km (131.7 miles)
Width: 1.8m (6.2ft)	Radio: EP3 mit UKE6
Height: 1.19m (3.9ft)	

▲ Panzerkampfwagen VI Ausf E (Sd Kfz 181)

I Battalion / Schwere Panzer Abteilung (Tiger-Fkl) 301 / 1st Company / tank
number 1 (Attached to 9th Panzer)

No fewer than 70 Allied tanks were claimed as kills by the guns of the Tigers of
the 301st Heavy Battalion while it operated with the 9th Panzer Division in the
last months of the war. This is a late version of the Tiger I, with all-steel wheels.

Specifications

Crew: 5	Engine: Maybach HL210P45
Weight: 62.8 tonnes (57 tons)	Speed: 38km/hr (23.6mph)
Length: 8.45m (27.7ft)	Range: 140km (87 miles)
Width: 3.7m (12.1ft)	Radio: FuG5
Height: 2.93m (9.6ft)	

▶ Panzerkampfwagen IV Ausf H (Sd Kfz 161/2)

Kampfgruppe / Pz. Rgt 33

As deployed in the Harz Region in 1945. During February 1945, the Division
unsuccessfully mounted an attack on the US forces in
possession of the Remagen Bridge.

Specifications

Crew: 5	Engine: Maybach HL120TRM
Weight: 27.6 tonnes (25 tons)	Speed: 38km/hr (23.6mph)
Length: 7.02m (23ft)	Range: 210km (130.5 miles)
Width: 2.88m (9.4ft)	Radio: FuG5
Height: 2.68m (8.8ft)	

▶ Panzerjäger 38(t) mit 7.5cm PaK40/3 Ausf M (Sd Kfz 138)

Kampfgruppe / 50th Panzerjäger Battalion

One of the Division's last operational vehicles, in action in the Cologne region in
1945. The 9th Panzer Division was trapped in the Ruhr Pocket in April 1945, where
it surrendered to US forces.

Specifications

Crew: 4	Engine: Praga AC
Weight: 11.6 tonnes (10.5 tons)	Speed: 42km/hr (26mph)
Length: 4.95m (16.2ft)	Range: 190km (118 miles)
Width: 2.15m (7ft)	Radio: FuG Spr d
Height: 2.48m (8.1ft)	

10th Panzer Division

The last of the pre-war armoured divisions to be formed, the 10th Panzer Division was also to have the shortest life of all of them.

THE 10TH PANZER DIVISION was created primarily as an occupation force in Czechoslovakia after the final takeover of that country early in 1939. Components of the new Division were provided by other formations, including the 4th Panzer Brigade.

Commanders

General der Panzertruppen F. Schaal
(1 Sept 1939 – 2 Aug 1941)

General der Panzertruppen W. Fischer
(2 Aug 1941 – 1 Feb 1943)

Generalleutnant F .von Broich
(1 Feb 1943 – 12 May 1943)

INSIGNIA

Possibly the simplest of all tactical symbols, the single oblique line was used by the 10th Panzer Division in 1939 and 1940.

Standard tactical symbol used by 10th Panzer in 1940.

Modified version of the standard 10th Panzer tactical insignia, used by the Division between 1941 and 1943.

Buffalo symbol used by 7th Panzer Regiment, and adopted by some other 10th Panzer units as a *Zusatzsymbol* between 1941 and 1943.

◀ **Defeat in Tunisia**
The men of the 10th Panzer Division were among 150,000 Axis troops who went into captivity in Tunisia following the Allied victory in 1943.

Fall Weiss: the invasion of Poland
1 SEPTEMBER 1939

Newly formed, the 10th Panzer Division was held in reserve for Army Group North during the early days of the Invasion of Poland.

WHEN HEINZ GUDERIAN needed reinforcement for his lightning assault through northern Poland, 10th Panzer was assigned to his XIX Army Corps. The division's first major action was at Wizna, where the Poles had fortified a position to cover the crossings of the Narev and the Biebrza Rivers, and to protect the roads from Bialystock and to Brest-Litovsk.

The fortifications were quickly smashed, and Guderian's Panzers advanced towards Wysokie Mazowieckie, encircling and destroying the Polish Narew Corps. After removing these obstacles, Guderian's panzers advanced to Brest Litovsk. Lead units made contact with XXII *Panzerkorps*, advancing from the south on 18 September, one day after the Red Army moved in from the east. The two conquerors then ruthlessly divided Poland.

ORGANIZATION

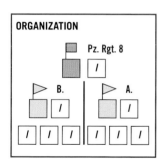

Panzer Unit	Pz. I	Pz. II	Pz. III	Pz. IV	Pz. Bef.
8th Pz. Rgt.	57	74	3	7	9

▶ Panzerkampfwagen II Ausf B (Sd Kfz 121)

Pz. Rgt 8 / A Battalion / 2nd Company / 3rd Zug / tank number 4

25 Ausf B models were produced between February and March 1937. Succeeding variants had a revised and much more effective suspension and tracks.

Specifications

Crew: 3	Engine: Maybach HL62TR
Weight: 8.7 tonnes (7.9 tons)	Speed: 40km/hr (24.9mph)
Length: 4.76m (15.6ft)	Range: 200km (124.3 miles)
Width: 2.14m (7ft)	Radio: FuG5
Height: 1.96m (6.4ft)	

▶ Panzerfunkwagen (Sd Kfz 263) 8-Rad

90th Nachrichten Kompanie (Signal Company)

Not intended as a combat vehicle, the Sd Kfz 263 served as a communications hub for Panzer divisions as well as at Corps and Army level. Some 240 examples were manufactured between April 1938 and April 1943.

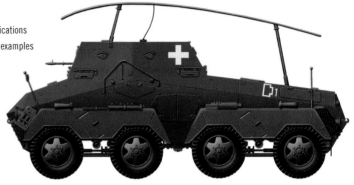

Specifications

Crew: 5	Engine: Büssing-NAG L8V
Weight: 8.9 tonnes (8.1 tons)	Speed: 100km/hr (62.1mph)
Length: 5.85m (19.2ft)	Range: 300km (186.4 miles)
Width: 2.2m (7.2ft)	Radio: 1 Satz Funkgerat fur (m)
Height: 2.9m (9.5ft)	Pz.Funktrupp b

Fall Gelb: the French campaign
10 May 1940

After the fall of Poland, 10th Panzer Division was assigned to Army Group A in the Eifel Mountains, as the *Wehrmacht* redeployed its forces westward.

FOR THE CAMPAIGN IN THE WEST, 10th Panzer was once again assigned to Guderian's *Panzerkorps*. Bursting through the Ardennes on 10 May, the corps was through Sedan and across the Meuse by 14 May. 10th Panzer, along with the elite *Grossdeutschland* infantry regiment, provided flank protection while 1st and 2nd Panzer Divisions raced westward. Guderian's corps reached the Channel a week later, cutting off the best of the Allied field armies.

Guderian was rewarded with a two-corps *Panzergruppe* for the next stage of the Battle of France, which saw the Germans strike south on a broad front on 5 June. By the time of the Armistice, Guderian's Panzers had reached the Swiss border and had cut off the French armies on the Maginot Line.

ORGANIZATION

Pz. Rgt. 8   Pz. Rgt. 7

I   I

B.   A.   B.   A.

St   St   St   St

m I I   m I I   m I I   m I I

Panzer Unit	Pz. I	Pz. II	Pz. III	Pz. IV	Pz. Bef.
7th Pz. Rgt.	22	58	29	16	9
8th Pz. Rgt.	22	55	29	16	9

▶ Panzerkampfwagen III Ausf E (Sd Kfz 141)

Pz. Rgt 7 / A Battalion / 1st Company / 2nd Zug / tank number 2

The 10th Panzer Division was part of *Panzergruppe* von Kleist during the Western campaign, advancing through Belgium to the Meuse.

Specifications

Crew: 5	Engine: Maybach HL120TRM
Weight: 24 tonnes (21.8 tons)	Speed: 40km/hr (24.9mph)
Length: 5.41m (17.7ft)	Range: 165km (102.5 miles)
Width: 2.95m (9.7ft)	Radio: FuG5
Height: 2.44m (8ft)	

▼ Panzerkampfwagen I Ausf A (Sd Kfz 101)

Pz. Rgt 7 / A Battalion / 1st Company / 3rd Zug / tank number 4

The early Ausf A had four road wheels, with the idler wheel touching the ground. The suspension was satisfactory at low speeds, but it pitched badly when moving faster. The turret was all welded, and was armed with two 7.92mm (0.3 in) MGs, which were operated by the commander who had to perform as the gunner as well.

Specifications

Crew: 2	Engine: Krupp M305
Weight: 6 tonnes (5.4 tons)	Speed: 37km/hr (23mph)
Length: 4.02m (13.2ft)	Range: 145km (90 miles)
Width: 2.06m (6.8ft)	Radio: FuG2
Height: 1.72m (5.6ft)	

▶ Panzerkampfwagen IV Ausf B (Sd Kfz 161)

Pz. Rgt 7 / B Battalion / 4th Company / 3rd Zug / tank number 2

The Ausf B had a straight front hull. It was fitted by a more powerful engine, the 300hp Maybach HL 120 T engine with a new ZF six-speed SSG 76 transmission.

Specifications

Crew: 5	Engine: Maybach HL120TR
Weight: 20.7 tonnes (18.8 tons)	Speed: 40km/hr (24.9mph)
Length: 5.92m (19.4ft)	Range: 200km (124.3 miles)
Width: 2.83m (9.3ft)	Radio: FuG5
Height: 2.68m (8.8ft)	

▶ Panzerkampfwagen II Ausf b (Sd Kfz 121)

Pz. Rgt 7 / B Battalion / 5th Company / 4th Zug / tank number 2

The Ausf B variant of the Panzer II incorporated numerous modifications to improve the vehicle compared to the first series. The main improvements involved a larger motor and strengthening the drive mountings and transmission.

Armament Specifications

Main gun: 2cm (0.8 in) KwK30 L/55 in left of turret	Sight: TZF4
Ammunition: 180 rounds	Secondary: 7.92mm (0.3in) MG34 in right of turret
Traverse: 360° (manual)	Ammunition: 2250 rounds
Elevation: -9.5° to +20°	MG sight: As for main armament

▼ **15cm sIG33 (Sf) auf Panzerkampfwagen I Ausf B**

706th Schwere Infanteriegeschütz Abteilung

Heavy Infantry Gun detachments were assigned to six of the Panzer divisions engaged in the Western campaign in 1940 .

The letter 'K' is used to identify units assigned to *Panzergruppe von Kleist*, which included the three panzer corps spearheading Germany's surprise attack through the Ardennes.

Specifications

Crew: 4	Engine: Maybach NL38TR
Weight: 9.4 tonnes (8.5 tons)	Speed: 40km/hr (24.9mph)
Length: 4.67m (15.3ft)	Range: 140km (87 miles)
Width: 2.06m (6.8ft)	Radio: Name
Height: 2.8m (9.2ft)	

Barbarossa: the attack on Russia
22 JUNE 1941

While 10th Panzer remained on occupation duties in France until February 1941, the 8th Panzer Regiment was detached and assigned to the 15th Panzer Division, destined for Africa.

THE 10TH PANZER DIVISION returned to Germany in March 1941, and was assigned to Army Group Centre for Operation *Barbarossa*. As part of Hoth's 3rd *Panzergruppe*, the division fought through Minsk, Smolensk and Vyasma before joining 4th *Panzerarmee* for the assault on Moscow.

Driven back from the gates of the Soviet capital, 10th Panzer remained with Army Group Centre until May 1942, when it was transferred to Army Group D in France. It was one of the units used to respond to the British and Canadian forces that raided Dieppe.

Panzer Unit	Pz. II	Pz. III(50)	Pz. IV	Pz. Bef
7th Pz. Rgt.	45	105	20	12

ORGANIZATION

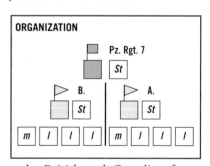

▶ **Panzerbefehlswagen III Ausf E (Sd Kfz 266-267-268)**

Pz. Rgt 7 / B Battalion / Stabskompanie / Signal Platoon / signal officer tank

The 7th Panzer Regiment used the letters 'A' and 'B' to identify its battalions, instead of the roman numerals used by other units.

Specifications

Crew: 5	Engine: Maybach HL120TR
Weight: 21.5 tonnes (19.5 tons)	Speed: 40km/hr (24.9mph)
Length: 5.38m (17.7ft)	Range: 165km (102.5 miles)
Width: 2.91m (9.5ft)	Radio: FuG6 plus FuG2 or
Height: 2.44m (8ft)	FuG7 or FuG8

▶ **Panzerkampfwagen III Ausf G (Sd Kfz 141)**

Pz. Rgt 7 / A Battalion / 3rd Company / 4th Zug / tank number 3

For Operation *Barbarossa,* the 10th Panzer was part of Army Group
Centre, assigned to *Panzergruppe Guderian.*

Specifications

Crew: 5	Engine: Maybach HL120TRM
Weight: 22.4 tonnes (20.3 tons)	Speed: 40km/hr (24.9mph)
Length: 5.41m (17.7ft)	Range: 165km (102.5 miles)
Width: 2.95m (9.7ft)	Radio: FuG5
Height: 2.44m (8ft)	

▶ **Panzerkampfwagen T-34 747 (r)**

Pz. Rgt 7

A Captured Russian T-34 model 1941. General
Guderian requested that German industry copy this
tank, but the Panther which emerged was a much more sophisticated vehicle.

Specifications

Crew: 4	Engine: V-2-34
Weight: 34.6 tonnes (31.39 tons)	Speed: 40km/hr (24.9mph)
Length: 6.58m (21.6ft)	Range: 430km (267 miles)
Width: 2.98m (9.8ft)	Radio: 10R
Height: 2.57m (8.4ft)	

▶ **Panzerkampfwagen III Ausf H (Sd Kfz 141)**

Pz. Rgt 7 / B Battalion / 6th Company / 2nd Zug / tank number 1

By October 1941, the 10th Panzer was 60km (37.3 miles) from Moscow.
By December, temperatures of -35°C (-31° F) had frozen it in place.

Specifications

Crew: 5	Engine: Maybach HL120TRM
Weight: 24 tonnes (21.8 tons)	Speed: 40km/hr (24.9mph)
Length: 5.41m (17.7ft)	Range: 165km (102.5 miles)
Width: 2.95m (9.7ft)	Radio: FuG5
Height: 2.44m (8ft)	

▶ **Panzerjäger 38(t) fur 7.62cm PaK36 (r) (Sd Kfz 139)**

*90th Panzerjäger Battalion / 1st Self-propelled Battery / 1st Zug / tank
number 3*

The 1st Self-propelled Battery was equipped with nine
'Marder III' armed with a Russian 76.2mm (3in) gun.

Specifications

Crew: 4	Engine: Praga EPA or EPA/2
Weight: 11.76 tonnes (10.67 tons)	Speed: 42km/hr (26mph)
Length: 5.85m (19.2ft)	Range: 185km (115 miles)
Width: 2.16m (7ft)	Radio: FuG Spr d
Height: 2.5m (8.2ft)	

Y. Defeat in North Africa

NOVEMBER – DECEMBER 1942

Rommel and the *Afrika Korps* had been fighting their own war in North Africa since February 1941. It was now in trouble, after the Battle of Alamein and the Allied landings in Algeria.

ROMMEL HAD LONG BEGGED for reinforcements and now, when it was almost too late, they were being poured into North Africa. The reinforcements included the 10th Panzer Division and the Tigers of sPzAbt 501 and 1/sPzAbt 504.

Rommel conducted a fighting retreat from Libya in the face of Montgomery's vastly more powerful 8th Army. Before leaving North Africa on sick leave, Rommel showed one more spark of his old genius, smashing the inexperienced American II Corps at Kasserine. However, Allied materiel superiority could not be stopped, and Tunisia fell on 12 May 1943.

Survivors of the 10th Panzer Division went into captivity along with the 15th and 21st Panzer Divisions and over 150,000 troops. The 10th Panzer Division was stricken on 30 June 1943. It was never to be reformed.

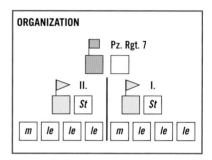

ORGANIZATION

Pz. Rgt. 7

Panzer Unit	Pz. II	Pz. III	Pz. IV(kz)	Pz. IV(lg)	Pz. Bef.
7th Pz. Rgt.	21	105	4	16	9

◀ **Panzerkampfwagen II Ausf F (Sd Kfz 121)**
Pz. Rgt 7 / Regiment Company / Light Platoon
The 10th Panzer was transferred to Tunis in response to Operation *Torch*, the Allied invasion of North Africa. It formed part of the newly created 5th *Panzerarmee* under the command of General von Arnim.

Specifications

Crew: 3	Engine: Maybach HL62TR
Weight: 10.5 tonnes (9.5 tons)	Speed: 40km/hr (24.9mph)
Length: 4.81m (15.8ft)	Range: 200km (124.3 miles)
Width: 2.28m (7.5ft)	Radio: FuG5
Height: 2.15m (7ft)	

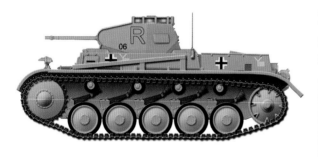

▶ **Panzerkampfwagen III Ausf L (Sd Kfz 141/1)**
Pz. Rgt 7 / II Battalion / 7th Company
653 Ausf L variants of the Panzer III were produced between June and December 1942. The Ausf L was armed with a long-barrelled 5cm (2in) KwK L/60, and its front turret armour had been increased from 30mm (1.2in) to 57mm (2.2in) thickness.

Specifications

Crew: 5	Engine: Maybach HL120TRM
Weight: 22.7 tons (25 tonnes)	Speed: 40km/hr (24.9mph)
Length: 6.28m (20.6ft)	Range: 155km (96.3 miles)
Width: 2.95m (9.7ft)	Radio: FuG5
Height: 2.5m (8.2ft)	

Specifications

Crew: 5	Engine: Maybach HL120TRM
Weight: 25.9 tonnes (23.5 tons)	Speed: 40km/hr (24.9mph)
Length: 6.62m (21.7ft)	Range: 210km (130.5 miles)
Width: 2.88m (9.4ft)	Radio: FuG5
Height: 2.68m (8.8ft)	

▲ Panzerkampfwagen IV Ausf G (Sd Kfz 161/1 und 161/2)

Pz. Rgt 7 / II Battalion / 8th Company / 2nd Zug / tank number 3

The Ausf G variant of the Panzer IV had one 7.5cm (3in) KwK40 L/48 cannon and carried a total of 87 antitank, high-explosive and smoke rounds. This is a late version of the Ausf G, with the vision port in the turret side removed. The cannon had the new-style muzzle brake and the turret carried a new cupola with thicker armour.

▶ Schwerer Panzerspähwagen (7.5cm) (Sd Kfz 233)

10th Motorcycle Battalion / 5th Heavy Company

In spite of its name, the 10th Motorcycle Battalion included the 1st Armoured Car Company, the 2nd Half-track Company and the 5th Heavy Company, as well as the 3rd and 4th Motorcycle Companies. The license plate carried by this close-support armoured car was WH 240815.

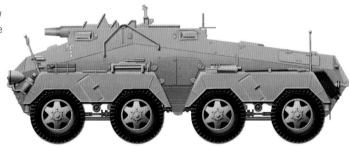

Specifications

Crew: 3	Engine: Büssing-NAG L8V
Weight: 9.6 tonnes (8.7 tons)	Speed: 80km/hr (49.7mph)
Length: 5.85m (19.2ft)	Range: 300km (186.4 miles)
Width: 2.2m (7.2ft)	Radio: FuG Spr Ger 'a'
Height: 2.25m (7.4ft)	

▶ 7.5cm Sturmgeschütz 40 Ausf F/8 (Sd Kfz 142/1)

I Battalion / Sturmgeschütz Abteilung 242 (Attached to division)

The Ausf F/8 variant of the StuG III was armed with one 7.5cm (3in) StuK40 L/48 cannon, and it carried 44 rounds of ammunition. Only one battery of the 242nd Battalion made it to North Africa; the rest of the unit was sent to the Eastern Front.

Specifications

Crew: 4	Engine: Maybach HL120TRM
Weight: 25.6 tonnes (23.2 tons)	Speed: 40km/hr (24.9mph)
Length: 6.77m (22.2ft)	Range: 140km (87 miles)
Width: 2.92m (9.6ft)	Radio: FuG15 or FuG16
Height: 2.15m (7ft)	

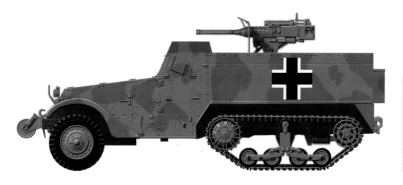

Specifications

Crew: 6	Engine: White 160AX
Weight: c. 9.9 tonnes (9 tons)	Speed: 72km/hr (44.7mph)
Length: 6.2m (20.3ft)	Range: 290km (180.2 miles)
Width: 2.24m (7.3ft)	Radio: (if fitted) FuG Spr Ger 1
Height: 2.28m (7.5ft)	

▲ Mittlerer Schützenpanzerwagen M3(a)

Unknown formation

The 10th Panzer Division captured several American vehicles in North Africa and pressed them into service immediately against their former owners. This example is a self-propelled anti-aircraft gun, with a French 3.7cm (1.5in) M1925 gun mounted onto an American M3 half-track. The M1925 was the primary light AA weapon in French warships. Its rate of fire was 30–42 rounds per minute.

▶ Infanterie Panzerkampfwagen Mk III 749(e)

Pz. Rgt 7

A Captured British Valentine Mk III infantry tank, armed with one 2pdr (40mm) gun. Two Valentines were among the 16 German tanks lost at the Kasserine Pass, when the *Afrika Korps* inflicted a stinging reverse and severe losses to the inexperienced American forces who had landed in North Africa.

 The National cross variant generally (but not always) used in North Africa was toned down to match the desert camouflage applied to vehicles in the theatre.

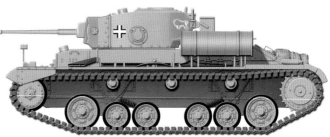

Specifications

Crew: 3	Engine: AEC or GMS 6-cyl diesel
Weight: 18.7 tonnes (17 tons)	Speed: 24km/hr (15mph)
Length: 5.89m (19.3ft)	Range: 145km (90 miles)
Width: 2.63m (8.6ft)	Radio: British No.9 set
Height: 2.273m (7.5ft)	

▶ Panzerkampfwagen III Ausf N (Sd Kfz 141/2)

Pz. Rgt 7 / II Battalion / 7th Company / 2nd Zug / tank number 3

The light companies of the 501st Heavy Tank Battalion, the first Tiger tank unit, were absorbed by the 7th Regiment and incorporated into the 7th and 8th Companies. The Ausf N Panzer III issued to the 501st Heavy Panzer Battalion were converted from Ausf L chassis.

Specifications

Crew: 5	Engine: Maybach HL120TRM
Weight: 25.4 tonnes (23 tons)	Speed: 40km/hr (24.9mph)
Length: 5.52m (18.1ft)	Range: 155km (96.3 miles)
Width: 2.95m (9.7ft)	Radio: FuG5
Height: 2.5m (8.2ft)	

Schwere Panzer Kompanie

The first Heavy Panzer Companies were formed early in 1942, providing the cores of the first Heavy Panzer Battalions later that year. The early organization of the companies saw the massive Pz.Kpfw VI Tiger serving in mixed platoons with Pz.Kpfw IIIs. The mobile Panzer IIIs provided flank protection for the ponderous Tigers. The 501st and 503rd Battalions were sent to North Africa at the end of 1942. In March 1943, the organization changed, with each battalion equipped only with Tigers.

1st *Zug*	2nd *Zug*	3rd *Zug*

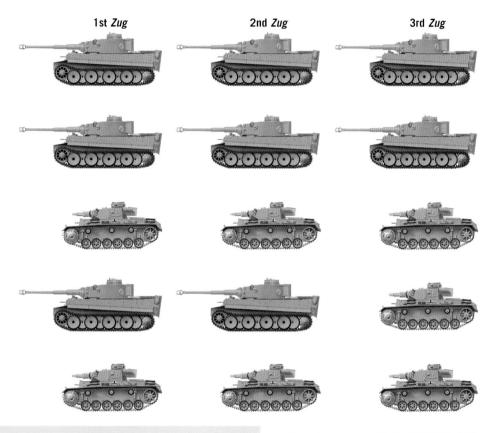

Specifications

Crew: 5

Weight: 62.8 tonnes (57 tons)

Length: 8.45m (27.7ft)

Width: 3.7m (12.1ft)

Height: 2.93m (9.6ft)

Engine: Maybach HL210P45

Speed: 38km/hr (23.6mph)

Range: 140km (87 miles)

Radio: FuG5

▼ Panzerkampfwagen VI Ausf E (Sd Kfz 181)

Pz. Rgt 7 / II Battalion / 8th Company / 2nd Zug / tank number 3

Until their surrender, the Tigers and Ausf N of the 501st claimed to have destroyed 170 Allied tanks. The remnants of the 10th Panzer Division surrendered with the rest of the *Afrika Korps* in May 1943, and was never reformed.

Chapter 3

1940–41
Panzer Divisions

The triumphant conquest of France and
the Low Countries in May and June 1940 proved that the
Panzer was the essential component of the modern,
Blitzkrieg-style of warfare. Ten Panzer divisions had
provided sufficient armoured power to complete the
conquest of France, but even as the Battle of Britain
commenced Hitler's eyes were looking eastwards. To win
a war with the Soviet Union, the *Wehrmacht* was going
to need more tanks, more motorized infantry
and more tank divisions.

◀ **Panzer Professionals**
By the time of Operation *Barbarossa* – the Invasion of the Soviet Union in June 1941 – the German
Panzerwaffe was the most experienced and most capable armoured force in the world.

11th Panzer Division

The massive expansion of the *Panzerwaffe,* which began after the Battle of France, placed a great strain on the *Wehrmacht*'s capacity to man the new Panzer formations.

THE 11TH PANZER DIVISION was established on 1 August 1940. The motorized infantry component of the formation was provided by the independent 11th *Schützen* Brigade, while the experienced 15th Panzer Regiment was transferred from the 5th Panzer Division to provide the armoured core. The motorcycle, reconnaissance and *Panzerjäger* battalions were newly formed, with men coming from the 231st Infantry Division.

Commanders

General der Panzertruppen L. Cruwell *(1 Aug 1940 – 15 Aug 1941)*	General der Infanterie D. von Choltitz *(4 Mar 1943 – 15 May 1943)*
Generalleutnant G. Angern *(15 Aug 1941 – 24 Aug 1941)*	Generalleutnant J. Mickl *(15 May 1943 – 10 Jul 1943)*
General der Panzertruppen H. von Esebeck *(24 Aug 1941 – 20 Oct 1941)*	Generalleutnant W. von Wietersheim *(10 Aug 1943 – 10 Apr 1945)*
Generalleutnant W. Scheller *(20 Oct 1941 – 16 May 1942)*	Generalmajor H. Freiherr Treusch und Buttlar – Brandenfels *(10 Apr 1945)*
General der Panzertruppen H. Balck *(16 May 1942 – 4 Mar 1943)*	

Signals units were provided by the 311th Infantry Division, the Pioneers or combat engineers were transferred from the 209th Infantry Division, and another *Schützen* battalion was organized from a regiment of the 4th Infantry Division.

War in the Balkans

6 APRIL 1941

After working up in Germany, 11th Panzer was assigned to XIV Corps of 12th Army in Poland. Early in 1941, it went with 12th Army to Romania and Bulgaria for the invasion of Yugoslavia.

THE 11TH PANZER DIVISION was attached to Kleist's 1st *Panzergruppe* for the invasion of Yugoslavia, attacking across the Bulgarian border on 7 April. After driving towards Skopje, 5th and 11th Panzer Divisions were detached from Kleist's force and directed northwards towards Nis in Serbia. After taking the town, 11th Panzer pushed on towards Belgrade.

Racing north, 11th Panzer units aimed to be first to reach the Yugoslav capital, but were chagrined to discover once they had entered the suburbs that they were hours too late. They had been beaten to Belgrade by 10 men from the motorcycle reconnaissance company of SS Division *Reich* (later to become the SS Panzer Division *Das Reich*), who had taken the surrender of the city.

The fall of Belgrade brought the conventional war in Yugoslavia to an end, but it marked the beginning of four years of brutal partisan war.

ORGANIZATION

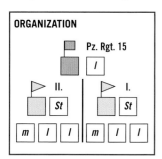

Panzer Unit	Pz. II	Pz. III(37)	Pz. III(50)	Pz. IV	Pz. Bef.
15th Pz. Rgt.	45	25	26	16	14

▶ **Kleiner Panzerbefehlswagen (Sd Kfz 265)**

Pz. Rgt 15 / II Battalion / Stabskompanie / Signal Platoon / tank number 4

The yellow circle indicates that this small command vehicle belonged to the 2nd Battalion. A yellow tactical number '04' was painted on the front of the vehicle.

Specifications

Crew: 3	Engine: Maybach NL38TR
Weight: 6.5 tonnes (5.9 tons)	Speed: 40km/hr (24.9mph)
Length: 4.42m (14.5ft)	Range: 170km (105.6 miles)
Width: 2.06m (6.8ft)	Radio: FuG2 and FuG6
Height: 1.99m (6.5ft)	

▶ **Panzerkampfwagen IV Ausf E (Sd Kfz 161)**

Pz. Rgt 15

The 11th Panzer Division used a two-digit tactical number (platoon/tank number). The 15th Regiment was also known as the *Gespenster,* or 'Ghost', Regiment after reports from prisoners taken during the invasion of France, to the effect that the 15th Regiment, then with the 5th Panzer Division, appeared from nowhere.

Specifications

Crew: 5	Engine: Maybach HL120TRM
Weight: 23.2 tonnes (21 tons)	Speed: 42km/hr (26mph)
Length: 5.92m (19.4ft)	Range: 200km (124.3 miles)
Width: 2.84m (9.3ft)	Radio: FuG5
Height: 2.68m (8.8ft)	

Leichte Panzerkompanie 'Gliederung'

The organization of the Light Panzer Company changed considerably after the fall of France. The pause in the fighting after July 1940 gave German industry the chance to build up production of modern tanks, allowing the German army to replace many of the obsolete vehicles with which it had fought from the outbreak of war. The light companies, originally equipped with a mix of Pz.Kpf Is and Pz.Kpfw IIs, now took delivery of large numbers of Pz.Kpfw IIIs. By early 1941, the Command troop of the company was exclusively equipped with Panzer IIIs, as were the 1st, 2nd and 3rd *Zugen* or Platoons. One *Zug* in each company was designated as a Light Platoon, and these retained the lightweight Panzer II. These were more suited to reconnaissance than the Panzer IIIs.

Company HQ

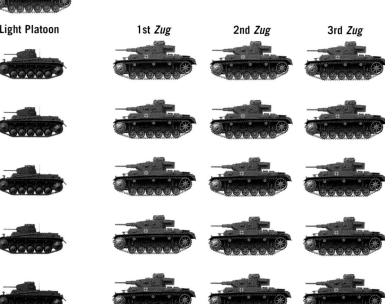

Light Platoon **1st** *Zug* **2nd** *Zug* **3rd** *Zug*

▶ **Mittlerer Gepanzerter Beobachtungskraftwagen (Sd Kfz 254)**

119th Panzer Artillery Regiment

This artillery observation vehicle was assigned to the 3rd Battery of a towed artillery battalion operating in Yugoslavia in 1941. One of the few diesel-powered vehicles in German service, the SdKfz 254 chassis, with its unique wheel-cum-track arrangement, was originally designed by Saurer for the Austrian army.

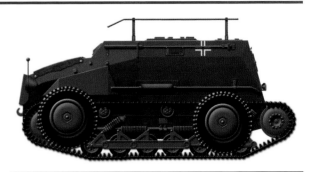

Specifications

Crew: 7	Engine: Saurer CRDv
Weight: 7 tonnes (6.4 tons)	Speed: 60km/hr (37.3mph)
Length: 4.56m (15ft)	Range (on wheels): 500km (310.7 miles)
Width (on wheels): 2.2m (7.2ft)	Radio: FuG4 plus FuG8 and FuG Spr Ger 'f'
Height: 1.88m (6.2ft)	

The vehicle carries the Divisional insignia and the military symbol for communications troops. Front plate licence plate WH-800920.

▶ **Mittlerer Schützenpanzerwagen Ausf B (Sd Kfz 251/1)**

11th Schützen Brigade / 110th Schützen Regiment

Markings on this standard troop carrier indicate that it was assigned to the Battalion's 2nd Motorized Infantry Company.

The vehicle carries the motorized infantry symbol on the left front mudguard, next to the shielded headlight.

Specifications

Crew: 2 plus 12 troops	with MG shield
Weight: 9.9 tonnes (9 tons)	Engine: Maybach HL42TUKRM
Length: 5.98m (19.6ft)	Speed: 53km/hr (32.9mph)
Width: 2.1m (6.9ft)	Range: 300km (186.4 miles)
Height: 1.75m (5.7ft) or 2.16m (7ft)	Radio: FuG Spr Ger f

Barbarossa: the attack on Russia
22 JUNE 1941

Following the Yugoslav campaign, 11th Panzer returned to Germany to refit, which meant that it missed the opening days of Operation *Barbarossa*.

ATTACHED TO ARMY GROUP SOUTH, the 11th Panzer Division entered combat in the Ukraine in July. After fighting through Zhitomir and Uman, it was in reserve for the great encirclement at Kiev.

On 11 October, Panzer transferred to the 4th *Panzergruppe*, which was part of Army Group Centre, for the delayed assault on Moscow. The division remained active with Army Group Centre until well into the summer of 1942.

Panzer Unit	Pz. II	Pz. III(37)	Pz. III(50)	Pz. IV	Pz. Bef.
15th Pz. Rgt.	44	24	47	20	8

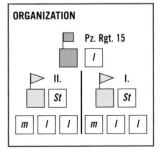

ORGANIZATION

▶ **Panzerkampfwagen III Ausf H (Sd Kfz 141)**

Pz. Rgt 15 / I Battalion / 1st Company

The Ausf H variant of the Pz.Kpfw III was the first to be armed with the 5cm (2in) KwK L/42 gun. It was introduced to service in October 1940. 1st Company vehicles were recognizable by the use of a white tank rhomboid on the turret side. It was fitted with an extra storage box on the back of the turret, commonly known as a 'Rommel' kit.

Markings on the 'Rommel' kit – extra storage attached to the rear of the turret – indicated that this tank belonged to the Battalion's 1st Company.

Specifications

Crew: 5	Engine: Maybach HL120TRM
Weight: 24 tonnes (21.8 tons)	Speed: 40km/hr (24.9mph)
Length: 5.41m (17.7ft)	Range: 165km (102.5 miles)
Width: 2.95m (9.7ft)	Radio: FuG5
Height: 2.44m (8ft)	

▶ **Panzerkampfwagen II Ausf F (Sd Kfz 121)**

Pz. Rgt 15 / II Battalion / 5th Company / 2nd Platoon

At the start of Operation *Barbarossa*, 11th Panzer still had 44 Panzer IIs in its inventory. The Ausf F was armed with one 2cm (0.8in) KwK30 L/55 automatic cannon and carried 180 PzGr and SpGr rounds. The white circle was used to identify units of the 2nd Platoon of one of the Light Panzer companies.

Specifications

Crew: 3	Engine: Maybach HL62TR
Weight: 10.5 tonnes (9.5 tons)	Speed: 40km/hr (24.9mph)
Length: 4.81m (15.8ft)	Range: 200km (124.3 miles)
Width: 2.28m (7.5ft)	Radio: FuG5
Height: 2.15m (7ft)	

▶ **Panzerkampfwagen IV Ausf D (Sd Kfz 161)**

Pz. Rgt 15

The 11th Panzer Division was part of the 1st *Panzergruppe*, Army Group South during the drive on Kiev in the summer of 1941. The Division had 20 Panzer IVs, which operated with the Medium Panzer companies of each battalion.

Specifications

Crew: 5	Engine: Maybach HL120TRM
Weight: 22 tonnes (20 tons)	Speed: 40km/hr (24.9mph)
Length: 5.92m (19.4ft)	Range: 200km (124.3 miles)
Width: 2.84m (9.3ft)	Radio: FuG5
Height: 2.68m (8.8ft)	

◑ *Fall Blau*: the Eastern Front
28 JUNE 1942

In July 1942, the 11th Panzer Division transferred with 4th *Panzerarmee* from Army Group Centre to Army Group South, where it was to support the summer offensive in southern Russia.

4TH *PANZERARMEE* struck westwards towards Voronezh, before being moved 500 km (310.7 miles) south to guard the flank of Paulus' 6th Army advancing on Stalingrad. Coming under the command of Manstein's Army Group Don, 11th

Panzer Unit	Pz. II	Pz. III(kz)	Pz. III(lg)	Pz. IV	Pz. Bef.
15th Pz. Rgt.	15	14	110	13	3

Panzer was detached once the Red Army encircled Stalingrad, being sent to support Romanian forces of the Chir River.

Under the command of one of the outstanding Panzer commanders of the war, Hermann Balck, 11th Panzer fought first to reach the forces trapped in Stalingrad, and then to counter the massive Soviet offensives which followed. The battles on the Chir saw the destruction of more than 700 Soviet tanks – but the understrength 11th Panzer Division was all but destroyed in the process.

ORGANIZATION

Pz. Rgt. 15 / I

III. St / II. St / I. St

m l l / m l l / m l l

◑ The last summer offensive
1 JULY 1943

11th Panzer Division's outstanding but costly performance in the Stalingrad campaign meant that Hitler ordered the Division's recreation almost immediately.

BY MAY OF 1943, the reconstituted 11th Panzer Division was working up to full strength at Kharkov. It fought at Belgorod, Kursk, Krivoj Rog and suffered heavy losses when it was encircled at Kresun, south of Kiev. In July 1943, it was attached to LXVIII *Panzerkorps* of the 4th *Panzerarmee* at Belgorod.

11th Panzer Division was one of Army Group South's lead formations during the Battle of Kursk. On 4 July, the division advanced, and after three days took the high ground around

Butovo while the *Grossdeutschland Panzergrenadier* Division attacked the town. However, LXVIII Corps became bogged down in fighting its way through the multi-layered Soviet defences, and progress slowed to a crawl. By 10 July, the German advance had come to a halt. The massive tank battle at Prokorovka was a victory for neither side, but it left LXVIII *Panzerkorps* exposed. When the Soviets launched a massive counterattack, the Germans had to withdraw. By 23 July they were back at their original positions. 11th Panzer Division had lost heavily in the fighting and had fewer than 20 tanks left.

ORGANIZATION

Pz. Rgt. 15 / I

II. St / I. St

m le le / m le le

Panzer Unit	Pz. II	Pz. III	Pz. IV	Pz. Bef.	Flammpz
15th Pz. Rgt.	8	62	26	4	13

▶ **Schwerer Panzerspähwagen (Sd Kfz 231)**

11th Reconnaissance Battalion / 1st Armoured Car Company

11th Panzer formed part of the southern pincer attack at Kursk in 1943, for which the *Wehrmacht* had concentrated 1035 older Panzers plus 45 Tigers and 200 Panthers. The Sd Kfz 231 seen here was armed with one 2cm (0.8in) cannon.

Specifications

Crew: 4	Engine: Büssing-NAG L8V
Weight: 9.1 tonnes (8.3 tons)	Speed: 85km/hr (52.8mph)
Length: 5.85m (19.2ft)	Range: 300km (186.4 miles)
Width: 2.2m (7.2ft)	Radio: FuG Spr Ger 'a'
Height: 2.35m (7.7ft)	

The Western Front

JUNE 1944

The 11th Panzer was sent to Bordeaux for refitting in June 1944, where it absorbed the 273rd Reserve Panzer Division. It was equipped with 79 Panthers and eight 3.7cm (1.5in) FlaK Panzer.

AFTER A YEAR OF FIGHTING RETREATS on the Eastern Front, culminating in fighting free of the Cherkassy Pocket in February 1944, 11th Panzer was in need of serious reconstruction. The 1st Battalion, 15th Panzer Regiment re-equipped with Pz.Kpfw V Panthers, while the 2nd Battalion continued to operate with long-barrelled Panzer IVs.

The division would probably have been ordered to the Normandy invasion front, had it not been for the Allied landings in the South of France. In July 1944, the Division was shifted to Toulouse, where its major mission was in countering Resistance sabotage. In August, it took part in delaying actions after the Allied landings, and later in the withdrawal to Alsace. There, it participated in the defence of the Belfort Gap in September 1944, and subsequently withdrew north into the Saar region, where the Division was again rebuilt.

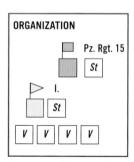

Leichte Panzerkompanie 'Gliederung'

By the last year of the war, there was no place for companies of light tanks in a Panzer division. However, there was a need for integrated air defence, given the superiority of Allied air power over the battlefield. Type 45 Divisions incorporated air defence into the Panzer units, each tank battalion having an armoured flak company of two platoons. One was armed with Flakvierling 2cm (0.8in) guns; the other, shown here, was equipped with the 3.7cm (1.5in) FlaK tanks nicknamed *Möbelwagens*.

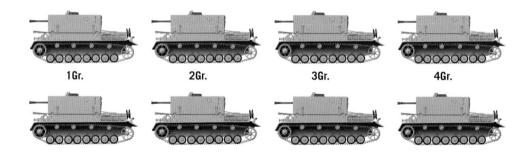

1Gr. 2Gr. 3Gr. 4Gr.

Ⓛ The Battle of the Bulge
14 DECEMBER 1944

The 11th Panzer Division conducted a fighting retreat through France, covering the escape of Army Group G from Provence, up the Rhone and into Alsace.

AFTER AGAIN REBUILDING from its base in the Belfort Gap, the 11th Panzer Division was placed in Army Group G's reserve in the Saarland. In December, the division was attached to XIII SS Corps, and was committed to action against the US Army near Biche. Based on the *Westwall* fortifications near Fort Simserhof and Fort Schiesseck, it fought alongside the 25th *Panzergrenadier* Division and the 361st *Volksgrenadier* Division.

Following the stalling of Operation *Wacht am Rhein* – the massive attack through the Ardennes, known now as the Battle of the Bulge – the 11th Panzer Division was pulled out of the line to be refitted. For this, there were only limited resources available, but the Division was then assigned as the mobile reserve of 7th Army, still embroiled on the southern flank of the Ardennes.

Panzer Unit	Pz. IV	Pz. V	FlkPz(20)	FlkPz(37)
15th Pz. Rgt.	31	47	8	7

Last Days

The division saw some action in the Ardennes, but was more heavily engaged in the 7th Army's defensive actions around the Trier area in January and February 1945. In March 1945, troops of the American 3rd Army seized the Ludendorff Bridge over the Rhine at Remagen before it could be blown. The 11th Panzer Division was attached to the 15th Army as it made an unsuccessful attempt to dislodge the Americans from this vital crossing. The remnants of the division retreated through Hesse and Thuringia, finally surrendering to the Americans in the Bavarian Forest on 4 May 1945.

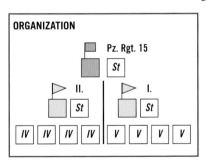

ORGANIZATION

Pz. Rgt. 15 / St

II. / St — I. / St

IV IV IV IV / V V V V

▼ **Panzerkampfwagen V Ausf G (Sd Kfz 171)**

Pz. Rgt 15 / I Battalion / 2nd Company / 3rd Zug / tank number 1

11th Panzer participated in the Ardennes offensive at the end of 1944 and saw combat at Remagen before surrendering to US forces in Bavaria, May 1945. In the last months of the war, it was equipped with four Panther companies and four companies of Panzer IVs.

Specifications

Crew: 5	Engine: Maybach HL230P30
Weight: 45.5 tons (50.2 tonnes)	Speed: 46km/hr (28.6mph)
Length: 8.86 m (29ft)	Range: 200km (124.3 miles)
Width: 3.4m (11.2ft)	Radio: FuG5
Height: 2.98m (9.8ft)	

12th Panzer Division

The 12th Panzer Division began forming at Stettin in northern Germany in October 1940, and its constituent units had been completely assembled by January 1941.

THE 2ND (MOT) INFANTRY DIVISION provided the structure for the new panzer formation. The 12 *Schützen* Brigade incorporated the 5th and 25th Infantry Regiments, while the three battalions of the 29th Panzer Regiment were new. Panzer strength in the spring of 1941 consisted of 40 Panzer Is, 33 Panzer IIs, 109 Panzer 38(t)s, 30 Panzer IVs and 8 Panzer 3(t) command tanks. The division was attached to the XLVI Corps of the 11th Army, part of Army Group C. The first divisional commander was *Generalmajor* (later *Generaloberst*) Josef Harpe, who had commanded the tank training school at Zossen.

Commanders

Generaloberst J. Harpe *(5 Oct 1940 – 15 Jan 1942)*	Generalmajor G. Muller *(28 May 1944 – 16 July 1944)*
Generalleutnant W. Wessel *(15 Jan 1942 – 1 Mar 1943)*	Generalleutnant E. von Bodenhausen *(16 July 1944 – 12 April 1945)*
Generalleutnant E. von Bodenhausen *(1 Mar 1943 – 28 May 1944)*	Oberst von Usedom *(12 April 1945 – 8 May 1945)*

▲ **Close support**

The Panzer IVs of the 12th Panzer Division provided close support to the smaller fighting tanks which made up the bulk of the division's inventory.

INSIGNIA

The 12th Panzer Division's tactical insignia was carried by divisional vehicles from 1941 to the end of the war in 1945.

Barbarossa: the attack on Russia

22 JUNE 1941

In July 1941, the 12th Panzer Division was transferred to Army Group Centre on the Eastern Front, where it formed part of 3rd *Panzergruppe's* XXXIX Corps.

THE *WEHRMACHT'S* TRIUMPHANT advance into Russia saw 12th Panzer playing its part in the operations to encircle Minsk, cross the Dnieper and to take Smolensk. In September 1941, XXXIX Corps was moved to the 16th Army of Army Group North. 12th Panzer was engaged in the Battle of Mga, and then suffered heavy losses during the Soviet winter counteroffensive on the Leningrad Front.

12th Panzer Division was withdrawn to Estonia to refit. In February 1942, it returned to the Volkhov Front to fight in the many battles south of Leningrad. In November 1942, the 12th Panzer Division was transferred to Army Group Centre, near Roslavl.

Panzer Unit	Pz I	Pz II	Pz. 38(t)	Pz. IV	Pz Bef 38(t)
29th Pz. Rgt.	40	33	109	30	8

ORGANIZATION

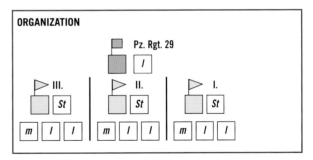

▶ **Panzerkampfwagen 38(t) Ausf C**

Pz. Rgt 29 / I Battalion / 1st Company / 2nd Zug / tank number 2

The Ausf C variant of this Czech-designed tank was armed with one 3.7cm (1.5in) KwK38 (t) L/48.8 cannon and two 7.92 MG37 (t) machineguns. Note the set of *Nebel* (smoke) grenade launchers attached to the rear deck.

Specifications

Crew: 4	Engine: Praga EPA
Weight: 10.5 tonnes (9.5 tons)	Speed: 42km/hr (26mph)
Length: 4.61m (15.1ft)	Range: 250km (155.3 miles)
Width: 2.14m (7ft)	Radio: FuG37(t)
Height: 2.4m (7.9ft)	

▼ **Panzerkampfwagen II Ausf b (Sd Kfz 121)**

12th Reconnaissance Battalion

A96 stands for *Aufklärungs* (Reconnaissance) Battalion, 9th Platoon, 6th vehicle. During the early phases of the invasion of the USSR, it was common for the *Panzertruppen* to carry extra fuel and supplies, neccessary because of the vast distances that had to be covered in Russia.

Specifications

Crew: 3	Engine: Maybach HL62TR
Weight: 8.7 tonnes (7.9 tons)	Speed: 40km/hr (24.9mph)
Length: 4.76m (15.6ft)	Range: 200km (124.3 miles)
Width: 2.14m (7ft)	Radio: FuG5
Height: 1.96m (6.4ft)	

▶ **Panzerkampfwagen IV Ausf E (Sd Kfz 161)**

Pz. Rgt 29

The 12th Panzer Division served initially with the 3rd *Panzergruppe*, Army Group Centre, before being transferred to the northern sector. The Panzer IV depicted here still used the old (1939–40) system of painting the tank tactical number in a black tank rhomboid on the hull.

Specifications

Crew: 5	Engine: Maybach HL120TRM
Weight: 23.2 tonnes (21 tons)	Speed: 42km/hr (26mph)
Length: 5.92m (19.4ft)	Range: 200km (124.3 miles)
Width: 2.84m (9.3ft)	Radio: FuG5
Height: 2.68m (8.8ft)	

The last summer offensive
1 JULY 1943

In 1942, the 3rd Panzer Battalion was transferred to the 13th Panzer Division. The 1st Battalion was redesignated as the 508th Panzer Battalion between May and July 1943.

FROM JANUARY 1943, the 12th Panzer Division was engaged in operations in and around Orel, Bryansk, Gomel and Zhlobin. During the Kursk battles of July 1943, 12th Panzer served with 2nd *Panzerarmee* on the northern sector. In the autumn of 1943, the Division was heavily engaged in defensive operations along the Dnieper.

In February 1944, the division was again moved north to take part in the desperate battles around Leningrad, but the *Wehrmacht* was not able to help stem the massive Soviet offensives against Army Group North. Over the next few months, 12th Panzer withdrew west along with the rest of the retreating German forces, until it was pushed into the Courland Pocket in September 1944.

Isolated until May 1945, the 12th Panzer Division surrendered to the Soviets early in that month, when *Festung Kurland* was forced to give in to the victorious Red Army.

Panzer Unit	Pz. II	Pz. III	Pz. III(75)	Pz. IV	Pz. Bef.
29th Pz. Rgt.	6	30	6	37	4

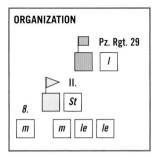

ORGANIZATION

▶ Panzerkampfwagen I Ausf F
Unknown formation

The heavily armoured Ausf F variant of the Panzer I was designed as a support weapon for infantry assaults – rather like a mobile pillbox. It was loved by its crews for its ability to survive mine explosions.

Specifications

Crew: 2	Engine: Maybach HL45P
Weight: 23.2 tonnes (21 tons)	Speed: 25km/hr (15.5mph)
Length: 4.38m (14.4ft)	Range: 150km (93.2 miles)
Width: 2.64m (8.7ft)	Radio: FuG5
Height: 2.05m (8.2ft)	

▶ Panzerkampfwagen IV Ausf H (Sd Kfz 161/2)
Pz. Rgt 29 / II Battalion / 5th Company / Company HQ tank

Late-war Panzer IVs in service with the 12th Panzer Division, with their long 7.5cm (3in) guns and extra armour, were immensely more powerful than the Panzer IVs of 1939.

Specifications

Crew: 5	Engine: Maybach HL120TRM
Weight: 27.6 tonnes (25 tons)	Speed: 38km/hr (23.6mph)
Length: 7.02m (23ft)	Range: 210km (130.5 miles)
Width: 2.88m (9.4ft)	Radio: FuG5
Height: 2.68m (8.8ft)	

13th Panzer Division

The 13th Panzer Division was formed in Vienna on 11 October 1940, using elements of the 13th Infantry Division (mot.) and the 4th Panzer Regiment, detached from the 2nd Panzer Division.

IN NOVEMBER 1940, 13th Panzer was sent to Romania as a *Lehrtruppe,* or demonstration unit, for the German military mission, nominally to teach Panzer tactics, but in fact to protect the Ploesti oil fields, which were vital to the German war effort. In May 1941, the Division was returned to Silesia for reinforcement and preparation for the war in Russia.

INSIGNIA

Like the 12th Panzer Division, vehicles of the 13th Panzer Division carried the same tactical insignia from 1941 to the end of the war.

Commanders

Generalleutnant F. von Rotkirch und Panthen *(11 Oct 1940 – 25 June 1941)*	Generalleutnant E. Hauser *(1 Sept 1943 – 26 Dec 1943)*
Generalleutnant W. Duvert *(25 June 1941 – 30 Nov 1941)*	Generalleutnant H. Mikosch *(26 Dec 1943 – 18 May 1944)*
General der Panzertruppen T. Herr *(1 Dec 1941 – 1 Nov 1942)*	Oberst F. von Hake *(18 May 1944 – 25 May 1944)*
Generalleutnant H. von der Chevallerie *(1 Nov 1942 – 1 Dec 1942)*	Generalleutnant H. Troger *(25 May 1944 – 9 Sept 1944)*
Generalleutnant W. Crisolli *(1 Dec 1942 – 15 May 1943)*	Generalmajor G. Schmidhuber *(9 Sept 1944 – 11 Feb 1945)*
Generalleutnant H. von der Chevallerie *(15 May 1943 – 1 Sept 1943)*	

◀ **Panzers across the Don**

During Germany's 1942 summer offensive, 13th Panzer provided the spearhead for Kleist's armoured thrust into the Caucasus.

⊕ *Barbarossa*: the attack on Russia
22 JUNE 1941

The 13th Panzer Division, commanded by *Generalmajor* Walther Düvert, was assigned to *Generaloberst* von Kleist's 1st *Panzergruppe* in Army Group South.

THE DIVISION CROSSED the river Bug on the Polish-Soviet frontier on 23 June 1941, behind the 44th Infantry Division. Advancing rapidly despite stiff Soviet resistance, it broke through the heavily fortified Stalin Line at Hulsk. The 13th Panzer Division captured Kremenchug, and on 25 August established the first bridgehead across the Dnieper river at Dniepropetrosvk. The advanced continued, reaching the Mius river by way of Mariopol and Taganrog, which had been taken by the SS-*Leibstandarte.*

On 13 November, 13th Panzer fought its way into Rostov-on-Don, but had to withdraw to the Mius Line, where it spent the next seven months over the severe winter of 1941/42. In the heavy defensive fighting that ensued, the Division was able to hold its own against repeated Soviet infantry assaults.

ORGANIZATION

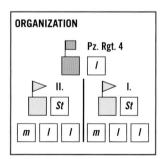

Panzer Unit	Pz. II	Pz. III(37)	Pz. III(50)	Pz. IV	Pz. Bef.
4th Pz. Rgt.	45	27	44	20	13

▶ **Panzerkampfwagen II Ausf F (Sd Kfz 121)**

Pz. Rgt 4 / II Battalion / Stabskompanie / Light Platoon / tank number 12

The Panzer II units were generally used for security patrols when the Division came to a halt. Their duties included blocking enemy reconnaissance patrols, repelling minor attacks and giving the main unit time to deploy in case of major attacks.

Specifications

Crew: 3	Engine: Maybach HL62TR
Weight: 10.5 tonnes (9.5 tons)	Speed: 40km/hr (24.9mph)
Length: 4.81m (15.8ft)	Range: 200km (124.3 miles)
Width: 2.28m (7.5ft)	Radio: FuG5
Height: 2.15m (7ft)	

▶ **Panzerkampfwagen III Ausf F (Sd Kfz 141)**

Pz. Rgt 4 / II Battalion / 8th Company / 3rd Zug / tank number 5

The 3.7cm (1.5in) gun could not penetrate the frontal armour of Soviet T-34s or KV-1s, even at point-blank range. But an expert crew could damage the enemy's gun barrel or turret ring at short ranges, forcing the Soviet tank to disengage.

Specifications

Crew: 5	Engine: Maybach HL120TR
Weight: 21.8 tonnes (19.8 tons)	Speed: 40km/hr (24.9mph)
Length: 5.38m (17.7ft)	Range: 165km (102.5 miles)
Width: 2.91m (9.5ft)	Radio: FuG5
Height: 2.44m (8ft)	

 # *Fall Blau*: the Eastern Front
28 JUNE 1942

The summer offensive of 1942 saw the 13th Panzer Division at the heart of the main German advance of that year, towards the vital Caucasus oilfields.

ALONG WITH SS DIVISION *WIKING*, 13th Panzer captured Rostov-on-Don in July. The next objective was Armavir on the Kuban river. The Division advanced in several columns, through corn and sunflower fields that stretched to the horizon. Huge dust clouds, lack of water and extreme heat put a tremendous strain on both soldiers and equipment, and supply lines were stretched almost to breaking point. Nevertheless, by the end of September, the Division was at Elchetovo, known as the 'Gateway to the Caucasus'. However, the Stalingrad catastrophe threatened the survival of entire Army Group, and it had to retreat back to Rostov and beyond.

ORGANIZATION

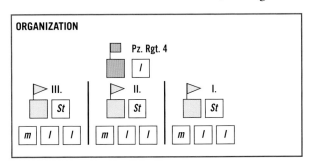

Panzer Unit	Pz. II	Pz. III(5kz)	Pz. III(5lg)	Pz. IV(kz)	Pz. Bef.
4th Pz. Rgt.	15	41	30	12	5

⊕ The last summer offensive
1 JULY 1943

While the offensive at Kursk was being planned, the German divisions that had fought their way to the Caucasus had to fight equally hard to get back to where they had started in 1942.

A<small>T THE BEGINNING OF JULY,</small> while German armies were launching their massive assault at Kursk, the tattered remnants of the 13th Panzer Division were being ferried across the Strait of Kerch to the Crimea. After refitting, in August the Division was moved to Stalino to support the weakened German divisions that were trying to hold the old Mius Line. These were gradually being pushed back toward the Dnieper by repeated Soviet attacks

The *Wehrmacht's* panzer divisions were employed as 'Fire Brigades' during the long German retreat from the Russia. 13th Panzer units now operated in individual mobile *Kampfgruppen*, made up of tanks, *Panzerjägers*, mobile artillery and armoured infantry. Their task was to delay the Soviets by actively engaging them in sharp local counterattacks, which caused significant Red Army losses.

Fighting Retreat

As 13th Panzer reached Cherson, near the mouth of the Dnieper, it was instructed to safeguard

Panzer Unit	Pz. II	Pz. III(kz)	Pz. III(lg)	Pz. IV(lg)	Pz. Bef.
4th Pz. Rgt.	5	4	10	50	2

the passage of the 4th *Gebirgs* Division as it retreated back across the river. On 3 November 1943, more than 15,000 vehicles of the two divisions made it safely across before the bridge was blown in the face of the enemy.

To help close the 150km (93-mile) gap torn by the Soviets in the German defences between Kremenchug and Dniepropetrovsk, the division was then ordered to the area of Krivoy Rog and Kirovograd, where it stemmed a number of potential Soviet breakthroughs in that sector of the front.

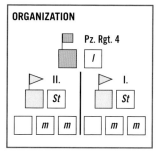

ORGANIZATION

Pz. Rgt. 4

Specifications

Crew: 5

Weight: 47.4 tonnes (43 tons)

Length: 8.86m (29ft)

Width: 3.4m (11.2ft)

Height: 2.95m (9.7ft)

Engine: Maybach HL230P30

Speed: 46km/hr (28.6mph)

Range: 200km (124.3 miles)

Radio: FuG5

▼ **Panzerkampfwagen V Ausf D (Sd Kfz 171)**

Pz. Rgt 4 / I Battalion / 3rd Company / 3rd Zug / tank number 2

The 1st Battalion of the 4th Panzer Regiment was re-equipped with 76 Pz.Kpfw V Panthers in January 1944. As with most Panther-equipped divisions at the time, the 2nd Battalion of the regiment continued to operate with Pz.Kpfw IVs.

Last battles
1944/1945

The 1st Battalion of the 4th Panzer Regiment was detached and sent to Italy to be part of an independent Panzer unit, with orders to drive the Allies from their beachhead at Anzio.

MEANWHILE, THE REST of the Division had been coming to the relief of the large German force trapped in the Cherkassy Pocket. By May, the division had been forced back as far as Kishinev, on the Romanian border.

The overwhelming power of the Soviet summer offensives forced them back further, some of the fighting units making their way into Hungary through the Carpathians. Others were interned when Romania changed sides, and many were handed over to the Red Army.

In September, those units which had escaped, assembled at Oerkeny, to the southeast of Budapest. Over the next six months, 13th Panzer Division defended the city, ultimately being wiped out in March 1945.

▸ **Panzerkampfwagen V Ausf A (Sd Kfz 171)**

Pz. Rgt 4 / I Battalion / Stabskompanie

The Allied landing at Anzio threatened Rome, but the Americans and British decided to dig in rather than break out, allowing the Germans to redeploy to attack the beachhead.

Specifications

Crew: 5	Height: 2.98m (9.8ft)
Weight: 49.4 tonnes	Engine: Maybach HL230P30
(44.8 tons)	Speed: 46km/hr (28.6mph)
Length: 8.86m (29ft)	Range: 200km (124.3 miles)
Width: 3.42m (11.2ft)	Radio: FuG5

▸ **Panzerkampfwagen V Ausf A (Sd Kfz 171)**

Pz. Rgt 4 / I Battalion / 1st Company / 2nd Zug / tank number 3

Under pressure by an eight-division German attack, the Allied VI Corps held firm. In spite of superior weapons, like the Panther, and greater combat experience gained in Russia, the *Wehrmacht* could not breach Allied defences at Anzio.

Weapon Specifications

Main: 7.5cm (3in) KwK42 L/70	Co-ax MG: 7.92mm (0.3in)
Ammunition: 79 rounds	MG 34
Traverse: 360° (hydraulic)	Hull MG: 7.92mm (0.3in)
Elevation: -8° to +18°	MG 34
Sight: TZF12a	Ammunition: 5100 rounds
	MG Sight: KgZF2

▶ 15cm Schweres Infanteriegeschütz 33/1 auf Selbstfahrlafette 38(t) (Sf) Ausf M (Sd Kfz 138/1)

93rd Panzergrenadier Battalion

282 SdKfz Ausf M were produced between April 1943 and September 1944. The self-propelled artillery piece was armed with one 15cm (6in) sIG33/2 cannon and carried 18 rounds of ammunition.

Specifications

Crew: 4	Engine: Praga AC
Weight: 13.2 tonnes (12 tons)	Speed: 35km/hr (21.7mph)
Length: 4.95m (16.2ft)	Range: 190km (118 miles)
Width: 2.15m (7ft)	Radio: FuG16
Height: 2.47m (8.1ft)	

▼ Panzer IV/70 (V) (Sd Kfz 162/1)

Unknown formation

An improved version of the Jagdpanzer IV, the first series Panzer IV/70 tank hunter entered production in August 1944. It was armed with a long-barrelled 7.5cm (3in) PaK42 L/70 cannon and carried 55 rounds of ammunition. The long gun and extra front armour made the vehicle nose-heavy, so the first two road wheels were steel rather than rubber-rimmed.

Specifications

Crew: 4	Engine: Maybach HL120TRM
Weight: 28.4 tonnes (25.8 tons)	Speed: 35km/hr (21.7mph)
Length: 8.5m (27.9ft)	Range: 210km (130.5 miles)
Width: 3.17m (10.4ft)	Radio: FuG Spr 1
Height: 1.85m (6ft)	

▼ Panzer IV/70 (V) (Sd Kfz 162/1)

Unknown formation

The vehicle depicted was from the second production series (September–November 1944), and was used at Budapest in January 1945. The 13th Panzer was sent to Hungary to take part in the futile defence of the city. The Division was destroyed early in 1945, and reformed as the *Panzer Division Feldherrnhalle 2*.

Weapons Specifications

Main: 7.5cm (3in) PaK42 L/70	Secondary: 7.92mm (0.3in) MG42
Ammunition: 55 (estimated)	Ammunition: 600 rounds
Traverse: 10° left and right (manual)	Sights: open
Elevation: -5° to +15°	
Sights: SflZF	

14th Panzer Division

The 14th Panzer Division actually predated the 12th and 13th Divisions, since it was first established at Koningsbruck/Milowitz in August of 1940.

THE 14TH PANZER DIVISION incorporated a mix of experienced and newly formed units. The 4th Infantry Division provided the basic structure and infantry strength, while the armoured component was provided by Panzer Regiment 36, from the 4th Panzer Division. By the time it went into action, 14th Panzer could deploy 45 Panzer IIs, 16 Panzer IIIs with 3.7cm (1.5in) guns, 35 Panzer IIIs with 5cm (2in) guns, 20 Panzer IVs, and eight command tanks.

▲ **War in Russia**
The Russian steppes offered almost perfect fighting terrain for tanks, and the Wehrmacht's panzers rampaged through the Soviet Union in the summer of 1941.

Commanders

General der Infanterie E. Hansen
(15 Aug 1940 – 1 Oct 1940)

Generalleutnant H. von Prittwitz und Gaffron
(1 Oct 1940 – 22 Mar 1941)

General der Panzertruppen F. Kuhn
(22 Mar 1941 – 1 July 1942)

Generalleutnant F. Heim
(1 July 1942 – 1 Nov 1942)

Generalleutnant H. von Falkenstein
(1 Nov 1942 – 16 Nov 1942)

Generalleutnant J. BaBler
(16 Nov 1942 – 26 Nov 1942)

Generalmajor M. Lattmann
(26 Nov 1942 – 31 Jan 1943)

Generalleutnant F. Seiberg
(1 Apr 1943 – 29 Oct 1943)

Generalleutnant M. Unrein
(29 Oct 1943 – 5 Sept 1944)

Generalmajor O. Munzel
(5 Sept 1944 – 1 Dec 1944)

Generalleutnant M. Unrein
(1 Dec 1944 – 10 Feb 1945)

Oberst F. Jurgen
(10 Feb 1945 – 15 Mar 1945)

Oberst K. GraBel
(15 Mar 1945 – 12 Apr 1945)

INSIGNIA

The standard tactical symbol carried by vehicles of the 14th Panzer Division. A similar, slightly elongated version was also used.

◇ War in the Balkans
6 APRIL 1941

In March 1941, 14th Panzer Division, by now part of the 17th Army, was transferred from its home base in Germany to new bases in Hungary, ready for the invasion of Yugoslavia.

FOR THE ASSAULT ON YUGOSLAVIA, the division was controlled by General Maximilian von Weichs' 2nd Army. 14th Panzer was part of XLVI Corps which attacked into Croatia, being welcomed by the pro-German Croats. After taking Zagreb, the Division pressed on through mountainous terrain into Bosnia, heading for Sarajevo. Racing through Banja Luka, Trovnik and Jajce, 14th Panzer reached Sarajevo from the west on 15 April, at the same time as 8th Panzer Division of von Kleist's command entered from the east.

On the same day, the Yugoslav government began negotiations with General von Weichs. The armistice was concluded and signed on 17 April, coming into effect the next day.

Panzer Unit	Pz. II	Pz. III(37)	Pz. III(50)	Pz. IV	Pz. Bef.
36th Pz. Rgt.	45	16	35	20	8

ORGANIZATION

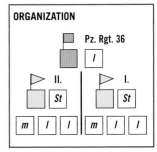

▶ Panzerkampfwagen I Ausf B (Sd Kfz 101)

Pz. Rgt 36 / Regiment Staff Company

Although no longer listed in the division inventory, a few Pz.Kpfw Is were retained for use as an 'armoured taxi' for the officers at Regimental level.

Specifications

Crew: 2	Engine: Maybach NL38TR
Weight: 6.4 tonnes (5.8 tons)	Speed: 40km/hr (24.9mph)
Length: 4.42m (14.5ft)	Range: 170km (105.6 miles)
Width: 2.06m (6.8ft)	Radio: FuG2
Height: 1.72m (5.6ft)	

▶ Panzerkampfwagen III Ausf H (Sd Kfz 141)

Pz. Rgt 36 / II Battalion / 7th Company / 2nd Zug / tank number 2

This tank retains the yellow dot after the tactical number on the turret that was used as an identification mark when the 36th Panzer Regiment was still part of the 4th Panzer Division.

Specifications

Crew: 5	Engine: Maybach HL120TRM
Weight: 24 tonnes (21.8 tons)	Speed: 40km/hr (24.9mph)
Length: 5.41m (17.7ft)	Range: 165km (102.5 miles)
Width: 2.95m (9.7ft)	Radio: FuG5
Height: 2.44m (8ft)	

Barbarossa: the attack on Russia
22 June 1941

The campaign in Yugoslavia had been relatively easy for those units which had not gone on to fight in Greece, and most were rapidly deployed to take part in the invasion of Russia.

IN MAY 1941, soon after the end of the Balkans campaign, the 14th Panzer Division was returned to Germany. In June 1941, it was assigned to III *Panzerkorps* of von Kleist's 1st *Panzergruppe*, which was the main strike force for Field Marshal Gerd von Rundstedt's Army Group South in Operation *Barbarossa*. Following the invasion of the Soviet Union, the 14th Panzer Division was engaged in nearly continuous combat through the summer, autumn and winter of 1941. The Division took part in the major battles at Kiev, Rostov and in the Chernigovka Pocket.

When the German offensive ground to a halt as winter set in, 14th Panzer was part of the force that took part in the defensive engagements along the Mius River after the first Soviet winter counter-offensive pushed the 1st *Panzergruppe* out of Rostov and back through Taganrog.

ORGANIZATION

Pz. Rgt. 36

II. St
I. St

m l l | m l l

Panzer Unit	Pz. II	Pz. III(37)	Pz. III(50)	Pz. IV	Pz. Bef.
36th Pz. Rgt.	45	15	56	20	11

▶ **Panzerkampfwagen III Ausf J (Sd Kfz 141)**

Pz. Rgt 36

The tank depicted used a two-digit tactical number indicating that it was tank number four of the medium company's 1st Platoon. The white rhomboid painted onto the turret side and rear was non-standard, and may have been an indication of the company to which it belonged.

By 1941, the Panzer rhomboid beneath the tank's identification number was becoming a less common tank marking.

Specifications

Crew: 5	Engine: Maybach HL120TRM
Weight: 24 tonnes (21.5 tons)	Speed: 40km/hr (24.9mph)
Length: 5.52m (18.1ft)	Range: 155km (96.3 miles)
Width: 2.95m (9.7ft)	Radio: FuG5
Height: 2.5m (8.2ft)	

▼ **Mittlerer Gepanzerter Beobachtungskraftwagen (Sd Kfz 254)**

4th Panzer Artillery Regiment

This vehicle was assigned to the 3rd Battery of a towed artillery battalion.

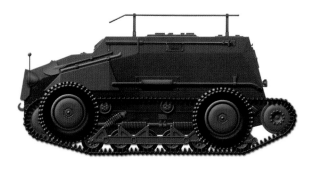

The front plate of the vehicle carried divisional and towed artillery tactical symbols.

Specifications

Crew: 7	Engine: Saurer CRDv diesel
Weight: 7 tonnes (6.4 tons)	Speed: 60km/hr (37.3mph)
Length: 4.56m (15ft)	Range: 500km (310.7 miles)
Width: 2.02m (6.6ft)	Radio: FuG8, FuG4, FuG Spr Ger 1
Height: 1.88m (6.2ft)	

⚐ *Fall Blau*: the Eastern Front
28 June 1942

14th Panzer raced through the Mius, Kharkov, Kupiansk and Don regions during the German Summer offensive of 1942.

I N NOVEMBER 1942, 14th Panzer was transferred to the 6th Army at Stalingrad – just in time to be cut off when a Soviet offensive completely encircled the city. All German relief attempts having failed, the Division was completely destroyed by February 1943.

Panzer Unit	Pz. II	Pz. III(5kz)	Pz. III(5lg)	Pz. IV(kz)	Pz. Bef.
36th Pz. Rgt.	14	41	19	24	4

ORGANIZATION

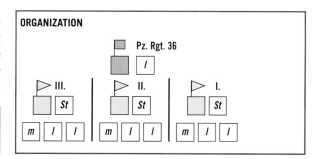

▶ Panzerkampfwagen IV Ausf F2 (Sd Kfz 161/2)

Pz. Rgt 36 / I Battalion / 4th Company / 3rd Zug / tank number 1

The Ausf F2 variant of the Panzer IV was armed with one 7.5cm (3in) KwK40 L/43
cannon, and it carried 87 rounds of ammunition. It was the first of the Panzer IVs
to be equipped with the long-barrelled, high-velocity
gun, and it went some way to redressing the balance
with the heavier Soviet tanks.

Specifications

Crew: 5	Engine: Maybach HL120TRM
Weight: 25.4 tonnes (23 tons)	Speed: 40km/hr (24.9mph)
Length: 5.62m (18.4ft)	Range: 200km (124.3 miles)
Width: 2.84m (9.3ft)	Radio: FuG5
Height: 2.68m (8.8ft)	

▶ Panzerkampfwagen III Ausf M (Sd Kfz 141/1)

Pz. Rgt 36

The number '10' indicates that this tank belonged to a company HQ section. The
Ausf M variant was the last Panzer III in series production to be armed with a 5cm
(2in) gun, and much of the production run was
cancelled in favour of flamethrower tanks, assault
guns, and the Ausf N with a short-barrelled 7.5cm (3in) gun.

Specifications

Crew: 5	Engine: Maybach HL120TRM
Weight: 25 tonnes (22.7 tons)	Speed: 40km/hr (24.9mph)
Length: 6.41m (21ft)	Range: 155km (96.3 miles)
Width: 2.95m (9.7ft)	Radio: FuG5
Height: 2.5m (8.2ft)	

▶ Mittlerer Schützenpanzerwagen Ausf C (Sd Kfz 251/1)

14th Schützen Brigade

The 14th *Schützen* Brigade had in their Order of Battle the 1/, 2/103rd *Schützen*
Regiment and the 1/, 2/108th *Schützen* Regiment. In June 1942, the motorized
infantry components of the *Panzerwaffe* were renamed, becoming known as
Panzergrenadiers. The 14th Panzer was destroyed at Stalingrad in February 1943.

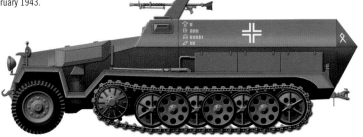

Specifications

Crew: 2 plus 12 troops	Engine: Maybach HL42TUKRM
Weight: 9.9 tonnes (9 tons)	Speed: 53km/hr (32.9mph)
Length: 5.98m (19.6ft)	Range: 300km (186.4 miles)
Width: 2.1m (6.9ft)	Radio: FuG Spr Ger f
Height: 2.16m (7ft) with MG shield	

The year of retreat

NOVEMBER 1943

Ordered to be reformed in March 1943, following its complete destruction at Stalingrad, the 14th Panzer Division was reborn in Brittany, France in April of that year.

NOW KNOWN AS the 'Stalingrad Division', 4th Panzer remained in France until November 1943, when it was sent back to the East. During the division's reconstruction, plans were made to equip a third Panzer Battalion with Pz.Kpfw VI Tiger tanks in addition to the Pz.Kpfw IVs equipping the two regular battalions. However, the scheme was quickly changed and the Third Battalion was given StuG assault guns.

By June 1943, the 36th Panzer Regiment consisted of two four-company battalions of Panzer IVs, each company having 22 tanks, and a third Assault Gun battalion. This included two Panzer companies and two StuG assault gun companies, each fielding 22 Sturmgeschütz IIIs.

By November 1943, 14th Panzer was back with Army Group South, attached to LVII *Panzerkorps* of the 1st *Panzerarmee* at Krivoi Rog. In December, it had been moved to XI *Panzerkorps* of the 8th Army at Kirovograd. Early in 1944, it was transferred to the 8th Army Reserve at around the time of the Cherkassy battles.

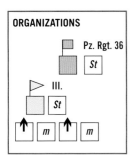

ORGANIZATIONS

Pz. Rgt. 36

Panzer Unit	Pz. IV	StuG	Pz. Bef	Flammpz
36th Pz. Rgt.	49	44	9	7

The last year on the Eastern Front

1944

The 14th Panzer Division remained in the Ukraine for the first six months of 1944. By August, the division's 1st Panzer Battalion had been refitted with 79 Pz.Kpfw V Panthers.

FROM JANUARY TO JUNE 1944, the 14th Panzer Division took part in actions in the Kirovograd, Zveningerodka, Kishinev and Jassy regions. The Division was pulled from the front in July 1944 for rest and refit at Ceterini, thus avoiding the massive series of offensives launched by nearly every Red Army Front or Army Group along more than 1000 km (621 miles) of battle lines.

In August 1944, the 14th Panzer Division was transported to the Army Group North sector of the Eastern Front, in order to take part in positional defensive actions in Courland ('Kurland' in German), an area that today includes the western parts of Latvia and Lithuania.

In January 1945, the Soviets launched a major offensive across four Fronts on the northern sector.

After four days, the Red Army broke through the German defences on the borders of the Reich and started flooding into Germany, moving 30–40 km (18.6–24.8 miles) a day. In quick succession, Soviet forces overran the Baltic states, Danzig, East Prussia and Poznan. The advance came to a halt on a line just 60 km (37.3 miles) east of Berlin along the Oder River.

Much of Army Group North had been bypassed in the offensive: Hitler renamed the substantial forces trapped in the pocket as Army Group Courland. The 14th Panzer Division, located near Libau, (now Liepaja, Latvia) remained intact until the collapse of Germany in May 1945.

ORGANIZATION

I. Pz. Rgt. 36

15th Panzer Division

The 15th Panzer Division was formed from the 33rd Infantry Division. It was shipped to Libya as part of Rommel's original *Deutsches Afrika Korps* in 1941.

THE 15TH PANZER DIVISION was authorized in October 1940, and was fully formed at Darmstadt/Landau by the middle of March 1941. It was based on the 33rd Infantry Division, with the 8th Panzer Regiment, originally from the 3rd Panzer Division, providing the tank component.

▲ **Advance towards Egypt**

15th Panzer arrived in Africa in time to play a part in Rommel's first offensive, which drove the British back through Libya to the Egyptian border.

INSIGNIA

The tactical insignia used by the 15th Panzer Division in North Africa from 1941 to 1943. It was also seen in black, and in white on a solid red circle.

Vehicles of the 15th Panzer Division were also seen carrying a variety of *Wolfsangel* (Wolf's Hook) or *Dopplehaken* (double hook) symbols.

The Wolf's Hook is an ancient runic symbol that was thought to protect against wolf attacks. Although used by several other army formations, it became infamous as part of the divisional insignia of a number of *Waffen-SS* units, including the 2nd SS Panzer Division *Das Reich*.

Commanders

General der Panzertruppen F. Kuhn
(1 Nov 1940 – 22 Mar 1941)

Generalleutnant H. von Prittwitz und Gaffron
(22 Mar 1941 – 10 Apr 1941)

General der Panzertruppen H. von Esebeck
(13 Apr 1941 – 13 May 1941)

Generalleutnant W. Neumann-Silkow
(26 May 1941 – 6 Dec 1941)

Generalleutnant E. Menny
(6 Dec 1941 – 9 Dec 1941)

General der Panzertruppen G. von Varst
(9 Dec 1941 – 26 May 1942)

Generalleutnant E. Crasemann
(26 may 1942 – 15 July 1942)

Generalleutnant H. von Randow
(15 July 1942 – 25 Aug 1942)

General der Panzertruppen G. von Varst
(25 Aug 1942 – 10 Nov 1942)

Generalleutnant W. Borowitz
(10 Nov 1942 – 13 May 1943)

◆ Enter the Desert Fox
1941

The 15th Panzer Division spent its entire combat existence as a Panzer division in North Africa, originally as part of the *Afrika Korps* and then as part of *Panzerarmee Afrika*.

ORGANIZATION

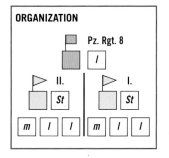

ERWIN ROMMEL ARRIVED in North Africa in February 1941. 5th *Leichte* Division arrived in February, and 15th Panzer was in North Africa by May. Rommel's first offensive drove the British back as far as Halfaya Pass on the Egyptian border. But by the end of the year, the *Afrika Korps* has been pushed back beyond Benghazi. The back-and-forth pattern that dominated the war in the desert had been established.

Panzer Unit	Pz. II	Pz. III(50)	Pz. IV	Pz. Bef
8th Pz. Rgt.	45	71	20	10

▶ Panzerkampfwagen III Ausf J (Sd Kfz 141)
Pz. Rgt 8 / I Battalion / 2nd Company

In 1941, an Italian Army of four corps had been annihilated by the British. 130,000 soldiers, 400 tanks and 1300 guns had been captured in North Africa, and Hitler was forced to come to aid of Germany's Fascist ally. He ordered two Panzer divisions, under the command of *Generalleutnant* Erwin Rommel, to be sent to Africa to stabilize the situation.

Specifications

Crew: 5	Engine: Maybach HL120TRM
Weight: 24 tonnes (21.5 tons)	Speed: 40km/hr (24.9mph)
Length: 5.52m (18.1ft)	Range: 155km (96.3 miles)
Width: 2.95m (9.7ft)	Radio: FuG5
Height: 2.5m (8.2ft)	

▶ Panzerkampfwagen II Ausf F (Sd Kfz 121)
Pz. Rgt 8 / I Battalion / 2nd Company

Reconnaissance in the desert could be performed effectively only during the morning and evening. During the day, the dazzling sun would blur the outlines of tanks and other targets. Additionally, reconnaissance had to be pushed right up to the enemy's frontline, and the thinly armoured Pz.Kpfw II, while having the mobility required, proved to be too vulnerable to enemy fire.

Specifications

Crew: 5	Engine: Maybach HL120TR
Weight: 21.8 tonnes (19.8 tons)	Speed: 40km/hr (24.9mph)
Length: 5.38m (17.7ft)	Range: 165km (102.5 miles)
Width: 2.91m (9.5ft)	Radio: FuG5
Height: 2.44m (8ft)	

▶ Panzerkampfwagen III Ausf G (Sd Kfz 141)
Pz. Rgt 8 / II Battalion / 8th Company

In June 1941, the British commander, General Wavell, initiated Operation *Battleaxe*, unaware that the 15th Panzer Division was now operational in North Africa. As British tanks were held up and channeled by minefields, they were engaged by 8.8cm (3.5in) Flak guns. Rommel then ordered the 8th Regiment to counterattack, catching the British off guard. After a six-hour battle, the British retreated, leaving 100 tanks destroyed or captured.

Specifications

Crew: 5	Engine: Maybach HL120TRM
Weight: 20.6 tonnes (20.3 tons)	Speed: 40km/hr (24.9mph)
Length: 5.41m (17.7ft)	Range: 165km (102.5 miles)
Width: 2.95m (9.7ft)	Radio: FuG5
Height: 2.44m (8ft)	

▶ Panzerkampfwagen IV Ausf F (Sd Kfz 161)

Pz. Rgt 8 / I Battalion / 4th Company

The tactical insignia depicted on this Panzer IV include the 15th Panzer Division symbol (a crossed triangle), the *Deutsches Afrika Korps* palm, the 4th *Kompanie* number and the *Wolfsangel*, or 'Wolf's Hook', of the 8th Regiment.

'Rommel' kit markings painted onto the back of the storage box added to the rear of the Panzer's turret.

Specifications

Crew: 5	Engine: Maybach HL120TRM
Weight: 24.6 tonnes (22.3 tons)	Speed: 42km/hr (26mph)
Length: 5.92m (19.4ft)	Range: 200km (124.3 miles)
Width: 2.84m (9.3ft)	Radio: FuG5
Height: 2.68m (8.8ft)	

▶ Panzerkampfwagen II Ausf C (Sd Kfz 121)

Pz. Rgt 8 / II Battalion / 8th Company

The Pz.Kpfw II could engage armoured targets beyond 600m (1968ft). The MG was used against soft targets at under 400m (1312ft) (200m (656ft) if on the move).

Specifications

Crew: 3	Engine: Maybach HL62TR
Weight: 9.8 tonnes (8.9 tons)	Speed: 40km/hr (24.9mph)
Length: 4.81m (15.8ft)	Range: 200km (124.3 miles)
Width: 2.22m (7.3ft)	Radio: FuG5
Height: 1.99m (6.5ft)	

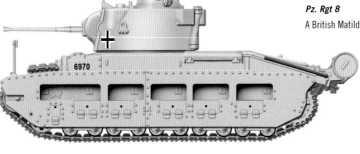

◀ Infanterie Panzerkampfwagen MkII 748(e)

Pz. Rgt 8

A British Matilda MkII infantry tank, captured during Operation *Battleaxe*.

Specifications

Crew: 4	Engine: Two AEC 6-cyl petrol
Weight: 29.7 tonnes (26.9 tons)	Speed: 24km/hr (15mph)
Length: 5.613m (18.4ft)	Range: 257km (159.7 miles)
Width: 2.59m (8.5ft)	Radio: British No.9 set
Height: 2.515m (8.3ft)	

▶ Panzerkampfwagen IV Ausf E (Sd Kfz 161)

Pz. Rgt 8 / II Battalion / 8th Company

When General Auchinleck launched Operation *Crusader* in 1942, Rommel was forced to retreat, lifting the siege of Tobruk and returning to El Agheila.

Specifications

Crew: 5	Engine: Maybach HL120TRM
Weight: 23.2 tonnes (21 tons)	Speed: 42km/hr (26mph)
Length: 5.92m (19.4ft)	Range: 200km (124.3 miles)
Width: 2.84m (9.3ft)	Radio: FuG5
Height: 2.68m (8.8ft)	

▶ **Leichter Panzerspähwagen (2cm) (Sd Kfz 222)**

33rd Reconnaissance Battalion / Armoured Car Company

The Sd Kfz 222 was armed with one 2cm (0.8in) KwK30 or 38 L/55 cannon and
carried 180 rounds of ammunition. All armoured reconnaissance units were
equipped with an antitank detachment to protect themselves from enemy armour.

Specifications

Crew: 3	Engine: Horch 3.5l or 3.8l
Weight: 5.3 tonnes (4.8 tons)	Speed: 85km/hr (52.8mph)
Length: 4.8m (15.7ft)	Range: 200km (124.3 miles)
Width: 1.95m (6.4ft)	Radio: FuG Spr Ger 'a'
Height: 2m (6.6ft)	

⛨ War in the desert
25 MAY 1942

**The 15th Panzer Division formed a key part of Erwin Rommel's armoury, as the German general
proved himself a master of continually-moving desert warfare.**

THE BRITISH CAPTURED BENGHAZI in January, but
a counterattack by the Germans retook the city
10 days later. Rommel's offensive ran out of steam on
7 February at
Gazala. Over
the next three
months, the
British built up
their forces at
Gazala, but in
May Rommel
attacked before
the British were
ready to launch their own offensive. After fierce
fighting at Gazala, the British were forced back
towards the Egyptian frontier, leaving the key port of
Tobruk under siege. Rommel captured Tobruk on
21 June, and continued to advance into Egypt.
However, by the time he reached the strong British
defensive positions at Alamein at the end of June, his
troops were exhausted, and further advances were
stopped after several weeks of fighting.

Panzer Unit	Pz. II	Pz. III(kz)	Pz. III(lg)	Pz. IV(kz)	Pz. Bef.
8th Pz. Rgt.	29	131	3	22	4

ORGANIZATION

Pz. Rgt. 8

II. / St / m le le le

I. / St / m le le le

▶ **Panzerkampfwagen III Ausf H (Sd Kfz 141)**

Pz. Rgt 8 / I Battalion / Stabskompanie / Signal Platoon

With the *Luftwaffe* putting pressure on Malta, Rommel's supplies started to arrive
safely, enabling him to quickly rebuild his forces – replacing Panzer IIs with more
effective Panzer IIIs and IVs. Not prepared for a sudden offensive, the
British lost Benghazi in January 1942 but held their defensive line at Gazala.

Specifications

Crew: 5	Engine: Maybach HL120TRM
Weight: 24 tonnes (21.8 tons)	Speed: 40km/hr (24.9mph)
Length: 5.41m (17.7ft)	Range: 165km (102.5 miles)
Width: 2.95m (9.7ft)	Radio: FuG5
Height: 2.44m (8ft)	

▶ Panzerkampfwagen III Ausf J (Sd Kfz 141/1)

Pz. Rgt 8 / I Battalion / 1st Company

In May 1942 Rommel attacked the British at Gazala. The
15th Panzer Division attacked from the south.

Specifications

Crew: 5	Engine: Maybach HL120TRM
Weight: 24 tonnes (21.5 tons)	Speed: 40km/hr (24.9mph)
Length: 5.52m (18.1ft)	Range: 155km (96.3 miles)
Width: 2.95m (9.7ft)	Radio: FuG5
Height: 2.5m (8.2ft)	

▶ Panzerkampfwagen III Ausf L (Sd Kfz 141/1)

Pz. Rgt 8 / I Battalion / 2nd Company

Recognizable by its long gun barrel, the Ausf L was
known by the British as the 'Mark III Special'.

Specifications

Crew: 5	Engine: Maybach HL120TRM
Weight: 24 tonnes (21.5 tons)	Speed: 40km/hr (24.9mph)
Length: 6.28m (20.6ft)	Range: 155km (96.3 miles)
Width: 2.95m (9.7ft)	Radio: FuG5
Height: 2.5m (8.2ft)	

▶ Panzerbefehlswagen III Ausf H

Pz. Rgt 8 / II Battalion / Stabskompanie / Signal Platoon

The standard crew of the command tank consisted of the commander, adjutant,
driver and two radio operators. By June 1942, the British had evacuated Bir
Hacheim, and Tobruk was once again under siege.

Specifications

Crew: 5	Engine: Maybach HL120TRM
Weight: 24 tonnes (21.8 tons)	Speed: 40km/hr (24.9mph)
Length: 5.4m (17.7ft)	Range: 165km (102.5 miles)
Width: 2.95m (9.7ft)	Radio: FuG6 plus FuG2 or FuG7 or
Height: 2.44m (8ft)	FuG8

▶ Panzerkampfwagen III Ausf J (Sd Kfz 141)

Pz. Rgt 8 / II Battalion / 5th Company / 3rd Zug / tank number 1

Rommel pretended to bypass Tobruk for Bardia, then launched a sudden attack
on 19 June. The British garrison of 30,000 soldiers along with large
quantities of fuel and supplies were captured.

Weapons Specifications

Main: 5cm (2in) KwK39 L/60	Co-axial: 7.92mm (0.3in) MG34
Ammunition: 92 rounds	Hull: 7.92mm (0.3in) MG34
Traverse: 360° (manual)	Ammunition: 4950 rounds
Elevation: -10° to +20°	MG sight: KgZF2
Sight: TZF5e	

▶ **Panzerkampfwagen III Ausf J (Sd Kfz 141/1)**

Pz. Rgt 8 / II Battalion / 6th Company / 3rd Zug / tank number 2

1067 Ausf J 'Long' were produced between December 1941
and July 1942. The long 5cm (2in) KwK39 L/60 was very
effective when engaging the American made 'Grant' and the British 'Valentine'.

Armour Specifications

Turret: 57mm (2.2in) front, 30mm
    (1.2in) side, 30mm (1.2in) rear,
    10mm (0.4in) top
Superstructure: 5mm (0.2in) front,
    30mm (1.2in) side, 50mm
    (2in) rear, 18mm (0.7in) top

Hull: 50mm (2in) front, 30mm (1.2in)
    side 50mm (2in) rear, 16mm
    (0.6in) bottom
Gun Mantlet: 50mm (2in) plus 20mm
    (0.8in) spaced armour

▶ **Panzerjäger 38(t) fur 7.62cm PaK36(r) (Sd Kfz 139)**

33rd Panzerjäger Battalion / Self-propelled Panzerjäger Company

Four Marder III were available in the Battalion inventory in August 1942. Based on
the obsolete Panzer 38(t) chassis, it carried a long-barrelled Soviet gun, hundreds
of which had been captured during Operation *Barbarossa*. In spite of its relatively
high profile, the powerful gun made the Marder an effective tank-hunter.

National insignia used on armoured vehicles between
1940 and 1942. In the desert, the areas around the
insignia were often not painted, leaving the original
grey colour scheme showing through.

Specifications

Crew: 4
Weight: 11.76 tonnes (10.67 tons)
Length: 5.85m (19.2ft)
Width: 2.16m (7ft)
Height: 2.5m (8.2ft)

Engine: Praga EPA or EPA/2
Speed: 42km/hr (26mph)
Range: 185km (115 miles)
Radio: FuG Spr 'd'

▶ **15cm sIG33 auf Fahrgestell Panzerkampfwagen II (Sf)**

115th Panzergrenadier Regiment / 707th Schwere Infanteriegeschütz Abteilung (Attached)

Only 12 were produced between November and December of 1941 and all were shipped to North Africa. The Sturmpanzer II was a poor design, the engine tended to
overheat and the chassis was overloaded. In its favour, it was armed with the well proven 150mm (6in) 3 L/12 heavy infantry gun.

Specifications

Crew: 4
Weight: 12.3 tonnes (11.2 tons)
Length: 5.41m (17.7ft)
Width: 2.6m (8.5ft)
Height: 1.9m (6.2ft)

Engine: Maybach HL62TRM
Speed: 40km/hr (24.9mph)
Range: 160km (99.4 miles)
Radio: FuG Spr 'f'

✠ El Alamein: Egypt denied
23 OCTOBER 1942

The British were given a new commander in August. General Bernard Law Montgomery was determined to use Allied material superiority to defeat Rommel in a battle of attrition.

IN NOVEMBER 1942, Montgomery launched his long-awaited offensive at El Alamein. The Germans were vastly outnumbered, resistance was futile, and Rommel's troops were soon reeling back. Not long afterwards, the Allies landed in Algeria, and the Germans in North Africa faced a two-front war.

Although fighting with their customary skill, *Panzerarmee Afrika* could not match the numbers of men, tanks, artillery pieces and aircraft available to the British and the Americans. Squeezed from east and west, the Axis forces were trapped in Tunisia, and eventually capitulated on 9 May 1943. The 15th Panzer Division was rebuilt, but as a *panzergrenadier* division.

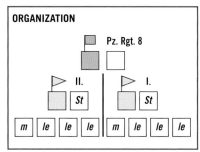

ORGANIZATION

Panzer Unit	Pz. II	Pz. III(kz)	Pz. III(lg)	Pz. IV	Pz. Bef.
8th Pz. Rgt.	14	43	44	18	2

▶ **Panzerkampfwagen IV Ausf F2 (Sd Kfz 161/1)**

Pz. Rgt 8 / II Battalion / 8th Company

The Panzer IV 'Special' was capable of destroying any American or British tank up to a range of 1500m (4921ft). That superiority made it one of the primary targets of Allied aircraft, artillery and antitank guns.

Specifications

Crew: 5	Engine: Maybach HL120TRM
Weight: 25.4 tonnes (23 tons)	Speed: 40km/hr (24.9mph)
Length: 5.62m (18.4ft)	Range: 200km (124.3 miles)
Width: 2.84m (9.3ft)	Radio: FuG5
Height: 2.68m (8.8ft)	

▶ **Mittlerer Gepanzerter Beobachtungskraftwagen (Sd Kfz 254)**

33rd Artillery Regiment

This vehicle was assigned to the 5th Battery of a towed artillery battalion. The frame aerial was for the FuG 8 radio set, intended for divisional use. It had a range of 40km (2.9-mile) transmitting by key, and a 10km (6.2-mile) voice telephony range. The unusual wheel-cum-track arrangement was complex, but it gave the SdKfz 254 good mobility both on roads and across country.

The vehicle front plate carried the artillery version of the *Afrika Korps* palm tree symbol. Licence plate WH-616664.

Specifications

Crew: 7	Engine: Saurer CRDv
Weight: 7 tonnes (6.4 tons)	Speed: 60km/hr (37.3mph)
Length: 4.56m (15ft)	Range (on wheels): 500km (310.7 miles)
Width (on wheels): 2.2m (7.2ft)	Radio: FuG4 plus FuG8 and FuG Spr Ger 'f'
Height: 1.88m (6.2ft)	

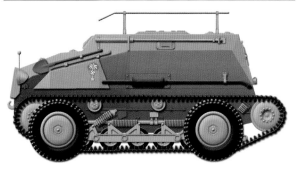

▶ 15cm sFH13/1 auf Geschützwagen Lorraine Schlepper (f) (Sd Kfz 135/1)

33rd Artillery Regiment / 4th Self-propelled Battalion

Initially 12 guns had been concentrated in a battery of three platoons, each with four guns and assigned to the 8th Panzer Regiment as artillery escorts. However, the captured French chassis lacked power: with a cross-country speed of only 8km/hr (5mph), it proved too slow to keep up with the panzers.

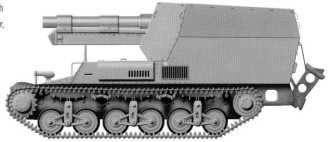

Specifications

Crew: 4	Engine: Delahaye 103TT
Weight: 9.4 tonnes (8.5 tons)	Speed (road): 34km/hr (21.1mph)
Length: 5.31m (17.4ft)	Range: 135km (83.9 miles)
Width: 1.83m (6ft)	Radio: FuG Spr 'f'
Height: 2.23m (7.3ft)	

▶ Fiat-Ansaldo Carro Armato M 14-41

Kampfgruppe Nord / II. 133rd Italian Panzer Battalion (Littorio)

The Italian Army used a blue rectangle to identify units belonging to the 2nd Company of an armoured battalion. The M14-41 was identical to the M13-40 tank with the exception of a more powerful 145hp Fiat diesel engine. Armament consisted of one 4.7cm (1.9in) Ansaldo 47/32 gun with 104 rounds.

Specifications

Crew: 4	Engine: Fiat 8 t diesel
Weight: 15.8 tonnes (14.3 tons)	Speed: 32km/hr (19.9mph)
Length: 4.92m (16.1ft)	Range: 200km (124.3 miles)
Width: 2.23m (7.3ft)	Radio: RF 1 CA
Height: 2.39m (7.8ft)	

▶ Fiat-Ansaldo Carro comando per semovente (M14-41 Chassis)

Kampfgruppe Sud / 554th Italian Assault Gun Battalion

The 15th Panzer Division had been broken up into three *kampfgruppe* (*Nord*, *Mitte*, *Sud*) just before the first battle of El Alamein. The attack started on 30 August. Soon afterwards, elements of 15th Panzer made contact with the British 8th Armoured Brigade. After a bitter fight, Rommel ordered a general withdrawal.

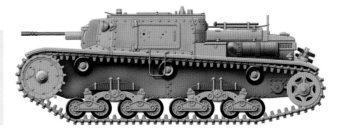

Specifications

Crew: 4	Engine: Fiat 15 TB V-8
Weight: 14.7 tonnes (13.3 tons)	Speed: 40km/hr (24.9mph)
Length: 5.04m (16.5ft)	Range: 200km (124.3 miles)
Width: 2.23m (7.3ft)	Radio: RF 1 CA plus RF 2 CA or RF 3M2
Height: 1.82m (6ft)	

▶ Fiat-Ansaldo Semovente da 75/18 (M13-40 Chassis)

Kampfgruppe Sud / 554th Italian Assault Gun Battalion

The British launched their own offensive at El Alamein on 23 October. The
Germans had 489 tanks, half of them Italian. They were faced by 1029 British
tanks. Under a massive artillery barrage, the British broke through and Rommel
was forced to retreat, abandoning 200 irreplaceable tanks.

Specifications

Crew: 3	Engine: Fiat 15 TB V-8
Weight: 16.5 tonnes (15 tons)	Speed: 38km/hr (23.6mph)
Length: 5.04m (16.5ft)	Range: 230 km (142.9 miles)
Width: 2.23m (7.3ft)	Radio: RF 1 CA
Height: 1.85m (6ft)	

▶ Panzerkampfwagen IV Ausf G (Sd Kfz 161/1 und 161/2)

Pz. Rgt 8 / II Battalion / 7th Company

Tunisia 1943: the 15th Panzer Division was forced to retreat to Tunisia and was
maintained in reserve until committed in the battle for the Mareth Line. There it
saw combat against the British, but by that time the
overwhelming Allied superiority in material made the
defence of North Africa hopeless.

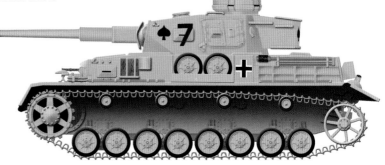

Specifications

Crew: 5	Engine: Maybach HL120TRM
Weight: 25.9 tonnes (23.5 tons)	Speed: 40km/hr (24.9mph)
Length: 6.62m (21.7ft)	Range: 210km (130.5 miles)
Width: 2.88m (9.4ft)	Radio: FuG5
Height: 2.68m (8.8ft)	

▶ Schwerer Panzerspähwagen I Ausf B (Sd Kfz 231)

33rd Reconnaissance Battalion / 1st Armoured Car Company

Tunisia 1943: the 15th Panzer Division surrendered along with other units of the
Panzerarmee Afrika in May 1943. It was later reformed as the 15th Division.

Specifications

Crew: 4	Engine: Büssing-NAG L8V
Weight: 9.1 tonnes (8.3 tons)	Speed: 85km/hr (52.8mph)
Length: 5.85m (19.2ft)	Range: 300km (186.4 miles)
Width: 2.2m (7.2ft)	Radio: FuG Spr Ger 'a'
Height: 2.35m (7.7ft)	

16th Panzer Division

The 16th Panzer Division was formed in 1940 at Munster. It was based on an already-existing infantry division, to which a Panzer regiment was added.

THE 16TH PANZER DIVISION was authorized in August 1940 and had formed at Munster by November. The Division was made up from elements of the 16th Infantry Division. The divisional Panzer strength was provided by the two veteran battalions of the 2nd Panzer Regiment, which had been detached from the 1st Panzer Division.

▶ **Attacking the Salerno Landings**
Assault guns pass through Naples on their way to Salerno. The 16th and 26th Panzer divisions almost defeated the Allied landings there in September 1943.

INSIGNIA

Divisional tactical insignia used between 1941 and 1942. A similar symbol was used in Italy in 1943, and in red was used in Russia in 1943 and 1944.

The divisional symbol enclosed within a yellow shield on a black field was a non-standard variant.

Commanders

Generaloberst H. Hube (1 Nov 1940 – 15 Sept 1942)	Generalmajor H. Back (1 Nov 1943 – 14 Aug 1944)
Generalleutnant G. Angern (15 Sept 1942 – 2 Feb 1943)	Generalleutnant D. von Muller (14 Aug 1944 – 19 Apr 1945)
Generalmajor B. Muller-Hillebrand (Mar 1943 – 5 May 1943)	Oberst K. Treuhaupt (19 Apr 1945 – 8 May 1945)
Generalmajor R. Sieckenius (5 May 1943 – 1 Nov 1943)	

 # *Barbarossa*: the attack on Russia
22 JUNE 1941

After being held in reserve in the Balkans, the 16th Panzer Division made its combat debut during Operation *Barbarossa*, the Axis invasion of the Soviet Union.

THE DIVISION WAS ASSIGNED to von Kleist's 1st *Panzergruppe*, part of Army Group South. The offensive was launched on 22 June, and made excellent progress. 16th Panzer fought with XIV *Panzerkorps* at Dubno in June, moving to LXVIII *Panzerkorps* at Zhitomir in July, and to XIV *Panzerkorps* at Uman and Nikolaev in August. In September, the Division fought in the battle of Kiev, when Army Groups Centre and South combined to encircle and capture over 650,000 Russian soldiers. However, the victory had diverted the *Wehrmacht* from its drive to the east, and when it resumed, winter was setting in. 16th Panzer ended the year on the Mius defensive line as the Soviets mounted their first winter attack.

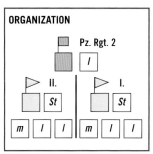

ORGANIZATION

Panzer Unit	Pz. II	Pz. III(37)	Pz. III(50)	Pz. IV	Pz. Bef.
2nd Pz. Rgt.	45	23	48	20	10

Fall Blau: the Eastern Front
28 JUNE 1942

Over the winter of 1941–42, the 16th Panzer Division was deployed in defensive positions along the Mius River, which reached the Sea of Azov at Taganrog.

SERVING WITH XIV *PANZERKORPS*, attached to 1st *Panzerarmee*, 16th Panzer was used in the fighting that took place after Kleist's Panzers had been forced out of Rostov on Don at the end of 1941. The Soviet Winter Offensive had forced the *Wehrmacht* back from Moscow far to the north. Here, in the south, Russian gains were much smaller, and by March Stalin had decided to call off the offensive.

In the spring, it was the Germans who began planning an offensive. In directive No. 41, dated 5 April, Hitler set out his objectives for the summer, an offensive codenamed *Fall Blau*. German forces were to concentrate in the south, annihilating Soviet forces on the Don before swinging north to take Stalingrad. This was to be followed by an assault on the vital oilfields in the Caucasus.

The offensive was launched on 28 June, with 16th Panzer being transferred from Kleist's *Panzerarmee* at

Panzer Unit	Pz. II	Pz. III(5kz)	Pz. III(5lg)	Pz. IV	Pz. Bef.
2nd Pz. Rgt.	13	39	18	27	3

Kharkov to 6th Army commanded by General Paulus, and then back to 1st *Panzerarmee*. The first attacks were successful, with the Russians being almost contemptuously swept aside. In July, Hitler became overambitious, splitting his forces to try to take Stalingrad and the Caucasus simultaneously, rather than in succession.

Advance to the Volga
From August 1942, 16th Panzer was attached to the XIV *Panzerkorps* of 6th Army. The Panzers led a headlong advance across the steppes towards the Volga, reaching the river on 23 August. All that was left was the assault on Stalingrad, and 6th Army began fighting through the outskirts of the sprawling city at the end of the month.

But the Soviets did not intend to give up the city. Over the next three months, 6th Army became bogged down in an increasingly bitter fight, in the kind of urban terrain in which tanks are most vulnerable. By November, Stalingrad appeared ready to fall to the Germans – until the Red Army unleashed a massive counteroffensive that trapped 6th Army in the city.

ORGANIZATION
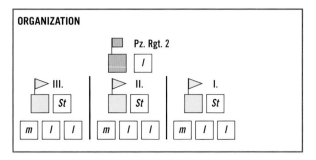

▶ **Mittlerer Schützenpanzerwagen Ausf C (Sd Kfz 251/1)**
16th Schützen Brigade / 64th Schützen Regiment
In the summer of 1942, the 16th Panzer Division served with Army Group South before transferring to Army Group B for the drive on Stalingrad. The offensive started well, but was to end in catastrophe.

Specifications
Crew: 2 plus 12 troops	Engine: Maybach HL42TUKRM
Weight: 9.9 tonnes (9 tons)	Speed: 53km/hr (32.9mph)
Length: 5.98m (19.6ft)	Range: 300km (186.4 miles)
Width: 2.1m (6.9ft)	Radio: FuG Spr Ger f
Height: 2.16m (7ft)	

Destroyed at Stalingrad

FEBRUARY 1943

The massive Red Army envelopment of Stalingrad surrounded 6th Army in the city in just four days, and prevented Hoth's Panzers from breaking through to its relief from the south.

FROM BEING A GRINDING battle of attrition, the fighting in Stalingrad now became a struggle for survival for the Germans. Over the next two months, 16th Panzer lost most of its vehicles, and its tank crews were fighting as infantrymen. Supplies of food, winter clothing, fuel, weapons and ammunition were short or non-existent. As the temperatures sank and blizzards raged across the steppe, fighting rations were reduced to 200g (7 ounces) of bread and 200g (7 ounces) of horsemeat per day. Non-combatants received half that – and Soviet prisoners were given nothing.

In January, Stalin ordered the pocket crushed. Only about a third of the 300,000 Germans who had been trapped were still alive. When another assault breached the perimeter west of the city, Stalingrad – and what was left of the 16th Panzer Division – was doomed. Paulus surrendered on 30 January.

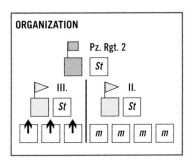

ORGANIZATION

Pz. Rgt. 2

Panzer Unit	Pz. IV	StuG	Pz. Bef
2nd Pz. Rgt.	98	42	12

 # The defence of Italy

1943/44

The 16th Panzer Division was ordered to be reformed on 17 February 1943, less than a fortnight after its destruction, and rebuilding began in Northern France soon afterwards.

IN JULY 1943, THE ALLIES LANDED in Sicily, and the Italian armistice forced the *Wehrmacht* to pull back to the Italian mainland. As British and American troops crossed to the toe of Italy, 16th Panzer was sent south to form part of XIV Corps. When the Allies tried to outflank the Germans by landing at Salerno near Naples, 16th Panzer along with 26th Panzer were close at hand, and were ordered into action against the Allies on the beachhead. For a week after 10 September, the two Panzer divisions and the Allied invasion force were engaged in a fierce battle. At one stage, the Allied commanders considered calling the landings off, so tough was the resistance. However, the British 8th Army was advancing northwards from the toe of Italy, and Allied naval gunfire was taking a fearsome toll of any German formations coming within 15 km (9.3 miles) of the coast. On 17 September, General von Vietinghoff, commander of German forces in southern Italy, requested permission to withdraw northwards to prepared defensive positions. 16th Panzer was sent to Termoli, then back towards the Sangro River and the defenses of the Gustav Line.

Panzer Unit	Pz. IV	Stug	Pz. Bef	Flammpz
2nd Pz. Rgt.	92	40	12	7

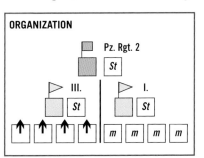

ORGANIZATION

Pz. Rgt. 2

▶ Panzerkampfwagen IV Ausf G (Sd Kfz 161/1 und 161/2)

Pz. Rgt 2 / I Battalion / 3rd Company / Company HQ tank

The 16th Panzer returned to the East at the end of 1943, fighting in the retreat from the Ukraine.

Specifications

Crew: 5	Engine: Maybach HL120TRM
Weight: 25.9 tonnes (23.5 tons)	Speed: 40km/hr (24.9mph)
Length: 6.62m (21.7ft)	Range: 210km (130.5 miles)
Width: 2.88m (9.4ft)	Radio: FuG5
Height: 2.68m (8.8ft)	

▶ 7.5cm Sturmgeschütz 40 Ausf G (Sd Kfz 142/1)

Pz. Rgt 2 / III Battalion / 10th Company / 2nd Zug / tank number 4

Some 7720 StuG 40 were produced from December 1942 to March 1945. A further 173 were converted from Pz.Kpfw III chassis in 1944. The Ausf G was armed with a 7.5cm (3in) StuG 40 L/48 cannon.

Specifications

Crew: 4	Engine: Maybach HL120TRM
Weight: 26.3 tonnes (23.9 tons)	Speed: 40km/hr (24.9mph)
Length: 6.77m (22.2ft)	Range: 155km (96.3 miles)
Width: 2.95m (9.7ft)	Radio: FuG15 and FuG16
Height: 2.16m (7ft)	

Panzer-Sturmgeschütz-Kompanie

During the rebuilding of the 16th Panzer Division in February 1943, it was intended that the 2nd Panzer Regiment should have three battalions – of Panthers, Panzer IVs and Tigers. However, by March it was decided to equip the third battalion with assault guns in place of the heavy Tigers, which were not yet available in any numbers, and the first battalion was to be equipped with Panzer IVs. Initial plans for the Sturmgeschütz companies to be equipped with four five-vehicle *Zugen* were modified over the course of the next few months, and in an order dated 18 November 1943 the High Command directed that the third battalion should consist of three companies of 14 assault guns, as depicted here, giving the battalion a total strength of 42 StuGs.

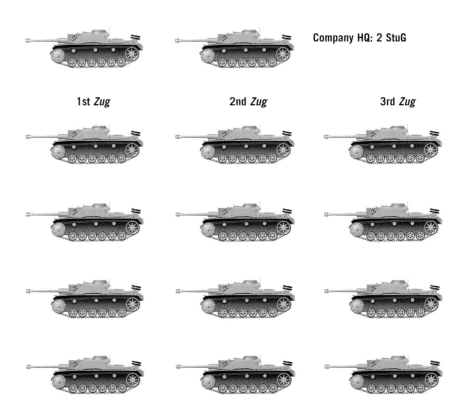

Company HQ: 2 StuG

1st *Zug*

2nd *Zug*

3rd *Zug*

▶ **Panzerkampfwagen III (FI) (Sd Kfz 141/3)**

Pz. Rgt 2

This vehicle was used against the Allied landings at Salerno in 1943. The Italian campaign was a hard-fought battle of attrition, as the Germans retreated up the Italian peninsula.

Specifications

Crew: 5	Engine: Maybach HL120TR
Weight: 25.4 tonnes (23 tons)	Speed: 40km/hr (24.9mph)
Length: 6.41m (21ft)	Range: 155km (96.3 miles)
Width: 2.95m (9.7ft)	Radio: FuG5, plus FuG2 in
Height: 2.5m (8.2ft)	commanders' tanks

 # Retreat from the Ukraine
NOVEMBER 1943–1945

At the end of 1943, 16th Panzer was withdrawn from Italy and sent back to Russia. Italy was essentially an infantryman's war, and tanks were more valuable on the Eastern Front.

THE 16TH PANZER DIVISION was shipped back to the Eastern Front through November and December 1943, arriving in Bobruisk in Army Group Centre's sector on 13 December. There it fought in a series of defensive actions, before moving south to the Ukraine, where it was used in support of the attempt to relieve the Cherkassy Pocket. It also saw action as the *Wehrmacht* was pushed back from Kiev. By the summer, the remnants of the 16th Panzer Division had withdrawn to the the Baranov area on the Vistula River.

During the summer of 1944, 16th Panzer was pulled back through Cholm and Lublin into Poland, where it was refitted. It was transferred to the Baranov region, where it remained in action until January 1945. As the Soviets advanced, the 16th Panzer Division was pushed back, and was located around Lauban and Brno in April 1945. The division was scattered. Some units surrendered to the Soviets, while others were taken by the US Army.

▲ **Leichter Schützenpanzerwagen (Sd Kfz 250/1)**

Unknown formation

After fighting the Americans at Salerno, the Division was sent to the southern sector of the Russian front. The 16th Panzer ended the war in Czechoslovakia, where some surrendered to the Soviets and others to the Americans.

Specifications

Crew: 2 plus 4 grenadiers	Engine: Maybach HL42TUKRM
Weight: 5.9 tonnes (5.38 tons)	Speed: 60km/hr (37.3mph)
Length: 4.61m (15.1ft)	Range: 300km (186.4 miles)
Width: 1.95m (6.4ft)	Radio: FuG Spr Ger 'f'
Height: 1.66m (5.4ft) without gun shield	

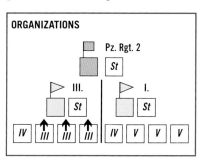

ORGANIZATIONS

Panzer Unit	Pz. IV	StuG	Pz. V	Pz. IV70V
2nd Pz. Rgt.	7	37	10	10

17th Panzer Division

The expansion of the *Panzerwaffe* continued in the autumn of 1940. In November of that year, four new divisions were formed. Among that number was the 17th Panzer Division.

FORMED AT AUGSBERG, the 17th Panzer Division, like its contemporaries, was created around a nucleus of already-existing units. Much of the troop strength came from the 27th Infantry Division, while the division's Panzer component was provided by the replacement battalions of the 4th and 33rd Regiments. The division was assigned to the 2nd Army while it worked up to operational levels, and it was assigned to Guderian's 2nd *Panzergruppe* in May 1941.

▲ **Fighting in Russia**

Although the steppe offered tanks almost perfect fighting terrain, the vast distances involved in the USSR was hard on both men and machinery.

Commanders

Generalmajor K. von Weber *(1 Nov 1940 – 17 July 1941)*	Generalleutnant W. Schilling *(16 June 1943 – 21 July 1943)*
General der Panzertruppen W. von Thoma *(17 July 1941 – 15 Sept 1941)*	Generalleutnant K. von der Meden *(21 July 1943 – 20 Sept 1944)*
Generaloberst H. von Arnim *(15 Sept 1941 – 11 Nov 1941)*	Generalmajor R. Demme *(20 Sept 1944 – 2 Dec 1944)*
Generalleutnant R. Licht *(11 Nov 1941 – 10 Oct 1942)*	Oberst A. Brux *(2 Dec 1944 – 19 Jan 1945)*
General der Panzertruppen F. von Senger und Etterlin *(10 Oct 1942 – 16 June 1943)*	Generalmajor T. Kretschmer *(1 feb 1945 – 8 May 1945)*

INSIGNIA

The tactical insignia used on vehicles of the 17th Panzer Division remained the same through the four and a half years of the formation's existence.

 # *Barbarossa*: the attack on Russia

22 JUNE 1941

As part of Guderian's 2nd *Panzergruppe*, the 17th Panzer Division formed part of the armoured spearhead of Army Group Centre during the attack on Russia in 1941.

AS PART OF GUDERIAN'S COMMAND, 17th Panzer fought through the battles for Smolensk and Kiev. However, it was unusual in that it was equipped with

Tauschpanzer, or 'diving tanks'. These submersible, snorkel-equipped Panzer IIIs and IVs had been designed for the cancelled invasion of Britain. They instead saw their combat debut at the opening of Operation *Barbarossa*, crossing the River Bug.

After the Kiev encirclement, 17th Panzer returned to the assault on Moscow. Fighting in the Tula area before pulling back to Orel, it suffered like all German units from the unforgiving Russian winter.

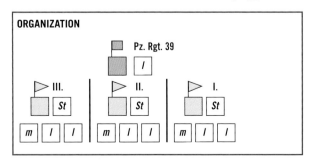

ORGANIZATION

Pz. Rgt. 39

Panzer Unit	Pz. I	Pz. II	Pz. III(50)	Pz. IV	Pz. Bef
39th Pz. Rgt.	12	44	106	40	10

Leichte PanzerKompanie K.St.N.1171

By the time of the invasion of the Soviet Union, the light panzer companies of Germany's panzer divisions had traded in their obsolete Panzer Is for much more powerful Panzer IIIs. However, the standard table of organization retained a platoon of lightweight Panzer IIs, which were primarily used for local reconnaissance when the unit was on the move, and to mount security patrols when it was stationary for any length of time. Security patrols became even more important as the war in Russia progressed, since partisan activity behind the lines was to become a major threat.

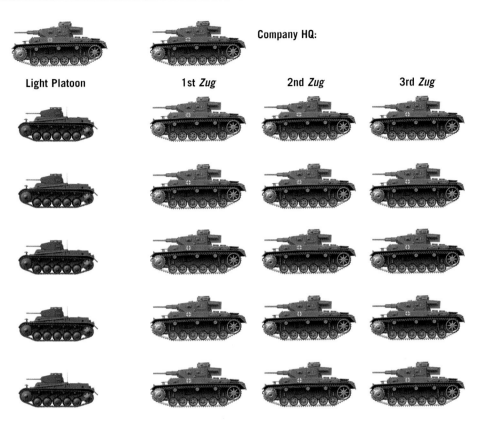

Light Platoon   **1st** *Zug*   **2nd** *Zug*   **3rd** *Zug*   Company HQ:

 # *Fall Blau*: the Eastern Front

28 JUNE 1942

The 17th Panzer Division played little part in the initial stages of the German summer offensive in 1942, though it would have an important role later in the campaign.

MOST *WEHRMACHT* REINFORCEMENT had gone south when *Fall Blau* got under way in June 1942. The 17th Panzer Division remained with Army Group Centre in the Orel Sector for much of the year. The primary mission was to hold the line, and to prevent any Soviet breakthrough while the German Army conquered the south of the USSR.

Initial stages of *Fall Blau* had gone very well for the

Panzer Unit	Pz. II	Pz. III(50)	Pz. IV	Pz. Bef
39th Pz. Rgt.	17	36	16	2

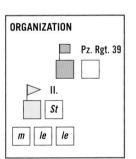

Germans, but the ill-advised attempt to take both major objectives of Stalingrad and the Caucasus simultaneously ran into serious trouble when the Soviets, who had learned to trade space for time, avoided any major action until they were ready. Stalin, unlike Hitler, allowed his generals to fall back when necessary – just as long as they had plans to mount a counterattack as quickly as possible. The attack came at Stalingrad.

Stalingrad and Kursk
DECEMBER 1942 – 1 JULY 1943

At the end of 1942, 17th Panzer Division was transferred to von Manstein's Army Group Don to take part in the attempt to relieve the beleaguered German 6th Army in Stalingrad.

MANSTEIN'S PLAN WAS SIMPLE. Hoth's 4th *Panzerarmee* would strike northwards from Kotelnikova, while the XLVIII *Panzerkorps* would attack eastwards from the Chir front, 65 km (40.4 miles) west of the city. Once the attackers got within range of Stalingrad, 6th Army would break out of the encirclement. However, the Soviets had been attacking all along the Chir River since 10 December, and the rescue would have to be performed by 4th *Panzerarmee* alone.

17th Panzer had been transferred down from Orel to take part in the operation, but on Hitler's direct orders, and over Manstein's objections, it was to be held in reserve. In the event, the 17th was available to cover the flanks of Hoth's Panzers as they became bogged down fighting towards Stalingrad in an attempt to relieve the beleaguered city. The entire *Panzerarmee* could have been destroyed had not 17th Panzer been there to protect the column's flanks when heavy Soviet attacks on the crumbling Romanian army threatened Hoth's advance. Even so, the relief effort had to be cancelled.

Kharkov, Kursk and after

The Soviet offensive after Stalingrad fell was countered in the south by Manstein's brilliant counterattack at Kharkov. 17th Panzer was part of 4th *Panzerarmee* for that operation. During the battle

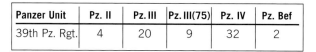

Panzer Unit	Pz. II	Pz. III	Pz. III(75)	Pz. IV	Pz. Bef
39th Pz. Rgt.	4	20	9	32	2

of Kursk, 17th Panzer was with 1st *Panzerarmee*, operating in the Donetz basin to the south of the main action. After the failure of the Kursk offensive, the Division remained with Army Group South for the long retreat through the Ukraine, from the Donetz back across the Dnieper River.

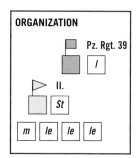

ORGANIZATION

Pz. Rgt. 39

In January 1944, 17th Panzer was with 4th *Panzerarmee* at Vinnitsa. It took part in operations around the Cherkassy Pocket, supporting III *Panzerkorps* as it broke through to relieve a force of 50,000 trapped German soldiers.

The Division remained with the 1st *Panzerarmee* until July, when it moved to 4th *Panzerarmee*. From Kamanetz-Pudolsk in March, the division retreated through Stanislav, Lemberg and Tarnow, and in September 1944 it had been driven back to Baranov, by which time it formed part of LXII *Panzerkorps*.

In November 1944, the Division was moved back into reserve for refitting.

▶ **Leichte Feldhaubitze 18/2 auf Fahrgestell Panzerkampfwagen II (Sf)**

27th Panzer Artillery Regiment / 1st (Self-propelled) Battalion

1st Battalion was equipped with two 'Wespe' batteries, each with six guns, together with a Heavy 'Hummel' battery with six guns.

Specifications

Crew: 4

Weight: 12.1 tonnes (11 tons)

Length: 4.81m (15.8ft)

Width: 2.28m (7.5ft)

Height: 2.3m (7.5ft)

Engine: Maybach HL62TR

Speed: 40km/hr (24.9mph)

Range: 220km (136.7 miles)

Radio: FuG Spr 'f'

In defence of the Fatherland
1945

The Division was organized in January 1945 as a *Kampfgruppe* with a mixed battalion armed with a Pz.Kpfw IV company of 16 tanks and two Pz.Kpfw IV/70(V) companies of 28 *panzerjägers*.

AT THE BEGINNING OF 1945, Germany's once victorious Panzer divisions had been driven right back to the borders of the Reich itself. As the Soviet armies began massing for a new offensive in January, the *Panzerwaffe* was no longer fighting to win, but for survival.

In February 1945, the 17th Panzer Division, by now reduced in size to a *Kampfgruppe,* was attached to Army Group Centre on the Oder River. By March 1945, it had been pushed back as far as Jägerndorf by the overwhelming might of the Red Army. Early in April, it had retreated southwest into Moravia, where in quick succession it came under the orders of 17th Army and 1st Army. The division finally surrendered to the Soviet army near Görlitz at the end of April 1945.

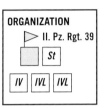

ORGANIZATION

II. Pz. Rgt. 39

St

IV | IVL | IVL

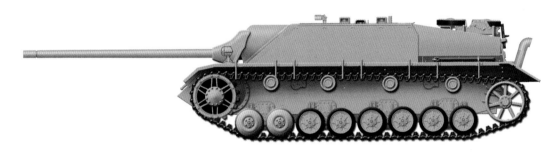

Specifications

Crew: 4	Engine: Maybach HL120TRM
Weight: 28.4 tonnes (25.8 tons)	Speed: 35km/hr (21.7mph)
Length: 8.5m (27.9ft)	Range: 210km (130.5 miles)
Width: 3.17m (10.4ft)	Radio: FuG Spr 1
Height: 1.85m (6ft)	

▲ **Panzer IV/70 (V) (Sd Kfz 162/1)**

17 Panzer Division Kampfgruppe / Pz. Rgt 39 / II Battalion

930 Pz.Kpfw IV/70 (V) were produced between August 1944 and March 1945. The powerful high-velocity 7.5cm (3in) L/70 cannon was capable of penetrating 194mm (7.6in) of armour at 100m (328ft) or 106mm (4.2in) at 2000m (6562ft).

▶ **Mittlerer Schützenpanzerwagen Ausf D (Sd Kfz 251/22)**

17 Panzer Division Kampfgruppe / Panzerjäger Battalion / 4th Half-track Company

This vehicle was used on the Vistula in January 1945. It was armed with a 7.5cm (3in) PaK40 L/46 cannon and carried 22 rounds of ammunition. The Division was overrun in Eastern Germany by the Soviets.

Specifications

Crew: 4	Engine: Maybach HL42TUKRM
Weight: 9.9 tonnes (9 tons)	Speed: 53km/hr (32.9mph)
Length: 5.98m (19.6ft)	Range: 300km (186.4 miles)
Width: 2.1m (6.9ft)	Radio: FuG Spr Ger 'f'
Height : 2.16m (7ft)	

18th Panzer Division

The 18th Panzer Division was formed at Chemnitz on 26 October 1940, with manpower being provided by parts of the 4th and 14th Infantry Divisions.

THE PANZER STRENGTH of the Division was drawn from the four battalions of 'diving' or submersible tanks created for Operation *Seelöwe* (Sea Lion), the planned invasion of England in the summer of 1940. Originally known as A, B, C and D battalions before the invasion was called off by Hitler, they were renamed as the 1st and 2nd Battalions, 18th Panzer Regiment and the 1st and 2nd Battalions, 28th Panzer Regiment, 18th Panzer Division.

In March 1941, as Panzer organizations were revised, the 28th Regiment was disbanded. The 1st Battalion became the 3rd Battalion, 18th Panzer Regiment, and the 2nd Battalion was transferred to the 3rd Panzer Division to become the 3rd Battalion, 6th Panzer Regiment.

Commanders

General der Panzertruppen W. Nehring
(26 Oct 1940 – 26 Jan 1942)

Generalleutnant K. von Thungen
(26 Jan 1942 – July 1942)

General der Nachrichtentruppen A. Praun
(July 1942 – 24 Aug 1942)

Generalleutnant K. von Thungen
(24 Aug 1942 – 15 Sept 1942)

Generalleutnant E. Menny
(15 Sept 1942 – Feb 1943)

Generalleutnant K. von Thungen
(Feb 1943 – 1 Apr 1943)

Generalleutnant K. von Schlieben
(1 Apr 1943 – 7 Sept 1943)

INSIGNIA

The standard tactical symbol for the 18th Panzer Division was related to those of the 16th and 17th Divisions, the number of crossbars on the 'Y' being the key recognition point.

The *Zusatzsymbols*, or additional marks, carried by panzers of the 18th were often much larger than the official tactical symbol. They showed a Panzer *Totenkopf*, or Death's Head, emerging from a stylized representation of the sea, recalling the division's origins as an amphibious assault unit.

Barbarossa: the attack on Russia
22 JUNE 1941

In May 1941, the 18th Panzer Division was assigned to the 2nd *Panzergruppe* then assembling in the *Reichsprotectorate* of Bohemia and Moravia.

THE 2ND *PANZERGRUPPE* was commanded by Heinz Guderian. Guderian's *Gruppe* formed the southern prong of Army Group Centre's advance into Russia in June 1941, and 18th Panzer used its diving tanks alongside those of the 17th Panzer in the crossing of the River Bug early in the campaign.

As part of the LXVII *Panzerkorps* of Guderian's Gruppe, 18th Panzer was in the central offensive drive through Russia, and over the next six months was involved in seizing the key Soviet cities of Smolensk, Bryansk and Tula. However, like much of Army Group Centre, the division was unprepared for the Soviet winter, and was driven back from Moscow to the Orel sector in January 1942.

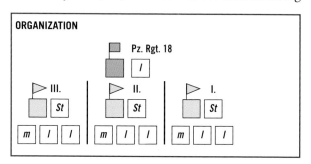

ORGANIZATION

Panzer Unit	Pz. I	Pz. II	Pz. III	Pz. IV	Pz. Bef
18th Pz. Rgt.	6	50	114	36	12

▶ **Panzerbefehlswagen III als Tauchpanzer**

Pz. Rgt 18 / Submersible battle tank

After the cancellation of the invasion of Britain, the *Tauchpanzer* of the 18th Panzer Division had their hose snorkel replaced by a steel one. Gyroscopes and radios were used to navigate under water.

Specifications

Crew: 5	Engine: Maybach HL120TR
Weight: 21.5 tonnes (19.5 tons)	Speed: 40km/hr (24.9mph)
Length: 5.38m (17.7ft)	Range: 165km (102.5 miles)
Width: 2.91m (9.5ft)	Radio: FuG6 plus FuG2 or FuG7 or
Height: 2.44m (8ft)	FuG8

▶ **Panzerkampfwagen II Ausf C (SdKfz 121)**

Pz. Rgt 18 / Regimental Staff Company

In March 1941, the division included six Panzer Is and 50 Panzer IIs in addition to the 'Diving' Panzer IIIs and Panzer IVs from which it had been formed.

Specifications

Crew: 3	Engine: Maybach HL62TR
Weight: 9.8 tonnes (8.9 tons)	Speed: 40km/hr (24.9mph)
Length: 4.81m (15.8ft)	Range: 200km (124.3 miles)
Width: 2.22m (7.3ft)	Radio: FuG5
Height: 1.99m (6.5ft)	

▶ **Panzerkampfwagen III Ausf H (Sd Kfz 141)**

Pz. Rgt 18 / II Battalion / 8th Company / 3rd Zug / tank number 2

The 18th Panzer was part of Guderian's 2nd *Panzergruppe* during Operation *Barbarossa*. Only 15 of the Pz.Kpfw IIIs listed on the Division's inventory at that time were armed with the 5cm (2in) cannon.

Specifications

Crew: 5	Engine: Maybach HL120TRM
Weight: 24 tonnes (21.8 tons)	Speed: 40km/hr (24.9mph)
Length: 5.41m (17.7ft)	Range: 165km (102.5 miles)
Width: 2.95m (9.7ft)	Radio: FuG5
Height: 2.44m (8ft)	

▶ **Panzerkampfwagen IV Ausf E (Sd Kfz 161)**

Pz. Rgt 18 / III Battalion / 9th Company / 3rd Zug / tank number 3

A tank with these markings was captured intact by Soviet troops in 1941 during the early stages of the war in Russia.

Specifications

Crew: 5	Engine: Maybach HL120TRM
Weight: 23.2 tonnes (21 tons)	Speed: 42km/hr (26mph)
Length: 5.92m (19.4ft)	Range: 200km (124.3 miles)
Width: 2.84m (9.3ft)	Radio: FuG5
Height: 2.68m (8.8ft)	

Fall Blau: the Eastern Front
28 JUNE 1942

In May 1942, the 18th Panzer Regiment became the 18th Panzer Battalion. Its staff and surplus combat units were allocated to other formations.

THE DIVISION REMAINED WITH Army Group Centre through 1942, mostly in the area around Orel. The Division's single tank battalion was commanded by the aristocratic Hyazinth Graf von Strachwitz, one of Germany's finest Panzer commanders, whose daring tactics and inspiring leadership led to his acquiring the nickname 'The Panzer Count'. In the summer of 1942, he was promoted to command a regiment of the 16th Panzer Division.

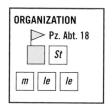

Panzer Unit	Pz. II	Pz. III(50)	Pz. IV	Pz. Bef
18th Pz. Rgt.	11	26	8	2

 The last summer offensive
1 JULY 1943

As 1943 progressed, 18th Panzer remained with Army Group Centre, where defensive fighting against the Soviet winter offensive was followed by planning for Operation *Zitadelle*.

THE 18TH PANZER DIVISION remained with 2nd *Panzerarmee* in the run up to the Battle of Kursk. 2nd *Panzerarmee* had a subsidiary role during the battle, providing flank protection to Model's 9th Army. However, just before the offensive began, 18th Panzer transferred to LXI *Panzerkorps* of 9th Army.

As part of the northern prong of the German pincer movement designed to destroy the Kursk Salient, 18th Panzer suffered heavy losses for very little gain. After Kursk, the 18th Panzer Division was disbanded. The 18th Panzer Battalion was to become the 504th Panzer Battalion, and the rest of the Division was used to build the 18th Artillery Division.

Panzer Unit	Pz. II	Pz. III	Pz. III(75)	Pz. IV	Pz. Bef
18th Pz. Rgt.	5	10	20	24	3

▶ **Panzerkampfwagen III Ausf M (Sd Kfz 141/1)**

Pz. Abt 18 / 2nd Company / HQ tank

The Ausf M was the last new production model of the PzKpfw III. Only 250 tanks out of an order of 1000 were completed: the production capacity released was to be used for assault guns.

Specifications

Crew: 5

Weight: 25 tonnes (22.7 tons)

Length: 6.41m (21ft)

Width: 2.95m (9.7ft)

Height: 2.5m (8.2ft)

Engine: Maybach HL120TRM

Speed: 40km/hr (24.9mph)

Range: 155km (96.3 miles)

Radio: FuG5

19th Panzer Division

Formed at Hanover in November 1940, the 19th Panzer Division was one of four new Panzer divisions created by the German Army in that month

CREATED AROUND A NUCLEUS provided by the combat-tested 19th Infantry Division, the divisional Panzer force was provided by the 10th, 11th and 25th *Ersatz* (Replacement) Panzer Battalions. As with four other Panzer divisions formed after the fall of France, the bulk of the 19th Division's tank inventory in June 1941 was provided by 110 Panzer 38(t)s. The Division also operated 42 Panzer Is, 35 Panzer IIs and 30 Panzer IVs.

> **Commanders**
>
> General der Panzertruppen O. von Knobelsdorff
> *(1 Nov 1940 – 5 Jan 1942)*
>
> Generalleutnant G. Schmidt
> *(5 Jan 1942 – 7 Aug 1943)*
>
> Generalleutnant H. Kallner
> *(7 Aug 1943 – 28 Mar 1944)*
>
> Generalleutnant W. Denkert
> *(28 Mar 1944 – May 1944)*
>
> Generalleutnant H. Kallner
> *(May 1944 – 22 Mar 1945)*
>
> Generalmajor H. Deckert
> *(22 Mar 1945 – 8 May 1945)*

> **INSIGNIA**
>
> The original tactical symbol of the 19th Panzer Division was a variant of the ancient runic *Wolfsangel*, or Wolf's Hook.
>
> Units involved at Kursk were given new tactical insignia, which during the battle itself were in black on white panels.

▲ **Combat in the Ukraine**
The winter of 1943–44 saw the 19th Panzer Division taking part in some of the toughest and most bitter fighting of the whole war.

Barbarossa: the attack on Russia
22 JUNE 1941

After being assigned to LXVII Corps in Germany while working up to operational readiness, 19th Panzer was transferred to the 3rd Panzer *Gruppe* for the invasion of the Soviet Union.

UNDER THE COMMAND OF General Hermann Hoth, the 3rd *Panzergruppe* operated with Guderian's 2nd *Panzergruppe* to surround the Soviet border armies, forming a pincer that met at Minsk on 27 June. Hoth's panzers had covered 350 km (217.5 miles) in just five days. The two *Panzergruppe* moved on towards Smolensk. Progress was delayed when Guderian was diverted south to Kiev. Some of Hoth's Panzers were sent to Army Group North, while the others, including 19th Panzer, were attached to 9th Army. 19th Panzer resumed the advance towards Moscow in November.

ORGANIZATION

Panzer Unit	Pz. I	Pz. II	Pz. 38(t)	Pz. IV	Pz.Bef38(t)
27th Pz. Rgt.	42	35	110	30	11

⚡ *Fall Blau*: the Eastern Front
28 JUNE 1942

In August 1941, the 3rd Battalion was disbanded. The next year, the 1st Battalion was also disbanded, leaving only the 2nd Battalion listed in the order of battle of the Division.

THE 19TH PANZER DIVISION'S strength was greatly reduced in 1941 and 1942. In August 1941, the 3rd Battalion was disbanded, while the 1st Battalion was disbanded in March 1942, leaving only the 2nd Battalion listed in the divisional order of battle.

Until August 1942, 19th Panzer served with 4th Army, which was trying to hold and expand a large German salient around Vyazma, which had been created after the Soviet winter offensive. Based initially at Juhno southeast of

Panzer Unit	Pz. II	Pz. III(50)	Pz. 38(t)	Pz. IV(kz)
27th Pz. Rgt.	6	12	35	4

Vyazma, the Division was moved back to Jelnja near Smolensk in May, going into reserve in July. In addition to fighting off regular Soviet attacks, the Division's troops had to be wary of intense partisan activity in the area between Smolensk and Vyazma.

In August 1942, the 19th Panzer Division was moved over 350 km (217.5 miles) south to the southern end of Army Group Centre's front. It was attached to the 2nd *Panzerarmee* at Orel, again going into reserve to refit in November of 1942.

ORGANIZATION

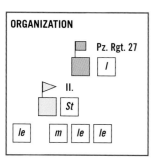

Pz. Rgt. 27

▶ **Panzerkampfwagen II Flamm Ausf A und B (Sd Kfz 122)**

27 Pz. Rgt (Attached)

155 flamethrower Panzer IIs were built or converted from Ausf D variants.

Specifications
Crew: 3
Weight: 13.2 tonnes (12 tons)
Length: 4.9m (16ft)
Width: 2.4m (7.9ft)
Height: 1.85m (6ft)

Engine: Maybach HL62TRM
Speed: 55km/hr (34.2mph)
Range: 250km (155.3 miles)
Radio: FuG2

When Germany went to war in the Soviet Union in 1941 all AFVs carried the same national insignia. However, by 1942, the Werhmacht was using low-visibility symbols in summer.

▼ **Panzerbefehlswagen mit 5cm KwK39 L/60**

27 Pz. Rgt

In 1943, the 18th Panzer Division had three command tanks in its inventory.

Specifications
Crew: 5
Weight: 24 tonnes (21.8 tons)
Length: 5.4m (17.7ft)
Width: 2.95m (9.7ft)
Height: 2.44m (8ft)

Engine: Maybach HL120TRM
Speed: 40km/hr (24.9mph)
Range: 165km (102.5 miles)
Radio: FuG6 plus FuG2 or FuG7
or FuG8

⚡ The last summer offensive
1 JULY 1943

The 19th Panzer Division moved south to stiffen the 8th Italian Army after Stalingrad. In February 1943, it was attached to III *Panzerkorps* of the 1st *Panzerarmee* on the Donetz.

THE DIVISION FORMED PART OF Army Detachment *Kempf* during the Battle of Kursk. Fighting alongside Hoth's 4th *Panzerarmee* on the southern flank of the Kursk Salient, 19th Panzer bridged the Donetz on the night of 5–6 July, taking its Panzers (which included a detachment of new Tiger heavy tanks) to the east bank. Kempf's Panzers were to support the flank of II SS *Panzerkorps*, but were unable to do so because of heavy Soviet resistance. As a consequence, the SS Panzers were halted themselves in the large tank battle at Prokorovka. 19th Panzer had advanced only a short distance from the River when Hitler called off the offensive.

Back to the Dniepr

As German forces were forced back through the Ukraine, 19th Panzer fought a delaying battle in September, with two Soviet brigades seeking to expand a bridgehead over the Dniepr south of Kiev. The Division continued fighting in the area around Kiev for the next two months before falling back towards Zhitomir.

ORGANIZATION

Pz. Rgt. 27

II. — I.
St — St
m m le — m m le le

Panzer Unit	Pz. II	Pz. III	Pz. III(75)	Pz. IV	Pz. Bef
27th Pz. Rgt.	2	27	11	38	14

▶ **Leichter Schützenpanzerwagen (Sd Kfz 250/9)**
19th Reconnaissance Battalion / 2nd Armoured Car (half-track) Company
The 'Caesar' is armed with one 2cm (0.8in) KwK38 L/55 cannon and carries 100 rounds of ammunition fed in ten 10-round box magazines.

Specifications
Crew: 3
Weight: 6.9 tonnes (6.3 tons)
Length: 4.56m (15ft)
Width: 1.95m (6.4ft)
Height: 2.16m (7ft)
Engine: Maybach HL42TRKM
Speed: 60km/hr (37.3mph)
Range: 32km (19.9 miles)
Radio: FuG Spr Ger 'f'

▶ **Mittlerer Schützenpanzerwagen I Ausf C (Sd Kfz 251/9)**
Unknown formation
The SdKfz 251 was built in a wide variety of variants. The SdKfz 251/9 was armed with a 7.5cm (3in) KwK37 L/24, and carried 52 rounds of ammunition.

Specifications
Crew: 3
Weight: 9.4 tonnes (8.53 tons)
Length: 5.98m (19.6ft)
Width: 2.83m (9.3ft)
Height: 2.07m (6.8ft)
Engine: Maybach HL42TUKRM
Speed: 53km/hr (32.9mph)
Range: 300km (186.4 miles)
Radio: FuG Spr Ger 'f'

✠ Last year on the Eastern Front
1944

The 19th Panzer Division took part in some of the most bitter fighting of the war in 1944, suffering heavy losses in the process.

THE ASSAULT ON ZHITOMIR at the end of 1943 was one of the *Wehrmacht's* last major successes on the Eastern Front. An armoured force comprising six Panzer and one infantry division under the command of General Herman Balck trapped a large Soviet force in a pocket at Zhitomir. 19th Panzer, part of Balck's XLVIII *Panzerkorps*, played a major part in the battle, which destroyed two Russian armies and badly mauled a third.

Over the next six months, 19th Panzer continued to fight with Army Group North Ukraine. After heavy losses, it was pulled out of the line in May 1944. In June, it was sent to the Netherlands, where it was to be rebuilt as a 'Type 44' Panzer Division, equipped with 81 long-barrelled Pz.Kpfw IVs, 79 Pz.Kpfw V Panthers, and eight 3.7cm (1.5in) Flakpanzer IVs.

Warsaw Uprising

No sooner had the Division re-equipped than it was sent back east, this time to Army Group Centre. It arrived outside Warsaw in August 1944, where its primary mission was to stabilize the defensive line on the Vistula, and its secondary mission to assist in putting down the Polish Home Army, which was then leading an uprising in the Polish capital

Panzer Unit	Pz. IV	Pz. V	Flk.Pz
27th Pz. Rgt.	81	79	8

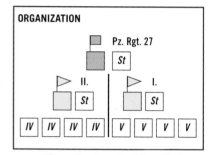

Along with the 3rd and 5th S S P a n z e r Divisions and the *Luftwaffe* H e r m a n n Göring Division, the 19th beat off an attack by a Soviet tank corps. The Soviets held off from attacking Warsaw itself for several months, giving the Germans time to deal with the rising. 19th Panzer dealt with the last Polish resistance in the suburbs of Sadyba and Sielce in the southern part of the city, followed by a powerful attack at Zoliborz on 29 September.

The division moved back though Poland in December 1944, ending the war in Czechoslovakia where it surrendered in May 1945.

Specifications

Crew: 6	Engine: HL120TRM
Weight: 26.5 tonnes (24 tons)	Speed: 42km/hr (26mph)
Length: 7.17m (23.5ft)	Range: 215km (133.6 miles)
Width: 2.97m (9.7ft)	Radio: FuG Spr 1
Height: 2.81m (9.2ft)	

▲ **15cm Schwere Panzerhaubitze auf Fahrgestell Panzerkampfwagen III/IV (Sf) (Sd Kfz 165)**

19th Panzer Artillery Regiment / Self-propelled Battalion / 3rd Self-propelled Battery

Also known as the 'Hummel', this powerful self-propelled artillery piece was issued to the armoured artillery detachments in several Panzer divisions, initially at a rate of one six-gun battery per division. The Hummel made its combat debut at Kursk in 1943.

20th Panzer Division

Last (numerically) of the divisions formed in the second phase of the *Panzerwaffe*'s expansion, the 20th Panzer Division began assembling at Erfurt in October 1940.

FORMED FROM ELEMENTS of the 19th Infantry Division not used in the creation of the 19th Panzer Division, the 20th Panzer Division incorporated the three battalions of the 21st Panzer Regiment, which had been supplied by the 7th and 35th Panzer Replacement Battalions. As with the 19th Division, the most numerous tank in 20th Panzer's inventory in its early days was the Panzer 38(t), providing 123 out of a total tank strength of 229 vehicles. Nearly all were destroyed or had been replaced by Panzer IIIs in the first few months of the war in Russia, but more of the Czech-built tanks were delivered in 1942. About nine Panzer 38(t)s were still in service with the 20th Panzer Division in July 1943 at the time of the Battle of Kursk.

INSIGNIA

Thought by some to be a stylized representation of the Brandenburg Gate, the tactical symbol of the 20th Panzer Division was probably chosen because it was simple and easy to remember.

From about the middle of 1941, 20th Panzer Division vehicles were seen bearing a new symbol, a vertical arrow crossing a line. Variants of the symbol had curved and straight lines. Sometimes the line and arrow were of equal thickness, while in other variants the arrow remained thick but the horizontal line was much thinner.

Commanders

General der Panzertruppen H. Stumpff *(13 Nov 1940 – 10 Sept 1941)*	General der Panzertruppen M. von Kessel *(5 May 1943 – 1 Jan 1944)*
Generalleutnant G. von Bismarck *(10 Sept 1941 – 14 Oct 1941)*	Generalleutnant W. Marcks *(1 Jan 1944 – 7 Feb 1944)*
General der Panzertruppen W. von Thoma *(14 Oct 1941 – 1 July 1942)*	General der Panzertruppen M. von Kessel *(7 Feb 1944 – 6 Nov 1944)*
Generalleutnant W. Duvert *(1 July 1942 – 1 Oct 1942)*	Generalmajor H. von Oppeln-Bronikowski *(6 Nov 1944 – 8 May 1944)*
General der Panzertruppen H. von Luttwitz *(1 Oct 1942 – 5 May 1943)*	

Barbarossa: the attack on Russia
22 JUNE 1941

The 20th Panzer Division fought with the 3rd *Panzergruppe* during the opening stages of Operation *Barbarossa* in June 1941.

LIKE THE 19TH PANZER DIVISION, 20th Panzer took part in the initial battles of encirclement at Minsk and Smolensk, during which tens of thousands of Soviet prisoners were captured. Remaining near Smolensk after part of the 3rd *Panzergruppe* had been diverted to assist Army Group North at Leningrad, it transferred to the 4th *Panzergruppe* at Vyasma for the delayed German push towards Moscow. The delay allowed the Soviets to improve Moscow's defences. It also meant that the *Wehrmacht* would have to contend with the Russian winter, for which it was far from well prepared.

ORGANIZATION

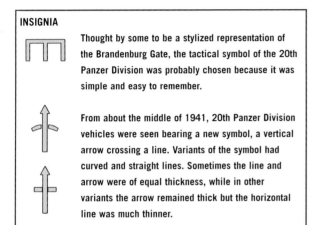

Pz. Rgt. 21

III. St | II. St | I. St

m / / | m / / | m / /

Panzer Unit	Pz. I	Pz. II	Pz. 38(t)	Pz. IV	Pz.Bef38(t)
21th Pz. Rgt.	44	31	121	31	2

▶ **Panzerkampfwagen 38(t) Ausf E/F**

Pz. Rgt 21

Some 525 Ausf E/F variants of the Pz.Kpfw 38(t) were produced for the *Wehrmacht* by Czech factories between November 1940 and October 1941. During Operation *Barbarossa,* the 20th Panzer Division used these tanks with Army Group Centre, seeing combat with *Panzergruppe* 3.

Specifications

Crew: 4	Engine: Praga EPA
Weight: 10.9 tonnes (9.85 tons)	Speed: 42km/hr (26mph)
Length: 4.61m (15.1ft)	Range: 250km (155.3 miles)
Width: 2.14m (7ft)	Radio: FuG37(t)
Height: 2.4m (7.9ft)	

▶ **Panzerkampfwagen 38(t) Ausf E/F**

Pz. Rgt 21

Manufactured by the BMM concern, the 525 examples of the Ausf E/F variant were used in Russia by the 7th, 8th, 12th and 19th Panzer Divisions in addition to the 20th. This model had more armour protection on the turret and hull front than the first Panzer 38(t)s, which had seen combat in Poland and France.

Weapons Specifications

Main: 3.7cm (1.5in) KwK38(t) L/47.8	Turret MG: 7.92mm (0.3in) MG37(t)
Ammunition: 42 rounds	Hull MG: 7.92mm (0.3in) MG37(t)
Traverse: 360° manual	Ammunition: 2400 rounds
Elevation: –10° to +25°	MG Sight: MGZF(t)
Sight: 0m TZF (t)	

▶ **Panzerkampfwagen 38(t) Ausf G**

Pz. Rgt 25 / II Battalion / 6th Company

90 Ausf G were produced between May and December 1941. The Ausf G was the final production model for the turreted version on the Pz.Kpfw 38(t). After 1941, the tank was considered obsolete and the Czech production lines were used to produce self-propelled antitank vehicles.

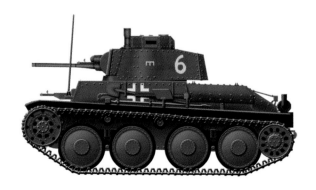

Specifications

Crew: 4	Engine: Praga EPA
Weight: 10.9 tonnes (9.85 tons)	Speed: 42km/hr (26mph)
Length: 4.61m (15.1ft)	Range: 250km (155.3 miles)
Width: 2.14m (7ft)	Radio: FuG5
Height: 2.4m (7.9ft)	

▶ **Panzerkampfwagen IV Ausf E (Sd Kfz 161)**

Pz. Rgt 21 / II Battalion

Built by Krupp-Gruson, the Ausf E variant of the Panzer IV had a new commander's cupola and increased armour protection. By the time Operation *Barbarossa* was launched, 438 Panzer IVs equipped the medium tank companies of the 17 Panzer divisions involved in the invasion of the USSR.

Specifications

Crew: 5	Engine: Maybach HL120TRM
Weight: 23.2 tonnes (21 tons)	Speed: 42km/hr (26mph)
Length: 5.92m (19.4ft)	Range: 200km (124.3 miles)
Width: 2.84m (9.3ft)	Radio: FuG5
Height: 2.68m (8.8ft)	

 # *Fall Blau*: the Eastern Front
28 June 1942

After the Battle of Moscow, the two battalions of the 21st Panzer Regiment, one battalion of the 112th *Schützen* Regiment and the 92nd Reconnaissance Battalion were disbanded.

EARLY IN 1942, AFTER THE FAILURE of the German assault on Moscow, the 20th Panzer Division's Panzer strength was reduced to a single battalion when the 1st and 2nd Battalions of the 21st Panzer Regiment were disbanded. Additionally, the 20th Panzer lost the 2nd Battalion of the 112th *Schützen* Regiment and the 92nd Reconnaissance Battalion.

20th Panzer served with Army Group Centre for most of its existence. In 1942, it was attached successively to 4th Panzer, 3rd Panzer and 9th Armies around Gshatsk (renamed Gagarin in the 1960s, after the first man in space). In August 1942, the Division was moved from the salient around Vyasma further south to the Orel sector, where it was attached to the 2nd *Panzerarmee*.

In November 1942, the Division was moved north again, and was dispersed around the small towns of Byelo and Toropets. In February 1943, it was placed in 9th Army reserve at Orel, before going back into the line with the 2nd *Panzerarmee*, where it would remain until just before the Battle of Kursk.

In spring 1943, the single battalion of the 21st Panzer Regiment was made up of a Regimental Staff Company equipped with a few flame-throwing tanks, and three medium Panzer companies, which were about to trade in their 3.7cm (1.5in) and 5cm (2in) armed Panzer IIIs for long-barrelled Panzer IVs and a single company of short-barrelled Panzer IVs. The battalion still had nine Panzer 38(t)s listed as operational.

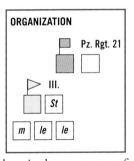

ORGANIZATION

Pz. Rgt. 21

III.

St

m   le   le

Divisional artillery was still towed equipment. Two battalions of the 92nd Panzer Artillery Regiment were equipped with 10.5cm (4.1in) leFH light field howitzers. Each battalion had three batteries: each battery had three guns. A third battalion was equipped with two batteries of three heavy 15cm (6in) sFH howitzers, and a single battery equipped with three long-range 10cm (4in) K18 cannon.

The reconnaissance battalion had one armoured car company and three motorcycle companies. The battalion's heavy company, designed to provide fire support, was equipped with four 7.5cm (3in) infantry guns, three 7.5cm (3in) antitank guns and three sPzBu 41 high velocity taper-bore guns.

Panzer Unit	Pz. II	Pz. 38(t)	Pz. III	Pz. IV	Pz. Bef
21st Pz. Rgt.	8	39	20	13	7

The last summer offensive
1 JULY 1943

In June 1943, the 3rd Battalion, 21st Panzer Regiment was renamed the 21st Panzer Battalion. Soon it was to be embroiled in the biggest tank battle of the war.

ATTACHED TO THE LXVIII Corps of Model's 9th Army, 20th Panzer saw intensive action in the northern assault on the Kursk Salient. Heavy losses meant that the Division went into reserve to refit after the battle.

Over the next year, 20th Panzer was forced back with the rest of Army Group Centre, retreating through cities which had been captured in the heady days of victory in 1941. By the summer of 1944,

20th Panzer was at Cholm when the largest offensive in history burst over Army Group Centre. During Operation Bagration, 20th Panzer was encircled with the rest of 9th Army near Bobruisk, and few of the 40,000 German soldiers in the pocket escaped being killed or captured.

What was left of the 20th Panzer Division had been reduced to a *Kampfgruppe* and was withdrawn to Romania for refitting. It returned to fight in East Prussia and later Hungary before being overrun by the Soviets in May 1945.

Panzer Unit	Pz. 38(t)	Pz. III	Pz. III(75)	Pz. IV	Pz. Bef
21st Pz. Rgt.	9	12	5	49	7

ORGANIZATION
- Pz. Abt. 21
- St
- m | le | le | le

▶ **Leichter Panzerspähwagen (2cm) (Sd Kfz 222)**
20th Reconnaissance Battalion

The SdKfz 222 was a modified version of the earlier SdKfz 221, with a larger turret designed to carry a 2cm (0.8in) automatic cannon. It was designed to act as an escort for larger armoured cars, which were equipped with longer-ranged radios. 989 Sd Kfz 222 were produced between 1936 and June 1943.

 The toned-down tactical insignia carried by this SdKfz 222 include a stylized representation of the divisional markings, together with a standard German map symbol for armoured reconnaissance units.

Specifications

Crew: 3
Weight: 5.3 tonnes (4.8 tons)
Length: 4.8m (15.7ft)
Width: 1.95m (6.4ft)
Height: 2m (6.6ft)

Engine: Horch 3.5 or 3.8
Speed: 85km/hr (52.8mph)
Range: 300km (186.4 miles)
Radio: FuG Spr Ger 'a'

▶ **Mittlerer Schützenpanzerwagen Ausf D (Sd Kfz 251/9)**
20th Reconnaissance Battalion / Half-track Gun Section

The SdKfz 251 was designed by Hanomag and built by eight other companies, and over 4600 examples were produced between 1939 and 1943. Built in dozens of variants, it was the principal carrier of *Panzergrenadiers* and their weapons.

Specifications

Crew: 3
Weight: 9.4 tonnes (8.53 tons)
Length: 5.98m (19.6ft)
Width: 2.1m (6.9ft)
Height: 2.07m (6.8ft)

Engine: Maybach HL42TUKRM
Speed: 53km/hr (32.9mph)
Range: 300km (186.4 miles)
Radio: FuG Spr Ger 'f'

21st Panzer Division

The creation of the 21st Panzer Division was authorized on 1 August 1941. It had already been in action in North Africa for several months as the 5th Light Division.

THE 5TH LIGHT DIVISION was formed on 18 February 1941 from German troops sent to Africa to help the Italians. The division staff came from the 3rd Panzer Brigade, the Panzers and artillery were drawn from the 3rd Panzer Division, and Infantry Regiment zbV 200 was created to control the infantry (zbV standing for *zur besonderen Verwendung*, 'For Special Duties'). 5th Light was in action as soon as it arrived in Africa. It first went into action as 21st Panzer during Operation *Crusader*, the British offensive launched at the end of 1941.

Commanders

Generalleutnant K. Bottcher
(1 Aug 1941 – 20 May 1941)

Generalleutnant J. von Ravenstein
(20 May 1941 – 29 Nov 1941)

Generalleutnant G. Knabe
(29 Nov 1941 – 1 Dec 1941)

Generalleutnant K. Bottcher
(1 Dec 1941 – 11 Feb 1942)

Generalleutnant G. von Bismarck
(11 Feb 1942 – 21 July 1942)

Oberst A. Bruer
(21 July 1942 – Aug 1942)

Generalleutnant G. von Bismarck
(Aug 1942 – 1 Sept 1942)

Generalleutnant C. Lungershausen
(1 Sept 1942 – 18 Sept 1942)

Generalleutnant H. von Randow
(18 Sept 1942 – 21 Dec 1942)

Generalleutnant H. Hiidebrandt
(1 Jan 1943 – 15 Mar 1943)

Generalmajor H. von Hulsen
(15 Mar 1943 – 15 May 1943)

Generalleutnant E. Feuchtinger
(15 May 1943 – 15 Jan 1944)

Generalmajor O. Grolig
(15 Jan 1944 – 8 May 1944)

Generalleutnant E. Feuchtinger
(8 May 1944 – 25 Jan 1945)

Oberst H. Zollenkopt
(25 Jan 1945 – 12 Feb 1945)

Generalleutnant W. Marcks
(12 Feb 1945 – Apr 1945)

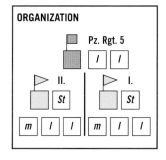 Enter the Desert Fox
1941

The 5th Light Panzer Division had been formed from troops sent to Africa together with the 5th Panzer Regiment, which had been detached from the 3rd Panzer Division.

ROMMEL LAUNCHED HIS FIRST attack against El Agheila in March 1941, only days after 5th Light's Panzers had arrived in the desert. The British, believing the Germans to be much stronger than they were, retreated. Rommel seized the initiative and chased the British through Mersa Braga, Mechili, Bardia, and reached the Halfaya Pass.

The British Operation *Battleaxe*, intended to push the Germans back, was a failure. But Rommel was at the end of a very long supply chain and could advance no further. On September 14 1941, units of the new 21st Panzer Division took part in Operation *Sommernachtstraum*, a reconnaissance in force eastwards across the Egyptian border. In November, the British Operation *Crusader* forced the Germans all the way back to Gazala, and then even further back to prepared positions at El Agheila.

ORGANIZATION

Panzer Unit	Pz. I	Pz. II	Pz. III(50)	Pz. IV	Pz. Bef
5th Pz. Rgt.	25	45	71	20	7

▶ Kleiner Panzerbefehlswagen (Sd Kfz 265)

5 Leichte Division / Pz. Rgt 5 / I Battalion / Stabskompanie / Signal Platoon

'I04' is one of the three kl.Pz.Bef.Wg that landed in Tripoli in March 1941. It still carries its original 3rd Panzer Division insignia.

Specifications	
Crew: 3	Engine: Maybach NL38TR
Weight: 6.5 tonnes (5.9 tons)	Speed: 40km/hr (24.9mph)
Length: 4.42m (14.5ft)	Range: 170km (105.6 miles)
Width: 2.06m (6.8ft)	Radio: FuG2 and FuG6
Height: 1.99m (6.5ft)	

▶ Panzerkampfwagen I Ausf A (Sd Kfz 101)

5 Leichte Division / Pz. Rgt 5 / I Battalion / Stabskompanie / Light Platoon

It was far from being a front-line weapon, but the mobility of the machine gun-armed Panzer I made it a useful weapon in the fluid, back-and-forth combat that was typical in North Africa.

Specifications	
Crew: 2	Engine: Krupp M305
Weight: 6 tonnes (5.4 tons)	Speed: 37km/hr (23mph)
Length: 4.02m (13.2ft)	Range: 145km (90 miles)
Width: 2.06m (6.8ft)	Radio: FuG2
Height: 1.72m (5.6ft)	

▶ Panzerkampfwagen II Ausf C (Sd Kfz 121)

5 Leichte Division / Pz. Rgt 5 / I Battalion / 2nd Company / 4th Zug / tank number 1

The Panzer II's 2cm (0.8in) cannon made it much more useful than the Panzer I.

Specifications	
Crew: 3	Engine: Maybach HL62TR
Weight: 9.8 tonnes (8.9 tons)	Speed: 40km/hr (24.9mph)
Length: 4.81m (15.8ft)	Range: 200km (124.3 miles)
Width: 2.22m (7.3ft)	Radio: FuG5
Height: 1.99m (6.5ft)	

▶ Panzerkampfwagen IV Ausf D (Sd Kfz 161)

5 Leichte Division / Pz. Rgt 5 / II Battalion / 8th Company / HQ tank

When it arrived in North Africa, the Panzer IV was the most powerfully armed tank in that theatre of combat, its 7.5cm (3in) armament being much more potent than the 2pdr (40mm) guns carried by most British tanks.

Specifications	
Crew: 5	Engine: Maybach HL120TRM
Weight: 22 tonnes (20 tons)	Speed: 40km/hr (24.9mph)
Length: 5.92m (19.4ft)	Range: 200km (124.3 miles)
Width: 2.84m (9.3ft)	Radio: FuG5
Height: 2.68m (8.8ft)	

▶ 4.7cm PaK (t) (Sf) auf Panzerkampfwagen I Ausf B

5 Leichte Division / 605th Panzerjäger Battalion

202 *Panzerjäger* I were converted from Pz.Kpfw I Ausf B between March 1940 and February 1941 by the addition of a Czech 4.7cm (1.9in) antitank gun.

Specifications

Crew: 3	Engine: Maybach NL38TR
Weight: 7 tonnes (6.4 tons)	Speed: 40km/hr (24.9mph)
Length: 4.42m (14.5ft)	Range: 140km (87 miles)
Width: 2.06m (6.8ft)	Radio: FuG2
Height: 2.25m (7.4ft)	

▶ Panzerkampfwagen I Ausf A (Sd Kfz 101)

5 Leichte Division / Pz. Rgt 5 / Regiment Staff

Some Pz.Kpfw I Ausf A were field modified to mount a *Kleine Flammwerfer* 42 (portable flamethrower) in place of the right-hand turret machine gun.

Specifications

Crew: 2	Engine: Krupp M305
Weight: 6 tonnes (5.4 tons)	Speed: 37km/hr (23mph)
Length: 4.02m (13.2ft)	Range: 145km (90 miles)
Width: 2.06m (6.8ft)	Radio: FuG2
Height: 1.72m (5.6ft)	

▶ Panzerkampfwagen III Ausf G (Sd Kfz 141)

5 Leichte Division / Pz. Rgt 5 / Regiment Staff / Signal Platoon / signal officer's tank

This vehicle was used during Operation *Battleaxe*, the British and Commonwealth offensive intended to relieve the siege of Tobruk.

Specifications

Crew: 5	Engine: Maybach HL120TRM
Weight: 22.4 tonnes (20.3 tons)	Speed: 40km/hr (24.9mph)
Length: 5.41m (17.7ft)	Range: 165km (102.5 miles)
Width: 2.95m (9.7ft)	Radio: FuG5
Height: 2.44m (8ft)	

▶ Panzerbefehlswagen III Ausf E (Sd Kfz 266-267-268)

5 Leichte Division / Pz. Rgt 5 / I Battalion / Stabskompanie

The 5th Light Division attempted to outflank the British during *Battleaxe*, a move typical of Rommel's tactics, which made great use of the wide expanses of desert and enabled his troops to move with lightning speed.

Specifications

Crew: 5	Engine: Maybach HL120TR
Weight: 21.5 tonnes (19.5 tons)	Speed: 40km/hr (24.9mph)
Length: 5.38m (17.7ft)	Range: 165km (102.5 miles)
Width: 2.91m (9.5ft)	Radio: FuG6 plus FuG2 or FuG7 or
Height: 2.44m (8ft)	FuG8

▶ Panzerkampfwagen I Ausf A (Sd Kfz 101)

5 Leichte Division / Pz. Rgt 5 / I Battalion / 1st Company / 2nd Zug / tank number 5

5th Light still had a number of early Panzer I Ausf As on strength. Long out of date, it had been the first German tank to go into mass production.

Specifications	
Crew: 2	Engine: Krupp M305
Weight: 6 tonnes (5.4 tons)	Speed: 37km/hr (23mph)
Length: 4.02m (13.2ft)	Range: 145km (90 miles)
Width: 2.06m (6.8ft)	Radio: FuG2
Height: 1.72m (5.6ft)	

▶ Panzerkampfwagen III Ausf G (Sd Kfz 141)

5 Leichte Division / Pz. Rgt 5 / I Battalion / 1st Coy. / 3rd Zug / tank number 1

Although the DAK (*Deutsches Afrika Korps*) had a number of battleworthy tanks in the shapes of the Panzer III and IV, its armoured vehicle laagers in 1941 still contained obsolete Pz.Kfw Is and IIs

Specifications	
Crew: 5	Engine: Maybach HL120TRM
Weight: 22.4 tonnes (20.3 tons)	Speed: 40km/hr (24.9mph)
Length: 5.41m (17.7ft)	Range: 165km (102.5 miles)
Width: 2.95m (9.7ft)	Radio: FuG5
Height: 2.44m (8ft)	

▶ Panzerkampfwagen I Ausf B (Sd Kfz 101)

5 Leichte Division / Pz. Rgt 5 / II Battalion / 8th Company / 3d Zug / tank number 3

The 5th Light Panzer Division was renamed 21st Panzer Division on August 1941.

Specifications	
Crew: 2	Engine: Maybach NL38TR
Weight: 6.4 tonnes (5.8 tons)	Speed: 40km/hr (24.9mph)
Length: 4.42m (14.5ft)	Range: 170km (105.6 miles)
Width: 2.06m (6.8ft)	Radio: FuG2
Height: 1.72m (5.6ft)	

▶ Kleiner Panzerbefehlswagen (Sd Kfz 265)

Pz. Rgt 5 / I Battalion / Stabskompanie / Signal Platoon / signal officer's tank

The 21st's first operation was a reconnaissance in force aimed at a British supply dump near the Egypt frontier. The Division took heavy casualties from air attacks.

Specifications	
Crew: 3	Engine: Maybach NL38TR
Weight: 6.5 tonnes (5.9 tons)	Speed: 40km/hr (24.9mph)
Length: 4.42m (14.5ft)	Range: 170km (105.6 miles)
Width: 2.06m (6.8ft)	Radio: FuG2 and FuG6
Height: 1.99m (6.5ft)	

Weapons Specifications

Main: 5cm (2in) KwK L/42

Ammunition: 99 rounds

Traverse: 360° manual

Elevation: -10° to +20°

Sights: TZF5d

Turret MG: 7.92mm (0.3in) MG34

Hull MG: 7.92mm (0.3in) MG34

Ammunition: 2700 rounds

MG sights: KgZF2

▲ Panzerkampfwagen III Ausf G (Sd Kfz 141)

Pz. Rgt 5 / I Battalion / 3rd Company / 2nd Zug / tank number 1

The Germans in Africa had a technological edge over the British, in that tanks like the Panzer III were combat-tested and reliable. British tanks built before 1943 were notoriously unreliable, and the situation did not change until large numbers of American M3s and M4s reached Commonwealth forces in the desert.

Specifications

Crew: 2 plus 10 troops

Weight: 8.8 tonnes (8 tons)

Length: 5.98m (19.6ft)

Width: 2.1m (6.9ft)

Height: 1.75m (5.7ft)

Engine: Maybach HL42TUKRM

Speed: 53km/hr (32.9mph)

Range: 300km (186.4 miles)

Radio: FuG Spr Ger 1

▲ Mittlerer Schützenpanzerwagen I Ausf B (Sd Kfz 251)

Unknown formation

The medium armoured troop carrier, the forerunner of the modern armoured personnel carrier, was proposed at the time the first armoured divisions were formed in 1935. However, the first production models of the SdKfz 251 did not enter service until 1939.

▶ Panzerkampfwagen IV Ausf D (Sd Kfz 161)

Pz. Rgt 5 / II Battalion / 8th Company / HQ tank

Headquarters Company tactical numbers indicated to whom a tank was assigned. The company commander's vehicle was 01; 02 was the adjutant's tank, while numbers from 03 onwards were used by other HQ vehicles.

Specifications

Crew: 5

Weight: 22 tonnes (20 tons)

Length: 5.92m (19.4ft)

Width: 2.84m (9.3ft)

Height: 2.68m (8.8ft)

Engine: Maybach HL120TRM

Speed: 40km/hr (24.9mph)

Range: 200km (124.3 miles)

Radio: FuG5

War in the desert
25 May 1942

After Rommel secured his supply lines, he decided to take the offensive against the British and Commonwealth forces in North Africa. He also wanted to capture the port of Tobruk.

THE GERMAN SUPPLY SITUATION started to change early in 1942. Air attacks on Malta prevented British aircraft and submarines from interfering with convoys, and for the first time, the *Afrika Korps* was receiving adequate support.

In May 1942, Rommel launched an assault on the British. 21st Panzer Division led a flanking manoeuvre around Gazala, where the British were dug in.

British tank losses in the Gazala fighting were huge. As the British withdrew, 21st Panzer was ready to lead the attack that finally took the port of Tobruk.

Pushing on towards Egypt, Rommel tried to outflank the heavily fortified position at El Alamein, but failed. Flanked by the sea on one side and the impassable Qattara Depression on the other, Alamein was just too tough. Rommel had more problems, however. At the end of a supply line stretching all the way to Benghazi and exposed to RAF air attack, the German troops were beginning to feel the pinch.

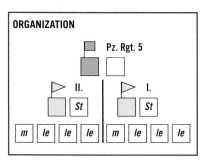

Panzer Unit	Pz. II	Pz. III(kz)	Pz. III(lg)	Pz. IV(kz)	Pz. Bef
5th Pz. Rgt.	29	131	3	22	4

▶ **Panzerkampfwagen II Ausf C (Sd Kfz 121)**

Pz. Rgt 5 / Regiment Staff

This Pz.Kpfw II was assigned to the Regimental Medical Officer. Note the caduceus painted by the tactical marking 'RA' (which stands for Regiment Arzt, or 'Doctor').

Specifications

Crew: 3	Engine: Maybach HL62TR
Weight: 9.8 tonnes (8.9 tons)	Speed: 40km/hr (24.9mph)
Length: 4.81m (15.8ft)	Range: 200km (124.3 miles)
Width: 2.22m (7.3ft)	Radio: FuG5
Height: 1.99m (6.5ft)	

▶ **Panzerkampfwagen I Ausf A (Sd Kfz 101)**

Pz. Rgt 5 / Regiment Staff

With regular supply convoys arriving in North Africa thanks to the aerial blockade of Malta by the *Luftwaffe* and the *Regia Aeronautica*, the *Deutsches Afrika Korps* could look forward to replacing old equipment like this early model Panzer I.

The front plate has both DAK and 21st Panzer Division symbols.

Specifications

Crew: 2	Engine: Krupp M305
Weight: 6 tonnes (5.4 tons)	Speed: 37km/hr (23mph)
Length: 4.02m (13.2ft)	Range: 145km (90 miles)
Width: 2.06m (6.8ft)	Radio: FuG2
Height: 1.72m (5.6ft)	

▶ **Panzerkampfwagen IV Ausf F2 (Sd Kfz 161/1)**
Pz. Rgt 5 / I Battalion / 4th Company / 1st Zug / tank number 2

Known to the British as the 'Mark IV Special', the long-barrelled 7.5cm (3in) variant of the Panzer IV was more than a match for any British or American tank in Africa.

Specifications

Crew: 5	Engine: Maybach HL120TRM
Weight: 25.4 tonnes (23 tons)	Speed: 40km/hr (24.9mph)
Length: 5.62m (18.4ft)	Range: 200km (124.3 miles)
Width: 2.84m (9.3ft)	Radio: FuG5
Height: 2.68m (8.8ft)	

▶ **Panzerfunkwagen (Sd Kfz 263) 8-Rad**
3rd Nachtrichten Abteilung (Signal Battalion)

Specialist communications vehicles were equipped with Enigma code machines. The Germans thought that their signals were secure, little realizing that Allied code-breakers could read much of what they sent.

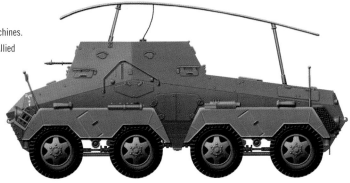

Specifications

Crew: 5	Engine: Büssing-NAG L8V
Weight: 8.9 tonnes (8.1 tons)	Speed: 100km/hr (62.1mph)
Length: 5.85m (19.2ft)	Range: 300km (186.4 miles)
Width: 2.2m (7.2ft)	Radio: 1 Satz Funkgerat fur (m)
Height: 2.9m (9.5ft)	Pz.Funktrupp b

El Alamein: Egypt denied
23 OCTOBER 1942

General Bernard Law Montgomery, the new commander of the British 8th Army, intended to use the sheer weight of Allied materiel to force the exhausted Axis troops into retreat.

OPENING THE ASSAULT on 23 October 1942 with an artillery barrage of World War I proportions, Montgomery launched a grinding attack that wore the German and Italian forces down. Progress was slow, but sheer Allied weight began to be felt. Rommel, who had been home on sick leave, arrived from Germany on the third day of the

attack, and realized that the situation was hopeless. Disobeying orders, he withdrew the *Afrika Korps*, using the 21st Panzer Division to fight a series of Rearguard actions.

El Alamein was the start of a long retreat for German troops in North Africa. By the time the Axis forces surrendered to the Allies in Tunisia in 1943, they had lost almost as heavily as they had done at Stalingrad. Among the German losses was the 21st Panzer Division.

ORGANIZATION

Pz. Rgt. 5

II.   I.
St   St

m le le le   m le le le

Panzer Unit	Pz. II	Pz. III(kz)	Pz. III(lg)	Pz. IV	Pz. Bef
5th Pz. Rgt.	14	43	44	18	2

▶ Panzerkampfwagen IV Ausf F2 (Sd Kfz 161/1)

Pz. Rgt 5 / I Battalion / 2nd Company / 1st Zug / tank number 5

Water is precious in the desert. Any of the ubiquitous
'Jerry Cans' intended for fresh water were marked with
a white cross, indicating that they should be used for no other liquids.

Specifications

Crew: 5	Engine: Maybach HL120TRM
Weight: 25.4 tonnes (23 tons)	Speed: 40km/hr (24.9mph)
Length: 5.62m (18.4ft)	Range: 200km (124.3 miles)
Width: 2.84m (9.3ft)	Radio: FuG5
Height: 2.68m (8.8ft)	

▶ Panzerkampfwagen II Ausf F (Sd Kfz 121)

Pz. Rgt 5 / II Battalion / Stabskompanie / Light Platoon

In October 1942, as the second battle of Alamein got under way, 21st Panzer still
had 19 Panzer IIs in its vehicle inventory.

Specifications

Crew: 3	Engine: Maybach HL62TR
Weight: 10.5 tonnes (9.5 tons)	Speed: 40km/hr (24.9mph)
Length: 4.81m (15.8ft)	Range: 200km (124.3 miles)
Width: 2.28m (7.5ft)	Radio: FuG5
Height: 2.15m (7ft)	

▶ Panzerkampfwagen III Ausf J (Sd Kfz 141)

Pz. Rgt 5 / I Battalion / 3rd Company / 3rd Zug / tank number 3

This Ausf J has been up-armoured, with a 20mm (0.8in) spaced armour
plate added to the front of the hull and turret.

Specifications

Crew: 5	Engine: Maybach HL120TRM
Weight: 24 tonnes (21.5 tons)	Speed: 40km/hr (24.9mph)
Length: 5.52m (18.1ft)	Range: 155km (96.3 miles)
Width: 2.95m (9.7ft)	Radio: FuG5
Height: 2.5m (8.2ft)	

▶ Panzerkampfwagen IV Ausf D (Sd Kfz 161)

Pz. Rgt 5 / I Battalion / 4th Company / 1st Zug / tank number 9

Captured by the British, this Ausf D has been upgunned with a 7.5cm (3in) KwK40
L/48 and has extra turret armour. These vehicles
were issued to training and replacement units.

Specifications

Crew: 5	Engine: Maybach HL120TRM
Weight: 22 tonnes (20 tons)	Speed: 40km/hr (24.9mph)
Length: 5.92m (19.4ft)	Range: 200km (124.3 miles)
Width: 2.84m (9.3ft)	Radio: FuG5
Height: 2.68m (8.8ft)	

▶ **Leichter Gepanzerter Beobachtungskraftwagen (Sd Kfz 253)**

115th Artillery Regiment

This light armoured observation post was based on the DEMAG 1 tonne tractor.

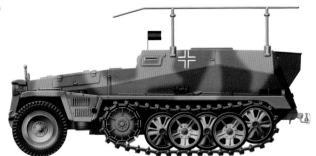

Specifications

Crew: 4	Engine: Maybach HL42TRKM
Weight: 6.3 tonnes (5.73 tons)	Speed: 65km/hr (40.4mph)
Length: 4.7m (15.4ft)	Range: 320km (198.8 miles)
Width: 1.95m (6.4ft)	Radio: FuG15 plus FuG16
Height: 1.8m (5.9ft)	

▶ **15cm sFH13/1 (Sf) auf Geschützwagen Lorraine Schlepper (f) (Sd Kfz 135/1)**

115th Artillery Regiment / 3rd Battalion

The German vehicle park was a quartermaster's nightmare, containing vehicles from all over Europe. This howitzer is mounted on a French Lorraine chassis.

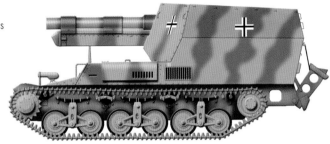

Specifications

Crew: 4	Engine: Delahaye 103TT
Weight: 9.4 tonnes (8.5 tons)	Speed (road): 34km/hr (21.1mph)
Length: 5.31m (17.4ft)	Range: 135km (83.9 miles)
Width: 1.83m (6ft)	Radio: FuG Spr 'f'
Height: 2.23m (7.3ft)	

▶ **Panzerkampfwagen IV Ausf F2 (Sd Kfz 161/1)**

Pz. Rgt 5

The first of the long-gunned Panzer IVs, the Ausf F2 was more than a match for tanks like the Sherman. But the few available could not match the sheer numbers of Allied tanks.

Weapons Specifications

Main: 7.5cm (3in) Kw40 L/43	Turret MG: 7.92mm (0.3in) MG34
Ammunition: 87 rounds	Hull MG: 7.92mm (0.3in) MG34
Traverse: 360° electric	Ammunition: 3000 rounds
Elevation: -8° to +20°	MG sights: KgZF2
Sights: TZF5f	

▶ **Panzerkampfwagen IV Ausf G (Sd Kfz 161/1 und 161/2)**

Pz. Rgt 5 / II Battalion / 8th Company / 5th Zug / tank number 2

Kasserine Pass was the last operation in divisional strength for 21st Panzer in North Africa. After that, it was split into *Kampfgruppen* until surrendering in May 1943.

Specifications

Crew: 5	Engine: Maybach HL120TRM
Weight: 25.9 tonnes (23.5 tons)	Speed: 40km/hr (24.9mph)
Length: 6.62m (21.7ft)	Range: 210km (130.5 miles)
Width: 2.88m (9.4ft)	Radio: FuG5
Height: 2.68m (8.8ft)	

The Western Front
JUNE 1944

Ordered to be rebuilt around a small nucleus of ex-African veterans, the 21st Panzer Division was reformed at Rennes in France on 15 July 1943.

INITIALLY EQUIPPED WITH captured French tanks, the recreated 21st was rapidly re-equipped with Panzer IIIs and Panzer IVs. On June 6 1944, the 21st Panzer Division was the only armoured formation close enough to the Normandy landings to have a chance to interfere with Allied consolidation of the beachhead. It was the only Panzer unit to attack on the day of the invasion, 6 June.

The slow German response to the Allied landings reflected a disagreement in the German High Command. Rommel wanted the Panzers deployed immediately to stop the Allies on the beach. Rundstedt, Guderian and others wanted to hold the Panzers inland, ready for a mobile campaign.

ORGANIZATION

Pz. Rgt. 22 / St

II. / St — I. / St

Pz.Kp. (Fkl) 315

Fkl | IV | IV | IV | IV | IV | IV | IV | IV

Panzer Unit	Pz. III(75)	Pz. IV	FlkPz	StuG	Pz. Bef
22nd Pz. Rgt.	4	117	12	10	2

▶ **Panzerkampfwagen IV Ausf H (Sd Kfz 161/2)**

Pz. Rgt 22 / II Battalion / 6th Company / 1st Zug / tank number 1

On 6 June, the 21st Panzer Division was the only armour formation in a position to influence the landings at Normandy. However, even veterans of the Eastern Front had not anticipated the devastating effects of Allied naval gunfire and air power.

Specifications

Crew: 5
Weight: 27.6 tonnes (25 tons)
Length: 7.02m (23ft)
Width: 2.88m (9.4ft)
Height: 2.68m (8.8ft)

Engine: Maybach HL120TRM
Speed: 38km/hr (23.6mph)
Range: 210km (130.5 miles)
Radio: FuG5

▶ **7.5cm PaK40 (Sf) auf Geschützwagen 39H (f)**

200th Sturmgeschütz Battalion

The 200th *Sturmgeschütz* Battalion engaged British tanks during Operation *Goodwood*. After early progress, the British were hit hard by fire from 88mm (3.2in) antitank guns and heavy tanks.

Specifications

Crew: 4
Weight: 13.8 tonnes (12.5 tons)
Length: 4.7m (15.4ft)
Width: 2.14m (7ft)
Height: 2.22m (7.3ft)

Engine: Hotchkiss 6-cylinder
Speed: 36 km/hr (22.3mph)
Range: 150 km (93 miles)
Radio: FuG Spr 'd'

▶ **10.5cm leFH18(Sf) auf Geschützwagen 39H (f)**
200th Sturmgeschütz Battalion
The Germans converted 48 French Hotchkiss tanks into a light self-propelled gun armed with a 10.5cm (4.1in) leFH18 cannon.

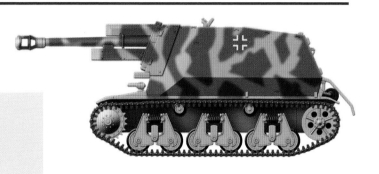

Specifications

Crew: 4	Engine: Hotchkiss 6-cylinder
Weight: 13.8 tonnes (12.5 tons)	Speed: 3 km/hr (22.4mph)
Length: 4.22m (13.8ft)	Range: 150km (93.2 miles)
Width: 2.14m (7ft)	Radio: FuG Spr 'd'
Height: 2.22m (7.3ft)	

▶ **7.5cm Sturmgeschütz 40 Ausf G (Sd Kfz 142/1)**
Panzer-Kompanie (Fkl) 315 (Attached)
The *Panzer-Kompanie (Fkl) 315* was attached to the 21st Panzer Division in January 1944. It was to use its force of assault guns in combat against the British and Canadians north of Caen.

Specifications

Crew: 4	Engine: Maybach HL120TRM
Weight: 26.3 tonnes (23.9 tons)	Speed: 40km/hr (24.9mph)
Length: 6.77m (22.2ft)	Range: 155km (96.3 miles)
Width: 2.95m (9.7ft)	Radio: FuG15 and FuG16
Height: 2.16m (7ft)	

Specifications

Crew: 1 (or 0 when remote-controlled)	Engine: Borgward 6M RTBV
Weight: 4 tonnes (3.6 tons)	Speed: 38km/hr (23.6mph)
Length: 3.65m (12ft)	Range: 212km (131.7 miles)
Width: 1.8m (6.2ft)	Radio: EP3 mit UKE6
Height: 1.19m (3.9ft)	

▲ **Schwerer Ladungstrager Ausf A (Sd Kfz 301)**
Panzer-Kompanie (Fkl) 315 (Attached)
Remote-controlled tracked demolition charge layer.

 # The Last Battles
14 DECEMBER 1944

After refitting, 21st Panzer was sent to the southern sector of the Western Front, where Germany and France shared a border.

ROMMEL'S FEARS OF ALLIED air power and of the devastating effect of naval gunfire were justified: in addition to normal combat losses and mechanical breakdowns, the constant fighter-bomber attacks and the hail of high explosive from battleships, cruisers and destroyers off the Normandy coast meant that most of the 21st's Panzers were destroyed in the first few days. However, the Division's grenadiers fought in and around Caen for many weeks.

Infantry losses could be made good by drafting in stragglers and remnants of other units: at the beginning of August, 21st Panzer received an influx of manpower when it absorbed surviving units of the 16th *Luftwaffe* Field Division. Many of these were killed or taken prisoner after the Allies broke out of the Beachhead in August, creating the Falaise pocket in which much of the German army lost its equipment. The battered remnants of 21st Panzer were withdrawn to Germany for rebuilding.

The 21st Panzer Division was rushed back to the Western Front after refitting with new tanks and drafting infantry from the 112th *Panzergrenadier* Regiment. It fought during the general withdrawal through France, mainly in the Saar and Alsace regions. In November, it was attached to LXIV Corps of the 19th Army near Lothringen.

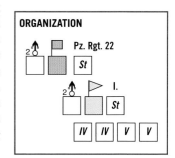

Panzer Unit	Pz. IV	Pz. V	FlkPz(20)	FlkPz(37)
22nd Pz. Rgt.	34	38	5	3

In defence of the Fatherland
1945

The Battle of the Bulge is well known as Germany's last offensive in the West – except that it was not. 21st Panzer took part in Operation *Nordwind*, launched two weeks later.

WITH THE SLOWING of the Ardennes offensive on 22 December 1944, Hitler ordered Army Group G to begin planning an attack on Alsace. Three days later, Hitler and von Rundstedt reviewed the plans and approved the attack, codenamed Operation *Nordwind*, for New Year's Eve. The primary target was Strasbourg. It had been annexed by the Germans in 1871, returned to France in 1918, retaken by the Germans in 1940 and was now again French. The offensive sparked off a three-week battle, but by 16 January Hitler's last reserves had been committed. The battle was over by 25 January.

In February 1945, the 21st Panzer Division was transported to the Oder front in Eastern Germany. There it fought in a series of hopeless defensive actions until surrendering to the Soviets at the end of April 1945.

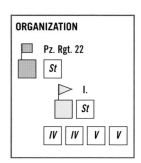

Panzer Unit	StuG	Pz. IV	Pz. IV(70)	Pz. V	FlkPz
22nd Pz. Rgt.	1	31	16	33	4

▶ **Panzerbeobachtungswagen IV (7.5cm) Ausf J**

155th Panzer Artillery Regiment

This armoured observation post is armed with a 7.5cm (3in) KwK40 L/48 cannon, and has been fitted with the cupola from a StuG assault gun. The 21st Panzer Division was overrun by the Soviets in April 1945.

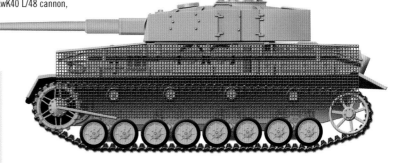

Specifications

Crew: 5	Engine: Maybach HL120TRM112
Weight: 27.6 tonnes (25 tons)	Speed: 38km/hr (23.6mph)
Length: 7.02m (23ft)	Range: 320km (198.8 miles)
Width: 2.88m (9.4ft)	Radio: FuG5
Height: 2.68m (8.8ft)	

22nd Panzer Division

Two new armoured formations were created in France in September 1941, the 22nd and 23rd Panzer Divisions. Both were to serve exclusively on the Eastern Front.

THE 22ND PANZER DIVISION was formed in Northern France by the upgrading of the 204th Panzer Regiment and by the addition of two newly formed *Schützen* Regiments making up the 22nd *Schützen* Brigade. 22nd Panzer was sent to southern Russia as part of Army Group South's reserve. In April 1942, it was attached to Manstein's 11th Army in Southern Russia.

On 8 May, Manstein launched an attack along the Kamenskoye Isthmus against Kerch. Although outnumbered, Manstein's Panzers attacked the weakest point of the Soviet defences. By 20 May, the Soviets had imploded and been driven back into the Black Sea.

As Manstein went on to invest Sevastopol, 2nd Panzer was transferred north to 6th Army.

Commanders

Generalleutnant W. von Apell
(25 Sept 1941 – 7 Oct 1942)

Generalleutnant H. von der Chevallerie
(7 Oct 1942 – 1 Nov 1942)

Generalleutnant E. Rodt
(1 Nov 1942 – 4 Mar 1943)

▲ **Graveyard for tanks**
The fighting in and around Stalingrad saw German panzers fighting through built-up terrain, where armoured vehicles are at their most vulnerable.

INSIGNIA

22nd Panzer's tactical sign was related to the symbol used by the 21st Panzer Division after its return from Africa, simply rotated clockwise through 45°.

Fall Blau: the Eastern Front

28 JUNE 1942

After the victory at Kerch, 22nd Panzer now took part in the German drive towards the Volga. Its primary target was the city of Stalingrad.

JOINING 6TH ARMY AT CHERSON, the 22nd Panzer Division operated with the 1st *Panzerarmee* against Rostov in July 1942. In August 1942, it was on the Chir River about 60km (37 miles) west of Stalingrad. The city was cut off after the launch of the Soviet Operation *Uranus* in November 1942, and 22nd Panzer was attached to Army Detachment *Hollidt*. This also included one Romanian tank division, three German and four Romanian infantry divisions. Although intended to relieve Stalingrad, strong Soviet forces prevented Hollidt from advancing beyond the Chir. In the fighting that followed, 22nd Panzer was almost destroyed. The remnants of the division were redesignated as *Kampfgruppe Brugsthaler* in March 1943, and the unit was disbanded and absorbed into the 23rd Panzer Division in April 1943.

Panzer Unit	Pz. II	38(t)	Pz. III	Pz. IV(kz)	Pz. IV(lg)
204th Pz. Rgt.	28	114	12	11	11

ORGANIZATIONS

Pz. Rgt. 204

I I

II.   I.

St   St

m le le   m le le

▶ Panzerkampfwagen 38(t) Ausf C

Pz. Rgt 204 / II Battalion / 5th Company / 2nd Zug / tank number 2

The 204th was the last unit to be issued with the Pz.Kpfw 38(t).

Specifications

Crew: 4	Engine: Praga EPA
Weight: 10.5 tonnes (9.5 tons)	Speed: 42km/hr (26mph)
Length: 4.61m (15.1ft)	Range: 250km (155.3 miles)
Width: 2.14m (7ft)	Radio: FuG37(t)
Height: 2.4m (7.9ft)	

▼ Panzerkampfwagen KV Ia 753(r)

Pz. Rgt 204

The 76mm (3in) gun on this captured Russian KV-1 tank has been replaced by a German 7.5cm (3in) KwK40 L/48 cannon.

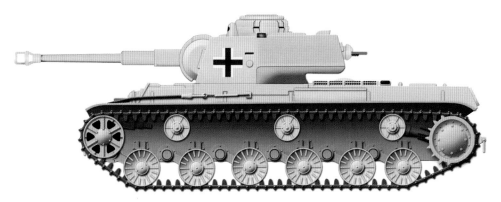

Specifications

Crew: 5

Weight: 46.6 tonnes (42.3 tons)

Length: 6.68m (21.9ft)

Width: 3.32m (10.9ft)

Height: 2.71m (8.9ft)

Engine: V-2K

Speed: 35km/hr (21.7mph)

Range: 180km (111.8 miles)

Radio: 10R

▶ Leichter Panzerspähwagen (Fu) (Sd Kfz 223)

140th Reconnaissance Battalion

The Sd Kfz 223 was designed to provide long-range radio communication for the far-ranging reconnaissance units equipped with light armoured cars.

Specifications

Crew: 3	Engine: Maybach Horch 3.5 or 3.8
Weight: 4.9 tonnes (4.4 tons)	Speed: 85km/hr (52.8mph)
Length: 4.8m (15.7ft)	Range: 300km (186.4 miles)
Width: 1.95m (6.4ft)	Radio: FuG10 + Spr Ger 'a'
Height: 1.75m (5.7ft)	

▶ Panzerkampfwagen 38(t) Ausf E/F

Pz. Rgt 204 / II Battalion / 7th Company / 1st Zug / tank number 1

22nd Panzer still used the Panzer 38(t) when it was shattered north of Stalingrad.

Specifications

Crew: 4	Engine: Praga EPA
Weight: 10.9 tonnes (9.85 tons)	Speed: 42km/hr (26mph)
Length: 4.61m (15.1ft)	Range: 250km (155.3 miles)
Width: 2.14m (7ft)	Radio: FuG37(t)
Height: 2.4m (7.9ft)	

23rd Panzer Division

The 23rd Panzer Division was formed in the Paris area in September 1941. Like the 22nd Division formed at the same time, it was sent to fight in the Soviet Union.

THE 23RD PANZER DIVISION incorporated the 101st Panzer Brigade, an occupation formation equipped with captured French armour. The French vehicles were only a temporary measure, however. By March 1942, when the division became fully operational, it had been re-equipped with 34 Panzer IIs, 112 Panzer IIIs, 32 short-barrel Panzer IVs and three command tanks.

In April 1942, the Division began the transfer to Army Group South on the Don River at Kharkov. In June 1942, the division was moved from the corps reserve and was assigned to LX *Panzerkorps* of Army Group A.

Attached to Kleist's 1st *Panzerarmee*, the Division fought through the searing heat towards the Caucasus. The Soviet attack at Stalingrad threatened to cut off the entire Army Group, and the Panzers made fighting retreat to the Don.

Commanders

Generalleutnant H. von Boineburg-Legsfeld
(25 Sept 1941 – 16 Nov 1941)

Generalmajor H. Werner-Ehrenfeucht
(16 Nov 1941 – 22 Nov 1941)

Generalleutnant H. von Boineburg-Legsfeld
(22 Nov 1941 – 20 July 1942)

Generalmajor E. Mack
(20 July 1942 – 26 Aug 1942)

Generalleutnant H. von Boineburg-Legsfeld
(26 Aug 1942 – 26 Dec 1942)

General der Panzertruppen N. von Vormann
(26 Dec 1942 – 25 Oct 1943)

Generalmajor E. Kraber
(25 Oct 1943 – 1 Nov 1943)

Generalmajor H. Werner-Ehrenfeucht
(1 Nov 1943 – 18 Nov 1943)

Generalmajor E. Kraber
(18 Nov 1943 – 9 June 1944)

Generalleutnant J. von Rodowitz
(9 June 1944 – 8 May 1945)

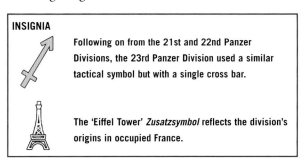

INSIGNIA

Following on from the 21st and 22nd Panzer Divisions, the 23rd Panzer Division used a similar tactical symbol but with a single cross bar.

The 'Eiffel Tower' *Zusatzsymbol* reflects the division's origins in occupied France.

From the Caucasus to Stalingrad
1942–43

Following the withdrawal from the Caucasus, 23rd Panzer was transferred to Hoth's 4th *Panzerarmee* in the failed attempt to relieve the besieged 6th Army at Stalingrad.

THE 23RD PANZER DIVISION had been battered by the hard fighting of the previous months, and more was to come as the Division's Panzer strength had been reduced to only 30 badly worn tanks.

After the relief force failed to get through to Paulus' trapped 6th Army at Stalingrad, 23rd Panzer was brought up to strength by absorbing what remained of the 22nd Panzer Division, which had been badly mauled in the fighting on the Chir.

By the spring of 1943, the Division's Panzer strength was in the process of being increased, with the 201st Panzer Regiment refitting to deploy one battalion with Panzer IVs and one battalion with Panzer V Panthers.

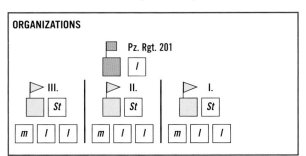

ORGANIZATIONS

Pz. Rgt. 201

Panzer Unit	Pz. II	Pz. III(5kz)	Pz. III(5lg)	Pz. IV	Pz. Bef
201st Pz. Rgt.	27	50	34	17	10

The last summer offensive
1 July 1943

After being attached to Army Detachment *Hollidt* during the withdrawal from Stalingrad, 23rd Panzer Division was reconstructed between April and June 1943.

THE DIVISION WAS BACK in action in July, as part of 1st *Panzerarmee's* reserve on the Mius River. Following the cancellation of the Kursk offensive by Hitler, the Soviets launched a series of offensives along the length of the front. It is believed that these were designed to force the Germans to disperse the powerful Panzer force, which was still a threat to the Red Army even after the losses in the battles in July.

23rd Panzer met the Soviet offensive on the Mius, where it was joined by the 3rd Panzer Division, the 2nd SS Panzer Division *Das Reich* and the 3rd SS Panzer Division *Totenkopf.* In August, 23rd Panzer was moved to Izium, where further reinforcements arrived in the shape of the 5th SS Panzer Division *Wiking* and the 17th Panzer Division.

Long retreat

The 23rd Panzer Division now began the long retreat through the Ukraine and Poland. In September 1943, it was involved in the heavy fighting on the Dnieper. At the end of the year, it was attached to LVII *Panzerkorps* at Dniepropetrovsk, initially with

Panzer Unit	Pz. III	Pz. III(75)	Pz. IV	Sturm-I.G	Pz. Bef
201st Pz. Rgt.	24	17	30	7	1

1st *Panzerarmee* and then with the rebuilt 6th Army. In March 1944, it was fighting at Nikolaev, before being withdrawn to Jassy for rest and recuperation at the end of April.

From August 1944, the 23rd Panzer Division fought as part of XLVIII *Panzerkorps* as the *Wehrmacht* tried to stabilize the front in the face of repeated Soviet offensives being launched from the Arctic to the Black Sea.

In October 1944, the Division was sent to Hungary after further Soviet advances threatened Budapest. The division continued to fight in Hungary and Slovakia before being destroyed by the Red Army in Austria in May 1945.

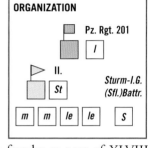

ORGANIZATION

Pz. Rgt. 201
I
II.
St
Sturm-I.G. (Sfl.)Battr.
m m le le S

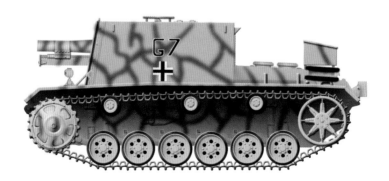

▲ **Sturminfanteriegeschütz 33B**

Pz. Rgt 201 / 9th Company

A vast improvement over the sIG33(SF), 24 of these infantry assault guns were produced between December 1941 and October 1942. The StuG33b is armed with one 15cm (6in) StuIG L/11 and has a fully enclosed fighting compartment.

Specifications

Crew: 5

Weight: 23.2 tonnes (21 tons)

Length: 5.4m (17.7ft)

Width: 2.9m (9.5ft)

Height: 2.3m (7.5ft)

Engine: Maybach HL120TRM

Speed: 40km/hr (24.9mph)

Range: 155km (96.3 miles)

Radio: FuG Spr 'd'

Staff Platoon, Medium Panzer Company, Type 44 Panzer Division

By the end of the war, Panzer Divisions were equipped with just two types of tank, the Pz.Kpfw IV and the Pz.Kpfw V Panther.
One of the platoons in the HQ company was tasked with reconnaissance.

Company HQ: 3 Pz.Bef V

Reconnaissance *Zug*: 5 Pz.Kpfw V

▶ **7.5cm PaK40/3 auf Panzerkampfwagen 38(t) Ausf H (Sd Kfz 138)**

128th Panzerjäger Battalion / Self-propelled Panzerjäger Company

Armed with a 7.5cm (3in) PaK40/3 L/46 cannon, it carried 38 rounds of ammunition.

Specifications

Crew: 4	Engine: Praga EPA/2
Weight: 11.9 tonnes (10.8 tons)	Speed: 35km/hr (21.7mph)
Length: 5.77m (18.9ft)	Range: 240km (149.1 miles)
Width: 2.16m (7ft)	Radio: FuG5
Height: 2.51m (8.2ft)	

▲ **Panzer IV/70 (V) (Sd Kfz 162/1)**

Unknown formation

The vehicle shown, from the second series built between September and November 1944, was in action in Hungary, mid-March 1945. The 23rd Panzer Division made a fighting retreat to Austria before it was overrun by the Soviets in May 1945.

Specifications

Crew: 4	Engine: Maybach HL120TRM
Weight: 28.4 tonnes (25.8 tons)	Speed: 35km/hr (21.7mph)
Length: 8.5m (27.9ft)	Range: 210km (130.5 miles)
Width: 3.17m (10.4ft)	Radio: FuG Spr 1
Height: 1.85m (6ft)	

Chapter 4

Later Wartime Panzer Divisions

The rapid expansion of the *Panzerwaffe* in the first three years of the war tailed off dramatically from 1943. The numerical sequence of panzer divisions ended after the establishment of the 27th Panzer Division in October 1942. Thereafter, only a few numbered divisions were formed. At the end of the war, with Germany assailed by enemies on all sides, several nominal Panzer divisions were created from remnants of other units destroyed in battle. They were usually given regional or historical names, but in the chaos into which the Reich had fallen, few were anything like true divisions in strength.

◀ **Panthers to the Fore**
Although the late war Panzer division had a third as many tanks as had those of 1939, its fighting power was much greater — because more than half of its panzers were the superb Panzerkampfwagen V Panther.

24th Panzer Division

The 24th Panzer Division began forming at Stablack in East Prussia in November 1941, working up to operational capacity at the *Truppenübungsplatz*, Ohrdruf, in February 1942.

THE CORE OF THE NEW DIVISION was provided by the 1st Cavalry Division. Cavalry had little place on the modern battlefield, but for political and sentimental reasons the German Army had retained a cavalry brigade when it expanded in the 1930s. The Brigade had been expanded to divisional size in February 1940, but its performance in the French campaign had been modest, especially in contrast to the astonishing success of the *Panzerwaffe*.

In April 1942, the 24th Panzer Division was sent to France to complete its training while acting as a reserve for 7th Army in Army Group D. Its primary equipment as a Panzer division included 32 Panzer IIs, 54 short-barrelled Panzer IIIs, 56 long-barrelled Panzer IIIs, 20 short-barrelled Panzer IVs and 12 long-barrelled Panzer IVs. Divisional units included the 24th *Schützen* Brigade, the 24th Panzer Regiment and the 89th Artillery Regiment.

Commanders

General der Kavallerie K. Feldt
(28 Nov 1941 – 15 Apr 1942)

General der Panzertruppen B. Ritter von Hauenschild
(15 Apr 1942 – 12 Sep 1942)

Generalleutnant A. von Lenski
(12 Sep 1942 – 31 Jan 1943)

General der Panzertruppen M. Freiherr von Edelsheim
(1 Mar 1943 – 1 Aug 1944)

Generalmajor G-A. von Nostitz-Wallwitz
(1 Aug 1944 – 25 Mar 1945)

Major R. von Knebel-Döberitz
(25 Mar 1945 – 8 May 1945)

INSIGNIA

The tactical insignia carried by 24th Panzer Division vehicles from 1942 to 1945 reflected the formation's cavalry orgins.

A simplified variant of the Divisional insignia was also seen on its vehicles from 1943 onwards.

Fall Blau: the Eastern Front

28 JUNE 1942

In preparing for the 1942 summer campaign in Russia, the *Wehrmacht* deployed as many Panzer units to Army Group South as it could gather.

ARRIVING ON THE EASTERN FRONT in June 1942, 24th Panzer made its combat debut with LXVIII *Panzerkorps* in the fighting around Voronezh, before being transferred to the 6th Army in August. After participating in the drive on the Volga, it transferred back to 4th *Panzerarmee* for the assault on Stalingrad. In October, it was returned to 6th Army control, and was tasked with leading the final assault on the city. The Division was trapped when the Soviets completed their encircling attack in November. By January, the remains of 24th Panzer had been combined with those of 16th Panzer and 94th Infantry Divisions to form a single *kampfgruppe*. The survivors surrendered on 2 February.

ORGANIZATION

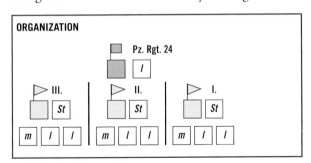

Panzer Unit	Pz. II	Pz. III(5kz)	Pz. III(5lg)	Pz. IV	Pz. Bef.
24th Pz. Rgt.	32	54	36	32	7

Specifications

Crew: 5

Weight: 24 tonnes (21.5 tons)

Length: 6.28m (20.6ft)

Width: 2.95m (9.7ft)

Height: 2.5m (8.2ft)

Engine: Maybach HL120TRM

Speed: 40km/hr (24.9mph)

Range: 155km (96.3 miles)

Radio: FuG5

▲ **Panzerkampfwagen III Ausf J (Sd Kfz 141/1)**

Pz. Rgt 24 / II Battalion / 5th Company / 2nd Zug / tank number 5

During the summer of 1942, before it was trapped in the Stalingrad pocket, the 24th Panzer Division numbered 56 Panzer IIIs with long-barrelled 5cm (2in) guns, out of a total strength of around 180 tanks.

◀ **Leichter Schützenpanzerwagen (Sd Kfz 250/1)**

Unknown formation

Designed to carry an *Halbgruppe,* or half-section, of four grenadiers, the crew of the Sd Kfz 251/1 consisted of a commander/gunner and driver.

Specifications

Crew: 2 plus 4 troops

Weight: 6.5 tonnes (5.89 tons)

Length: 4.7m (15.4ft)

Width: 1.94m (6.4ft)

Height: 1.52m (5ft)

Engine: Maybach HL42 TRKM

Speed: 59.5km/hr (37mph)

Range: 198km (123 miles)

Radio: FuSpr Ger 5

Specifications

Crew: 5

Weight: 25 tonnes (22.7 tons)

Length: 6.41m (21ft)

Width: 2.95m (9.7ft)

Height: 2.5m (8.2ft)

Engine: Maybach HL120TRM

Speed: 40km/hr (24.9mph)

Range: 155km (96.3 miles)

Radio: FuG5

▲ **Panzerkampfwagen III Ausf M (Sd Kfz 141/1)**

Pz. Rgt 24 / I Battalion / 2nd Company / 3rd Zug / tank number 4

A vehicle with these markings was captured by the Russians in the autumn of 1943. The *Schürzen,* or side skirts, offered extra protection against both armour-piercing and shaped charge high-explosive warheads.

Defence of Italy
1944

After the 24th Panzer Division was wiped out at Stalingrad in February 1943, the decision was taken to recreate it from scratch, based on the 891st *Panzergrenadier* Regiment.

BETWEEN APRIL AND AUGUST of 1943, the component parts of the new 24th Panzer Division were assembled in Northern France. The 1st, 2nd and 3rd Panzer Battalions received Pz.Kpfw IVs, Panthers and assault guns respectively.

In August 1943, the Division was ordered to join the II SS *Panzerkorps* in Italy as German forces occupied their former ally following Mussolini's downfall. Their first task was to disarm the Italian army. The Division remained in Northern Italy, fighting partisans and helping to man the series of defensive lines that Army Group B was preparing for the Allied armies advancing up the Italian peninsula.

Too far away to influence the Salerno landings, 24th Panzer was transferred to LI *Panzerkorps* in October, before being ordered back to the Eastern Front in November.

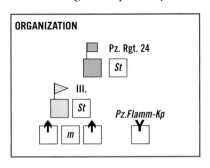

ORGANIZATION

Pz. Rgt. 24
St
III.
St
Pz.Flamm-Kp
m

Panzer Unit	Pz. IV	StuG	Pz. Bef	Flammpz
24th Pz. Rgt.	49	42	9	14

▶ **Panzerkampfwagen IV Ausf H (Sd Kfz 161/2)**
Pz. Rgt 24 / III Battalion / 12th Company / 4th Zug / tank number 1

As the war progressed, the shortage of resources was so critical that vehicles left for the front in the basic factory colour and rarely received any other treatment.

Specifications

Crew: 5	Engine: Maybach HL120TRM
Weight: 27.6 tonnes (25 tons)	Speed: 38km/hr (23.6mph)
Length: 7.02m (23ft)	Range: 210km (130.5 miles)
Width: 2.88m (9.4ft)	Radio: FuG5
Height: 2.68m (8.8ft)	

▶ **Sturmpanzer IV (Sd Kfz 166)**
89th Panzer Artillery Regiment

Seen here in Russia in September 1944, the Sturmpanzer IV was also known as *Brummbar*, or 'grizzly bear'. It was armed with a 15cm (6in) StuH43 L/12 demolition gun. Some 298 Sd Kfz 166 were produced from April 1943.

Specifications

Crew: 5	Engine: Maybach HL120TRM plus
Weight: 31 tonnes (28.2 tons)	TRM112
Length: 5.93m (19.5ft)	Speed: 40km/hr (24.9mph)
Width: 2.88m (9.4ft)	Range: 210km (130.5 miles)
Height: 2.52m (8.3ft)	Radio: FuG5 plus FuG2

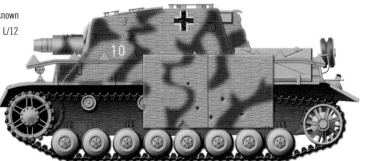

Defence of the Fatherland
1944/45

The 24th Panzer Division had been outfitted with Panthers in addition to its Pz.Kpfw IVs. It was ordered to the Eastern Front in October 1943, where it remained to the end of the war.

THE DIVISION ARRIVED in Army Group South's area of operations in November 1943, and was attached to XL *Panzerkorps* of the 1st *Panzerarmee* at Nikopol. In December, 24th Panzer transferred to IV *Panzerkorps* at Krivoi Rog. The city had been under attack by the Soviet 46th Army since October, as Malinovsky's 3rd Ukrainian Front and Konev's 2nd Belorussian Front launched an autumn offensive from its bridgeheads on the Dnieper River.

The battle for Krivoi Rog lasted until February as the Soviets maintained the pressure all along the Front. Threatened with encirclement like their comrades at Cherkassy, the Germans retreated before being cut off. In March, 24th Panzer fought to relieve German forces in Nikolaev, before retreating to Jassy and across the San and Weichsel rivers into Poland.

Soviet Summer Offensive

The massive Soviet offensives in the summer of 1944 continued to force the *Wehrmacht* westward. In

ORGANIZATION
I. Pz. Rgt. 24
St
V V V V

October 1944, 24th Panzer retreated into Hungary with Army Group South. As the Red Army juggernaut continued to attack, the Division fought defensive actions in Hungary until the end of November, being driven back into Slovakia in December. After operating with the 8th Army until January, 24th Panzer was transferred to East Prussia, where further Soviet attacks threatened to pour across the German border. In February, it joined the *Luftwaffe*'s *Hermann Göring* Parachute-Panzer Corps.

By now, the Division had been reduced to a *kampfgruppe* consisting of two Panther companies, the 21st *Panzergrenadier* Regiment and a single antitank battalion. As the Soviets pressed forward into Germany, 24th Panzer withdrew westward, eventually surrendering to the British Army in Schleswig-Holstein on 4 May 1945.

▲ **Panzerkampfwagen V Ausf G (Sd Kfz 171)**

Kampfgruppe / Pz. Rgt 24 / I Battalion / 3rd Company / 3rd Zug / tank no. 2

The Pz.Kpfw Ausf G was the final production version of the Panther, incorporating extra armour and a redesigned hull. By the end of the war, it made up more than half the tank strength of the *Wehrmacht*'s panzer divisions.

Specifications

Crew: 5	Engine: Maybach HL230P30
Weight: 50.2 tonnes (45.5 tons)	Speed: 46km/hr (28.6mph)
Length: 8.86m (29ft)	Range: 200km (124.3 miles)
Width: 3.4m (11.2ft)	Radio: FuG5
Height: 2.98m (9.8ft)	

25th Panzer Division

The 25th Panzer Division was formed in February 1942 in Eberswalde and was to remain in Norway until August 1943. It was equipped with 108 Panzer IV tanks.

PANZERS HAD NOT PLAYED a major part in the Norwegian campaign, but from 1940 to 1942 the *Panzer Abteilung zur besonderer Vervendung 40* provided what little armoured support was needed in the country. In February 1942, it became one of the constituent parts of the newly formed 25th Panzer

Division. In September 1943, the Division was transferred to France, before being moved to the Eastern Front. The Division fought at Zhitomir and at Kamanets-Podolsk, suffering heavy losses.

Commanders

Generalleutnant J. Haarde	Generalleutnant H. Tröger
(25 Feb 1942 – 31 Dec 1942)	*(20 Nov 1943 – 10 May 1944)*
Generalleutnant A. von Schell	Generalmajor O. Grolig
(1 Jan 1943 – 15 Nov 1943)	*(1 June 1944 – 18 Aug 1944)*
General der Panzertruppen G. Jauer	Generalmajor O. Audörsch
(15 Nov 1943 – 20 Nov 1943)	*(18 Aug 1944 – 8 May 1945)*

INSIGNIA

As a panzer division with non-standard origins, it is not surprising that 25th Panzer should also make use of non-standard tactical insignia.

After moving from Norway to the Eastern Front, the division adopted a simplified version of its symbol. It was also seen in yellow.

Retreat and defence of the Fatherland

NOVEMBER 1943 – 1945

In June 1944, the Division was sent to be reformed in Denmark, being redeployed as a *kampfgruppe* to the Polish sector of the Eastern Front in August and September 1944.

ALTHOUGH THE MAIN CHARGES for the violent and brutal suppression of the Warsaw Rising can be laid against SS units, *Obergruppenführer* Erich von dem Bach Zalewski also made use of detachments from the 25th, 19th and *Hermann Göring* Panzer Divisions to crush the Polish Home Army, which had risen in revolt in August 1944. The Poles were forced to surrender to the Germans at the beginning of October.

Soviet inactivity on the other side of the Vistula allowed the Germans to deal with Warsaw without any distractions. But once the Soviet Armies resumed their advance, 25th Panzer was forced to retreat through Poland, eventually fighting on the Oder River in February 1945. Heavy losses meant that the Division had to be reorganized as a *kampfgruppe*, featuring a mixed battalion equipped with two Pz.Kpfw IV companies that had 21 tanks and a company of Pz.Kpfw IV/70(V) with 10 powerfully armed tank destroyers.

Through February and into March 1945, the division continued to fight on the Oder Front, before being transferred south to Austria to fight with the 8th Army on the Lower Danube. The 25th Panzer Division had fewer than 30 armoured vehicles left when it was overrun by the Soviets in May 1945.

ORGANIZATION

ORGANIZATIONS

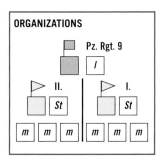

ORGANIZATIONS

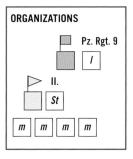

26th Panzer Division

The 26th Panzer Division was formed in September 1942 in France and Belgium from elements of the 23rd Infantry Division, with Panzers provided by the 202nd Panzer Regiment.

IN OCTOBER 1942, THE DIVISION was moved to Amiens. There it remained, continuing to train and to act as a coastal defence force, until July 1943. The Allied invasion of Sicily and the Italian Armistice forced Germany to take control of Italy. 26th Panzer was one of a number of units sent south to reinforce Army Group South (later Army Group C).

Commanders

General der Panzertruppen S. Frh von Lüttwitz	(6 July 1944 – 29 Jan 1945)
(Sep 1942 – Jan 1944/ Feb 1944 – July 1944)	Generalmajor A. Kuhnert
Generalmajor H. Hecker	(29 Jan 1945 – 19 Apr 1945)
(22 Jan 1944 – 20 Feb 1944)	Generalleutnant V. Linnarz
Generalleutnant E. Crasemann	(19 Apr 1945 – 8 May 1945)

INSIGNIA

The tactical symbol of the 26th Panzer Division was a representation of a Grenadier from the time of Frederick the Great.

 # Defence of Italy and the Eastern Front
1944

While the Division was fighting in Italy, the 1st Battalion had been detached and sent to the Eastern Front. It was equipped with 76 Panthers.

ORGANIZATIONS

SENT TO CALABRIA in Southern Italy, 26th Panzer saw action against the Allied landings at Salerno and on the Volturno. At the beginning of 1944, the Division was thrown into the fight against the Allied landings at Anzio and Nettuno. It remained at Anzio until the Germans were forced to retreat by the Allied success in outflanking Monte Cassino. Retreating through Tuscany and Rimini, it surrendered in Northern Italy in 1945.

ORGANIZATION

Panzer Unit	Pz. III(75)	Pz. IV(kz)	Pz. IV(lg)	Pz. Bef	Flammpz
26th Pz. Rgt.	16	17	36	9	14

▶ **Panzerkampfwagen V Ausf G (Sd Kfz 171)**
Pz. Rgt 26 / I Battalion / 2nd Company / 1st Zug / tank number 1
Some 3126 Ausf G were produced between March 1944 and April 1945.

Specifications

Crew: 5	Engine: Maybach
Weight: 50.2 tonnes	HL230P30
(45.5 tons)	Speed: 46km/hr (28.6mph)
Length: 8.86m (29ft)	Range: 200km
Width: 3.4m (11.2ft)	(124.3 miles)
Height: 2.98m (9.8ft)	Radio: FuG5

116th Panzer Division

The 116th Panzer Division was formed at the end of March 1944 from the remnants of the 16th *Panzergrenadier* Division, absorbing the 179th Reserve Panzer Division in the process.

APART FROM THE SHORT-LIVED 27th Panzer Division (which had been formed in October 1942 in southern Russia from *Kampfgruppe* Michalik and had been disbanded on 15 February 1943), the 26th Panzer Division was the last of the sequentially numbered Panzer formations to be formed. The next division to be created was the 116th, which began assembling in the Rhineland and Westphalia in February 1944. It included troops from the 16th *Panzergrenadier* Division, which had been badly mauled in Southern Russia, and from the second-line 179th Reserve Panzer Division, which had been on occupation duty in France since 1943.

INSIGNIA
The 116th Panzer Division was known as 'The Greyhound Division', and the formation's tactical symbol was chosen accordingly.

Commanders

Generalmajor G. Müller
(28 Mar 1944 – 1 May 1944)

General der Panzertruppen G. Graf
von Schwerin
(1 May 1944 – 1 Sep 1944)

Generalmajor H. Voigtsberger
(1 Sep 1944 – 14 Sep 1944)

Generalmajor S. von Waldenburg
(14 Sep 1944 – ? Apr 1945)

▲ **Through the Ardennes**
The 116th Panzer Division penetrated deep into Allied lines during the Battle of the Bulge, but the Germany's last panzer offensive was ultimately a failure.

The Western Front

JUNE 1944

The 116th Panzer Division was sent to the Pas-de-Calais in France immediately after its formation. Calais was where the German High Command expected the imminent Allied landings.

STILL NORTH OF THE SEINE when the Allies landed in Normandy, the Division was not sent to the front until July. It was thrown into action during Operation *Luttich*, the German offensive at Mortain, which resulted in the largest tank battle of the Normandy campaign.

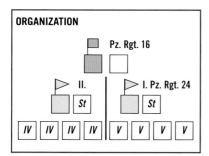

Unable to block the US 3rd Army from breaking out of the beachhead, the Division was caught in the Falaise Pocket. It broke out with tremendous losses when Hitler finally allowed a general withdrawal on 16 August 1944. By 21 August 1944, the division numbered just 600 men, 12 tanks and no artillery.

Retreating to Aachen, it was the only German unit defending the city when the US 1st Army began its assault on the *Westwall* in September 1944.

Panzer Unit	Pz. III	Pz. IV	Pz. V	FlkPz(37)
116th Pz. Div.	6	73	79	8

▶ **Sturmgeschütz neuer Art mit 7.5cm PaK I/48 auf Fahregestell Panzerkampfwagen IV (Sd Kfz 162)**

228th Panzerjäger Battalion

An early Jagdpanzer IV. The gun on later production vehicles had a muzzle brake.

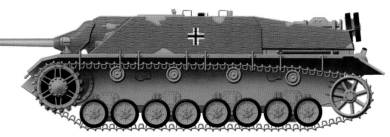

Specifications

Crew: 4	Engine: Maybach HL120TRM
Weight: 26.5 tonnes (24 tons)	Speed: 40km/hr (24.9mph)
Length: 6.85m (22.5ft)	Range: 210km (130.5 miles)
Width: 3.17m (10.4ft)	Radio: FuG Spr 'f'
Height: 1.85m (6ft)	

▶ **3.7cm FlaK auf Fahrgestell Panzerkampfwagen IV (Sf) (Sd Kfz 161/3)**

Pz. Rgt 16

Known as the *Möbelwagen,* or 'moving van', the four-sided superstructure folded down to provide a firing platform.

Specifications

Crew: 6	Engine: Maybach HL120TRM
Weight: 26.5 tonnes (24 tons)	Speed: 38km/hr (23.6mph)
Length: 5.92m (19.4ft)	Range: 200km (124.3 miles)
Width: 2.95m (9.7ft)	Radio: FuG5 + FuG2
Height: 2.73m (9ft)	

 # The Battle of the Bulge
14 DECEMBER 1944

After refitting at Düsseldorf, the division returned to defend Aachen, and was then involved in the bloody battle of the Hürtgen Forest early in November.

ASSIGNED TO THE 5TH *PANZERARMEE* in December 1944, 116th Panzer was one of the spearhead formations that ripped through the Allied lines in the Ardennes during the Battle of the Bulge. 5th Panzerarmee almost reached the Meuse at Dinant, where Rommel's 7th Panzer had crossed only four years previously. However, lack of fuel, Allied air power along with the arrival of American reinforcements brought the offensive to an end. After again suffering heavy casualties, 116th Panzer was withdrawn to Cleves, on the Dutch-German border.

Defending the Roer River dams against an Anglo-Canadian Offensive, 116th Panzer was trapped in the Wesel Pocket in February 1945. In March 1945, the division withdrew across the Rhine. Fighting in the Ruhr Pocket, it surrendered to the US 9th Army on 18 April 1945.

Panzer Unit	Pz. IV	Pz. V	StuG	FlkPz(37)
116th Pz. Div.	21	41	14	3

ORGANIZATION

Pz. Rgt. 16

St

II.

St

I.

St

IV IV   V V V V

▲ Panzerkampfwagen V Ausf G (Sd Kfz 171)

Pz. Rgt 16 / I Battalion / 3rd Company / 2nd Zug / tank number 1

The Pz.Kpfw V Panther equipped the four medium companies of the 1st Battalion, 16th Panzer Regiment, which had been formed around the remnants of the 16th *Panzergrenadier* Divisions 116th Panzer Regiment.

Weapons Specifications

Main: 7.5cm (3in) KwK42 L/70	Turret MG: 7.92mm (0.3in) MG 34
Ammunition: 81 rounds	Hull MG: 7.92mm (0.3in) MG 34
Traverse: 360° (hydraulic)	Ammunition: 4800 rounds
Elevation: -8° to +18°	MG Sight: KgZF2
Sight: TZF12a	

▲ 38cm RW61 auf Sturmmörser Tiger

Kampfgruppe / Pz. Rgt 16

Assault mortar-firing rocket-assisted projectiles mounted on a Tiger chassis. It was designed to destroy strongpoints and fortifications at close quarters. In April 1945, the remnants of 116th Panzer were formed into a *Kampfgruppe*. It had a single Panzer company with 14 PzKpfw V Panthers and a platoon of 4 Sturmtigers.

Specifications

Crew: 5	Engine: Maybach HL230P45
Weight: 71.7 tonnes (65 tons)	Speed: 40km/hr (24.9mph)
Length: 6.28m (20.6ft)	Range: 120km (74.6 miles)
Width: 3.57m (11.7ft)	Radio: FuG5
Height: 2.85m (9.4ft)	

(130th) Panzer *Lehr* Division

Although it existed for only a year from its formation early in 1944, the Panzer *Lehr* Division proved itself to be one of the crack armoured units in the German Army.

Commanders

Generalleutnant F. Bayerlein
(10 Jan 1944 – 20 Jan 1944)

Generalmajor H. Niemack
(20 Jan 1944 – Apr 1945)

THE PANZER LEHR Division was formed in the area around Nancy and Verdun in January 1941. The word *Lehr* means 'teaching' or 'demonstration', and the Division's cadre was provided by German Army training and demonstration units. Led by instructors and combat veterans, the Division was considered an elite unit from its foundation. In March 1944, the Division was sent to Hungary, but returned to the West in May. It was part of the High Command's reserve Panzer force, which they intended using to throw the expected Allied invasion back into the sea.

▲ **Destroyed in Normandy**

Panzer Lehr Division fought hard against Allied armies in Normandy, but in the process it lost most of its vehicles in bloody battles of attrition.

INSIGNIA

The tactical symbol used by the 130th Panzer Division included the letter 'L' for *Lehr*, or demonstration, carried within the rhomboidal military map symbol for armour.

Variants of the insignia usually did away with the rhomboid.

The Western Front

JUNE 1944

The *Lehr,* or demonstration, units were led by the most expert troops in the German Army, and the Panzer-Lehr Division was one of the largest and best equipped Panzer formations.

WHEN THE FULL FURY of the Allied landings in Normandy finally hit in June 1944, Panzer Lehr, officially known as the 130th Panzer Division, was one of the strongest units in the West. Ordered north on 6 June, it suffered heavily from Allied air attacks. After entering the battle at Bayeux on 9 June, Panzer-Lehr continued to fight the British in bloody battles of attrition around Caen before being switched to fight the Americans at St Lo. Weeks of fighting against the odds left Panzer-Lehr so depleted that it had only a fraction of the armour it had started with. The shattered division withdrew across France, reaching Luxembourg as an understrength *kampfgruppe.* It was pulled out of the lines and reformed and re-equipped at Sennelager.

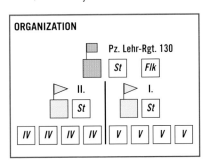

ORGANIZATION

Panzer Unit	StuG	Pz. IV	Pz. V	Pz. VI	FlkPz38
130th Pz. Rgt.	9	101	89	8	12

▶ **Panzerkampfwagen IV Ausf H
(Sd Kfz 161/2)**

*Pz.Lehr Rgt 130 / II Battalion / 6th Company /
3rd Zug / tank number 4*

The original Panzer-Lehr Battalion was renamed the
2nd Battalion, Panzer-Lehr Regiment early in 1944.
It was composed of four companies, each with 22
Pz.Kpfw IV.

Specifications

Crew: 5	Engine: Maybach HL120TRM
Weight: 27.6 tonnes (25 tons)	Speed: 38km/hr (23.6mph)
Length: 7.02m (23ft)	Range: 210km (130.5 miles)
Width: 2.88m (9.4ft)	Radio: FuG5
Height: 2.68m (8.8ft)	

 The crest of the CO of the 2nd Battalion, Prince
Schoenburg-Waldenburg (KIA June 1944) was used
as a memorial by tanks of his unit.

 The Gothic letter 'L' carried as an identification sign
by the vehicles of the Panzer-Lehr Division.

Specifications

Crew: 5
Weight: 49.4 tonnes (44.8 tons)
Length: 8.86m (29ft)
Width: 3.42m (11.2ft)
Height: 2.98m (9.8ft)
Engine: Maybach HL230P30
Speed: 46km/hr (28.6mph)
Range: 200km (124.3 miles)
Radio: FuG5

▲ **Panzerkampfwagen V Ausf A (Sd Kfz 171)**

1st Battalion 6th Pz. Rgt

As with most frontline Panzer formations in 1944, the Panzer-Lehr Division operated a mixed tank force with one
battalion of Panzer IVs and one of Panzer V Panthers.

▶ **Flakpanzer 38(t) auf Selbstfahrlafette 38(t) Ausf M (Sd Kfz
140)**

Pz.Lehr Rgt 130

The Flakpanzer 38(t) was armed with one 2cm (0.8in) FlakK38 L/112.5 AA gun.

Specifications

Crew: 4	Engine: Name
Weight: 10 tonnes (9.8 tons)	Speed: 42km/hr (26mph)
Length: 4.61m (15.1ft)	Range: 210km (130.5 miles)
Width: 2.15m (7ft)	Radio: FuG5 or FuG2
Height: 2.25m (7.4ft)	

The Battle of the Bulge
14 DECEMBER 1944

Destroyed in Normandy, Panzer *Lehr* was reorganized in October 1944. Even after rebuilding, the once elite unit was not as powerful as it had been before the Allied invasion.

IN NOVEMBER 1944, PANZER *LEHR* returned to defend the Saar, which was threatened by the advancing Americans. However, in December the division became part of LXVII *Panzerkorps* in Hasso von Manteuffel's 5th *Panzerarmee*. This was the southern prong of *Wacht am Rhein*, Hitler's last throw of the dice in the west. Along with Sepp Dietrich's 6th *Panzerarmee*, 5th Panzer was to smash through the Ardennes, aiming for Antwerp.

Battle of the Bulge

The German attack came as a complete surprise to the Allies, and Manteuffel's Panzers penetrated deep into the Allied rear. However, Panzer-Lehr was held up by the stubborn resistance of the American defenders of Bastogne. As fuel supplies became critically low, the weather cleared, allowing Allied fighter bombers to wreak havoc on the advancing panzers. Once the Allies regrouped and started bringing numbers to bear on the battle, there was nowhere for the Germans to go but backwards.

When the Ardennes offensive failed, Panzer-Lehr saw further defensive action in the battles for the Maas Line in the Netherlands. Early in March, it was used in an attempt to smash the American Rhine bridgehead at Remagen, which also failed.

Short of men and ammunition and with few tanks left, Panzer-Lehr was trapped in the Ruhr Pocket at the end of March. Unable to put up more than a token resistance, the division surrendered to the US Army when the Ruhr Pocket finally fell at the end of April 1945.

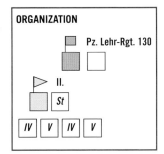

ORGANIZATION

Pz. Lehr-Rgt. 130

II.

St

IV V IV V

Panzer Unit	Pz. IV	Pz. V	FlkPz(20)	FlkPz(37)
130th Pz. Rgt.	27	30	3	4

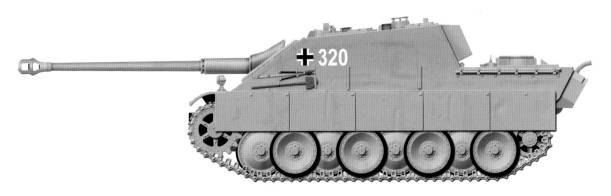

▲ **Jagdpanther (Sd Kfz 173)**
559th Schwere Panzerjäger Abteilung (Attached from Army Reserve)
This was one of the most powerful and effective tank destroyers of the war, and 392 SdKfz 173 Jagdpanthers were produced between January 1944 and March 1945. This is a late production model, with a two-piece barrel.

Specifications

Crew: 5	Engine: Maybach HL230P30
Weight: 50.7 tonnes (46 tons)	Speed: 46km/hr (28.6mph)
Length: 9.9m (32.5ft)	Range: 160km (99.4 miles)
Width: 3.42m (11.2ft)	Radio: FuG5 plus FuG2
Height: 2.72m (8.9ft)	

Volume Two:
Waffen-SS
Divisions

Introduction

The history of the SS (*Schutzstaffel*) falls into distinct phases. Formed as a security force to keep order at party meetings, then developing into the *Führer's* bodyguard, the SS was not a large organization in the 1920s. By the time Hitler came to power, however, it had grown to around 25,000 men, a tiny number compared to the millions of SA (*Sturmabteilung*) members.

AFTER 1933, THE SS GREW RAPIDLY, in the process splitting into three main groups. The *Allgemeine-SS*, or 'General' SS, initially took control of the police and security forces. It was also responsible for administering the rapidly growing SS economic empire, and took a leading role in investigating and promoting Himmler's racial theories. The *Allgemeine-SS* retained the characteristic black unifom long after other SS branches had switched to grey.

Separate from the *Allgemeine-SS*, the *Totenkopf-verbände* were the camp guards and have been most responsible for the horrible reputation the SS has kept since the end of the war. These brutal units were created after the SS won a turf fight with the SA for control of the concentration camps. The first camps were being built almost as soon as the Nazis came to power, and at Dachau the *Totenkopf* guards evolved many of the systems and techniques by which the SS terrorized Europe.

Armed SS

The Armed SS was established after Hitler came to power in 1933. Neither Hitler nor Himmler trusted the German generals, and they saw the SS as a military force personally loyal to the *Führer*, which he could use as a counterweight to the Army. Composed of well-trained troops of unquestioned loyalty to the party and the *Führer*, the Armed SS initially comprised the members of Hitler's bodyguard and the *Leibstandarte*, together with a number of *Politischen Bereitschaften*, or Political Emergency Squads, whose primary function had been to use

◀ **Ardennes offensive**
A PzKpfw V 'Panther' Ausf E from the II SS Panzer Corps advances down a snow-covered Belgian road as part of the attempt to push the Allies back to the English Channel, December 1944.

▲ Cherkassy encirclement

Men from the 5th SS Division *Wiking* man a PzKpfw IV amidst the fighting in the Cherkassy pocket, January 1944. More than 75,000 German troops were trapped in the encirclement, with some 35,000 – including troops from the *Wiking* Division – managing to break out in February.

violent measures against party opponents. These became the *SS-Verfügungstruppe*, or SS-VT.

By the time of the *Anschluss* with Austria in March 1938, the Armed SS had grown dramatically. In addition to the 2600 men of the *Leibstandarte*, there were three SS-VT *Standarten*, or regiments, derived from the *Politischen Bereitschaften*. The three regiments were given the names *Deutschland*, *Germania* and *Der Führer*, and were trained and equipped as motorized infantry.

Becoming known as the *Waffen-SS* in 1940, the Armed SS would be by far the largest branch of Himmler's personal empire, eventually numbering 38 divisions. Through its ranks passed nearly one million men of 15 nationalities. The premier formation of the *Waffen-SS*, the *Leibstandarte Adolf Hitler*, provided guards of honour for visiting VIPs before the war, but they were more than parade-ground warriors. The *Waffen-SS* took part in 12 major campaigns and were noted for their tough fighting qualities and aggressive leadership.

Chain of command

Assigned to Army control in combat, the SS had an entirely separate chain of command away from the battlefield. Answering to the *Reichsführer-SS* Heinrich Himmler, and through him to the *Führer*, the Armed SS was controlled by the *SS-Führungshauptamt* (FHA), the SS Operations Department. This was one of a dozen or so Main Offices via which the SS spread its tentacles throughout German society.

Headed by *SS-Obergruppenführer und General der Waffen-SS* Hans Jüttner, the FHA was split into four main groups. *Amtsgruppe* A was responsible for organization, personnel and supply. *Amtsgruppe* B was responsible for training. *Amtsgruppe* C controlled the inspectorates for various branches of the service, including infantry and mountain troops, cavalry, artillery, combat engineers, armoured troops, signals troops and various support and training services. *Amtsgruppe* D controlled SS medical services.

Surprisingly, the *Waffen-SS* had great difficulty in acquiring adequate equipment, at least in the early years of the war. Although classed as motorized formations, large parts of the SS went into battle on foot, with horsedrawn supplies – although in this they were hardly any different from the bulk of the German Army.

SS equipment was procured through the Army, and since the Army saw the SS as a potential rival, it was reluctant to supply the latest weapons. Some SS units used commandeered Czech weapons, and as the war progressed they also made extensive use of captured equipment. It was not until the last years of the conflict that the *Waffen-SS* received any preferential treatment, and by then they were hardly a separate organization.

Combat role

Originally looked on with distrust by the Army, the SS became more and more a part of the *Wehrmacht*. Armed SS units had always been under Army control on the battlefield; now, *Waffen-SS* equipment and organization were the same as those of the Army. SS units were interchangeable with Army units, and senior SS officers adopted Army ranks.

By the end of the war, first-line SS Panzer and Panzergrenadier divisions were among the largest and most powerful in the German armed forces. SS cavalry and mountain divisions had been formed, and hundreds of thousands of foreign volunteers found a home in the SS, until parts of it were more like a German 'Foreign Legion' than the elite of the German race.

The *Waffen-SS* had moved a long way in 20 years. Hitler's personal thugs became the parade soldiers of the 1930s, who in turn evolved into the well-equipped, million-strong army of 1944.

In the early days at least, Armed SS members retained the fanaticism that had been bred into them, which they translated into fighting spirit. They were regarded as an elite, only the best physical specimens being allowed to join. They were tough, and they were dedicated, influencing the course of World War II out of all proportion to their numbers.

They were also fanatical and ruthless. Being fanatics, they were responsible for many atrocities.

▶ **SS Panzer commander**

SS-Gruppenführer Paul Hausser (centre, inside turret), shown here inspecting a PzKpfw III from the *Das Reich* Division, led that division from its formation until October 1941, when he became commander of the I SS Panzer Corps.

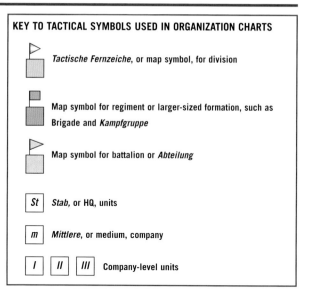

KEY TO TACTICAL SYMBOLS USED IN ORGANIZATION CHARTS

Tactische Fernzeiche, or map symbol, for division

Map symbol for regiment or larger-sized formation, such as Brigade and *Kampfgruppe*

Map symbol for battalion or *Abteilung*

St | *Stab*, or HQ, units

m | *Mittlere*, or medium, company

I | *II* | *III* | Company-level units

But as the war went on, it became harder to distinguish the SS from the soldiers alongside whom they served. By 1945, the survivors were a close-knit, battle-wise force with a full range of modern weapons, including tanks and artillery.

Chapter 5

The First SS Divisions

Hitler's bodyguard, the *Leibstandarte,* was the first unit of what would eventually become the Armed, or *Waffen-*, SS. Hitler and Himmler did not trust the German Army, and saw the SS as a military force personally loyal to the *Führer,* which he could use as a counterweight to the Army. The Armed SS was the largest branch of the organization. It would eventually number some 39 divisions, and one million men of 15 nationalities passed through its ranks. Taking the name *Waffen-SS* in the spring of 1940, it took part in 12 major campaigns and was noted for its tough fighting qualities and aggressive leadership.

◀ **Kharkov defence**
Panzergrenadiers from the *Das Reich* Division climb on board a StuG assault gun amidst the protracted fighting around Kharkov in March 1943. The II SS *Panzerkorps*, which included divisions *Das Reich, Leibstandarte* and *Totenkopf*, was used to stem the Soviet advance following the retreat from the Volga and Caucasus after the defeat at Stalingrad.

1st SS Panzer Division LSSAH

Between March 1933 and May 1945, the *Leibstandarte SS Adolf Hitler* grew from a bodyguard of 120 men protecting the *Führer* to the 1st SS Panzer Division, an outsized and immensely powerful armoured formation more than 20,000 strong.

EQUIPPED WITH THE most modern weapons that German industry could produce, it was led by some of the toughest and most controversial figures in German military history – men like *SS-Oberführer* Kurt 'Panzer' Meyer, *SS-Obersturmbannführer* Joachim 'Jochen' Peiper and *SS-Obersturmbannführer*

Max Wunsche. But the man who did most to shape the character of *Leibstandarte* was its first commanding officer, Josef 'Sepp' Dietrich. Dietrich, one of the earliest members of the SS, had been Hitler's driver and bodyguard, and was to rise to become an Army commander.

The *Leibstandarte* initially wore the black uniform of the *Allgemeine-SS* with the *Totenkopf* cap badge. The first armed SS guard unit was the *SS-Stabswache Berlin*, later renamed the *Wachtbataillon Berlin*. This became the *Leibstandarte SS Adolf Hitler* (SS Bodyguard Regiment Adolf Hitler) in

ORGANIZATION

Inf.Rgt LSSAH
St

I.	II.	III.	IV.
St	St	St	St
I II III	I II III	I II III	I II III

IG.Kp	Pzjr.Kp	Krd.Kp
St	St	St
I II III	I II III	I II III

HQ ORGANIZATION

Inf.Rgt LSSAH
HQ

Auf | Pnr | Krd | Nch | Mu | le.I

Commanders

Obergruppenführer Josef 'Sepp' Dietrich
1933 – July 1943

Brigadeführer Theodor Wisch
July 1943 – August 1944

Brigadeführer Wilhelm Mohnke
August 1944 – February 1945

Brigadeführer Otto Kumm
February 1945 – May 1945

INSIGNIA

In German, 'dietrich' is slang for a skeleton key, so to honour their commander the division adopted a shield with a key as its insignia.

Waffen-SS Divisional insignia were usually enclosed within a standard shield although this was not always applied on vehicles.

Because insignia were often painted on to vehicles in the field, they occasionally varied from the standard, sometimes being modified to fit a specific space.

When Dietrich was awarded the Oakleaves to the Knight's Cross in 1941, the division honoured their commander by adding oakleaves to its insignia.

As a security measure in the build up to Kursk, units involved in the operation used special formation markings to replace their standard insignia.

Divisional History	Formed
SA Stabswache	1923
SA Stosstrupp Adolf Hitler	1923
Stabswache	1925
Schutzstaffel	1925
SS-Stabswache Berlin	1933
SS-Sonderkommando Berlin	1933
Adolf Hitler-Standarte	1933
Leibstandarte Adolf Hitler	1933
Leibstandarte-SS Adolf Hitler	1934
Infanterie-Regiment Leibstandarte SS Adolf Hitler (mot)	1938
SS-Division Leibstandarte-SS Adolf Hitler	1941
SS-Panzergrenadier-Division Leibstandarte-SS Adolf Hitler	1942
1.SS-Panzer-Division Leibstandarte-SS Adolf Hitler	1944

▶ **Motorcycle reconnaissance company**
Although *Leibstandarte* was originally a ceremonial unit, from 1936 it was equipped as a motorised infantry formation as its combat role developed.

September 1933. Two months later, on the tenth anniversary of the Munich Putsch, its members took an oath of personal allegiance to Adolf Hitler.

In the early days, the purpose of the *Leibstandarte* was ceremonial – standing like black statues outside the main buildings in Berlin or executing crisp drill movements as honour guards for visiting VIPs. But its capacity for violent action was never far from the surface. In June 1934, Dietrich and his men – using weapons and transport supplied by the Army – were used by the Nazi party in the 'Night of the Long Knives', the bloody purge that eliminated senior *Sturmabteilung* leaders and other political enemies.

Armed SS

When it was decided to set up a private Nazi army, the *Leibstandarte* provided the core of the new 'Armed SS'. In December 1934, it was expanded to regimental size and began to move away from its political bodyguard function to a more conventional military role. It participated in the bloodless occupation of the Rhineland in March 1936, and a motorized battalion under Sepp Dietrich took part in the invasion of Austria in March 1938.

▶ **Leichte Lkw 1t Opel Blitz 2.0-12**
Leibstandarte SS Adolf Hitler / I.Bataillon
In 1934, the LSSAH had to borrow trucks from the Army to take part in the 'Night of the Long Knives'. By 1938, it was a fully motorized formation, though many of its vehicles were commercial models like the Opel Blitz introduced in that year.

Specifications

Crew: 1	Engine: Opel 1920cc 6-cylinder petrol
Weight: 3.29 tonnes (3 tons)	(36hp)
Length: 6.02m (19ft 9in)	Speed: 80km/h (50mph)
Width: 2.27m (7ft 5in)	Range: 410km (255 miles)
Height: 2.18m (7ft 2in)	Radio: None

▶ **Schwerer Panzerspähwagen 6-Rad (SdKfz 231)**
Spähpanzerwagen-Zug LSSAH
Although nominally an infantry regiment, the LSSAH was in effect a motorized division in miniature, with artillery, reconnaissance, pioneers and support units. In addition to a motorcycle company, LSSAH had its own armoured car platoon.

Specifications

Crew: 4	Magirus petrol (60–80hp)
Weight: 5.9 tonnes (5.35 tons)	Speed: 70km/h (43mph)
Length: 5.57m (18 ft 7in)	Range: 300km (186 miles)
Width: 1.82m (5ft 11.5in)	Radio: FuG Spr Ger 'a'
Height: 2.25m (7ft 4.5in)	Armament: 1 x 20mm (0.7in) cannon;
Engine: Daimler-Benz, Büssing-NAG or	1 x 7.62mm (0.3in) MG (coaxial)

Poland and France
1939–1940

As a regimental formation, *Leibstandarte* was the first *Waffen-SS* unit to see combat action in World War II – first in Poland in September 1939, then in Holland and France in May 1940.

WHEN WAR BROKE OUT in September 1939, the *Leibstandarte* was organized as a motorized infantry regiment. By this time, the Armed, or *Waffen-*, SS was wearing field grey uniform like the Army. Unlike Army units, however, its soldiers were also equipped with a range of well-designed camouflaged smocks and helmet covers – which were later to become complete camouflage uniforms.

The *Leibstandarte* was distinguished from other *Waffen-SS* formations by cuff titles worn on the left sleeve of uniform jackets. The *Leibstandarte* cuff title consisted of a strip of black ribbon with a woven silver border and facsimile of the signature 'Adolf Hitler'. In day-to-day usage, the full title *Leibstandarte SS Adolf Hitler* was usually contracted to 'LSSAH' or 'LAH'.

On 1 September 1939, Hitler unleashed his forces against Poland, with the Armed SS operating under Army control. The *Leibstandarte* in particular, now expanded to regimental size, fought hard, serving as a motorized regiment attached to von Rundstedt's Army Group South. *Leibstandarte* was part of the Tenth Army, under the command of fanatical Nazi General von Reichenau.

Casualties were high, however, as the attacking philosophy instilled into the SS by Felix Steiner meant that commanders often threw caution to the wind in order to achieve their aims. Army

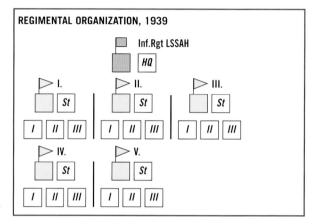

commanders were particularly critical of the leadership capabilities of junior SS officers.

War in the West

When the war moved west, the bulk of the Armed SS was deployed. *Leibstandarte* was attached to the right flank of the 227th Infantry Division with von Bock's forces, which also controlled the SS-VT Division.

The *Leibstandarte* was the first SS unit into action, crossing the Dutch border just after dawn on 9 May. LAH linked up with German paratroopers in the Dutch city of Rotterdam.

After Holland, it was deployed to France. The SS had no part to play in the opening stages of the drive

▶ **Gepanzerter Selbstfahrlafette für Sturmgeschütz 7.5-cm Ausf B (SdKfz 142)**

Panzersturmbatterie LSSAH

At the end of April 1940, a battery of six 7.5cm (3in) assault guns was assigned to the LSSAH's 5th Battalion, though it was not formally incorporated into the unit until July, after France had been defeated.

Specifications

Crew: 4	Engine: Maybach HL120TR
Weight: 21.6 tonnes (21.1 tons)	Speed: 40km/h (25mph)
Length: 5.38m (17.7ft)	Range: 160km (99.4 miles)
Width: 2.92m (9.6ft)	Radio: FuG15 or FuG16
Height: 1.95m (6.4ft)	

through the Ardennes. However, the *Leibstandarte* was one of the regiments attached to the 1st Panzer Division, which drove across northern France to the sea at Boulogne.

After Dunkirk, the three SS units were withdrawn for a couple of days of rest, before being moved yet again to take part in the Battle of France. *Leibstandarte* and the two SS divisions were attached to *Panzergruppe Kleist*, which was planning its advance towards the Marne. On 8 June, the *Leibstandarte* drove through Soissons towards the Aisne. The *Leibstandarte* continued the chase through central France, taking Clermont-Ferrand on 20 June. They overran the large French airbase near the city, capturing hundreds of *Armée de l'Air* aircraft as well as a number of Polish Air Force machines that had fled westwards the year before. LSSAH ended the campaign at St Etienne on 24 June.

LAH was expanded to brigade strength in August 1940, and at this time its members were told by their *Führer*, 'It will be an honour for you, who bear my name, to lead every German attack.'

▼ LSSAH Artillery Regiment

By May 1940, the *Leibstandarte* had grown to the size of a brigade, and had been redesignated as the Reinforced LSSAH. The unit's artillery assets originally came from the 4th Battalion, SS Artillery Regiment, but by August of 1940 this had grown to the size of a regiment itself, with two battalions of light and heavy field howitzers and an anti-aircraft, or Flak, battery attached to the 2nd Battalion.

I.*Bataillon*

II.*Bataillon*

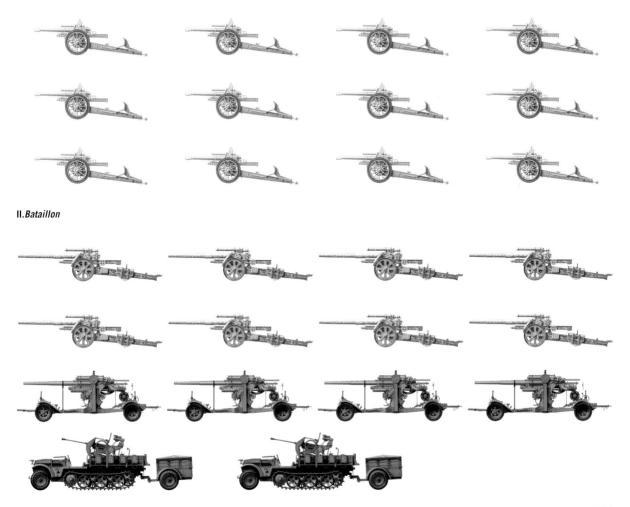

▶ Panzerspähwagen (Fu) 8-Rad (SdKfz 232)

Aufklärungs-Abteilung LSSAH

The SdKfz 232 was the radio version of the heavy SdKfz 231 eight-wheeled armoured car introduced in the late 1930s. It usually operated in support of the lighter and more numerous four-wheeled reconnaissance vehicles.

Specifications

Crew: 4	Speed: 85km/h (52.8mph)
Weight: 9.1 tonnes (8.3 tons)	Range: 300km (186 miles)
Length: 4.67m (15ft 4in)	Radio: FuG12 plus FuG Spr Ger 'a'
Width: 2.2m (7ft 2in)	Armament: 1 x 20mm (0.7in) KwK
Height: 2.35m (7ft 8in)	30/38 L/55 cannon; 1 x 7.92mm
Engine: Büssing-NAG L8V	(0.3in) MG (coaxial)

Balkans and Greece
APRIL–MAY 1941

The *Wehrmacht's* plans to invade the USSR were interrupted by the Balkans campaign, in which German troops were called upon to come to the aid of Mussolini's Italian forces.

IN FEBRUARY 1941, THE *LEIBSTANDARTE,* which by now had grown from an outsized regiment into a mechanized brigade, was moved from its winter quarters at Metz. It travelled by rail to Sofia in Bulgaria, where it would join Field Marshal Wilhelm List's Twelfth Army. On 6 April 1941, it crossed the border as one of the lead elements in the invasion of southern Yugoslavia.

Most of the Twelfth Army would attack southwards out of southern Bulgaria into Greece, while the rest of the army, led by the *Leibstandarte*, drove westwards into Kosovo and Macedonia.

Along with the 9th Panzer Division, the LSSAH formed General Stumme's XL Panzer Corps. The *Leibstandarte* and the Panzers headed westwards, driving through Macedonia towards Skopje. This force overran southern Yugoslavia to reach the Greek frontier at Monastir on 10 April. Their aim was to put a barrier in the way of any Greek armies coming to help the Yugoslavs.

South into Greece

Only one corps of List's Twelfth Army had entered Yugoslavia: the other two corps would attack though Macedonia, piercing or bypassing the Greek defences. The XXX and XLVIII Corps drove directly to the Aegean, punching clean through the Greek defences. A British armoured brigade deployed in the north was ordered to fall back along the eastern coast.

Meanwhile, *Leibstandarte* and the 9th Panzer Division were ordered south along the Albanian border. A smaller German force presented a further threat to the Greek defenders, making a series of landings on the Greek islands along the Turkish coast.

REGIMENTAL ORGANIZATION, EARLY 1941

Inf.Rgt LSSAH

St | Mu

▷ I.
St
I | II | III

▷ II.
St
I | II | III

▷ III.
St
I | II | III

▷ IV.
St
I | II | III

▷ Auf.Abt
St
I | II | III

▷ Art.Rgt
St
I | II | III

▷ Pnr.Btl
St
I | II | III

▷ Nach.Abt
St
I | II | III

▷ Nsch.Die
St
I | II | III

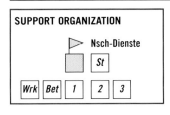

SUPPORT ORGANIZATION

Nsch-Dienste

St

Wrk | Bet | 1 | 2 | 3

The Italian Army undertook a new offensive that was timed to coincide with the *Führer*'s intervention. The Greek 'Army of Epirus', outgunned, started to give way.

The *Leibstandarte* performed outstandingly well. On 11 April, it had forced its way through the Monastir gap after a close-quarter, hand-to-hand battle with the small force of Australian and New Zealand troops who had been rushed north. By the 14th, the brigade was engaging the Greek 21st Division defending the Klissura Pass. The Greek resistance was extremely tough, and it was not until a young *Sturmbannführer* named Kurt Meyer infiltrated the LSSAH reconnaissance company along goat tracks over the mountains that the tide turned.

Victory

The Greek Government accepted defeat on 19 April, and the British announced their withdrawal from the mainland, although Crete would continue to be held. An orderly evacuation was imperiled on 26 April by a daring *coup de main*. German paratroops attacked the bridge over the Corinth Canal.

By this time, the *Leibstandarte* had reached the Gulf of Corinth, where Kurt Meyer commandeered two caiques (Greek fishing boats) and organized a ferry across the gulf. Swinging eastwards, the SS troops cleared the southern edge of the gulf before linking up with the paratroopers of the 2nd Fallschirmjäger Regiment.

However, the bridge was blown up and the British retreat continued into the Peloponnese, where a last stand at Kalamata ended with 7000 British and Commonwealth troops laying down their arms after exhausting their ammunition.

During the Greek campaign, the *Leibstandarte* won a reputation for being hard but fair – a reputation that was to change dramatically on the Eastern Front. Following a victory parade in Athens, the unit returned to barracks in Czechoslovakia.

▼ Panzerjäger I

V.Bataillon LSSAH / Panzerjäger-Kompanie (Sf)

The Czech 47mm (1.8in) anti-tank gun was fitted to the chassis of the tiny Panzer I to create one of the first self-propelled tank-hunters. From May 1940 until at least the end of 1941 or early 1942, the 5th Battalion of the *Leibstandarte* had nine of these vehicles in its *Panzerjäger* company.

Specifications	
Crew: 3	Engine: Maybach HL62TR
Weight: 8.9 tonnes (8.1 tons)	Speed: 40km/h (25mph)
Length: 4.8m (15ft 8in)	Range: 200km (124 miles)
Width: 2.22m (7ft 4in)	Radio: FuG5
Height: 1.99m (6ft 6in)	Arament: 1 x 47mm (1.8in) gun

▶ Panzerkampfwagen I Ausf B (SdKfz 101)

Panzerjäger-Abteilung LSSAH / 1.Kompanie / Stab

By the time the LSSAH was authorized to raise a three-company Panzer troop in February 1942, the Panzer I was long out of frontline service. However, it was issued to the commanders of *Panzerjäger* companies and battalions.

Specifications	
Crew: 3	Engine: Maybach HL62TR
Weight: 8.9 tonnes (8.1 tons)	Speed: 40km/h (25mph)
Length: 4.8m (15ft 8in)	Range: 200km (124 miles)
Width: 2.22m (7ft 4in)	Radio: FuG5
Height: 1.99m (6ft 6in)	

On the Eastern Front
1941–1942

Thanks to its involvement in the Balkans, *Leibstandarte* was still refitting when the invasion of the Soviet Union was launched in June 1941. However, it was quickly sent to the front.

BY THE OPENING OF Operation *Barbarossa* in June 1941, LAH was a division in strength, but not in name (although by September 1941 it was unofficially being referred to as the *SS-Division LSSAH*, and by the end of the year it had in fact been redesignated).

Waffen-SS units were deployed among the various Army commands. Field Marshal Gerd von Rundstedt, commanding Army Group South, was allocated the *Leibstandarte SS Adolf Hitler* and the *Wiking* Division, which were with General Ewald von Kleist's 1st Panzer Group.

Between July and November 1941, *Leibstandarte* fought non-stop from the Polish border to Kherson near the Black Sea and then along the Sea of Azov to Rostov on the Don.

In mid-November, when the majority of III Panzer Corps had caught up with the spearhead units, the assault on Rostov began. The capture of this essential communications link by the *Leibstandarte* Division was assured when it took a vital bridge over the River Don. Soviet engineers had mined the rail bridge with demolition charges, but it was still intact. Its imminent destruction was, apparently, being

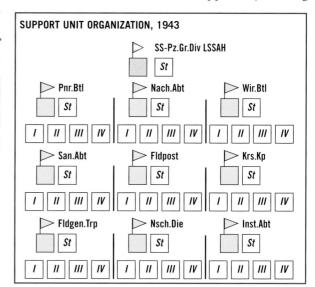

▶ **PzKpfw II für 7.62-cm Pak36(r) (SdKfz 139)**
Panzerjäger-Abteilung LSSAH / 1.Kompanie
Known as the Marder III, the combination of a captured Soviet gun mounted on a modified Czech tank chassis saw service on the Eastern Front from April 1942 until phased out in the summer of 1944.

Specifications

Crew: 4	Engine: Praga EPA or EPA/2
Weight: 11.76 tonnes (10.67 tons)	Speed: 42km/h (26mph)
Length: 5.85m (19ft 2in)	Range: 185km (115 miles)
Width: 2.16m (7ft 0in)	Radio: FuG Spr 'd'
Height: 2.50m (8ft 2in)	Armament: 1 x 76.2mm (3in) FK296

considered by Soviet engineers. Seeing a locomotive standing by the bridge with a full head of steam, *SS-Hauptsturmführer* Springer, commanding the 3rd Company, SS-Panzergrenadier Regiment of the *Leibstandarte* Division, ordered his men to open fire with every weapon available, peppering the engine and releasing high-pressure steam from countless holes. The ensuing confusion provided the cover required to storm the bridge. Springer and his men went on to remove the demolition charges, ensuring the bridge's safety.

Pushed back for the first time

However, the Soviet winter counteroffensive pushed LAH out of the city and back over the River Mius, all but destroying the division in the process. Its performance in the fierce fighting on the Eastern

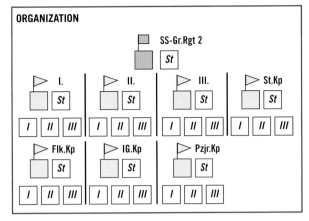

ORGANIZATION

National markings were enlarged on captured tanks to reduce the risk of 'friendly fire' incidents, though not always successfully since troops often fired at the shapes of tanks long before seeing any markings.

Front won the *Leibstandarte* considerable respect from the Army for its combat ability, but the hardness of its men was also reflected in the increasing number of atrocities they committed.

Vengeance was a major motive for slaughter: over three days in April 1942, the *Leibstandarte* murdered 4000 Soviet POWs in retaliation for the killing of six of their own.

▶ **Panzerkampfwagen T-34 747(r)**

Panzer-Regiment LSSAH / I.Bataillon

Captured Soviet T-34s were pressed into service by most German formations. When the LSSAH 1st Panzer Battalion was transferred west to be reorganized in April 1943, it took six damaged Panzers and two T-34s.

Specifications

Crew: 4	Engine: V-2-34
Weight: 24 tons (23.6 tonnes)	Speed: 40km/h (25mph)
Length: 6.58m (21ft 6in)	Range: 430km (267 miles)
Width: 2.98m (9ft 8in)	Radio: 10R
Height: 2.57m (8ft 4in)	

▶ **Mittlere Schützenpanzerwagen (SdKfz 251/1)**

2.Panzergrenadier-Regiment LSSAH / III.Bataillon

The three *Schützen* companies and the heavy company of the 3rd Battalion of the 2nd Regiment were issued with half-tracks when the division was upgraded to Panzergrenadier status in November 1942.

Specifications

Crew: 2 plus 12 troops	Engine: Maybach HL42TUKRM
Weight: 9.9 tonnes (9 tons)	Speed: 53km/h (33mph)
Length: 5.98m (19ft 7in)	Range: 300km (186 miles)
Width: 2.1m (6ft 11in)	Radio: FuG Spr Ger 1
Height: 1.75m (5ft 8in) or 2.16m	Armament: 1/2 x 7.62mm
(7ft) including MG shield	(0.3in) MG

⊥ Kharkov and Kursk
1943

The mauled LAH was withdrawn to France in June 1942. There it was partly re-equipped with armour and designated a *Panzergrenadier,* or armoured infantry, division.

IN THIS NEW ROLE, IT RETURNED to Russia in January 1943 as part of the XXXVIII Panzer Corps under Field Marshal von Manstein. In February 1943, after the fall of Stalingrad, the LAH played a critical part in the battle for Kharkov. Following the battle – Germany's last major victory on the Eastern Front – Josef Goebbels recorded in his diary that Hitler 'was exceptionally happy about the way the *Leibstandarte* was led by Sepp Dietrich. This man has personally performed real feats of heroism.'

Leibstandarte was part of the southern pincer attempting to pinch off the Kursk salient in July 1943. It bypassed Belgorod and reached Teterevino

before being forced to withdraw. In the intense fighting, the division knocked out about 500 Soviet tanks. The Soviet forces moved from the defensive at Kursk to a huge rolling summer and winter offensive.

2nd SS Panzer Regiment, July 1943	Strength
PzKpfw II	4
PzKpfw III (short barrel)	3
PzKpfw III (long barrel)	10
PzKpfw IV (long barrel)	67
PzKpfw VI Tiger	13

▶ **Panzerkampfwagen III Ausf M (SdKfz 141/1)**

Panzer-Regiment LSSAH / II.Bataillon / Battalion Adjutant

There were more than 400 long-barrelled Panzer IIIs serving in German frontline units at the start of the Kursk offensive in July 1943.

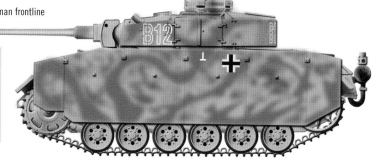

Specifications

Crew: 4
Weight: 25.4 tonnes (23 tons)
Length: 6.41m (21ft)
Width: 2.95m (9ft 7in)
Height: 2.44m (8ft)
Engine: Maybach HL120TRM petrol
(300hp)
Speed: 40km/h (25mph)
Range: 155km (96 miles)
Radio: FuG5

▶ **Panzerkampfwagen IV Ausf H (SdKfz 161/2)**

Panzer-Regiment LSSAH / II.Bataillon / 1.Kompanie

At the beginning of the Kursk action, the *Leibstandarte*'s 2nd Panzer Battalion had three medium Panzer companies with a total of 10 Panzer IIIs and 52 Panzer IVs, and a heavy company with nine Panzer VI Tigers.

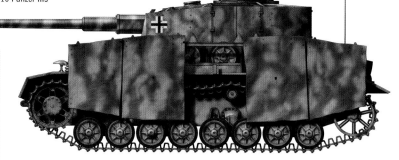

Specifications

Crew: 5
Weight: 27.6 tonnes (25 tons)
Length: 7.02m (23ft 0in)
Width: 2.88m (9ft 5in)
Height: 2.68m (8ft 10in)
Engine: Maybach HL120TRM
Speed: 38km/h (23.6mph)
Range: 210km (130.5 miles)
Radio: FuG5
Armament: 1 x 75mm (3in) KwK
40/43; 2 x 7.92mm (0.3in) MG
(one hull-mounted, one coaxial)

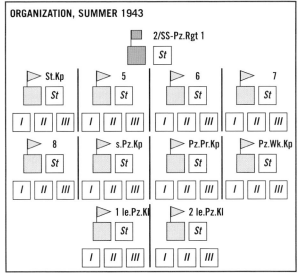

ORGANIZATION, SUMMER 1943

To Italy

After being stopped by fierce Soviet resistance at Kursk, *Leibstandarte* was sent to Italy. Re-equipped and redesignated as a full Panzer division, the LAH was again sent to rescue the crumbling situation on the Eastern Front.

The LAH played a significant part in the relief of the Cherkassy pocket, where 50,000 Germans, including men of the *Waffen-SS* Division *Das Reich*, had been trapped by the Soviet advance. About 35,000 survivors were able to break out and link up with advanced guards of the *Leibstandarte*.

▼ Medium Panzer Company

At the time of the Battle of Kursk, the 1st Battalion of *Leibstandarte's* Panzer regiment had been returned to the West to re-equip with new Panzer V Panthers. The unit had transferred all of its tanks to the 2nd Battalion, which had four medium Panzer companies plus a company of Tigers. Most of the Panzer strength was provided by long-barrel Panzer IVs with a small number of Panzer IIs and IIIs serving in staff companies and platoons.

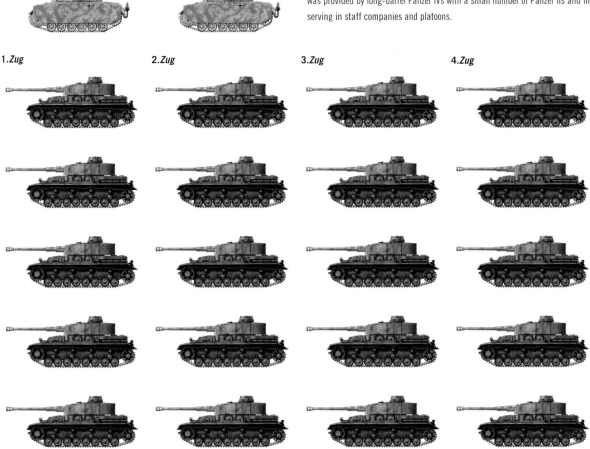

Stab

1.*Zug*   2.*Zug*   3.*Zug*   4.*Zug*

▶ **Panzerkampfwagen V Ausf A (SdKfz 171)**

1.SS-Panzer-Regiment / I.Panzer-Abteilung

The LSSAH sent the men of its 1st Panzer Battalion back to Germany, where they were to re-equip with the new PzKpfw V Panther tank.

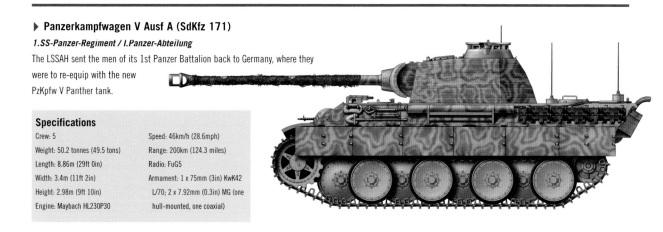

Specifications

Crew: 5	Speed: 46km/h (28.6mph)
Weight: 50.2 tonnes (49.5 tons)	Range: 200km (124.3 miles)
Length: 8.86m (29ft 0in)	Radio: FuG5
Width: 3.4m (11ft 2in)	Armament: 1 x 75mm (3in) KwK42
Height: 2.98m (9ft 10in)	L/70; 2 x 7.92mm (0.3in) MG (one
Engine: Maybach HL230P30	hull-mounted, one coaxial)

▶ **Panzerkampfwagen VI Ausf E (SdKfz 181)**

1.SS-Panzer-Regiment / II.Panzer Abteilung / 13.schwere Kompanie / Stab

The 13th (Heavy) Tank Company of the LSSAH's Panzer regiment at Kursk was equipped with Tiger I heavy tanks.

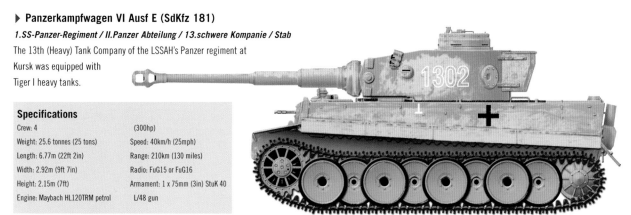

Specifications

Crew: 4	(300hp)
Weight: 25.6 tonnes (25 tons)	Speed: 40km/h (25mph)
Length: 6.77m (22ft 2in)	Range: 210km (130 miles)
Width: 2.92m (9ft 7in)	Radio: FuG15 or FuG16
Height: 2.15m (7ft)	Armament: 1 x 75mm (3in) StuK 40
Engine: Maybach HL120TRM petrol	L/48 gun

Normandy

JUNE 1944

By the beginning of 1944, the *Leibstandarte* Division was a shadow of the well-armed, nearly full-strength force that had spearheaded Operation *Citadel* at Kursk in 1943.

IT WAS WITHDRAWN to western Europe to rest and refit, becoming a fully fledged Panzer division in the process. In the summer of 1944, the 1st SS Panzer Division *Leibstandarte* was based near Bruges in Belgium. Following the D-Day landings in Normandy, it was ordered to northwest France to form part of the I SS Panzer Corps.

By 17 June, the *Leibstandarte* had arrived from Bruges to join the battle for Caen. It suffered badly at the hands of Allied aircraft, as well as from naval gunfire and continuous action against overwhelming British, Canadian and US forces.

On 6 July, one month after the Allied landings, the LSSAH was fully committed to the campaign. Over the next three days, it would repulse a British assault, and when the 12th SS Division was pulled out of the line for a rest, the *Leibstandarte* took over the defence of the Caen sector. Between 18 and 21 July, the 1st SS Panzer Division met the major Allied offensive known as Operation *Goodwood*, driving back the British 7th and 11th Armoured Divisions and inflicting heavy casualties in the process.

The constant battering against the German right flank had been costly to the Anglo-Canadian forces, and seemed to have made little progress. The *Leibstandarte* men were still holding their positions on the Caen-Falaise highway, standing firm against repeated attacks from Montgomery's 21st Army Group. By this time, the formation's Panzer strength had fallen to 33 Panthers, 30 Mark IV Panzers and 22 *Sturmgeschütz* assault guns. Around 1500 men had been killed, wounded, captured or were missing.

The relative weakness of the German units in the western sector of the front was fairly obvious to the Americans, who were far from being the amateur incompetents imagined by Rommel. And General Omar N. Bradley was certainly not going to pass up this opportunity.

At the end of July, in spite of bad weather, Bradley readied the US First Army to punch through the German lines west of St Lô. Known as Operation *Cobra,* the breakout began on 24 July 1944.

Mortain counterattack

Obergruppenführer Paul Hausser's Seventh Army was ordered to counterattack. On 4 August, they struck westwards. The attack was reinforced on 6 August by the 1st SS Panzer Division. *Leibstandarte* had been relieved on the Caen sector and had marched across the battlefield to continue the thrust. Bradley, now promoted to command the 7th Army Group, sensed the danger and threw in two corps from the US First Army. There was bitter fighting at Mortain, but Avranches was not reached by the Germans.

The attacks were finally stopped by artillery fire and by a devastating series of attacks by Allied fighter bombers. On 7 August, the LSSAH attack was shattered by Hawker Typhoons of the RAF's 245th Squadron. By the 10th, the *Leibstandarte* was on the defensive at St Barthelemy, and Sepp Dietrich was

asking the *Führer* for permission to pull back. Permission was refused.

Waffen-SS losses had been appalling. Divisions that had entered the fray with hundreds of tanks and thousands of men were reduced to little more than battalion strength: the *Leibstandarte* lost all its tanks and artillery. The Battle of Normandy finally ended on 21 August, with surviving German divisional units pulling back to the Seine.

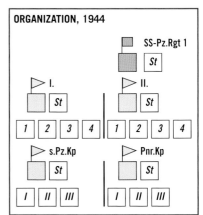

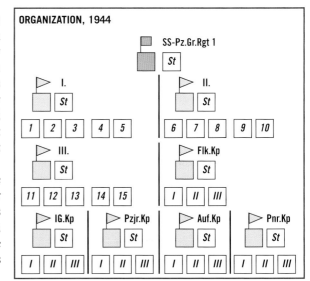

▶ **7.5cm Sturmkanone 40 Ausf F/8 (SdKfz 142/1)**

SS Sturmgeschütz Abteilung 1 / I. Kompanie

The *Leibstandarte* had been operating assault guns in small numbers since 1940. These had been organized into a *Sturmgeschütz-Abteilung* in 1942, and in 1943 it was designated as the 1st SS StuG Battalion.

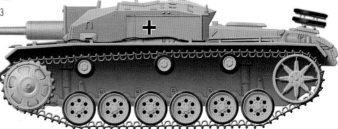

Specifications

Crew: 4	Engine: Maybach HL120TRM petrol (300hp)
Weight: 25.6 tonnes (23.3 tons)	Speed: 40km/h (25mph)
Length: 6.77m (22ft 2in)	Range: 210km (130 miles)
Width: 2.92m (9ft 7in)	Radio: FuG15 or FuG16
Height: 2.15m (7ft)	Armament: 1 x 75mm (3in) StuK 40 L/48 gun

▶ **15cm sIG33 (Sf) auf PzKpfw I Ausf B (SdKfz 101)**

1.SS-Panzergrenadier-Regiment / 17.sIG-Kompanie

Late in 1943, LSSAH's Panzergrenadier regiments had a heavy infantry gun company, but by the summer of 1944 these had been transferred into the regiments' heavy infantry companies.

Specifications

Crew: 4	Engine: Maybach NL38TR
Weight: 9.4 tonnes (8.5 tons)	Speed: 40km/h (25mph)
Length: 4.67m (15.3ft)	Range: 140km (87 miles)
Width: 2.06m (6.8ft)	Armament: 1 x 150mm (5.9in) sIG33 L/11
Height: 2.8m (9.2ft)	

◀ **Leichte Schützenpanzerwagen (SdKfz 250/9)**

SS-Panzer-Aufklärungs-Abteilung LSSAH / 2.Kompanie (Skw)

Late in 1944, the reconnaissance battalion had three half-track companies.

Specifications

Crew: 3	Speed: 60km/h (37mph)
Weight: 6.9 tonnes (6.3 tons)	Range: 320km (199 miles)
Length: 4.56m (14ft 11.5in)	Radio: FuG Spr Ger 'f'
Width: 1.95m (6ft 5in)	Armament: 1 x 20mm (0.7in) KwK 30/38 L/55
Height: 2.16m (7ft 1in)	cannon; 1 x 7.92mm (0.3in) MG (coaxial)
Engine: Maybach HL42TRKM 6-cylinder (100hp)	

The Ardennes
DECEMBER 1944

The defeat in Normandy did not mean that the fighting days of the LAH were over. From 16 December 1944 to 1 January 1945 it played a key part in the Ardennes against the US Army.

BY THE CLOSE OF THE Battle of Normandy, it had been reduced to less than 30 serviceable armoured vehicles. Among the casualties was the seriously wounded Teddy Wisch. From August 1944 to February 1945, command of LAH passed to *SS-Oberführer* Wilhelm Mohnke.

By now, the *Waffen-SS* had grown to nearly a million men, enough to provide an entire armoured

▶ **Mittlere Schützenpanzerwagen (SdKfz 251/9)**

1.SS-Panzergrendier-Regiment LSSAH / I.Battalion / 1.Kompanie

In December 1944, one battalion in each of the *Leibstandarte*'s 1st and 2nd SS Panzergrenadier Regiments were mounted on half-tracks. The three Panzergrenadier companies in each battalion had two SdKfz 251/9s in their heavy platoons.

Specifications

Crew: 3	Engine: Maybach HL42TUKRM
Weight: 9.4 tonnes (8.53 tons)	Speed: 53km/h (33mph)
Length: 5.98m (19ft 7in)	Range: 300km (186 miles)
Width: 2.83m (9ft 4in)	Radio: FuG Spr Ger 'f'
Height: 2.07m (6ft 10in)	Armament: 1 x 75mm (3in) KwK L/24 gun

army for the campaign, the Sixth Panzer Army. However, the SS and the *Leibstandarte* were no longer the elite formation of the early 1940s. Conscription had been brought in, and the division included among its reluctant recruits men from factories, the *Kriegsmarine* and the *Luftwaffe*.

SS Panzer Army

Leibstandarte was the most powerful unit in the Sixth SS Panzer Army. It had just re-equipped with massive King Tiger tanks serving alongside Panthers and long-barrel Panzer IVs. Spearheading the attack in the Ardennes was an LAH *Kampfgruppe,* or battle

group, under the command of *SS-Obersturmbannführer* Jochen Peiper. The 5000 men of *Kampfgruppe Peiper* pushed forward nearly 60km (37 miles), but their attack was eventually blunted. It was during this thrust that the *Leibstandarte* was held responsible for the murder of 71 American prisoners of war at the Malmedy crossroads.

Steady Allied pressure and air power freed by clearing weather halted and finally broke the German attack. The remnants of the *Leibstandarte* were withdrawn to Bonn to refit. The Ardennes offensive had cost the Germans nearly 100,000 dead and the Americans 76,000.

▶ **Medium Panzer Company**

In 1944, the nominal strength of a Panther company was 21 or 22 tanks as seen here. However, by February 1945 the four companies of the *Leibstandarte*'s 1st Battalion had only 34 Panthers, an average of only eight or so tanks per company.

Stab

1.*Zug*   2.*Zug*   3.*Zug*   4.*Zug*

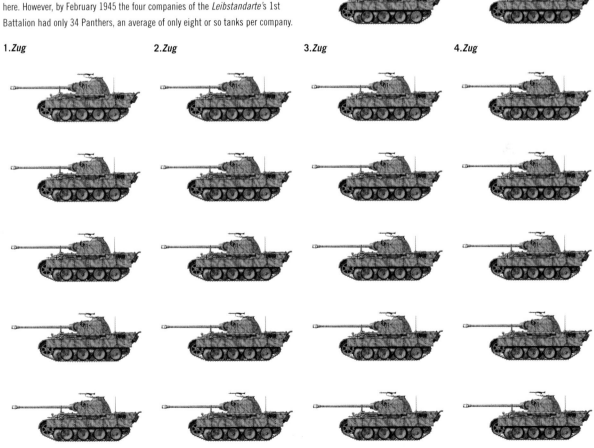

▶ 10.5cm leFH 18/2 auf PzKpfw II (Sf) Wespe (SdKfz 124)

1.SS-Panzer-Artillerie-Regiment LSSAH / I.Bataillon / 3.Batterie

Even for such a favoured formation as the *Leibstandarte*, there were not enough resources to equip more than one out of the LSSAH's four artillery battalions with self-propelled artillery pieces.

Specifications

Crew: 5	Speed: 40km/h (25mph)
Weight: 12.1 tonnes (11 tons)	Range: 220km (136.7 miles)
Length: 4.81m (15ft 10in)	Radio: FuG Spr 1
Width: 2.28m (7ft 6in)	Armament: 1 x 105mm (4.1in) LeFH 18M
Height: 2.25m (7ft 4.5in)	L/28 howitzer
Engine: Maybach HL62TR	

▶ 15cm schw. Panzerhaubitze auf Geschützwagen III/IV Hummel (SdKfz 165)

1.SS-Panzer-Artillerie-Regiment LSSAH / I.Bataillon / 1.Batterie

At the end of 1944, the LSSAH artillery regiment's 1st Battalion had one battery of 15cm (5.9in) Hummel howitzers and two batteries of 10.5cm (4.1in) Wespe light field howitzers.

Specifications

Crew: 6	Speed: 42km/h (26mph)
Weight: 26.5 tonnes (24 tons)	Range: 215km (133.6 miles)
Length: 7.17m (23ft 6in)	Radio: FuG Spr 1
Width: 2.97m (9ft 8in)	Armament: 1 x 150mm (5.9in)
Height: 2.81m (9ft 2in)	sFH 18/1 L/30;
Engine: Maybach HL120TRM (265hp)	1 x 7.92mm (0.3in) MG

 # The end in Hungary

FEBRUARY–MAY 1945

The final battle for the *Leibstandarte* came in January 1945, when the Russian winter offensive pushed into Hungary and the Sixth SS Panzer Army was deployed to retake the Balaton oilfields.

▶ 3.7cm Flak auf Pz IV (Sf) Möbelwagen (SdKfz 161/3)

1.SS-Panzer-Regiment LSSAH / Stab-Kompanie / Flak-Zug

At the beginning of February 1945, the *Leibstandarte* had eight 3.7cm (1.5in) Flak Panzers in its Panzer regiment's HQ company.

Specifications

Crew: 6	Engine: Maybach HL120TRM
Weight: 26.5 tonnes (24 tons)	Speed: 38km/h (23.6mph)
Length: 5.92m (19.4ft)	Range: 200km (124 miles)
Width: 2.95m (9.7ft)	Radio: FuG5 and FuG2
Height: 2.73m (9ft)	

AFTER A FRUITLESS ATTEMPT to recapture the oilfields and to relieve the besieged Hungarian capital of Budapest, the Germans withdrew into Austria but were ordered to hold Vienna. When Hitler heard of the withdrawals, he flew into a rage. He ordered that the men of SS divisions should remove their cuff titles and that all promotions and decorations were to be cancelled.

Sepp Dietrich's reaction was typical and robust. When the commander of the Sixth SS Panzer Army received the signal, he considered putting all the honours into a chamber pot and sending them to Hitler, but then he simply ignored the order.

Following the news of Hitler's death, Dietrich ensured that most of the *Waffen-SS* divisions in the East were able to break contact with the advancing Russians and surrender to the Americans at Steyr in upper Austria. But the war was not over for the men of the *Leibstandarte.* They might have considered themselves the elite of the German armed forces, but to the Allies, they were all members of the SS. They faced years of captivity in POW cages after the International Military Tribunal at Nuremberg determined that the SS was an illegal organization. Many of its leading lights were tried and sentenced as war criminals, though few served their full terms.

Specifications

Crew: 5	Speed: 38km/h (23.6mph)
Weight: 62.8 tonnes (61 tons)	Range: 140km (87 miles)
Length: 8.45m (27ft 8in)	Radio: FuG5
Width: 3.7m (12ft 1in)	Armament: 1 x 88mm (3.5in) KwK 36 L/56;
Height: 2.93m (9ft 7in)	2 x 7.92mm (0.3in) MG (one hull-mounted,
Engine: Maybach HL210P45 (700hp)	one coaxial)

▲ Panzerkampfwagen VI Ausf E (SdKfz 181)

501.schwere Panzer-Abteilung

In November 1944, the 101st Corps' heavy tank battalion was attached to LAH as the 501st Heavy Tank Battalion.

Specifications

Crew: 5	Speed: 46km/h (28.6mph)
Weight: 47.4 tonnes (43 tons)	Range: 200km (124 miles)
Length: 8.86m (29ft 0in)	Radio: FuG5
Width: 3.4m (11ft 2in)	Armament: 1 x 75mm (3in) KwK 42 L/70;
Height: 2.95m (9ft 8in)	2 x 7.92mm (0.3in) MG (one hull-mounted,
Engine: Maybach HL230P30	one coaxial)

▼ Panzerkampfwagen V Ausf D (SdKfz 171)

1.SS-Panzer-Regiment LSSAH / I.Abteilung / 1.Kompanie / Stab

Although early Panther D models had largely been replaced by 1944, some survived into 1945.

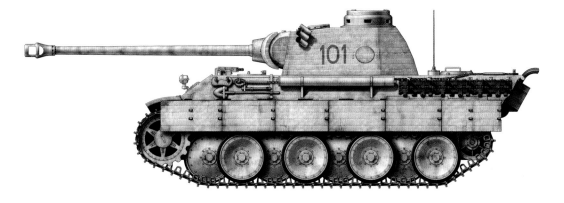

2nd SS Panzer Division *Das Reich*

The *Schutzstaffel*, or SS, split into three main branches after the Nazis came to power: the *Allgemeine-*, or General SS, the *Totenkopf* concentration camp guards and the Armed SS.

THE ARMED SS WAS the largest branch of the organization. It would eventually number some 39 divisions, and one million men of 15 nationalities passed through its ranks.

Taking the name *Waffen-SS* in the spring of 1940, it took part in 12 major campaigns and was noted for its tough fighting qualities and aggressive leadership.

The premier formation of the *Waffen-SS*, the *Leibstandarte Adolf Hitler*, provided guards of honour for visiting VIPs before the war.

Initially the Armed SS was made up from Hitler's bodyguard, the *Leibstandarte*, together with a number of *Politsiche Bereitschaften*, or political emergency squads. These had been established in the 1930s as strong-arm units designed to use violent measures against political opponents.

INSIGNIA

The *Wolfsengel* or Wolf's Hook is a germanic symbol dating back to the Middle Ages, thought in folklore to represent a kind of iron trap used to catch wolves.

The horizontal version of the symbol as used by *Das Reich* was known as 'the werewolf'. It was often painted onto vehicles without a surrounding shield.

As the second SS Division, at Kursk *Das Reich* was given a symbol with two vertical uprights compared to the single upright of *Leibstandarte*.

Commanders

Gruppenführer Paul Hausser *October 1939 – October 1941*	Obersturmbannführer Christian Tychsen *July 1944*
Brigadeführer Wilhelm Bittrich *October 1941 – December 1941*	Oberführer Otto Baum *July 1944 – October 1944*
Brigadeführer Matthias Kleinheisterkamp *December 1941 – April 1942*	Brigadeführer Heinz Lammerding *October 1944 – January 1945*
Gruppenführer Georg Keppler *April 1942 – February 1943*	Standartenführer Karl Kreutz *January 1945 – February 1945*
Oberführer Hebert-Ernst Vahl *February 1943 – March 1943*	Gruppenführer Werner Ostendorff *February 1945 – March 1945*
Standartenführer Kurt Brasack *March 1943 – April 1943*	Standartenführer Rudolf Lehmann *March 1945 – April 1945*
Gruppenführer Walter Krüger *April 1943 – October 1943*	Standartenführer Karl Kreutz *April 1945 – May 1945*
Brigadeführer Heinz Lammerding *November 1943 – July 1944*	

▼ **Armoured column**

A mixture of armoured fighting vehicles from the *Das Reich* Division, including a Panzer IV (right) and a Tiger I (left), prepare to move, southern Russia, late 1943.

Members of the Armed SS were originally designated as *SS-Verfügungstruppe,* or special duty troops. The name was usually shortened to SS-VT.

By the time of the *Anschluss,* the Armed SS had grown dramatically. In addition to the 2600 men of the *Leibstandarte,* there were three SS-VT *Standarten,* or regiments, derived from the *Politische Bereitschaften.* The three regiments were given the names *Deutschland, Germania,* and *Der Führer,* and were trained and equipped as motorized infantry.

Divisional History	Formed
Die SS-Verfügungstruppe	1934
SS-Division Verfügungstruppe	1940
SS-Division Deutschland	1940
SS-Division (mot) Reich	1940
SS-Division (mot) Das Reich	1942
SS-Panzergrenadier-Division Das Reich	1942
2.SS-Panzer-Division Das Reich	1943

▶ Schwere Panzerspähwagen (SdKfz 231)

SS-Verfügungstruppe / SS-Standarte Germania / Spähpanzerwagen-Zug

The SdKfz 231 was the standard pre-war heavy armoured car that was used by motorized reconnaissance troops in Austria, Czechoslovakia, Poland and France.

Specifications

Crew: 2

Weight: 2.45 tonnes (2.23 tons)

Length: 5.10m (16ft 8in)

Width: 1.93m (6ft 4in)

Height: 1.96m (6ft 5in)

Engine: Krupp 3.3L 4-cylinder (60hp)

Speed: 70km/h (43mph)

Range: 450km (280 miles)

Radio: None

▶ Mittlere Lkw Henschel 33 3t

SS-Verfügungstruppe / SS-Standarte Der Führer

The *Der Führer* Regiment, of the SS-VT was originally raised in Vienna in 1938 after the German *Anschluss.* From the start, the *Standarte* was motorized, its troops being lorry-borne.

Specifications

Crew: 1

Weight: 6.1 tonnes (6 tons)

Length: 7.4m (24ft)

Width: 2.25m (7ft 4in)

Height: 3.2m (10ft 6in)

Engine: 10.7 L (650ci),
    6-cylinder petrol (100hp)

Speed: 60km/h (37mph)

Payload: 3 tonnes (2.95 tons)
    or 18 troops

▶ Leichte Lkw Krupp L2H143 (Kfz 69)

SS-Verfügungstruppe / SS-Standarte Deutschland

The light artillery tractor variant of the Krupp L2H43 and L2H143 was used by the Panzerjäger and infantry gun companies of the *SS-VT* regiments to tow 3.7cm (1.5in) Pak 36 anti-tank guns and 7.5cm (3in) light infantry guns.

Specifications

Crew: 2

Weight: 2.45 tonnes (2.23 tons)

Length: 5.10m (16ft 8in)

Width: 1.93m (6ft 4in)

Height: 1.96m (6ft 5in)

Engine: Krupp 3.3L 4-cylinder (60hp)

Speed: 70km/h (43mph)

Range: 450km (280 miles)

Radio: None

Poland and France
1939–1940

The motorized *Der Führer*, *Deutschland* and *Germania* Regiments of the Armed SS were attached to and under the command of German Army units in the invasion of Poland in September 1939.

BEFORE THE WAR, the SS was an exclusively volunteer force, and its physical entry standards were high. Training was along Army lines; aggression was highly prized, and exercises emphasized speed and ferocity of attack.

The three SS-VT *Standarten* displayed all of that aggression when they fought in Poland, as individual regiments attached to Army formations. *Reichsführer-SS* Himmler was unhappy about this, and won a concession from the Army that SS units would serve in SS formations, though remaining under *Wehrmacht* control when in combat.

SS-VT Division in France
After the campaign in Poland, the SS-VT units were withdrawn to East Prussia, where they were to be merged into a new division. Although the *Leibstandarte* remained separate, the three other *Standarten* would become the nucleus of the SS-VT Division, which saw action in Poland and France.

In the early stages of the campaign in the West, the SS-VT Division had been split. *Der Führer* fought alongside the *Leibstandarte* as the German X Corps

pushed through the Grebbe defensive lines en route to Amsterdam.

The other two regiments, *Deutschland* and *Germania,* were attached to the 9th Panzer Division. Operating further south, the units were tasked with pushing through heavily mined polders on the approach to Rotterdam. First combat came against Dutch units reinforced by French troops that had driven through Belgium, and the *Deutschland* Regiment performed very well in heavy fighting around the port of Flushing.

All three regiments suffered heavy casualties in unsuccessfully trying to prevent the British retreat into Dunkirk. After Dunkirk, the three SS units were withdrawn for a couple of days of rest, before being moved yet again to take part in the Battle of France. *Leibstandarte* and the SS-VT Division were attached to *Panzergruppe Kleist.*

The SS-VT Division reached the Aire River on 7 June, where it encountered some of the fiercest French resistance of the campaign. The badly mauled SS-VT retired over the Somme, before returning to prevent a breakout of French forces in Alsace.

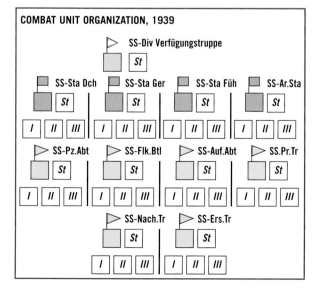

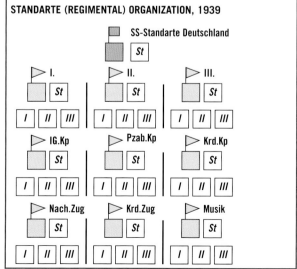

▶ Panzerkampfwagen II Ausf C (SdKfz 121)

SS-Panzertruppe Reich

The *Reich* Division was given its own Panzer troop in May 1941, soon after the division was withdrawn from the Balkans.

Specifications

Crew: 3	Engine: Maybach HL62TR
Weight: 9.8 tonnes (8.9 tons)	Speed: 40km/h (25mph)
Length: 4.81m (15.8ft)	Range: 200km (124.3 miles)
Width: 2.22m (7.3ft)	Radio: FuG5
Height: 1.99m (6.5ft)	

▶ 15cm sIG33 auf PzKpfw I Ausf B

SS-Division VT / SS-Standarte Germania / Infanteriegeschütz-Kompanie

Mounting light howitzers onto tracked chassis gave German infantry units a considerable amount of dedicated firepower, which meant that they did not have to wait for regimental or divisional assets to be assigned for their use.

Specifications

Crew: 4	Engine: Maybach NL38TR
Weight: 9.4 tonnes (8.5 tons)	Speed: 40km/h (25mph)
Length: 4.67m (15.3ft)	Range: 140km (87 miles)
Width: 2.06m (6.8ft)	Armament: 1 x 150mm (5.9in) sIG33 L/11
Height: 2.8m (9.2ft)	

▶ Leichte Panzerspähwagen MG (SdKfz 221)

SS-Aufklärungs-Abteilung

Manufactured from 1935 to 1940, the lightweight SdKfz 221 was issued to light, Panzer and motorized divisions in the early years of the war.

Specifications

Crew: 2	Engine: Horch 3.5 L petrol (75hp)
Weight: 4 tonnes (3.61 tons)	Speed: 90km/h (56mph)
Length: 4.80m (15ft 8in)	Range: 320km (199 miles)
Width: 1.95m (6ft 5in)	Radio: None
Height: 1.70m (5ft 7in)	Armament: 1 x 7.92mm (0.3in) MG

▶ Personenkraftwagen VW (Kfz 1)

SS-Division Reich

The mass-produced Volkswagen Model 82 fitted with standard military bodywork became one of the most used light vehicles in the whole *Wehrmacht*.

Specifications

Crew: 1	Engine: Volkswagen 998cc petrol (24hp). Later
Weight: 0.64 tonnes (0.58 tons)	Volkswagen 1131cc petrol (25hp)
Length: 3.73m (12 ft 3in)	Speed: 100km/h (62mph)
Width: 1.60m (5ft 3in)	Range: 600km (375 miles)
Height: 1.35m (4ft 5in)	Radio: None

Invasion of the Balkans
APRIL 1941

After a period on occupation duties, training for an invasion of Britain which never came, the SS-VT Division lost some of its units to form a new SS division, later known as *Wiking*.

FOR A SHORT TIME, the SS-VT Division was given the new title *SS-Division Deutschland,* but this was too close to the name of the Army's showpiece *Grossdeutschland* Regiment, so in January 1941 it was again renamed, becoming the *SS-Division Reich.*

The German campaign against the Balkans in 1941 would involve both *Leibstandarte* and the *Reich* Division. General Ewald von Kleist's 1st Panzer Group, an armoured army in all but name, would attack westwards from southern Romania and northern Bulgaria, directed towards Belgrade. The *SS-Division Reich* would be one of his spearhead formations.

Panzers drove westwards, the *SS-Division Reich* racing the Army's elite *Grossdeutschland* Regiment for their objectives. The SS men reached the town of Alibunar first, but heavy rains, marshy terrain and muddy roads slowed progress. On 12 April, the Germans reached the Tamis River where it joined the Danube (known as the Dunay in Yugoslavia). The delays in reaching their objectives meant that *Reich* and *Grossdeutschland* were halted on the banks of the Danube while new plans were being made.

SS-Hauptsturmführer Fritz Klingenberg, the commander of *Reich's* motorcycle reconnaissance company, had other ideas, however. Using rubber boats to cross the Danube on 14 May, Klingenberg took 10 men into Belgrade, quickly realizing that the city was very lightly defended. The inventive SS officer claimed to be the forerunner of a powerful assault. He threatened the city's mayor with further massive aerial bombardments unless the city surrendered – neglecting to point out that his radios were not working and that his 10 men were all the assault force that there was.

The 11th Panzer Division arrived in the city a few hours later. Much to their chagrin, the Army troops found Belgrade already in the possession of one SS officer and 10 of his men.

SS arrogance

Relations between the *Reich* Division and their fellows were not good, however. All would admit that the SS men fought with vigour and great dash, but their arrogance rubbed most of the *Wehrmacht* up the wrong way. Relations were not helped by friction in the field: in one incident, a fast-moving Army convoy was about to overtake a column of SS vehicles. Wanting a clear road ahead, and not wanting to eat the Army's dust, the SS

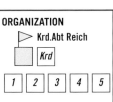

▶ **Panzerkampfwagen III Ausf F (SdKfz 141)**

SS-Panzergrenadier-Division Das Reich / Panzer-Abteilung / Stab

The *Reich* Division acquired a Panzer troop after the Balkans campaign. By 1942, this had grown to battalion size, and in November 1942 it became a two-battalion regiment in the Panzergrenadier Division *Das Reich*.

Specifications

Crew: 5	Engine: Maybach HL120TRM
Weight: 21.8 tonnes (19.8 tons)	Speed: 40km/h (25mph)
Length: 5.38m (17.7ft)	Range: 165km (102.5 miles)
Width: 2.91m (9.5ft)	Radio: FuG5
Height: 2.44m (8ft)	

commander threatened to open fire if the Army vehicles did try to pass.

After a war that had lasted only 12 days, Yugoslavia ceased to exist as a nation. Italy and Germany annexed parts of Slovenia, while Hungary received territory northwest of Belgrade. To the east, Bulgaria acquired a large piece of land that included parts of Macedonia and northeastern Greece. Italy also received a section of the Dalmatian coast and the Bay of Kotor.

The units involved in the campaign, including the *Reich* Division, were quickly pulled out for refitting. A much larger campaign, against the Soviet Union, was about to get under way.

▼ Aufklärungs-Abteilung SS-Division Reich, Spähpanzerwagen-Kompanie

The purpose of a reconnaissance company was to discover information about the enemy, and to get that information back to higher command levels. As a result, armoured car platoons always featured vehicles with long-range radios, operating together with gun-armed vehicles which served as protection.

Schwere Zug

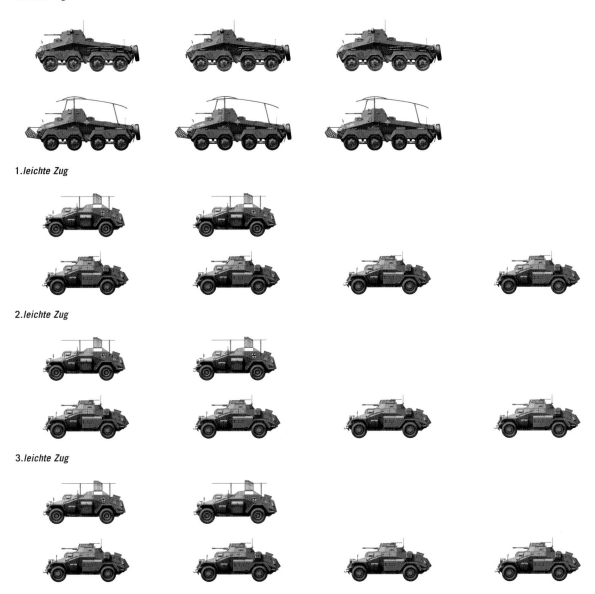

1.leichte Zug

2.leichte Zug

3.leichte Zug

▶ **Panzerkampfwagen IV Ausf H (SdKfz 161/2)**

2.SS-Pz.Rgt Das Reich / II.Abteilung / 6.Kompanie

Production of the Ausf H variant of the
Panzer IV began early in 1943, and the 2nd
SS Panzer Regiment had started replacing Panzer IIIs with the type
by the summer.

Specifications

Crew: 5	Engine: Maybach HL120TRM
Weight: 27.6 tonnes (25 tons)	Speed: 38km/h (23.6mph)
Length: 7.02m (23ft 0in)	Range: 210km (130.5 miles)
Width: 2.88m (9ft 5in)	Radio: FuG5
Height: 2.68m (8ft 10in)	

▶ **Schwere Spähpanzerwagen 8-Rad (SdKfz 231)**

SS-Aufklärungs-Regiment Langemark / Spähpanzerwagen-Kompanie

With a maximum speed of 85km/h (52.8mph), the SdKfz 231 had duplicate driving
controls at the rear of the vehicle. With six reverse gears matching its six forward
gears, it was just as fast going backwards as it was in advancing.

Specifications

Crew: 4	Engine: Büssing-NAG 8-cylinder petrol
Weight: 9.1 tonnes (8.3 tons)	Speed: 85km/h (52.8mph)
Length: 5.85m (19ft 2in)	Range: 300km (186 miles)
Width: 2.20m (7ft 2.5in)	Radio: FuG Ger 'a'
Height: 2.35m (7ft 8in)	Armament: 1 x 20mm (0.7in) cannon

With Army Group Centre
1941–1942

SS-Division Reich was one of the *Wehrmacht's* spearhead formations in the invasion of the
Soviet Union. It would take its final and most famous name of *Das Reich* early in 1942.

T HE *REICH* DIVISION was allotted to General Heinz
Guderian's 2nd Panzer Group and formed part of
Army Group Centre, which comprised nine Panzer
divisions, five motorized and 31–35 infantry
divisions, as well as two to three security divisions,
a cavalry division and the *Grossdeutschland* Regiment,
all under Field Marshal Fedor von Bock.

The *Reich* Division experienced considerable
difficulty in its advance. Because Army Group Centre
had not allocated it any space on the road leading to
the front line, most of its soldiers had to march on
foot through the countryside, although some of them
were able to hitch rides with Army convoys.

However, these unpromising
beginnings were soon forgotten
as *Reich* took part in the Battle
of Yelnya near Smolensk, and
then in the spearhead of the
drive to capture Moscow. *Reich*
came within a few kilometres of
the Soviet capital in November
1941. However, with Moscow
within sight of the division's
reconnaissance units, the
offensive ground to a halt in the
fierce Russian winter. *Reich* then

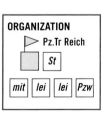

ORGANIZATION

▷ Pz.Tr Reich

St

| mit | lei | lei | Pzw |

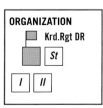

ORGANIZATION

Krd.Rgt DR

St

| I | II |

ORGANIZATION

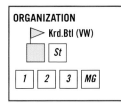

suffered massive losses as the Soviet counterattack pushed the Germans back from Moscow.

After a period of heavy combat and serious losses for the division, by now named *Das Reich,* it was pulled out of the fighting and sent to France to refit, where it would eventually be upgraded as a Panzergrenadier division. Some units remained in the East under the command of *Standartenführer* Werner Ostendorf as *Kampfgruppe Ostendorf.*

▶ **Panzerkampfwagen KV-1a 753(r)**

2.SS-Panzer-Regiment Das Reich

Although most captured Soviet KV-1 tanks were operated by Army divisions, formations like *Das Reich* would use any captured tanks in working order to supplement their own armour.

Specifications

Crew: 5	Height: 2.7m (8ft 11in)
Weight: 46.6 tonnes	Engine: V-2K
(42.3 tons)	Speed: 35km/h (22mph)
Length: 6.7m (22ft)	Range: 180km (112 miles)
Width: 3.32m (10ft 11in)	Radio: 10R

 # Kharkov and Kursk

1943

While *Das Reich* was refitting in France over the summer of 1942, the decision was taken to upgrade it further. In November, it became the *SS-Panzergrenadier-Division Das Reich*.

IN THE SAME MONTH, as Germany occupied the Vichy-controlled zone of France, parts of the division took part in an attempt to prevent the scuttling of the French Fleet at Toulon. Early in 1943, *Das Reich* was transferred back to the Eastern Front, where it helped reclaim the crumbling central front around Kharkov.

Kharkov was the first major Soviet city to be liberated by the Red Army after Stalingrad. Two weeks later on 17 February, the Red Army was at Pavlograd, only 40km (25 miles) from the Dnieper – and quite close to Hitler, who was paying a flying visit to Zaporozhye. Field Marshal von Manstein had a clear plan for stabilizing the desperate situation in the East, and he persuaded the *Führer* to let him conduct the battle his way, instead of conducting the rigid defence that Hitler usually favoured. The result was a tactical masterstroke, which continues to be studied in military academies today.

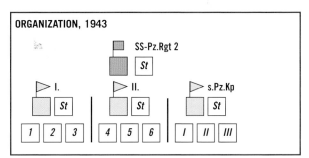

SS-Panzergrenadier-Division *Das Reich*, July 1943	Strength
PzKpfw II	1
PzKpfw III (long-barrel)	62
PzKpfw IV (long barrel)	33
PzKpfw VI Tiger	14
PzKpfw T-34(r)	25
Befehls	10

Manstein let the Soviet advance continue while he assembled a powerful striking force on its flanks, consisting of SS Panzergrenadier Divisions *Leibstandarte, Das Reich* and *Totenkopf* combined with five Army Panzer divisions and the *Grossdeutschland* Division. Manstein sprang his first trap on 20 February. On the day that the forward Soviet patrols reached Pavlograd, Panzers were driving up the west bank of the Donets behind them. In what he dubbed his 'backhand blow', Manstein drove east to cut off all the Soviet forces that had broken over the Donets.

▶ Panzerkampfwagen VI Ausf E (SdKfz 181)

2.SS-Panzer-Regiment Das Reich / II.Battalion / 8.Kompanie

Early in 1943, each of the *Das Reich* Panzer battalions was assigned a heavy company of Tiger tanks.

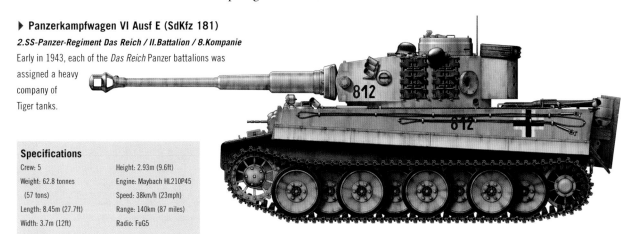

Specifications

Crew: 5	Height: 2.93m (9.6ft)
Weight: 62.8 tonnes	Engine: Maybach HL210P45
(57 tons)	Speed: 38km/h (23mph)
Length: 8.45m (27.7ft)	Range: 140km (87 miles)
Width: 3.7m (12ft)	Radio: FuG5

▶ Panzerkampfwagen V Ausf A (SdKfz 171)

2.SS-Panzer-Regiment Das Reich / I.Battalion / 1.Kompanie

In May 1943, *Das Reich*'s 1st Panzer Battalion was returned to Germany to convert to the new PzKpfw V Panther.

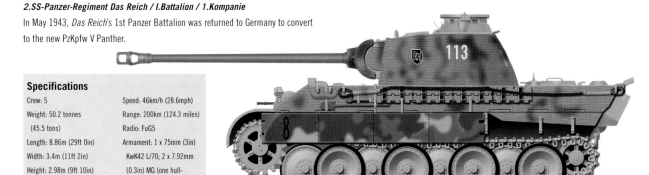

Specifications

Crew: 5	Speed: 46km/h (28.6mph)
Weight: 50.2 tonnes	Range: 200km (124.3 miles)
(45.5 tons)	Radio: FuG5
Length: 8.86m (29ft 0in)	Armament: 1 x 75mm (3in)
Width: 3.4m (11ft 2in)	KwK42 L/70; 2 x 7.92mm
Height: 2.98m (9ft 10in)	(0.3in) MG (one hull-
Engine: Maybach HL230P30	mounted, one coaxial)

▶ Panzerkampfwagen III Ausf M (SdKfz 141/1)

2.Pz.Rgt Das Reich / I.Bataillon / 3.Kompanie

Das Reich still had more than 60 Panzer IIIs on strength in July 1943, at the opening of the Battle of Kursk. Most had been replaced by Panthers by the end of the year.

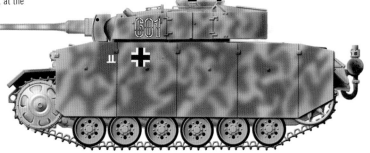

Specifications

Crew: 4	Engine: Maybach HL120TRM petrol
Weight: 25.4 tonnes (23 tons)	(300hp)
Length: 6.41m (21ft)	Speed: 40km/h (25mph)
Width: 2.95m (9ft 7in)	Range: 155km (96 miles)
Height: 2.44m (8ft)	Radio: FuG5

By 3 March, the Soviets had been forced to abandon nearly 15,500 square kilometers (6000 square miles) of their recent gains. The SS Panzer Corps stormed Kharkov in mid-March, and Belgorod was retaken. By the end of the month, the four Soviet tank corps strung out between the Donets and Zaporozhye were annihilated.

Kursk

After the Third Battle of Kharkov, *Das Reich* along with other divisions was thrown into an assault into the Kursk salient, a bulge in the Soviet front line around the area of Kursk. *Das Reich* pushed 64km (40 miles) into the southern sector of the bulge, but was pulled out of the battle when the offensive was called off. *Das Reich* was again withdrawn to France, this time to refit as *SS-Panzer-Division Das Reich*.

Part of the division was left in the East as *Kampfgruppe Lammerding*. The *Kamfgruppe* was one of the units encircled by the Soviets at Cherkassy. In February 1944, the *Kampfgruppe* was transferred to France to join the rest of the division.

▲ **Kursk tank battle**

Sitting in the rear of an SdKfz 251, young Panzergrenadiers from the *Das Reich* Division prepare to engage Soviet forces at Kursk, July 1943.

▼ **Mittlere Pionierpanzerwagen Ausf D (SdKfz 251/7)**

2.SS-Panzer-Pionier-Bataillon / 1.(Skw) Kompanie

Introduced in September 1943, the Ausf D variant of the SdKfz 251 had a simplified armoured body made from fewer armoured plates, which was quicker and easier to manufacture.

Specifications

Crew: 7 or 8	Engine: Maybach HL42TUKRM
Weight: 8.9 tonnes (8.7 tons)	6-cylinder (100hp)
Length: 5.80m (19ft 0in)	Speed: 50km/h (31mph)
Width: 2.10m (6ft 11in)	Range: 300km (186 miles)
Height: 2.70m (8ft 10in)	Radio: FuG Spr Ger 1

France
1944

The Allied landings in Normandy caught the German high command by surprise, with few of its Panzer divisions in position to attack the Allied beachhead.

QUICKLY GETTING OVER ITS surprise, OKW quickly began to move reserves to block the Allied advance. Among them were the *Waffen-SS* divisions, most with a hard core of troops seasoned in the bitter fighting on the Eastern Front.

The *Waffen-SS* Panzer divisions that took part in the Normandy battles brought with them a wealth of combat experience gained in years of vicious fighting on the Eastern Front, and many were survivors of the greatest tank battle of all time – Kursk. One division that had further to travel than most was *Das Reich*. On 6 June, it had been on occupation duty around Cahors, near Bordeaux. By 9 June, it was on the march through the Massif Central, skirmishing with and being delayed by the Resistance all the way. On 10 June, a company of *Das Reich* men committed a massacre at Oradour-sur-Glane in reprisal for the apparent kidnapping of *Sturmbannführer* Kampfe.

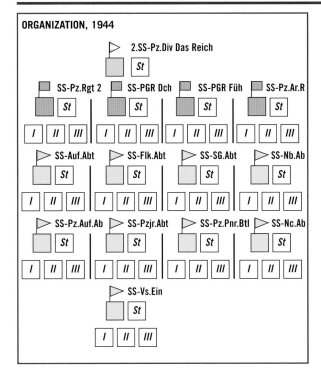

ORGANIZATION, 1944

Divisional strength – Normandy, May 1944	Strength
PzKpfw IV	78
PzKpfw V	79
StuG III	13
FlakPz 38	12

The SS men massacred 642 civilians, including 207 children, in one of the worst outrages to have taken place in Western Europe. Such events were far from unusual in Russia, however, and many of the *Das Reich* troopers still had an Eastern Front mindset.

Under the command of *Gruppenführer* Heinz Lammerding, *Das Reich* units began reaching the combat zone early in July, and were immediately engaged in combat with American forces at Coutances, St Lô, Percy and Mortain.

The relative weakness of the German units in the western sector of the front was obvious to the Americans, an enemy hitherto underestimated by the Germans. General Omar N. Bradley saw a chance – and prepared to take it. At the end of July, in spite of bad weather, he readied the US First Army to punch through the German lines west of St Lô; from there, they would break out into the interior of France.

Mortain counterattack

Known as Operation *Cobra,* the breakout began on 24 July 1944 after heavy bombers of the Eighth US Air Force had carpet-bombed the German forward positions. To their amazement, given the sheer scale of the bombardment, the Americans encountered resistance – but it was only a thin grey line. By 28 July, the VII Corps under the dynamic General L. J. (Lightning Joe) Collins, together with General Troy Middleton's VIII Corps, had pushed the Germans back over 20km (12 miles).

The four Panzer divisions of Paul Hausser's Seventh Army struck westwards on 4 August, but in spite of bitter fighting the target of Avranches was not reached. The attacks were finally stopped by artillery fire and Allied fighter bombers. Most of the German armies in Normandy were now trapped in a pocket at Falaise. Many men escaped, but tens of thousands were either killed or taken prisoner. By the end of the battle, *Das Reich*'s strength had been reduced to just 450 men and 15 tanks.

▶ **Panzerkampfwagen V Ausf A (SdKfz 171)**

2.SS-Pz.Rgt / I.Abteilung / 1.Kompanie

Most of the Panther units in service in France in 1944 were equipped with Panther Ausf A tanks.

Specifications

Crew: 5
Weight: 50.2 tonnes (45.5 tons)
Length: 8.86m (29ft 0in)
Width: 3.4m (11ft 2in)
Height: 2.98m (9ft 10in)
Engine: Maybach HL230P30
Speed: 46km/h (28.6mph)
Range: 200km (124.3 miles)
Radio: FuG5
Armament: 1 x 75mm (3in) KwK42 L/70; 2 x 7.92mm (0.3in) MG (one hull-mounted, one coaxial)

▶ 10.5cm IFH 18/2 auf PzKpfw II (Sf) Wespe (SdKfz 124)

2.SS-Panzer-Artillerie-Regiment Das Reich / I.Bataillon (Sf) / 2.Batterie

The *Das Reich* Division's artillery regiment had the standard late-war table of equipment, with its 1st Battalion operating self-propelled howitzers and the 2nd, 3rd and 4th Battalions using towed guns and howitzers.

Specifications

Crew: 5	Speed: 40km/h (25mph)
Weight: 12.1 tonnes (11 tons)	Range: 220km (136.7 miles)
Length: 4.81m (15ft 10in)	Radio: FuG Spr 1
Width: 2.28m (7ft 6in)	Armament: 1 x 105mm (4.1in) LeFH
Height: 2.25m (7ft 4.5in)	18M L/28 howitzer
Engine: Maybach HL62TR	

▶ Mittlere Schützenpanzerwagen (SdKfz 251/9)

4.SS-Panzergrenadier-Regiment Der Führer / III.Bataillon / 11.Kompanie

Known unofficially as the *Stummel*, or Stump, the SdKfz 251/9 was designed to provide flexible short-range fire support for the heavy companies of Panzergrenadier battalions.

Specifications

Crew: 3	Speed: 53km/h (33mph)
Weight: 9.4 tonnes (8.53 tons)	Range: 300km (186 miles)
Length: 5.98m (19ft 7in)	Radio: FuG Spr Ger 'f'
Width: 2.83m (9ft 4in)	Armament: 1 x 75mm (3in) KwK
Height: 2.07m (6ft 10in)	L/24 gun
Engine: Maybach HL42TUKRM	

▲ King Tigers, Normandy 1944

Tiger IIs from an SS division rest between actions amidst the heavy fighting in Normandy following the Allied landings on 6 June 1944.

Battle of the Bulge
DECEMBER 1944

After being all but destroyed in Normandy, *Das Reich* was rebuilt in the Eifel region of Germany, in readiness to take part in Germany's last major offensive in the West.

PULLED BACK ACROSS THE SEINE and then into positions behind the West Wall fortifications along the German-French border, the 2nd SS Panzer Division prepared for the operation to punch through the Ardennes Forest in December 1944.

Led by *SS-Oberstgruppenführer* Josef 'Sepp' Dietrich, the newly established Sixth SS Panzer Army contained I and II SS Panzer Corps. Attached to II Corps, the *Das Reich* Division had finished crossing the Rhine by 24 November and, along with the 9th SS Panzer Division *Hohenstaufen,* took up positions south of I Corps near Losheim. I Corps consisted of the 1st and 12th SS Panzer Divisions, along with three Army formations. In addition, Dietrich commanded LXVII Corps of two more *Heer* divisions.

Problems bedevilled *Das Reich* and other divisions, even in the early stages of the offensive. Rushing into the battle zone, the SS units quickly became bogged down in traffic jams induced by petrol shortages. To reach Antwerp, the Germans needed to refuel their vehicles at least five times. However, Hitler provided his forces with enough petrol for only two refuellings. To maintain the secrecy of the operation, the *Führer* had forbidden the establishment of fuel dumps close to the front line.

On 20 December, *Obergruppenführer* Bittrich, commander of II SS Corps, directed *Das Reich* to relieve the 560th Volksgrenadier Division, which was attempting to capture the Baraque de Faiture crossroads. After accomplishing this task, the SS division was to push northwest through Manhay and establish a bridgehead across the River Ourthe at Bomal. By this time, Heinz Lammerding had resumed command of *Das Reich.* Coming within sight of the River Meuse, the division was halted, and then slowly smashed by fierce Allied counterattacks.

REGIMENTAL ORGANIZATION, 1944

3.SS-Pz.Gren.Rgt Deutschland

St

| I | II | III | Flk | sIG | Pnr |

2.SS-Panzer-Division *Das Reich*	Strength
PzKpfw IV	28
PzKpfw V	58
StuG III/IV	28
FlakPz IV (2-cm)	4
FlakPz IV (3.7-cm)	4

▶ **7.5cm Sturmgeschütz 40 Ausf G (SdKfz 142/1)**

2.SS-Panzer-Regiment Das Reich / II.Battalion / 8.Kompanie

One company of *Das Reich*'s 2nd Panzer Battalion was equipped with assault guns in May 1944; the other three companies had Panzer IVs.

Specifications

Crew: 4
Weight: 26.3 tonnes (23.9 tons)
Length: 6.77m (22ft 2in)
Width: 2.95m (9ft 8in)
Height: 2.16m (7ft 0in)
Engine: Maybach HI120TRM

Speed: 40km/h (25mph)
Range: 155km (96.3 miles)
Radio: FuG 15 and FuG 16
Armament: 1 x 75mm (3in) StuG L/48 cannon

On 4 January, Bittrich ordered the 2nd SS Panzer Division *Das Reich* to leave the battle zone and serve as a reserve unit.

However, many of the division's regiments and battalions, which had been dispersed to other organizations at various sectors throughout the Ardennes, did not initially hear about this order and remained at the front lines. As a result, some of them suffered more losses when the Americans opened a major offensive five days later.

▶ **Mittlere Schützenpanzerwagen Ausf D (SdKfz 251/22)**

2.SS-Panzerjäger-Abteilung Das Reich / 1.Kompanie

Towards the war's end, Adolf Hitler ordered that every vehicle capable of carrying a 7.5cm (3in) Pak 40 be put into production. The SdKfz 251 was easy to modify: the entire Pak 40 (minus its wheels) was simply bolted on the half-track's loadbed.

Specifications

Crew: 4 or 5	Speed: 50km/h (31mph)
Weight: 8 tonnes (7.28 tons)	Range: 300km (186 miles)
Length: 5.98m (19ft 7in)	Radio: None
Width: 2.1m (6ft 11in)	Armament: 1 x 75mm (3in) PaK 40
Height: 2.25m (7ft 4.5in)	L/46 anti-tank gun; 1 x 7.92mm
Engine: Maybach HL42TUKRM	(0.3in) MG (rear-mounted)
6-cylinder petrol (100hp)	

▶ **Sanitätswagen Opel Blitz S (Kfz 31)**

2.SS-Krankenwagen-Kompanie

Das Reich's ambulance company had three detachments, which operated with the 1st and 2nd SS Medical Companies and the 1st SS Field Hospital.

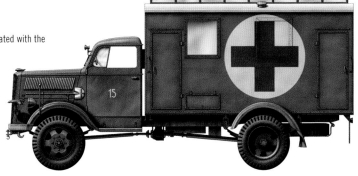

Specifications

Crew: 1	Engine: Opel 6-cylinder petrol
Weight: 3.29 tonnes (3 tons)	(73.5hp)
Length: 6.02m (19ft 9in)	Speed: 80km/h (50mph)
Width: 2.27m (7ft 5in)	Range: 410km (255 miles)
Height: 2.18m (7ft 2in)	

 # End of the Reich
1945

Pulled out of the Ardennes, *Das Reich* was transferred into Germany to refit once again. However, in February it received orders to take part in the last German offensive of the war.

E ARLY IN DECEMBER 1944, the Red Army invaded Hungary and reached a point along the River Danube 30km (18.6 miles) south of Budapest. Before the bulk of the Communist forces could cross the river, German formations arrived in time to stall the advance and establish the 'Margarethe Positions', a series of defensive lines arrayed from the Plattensee (Lake Balaton) to the Hungarian capital. In response, Stavka redirected the Soviet offensive and concentrated its forces at a bend in the Danube north of Budapest.

The Red Army took the Hungarian capital on 12 February. With this task accomplished, the Soviets were now able to commit most of their forces to an invasion of the oil-refining region of southern Hungary. If this area were to fall into Russian hands, the Third *Reich* would forfeit its only remaining source of fuel and thus be unable to continue the war. The loss of Hungary would also deprive the Germans of a vital grain-producing area.

To prevent such a catastrophe from befalling Germany, Hitler pulled his *Waffen-SS* divisions from the Western Front and dispatched them to the 'Margarethe Positions'. In fact, the Sixth SS Panzer Army had received orders to that effect even before the fall of Budapest. For the last time in the war, the *Das Reich* Division and other SS formations were to participate in a desperate counteroffensive that stood little chance of success against powerful and determined adversaries. Hitler called the attack Operation *Spring Awakening*.

Operation *Spring Awakening*

Unfortunately for the Germans, the Red Army would not be surprised by Operation *Spring Awakening*. When intelligence reports indicated the presence of

Das Reich and other SS divisions within the area, Stavka advised its field commanders to expect an attack that would be launched sometime between late February and early March.

Because of the soft terrain, the grenadiers had to attack on 6 March without aid from the divisional armoured units. Despite this, the SS battalions overran several lines of trenches and captured useful high ground. But as the German grenadiers pressed forward, the Red Army threw more reinforcements in their way, and the advance gradually slowed down and stalled.

Although the SS infantry units continued to press forward into the Red Army, senior officers in Army Group South eventually realized that the offensive did not stand any realistic chance of success.

On 16 March, the Soviets counterattacked with overwhelming force. It effectively brought Operation *Spring Awakening* to an inglorious end. Suddenly, the soldiers of the *Das Reich* Division found themselves fighting enemies that were attacking from three directions. After pushing back the Sixth *(Wehrmacht)*

▶ Panzerkampfwagen IV Ausf H (SdKfz 161/2)

2.SS-Pz.Rgt Das Reich / II.Battalion / 5.Kompanie

In December 1944, just before the beginning of the Ardennes offensive, *Das Reich* had 28 Panzer IVs in two companies of its 2nd Battalion. The other two companies had StuGs.

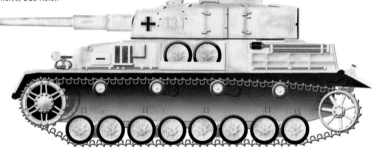

Specifications

Crew: 5	Speed: 38km/h (23.6mph)
Weight: 27.6 tonnes (25 tons)	Range: 210km (130.5 miles)
Length: 7.02m (23ft 0in)	Radio: FuG5
Width: 2.88m (9ft 5in)	Armament: 1 x 75mm (3in) KwK
Height: 2.68m (8ft 10in)	40/43; 2 x 7.92mm (0.3in) MG
Engine: Maybach HL120TRM	(one hull-mounted, one coaxial)

▶ Flakpanzer IV/2-cm Flakvierling Wirbelwind

2.SS-Panzer-Artillerie-Regiment Das Reich / Stab / Flak-Zug

The Whirlwind was allocated to the anti-aircraft platoons attached to the staff companies of Panzer regiments and divisions. The quad 2cm (0.7in) turrets were mounted on obsolescent Panzer IV Ausf F and G chassis.

Specifications

Crew: 5	Engine: Maybach HL120TRM
Weight: 24.3 tonnes (22 tons)	Speed: 38km/h (23.6mph)
Length: 5.9m (19ft 5in)	Range: 210km (130 miles)
Width: 2.9m (9ft 6in)	Radio: FuG2 and FuG5
Height: 2.76m (9ft)	

Army, Soviet armoured forces drove around Szekesfehervar and practically encircled the Sixth SS Panzer Army.

Das Reich spent the rest of the war fighting for survival from Dresden to Prague and on to Vienna. In the end, most of the division managed to escape to the West to surrender to the Americans. Before surrendering, elements of *Das Reich* helped large numbers of civilians in Prague escape the Red Army.

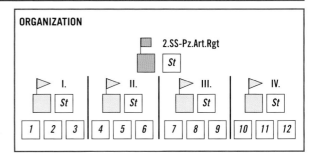

▼ Panzer Artillery Regiment, Self-propelled Battalion

Das Reich's artillery regiment had four artillery battalions. Even at the height of the war, German production bottlenecks meant that all but the 1st Battalion were equipped with towed artillery pieces, with 10.5cm (4.1in) lFH18s in the 2nd and 3rd Battalions and 15cm (5.9in) sFH18 howitzers and 10cm (3.9in) sK18/40 long-range guns in the 4th Battalion. The 1st Battalion, however, was fully self-propelled. In May 1944, when it was at its peak strength just before the Normandy landings, the battalion had 12 Wespes in two batteries and six Hummels in a third heavy battery. The battalion's staff battery had no guns.

1.*Batterie*

2.*Batterie*

3.*Batterie*

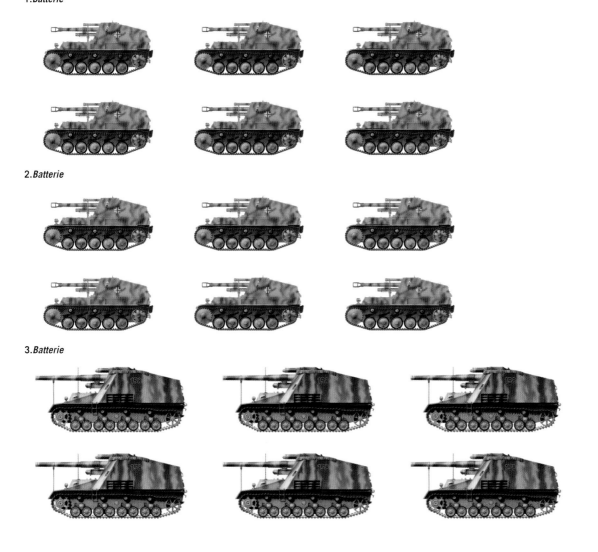

3rd SS Panzer Division *Totenkopf*

Even before the outbreak of World War II, *Reichsführer-SS* Heinrich Himmler had been pressing to expand the Armed SS against fierce opposition from the German Army.

THE PERFORMANCE OF THE SS UNITS in Poland meant that in October 1939 Hitler gave Himmler permission to raise two new divisions. However, Army opposition remained intense, and since in law the Army had first right to conscript all German nationals, the SS struggled to find the manpower it needed. There were two sources of recruits that were under Himmler's control – the police and the concentration camp guards.

Originally classed as being part of the armed SS, Theodore Eicke's *Totenkopfverbände* had in effect become a separate organization, very different from the ferociously disciplined members of the Armed SS. Tasked with guarding and running Nazi concentration camps, the *Totenkopf* men took pride in their total lack of military virtues. The guards took their cue from their commander, Theodor Eicke.

Eicke, a psychopathic killer before being recruited by Himmler, had been a failure as a soldier and a policeman. Eicke hated professional army officers almost as much as he hated Marxists and Jews.

Death's Head Guards

In his Death's Head guards – recruited from unemployed malcontents, embittered farmhands and simple thugs – Eicke found pupils eager to learn his personal brand of brutality.

In October 1939, Eicke was ordered to raise a division from the Death's Head *Standarten*, five of which were then in existence at Dachau,

Commanders

Gruppenführer Theodor Eicke *1 November 1939 – 7 July 1941*	Gruppenführer Heinz Lammerding *27 April 1943 – 15 May 1943*
Oberführer Matthias Kleinheisterkamp *7 July 1941 – 18 July 1941*	Brigadeführer Max Simon *15 May 1943 – 22 October 1943*
Brigadeführer Georg Keppler *18 July 1941 – 19 September 1941*	Gruppenführer Herman Priess *22 October 1943 – 21 June 1944*
Obergruppenführer Theodor Eicke *19 September 1941 – 26 February 1943*	Brigadeführer Hellmuth Becker *21 June 1944 – 8 May 1945*
Brigadeführer Herman Priess *26 February 1943 – 27 April 1943*	

▲ **Pak 36 anti-tank training**

Soldiers from the *Totenkopf* division take part in an anti-tank drill in France, May 1940. *Totenkopf* troops would soon discover that this versatile weapon was ineffective against heavily-armoured British Matilda tanks near Arras.

▶ **Mittlere Lkw Opel Blitz 3000S Type S**

SS Totenkopf Infanterie Regiment 1 (mot) / II Bataillon

Built as a result of the Schell Program of 1938, examples of the Type S commercial standard 4x2 truck were constructed by Borgward, Magirus and Mercedes-Benz as well as by Opel.

Specifications

Crew: 1	Engine: Opel 6-cylinder petrol
Weight: 3.29 tonnes (3 tons)	(73.5hp)
Length: 6.02m (19ft 9in)	Speed: 80km/h (50mph)
Width: 2.27m (7ft 5in)	Range: 410km (255 miles)
Height: 2.18m (7ft 2in)	Radio: None

Mauthausen, Sachsenhausen, Buchenwald and Frankenberg.

On 1 November 1939, the *SS-Division Totenkopf* was officially raised, and began training at Dachau. A number of SS-VT troops were transferred into the division to provide a core of well-trained, combat-experienced troops. They were needed, since the new division was plagued with disciplinary problems. In December 1939, further reinforcements came from the former *Totenkopf-Standarte Götze,* which had seen combat with the *SS-Heimwehr Danzig* in the early stages of the Polish campaign.

The *Totenkopf* Division had to struggle to acquire weapons from the Army. The generals had to some extent come to accept the *Leibstandarte* and the SS-VT as real fighting men. They saw the *Totenkopf's* former concentration camp guards as paramilitaries or police at best, and as simple thugs lacking in any military virtue at worst. It took a direct order from Hitler before the Army could be persuaded to supply the new SS unit with artillery and anti-tank guns.

Divisional History	Formed
Totenkopf-Standarten 1, 2 and 3	1937
SS-Division Totenkopf	1939
SS-Panzergrenadier-Division Totenkopf	1942
3.SS-Panzer-Division Totenkopf	1943

INSIGNIA

An ancient military symbol appropriated by the SS, the *Totenkopf* or Death's head was naturally used by the *Totenkopf* Division on its vehicles.

As the third SS division, the *Totenkopf's* temporary divisional identification symbol used on its tanks at Kursk had three upright 'fingers'.

▶ **Leichte Panzerspähwagen 2cm (SdKfz 222)**

SS-Aufklärungs-Abteilung Totenkopf

In France in 1940, *Totenkopf* had a single light armoured car platoon, but by the time of Operation *Barbarossa* in June 1941 it had an armoured car company and by 1944 the reconnaisance battalion also had an extra armoured car platoon.

Specifications

Crew: 3

Weight: 5.3 tonnes (4.8 tons)

Length: 4.8m (15ft 8in)

Width: 1.95m (6ft 5in)

Height: 2.00m (6ft 7in)

Engine: Horch 3.5L or 3.8L petrol

Speed: 85km/h (52.8mph)

Range: 300km (186 miles)

Radio: FuG Spr Ger 'a'

Armament: 1 x 20mm (0.7in) KwK 30 L/55 cannon; 1 x 7.92mm (0.3in) MG (coaxial)

Battles in France
MAY 1940

In the opening stages of the campaign in the West, the *Totenkopf* Division of the SS was held back as part of von Rundstedt's reserves in Army Group A.

THE *TOTENKOPF* DIVISION had been assigned to General Max Weichs's Second Army, but the army commanders felt that a newly formed, untried division would be of little use in the campaign, and in the early phases of planning it was expected that the SS men would never play more than a reserve role. However, when Weichs inspected the division early in April, he was pleasantly surprised. Theodor Eicke, the divisional commander, had put the *Totenkopf* through an intensive period of training in February and March. By April, he had begged, stolen and borrowed enough modern equipment to ensure

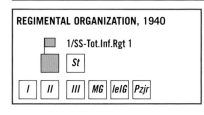

that *Totenkopf* could match the best Army mechanized unit. The hard training had another effect on the thuggish former camp guards who made up much of the division: disciplinary cases, which had been running higher than in any other SS unit, were reduced considerably.

On 16 May, the *Totenkopf* Division was ordered into Belgium. As a mechanized force, it could keep up with the fast-moving Panzers, so it was sent to join General Hermann Hoth's XV Panzer Corps, consisting of the 5th and 7th Panzer Divisions.

Struggling though roads crowded with military traffic and fleeing refugees, Eicke's men made slow going. Reaching Le Cateau on the 19th, they entered combat against French tanks and Moroccan troops the next day. In a series of hard engagements, the *Totenkopf* lost 16 killed and 53 wounded. However, any respect due to the division's fighting abilities had

to be tempered by the *Totenkopf's* attitude to the French colonial troops they faced: refusing to take 'subhuman Negroes' prisoner, they shot surrendering Moroccan soldiers out of hand.

Arras tank attack

The extended German formations were moving fast, but stretched thin, meaning that they were vulnerable to a determined Allied counterattack. On 21 May, five British brigades attacked out of Arras, the counterthrust being led by 74 Matilda infantry tanks. After a period of unbroken success, the British attack came as an unwelcome shock. Eicke ordered his artillery to engage the British over open sights, but a number of inexperienced *Totenkopf* men fled in panic. The British were eventually forced back by a combination of Ju-87 *Stuka* attacks and by Rommel's use of the powerful 8.8cm (3.5in) Flak gun in the anti-tank role, but German confidence had been severely dented, and the poor performance of some *Totenkopf* units was an embarrassment to the SS.

Over the next five days, the *Totenkopf* pressed forward towards the Lys Canal at Bethune, stubborn

▶ Panzerkampfwagen III Ausf F (SdKfz 141)

Panzer-Truppe Totenkopf / I.Bataillon / Stab

Totenkopf acquired an armoured troop of one medium company and two light companies when the division was reorganized in May 1941. The A12 marking indicates that this was the battalion adjutant's vehicle.

Specifications

Crew: 5	Engine: Maybach HL120TRM
Weight: 21.9 tonnes (19.8 tons)	Speed: 40km/h (25mph)
Length: 5.38m (17ft 8in)	Range: 165km (103 miles)
Width: 2.84m (9ft 4in)	Radio: FuG5
Height: 2.44m (8ft)	

▶ Leichte Personenkraftwagen VW (Kfz 1)

SS-Kraftrad-Regiment (VW) Totenkopf

Under the 1941 reorganization, the motorized infantry companies of the division's motorcycle regiment were re-equipped in part with Volkswagen *Kübels* in place of motorcycles with sidecars.

Specifications

Crew: 1	Engine: Volkswagen 998cc petrol (24hp). Later
Weight: 0.64 tonnes (0.58 tons)	Volkswagen 1131cc petrol (25hp)
Length: 3.73m (12ft 3in)	Speed: 100km/h (62mph)
Width: 1.60m (5ft 3in)	Range: 600km (375 miles)
Height: 1.35m (4ft 5in)	Radio: None

British opposition inflicting significant casualties in the process. On 27 May, they reached the hamlet of Le Paradis, which was being held by 100 members of the Royal Norfolk Regiment.

The British defended their positions with vigour, retreating through a farm complex to make a stand from a large cowshed. The British fought hard, and when they surrendered, the *Totenkopf* men herded their prisoners down to a field alongside another barn. Two machine guns opened up, mowing down the 100 British soldiers in cold blood.

After Dunkirk, all three SS formations were assigned to von Kleist's *Panzergruppe.* After attacking across the Aisne, the *Panzergruppe* aimed southeast towards Dijon, its purpose being to cut off any French armies in Alsace. The *Totenkopf* Division was capturing many prisoners, though colonial troops were often slaughtered out of hand. The division encountered serious resistance only once, at Tarare near Lyon, where the reconnaissance battalion fought a vicious little action with African troops before taking several thousand prisoners.

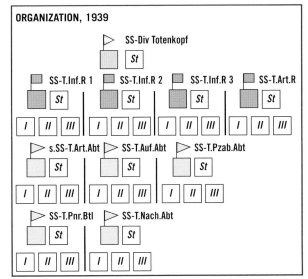

Totenkopf ended the campaign in southwest France. There they were to remain on occupation duties until being transferred east to form part of Operation *Barbarossa.*

 # Operation *Barbarossa*

JUNE–SEPTEMBER 1941

In April 1941, the *Totenkopf* Division was ordered east to join *Generalfeldmarschall* Wilhelm Ritter von Leeb's Army Group North, which was the northern wing of Operation *Barbarossa*.

EICKE USED THE YEAR between the French campaign and the Russian campaign to strengthen the firepower of his division. He converted the motorized infantry regiments into self-contained *Kampfgruppen,* or battle groups, thus giving them a greater degree of independence and flexibility. *Totenkopf*'s Flak capability was expanded and Eicke gained the long-promised allotment of enough 150mm (5.9in) heavy artillery pieces to assemble a heavy battalion in *Totenkopf*'s artillery regiment.

For the Russian campaign, the division was attached to Erich Höpner's 4th Panzer Group, the vanguard of Field Marshal Wilhelm Ritter von Leeb's Army Group North, which was tasked with advancing on Leningrad. Höpner's group, which contained XLI and LVI Panzer Corps led by Max Reinhardt and Erich von Manstein respectively,

would lead the attack through the Baltic States to Leningrad.

Russian combat

The division entered combat mopping up Soviet stragglers behind the advancing German Panzers, and was then used to plug the widening gap between Höpner's Panzers and the Sixteenth Army. *Totenkopf* smashed its way into the Stalin Line on 6 July and found the defensive network was particularly extensive in its sector. Heavy losses were sustained, but it forced its way through,

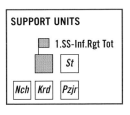

establishing a bridgehead over the River Velikaya by nightfall. On 12 July, the *Totenkopf* Division moved into reserve at Porkhov. On 21 July, the advance began once again, moving through the dark forests and swamps of the region to the west of Lake Ilmen. From 8 August, the Soviets began a morale-sapping campaign, initiating night-time counterattacks. Rest in any form was all but impossible, as the *Totenkopf's* troops had to use all of their efforts during the day to force the determined defenders back.

On 22 August, the advance resumed as the *Totenkopf* Division crossed the Polist River and pushed eastwards towards the Rivers Lovat and Pola. The *Totenkopf* Division's advance continued, with its reconnaissance battalion reaching the Pola River at Vasilyevschina just as the rains commenced. Almost immediately, the division's vehicles were bogged down in the mud. The Soviets hit the *Totenkopf* Division with determined assaults, which it then spent two days desperately beating off. But the advance was being slowed all the time.

By 12 September, in the face of considerable stiffening resistance and ferocious counterattacks by the Soviet forces, the *Totenkopf* Division was once more forced onto the defensive. It became clear that *Barbarossa* would not defeat the Red Army. As the weather deteriorated, the *Waffen-SS* braced itself for its first winter in Russia.

▼ **10.5cm leichte Feldhaubitze (leFH18)**

SS-Artillerie-Regiment Totenkopf / I.Bataillon / 1.Batterie

Until the division was upgraded to Panzergrenadier status at the end of 1942, its artillery regiment was exclusively equipped with towed artillery. Three battalions used leFH18s; the fourth was equipped with heavy howitzers.

Specifications

Crew: 3	Muzzle Velocity (AP): 540m/s (1770fps)
Weight: 2 tonnes (1.8 tons)	Range: HE: 12,325m (13,478 yards)
Length: 3.3m (10ft 11in)	Ammunition: Armour-piercing, high explosive
Calibre: 105mm (4.1in)	

▶ **Kleine Panzerbefehlsfwagen (SdKfz 265)**

Panzer-Truppe Totenkopf / Stab

Initially issued to Panzer staff units at all levels from company to brigade, the small command tank based on the Panzer I was used only at regimental and divisional level from 1941 to 1942.

Specifications

Crew: 3	Engine: Maybach NL38TR
Weight: 6.5 tonnes (6 tons)	Speed: 40km/h (25mph)
Length: 4.42m (14ft 6in)	Range: 170km (105 miles)
Width: 2.06m (6ft 8in)	Radio: FuG2 and FuG6
Height: 1.99m (6ft 6in)	

▶ **5cm Panzerabwehrkanone (Pak 38)**

1.SS-Infanterie-Regiment Totenkopf / Stab-Kompanie / Panzerjäger-Zug

The Panzerjäger platoons attached to the headquarters companies of the division's two motorized infantry regiments in 1941 and 1942 each had three Pak 38s to provide last-ditch protection against enemy tanks.

Specifications

Crew: 3	Muzzle Velocity (AP): 835m/s (2900fps)
Weight: 1.2 tonnes (1.13 tons)	Range: AP: 1800m (1968 yards), HE: 2.6km
Length: 3.2m (10ft 5in)	(1.6 miles)
Calibre: 50mm (2in)	Ammunition: Armour-piercing, high explosive

Soviet Union
1941–1942

The early advances through the Baltic States soon began to slow down. By the end of 1941, a fierce series of counterattacks saw the *Totenkopf* surrounded in the Demjansk pocket.

DURING THE AUTUMN AND WINTER OF 1941, the Soviets launched a number of operations against the German lines in the northern sector of the front. During one of these operations, the division was encircled for several months near Demjansk in what would come to be known as the Demjansk pocket.

Under orders from the German Sixteenth Army, the *Totenkopf* Division was divided up and deployed at various crisis points piecemeal. With the objective of strengthening the Sixteenth Army's flanks, two infantry battalions were sent to Demjansk. The *Totenkopf* Division's infantry reconnaissance battalions were deployed at Staraya Russia, which they were ordered to hold at all costs.

Kessel battles

During these *Kessel,* or 'kettle', battles, *Totenkopf* suffered so greatly that, due to its reduced size, it was re-designated *Kampfgruppe Eicke.* The division was involved in ferocious fighting to hold the pocket. *SS-Hauptscharführer* Erwin Meierdress of the *Sturmgeschütz-Batterie Totenkopf* formed a *Kampfgruppe* of about 120 men and held the strategic town of Bjakowo despite repeated determined enemy attempts to capture the town.

During these battles, Meierdress personally destroyed several enemy tanks in his StuG III. He was

awarded the Iron Cross for his actions during this period. In April 1942, the division broke out of the pocket and managed to reach friendly lines.

Once the Soviet ring around Demjansk finally closed, General Graf von Brockdorff-Ahlefeldt took command of the troops within the pocket. The remaining *Totenkopf* Division units within the pocket were split into two battle groups, which were constructed from *Totenkopf* Division and Army

ORGANIZATION, 1942

SS-Div Totenkopf / St

SS-T.Inf.R 1 / St — I II III
SS-T.Inf.R 2 / St — I II III
SS-T.Art.R / St — I II

s.SS-T.Art.Abt / St — I II III
SS-T.Auf.Abt / St — I II III
SS-T.Krd.Btl / St — I II III
SS-T.Pzab.Abt / St — I II III

SS-T.Pnr.Btl / St — I II III
SS-T.Flk.Abt / St — I II III
SS-T.Nach.Abt / St — I II III

▶ **Panzerkampfwagen II Ausf C (SdKfz 121)**

3.SS-Panzer-Regiment / 2.leichte Kompanie

In June 1942, the *Totenkopf*'s Panzer troop was enlarged to become the 3rd SS Panzer Regiment *Totenkopf*. A handful of Panzer IIs served with the regimental staff and with company headquarters.

Specifications

Crew: 3	Speed: 40km/h (25mph)
Weight: 9.8 tonnes (8.9 tons)	Range: 200km (124.3 miles)
Length: 4.81m (15ft 10in)	Radio: FuG5
Width: 2.22m (7ft 4in)	Armament: 1 x 20mm (0.7in) KwK 30 or 38
Height: 1.99m (6ft 6in)	L/55 cannon; 1 x 7.92mm (0.3in) MG (coaxial)
Engine: Maybach HL62TR (140hp)	

personnel. The troops were supplied from the air by the *Luftwaffe*, and in spite of fierce Soviet attacks, the pocket held out until relieved in April 1942.

Huge losses

At Demjansk, about 80 per cent of its soldiers were killed in action. The remnants of the division were pulled out of action in late October 1942 and sent to France to be refitted. While there, the division took part in Case *Anton*, the takeover of Vichy France in November 1942. For this operation, the division was supplied with a Panzer regiment and redesignated *3.SS-Panzergrenadier-Division Totenkopf.*

Thanks to the persuasive efforts of Himmler and *SS-Obergruppenführer* Paul Hausser, all SS Panzergrenadier divisions received a full regiment of Panzers, so were full strength Panzer divisions in all but name. The division remained in France until February 1943, when its old commander, Theodor Eicke, resumed control.

ORGANIZATION, LATE 1942

SS-Pz.Gr.Div Totenkopf
St

SS-Pz.Gr.R 1 — SS-Pz.Gr.R 2 — Pz.Rgt 3
St — St — St
I II III — I II III — I II III

SS-T.SG.Abt — SS-T.Auf.Abt — SS-T.Krd.Btl — SS-T.Pzjr.Abt
St — St — St — St
I II III — I II III — I II III — I II III

SS-T.Pnr.Btl — SS-T.Flk.Abt — SS-T.Nach.Abt
St — St — St
I II III — I II III — I II III

▶ **Panzerkampfwagen III Ausf H (SdKfz 141)**

3.SS-Panzer-Regiment / I.Abteilung / 2.Kompanie

The Panzer III provided the bulk of *Totenkopf's* Panzer strength in 1942 and 1943, Over 80 were in operation at the end of 1942, with 63 remaining on strength in July 1943 at the time of the Kursk offensive.

Specifications

Crew: 5	Speed: 40km/h (25mph)
Weight: 24 tonnes (21.8 tons)	Range: 165km (103 miles)
Length: 5.4m (17ft 7in)	Radio: FuG5
Width: 2.95m (9ft 7in)	Armament: 1 x 75mm (3in) KwK 37
Height: 2.44m (8ft)	L/24 gun; 2 x 7.92mm (0.3in) MG
Engine: Maybach HL120TRM	(one hull-mounted, one coaxial)

▶ **Schwere Panzerspähwagen 7.5cm (SdKfz 233)**

SS-Panzer-Aufklärungs-Abteilung Totenkopf / Stab

In September 1942, *Totenkopf* became a Panzergrenadier division. By 1944, the reconnaissance battalion's staff company was operating three close-support armoured cars equipped with obsolete 7.5cm (3in) tank guns.

Specifications

Crew: 3	Engine: Büssing-NAG L8V
Weight: 9.6 tonnes (8.7 tons)	Speed: 80km/h (50mph)
Length: 5.8m (19ft)	Range: 300km (186 miles)
Width: 2.2m (7ft 2in)	Radio: FuG Spr Ger 'a'
Height: 2.25m (7ft 5in)	

▶ Panzerkampfwagen IV Ausf E (SdKfz 161)

3.SS-Panzer-Regiment / I.Abteilung / 1.Kompanie

Early short-barrelled Panzer IVs served with *Totenkopf*'s Panzer troop and the 3rd SS Panzer Regiment
in 1942, but they were soon replaced by variants with longer high-velocity 7.5cm (3in) guns.

Specifications

Crew: 5	Speed: 40km/h (25mph)
Weight: 25.9 tonnes (23.5 tons)	Range: 210km (130.5 miles)
Length: 5.92m (19ft 5in)	Radio: FuG5
Width: 2.84m (9ft 4in)	Armament: 1 x 75mm (3in) KwK 37
Height: 2.68m (8ft 9.5in)	L/24 gun; 2 x 7.92mm (0.3in) MG
Engine: Maybach HL120TRM	(one hull-mounted, one coaxial)

▶ Panzerkampfwagen III Ausf N (SdKfz 141/2)

3.SS-Panzer-Regiment Totenkopf / II.Battalion / 6.Kompanie

The Panzer III equipped with a short-barrelled 7.5cm (3in) gun was designed
to provide close support to medium and heavy (Tiger) companies. There were
155 Ausf Ns in service with the *Wehrmacht* at Kursk.

Specifications

Crew: 5	Engine: Maybach HL120TRM
Weight: 25.4 tonnes (23 tons)	Speed: 40km/h (25mph)
Length: 5.52m (18ft 1in)	Range: 155km (96 miles)
Width: 2.95m (9ft 7in)	Radio: FuG5
Height: 2.5m (8ft 2in)	

 # Kharkov and Kursk
1943

**Early in February 1943, *SS-Panzergrenadier-Division Totenkopf* was transferred back to the
Eastern Front as part of Erich von Manstein's Army Group South.**

THE DIVISION, AS A PART of SS-*Obergruppenführer*
Paul Hausser's *SS-Panzerkorps,* took part in the
Third Battle of Kharkov, helping to blunt the Soviet
offensive led by General Konev. During this
campaign, Theodor Eicke was killed when his plane
was shot down.

The *SS-Panzerkorps,* including *Totenkopf,* was then
shifted north to take part in Operation *Citadel,* the
offensive to reduce the Kursk salient. It was during

REGIMENTAL ORGANIZATION

SS-Panzergrenadier-Division *Totenkopf*, July 1943	Strength
PzKpfw III (long barrel)	63
PzKpfw IV (short barrel)	8
PzKpfw IV (long barrel)	44
PzKpfw VI Tiger	15
Befehls	9

this period that the 3.*SS-Panzer-Regiment* received a company of Tiger I heavy tanks *(9.SS-Panzer-Regiment 3).*

The *Totenkopf* covered the advance on the *SS-Panzerkorps* left flank, with the *Leibstandarte* forming the spearhead. *SS-Panzer-Regiment 3* advanced in a *Panzerkeil* (armoured wedge) across the hot and dusty steppe.

In the afternoon of 12 July, near the village of Andre'evka on the south bank of the Psel, the Soviets launched a counterattack against *Regiment Thule* and the division's *StuG-Abteilung*. The division managed to halt the Soviet assault, destroying many Soviet T-34s, but at the cost of most of the division's remaining operational Panzers.

On 14 July, Hitler called off the operation.

▶ **Panzerkampfwagen IV Ausf H (SdKfz 161/2)**
3.SS-Panzer-Regiment Totenkopf / I.Abteilung / 2.Kompanie

At the start of the Kursk campaign, the 3rd SS Panzer Regiment had two battalions, each with two medium and one light company. A total of 44 Panzer IVs were on strength.

Specifications

Crew: 5	Speed: 38km/h (23.6mph)
Weight: 27.6 tonnes (25 tons)	Range: 210km (130.5 miles)
Length: 7.02m (23ft 0in)	Radio: FuG5
Width: 2.88m (9ft 5in)	Armament: 1 x 75mm (3in) KwK
Height: 2.68m (8ft 10in)	40/43; 2 x 7.92mm (0.3in) MG
Engine: Maybach HL120TRM	(one hull-mounted, one coaxial)

▶ **Panzerkampfwagen V Ausf A (SdKfz 171)**
SS-Panzer-Regiment Totenkopf/ I.Abteilung / 3.Kompanie

In July 1944, the *Totenkopf* Division's 1st Panzer Battalion was equipped with four companies of Panzer V Panthers.

Specifications

Crew: 5	Range: 200km (124.3 miles)
Weight: 50.2 tonnes (45.5 tons)	Radio: FuG5
Length: 8.86m (29ft 0in)	Armament: 1 x 75mm (3in)
Width: 3.4m (11ft 2in)	KwK42 L/70; 2 x 7.92mm
Height: 2.98m (9ft 10in)	(0.3in) MG (one hull-mounted,
Engine: Maybach HL230P30	one coaxial)
Speed: 46km/h (28.6mph)	

◀ **Mittlerer Kommandopanzerwagen Ausf B (SdKfz 251/6)**
1.SS-Panzergrenadier-Regiment Totenkopf / I.Battalion / Stab

In the summer of 1944, the 1st Battalion of *Totenkopf*'s 1st Panzergrenadier Regiment was mounted on half-tracks. The *Kommandopanzerwagen* was a fully equipped command post with both long-range and short-range radios.

Specifications

Crew: 8	Engine: Maybach
Weight: 9.4 tonnes (8.5 tons)	Speed: 53km/h (32.9mph)
Length: 6m (19ft 6in)	Range: 300km (186 miles)
Width: 2.1m (6ft 9in)	Radio: FuG11 plus FuG Tr 100W.
Height: 1.75m (5ft 7in)	Later FuG19 plus FuG12

Retreat from Russia
1943–1944

After Kursk, *Totenkopf* was reassigned along with *Das Reich* to the re-formed Sixth Army commanded by *General der Infanterie* Karl-Adolf Hollidt in the southern Ukraine.

TOTENKOPF WAS INVOLVED in heavy fighting over the next several weeks, as Sixth Army attempted to eliminate the Soviet bridgehead over the Mius River. During the battles of July and August 1943, the division suffered heavy losses, and over the course of the campaign on the Mius Front it suffered more casualties than it had during Operation *Citadel*. By the time the Soviet bridgehead was eliminated, the division had lost 1500 men dead and the Panzer regiment was reduced to a strength of 20 tanks.

The *Totenkopf* was then moved north, back to Kharkov. Along with *Das Reich, Totenkopf* took part in the battles to halt Operation *Rumyantsev* and to prevent the Soviet capture of the city. Although the two divisions managed to halt the offensive, inflicting heavy casualties and destroying over 800 tanks, the Soviets outflanked the defenders, forcing them to abandon the city on 23 August.

By early September, the *Totenkopf* had been forced back as far as the the Dnieper. The Soviet Fifth Guards Tank Army had forced a crossing at Kremenchug and threatened to break through the German defensive line. *Totenkopf* was now thrown into action against the bridgehead.

Totenkopf Panzer Division
In October 1943, the division was reorganized and upgraded to become a full Panzer division, and was renamed the 3.*SS-Panzer-Division Totenkopf*. The

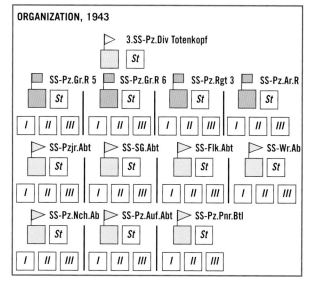

Panzer battalion became a regiment, and the division's two Panzergrenadier regiments were given the honorary titles *Theodor Eicke* and *Thule*. The *Thule* Regiment had been raised in 1942 from the remains of *SS-Infanterie-Regiment 9 Thule,* an independent formation based on the *Totenkopf-Standarte K,* which was merged with the *Totenkopf* Motorcycle Battalion.

After holding the Kremenchug bridgehead for several months, the Soviets broke out, pushing the Germans back towards the Romanian border. By

▶ **2cm Flakvierling 38 auf Zugkraftwagen 8t (SdKfz 7/1)**

3.SS-Panzer-Division Totenkopf / Divisionsstab / Flak-Batterie (Sf)

Initially equipped with single 2cm (0.7in) guns, divisional headquarters later received *Flakvierling* quad guns, which were replaced by 3.7cm (1.5in) guns.

Specifications

Crew: 7	Engine: Maybach HL62TUK
Weight: 1.16 tonnes (1.06 tons)	6-cylinder (140hp)
Length: 6.55m (21ft 6in)	Speed: 50km/h (31mph)
Width: 2.40m (7ft 10.5in)	Range: 250km (156 miles)
Height: 3.20m (10ft 6in)	Radio: None

November, *Totenkopf* was engaged fighting intense defensive actions against Soviet attacks over the vital town of Krivoi Rog to the west of the Dnieper.

In January 1944, *Totenkopf* was still engaged in heavy defensive fighting alongside the Army's *Grossdeutschland* Division. In February 1944, 56,000 German troops were trapped in the Korsun pocket. *Totenkopf* was sent towards Cherkassy to assist in the relief attempts. The division attacked towards the city of Korsun, attempting to secure a crossing across the Gniloy-Tilkich River. The 1st Panzer Division, fighting alongside the *Totenkopf*, eventually reached the encircled forces, enabling them to break out.

Withdrawn to refit in Romania, the division was ordered to Poland late in July 1944 as part of the German response to the destruction of Army Group Centre in Operation *Bagration*. There it would cover the approaches to Warsaw as part of *SS-Obergruppenführer* Gille's IV SS Panzer Corps. In August, the *Totenkopf*, fighting alongside the 5th SS Panzer Division *Wiking* and the 1st Fallschirm-Panzer Division *Hermann Göring*, virtually annihilated the Soviet III Tank Corps. The Soviets, having pushed forwards more than 482km (300 miles), were exhausted, and the crack German divisions managed to hold the line of the Vistula until December.

▼ 5th Company, 2nd Panzer Battalion *Totenkopf*

In the fierce fighting around Modlin in August 1944, the terrain suited German armour. *Totenkopf*'s Panzers exploited this to their advantage, engaging Soviet tanks at long range, allowing the superiority of the German sights and the power of the 7.5cm (3in) high-velocity gun to tell. In such combat, Panthers were superior to the T-34, and in well-trained hands the long-barrelled Panzer IVs that equipped the division's 2nd Panzer Battalion were a match for the Soviet tank.

Stab

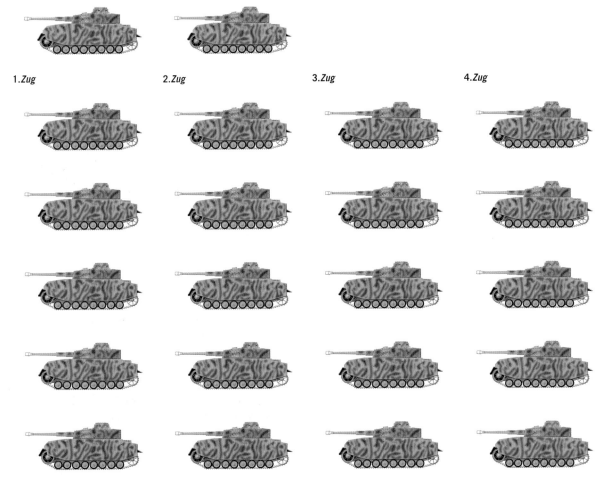

1.*Zug*   2.*Zug*   3.*Zug*   4.*Zug*

▶ **Mittlere Schützenpanzerwagen 7.5cm Ausf C (SdKfz 251/9)**

SS-Panzer-Aufklärungs-Abteilung Totenkopf / 1.Aufklärungs-Kompanie (Spw)

Ordinary Panzergrenadier units had towed 7.5cm (3in) infantry guns for close support. Reconnaissance units were issued with self-propelled equipment, which used old 7.5cm (3in) tank guns formerly mounted in Panzer IVs.

Specifications

Crew: 3	Speed: 53km/h (33mph)
Weight: 9.4 tonnes (8.53 tons)	Range: 300km (186 miles)
Length: 5.98m (19ft 7in)	Radio: FuG Spr Ger 'f'
Width: 2.83m (9ft 4in)	Armament: 1 x 75mm (3in) KwK
Height: 2.07m (6ft 10in)	L/24 gun
Engine: Maybach HL42TUKRM	

Specifications

Crew: 5	Speed: 46km/h (28.6mph)
Weight: 50.2 tonnes (45.5 tons)	Range: 200km (124 miles)
Length: 8.86m (29ft 0in)	Radio: FuG5
Width: 3.4m (11ft 2in)	Armament: 1 x 75mm (3in) KwK42 L/70;
Height: 2.98m (9ft 10in)	2 x 7.92mm (0.3in) MG (one hull-mounted,
Engine: Maybach HL230P30	one coaxial)

▲ **Panzerkampfwagen V Ausf A (SdKfz 171)**

SS-Panzer-Regiment Totenkopf/ I.Abteilung / 4.Kompanie

By 1944, the standard Panzer division organization included one battalion of Panthers and one battalion of long-barrelled Panzer IVs .

 # Last stand of the *Waffen-SS*
1944–1945

While the position along the line of the Vistula in Poland might have stabilized at the end of 1944, the rest of the German situation in Europe did not look good.

THE OFFENSIVE IN THE ARDENNES had been pushed back, German armies were retreating in Italy and the Balkans, and Romania and Bulgaria had fallen to the Red Army. In Hungary, the situation was no better. In October 1944, it was clear to the Germans that the Hungarian head of state, Admiral Horthy, was about to abandon his German allies and attempt to negotiate terms with the Soviets. And so *SS-Obersturmbannführer* Otto Skorzeny led a spectacular coup against the Horthy government. A pro-German puppet regime was installed.

This did not halt the Red Army's advance, however, and the Soviets established bridgeheads on the west bank of the Danube. The German defensive

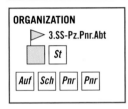

ORGANIZATION
▷ 3.SS-Pz.Pnr.Abt
St
Auf | Sch | Pnr | Pnr

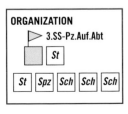

ORGANIZATION
▷ 3.SS-Pz.Auf.Abt
St
St | Spz | Sch | Sch | Sch

positions at Lake Balaton, southwest of Budapest, slowed the Soviet advance for a time. Nonetheless, on 24 December, the Soviets had managed to encircle Budapest, garrisoned by the remnants of 8th SS Cavalry Division *Florian Geyer*, 22nd SS Volunteer Cavalry Division *Maria Theresia* and 18th SS Volunteer Panzergrenadier Division *Horst Wessel.*

The *Führer* decided that Budapest must be relieved. At his personal order, *SS-Gruppenführer* Herbert Gille's IV SS Panzer Corps was selected to lead the assault on the Hungarian capital. *Totenkopf* and *Wiking* were pulled out of the line west of Warsaw and sent by train via Prague, Vienna and Bratislava to western Hungary, where they moved to jumping-off points ready for the drive on Budapest.

Budapest attack

Totenkopf and *Wiking* launched their attack towards Budapest on New Year's Day 1945. The advance stalled in the face of resistance from the Soviet Fourth Guards Army and Sixth Guards Tank Army. By 11 January, fierce Soviet counterattacks had stopped the SS Corps and forced it onto the defensive.

On 8 January, Hitler ordered Sepp Dietrich's Sixth SS Panzer Army to be moved from the Western Front to Hungary. In the meantime, he ordered the

exhausted IV SS Panzer Corps to attack towards Budapest again, without waiting for Dietrich. The second attack began on 18 January. Early success was only temporary, and by 20 January the Soviets had held the German attack.

A Soviet counterattack on 27 January drove the SS divisions back in confusion, although they

▲ **King Tigers in Hungary**

An SS Panzergrenadier shares a cigarette with a Hungarian soldier in a remarkably cheerful scene from Hungary, March 1945.

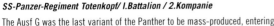

▶ **Panzerkampfwagen V Ausf G (SdKfz 171)**

SS-Panzer-Regiment Totenkopf/ I.Battalion / 2.Kompanie

The Ausf G was the last variant of the Panther to be mass-produced, entering service in March 1944.

Specifications

Crew: 5	Speed: 46km/h (28.6mph)
Weight: 47.4 tonnes	Range: 200km (124 miles)
(43 tons)	Radio: FuG5
Length: 8.86m (29ft 0in)	Armament: 1 x 75mm (3in)
Width: 3.4m (11ft 2in)	KwK 42 L/70; 2 x 7.92mm
Height: 2.95m (9ft 8in)	(0.3in) MG (one hull-
Engine: Maybach HL230P30	mounted, one coaxial)

managed to re-establish themselves in the Bakony Forest north of Lake Balaton. In these dense woods, *Totenkopf* dug in and awaited the arrival of Sixth SS Panzer Army.

Dietrich's Panzer divisions reached Hungary at the beginning of March 1945. The offensive, codenamed *Spring Awakening (Frühlingserwachen),* was intended to drive the Soviets from the last oilfields in German possession around Lake Balaton, knock them back across the Danube and retake Budapest, which had finally fallen on 11 February.

Final offensive

The offensive opened on 6 March in heavy snow. Despite the appalling conditions, the *Waffen-SS* threw themselves into the battle with their customary determination and elan. However, they ran into trouble almost immediately. On 13 March, the offensive halted due to Soviet resistance and the thaw that turned the roads and surrounding countryside into a quagmire. On 16 March, Marshal Tolbukhin's 3rd Ukrainian Front shifted to the offensive. The

Ninth Guards Tank Army smashed into the *Totenkopf* Division, overwhelmed them and drove into the rear of the IV SS Panzer Corps.

What was left of *Totenkopf* withdrew up the main road to Bratislava and Vienna, with the remnants of Sixth SS Panzer Army. On 3 April, *Totenkopf* halted in the southern suburbs of Vienna and, with the rest of what once had been elite SS divisions, put up largely symbolic resistance to the two Soviet fronts converging on the city.

Final surrender

Meanwhile, the Third US Army was driving towards Regensburg, threatening the rear of Army Group South's position. *Brigadeführer* Becker tried to surrender *Totenkopf* to the Third US Army – which insisted that the division disarmed the camp guards at the Mauthausen concentration camp. This they did, before turning themselves over to the Americans. The SS men were then handed over to the Soviets and transported to detention camps. Those who survived spent many years in Soviet labour camps.

▶ **Jagdpanzer IV (SdKfz 162)**

SS-Panzerjäger-Abteilung Totenkopf / Stab

Nearly 800 Jagdpanzer IVs were built between January and November 1944. The type entered service with tank-destroyer detachments of Panzer divisions in March 1944.

Specifications

Crew: 4	Engine: Maybach HL120TRM
Weight: Up to 27.6 tonnes (25 tons)	Speed: 38km/h (23.6mph)
Length: 6.85m (22.5ft)	Range: 210km (130.5 miles)
Width: 6.7m (22ft)	Radio: FuG15 and FuG160
Height: 1.85m (6ft)	

▶ **Leichte Schützenpanzerwagen (SdKfz 250/9)**

SS-Panzer-Aufklärungs-Abteilung Totenkopf / 2.Aufklärungs-Kompanie (Spw)

Vastly more capable across country than light armoured cars, the reconnaissance variant of the SdKfz 250 began to replace the SdKfz 222 from 1943. *Totenkopf*'s armoured reconnaissance battalion had three half-track companies by late 1944.

Specifications

Crew: 3	Speed: 60km/h (37mph)
Weight: 6.9 tonnes (6.3 tons)	Range: 320km (199 miles)
Length: 4.56m (14ft 11.5in)	Radio: FuG Spr Ger 'f'
Width: 1.95m (6ft 5in)	Armament: 1 x 20mm (0.7in) KwK 30/38 L/55
Height: 2.16m (7ft 1in)	cannon; 1 x 7.92mm (0.3in) MG (coaxial)
Engine: Maybach HL42TRKM 6-cylinder (100hp)	

4th SS-Polizei-Panzergrenadier-Division

Never one of the first-line SS divisions, the *Polizei* Division was not officially part of the SS until 1942. It was a product of the expansion of the SS at the outbreak of war in 1939.

FOR SOME TIME BEFORE THE WAR, the *Reichsführer* together with the head of the *SS-Hauptamt*, *Obergruppenführer* Gottlob Berger, who was responsible for recruiting, had been pressing to expand the Armed SS.

In law, the Army had first right to conscript all German nationals, so the SS struggled to find the manpower it needed. The two sources of recruits that were under Himmler's control were the camp guards and the police. The camp guards provided the men for the 3rd SS Division.

The expansion of Nazi control

The other source of at least partially trained manpower under Himmler's control was the police. The *Ordnungspolizei,* or Order Police, was the uniformed branch of German law enforcement under the Third *Reich*. Prior to the Nazi takeover in 1933,

there was no central police organization in Germany, each of the *Länder* controlling its own forces. The main branches of the uniformed police usually comprised the *Schutzpolizei* in the cities and the *Landespolizei* and the *Gendarmerie* in rural areas,

Divisional History	Formed
Polizei-Division	1939
SS-Polizei-Division	1942
SS-Polizei-Panzergrenadier-Division	1943
4.SS-Polizei-Panzergrenadier-Division	1943

Commanders

Generalleutnant der Polizei Konrad Hitschler
September 1940

SS-Obergruppenführer Karl von Pfeffer-Wildenbruch
September 1940 – November 1940

SS-Gruppenführer Arthur Mülverstadt
November 1940 – August 1941

SS-Obergruppenführer Walter Krüger
August 1941 – December 1941

Generaloberst der Polizei Alfred Wünnenberg
December 1941 – April 1943

SS-Brigadeführer Fritz Freitag
April 1943 – June 1943

SS-Brigadeführer Fritz Schmedes
June 1943 – August 1943

SS-Brigadeführer Fritz Freitag
August 1943 – October 1943

SS-Oberführer Friedrich-Wilhelm Bock
October 1943 – April 1944

SS-Brigadeführer Jürgen Wagner
April 1944 – May 1944

SS-Oberführer Friedrich-Wilhelm Bock
May 1944

SS-Brigadeführer Hebert-Ernst Vahl
May 1944 – July 1944

SS-Standartenführer Karl Schümers
July 1944 – August 1944

SS-Oberführer Helmuth Dörnder
August 1944

SS-Brigadeführer Fritz Schmedes
August 1944 – November 1944

SS-Standartenführer Walter Harzer
November 1944 – March 1945

SS-Standartenführer Fritz Göhler
March 1945

SS-Standartenführer Walter Harzer
March 1945 – May 1945

INSIGNIA

The *Polizei* Division used a variant of the Germanic and heraldic Wolf's hook symbol, but unlike the *Totenkopf* version this was vertical rather than horizontal. In this form it was also known as the *Donnerkeil* or 'thunderbolt'. The division would not have used the shield until it became a fully integrated SS formation in 1942.

▶ **Mannschafts Kraftwagen Krupp L2H-143 (Kfz 70)**

1.Polizei-Schützen-Regiment / I.Battalion / Infanteriegeschütz-Kompanie

When formed in 1939, the *Polizei* Division was very much the poor relation of the other SS divisions when it came to equipment, having only minimal supplies of motor transport and with much of its equipment being horse-drawn.

Specifications

Crew: 2	Engine: Krupp 3.3L 4-cylinder (60hp)
Weight: 2.45 tonnes (2.23 tons)	Speed: 70km/h (43mph)
Length: 5.10m (16ft 8in)	Range: 450km (280 miles)
Width: 1.93m (6ft 4in)	Radio: None
Height: 1.96m (6ft 5in)	

although the uniformed police also controlled the fire service and administrative legal officers such as health inspectors and building inspectors.

In 1933, Wilhelm Frick proposed that all German police units should come under the control of the Ministry of the Interior, but unification did not begin until Heinrich Himmler became *Chef der Deutschen Polizei* in 1936.

After Hitler came to power in 1933, Himmler was appointed police chief in Bavaria, a position that he used as a launching platform to eventually bring all German law enforcement agencies, both uniformed and plain-clothed, under SS control. Uniformed police now came under the control of the *Hauptamt Ordnungspolizei,* headed by Kurt Daluege, while the detectives of the *Kriminalpolizei* and the secret police of the *Gestapo* were made part of Heydrich's *Sicherheitspolizei,* or *Sipo.* Although Himmler's aim was to merge the uniformed police with the SS, they remained separate organizations until midway through the war.

On 17 June 1936, the *Reichsführer-SS* had taken control of the unified German police service. Now he used that control to transfer 15,000 members of the uniformed *Ordnungspolizei* into a new division. Raised as the *Polizei-Division* at *Truppenübungsplatz* Wandern, near the Black Forest, the unit was not strictly part of the SS at this stage.

▲ A soldier from the *Polizei* Division braves the harsh northern Russian winter, Leningrad sector, January 1942.

◀ **3.7cm Panzerabwehrkanone (Pak 36)**

Polizei-Panzerabwehr-Abteilung

Although quickly found to be ineffective against modern armour, the 3.7cm (1.5in) Pak 36 remained in use in the *Polizei* Division's Panzerjäger units well into 1943.

Specifications

Crew: 3	Muzzle Velocity: 762m/s (2500fps)
Weight: 0.43 tonnes (0.39 tons)	Range: 600m (656 yards)
Length: 1.67m (5ft 5.5in)	Ammunition: Armour-piercing
Calibre: 37mm (1.5in)	

▶ **Mittlere Nachrichten Kraftwagen (Kfz 15)**

Polizei-Nachrichten-Abteilung

The *Polizei* Signals Battalion was formed in June 1940. By the time the division was in action in the siege of Leningrad over the winter of 1941/42, the battalion had been fully motorized.

Specifications

Crew: 1	Engine: Mercedes-Benz 6-cylinder petrol
Weight: 2.4 tonnes (2.2 tons)	(90hp)
Length: 4.44m (14ft 7in)	Speed: 88km/h (55mph)
Width: 1.68m (5ft 6in)	Range: 400km (250 miles)
Height: 1.73m (5ft 8in)	Radio: Various depending on deployment

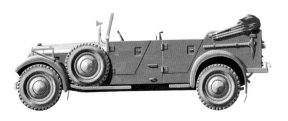

Poland and France
1940

The *Polizei* Division was formed in October 1939. It had only just completed its training when orders were given for the division to join Army Group C for the attack in the West.

USED AS OCCUPATION TROOPS in Poland, the *Polizei* Division began to receive more intensive military training in February 1940. However, the men were older, less fit and much less ideologically inspired than other SS units, and the division was only partially equipped – with obsolete and captured weapons.

Attack in the West

On 9 May 1940, all German forces received the codeword *Danzig,* which set in motion one of the most devastating advances in military history. Shortly after 02.30 on 10 May, 64 German troops crossed the Dutch frontier – the spearhead of Germany's invasion of the Low Countries. Some three hours later, glider-borne troops dropped over the Belgian border to capture and demolish the huge fortifications at Eben-Emael. The imposing concrete and steel fortress fell to a crack unit of Fallschirmjäger – paratroops – who landed by glider right on the roof of the fortress.

At 05.45, the 30 infantry divisions of General Fedor von Bock's Army Group B moved out of the Rhineland, heading for the Low Countries. In the centre, the 44 divisions of General Gerd von Runstedt's Army Group A staged through towards the Ardennes, with the lead being taken by seven Panzer divisions under General Ewald von Kleist.

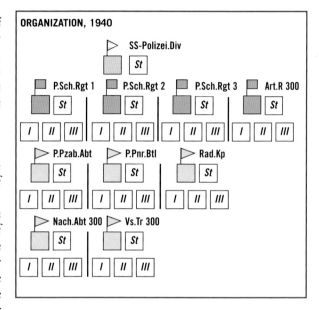

Army Group C, commanded by General Wilhelm Ritter von Leeb, faced the strongest French defences in the south, its primary task being to pin down the 400,000 French troops manning the Maginot Line.

The bulk of the Armed SS was deployed in this operation. *Leibstandarte* was attached to the right flank of the 227th Infantry Division with von Bock's forces, which also controlled the SS-VT Division. The *Totenkopf* Division was held back as part of von

▶ **3.7cm Fliegerabwehrkanone (Flak 36)**

SS-Polizei-Flak-Abteilung / 2.Batterie

When formed, the *Polizei* Division had no attached Flak unit. By the summer of 1941, however, a Flak battalion was on strength, and by 1942 when the division became an SS unit it had motorized light, medium and heavy batteries.

Specifications

Crew: 5	Muzzle Velocity: 820m/s (2690fps)
Weight: 1.5 tonnes (1.4 tons)	Range: 4800m (5250 yards)
Length: 3.5m (11ft)	Ammunition: High explosive or smoke
Calibre: 37mm (1.5in)	

Rundstedt's reserves, while the *Polizei* Division was assigned to Army Group C, where it would remain largely inactive for more than a month.

On 9/10 June, the *Polizei* Division crossed the Aisne River and the Ardennes Canal with Army Group A. The French counterattacked with armour, and the fighting see-sawed back and forwards for some time, until the French were eventually overcome by the sheer pressure of the German advance. The *Polizei* Division was heavily engaged during this time, and after securing its objectives, was moved on to the old World War I battlefield of the Argonne Forest.

In the Argonne Forest, the division was again involved in heavy fighting, engaged with rearguard units of the retreating French. In the process, the division captured the small town of Les Islettes. Late in June 1940, the unit was pulled out of combat and placed into reserve.

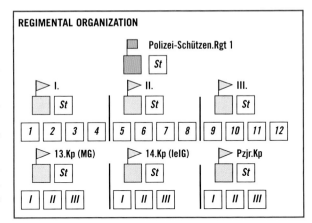

REGIMENTAL ORGANIZATION

Polizei-Schützen.Rgt 1

▶ **10.5cm leichte Feldhaubitze (leFH18)**

Polizei-Artillerie-Regiment / II. (leichte) Bataillon

The *Polizei* Division's artillery regiment was formed in May 1940. It used towed equipment for the entire war, with three light howitzer batteries (later reduced to two) and a single heavy howitzer battery.

Specifications

Crew: 5	Muzzle Velocity: 540m/s (1770fps)
Weight: 1.95 tonnes (1.85 tons)	Range: 12,325m (13,480 yards)
Length: 3.3m (10ft)	Ammunition: High explosive or smoke
Calibre: 105mm (4.3in)	

Operation *Barbarossa*

JUNE–DECEMBER 1941

After almost a year on garrison duties in Burgundy, Paris and elsewhere in occupied France, the *Polizei* Division was ordered to move east to take part in Operation *Barbarossa*.

ON 27 JUNE 1941, the *Polizei* Division was transferred to the Eastern Front and put into Army Group North reserve. Commanded by Field Marshal Ritter von Leeb, the army group was aimed at the Baltic States and Leningrad. Group North consisted of two infantry armies containing 15 infantry divisions between them.

The armoured punch was provided by 4.Panzergruppe, which comprised three Panzer divisions, three motorized infantry divisions and two infantry divisions. Three infantry divisions were held in support.

The *Polizei* Division saw little action in the opening stages of the campaign, not being called upon to fight for almost two months. In August 1941, the division finally saw action near Luga. It was during heavy fighting for the Luga bridgehead held by a number of Soviet divisions that the *Polizei* Division lost over 2000 soldiers in bloody frontal assaults. The fighting was very difficult, taking place

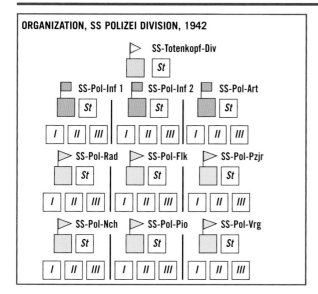

ORGANIZATION, SS POLIZEI DIVISION, 1942

across swamp and forest land. After a number of bloody assaults, the *Polizei* Division was one of the formations that managed to fight into the northern

edge of Luga, where the Germans encircled and destroyed the Soviet defenders. After the battles for Luga, the division was moved to the fighting around Leningrad. From January to March 1942, the division saw action along the Wolchow River and helped in the encirclement and destruction of the Second Soviet Assault Army.

Officially part of the SS

Even though the division was definitely under Himmler's control, it was still known as the Police Division. Its members continued to use police insignia and rank badges until the division came fully under SS administration early in 1941. It was not until January 1942, while its troops were heavily engaged in the fighting around Leningrad, that the division was finally given official *Waffen-SS* status. Its title was changed to the *SS-Polizei-Division* as the formation was absorbed into the *Waffen-SS,* and all of the division's subordinate units received SS rather than police designations.

▶ **Protz Kraftwagen (Kfz 69)**

SS-Polizei-Flak-Abteilung

In 1943, the *Polizei* Division's Flak battalion was fully motorized. The earlier Krupp Protz used to tow light anti-aircraft weapons had been supplanted by variants of the *Wehrmacht*'s standard heavy car.

Specifications

Crew: 1	Engine: Horch 6-cylinder petrol (90hp)
Weight: 2.4 tonnes (2.2 tons)	Speed: 88km/h (55mph)
Length: 4.44m (14 ft 7in)	Range: 400km (250 miles)
Width: 1.68m (5ft 6in)	Radio: None usually fitted
Height: 1.73m (5ft 8in)	

▶ **Leichte Schützenpanzerwagen (SdKfz 250/1)**

4.SS-Aufklärungs-Abteilung / 1.Aufklärungs-Kompanie (Spw)

Originally a bicycle reconnaissance battalion, the *Polizei*'s recce force was converted into a motorcycle unit while in the Balkans in 1944, and by May 1944 it had one company equipped with half-tracks.

Specifications

Crew: 2 plus 4 troops	(100hp)
Weight: 5.9 tonnes (5.38 tons)	Speed: 60km/h (37mph)
Length: 4.61m (15ft 1in)	Range: 300km (186 miles)
Width: 1.95m (6ft 5in)	Radio: FuG Spr Ger 'f'
Height: 1.66m (5ft 5in)	Armament: 1 x 7.92mm (0.3in) MG
Engine: Maybach HL42TRKM 6-cylinder	

▶ **Leichte Personenkraftwagen VW (Kfz 1)**

1.Polizei-Schützen-Regiment

The three infantry regiments of the *Polizei* Division were designated *Schützen* regiments until October 1942, when they were redesignated as *SS-Polizei-Infanterie* regiments. Early in 1943, they became grenadier regiments.

Specifications

Crew: 1	Engine: Volkswagen 998cc petrol (24hp). Later
Weight: 0.64 tonnes (0.58 tons)	Volkswagen 1131cc petrol (25hp)
Length: 3.73m (12ft 3in)	Speed: 100km/h (62mph)
Width: 1.60m (5ft 3in)	Range: 600km (375 miles)
Height: 1.35m (4ft 5in)	Radio: None

Siege of Leningrad
1941–1943

By early December 1941, the German armies that had steamrollered into the Soviet Union in June of that year had all but run out of momentum.

SUPPLY LINES WERE OVERSTRETCHED, the troops were exhausted and the full horrors of the Russian winter were being visited upon German soldiers who, in the main, were still equipped with little more than the summer-weight clothing with which they had begun the campaign. However, on the northern front, it seemed only a matter of time before Leningrad was taken.

Stalin's failure to relieve besieged Leningrad appeared to have doomed the city. Since Hitler had ordered that the cradle of the Bolshevik revolution be levelled, it seemed only a matter of time before it fell.

Its population swollen to over three million by refugees flooding into the city, Leningrad was cut off by Germans to the south and to the north by the Finns, eager to avenge the Winter War.

Communist Party chiefs anxiously calculated their food reserves: on 1 November, they realized there was only enough food for another week. And with winter approaching, there was so little fuel that buildings could not be heated – electricity was rationed to an hour a day.

What followed was the most appalling siege in history, a long-drawn-out agony in which nearly a

Specifications

Crew: 2	Engine: Maybach HL62 6-cylinder (140hp)
Weight: 1.16 tonnes (1.06 tons)	Speed: 50km/h (31mph)
Length: 6.85m (20ft 3in)	Range: 250km (156 miles)
Width: 2.40m (7ft 10.5in)	Radio: None
Height: 2.62m (8ft 7.1in)	

▲ **8.8cm Fliegerabwehrkanone (Flak 18)**

SS-Polizei-Flak-Abteilung / 8.8cm Flak-Batterie (mot)

Flak battalions attached to German divisions had one light (2cm/0.7in) battery, one medium (3.7cm/1.5in) battery, and one heavy battery equipped with four 8.8cm (3.5in) Flak guns towed by SdKfz 7 half-tracks.

million men, women and children died of cold and slow starvation – three times the total war dead suffered by Britain or the United States in the whole of World War II.

For the next two years, the *SS-Polizei-Division* would be engaged on the Leningrad Front. As part of the Eighteenth Army, it would be attached to I Corps until July 1942, then switch between L Corps and LIV Corps until the middle of 1943.

Soviet pressure

In January 1943, the *SS-Polizei-Division*, then situated south of Lake Ladoga, became the subject of fierce Soviet counterattacks that punched a hole in the German defences. The breakthrough occurred south of Schlüsselburg, near the 170th Infantry Division. By early February 1943, the retreating *SS-Polizei-Division* took over its newly assigned position west of Kopino, where it had to repulse a number of fierce Soviet onslaughts.

That month, the division was reduced to a *Kampfgruppe* while the bulk of the division was

transferred westwards to be upgraded to a Panzergrenadier division. The *Kampfgruppe SS-Polizei* was disbanded in May 1944, after serving independently on the Eastern Front since April 1943.

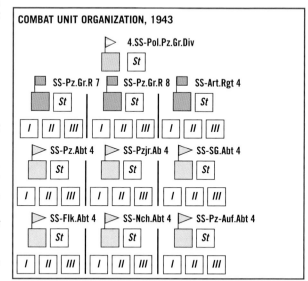

COMBAT UNIT ORGANIZATION, 1943

▸ **Mittlere Lkw Henschel 33D1**

4.SS-Polizei-Panzergrenadier-Division / Versorgungsdienste

Produced from 1933 to 1942, around 22,000 Henschel medium trucks were made for the *Wehrmacht*. The standard cargo/personnel body was most common, but other open and closed bodies were built.

Specifications

Crew: 1	Engine: 10.7 litre (650ci),
Weight: 6.1 tonnes (6 tons)	6-cylinder petrol (100hp)
Length: 7.4m (24ft)	Speed: 60km/h (37mph)
Width: 2.25m (7ft 4in)	Payload: 3 tonnes (2.95 tons)
Height: 3.2m (10ft 6in)	or 18 troops

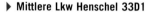

▸ **Panzerkampfwagen Opel Blitz 3000S**

4.SS-Polizei-Panzergrenadier-Division / Versorgungsdienste

Produced under the Schell Program, which simplified the German automotive industry before the war, the 'S' type Opel Blitz was a commercial 4x2 truck that was used extensively by the supply columns of German divisions.

Specifications

Crew: 1	Engine: Opel 6-cylinder petrol
Weight: 3.29 tonnes (3 tons)	(73.5hp)
Length: 6.02m (19ft 9in)	Speed: 80km/h (50mph)
Width: 2.27m (7ft 5in)	Range: 410km (255 miles)
Height: 2.18m (7ft 2in)	Radio: None

▼ SS-Polizei-Panzerjäger-Abteilung

In 1941 and 1942, the Panzerjäger Battalion of the *Polizei* Division was equipped with a mix of 3.7cm (1.5in) Pak 36 and 5cm (2in) Pak 38 guns. The Pak 36 was the standard German anti-tank gun at the outbreak of war. Light and handy to use in the field, it was a very influential design when first produced between the wars. By World War II, however, its performance was inadequate. It could penetrate up to 38mm (1.5in) of armour at a range of 350m (383 yards).

The 5cm (2in) Pak 38 was more powerful. It was introduced too late to be used in the early campaigns, but on the Eastern Front in 1941 it was the only German anti-tank gun powerful enough to knock out a T-34 tank. With tungsten-cored AP40 projectiles, it could penetrate over 100mm (4in) of armour at 740m (809 yards).

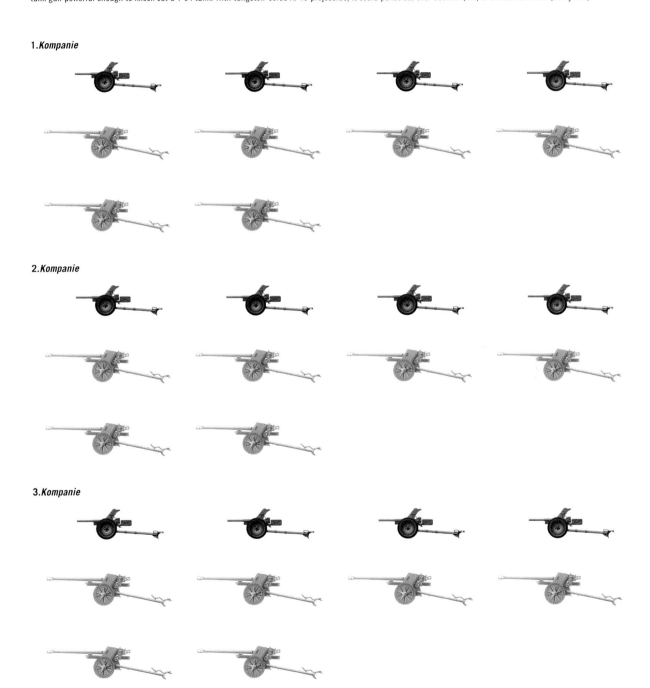

1.*Kompanie*

2.*Kompanie*

3.*Kompanie*

Greece and the Balkans
1943–1944

In April 1943, the division began to upgrade to an armoured infantry formation with the establishment of *Polizei* Panzergrenadier Regiments 1 and 2 at Cracow in Poland.

BOTH REGIMENTS WERE SENT to the Balkans in mid-July 1943, where they were attached to Army Group E. The complete *SS-Polizei-Division* finally arrived in Thessaloniki in December 1943.

After the conquest of Greece in 1941, the country was divided between Germany, Italy and Bulgaria. German forces occupied the strategically important areas, including Athens, Thessaloniki, central Macedonia, and some key Aegean islands.

Responsibility for internal security was initially in the hands of the *Wehrmacht,* which was primarily interested in keeping open lines of communication to Greek ports to supply German troops fighting the British in North Africa. After the fall of Tunisia, German troops were mainly used in anti-partisan operations.

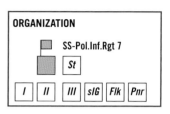

ORGANIZATION

- SS-Pol.Inf.Rgt 7
  - St
  - I | II | III | sIG | Flk | Pnr

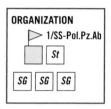

ORGANIZATION

- 1/SS-Pol.Pz.Ab
  - St
  - SG | SG | SG

Partisan war

The increasing frequency of attacks by partisans in the Balkans resulted in executions and the slaughter of civilians in reprisal. The 4th SS *Polizei* Panzergrenadier Division saw action in Greece on anti-partisan duties between January and September 1944, before Soviet advances on the Eastern Front threatened to cut off Army Group E in the Balkans. In September and October 1944, the division retreated through Yugoslavia and southern Romania, seeing combat around Belgrade. It continued its anti-partisan duties in the Banat, the region straddling the borders of Serbia, Romania and Hungary.

▲ **Schwere Kraftrad mit Seitenwagen BMW R75 750-cc**

4.SS-Polizei-Panzergrenadier-Division / Kraftrad-Aufklärungs-Abteilung

In February 1944, the *Polizei* Division was ordered to form a motorcycle battalion in place of its bicycle reconnaissance battalion. While it was being formed, the unit was upgraded to become a full reconnaissance battalion.

Specifications

Crew: 2	Engine: BMW 750cc petrol (26hp)
Weight: 0.67 tonnes (0.61 tons)	Speed: 92km/h (57mph)
Length: 2.4m (7ft 10in)	Range: 340km (211 miles)
Width: 1.73m (5ft 8in)	Radio: None
Height: 1m (3ft 3in)	Armament: 1 x 7.92mm (0.3in) MG (if fitted)

▶ **2cm Flak 38 auf Fahrgestell Zugkraftwagen 1t (SdKfz 10/5)**

4.SS-Polizei-Panzergrenadier-Division / Stab / Flak-Zug (Sf)

In the summer of 1944, the 4th Division's headquarters was protected by a Flak platoon with four self-propelled 2cm (0.7in) guns. These were just as likely to be used against partisans on the ground as against attacking aircraft.

Specifications

Crew: 7	6-cylinder (100hp)
Weight: 5.5 tonnes (5 tons)	Speed: 65km/h (40mph)
Length: 4.75m (15ft 7in)	Range: 300km (186 miles)
Width: 2.15m (7ft 1in)	Radio: None
Height: 3.20m (10ft 6in)	Armament: Twin 20mm (0.7in)
Engine: Maybach HL42TRKM	Flak 38 L/112.5

▼ 4.SS-Sturmgeschütz-Abteilung, 1.Kompanie

In May 1944, after re-equipping to bring the formation up to Panzergrenadier strength in fact as well as name, the *Polizei* Division had been assigned an armoured detachment for the first time. The 4.*SS-Polizei-Panzer-Abteilung* was a three-battalion unit equipped with *Sturmgeschütz* assault guns rather than tanks. By August 1944, the unit had been redesignated as 4.*SS-Polizei-Sturmgeschütz-Abteilung*.

The 4.*SS-Polizei-Sturmgeschütz-Abteilung* had a staff company, which was equipped with two self-propelled *Flakvierling* anti-tank guns, and three *Sturmgeschütz* companies. The standard table of equipment was for each company to have a staff platoon with two guns and three platoons with four guns each. However, at the time the battalion was established the third company was one gun short with only 13 vehicles.

Stab

1.Zug

2.Zug

3.Zug

▶ Mittlere Zugkraftwagen 8t (SdKfz 7)

4.SS-Polizei-Flak-Abteilung (mot)

The standard tractor for the 8.8cm (3.5in) Flak 18 anti-aircraft gun and the 15cm (5.9in) sFH18 howitzer, the SdKfz 7 was designed by Krauss-Maffei. It was also manufactured by Mercedes, Büssing-NAG and Borgward.

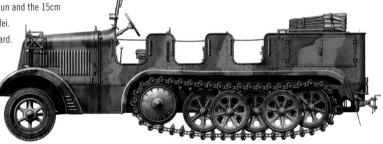

Specifications

Crew: 2	Engine: Maybach HL62
Weight: 1.16 tonnes (1.06 tons)	6-cylinder (140hp)
Length: 6.85m (20ft 3in)	Speed: 50km/h (31mph)
Width: 2.40m (7ft 10.5in)	Range: 250km (156 miles)
Height: 2.62m (8ft 7.1in)	Radio: None

Hungary and Prussia
1945

In January 1945, the Red Army's main priority was to drive the Germans out of Poland, and to take the offensive into Germany's heartlands of Saxony and Prussia.

MARSHAL ZHUKOV AND HIS 1st Belorussian Front was to aim for Poznan, while Marshal Konev would direct his assault towards Breslau to the south. Each massive force comprised over one million men, with over 30,000 guns and 7000 tanks between them. Opposing them was Army Group Centre with only 400,000 men and just over 1000 tanks. The Germans, however, still had some 580,000 troops in East Prussia, which could cause the Soviets considerable problems.

In January 1945, the *Polizei* Division had been pushed into Slovakia. From there, it was moved north to join the still substantial German forces on the Baltic coast.

Fighting in Prussia

Arriving in Pomerania, as part of *SS-Obergruppenführer* Felix Steiner's Eleventh Panzer Army, the division was pushed into action against the advancing Red Army. After a series of battles, the 4th SS Division was moved to Danzig, where it was

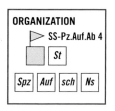

ORGANIZATION
SS-Pz.Auf.Ab 4
St
Spz | Auf | sch | Ns

ORGANIZATION
SS-Flk.Abt 4
St
Bat | Bat | Bat | Bat | Sw

▼ **4.SS-Polizei-Panzerjäger-Abteilung, 1.Kompanie**

For a long period one of the poorest-equipped of the early SS divisions, the *Polizei* Division began to become a formation of real power by the time it was brought up to Panzergrenadier division strength in 1944. The division's Panzerjäger battalion was equipped with two companies of 14 *Jagdpanzers*, together with a motorized company equipped with 17 towed 7.5cm (3in) Pak 40 anti-tank guns. However, by the end of 1944 these were no longer in the division's table of organization.

Stab

1.Zug

2.Zug

3.Zug

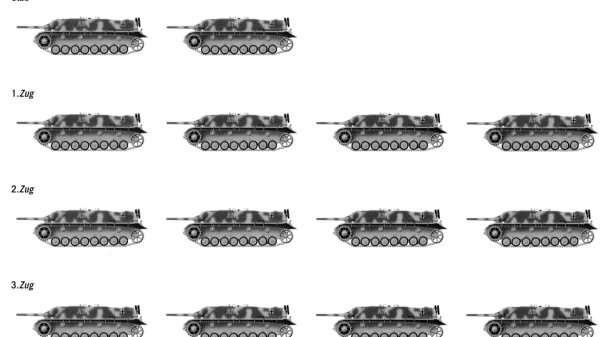

trapped when the city was bypassed by Soviet forces. After intense fighting on the Vistula River, the division was shipped across the Hela Peninsula. It was evacuated by sea to Swinemünde in April and fought on the Oder Front north of Berlin. The wounded were sent to Copenhagen along with the division's 1st Medical Company. The division surrendered to US forces in May near Wittenberge-Lenzen.

▲ 15cm Schwere Infanterie Geschütz (sIG33)

7.SS-Polizei-Grenadier-Regiment (mot) / 13.Kompanie

The *Polizei* Division's two grenadier regiments each had a heavy infantry gun company to support each regiment's three infantry battalions.

Specifications

Crew: 5	Muzzle Velocity: 241m/s (783fps)
Weight: 1.75 tonnes (1.71 tons)	Range: 5504m (6000 yards)
Length: 1.64m (64.57in)	Ammunition: High explosive or smoke
Calibre: 150mm (5.9in)	

▲ 7.5cm Panzerabwehrkanone (Pak 40)

8.SS-Polizei-Grenadier-Regiment / Stab / Panzerjäger-Zug

The HQs of the 7th and 8th SS Grenadier Regiments each had a three-gun anti-tank platoon, as did the heavy companies of the division's six infantry battalions.

Specifications

Crew: 3	Muzzle Velocity (AP): 990m/s (3248fps)
Weight: 1.5 tonnes (1.37 tons)	Range: AP: 2000m (2190 yards), HE: 7.5km
Length: 3.7m (12ft 1.5in)	(4.66 miles)
Calibre: 75mm (3in)	Ammunition: Armour-piercing, high explosive

▶ Schwere Panzerspähwagen (SdKfz 231)

4.SS-Polizei-Aufklärungs-Abteilung / Spähpanzerwagen-Kompanie

A reconnaissance battalion was raised for the *Polizei* Division when it was upgraded in 1943/44. It had one armoured car company and three light reconnaissance companies equipped with soft-skin vehicles.

Specifications

Crew: 4	petrol (150hp)
Weight: 9.1 tonnes (8.3 tons)	Speed: 85km/h (52.8mph)
Length: 5.85m (19ft 2in)	Range: 300km (186 miles)
Width: 2.20m (7ft 2.5in)	Radio: FuG Ger 'a'
Height: 2.35m (7ft 8in)	Armament: 1 x 20mm (0.7in)
Engine: Büssing-NAG 8-cylinder	cannon

▶ Sturmgeschütz 40 Ausf G (SdKfz 142/1)

4.SS-Sturmgeschütz-Abteilung / 1.Kompanie

Designed to serve as mobile artillery providing close support to the infantry, the *Sturmgeschütz* evolved into a versatile weapon system able to substitute for tanks or for tank-destroyers.

Specifications

Crew: 4	Engine: Maybach HL120TRM
Weight: 26.3 tonnes (23.9 tons)	Speed: 40km/h (25mph)
Length: 6.77m (22ft 2in)	Range: 155km (96.3 miles)
Width: 2.95m (9ft 8in)	Radio: FuG15 and FuG16
Height: 2.16m (7ft 0in)	Armament: 1 x 75mm (3in) cannon

Chapter 6

The Expansion of the SS

During the course of World War II, the *Waffen-SS* grew from an elite force of four regiments composed solely of Germans meeting Heinrich Himmler's exacting physical and racial standards to a polyglot force of 900,000 men in 39 divisions, with over half of its troops being either foreign volunteers or conscripts. Even so, at its peak the *Waffen-SS* represented only one-tenth of the strength of the *Wehrmacht* – although it provided a quarter of German Panzer strength.

◀ **Warriors of the *Reich***
An SS flamethrower crew prepares for battle. The exceptional physical standards of the early SS divisions could not be maintained in the massive expansion of the *Waffen-SS*, but SS troops remained highly motivated long after other Germans believed the war was lost.

5th SS Panzer Division *Wiking*

The first of the 'international' SS divisions, *Wiking* was one of the most effective fighting formations to have seen combat in World War II.

AFTER THE MAY 1940 *Sieg im Westen,* or Victory in the West, the SS began an active programme to recruit suitably 'Nordic' or 'Germanic' volunteers from northern and western Europe to join a number of *Waffen-SS Freiwilligen* (volunteer) legions. This effort intensified after June 1941, as the SS exhorted volunteers to join the campaign in the Soviet Union.

However, all this was still in the future and standards were still high in September 1940, when Hitler consented to the raising of a new *Waffen-SS* division. Originally to be named *SS-Division Germania,* the backbone of the unit was to be provided by the experienced and combat-tested *Germania* Regiment of the SS-VT Division.

It was hoped that the bulk of its strength would be provided by Dutch, Flemish, Danish and Norwegian volunteers serving in the volunteer *SS-Regiment Westland.* This was a sop to the Army, which had been complaining about the SS poaching the best German recruits. *SS-Infanterie-Regiment* 11, one of the *SS-Totenkopfstandarten,* replaced *Germania* in the

▼ **Eastern Front, early 1943**
Wiking was one of the hardest-fighting, most successful combat units on the Eastern Front, where it served from 1941 to 1945.

INSIGNIA

The sun cross, a cross inside a circle, is one of the oldest mythic symbols. The Nazis used a swastika variant of the sun cross as the *Wiking* insignia.

Insignia varied depending on the background. A dark-painted vehicle necessitated the use of a white shield to make the divisional symbol identifiable.

Commanders

Obergruppenführer Felix Steiner
1940 – January 1943

Obergruppenführer Herbert Gille
January 1943 – August 1944

Oberführer Edmund Deisenhofer
August 1944

Standartenführer Rudolf Mühlenkamp
August 1944 – September 1944

Oberführer Karl Ullrich
September 1944 – May 1945

Divisional History	Formed
Nordische Division (Nr. 5)	1940
SS-Division Germania (mot)	1940
SS-Division Wiking	1941
SS-Panzergrenadier-Division Wiking	1942
5.SS-Panzer-Division Wiking	1943

SS-VT. Further strength was supplied by the transfer of the *SS-Standarte Nordland.* Early 1941 saw the addition of a volunteer unit of Finns, the *Finnisches Freiwilligen-Bataillon der Waffen-SS Nordost,* which had been raised in February 1941.

On 20 December, Hitler ordered that the division should be known as the *SS-Division Wiking.* Commanded by Felix Steiner, one of the most influential officers in the *Waffen-SS, Wiking* was the first 'international' *Waffen-SS* division. It proved to be an excellent fighting unit, and as the 5.*SS-Panzer-Division Wiking* it gained a combat reputation second to none. However, in spite of the hopes of the SS to make it a Germanic volunteer formation, Germans always outnumbered Nordic volunteers in its ranks.

▶ Leichte Spähpanzerwagen (SdKfz 222)

SS-Aufklärungs-Abteilung Wiking / leichte Spähpanzerwagen-Kompanie

As originally authorized in May 1940, the *Wiking* Division (then known as *Germania*) was to have a single light armoured car company as part of its reconnaissance battalion.

Specifications

Crew: 3	Speed: 85km/h (52.8mph)
Weight: 5.3 tonnes (4.8 tons)	Range: 300km (186 miles)
Length: 4.8m (15ft 8in)	Radio: FuG Spr Ger 'a'
Width: 1.95m (6ft 5in)	Armament: 1 x 20mm (0.7in) KwK 30 L/55
Height: 2.00m (6ft 7in)	cannon; 1 x 7.92mm (0.3in) MG (coaxial)
Engine: Horch 3.5L or 3.8L petrol	

Specifications

Crew: 5	Muzzle Velocity: 520m/s (1706fps)
Weight: 6.3 tonnes (5.7 tons)	Range: 13km (8 miles)
Length: 4.4m (14 ft 5in)	Ammunition: High explosive or smoke
Calibre: 150mm (5.9in)	

▲ 15cm schwere Feldhaubitze (sFH18)

SS-Artillerie-Regiment Wiking / 4.Bataillon

Wiking was formed with an artillery regiment consisting of three motorized battalions of 10.5cm (4.1in) light field howitzers and a single battalion of 15cm (5.9in) heavy howitzers.

▶ Panzerfunkwagen 8-Rad (SdKfz 263)

SS-Nachrichten-Abteilung Wiking

Developed in the 1930s, the *Panzerfunkwagen* was a heavy armoured radio car issued to the radio companies and communications detachments of the signals battalions of Panzer and motorized divisions.

Specifications

Crew: 4	petrol (150hp)
Weight: 9.1 tonnes (8.3 tons)	Speed: 85km/h (52.8mph)
Length: 5.85m (19ft 2in)	Range: 300km (186 miles)
Width: 2.20m (7ft 2.5in)	Radio: FuG Ger 'a'
Height: 2.35m (7ft 8in)	Armament: 1 x 20mm (0.7in)
Engine: Büssing-NAG 8-cylinder	cannon

With Army Group South
SUMMER 1941

Formation of the division began in late 1940, and by the time of the invasion of the Soviet Union in June 1941, *Wiking* was a fully fledged, fully trained SS motorized infantry division.

THE DIVISION FIRST SAW ACTION on 29 June 1941. Assigned to Army Group South, it took part in the fighting for Tarnopol in Galicia. Opposition from isolated pockets of resistance and guerrilla groups aside, the progress of the division's tanks over the roads of the Ukraine from Dubno to the outskirts of Zhitomir was relatively free of problems, as seemingly endless lines of Soviet prisoners captured in the pocket of Lvov were marching towards the rear. Abandoned tanks and guns cluttered the roads.

Across the Dnieper

In August, 1941, the division was at the head of the army group as it fought to establish a bridgehead across the Dnieper River. Continuing the drive, *Wiking* fought its way through Dnepropetrovsk and on to Rostov.

According to one SS man, the fall of Rostov was greeted by its inhabitants with 'tremendous enthusiasm'. As far as the Red Army was concerned, the truth was otherwise. First, the Germans had been slowed by anti-tank obstacles, ditches and minefields. *Wiking* troops faced not Red Army soldiers but fanatical NKVD men, the shock troops of the Communist state. These men fought hand-to-hand in the streets, where they ripped up paving blocks to serve as thick barricades.

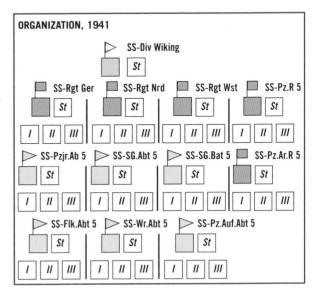

ORGANIZATION, 1941

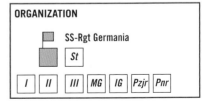

ORGANIZATION

First reverses

Almost every door concealed booby traps and tripwires. Pillboxes spat fire amid flamethrowers, grenades, machine guns, rifles and bayonets. The *Wiking* wounded were either

▶ **Mittlere Lkw Opel Blitz 3000S**

Versorgungsdienste Wiking / 30t Kolonne

The motorized transport columns attached to divisional support services were rated by their total load capacity: a 30-tonne (29.4-ton) column controlled two sections each with five medium, or 3-tonne (2.94-ton), trucks.

Specifications	
Crew: 1	Engine: Opel 6-cylinder petrol
Weight: 3.29 tonnes (3 tons)	(73.5hp)
Length: 6.02m (19ft 9in)	Speed: 80km/h (50mph)
Width: 2.27m (7ft 5in)	Range: 410km (255 miles)
Height: 2.18m (7ft 2in)	Radio: None

bayoneted as they lay in the street or were dragged from troop-carriers serving as makeshift ambulances.

Within days, the Soviets had driven the Germans out of the town and they fell back to defensive positions across the Mius, leaving behind piles of dead. Against furious onslaughts, the *Leibstandarte*

and the *Wiking* Division held on, but their men knew that the position was hopeless. When the Germans were pushed out of Rostov by the first truly successful Red Army counterattack, *Wiking* moved back to the line of the Mius River, where the division spent the winter months.

Advance to the Causasus
MAY–SEPTEMBER 1942

Although it suffered heavy losses in its first year, *Wiking* acquired an excellent reputation, even earning the grudging respect of the Soviets in several battle reports for its pugnacious fighting spirit. Soviet commanders were always concerned to learn that their troops were facing the soldiers of the *Wiking* Division.

WHEN THE GERMANS LAUNCHED their major offensive in the summer of 1942, *Wiking* was again one of the spearhead divisions. Its make-up had changed, however, as individual elements of the *Wiking* Division were added and removed many times in its existance. As a replacement for the disbanded Finnish battalion of the *Nordland* Regiment, the *Estonian Narwa* Regiment was transferred to *Wiking*. The *Nordland* Regiment itself was detached to help establish a new *Waffen-SS* Division, the *Nordland* Division.

Army Group South, renamed Army Group B, was to advance into the bend of the Don River then on to the Volga at Stalingrad. The other claw in a gigantic pincer movement would be a new formation. Army Group A, comprising First Panzer Army, Seventeenth Army and Third Romanian Army, would link up

ORGANIZATION, 1942

▷ 5.SS-Pz.Gr.Div Wiking — St

SS-PG.R Ger	SS-PG.R Nrd	SS-PG.R Wst	Art.Rgt 5
St	St	St	St
I II III	I II III	I II III	I II III

▷ Fin.W-SS.Btl | ▷ SS-Pz.Abt Wik | ▷ Pzjr.Abt | ▷ Auf.Abt
St | St | St | St
I II III | I II III | I II III | I II III

▷ Flk.Abt | ▷ Pnr.Btl | ▷ Div Sup
St | St | St
I II III | I II III | I II III

▶ **Panzerkampfwagen III Ausf J (SdKfz 141)**

5.SS-Panzer-Regiment Wiking / II.Abteilung

In the summer of 1942, the *Wiking* Division added a Panzer battalion to its order of battle. *Wiking* was one of the first divisions to be issued with the long-barrelled Panzer III Ausf J.

Specifications

Crew: 5	Speed: 40km/h (25mph)
Weight: 24 tonnes (21.5 tons)	Range: 155km (96.3 miles)
Length: 6.28m (20ft 7in)	Radio: FuG5
Width: 2.95m (9ft 9in)	Armament: 1 x 50mm (2in) KwK 39
Height: 2.50m (8ft 2in)	L/60 gun; 2 x 7.92mm (0.3in) MG
Engine: Maybach HL120TRM	(one coaxial, one hull-mounted)

with Army Group B somewhere on the steppe west of the Volga, hopefully trapping another vast haul of Soviet prisoners. Army Group A would then lunge south and east to overrun the Soviet oilfields.

Six months after they had endured winter temperatures of -30°C (-22°F), *Wiking* soldiers found themselves leading the First Panzer Army on the Kuban steppe, where the thermometer topped 40°C (104°F) in the shade. Inside the tanks and fighting vehicles, the heat was simply unbearable. The terrain slowed up fighting troops as well as supplies. Roads were rivers of dust, and the rivers were wide, with unpredictable currents.

Nevertheless, the SS *Wiking* Division forced the

▶ 7.5cm Panzerjäger Marder II (SdKfz 131)
SS-Panzerjäger-Abteilung Wiking / Panzerjäger-Kompanie (Sf)

Mounting the powerful Pak 40 anti-tank gun onto a late-model Panzer II chassis produced a highly effective tank-hunter. In October 1942, the division had one self-propelled company and two companies with towed Pak 40s.

Specifications

Crew: 4	Speed: 42km/h (26mph)
Weight: 11.76 tonnes (10.67 tons)	Range: 185km (115 miles)
Length: 5.85m (19ft 2in)	Radio: FuG Spr 'd'
Width: 2.16m (7ft 0in)	Armament: 1 x 76.2mm (3in) FK296
Height: 2.50m (8ft 2in)	anti-tank gun
Engine: Praga EPA or EPA/2	

▶ Mittlere Flammpanzerwagen (SdKfz 251/16)
SS-Pionier-Abteilung Wiking / Panzer-Pionier-Kompanie (Spw)

One of the division's three combat engineer companies was half-track-equipped. Each pioneer company had six flamethrowers, either as individual man-portable equipment or mounted in pairs aboard flamethrower half-tracks.

Specifications

Crew: 5	(0.3in) MG34 or MG42; earlier
Weight: 9.5 tonnes (8.6 tons)	models also carried a single 7mm
Armament: 2 x 14mm (0.6in)	(0.3in) man-portable
Flammenwerfer: 2 x 7.62mm	Flammenwerfer 42

▶ Panzerkampfwagen IV Ausf G (SdKfz 161/1)
5.SS-Panzer-Regiment Wiking / I.Abteilung

While short-barrel Panzer IIIs were taking over the fire-support role, Panzer IVs traded in their short guns for the powerful long-barrelled 7.5cm (3in) KwK40 L/43 gun.

Specifications

Crew: 5	Speed: 40km/h (25mph)
Weight: 25.9 tonnes (23.5 tons)	Range: 210km (130.5 miles)
Length: 6.62m (21ft 8in)	Radio: FuG5
Width: 2.88m (9ft 5in)	Armament: 1 x 75mm (3in) KwK 40/43;
Height: 2.69m (8ft 10in)	2 x 7.92mm (0.3in) MG (one hull-
Engine: Maybach HL120TRM	mounted, one coaxial)

River Kuban in the face of intense Soviet resistance early in August. On 9 August, 1.*Panzerarmee* took Pyatigorsk at the bottom of the first foothills of the Caucasus, and patrols were sent out towards Astrakhan.

Fighting through the steppes

However, this was as far as it went. The *Wiking* Division had fought its way into and through the Caucasus. It would remain in the area until von Kleist's army group was forced to pull back after the fall of Stalingrad early in 1943.

By this time, it had been converted from a motorized infantry division into a Panzergrenadier, or armoured infantry, division.

▶ **SS Camouflage**
SS troopers were among the first soldiers to be issued with camouflage smocks and helmet covers as standard combat clothing.

▼ **SS-Panzer-Abteilung Wiking light tank company**
As late as the invasion of the Soviet Union in 1941, the light tank companies of Panzer battalions still had large numbers of Panzer IIs. By the beginning of 1943, however, the few survivors were being used as commander's tanks or for reconnaissance, with the bulk of the company strength being provided by Panzer IIIs with short and long barrels.

Stab

1.*Zug*

2.*Zug*

3.*Zug*

Korsun encirclement
MARCH–DECEMBER 1943

Wiking avoided the cataclysmic battles at Kursk, serving further south with 4.*Panzerarmee* on the Don, fighting a defensive campaign through the summer and autumn of 1943.

IN OCTOBER 1943, the division was again upgraded, being converted from a Panzergrenadier division to a fully armoured Panzer division.

In the summer and autumn of 1943, the division fought in defensive operations in the area of Kharkov and the Dnieper River. By the end of of 1943, *Wiking* was one of six divisions occupying a 96km (60-mile) salient at Korsun, on the east of the Dnieper.

Hitler had the unrealistic belief that the 56,000 men in the salient could thrust in an offensive towards Kiev. He had not reckoned on the Soviets. General Konev's 2nd Ukrainian Front punched

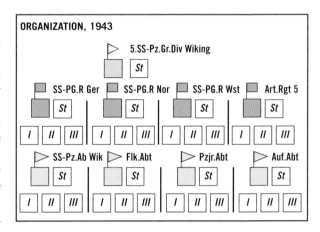

ORGANIZATION, 1943

▷ 5.SS-Pz.Gr.Div Wiking

▶ Panzerkampfwagen III Ausf N (SdKfz 141/2)
5.SS-Panzer-Regiment Wiking

In July 1943, *Wiking* had eight Panzer III Ausf N tanks on strength. The short-barrelled 7.5cm (3in) gun was used to support other tanks by engaging enemy fortifications and infantry positions with high-explosive rounds.

Specifications

Crew: 5	Engine: Maybach HL120TRM
Weight: 25.4 tonnes (23 tons)	Speed: 40km/h (25mph)
Length: 5.52m (18ft 1in)	Range: 155km (96 miles)
Width: 2.95m (9ft 7in)	Radio: FuG5
Height: 2.5m (8ft 2in)	

▶ Leichte Feldhaubitze 18/2 auf fahrgestell PzKpfw II (Sf) Wespe (SdKfz 124)
5.SS-Artillerie-Regiment / I.Abteilung

The *Wiking* Division began to trade in some of its towed artillery pieces for Wespe self-propelled guns in August 1943. Only one battalion was given the new equipment; the other three used towed guns until the end of the war.

Specifications

Crew: 5	Speed: 40km/h (25mph)
Weight: 12.1 tonnes (11 tons)	Range: 220km (136.7 miles)
Length: 4.81m (15ft 10in)	Radio: FuG Spr 1
Width: 2.28m (7ft 6in)	Armament: 1 x LeFH18M L/28 105mm
Height: 2.25m (7ft 4.5in)	(4.1in) howitzer
Engine: Maybach HL62TR	

through the bridgehead lying between Kremenchug, which lay far to the southwest of Kharkov, and Dnepropetrovsk to the east of Kremenchug. Konev's objective was to form a wedge between First Panzer Army and Eighth Army. The latter was no match for the strong Soviet muscle and was forced to pull back in the face of the steady advance of the 2nd Ukrainian Front.

Kiev

In the north, things were no better, with ever more powerful Soviet forces throwing the Germans out of Kiev on 6 November after they had established a bridgehead there. Soviet pride was further restored with the recapture, after a temporary loss, of the town of Zhitomir on 20 November.

Buildings there were reduced to rubble and the streets were littered with the burnt-out hulks of vehicles. Of considerable compensation were the large supply dumps and foodstuff depots of Fourth Panzer Army, which the Germans had established in the high summer of triumph two years before.

Encirclement

The men of *Wiking* were assigned to territory where the prospects were bleak for the Germans. Four divisions were encircled in this flat countryside under snow with the temperature in Kirovograd itself at -20°C (-4°F). On 5 January, Konev's 2nd Ukrainian Front launched its attack and took the city. A breakout was eventually achieved by 3rd Panzer Division with fire cover from the artillery; engineers and Panzergrenadiers followed, while the Soviets were pinned down in local fighting.

For all the efforts of the Panzer units and the SS, the truth was that the Soviet advance had become a flood with the great winter offensive dealing the decisive blow.

▶ **Mittlere Schützenpanzerwagen Ausf D (SdKfz 251)**

Panzergrenadier-Regiment Germania / Spw Bataillon

In the summer of 1943, one battalion of the *Germania* Panzergrenadier Regiment was mounted in half-tracks. The *Germania* Regiment, one of the original Armed SS units, was later redesignated as the 9th SS Panzergrenadier Regiment *Germania*.

Specifications

Crew: 2 plus 12 troops	Engine: Maybach HL42TUKRM
Weight: 9.9 tonnes (9 tons)	Speed: 53km/h (33mph)
Length: 5.98m (19ft 7in)	Range: 300km (186 miles)
Width: 2.1m (6ft 11in)	Radio: FuG Spr Ger 1
Height: 1.75m (5ft 8in) or 2.16m	Armament: 1/2 x 7.62mm
(7ft) including MG shield	(0.3in) MG

▶ **Leichte Schützenpanzerwagen (SdKfz 250/9)**

5.SS-Panzer-Aufklärungs-Abteilung / 2.Spähpanzerwagen-Kompanie (Spw)

In 1944, only one of *Wiking's* five reconnaissance companies used armoured cars. The 2nd Armoured Car Company was actually equipped with reconnaissance half-tracks.

Specifications

Crew: 3	Speed: 60km/h (37mph)
Weight: 6.9 tonnes (6.3 tons)	Range: 320km (199 miles)
Length: 4.56m (14ft 11.5in)	Radio: FuG Spr Ger 'f'
Width: 1.95m (6ft 5in)	Armament: 1 x 20mm (0.7in) KwK 30/38
Height: 2.16m (7ft 1in)	L/55 cannon; 1 x 7.92mm (0.3in) MG (coaxial)
Engine: Maybach HL42TRKM 6-cylinder (100hp)	

▼ SS-Panzer-Artillerie-Regiment 5 : I.Bataillon

When formed, the *Wiking* Division's artillery regiment was equipped with towed artillery. By 1943, th 1st Artillery battalion had re-equipped with Wespe self-propelled howitzers.

1.*Batterie*

2.*Batterie*

3.*Batterie*

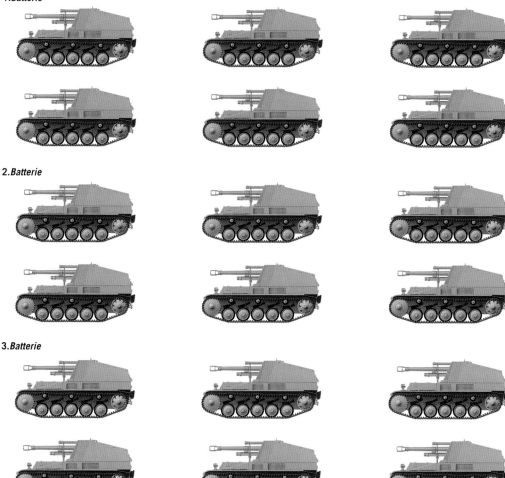

☸ Retreat from Cherkassy

JANUARY 1944

Wiking's position in the Korsun salient was perilous. Overwhelming Soviet forces were assembling, clearly ready to pinch off and destroy the German divisions in the area.

THE CONQUEST OF KIROVOGRAD still left unfinished business for the Soviets. To the north lay the salient around Korsun and Cherkassy, a position that Hitler was determined to hold and which was defended by six-and-a-half divisions with around 56,000 men.

The German positions south of the Korsun bulge took the full bombardment. Fourth Guards, Fifty-Third and Fifth Tank Armies struck at the heart of the German line. From the north of the bulge came the 1st Ukrainian Front. By 28 January, it had met up with Konev's 2nd Ukrainian Front, which had advanced from the south. Men of 5.*SS-Panzer-Division Wiking* were among the 56,000 German troops trapped there.

Breakout

Being the only Panzer unit in the pocket, *Wiking* spearheaded the operation to break out of the encirclement. Included under its orders at the time was an independent SS formation of Belgian volunteers, 5.*SS-Freiwilligen-Sturmbrigade Wallonien*, which would later become 28.*SS-Freiwilligen-Grenadier-Division Wallonien*. The breakout was successful, but casualties were heavy – some 30,000 of the 56,000 German troops escaped. The *Wiking* Division lost all of its armour and much of its equipment in the process.

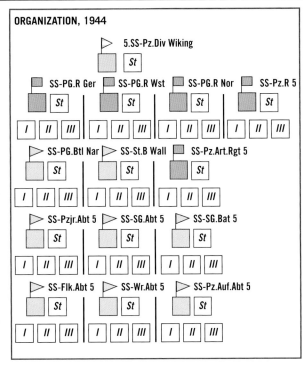

ORGANIZATION, 1944

▶ **7.5cm Panzerspähwagen 8-Rad (SdKfz 234/3)**

5.SS-Panzer-Aufklärungs-Abteilung / schwere Zug

The heavy platoon of the Panzer reconnaissance battalion in the last months of the war was equipped with six heavy eight-wheeled armoured cars armed with short-barrelled KwK51 tank guns.

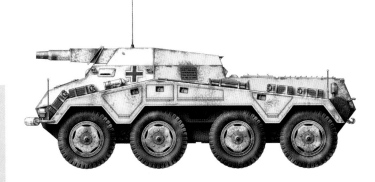

Specifications

Crew: 4	Speed: 80km/h (50mph)
Weight: 11.50 tonnes (10.47 tons)	Range: 900km (559 miles)
Length: 6.0m (19ft 8in)	Radio: FuG Spr Ger 'a'
Width: 2.40m (7ft 10.5in)	Armament: 1 x 75mm (3in) PaK 40 L/46
Height: 2.21m (7ft 4in)	cannon; 1 x 7.92 mm (0.3in) MG
Engine: Tatra 103 12-cylinder (220hp)	

▶ **Panzerkampfwagen IV Ausf H (SdKfz 161/2)**

5.SS-Panzer-Regiment / II.Abteilung / 5.Kompanie

Wiking was equipped with the standard late-war Panzer regiment, comprising one battalion with Panthers and one with Panzer IVs.

Specifications

Crew: 5	Engine: Maybach HL120TRM
Weight: 27.6 tonnes (25 tons)	Speed: 38km/h (23.6mph)
Length: 7.02m (23ft)	Range: 210km (130.5 miles)
Width: 2.88m (9ft 5in)	Radio: FuG5
Height: 2.68m (8ft 10in)	

Specifications

Crew: 5

Weight: 50.2 tonnes (45.5 tons)

Length: 8.86m (29ft)

Width: 3.4m (11ft 2in)

Height: 2.98m (9ft 8in)

Engine: Maybach HL230P30

Speed: 46km/h (29mph)

Range: 200km (124 miles)

Radio: FuG5

▲ **Panzerkampfwagen V Ausf G (SdKfz 171)**

5.SS-Panzer-Regiment / I.Abteilung / 3.Kompanie

In October 1943, the *Wiking* Division was upgraded to become a full Panzer division. In May 1944, the records of the German high command showed that the 1st Battalion of the 5th Panzer Regiment had completed re-equipping with *Panzerkampfwagen* V Panthers.

▼ **5.SS-Panzer-Regiment, I.Abteilung, 1.Kompanie**

In 1943, with the large-scale introduction of the PzKpfw V Panther into service, a major reorganization of German Panzer forces was undertaken. Some Panzer divisions had one tank battalion of three companies, each company being formed of a command troop with two tanks and four platoons each with five tanks. In the summer of 1944, the Panzer divisions were again reorganized. The Panzer regiments in the Type 44 Division now consisted of two battalions, one equipped with Panthers and the second with Panzer IVs. Some companies retained 22 tanks, but in many divisions the number of tanks in a company was reduced from 22 to 17.

Stab

1.Zug

2.Zug

3.Zug

Hungary and Austria
1944–1945

The losses suffered by *Wiking* in the fierce fighting at Korsun and Cherkassy meant that by the spring of 1944 the division was in need of complete rebuilding.

THE REMNANTS OF THE *WIKING* DIVISION fought on as a *Kampfgruppe,* before being transferred to Poland where they would form the nucleus of a new *5.SS-Panzer-Division Wiking*. Because it was out of the line, it missed the massive Soviet summer offensive known as Operation *Bagration*. Perhaps the most powerful military attack in history, *Bagration* smashed the German Eastern Front and virtually destroyed Army Group Centre.

By the time *Wiking* was again in action, the Soviets had pushed all the way to the Vistula River and to Warsaw. Along with the 3.*SS-Panzer-Division Totenkopf* and the Army's 19th Panzer Division,

Wiking fought to stem the Soviet advance, stabilizing the front along the line of the Vistula.

As the vast Soviet wave of destruction rolled onwards towards Germany, north of the Carpathians, Hitler found himself obsessed with Hungary. *Wiking* was pulled from Warsaw in December 1944, and transferred south to relieve 60,000 German soldiers and more than 800,000 civilians trapped in the Hungarian capital, Budapest.

Attached to IV SS Panzer Corps, *Wiking* pushed forward for two weeks, but could not penetrate the massed Soviet armies which were besieging the city. Even though units of the Red Army were now in

▲ **Retreat from the East**

Hammered almost into oblivion in the escape from the Cherkassy pocket, the men of the *Wiking* Division were pulled out of the line early in 1944. The division had left most of its equipment behind, so surviving troops were used as a *Kampfgruppe* until more Panzers could be delivered.

sight of the suburbs of the Hungarian capital, IV SS Panzer Corps received orders to shift position to the industrial and farming area of Szekesfehervar in the southwest. This is believed to have been on the personal orders of Hitler himself. It was from here that the next attempt to break the stranglehold on Budapest would be made.

The overall loss of men and materiel to the *Wiking* and *Totenkopf* Divisions was bleeding the *Waffen-SS* formations dry. A slow countermove was set at naught by the strength of enemy fire, and the command post at Szekesfehervar had to be moved back and all resistance collapsed.

The next attack was to be made by Sepp Dietrich's Sixth SS Panzer Army, withdrawn from the fighting in the Ardennes and moved across Europe to Hungary. On 25 March, the Soviet breakthrough was all but complete, and the next day the Soviets went into the final phase which was the drive into Austria. With the failure of the final attempt to relieve the city, *Wiking* was withdrawn into Austria, where it fought in the final battles to defend Vienna in 1945.

Defence of Vienna

High priority was given to the defence of Vienna by the *Waffen-SS,* although there was nothing that even remotely compared with the defensive systems that had existed at Budapest. Rearguard detachments of Sixth SS Panzer Army, with elements of *Wiking, Leibstandarte* and the 17th Infantry Division, set up frequent ambushes, mined roads and blew bridges to hold off the Soviet Army.

▶ **2cm Flak 38 auf Fahrgestell Zugkraftwagen 1t (SdKfz 10/5)**

5.SS-Panzer-Division Wiking / Divisionsstab-Kompanie

Wiking's divisional staff company included Flak, infantry gun and Panzerjäger platoons. The Flak battery was equipped with four self-propelled 2cm (0.7in) anti-aircraft guns.

Specifications

Crew: 7	6-cylinder (100hp)
Weight: 5.5 tonnes (5 tons)	Speed: 65km/h (40mph)
Length: 4.75m (15ft 7in)	Range: 300km (186 miles)
Width: 2.15m (7ft 1in)	Radio: None
Height: 3.20m (10ft 6in)	Armament: Twin 20mm (0.7in)
Engine: Maybach HL42TRKM	Flak 38 L/112.5

Specifications

Crew: 6	Speed: 42km/h (26mph)
Weight: 26.5 tonnes (24 tons)	Range: 215km (133.6 miles)
Length: 7.17m (23ft 6in)	Radio: FuG Spr 1
Width: 2.97m (9ft 8in)	Armament: 1 x 150mm (5.9in) sFH 18/1 L/30; 1 x
Height: 2.81m (9ft 2in)	7.92mm (0.3in) MG
Engine: Maybach HL120TRM (265hp)	

▲ **15cm schwere Panzerhaubitze Hummel (SdKfz 165)**

5.SS-Panzer-Artillerie-Regiment / II.Bataillon / 3.Batterie

The 15cm (5.9in) sFH18 heavy field howitzer mounted in the Hummel could fire a 43.5kg (96lb) shell out to a maximum range of 13,325m (14,572 yards).

However, nothing could stop the Soviet juggernaut, and orders were given for the remnants of the division to retreat towards Graz. On the River Mur, the Soviets were waiting with cavalry and T-34 tanks. Those who survived the onslaught made for the American lines at Rastad, where they surrendered.

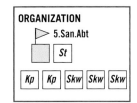

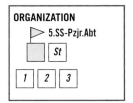

5.SS-Panzerjäger-Abteilung, 1.Kompanie

Anti-tank units in German divisions were equipped at the beginning of the war with a few 3.7cm (1.5in) anti-tank guns, which were of little use against even moderately armed vehicles. By the end of the war, anti-tank guns had grown enormously. These were more versatile, since many were mounted on self-propelled platforms. At the end of the war, *Wiking*'s three Panzerjäger companies were all self-propelled. Platforms ranged from the SdKfz 251/22, known as the *Kanonen Spw*, to the long-serving Marder III. The latter was introduced in 1942, and there were more than 350 Marders operational throughout the *Wehrmacht* in February 1945.

Stab

1.Zug

2.Zug

3.Zug

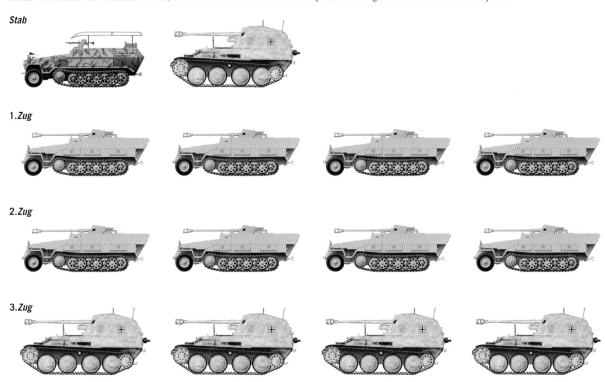

▶ 7.5cm Mittlere Schützenpanzerwagen (SdKfz 251/22)

5.SS-Panzerjäger-Abteilung / 1.Kompanie

Built in large numbers in the last year of the war, the SdKfz 251/22 simply mounted the 7.5cm (3in) Pak 40 onto the loadbed of the *mittlere Schützenpanzerwagen*.

Specifications

Crew: 4 or 5	Engine: Maybach HL42TUKRM
Weight: 8 tonnes (7.28 tons)	6-cylinder petrol (100hp)
Length: 5.98m (19ft 7in)	Speed: 50km/h (31mph)
Width: 2.1m (6ft 11in)	Range: 300km (186 miles)
Height: 2.25m (7ft 4.5in)	Radio: None

6th SS Gebirgs Division *Nord*

Formed in Norway from members of the *Allgemeine-,* or General, SS, the *Nord* Division was the first of the *Waffen-SS Gebirgs,* or mountain, divisions.

IN JUNE 1940, the capitulation of Norway left a large border with Finland and the Soviet Union unguarded. To replace the two Norwegian infantry battalions and the motorized artillery battery that had been deployed in the area, the Germans decided to deploy SS units rather than regular Army formations. The *Totenkopfstandarten* that would provide the manpower for the new force were composed of military-age members of the *Allgemeine-SS*. SS-*Totenkopf-Standarte* 9, commanded by SS-*Obersturmbannführer* Ernst Deutsch, was ordered north, with the first unit – *SS-Bataillon Reitz,*

commanded by *Obersturmbannführer* Wilhelm Reitz – arriving at Kirkenes in the late summer.

In February 1941, two further SS regiments arrived in northern Norway: the 6th and 7th *SS-Totenkopf-Standarten*. Soon afterwards, most of the 6th *Standarte,* reinforced by elements of the 9th, moved forwards to defensive positions at Salla in northern Finland. The German commander in Norway, General von Falkenhorst, was not impressed with the SS men, however. Although well equipped, the *Totenkopf-Standarten* were not made up from highly trained *Waffen-SS* men: the volunteers transferred from the *Allgemeine-SS* lacked the fitness and spirit of the Armed SS men.

Action in Russia

With the attack on Russia in June 1941, the units, now brigaded as *SS-Kampfgruppe Nord,* were launched into battle against veteran Soviet troops on

---

INSIGNIA

Formed to fight in the harsh terrain north of the Arctic Circle, the *Nord* Division adopted a stylised snowflake as its divisional symbol.

As a mountain division, the shield used on the *Nord* divisional insignia was notched at the top. Panzer division shields were notched at the top right.

Divisional History	Formed
SS-Kampfgruppe Nord	1941
SS-Division Nord (mot)	1941
SS-Gebirgs-Division Nord	1942
6.SS-Gebirgs-Division Nord	1943

Commanders

Brigadeführer Karl Herrmann *February 1941 – May 1941*	Gruppenführer Lothar Debes *January 1943 – June 1943*
Obergruppenführer Karl-Maria Demelhuber *May 1941 – April 1942*	Obergruppenführer Friedrich-Wilhelm Krüger *June 1943 – August 1943*
Obergruppenführer Matthias Kleinheisterkamp *April 1942*	Brigadeführer Gustav Lombard *August 1943 – January 1944*
Oberführer Hans Scheider *April 1942 – June 1942*	Gruppenführer Karl Brenner *January 1944 – April 1945*
Obergruppenführer Matthias Kleinheisterkamp *June 1942 – January 1943*	Standartenführer Franz Schreiber *April 1945 – May 1945*

▶ **Mittlere Lkw Henschel 33D1**

Kampfgruppe Nord / 6.SS-Infanterie-Regiment

As originally created, *Nord* was primarily an infantry formation with minimal motorization. However, by the time the *Kampfgruppe* became a brigade in 1941, its two infantry regiments had been motorized.

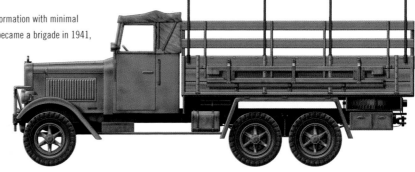

Specifications

Crew: 1	Engine: 10.7L (650ci),
Weight: 6.1 tonnes (6 tons)	6-cylinder petrol (100hp)
Length: 7.4m (24ft)	Speed: 60km/h (37mph)
Width: 2.25m (7ft 4in)	Payload: 3 tonnes (2.95 tons)
Height: 3.2m (10ft 6in)	or 18 troops

the Finnish border at Markajärvi-Salla. This was in spite of the fact that the *Kampfgruppe's* former commander, *Brigadeführer* Hermann, had asked for at least two months' further training to bring the unit up to standard.

The poorly trained SS men made a poor showing in the fighting, suffering 300 killed and more than 400 wounded in two days. *Nord* eventually rallied, however, and took part in the failed drive to interdict the Murmansk railway at Louhi. In July and August 1941, units of *Nord* were re-equipped, and their shortcomings were addressed by a period of intensive training. Between July and September *Nord,* now classed as a motorized division, was gradually withdrawn from the front and moved 140km (87 miles) south to the Kiestinki–Uhtua area.

▲ **3.7cm Panzerabwehrkanone (Pak 36)**

9.SS-Infanterie-Regiment / 14.leichte Panzerjäger-Kompanie

The only anti-tank assets controlled by *Nord* in 1941 were the single light motorized tank companies assigned to the 6th, 7th and 9th SS Infantry Regiments. These were each equipped with 12 Pak 36 guns.

Specifications	
Crew: 3	Muzzle Velocity: 762m/s (2500fps)
Weight: 0.43 tonnes (0.39 tons)	Range: 600m (656 yards)
Length: 1.67m (5ft 5.5in)	Ammunition: Armour-piercing
Calibre: 37mm (1.5in)	

▲ **15cm schwere Infanteriegeschütz (sIG33)**

7.SS-Infanterie-Regiment / 13.Infanteriegeschütz-Kompanie

Each of *Nord's* three infantry regiments included three infantry battalions. The 13th Company in each regiment was equipped with three light infantry gun platoons and a single heavy platoon with two 15cm (5.9in) sIG33s.

Specifications	
Crew: 5	
Weight: 1.75 tonnes (1.71 tons)	Muzzle Velocity: 241m/s (783fps)
Length: 1.64m (64.57in)	Range: 5504m (6000 yards)
Calibre: 150mm (5.9in)	Ammunition: High explosive or smoke

Combat in Soviet Russia

SEPTEMBER 1941 – SEPTEMBER 1944

Although not an *SS-Freiwilligen,* or volunteer, formation in the classic sense, the 6th SS Division did have a significant foreign volunteer component.

IN SEPTEMBER 1941, the *Kampfgruppe* acquired an artillery regiment, and further reinforcements were planned to bring the *Kampfgruppe* up to full divisional status. Hitler directed that 'a new *SS-Gebirgsbrigade* is to be formed by volunteering Norwegians and Finns. An Austrian *SS-Regiment* is to be attached, and the remaining units are to be deployed from *Kampfgruppe Nord.*'

Although the promised Finnish regiment did not appear, the new *SS-Division Nord* did later include the *Freiwilligen-Schikompanie Norwegen,* later enlarged to become the *Schibataillon Norwegen.*

In the meantime, the unit was placed under the temporary command of the veteran Finnish General Siilasvuo – the only time an SS unit was placed under foreign command. As part of the temporary 'Division J', it was assigned to Siilasvuo's III Finnish Army Corps.

Mountain division

In January 1942, it was decided that the *Nord* Division should be redesignated as a mountain division in the near future, and plans were set afoot to create new units for the division. These were assigned

ORGANIZATION, 1941

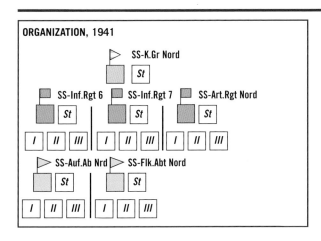

in June and arrived in September 1942, when the division was redesigned *SS-Gebirgs-Division Nord*.

By now detached from 'Division J', *Nord* was assigned to fight alongside the Army's 7.*Gebirgs-Division* in the new German XVIII *Gebirgs-Armee-Korps,* which had arrived in Finland during the winter of 1941 and spring of 1942. In August 1942, the division returned to Finland.

Nord was deployed to hold the line around the Kiestinki area, where it would remain until autumn of 1944. Early in 1943, the Norwegian Ski Battalion was attached to the division, which became 6.*SS-Gebirgs-Division Nord* on 22 October 1943.

 SS-Division *Nord*, Kradschützen-Aufklarungs-Kompanie, schwere Zug

The heavy platoon of the motorcycle reconnaissance company was equipped with heavy machine guns and with two 8.1cm (3.2in) mortars carried by the mortar section.

Stab

1.Gruppe

2.Gruppe

Granatewerfer Gruppe

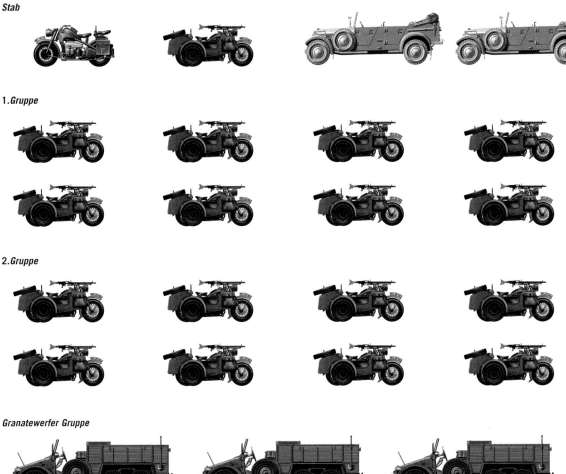

At the same time, a company raised by the Norwegian police was attached to the ski battalion. Also in October, the division provided a cadre of officers for the newly forming 13. *Waffen-Gebirgs-Division der SS Handschar (kroatische Nr. 1)*.

In March 1944, the 2nd Norwegian Police Company, which had been operating with the division, was withdrawn. It was replaced by the 3rd Company of 150 men, assigned to the ski battalion.

On 25 June 1944, after a Soviet assault at Kaprolat, the Norwegian volunteers lost 135 men from a total of 300 in the battalion. The survivors were absorbed by *SS-Polizei-Grenadier-Bataillon (mot) 506*.

▶ Mittlere Nachrichten Kraftwagen (Kfz 15)

SS-Aufklärungs-Abteilung Nord / Kradschützen-Aufklärungs-Kompanie

The headquarters section in each of the motorcycle reconnaissance company's four platoons had two Kfz 15 radio cars.

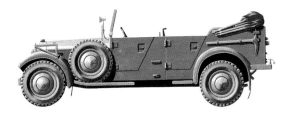

Specifications

Crew: 1	Engine: Mercedes-Benz 6-cylinder petrol
Weight: 2.4 tonnes (2.2 tons)	(90hp)
Length: 4.44m (14ft 7in)	Speed: 88km/h (55mph)
Width: 1.68m (5ft 6in)	Range: 400km (250 miles)
Height: 1.73m (5ft 8in)	Radio: Various depending on deployment

▶ 21cm Wurfgranate 42

SS-Gebirgs-Infanterie-Regiment Reinhard Heydrich / Nebelwerfer-Batterie

Designed originally as a smoke projector, the *Nebelwerfer* was used almost exclusively as an artillery weapon. It could fire a 10kg (18lb) high-explosive warhead out to a range of nearly 8km (5 miles).

Specifications

Crew: 3	Calibre: 21cm (8.27in)
Weight: 109kg (240lb) overall; 18.27kg	Muzzle Velocity: 320m/s (1050fps)
(40.25lb) propellant	Range: 7850m (8580 yards)
Length: 1.25m (4ft 1in)	Ammunition: High-explosive

▲ 8.8cm Flak 18/Mittlere ZgKw (SdKfz 7)

SS-Gebirgs-Division Nord / Flak-Abteilung / 3.Batterie

Nord's Flak battalion's 1st Battery operated 12 self-propelled 2cm (0.7in) Flak 36 guns; the 2nd Battery had 12 towed 2cm (0.7in) guns (later replaced by 3.7cm/1.5in weapons) and the heavy 3rd Battery was equipped with four towed 8.8cm (3.5in) Flak 18 weapons.

Specifications

Crew: 2	Engine: Maybach HL62 6-cylinder (140hp)
Weight: 1.16 tonnes (1.06 tons)	Speed: 50km/h (31mph)
Length: 6.85m (20ft 3in)	Range: 250km (156 miles)
Width: 2.40m (7ft 10.5in)	Radio: None
Height: 2.62m (8ft 7.1in)	

Arctic operations
JULY 1941 – AUGUST 1944

The border between Russia and Finland offered some of the hardest combat of the war, and after a shaky start the 6th SS Division played a major part in the action north of the Arctic Circle.

FORMED SOON after the creation of the 5th SS Division *Wiking*, the SS *Nord* formation was not to become a division for some time. Constructed around members of the *Totenkopfstandarten* of the *Allgemeine-SS*, *SS-Kampfgruppe Nord* was transferred to Norway for garrison duty.

Trained by the Finns

The *Kampfgruppe* participated in Operation *Silver Fox*, the liberation of part of Soviet-occupied Finland, and the invasion of Soviet Karelia. Routed by the Soviets at Salla in the summer of 1941, it was retrained by the Finns, and operating with the German Army's 7th Mountain Division it performed well for the rest of the war.

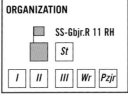

ORGANIZATION

SS-Gbjr.R 11 RH
St
I | II | III | Wr | Pzjr

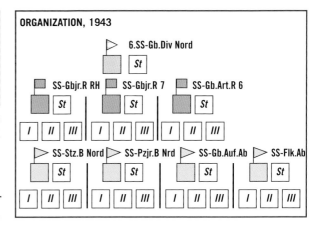

ORGANIZATION, 1943

6.SS-Gb.Div Nord — *St*

SS-Gbjr.R RH — *St* | SS-Gbjr.R 7 — *St* | SS-Gb.Art.R 6 — *St*
I | II | III || I | II | III || I | II | III

SS-Stz.B Nord — *St* | SS-Pzjr.B Nrd — *St* | SS-Gb.Auf.Ab — *St* | SS-Flk.Ab — *St*
I | II | III || I | II | III || I | II | III || I | II | III

As 6.*SS-Gebirgs-Division Nord*, the formation fought in the Arctic for 1214 consecutive days from 1 July 1941. One of its most effective units was the *SS-Freiwilligen-Schusskompanie Norwegen* – expert skiers from Norway, Sweden and Denmark, who were used on long-range reconnaissance patrols.

▲ **Leichte Pkw Stoewer 40 (Kfz 2)**
SS-Gebirgsjäger-Regiment Reinhard Heydrich / Stab

The motor pool assigned to the divisional staff usually had five light cars like the Stoewer or the VW *Kübel*, five medium cars and an assortment of motorcycles, trucks and specialist communications and maintenance vehicles.

▲ **5cm Panzerabwehrkanone (Pak 38)**
7.SS-Gebirgs-Regiment / Gebirgs-Panzerjäger-Kompanie

The regimental anti-tank companies were reorganized in the summer of 1942, each company receiving a pair of 5cm (2in) Pak 38s to supplement the 3.7cm (1.5in) Pak 36 guns that had been the division's only anti-tank weapons.

Specifications

Crew: 1	Engine: Stoewer AW2 or R180W petrol (50hp)
Weight: 1.81 tonnes (1.65 tons)	Speed: 100km/h (62.5mph)
Length: 3.58m (11ft 9in)	Range: 500km (311 miles)
Width: 1.57m (5ft 2in)	Radio: None
Height: 1.78 (5ft 10in)	

Specifications

Crew: 3	Muzzle Velocity (AP): 835m/s (2900fps)
Weight: 1.2 tonnes (1.13 tons)	Range: AP: 1800m (1968 yards), HE: 2.6km
Length: 3.2m (10ft 5in)	(1.6 miles)
Calibre: 50mm (2in)	Ammunition: Armour-piercing, high explosive

▶ **Panzerjäger 38(t) fur 7.62cm Pak 36(r) (SdKfz 139)**

7.SS-Gebirgs-Regiment / Gebirgs-Panzerjäger-Kompanie

The division received nine Marder tank-hunters in April 1943. Equipped with Soviet guns, they only served in the division for a month.

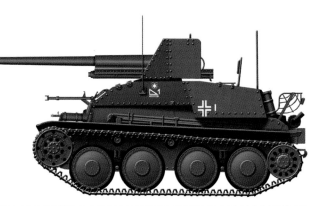

Specifications

Crew: 4	Speed: 42km/h (26mph)
Weight: 11.76 tonnes (10.67 tons)	Range: 185km (115 miles)
Length: 5.85m (19ft 2in)	Radio: FuG Spr 'd'
Width: 2.16m (7ft 0in)	Armament: 1 x 76.2mm (3in) FK296
Height: 2.50m (8ft 2in)	anti-tank gun
Engine: Praga EPA or EPA/2	

 # Retreat from the north
SEPTEMBER 1944 – MAY 1945

When the Finns made a separate peace with the Soviets in the autumn of 1944, German forces in Finland were faced with a fighting retreat through what was now hostile territory.

O N 2 SEPTEMBER 1944, the Finns withdrew from the war. The next day, all German units received the message: *Birke anschlagen,* or 'Cut the birch'. The message was a warning to prepare for the evacuation of Finland. Two days later, the message *Birke fällen* ('Birch has fallen') ordered the evacuation to begin.

During August and September, the Germans had activated two temporary units called *Kampfgruppe West* and *Ost* to secure their southern flank. Units from *Nord,* together with *Divisiongruppe Kräutler,* formed the bulk of thezse two battle groups.

At the end of September, the two *Kampfgruppen* fought several short engagements with their erstwhile Finnish allies, but the retreat was not slowed to any great degree.

Nord reached Norway in October 1944. At the end of the year, it was transferred to Germany, where it took part in Operation *Nordwind.* This was an

▲ **7.5cm Panzerabwehrkanone (Pak 40)**

SS-Panzerjäger-Abteilung Nord

Briefly equipped with self-propelled Marder I tank-hunters, the anti-tank battalion was to have had them replaced by towed Pak 40s in May 1943.

Specifications

Crew: 3	Muzzle Velocity (AP): 990m/s (3248fps)
Weight: 1.5 tonnes (1.37 tons)	Range: AP: 2000m (2190 yards), HE: 7.5km
Length: 3.7m (12ft 1.5in)	(4.66 miles)
Calibre: 75mm (3in)	Ammunition: Armour-piercing, high explosive

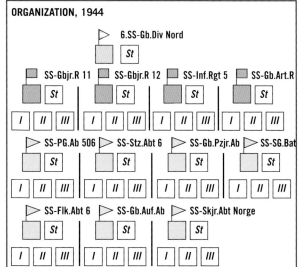

ORGANIZATION, 1944

abortive attack mounted south of the Ardennes in January 1945, the last major German offensive in the West. Designed to take pressure off the main Ardennes offensive, the action saw *SS-Kampfgruppe Schreiber*, made up from *SS-Gebirgsjäger-Regiment* 12, pass through US VI Corps lines to seize Wingen-sur-Moder. Promised panzer back-up having been diverted elsewhere, the *Kampfgruppe* had to fight its way back to German lines, losing 500 out of 725 men in the process.

ORGANIZATION

SS-Skjr.Abt Nrg

St

1 2 3 MG

Final actions

After a period on the defensive in the Vosges Mountains, *Nord* was transferred to the Saar, where it was employed against Patton's Third Army. In April 1945, *Nord* retreated south to Bavaria, where it surrendered to the Americans in May 1945.

▲ *Nebelwerfer* **artillery**

Although not particularly accurate, a battery of *Nebelwerfer* firing salvos of high-explosive rockets was a very effective area weapon against unprotected troops.

▶ **2cm Flakvierling auf ZgKw 8t (SdKfz 7/1)**

SS-Flak-Abteilung Nord

The *Nord* Flak battalion was equipped with the usual mix of 2cm (0.7in), 3.7cm (1.5in) and 8.8cm (3.5in) towed weapons but by 1944 had also taken on strength two self-propelled light Flak batteries.

Specifications

Crew: 7	Engine: Maybach HL 62 TUK
Weight: 1.16 tonnes	6-cylinder (140hp)
(1.06 tons)	Speed: 50km/h (31mph)
Length: 6.55m (21ft 6in)	Range: 250km (156 miles)
Width: 2.40m (7ft 10.5in)	Radio: None
Height: 3.20m (10ft 6in)	Armament: Quad 20mm
	(0.7in) Flak 38

▶ **Mittlere Lkw Opel Blitz S 3t**

6.SS-Gebirgs-Division Nord

In 1944, as the division retreated through Finland, it was supported by two truck parks, which supplied the division's transport and supply columns. The 120-tonne (109-ton) supply column operated up to 40 medium trucks like this Opel Blitz.

Specifications

Crew: 1	Engine: Opel 6-cylinder petrol
Weight: 3.29 tonnes (3 tons)	(73.5hp)
Length: 6.02m (19ft 9in)	Speed: 80km/h (50mph)
Width: 2.27m (7ft 5in)	Range: 410km (255 miles)
Height: 2.18m (7ft 2in)	Radio: None

7th SS Freiwilligen Gebirgs Division *Prince Eugen*

One of the most effective of all German anti-partisan units, the *Prinz Eugen* Mountain Division was also one of the most feared for its brutal tactics in an already brutal war.

THE 7.*SS-FREIWILLIGEN-GEBIRGS-DIVISION* Prinz *Eugen* was created for partisan operations in the Balkans, and the bulk of its strength consisted of ethnic German *Volksdeutsche* volunteers and conscripts from Romania, Hungary and Yugoslavia.

Formed as a mountain division, *Prinz Eugen* was equipped with obsolete and captured equipment such as Czech-made machine guns and French light tanks. Despite the limited equipment, it was one of the most effective counterinsurgency units the Germans fielded in Yugoslavia during the war, and was greatly feared by the partisans. However, that reputation was gained primarily by brutality and utter ruthlessness.

Volksdeutsche volunteers

The origins of the *Prinz Eugen* Division can be found in Himmler's desire to form entire SS units from the massive manpower resource that was the large *Volksdeutsche* community living outside Germany's borders. Many *Volksdeutsche* were already serving in the *Wehrmacht,* but they had primarily joined as individual volunteers.

Gottlob Berger, head of the SS recruiting office, proposed to form a new SS division early in 1942. It was to be made up of volunteers from the large *Volksdeutsche* community living in Serbia, Croatia and the Banat.

The new *Freiwilligen-Gebirgs-Division* was initially established in March 1942. At its core were two Croatian units, an *SS-Selbstschutz* (a locally recruited SS protection force) and a unit known as the *Einsatz-Staffel Prinz Eugen.*

Commanders

Obergruppenführer Arthur Phleps
January 1942 – May 1943

Brigadeführer Karl Reichsritter von Oberkamp
May 1943 – January 1944

Brigadeführer Otto Kumm
January 1944 – January 1945

Brigadeführer August Schmidthuber
January 1945 – May 1945

INSIGNIA

Prinz Eugen used an ancient symbol from the Futharc Runic alphabet, modified with extra 'feet' to distinguish it from the symbol used by the 4th Infantry Division.

Divisional History	Formed
SS-Selbstschutz	1941
Einsatz-Staffel Prinz Eugen	1941
Freiwilligen-Gebirgs-Division	1942
SS-Freiwilligen-Division Prinz Eugen	1942
SS-Freiwilligen-Gebirgs-Division Prinz Eugen	1942
7.SS-Freiwilligen-Gebirgs-Division Prinz Eugen	1943

▼ **Mittlere Lkw Henschel 33D1**

7.SS-Division / Versorgungsdienst

As formed, the *Prinz Eugen* Division's supply service was largely horse-drawn, but by March 1943 it was split almost equally between horse-drawn and motorized transport.

Specifications

Crew: 1

Weight: 6.1 tonnes (6 tons)

Length: 7.4m (24ft)

Width: 2.25m (7ft 4in)

Height: 3.2m (10ft 6in)

Engine: 10.7L (650ci),
6-cylinder petrol (100hp)

Speed: 60km/h (37mph)

Payload: 3 tonnes (2.95 tons)
or 18 troops

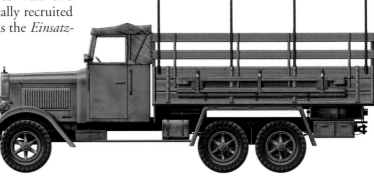

▶ Panzerkampfwagen B2 740(f)

SS-Panzer-Abteilung Prinz Eugen

Large numbers of Char B tanks were captured in France in 1940.

Specifications

Crew: 4	Engine: Renault 6-cylinder petrol
Weight: 31 tonnes (30.5 tons)	(307bhp)
Length: 6.37m (20ft 10in)	Speed: 28km/h (17.5mph)
Width: 2.5m (8ft 2in)	Range: 180km (112 miles)
Height: 2.79m (9ft 2in)	Armament: 1 x 75mm (2.95in) cannon

▶ Panzerkampfwagen 35-S 739(f)

SS-Panzer-Abteilung Prinz Eugen

About half of *Prinz Eugen*'s Panzer strength was provided by captured tanks. The Somua S-35 was one of the best of the French tanks pressed into service.

Specifications

Crew: 3	Engine: SOMUA V-8 petrol engine
Weight: 19.5 tonnes (18.7 tons)	(190bhp)
Length: 5.38m (17ft 8in)	Speed: 40km/h (25mph)
Width: 2.12m (7ft)	Range: 230km (143 miles)
Height: 2.62m (8ft 7in)	Armament: 1 x 47mm (1.8in) cannon

Anti-partisan operations
1942

Early hopes that there would be a flood of ethnic German volunteers to make up the numbers for the new division proved unrealistic.

THE SS HAD to introduce conscription from among the *Volksdeutsche* community to reach a target divisional strength of 21,500 men for *Prinz Eugen*. This did not please the Pavelic government in Croatia, which felt that its German allies were poaching on national preserves.

Action in Serbia

The new SS division was intended for use in anti-partisan warfare in the Balkans. In October 1942, it saw its first major action in the south of Serbia, in mountainous terrain east of the Ibar River, near the Montenegro border. By now, it had been reclassified as a mountain division, and its designation changed to the *SS-Freiwilligen-Gebirgs-Division Prinz Eugen*.

Late in 1942, *Prinz Eugen* was transferred to the Zagreb–Karlovac area. There it was one of several

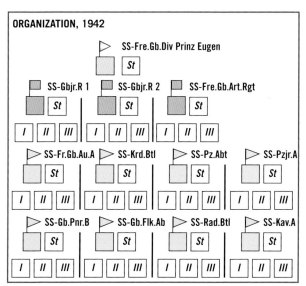

units that were taking part in the massive anti-partisan operation known as Operation *White*. This was one of a series of major anti-partisan operations conducted in the region, whose primary aim was to destroy the Communist resistance movement led by Tito. Some partisans were indeed killed, but for the most part the operation proved to be a failure, since the bulk of Tito's forces managed to evade the German offensive.

In 1942, *Prinz Eugen* was assigned to the *Wehrmacht*'s Army Group E. In May of that year, the division took part in another major anti-partisan campaign, known as Operation *Black*. Later in the year, elements of the division were sent to Bosnia, operating to the north of Sarajevo. After that, the division was deployed around Mostar, and for the next year it would continue to play its part in the fiercely fought, no-quarter-given partisan war.

▲ 3.7cm Panzerabwehrkanone (Pak 36)

13.Waffen-SS-Gebirgsjäger-Regiment / I.Bataillon / schwere Kompanie

The heavy company attached to each Gebirgsjäger battalion had a pioneer platoon, an infantry gun platoon, a mortar platoon and a Panzerjäger platoon that was equipped with two light 3.7cm (1.5in) Pak 36 guns.

Specifications

Crew: 3	Muzzle Velocity: 762m/s (2500fps)
Weight: 0.43 tonnes (0.39 tons)	Range: 600m (656 yards)
Length: 1.67m (5ft 5.5in)	Ammunition: Armour-piercing
Calibre: 37mm (1.5in)	

▲ 15cm schwere Feldhaubitze (sFH18)

7.SS-Gebirgs-Artillerie-Regiment / IV.Abteilung / 1.Batterie

The mountain artillery regiment had a mixed bag of artillery pieces, ranging from light mountain pack howitzers to two batteries of long-range 10cm (3.9in) K18 guns and two batteries of 15cm (5.9in) heavy howitzers.

Specifications

Crew: 5	Muzzle Velocity: 520m/s (1706fps)
Weight: 6.3 tonnes (5.7 tons)	Range: 13km (8 miles)
Length: 4.4m (14 ft 5in)	Ammunition: High explosive or smoke
Calibre: 150mm (5.9in)	

▲ 7.5cm Panzerabwehrkanone (Pak 40)

SS-Panzerjäger-Abteilung Prinz Eugen / 1.Kompanie

In July 1944, the 1st Company of the division's tank-hunter battalion had been re-equipped with towed 7.5cm (3in) Pak 40s. The 2nd Company used 5cm (2in) Pak 38s, and the 3rd Company was a self-propelled Flak unit.

Specifications

Crew: 3	Muzzle Velocity (AP): 990m/s (3248fps)
Weight: 1.5 tonnes (1.37 tons)	Range: AP: 2000m (2190 yards), HE: 7.5km
Length: 3.7m (12ft 1.5in)	(4.66 miles)
Calibre: 75mm (3in)	Ammunition: Armour-piercing, high explosive

▲ 5cm Panzerabwehrkanone (Pak 38)

Panzerjäger-Abteilung Prinz Eugen

In its March 1943 table of organization and equipment, the *Prinz Eugen* Division's tank-hunter battalion consisted of three motorized companies, each equipped with nine 5cm (2in) Pak 38 towed guns.

Specifications

Crew: 3	Muzzle Velocity (AP): 835m/s (2900fps)
Weight: 1.2 tonnes (1.13 tons)	Range: AP: 1800m (1968 yards), HE: 2.6km
Length: 3.2m (10 ft 5in)	(1.6 miles)
Calibre: 50mm (2in)	Ammunition: Armour-piercing, high explosive

▼ 7.SS-Panzer-Abteilung, 2.Panzer-Kompanie

Captured armour was mainly used for training or for occupation duties. However, the inability of German industry to provide an adequate supply of tanks meant that such vehicles were pressed into operational use in areas where they were unlikely to meet first-line Allied armour. *Prinz Eugen*'s Panzer battalion had two companies, the first being equipped with German tanks. The 2nd Company was exclusively equipped with foreign, mostly French, tanks.

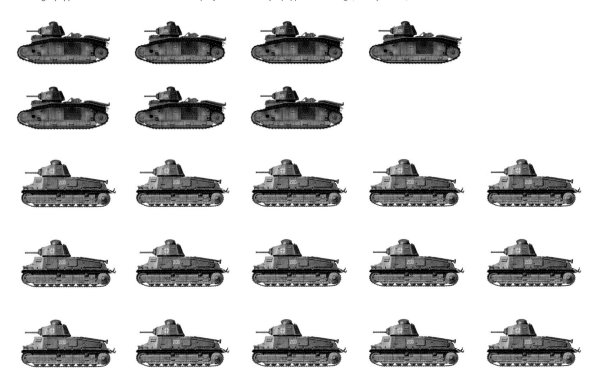

Target Tito
1943–1944

In the summer of 1943, the *Prinz Eugen* Division was sent to the Dalmatian coast, where in September it disarmed Italian units in the region after the Badoglio government signed an armistice with the Allies.

P*RINZ EUGEN* WAS THEN USED to occupy former Italian positions on Brac, Hvar and Korcula Islands and on the Peljesac Peninsula.

In August 1943, *Prinz Eugen* came under the control of the *Wehrmacht*'s XV.*Gebirgs-Korps* (XV Mountain Corps), part of the Second Panzer Army under Army Group F.

In November 1943, *Prinz Eugen* was transferred to V.*SS-Gebirgs-Korps*. In December, the *Prinz Eugen*

Division fought with the mountain corps from the area northwest of Sarajevo south to Gorazde.

On 21 September 1944, the former divisional commander, *SS-Obergruppenführer* and General of the *Waffen-SS* Arthur Phleps, was killed en route from Montenegro to Transylvania, where he was to form a front against the Red Army. In October 1943, *Prinz Eugen* officially became the 7.*SS-Freiwilligen-Gebirgs-Division Prinz Eugen*. In December 1943, the 7th SS Division once more moved inland, where actions against Tito's forces, as before, proved to be less than effective.

Partisan battles

In January 1944, the 7th SS Division was transferred to the area around Split and Dubrovnik for training, recuperation and re-equipment. In March, it was back in Bosnia, where it again took up the fight against Tito's partisans, with a major battle being fought at Drvar in May.

The goal of this operation was to kill or capture Tito himself on Drvar Island. *Prinz Eugen* played a supporting role; the actual snatch was to be made by the *SS-Fallschirmjäger-Bataillon* 500 and the 1st *Brandenburg* Regiment. However, the assault missed Tito.

After Drvar, the 7th SS Division was sent on further anti-partisan operations. In May, the division saw action in Operation *Waldrausch*, then took part in Operation *Freie Jagd* in June and July; between 12

and 30 August, it was part of Operation *Rübezahl*, which was designed to prevent partisan forces from moving into Montenegro.

```
COMBAT UNITS ORGANIZATION, 1944

                         7.SS-Fre.Gb.Div Prinz Eugen
                         St

  SS-Fr.Gbjr.R 13   SS-Fr.Gbjr.R 14   SS-Fr.Gb.Art.Rgt 7
  St                St                St
  I   II   III      I   II   III      I   II   III

  SS-Fr.Gb.Au.A   SS-Pz.Abt      SS-Gb.Pnr.B   SS-Pzjr.A
  St              St             St            St
  I   II   III    I   II   III   I   II   III  I   II   III

  SS-Gb.Flk.A   SS-Rad.Btl   SS-Kav.Abt
  St            St           St
  I   II   III  I   II   III  I   II   III
```

▶ Panzerkampfwagen II Ausf F (SdKfz 121)

7.SS-Freiwilligen-Gebirgs-Division Prince Eugen / Divisionsstab / Panzer-Aufklärungs-Zug

In July 1944, the divisional HQ had one Panzer reconnaissance platoon equipped with old Panzer II light tanks.

Specifications

Crew: 4	Speed: 40km/h (25mph)
Weight: 21.8 tonnes (19.8 tons)	Range: 165km (102 miles)
Length: 5.38m (17ft 7in)	Radio: FuG5
Width: 2.91m (9ft 5in)	Armament: 1 x 20mm (0.7in) cannon;
Height: 2.44m (8ft)	1 x 7.92mm (0.3in) MG
Engine: Maybach HL120TR	

▶ Leichte Schützenpanzerwagen (SdKfz 250/1)

7.SS-Freiwilligen-Gebirgs-Division Prince Eugen / Divisionsstab / Spw Aufklärungs-Zug

Alongside the Panzer IIs, the HQ reconnaissance element included a platoon of light reconnaissance SdKfz 250 half-tracks.

Specifications

Crew: 2 plus 4 troops	(100hp)
Weight: 5.9 tonnes (5.38 tons)	Speed: 60km/h (37mph)
Length: 4.61m (15ft 1in)	Range: 300km (186 miles)
Width: 1.95m (6ft 5in)	Radio: FuG Spr Ger 'f'
Height: 1.66m (5ft 5in)	Armament: 1 x 7.92mm (0.3in) MG
Engine: Maybach HL42TRKM 6-cylinder	

▶ **Leichte Schützenpanzerwagen (SdKfz 250/9)**

7.SS Aufklärungs-Abteilung / Stab-Kompanie

Prinz Eugen's reconnaissance assets in August 1944 ranged from horse cavalry and bicycle-mounted troops to modern half-track reconnaissance vehicles like the SdKfz 250/9, four of which were used by the reconnaissance battalion staff.

Specifications

Crew: 3	(100hp)
Weight: 6.9 tonnes (6.3 tons)	Speed: 60km/h (37mph)
Length: 4.56m (14ft 11.5in)	Range: 320km (199 miles)
Width: 1.95m (6ft 5in)	Radio: FuG Spr Ger 'f'
Height: 2.16m (7ft 1in)	Armament: 1 x 20mm (0.7in) KwK 30/38 L/55
Engine: Maybach HL42TRKM 6-cylinder	cannon; 1 x 7.92mm (0.3in) MG (coaxial)

 # Retreat from Bosnia
1944–1945

The battle against the partisans came to an end only when Soviet advances threatened to cut off German forces in the Balkans, and the *Wehrmacht* had to retreat into Croatia and Hungary.

THE RED ARMY'S SUMMER OFFENSIVE was unleashed in June 1944, and the Soviet steamroller threatened to smash through the Axis forces without stopping. In August, *Prinz Eugen* was transferred north to Bulgaria, where it suffered great losses fighting against the Red Army.

Holding the corridor

The Soviet advance threatened to cut off *Heeresgruppe* E in Greece, so in September *Prinz Eugen* and other *Waffen-SS* units were moved south to Macedonia. Linking up with 13.*Waffen-Gebirgs-Division der SS Handschar (kroatische Nr. 1),* the remnants of the 23.*Waffen-Gebirgs-Division der SS Kama (kroatische Nr. 2)* and 21.*Waffen-Gebirgs-Division der SS Skanderbeg (albanische Nr. 1), Prinz Eugen* created the Vardar corridor in Macedonia, allowing the retreat north of 350,000 German soldiers from occupation duties in the Aegean and

Greek regions. While fighting on the flanks of the Vardar corridor, they were subordinated to *Armeekorps Müller,* part of *Generaloberst* Alexander Löhr's *Heeresgruppe* E.

Once again, the 7th SS Division was badly mauled, but the operation succeeded in its main aim. Even though the Red Army had captured Belgrade, the corridor had been held open long enough for the bulk of the trapped German troops to escape. Now the *Prinz Eugen* Division was free to retreat itself, moving from Cacak to Brcko and over the Drina. In

▼ **Leichte Pkw VW (Kfz 1)**

13.Waffen-SS-Gebirgsjäger-Regiment / Stab-Kompanie

Cars had all but replaced motorcycles in staff units by 1944, although solo motorbikes were still used as messengers. The ubiquitous VW *Kübel* was also used as a reconnaissance vehicle.

Specifications

Crew: 1	Engine: Volkswagen 998cc petrol (24hp). Later
Weight: 0.64 tonnes (0.58 tons)	Volkswagen 1131cc petrol (25hp)
Length: 3.73m (12ft 3in)	Speed: 100km/h (62mph)
Width: 1.60m (5ft 3in)	Range: 600km (375 miles)
Height: 1.35m (4ft 5in)	Radio: None

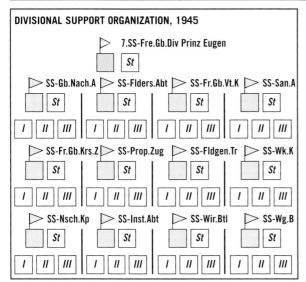

DIVISIONAL SUPPORT ORGANIZATION, 1945

November, the division absorbed the remnants of the disbanded *Skanderbeg* Division.

Final battles

In January 1945, the division fought partisans near Otok, and later was sent to the area of Vukovar, where it fought again against advancing Soviet forces and Tito's partisans. From February 1945 to April 1945, the division was in action against the partisans and the Soviets, retreating from Bosnia through Croatia to defensive positions south of Karlovac.

The division began its final retreat on 10 May 1945, heading towards Celje in Slovenia. Even though the war had officially ended, the division did not surrender to Yugoslav forces on 11 May.

The *Prinz Eugen* SS Division was accused by the Yugoslavs of committing some of the worst atrocities of World War II. In the vicious action against the partisans, the division murdered unarmed civilians, burned and looted entire villages and tortured and massacred men, women and children.

▲ ***Sturmbannführer, Prinz Eugen* Division**

A *Sturmbannführer* (major) from the *Prinz Eugen* Division poses proudly for a portrait photograph, his sleeve demonstrating his divisional identity. Despite the large numbers of *Volksdeutsche* in the division, most officers were German.

▼ **7.5cm Sturmgeschütz 40 Ausf G (SdKfz 142/1)**

SS-Panzerjäger-Abteilung Prinz Eugen / Sturmgeschütz-Kompanie

Before the division suffered heavy losses in the autumn of 1944, one company of the tank-destroyer battalion was issued with 12 assault guns to be used as tank-hunters.

Specifications

Crew: 4	Engine: Maybach HL120TRM
Weight: 26.3 tonnes (24 tons)	Speed: 40km/h (25mph)
Length: 6.77m (22ft 2in)	Range: 155km (96 miles)
Width: 2.95m (9ft 7in)	Radio: FuG15 and FuG16
Height: 2.16m (7ft)	

8th SS Kavallerie Division
Florian Geyer

Cavalry had always been highly regarded by the German armed forces, so it is no surprise that with the expansion of the Armed SS Himmler's private army also formed cavalry units.

T HE *FLORIAN GEYER* Division was one of several SS units that started out as purely German, but which during the course of the war increasingly numbered ethnic-Germans, or *Volksdeutsche*, among its units. It was named after Florian Geyer (1490–1525), a Franconian knight. Geyer was a supporter of Martin Luther (1483–1546), and led the German Peasants' War of 1522–1525.

SS cavalry units

The origins of the *Florian Geyer* Division date back to the original SS cavalry units. The cavalry components of the *SS-Totenkopf-Standarten*, or regiments, were formed in the winter of 1939. As part of the *Allegemeine-*, or General, *SS*, their primary mission was to teach horse-handling, although they had an important secondary role in policing.

In the summer of 1941, the *Totenkopf* cavalry detachments were combined as an *SS-Kavallerie-Regiment* under the aegis of the *Kommandostab-Reichsführer-SS* (RFSS). The cavalry so gathered were

INSIGNIA

Many divisions adopted symbols indicative of the formation's origins. The *Florian Geyer* Division used a horse's head to indicate its cavalry history.

Commanders

Brigadeführer Gustav Lombard
March 1942 – April 1942

Gruppenführer Hermann Fegelein
April 1942 – August 1942

Obergruppenführer Willi Bittrich
August 1942 – February 1943

Brigadeführer Fritz Freitag
February 1943 – April 1943

Brigadeführer Gustav Lombard
April 1943 – May 1943

Gruppenführer Hermann Fegelein
May 1943 – September 1943

Gruppenführer Bruno Streckenbach
September 1943 – October 1943

Gruppenführer Hermann Fegelein
October 1943 – January 1944

Gruppenführer Bruno Streckenbach
January 1944 – April 1944

Brigadeführer Gustav Lombard
April 1944 – July 1944

Brigadeführer Joachim Rumohr
July 1944 – February 1945

Divisional History	Formed
SS-Kavallerie-Brigade	1941
SS-Kavallerie-Division	1942
8.SS-Kavallerie-Division	1943
8.SS-Kavallerie-Division Florian Geyer	1944

▲ **SS cavalry**

This rare colour photograph shows men of the *SS-Kavallerie-Brigade* on the Eastern Front in the summer of 1942.

formed into an official unit in August 1941, known variously as the *SS-Kavallerie-Brigade* or the *SS-Reiter-Brigade*. It was commanded by Hermann Fegelein, and it was often referred to as the *Fegelein* Brigade or *Kampfgruppe Fegelein*.

Hermann Fegelein

Fegelein began his career in Middle Franconia as a groom and then became a jockey. A chance contact with a horse-fancier who was a Nazi led him into the National Socialist Party. Fegelein's knowledge of horses led the *Waffen-SS* to select him as the commanding officer of the *SS-Kavallerie* units, and he became commander of the new brigade. on its formation in 1941.

He was wounded in September 1943 south of Kharkov and posted to the Führer's HQ as Himmler's official SS liaison officer.

Specifications

Crew: 3	Muzzle Velocity: 762m/s (2500fps)
Weight: 0.43 tonnes (0.39 tons)	Range: 600m (656 yards)
Length: 1.67m (5ft 5.5in)	Ammunition: Armour-piercing
Calibre: 37mm (1.5in)	

▼ **Leichte Panzerspähwagen (SdKfz 222)**

8.Panzer-Aufklärungs-Abteilung

The Cavalry Division's reconnaissance unit was originally a bicycle battalion, but early in 1944 this was converted into an armoured car unit equipped with 18 SdKfz 222 light armoured cars.

▲ **3.7cm Panzerabwehrkanone (Pak 36)**

4.Bataillon / Panzerabwehr-Zug

As formed, the SS Cavalry Brigade was known as the *SS-Totenkopf-Reiterstandarte*. It consisted of 12 squadrons organized into four battalions plus attached horse artillery batteries.

Specifications

Crew: 3

Weight: 5.3 tonnes (4.8 tons)

Length: 4.8m (15ft 8in)

Width: 1.95m (6ft 5in)

Height: 2.00m (6ft 7in)

Engine: Horch 3.5L or 3.8L petrol

Speed: 85km/h (52.8mph)

Range: 300km (186 miles)

Radio: FuG Spr Ger 'a'

Armament: 1 x 20mm (0.7in) KwK 30 L/55 cannon;
1 x 7.92mm (0.3in) MG (coaxial)

▶ **Leichte Panzerspähwagen (Fu) (SdKfz 223)**

8.Panzer-Aufklärungs-Abteilung

Manufactured until 1944, the SdKfz 223 was designed to provide a communications capability for armoured reconnaissance units. The FuG10 radio had a range of 40km (25 miles) reduced to 10km (6.2 miles) for voice telephony.

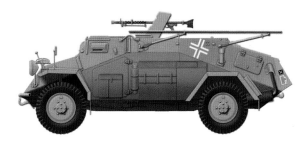

Specifications

Crew: 4	Engine: Horch 3.5L
Weight: 4.7 tonnes (4.3 tons)	Speed: 85km/h (53mph)
Length: 4.83m (15ft 8in)	Range: 310km (192 miles)
Width: 1.99m (6ft 5in)	Radio: FuG Spr Ger 'a' plus FuG7 or FuG12
Height: 1.78m (5ft 8in)	

Combat operations in Russia
1941–1942

The SS Cavalry Brigade operated largely in the front line of the central and southern sectors of the Eastern Front, although its duties also included mounting rear area security patrols.

IN JUNE 1942, the *SS-Kavallerie-Brigade* was upgraded to divisional status with the addition of 9000 Hungarian *Volksdeutsche* volunteers. One month later, the division went into action with the Ninth Army, part of Army Group Centre. It was used to destroy pockets of Soviet resistance around the Vyazma-Bryansk-Rzhev salient. It continued to fight under Ninth Army control until December 1942, when most of the division was sent south to Army Group South. In the Don Basin, it was assigned to the Second Panzer Army as *Kampfgruppe Fegelein*.

In January 1943, the division's reserve and training battalion had been ordered to Warsaw, where it took part in the suppression of the Ghetto uprising. On 18 January, the Jews of the Warsaw Ghetto rose in rebellion as the Germans began deporting the inhabitants, who were ultimately destined for the extermination camps.

Jewish insurgent groups took control of the Ghetto, building dozens of fighting posts and killing Jews they considered to be Nazi collaborators, including Jewish police officers and *Gestapo* agents.

Specifications

Crew: 2	Engine: Maybach HL62 6-cylinder (140hp)
Weight: 1.16 tonnes (1.06 tons)	Speed: 50km/h (31mph)
Length: 6.85m (20ft 3in)	Range: 250km (156 miles)
Width: 2.40m (7ft 10.5in)	Radio: None
Height: 2.62m (8ft 7.1in)	

▲ **Mittlere Zugraftwagen 8t / 8.8cm Flak 18 (SdKfz 7)**

8.SS-Flak-Abteilung / schwere Batterie

Florian Geyer had been operating with a heavy Flak battery since the days of the SS Cavalry Brigade in 1941. The battery was equipped with four towed Flak 18 guns, the famous 'Eighty-Eight' that could also be used as an anti-tank gun.

▶ **Mittlere Zugkraftwagen 8t 3.7cm Flak 36 Sf (SdKfz 7/2)**

SS-Flak-Abteilung

In the summer of 1942, the SS Cavalry Division's Flak battalion had two self-propelled batteries with 2cm (0.7in) and 3.7cm (1.5in) guns. Later in the war, these were replaced by motorized units with towed guns.

Specifications

Crew: 7	Engine: Maybach HL62TUK
Weight: 1.16 tonnes	6-cylinder (140hp)
(1.06 tons)	Speed: 50km/h (31mph)
Length: 6.55m (21ft 6in)	Range: 250km (156 miles)
Width: 2.40m (7ft 10.5in)	Armament: Twin 37mm (1.5in)
Height: 3.20m (10ft 6in)	Flak 36/37/43 L/89

▲ **7.5cm Panzerabwehrkanone (Pak 40)**

15.Waffen-SS-Kavallerie-Regiment / schwere Schwadrone / Pzjr.Zug

The heavy squadrons of the division's four cavalry regiments each had an anti-tank platoon equipped with three towed Pak 40s.

Specifications

Crew: 3	Muzzle Velocity (AP): 990m/s (3248fps)
Weight: 1.5 tonnes (1.37 tons)	Range: AP: 2000m (2190 yards), HE: 7.5km
Length: 3.7m (12ft 1.5in)	(4.66 miles)
Calibre: 75mm (3in)	Ammunition: Armour-piercing, high explosive

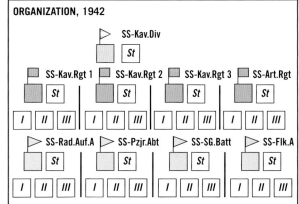

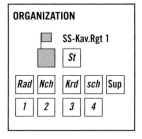

Suppression of the Warsaw Ghetto

Over the next three months, the Ghetto fought off increasingly heavy German attacks as SS troops, *Ordnungspolizei, Sicherheitsdienst* units, Army troops and Ukrainian, Latvian and Lithuanian auxiliaries sought to end the stalemate. The final battle began on 19 April as the Germans used smoke grenades and gas to force the Jews from their bunkers. The uprising ended on 16 May 1943. Most of the 50,000 survivors of the Ghetto were sent to the death camp at Treblinka, northeast of Warsaw.

In January and February 1943, the rest of the division was again under the control of Ninth Army, where it saw extensive combat south of Orel. In March, it was part of XLVII Armoured Corps. In April 1943, it was moved to Bobruysk for refitting. The Cavalry Division's primary mission was now security, its units being increasingly used behind the front lines to mop up bypassed Soviet units.

In May 1943, the *SS-Kavallerie-Division* began the anti-partisan campaign that it would fight until the end of the war. Successful in this brutal form of combat, the division was transferred to Army Group South in July 1943. It was ordered to Croatia, where it would be used for combat against Tito's Communist partisans.

Czechoslovakia and Poland
1943–1944

As a mounted formation, the division was effective against the partisans, having the advantage over them on foot and able to operate more rapidly over terrain impassable to vehicles.

THE DIVISION SAW A CONSIDERABLE amount of action at Bespalowka and Bol-Gomolscha before being withdrawn to Croatia for rest and refitting. On 23 October, the unit was redesignated as *8.SS-Kavallerie-Division*. At the end of the year, the division had over 9300 men on strength, the bulk being Hungarian *Volksdeutsche*.

In January and February 1944, the division continued anti-partisan operations. In March, the divisional units were dispersed, being used for anti-partisan operations in the Balkans, Hungary and Poland. On 12 March, the division received the honour title 'Florian Geyer', becoming the *8.SS-Kavallerie-Division Florian Geyer*.

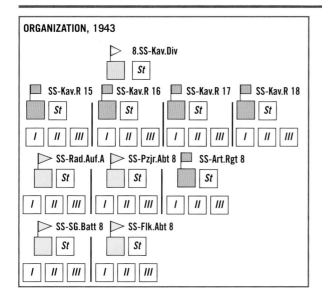

ORGANIZATION, 1943

Budapest. In April, one of the division's regiments – *SS-Kavallerie-Regiment* 17 – was dispatched to Kisber, Hungary, for rest and refitting. From there, the unit would form the nucleus of *22.SS-Freiwilligen-Kavallerie-Division Maria Theresia*, made up largely of Hungarian *Volksdeutche* troops.

While it operated in small groups against Yugoslav partisans, the 8th SS Cavalry Division nevertheless retained its supporting arms. These included artillery assets of 32 10.5cm (4.1in) field howitzers and four 15cm (5.9in) howitzers; Flak units with 2cm (0.7in) and 3.7cm (1.5in) guns; as well as 35 7.5cm (3in) and 8.8cm (3.5in) anti-tank guns. Infantry weapons included 30 8.1cm (3.2in) mortars, four Soviet 12cm (4.7in) mortars, 213 light machine guns and 42 heavy machine guns. The two SS cavalry divisions operated together in the defensive battles in the difficult terrain of Transylvania. The SS probably intended to organize them into a cavalry corps, but due to the continuous combat they experienced this was never accomplished and they came under the control of the IX SS Mountain Corps.

On 19 March, elements of the *Florian Geyer* Division became part of *Kampfgruppe Streckenbach* under *SS-Gruppenführer* Bruno Streckenbach. The unit was transferred north from Osijek, Yugoslavia, to

▶ **7.5cm Pak 40 auf PzJäg 38 (t) Marder III**

8.SS-Panzerjäger-Abteilung / Panzerjäger-Kompanie (Sf)

When fighting on the Eastern Front, the Cavalry Division's tank-hunting battalion had one self-propelled company equipped with Marders. These were replaced by towed guns when the division switched to anti-partisan operations.

Specifications

Crew: 4	Speed: 35km/h (22mph)
Weight: 10.8 tonnes (9.8 tons)	Range: 240km (150 miles)
Length: 5.77m (19ft 11in)	Radio: FuG Spr Ger 1
Width: 2.16m (7ft 1in)	Armament: 1 x 75mm (3in) Pak 40/3 L/46
Height: 2.51m (8ft 3in)	anti-tank gun; 1 x 7.92mm (0.3in) MG
Engine: Praga EPA 6-cylinder (140hp)	

▶ **Sturmgeschütz 7.5cm Sturmkanone 40 Ausf F8 (SdKfz 142/1)**

8.SS-Sturmgeschütz-Abteilung / 1.Kompanie

In October 1943, the divison had a single assault gun battalion assigned. In June 1944, this was absorbed by the division's *Panzerjäger-Abteilung.*

Specifications

Crew: 4	Engine: Maybach HL120TRM petrol (300hp)
Weight: 25.6 tonnes (23.3 tons)	Speed: 40km/h (25mph)
Length: 6.77m (22ft 2in)	Range: 210km (87 miles)
Width: 2.92m (9ft 7in)	Radio: FuG15 or FuG16
Height: 2.15m (7ft)	Armament: 1 x 75mm (3in) StuK 40

▶ **Anti-partisan cavalry**
Both the German Army and the SS used cavalry in the partisan war, such troops
being particularly effective in difficult terrain.

The reverses in the Balkans in the summer of 1944 convinced Hungary that the Axis had lost the war. In October 1944, the government of Admiral Horthy decided to follow the examples of Romania and Bulgaria and sought to come to terms with the Soviets. To stop the Hungarian defection, Hitler ordered that Hungary be occupied, and an SS team led by *Obersturmbannführer* Otto Skorzeny kidnapped Horthy's son to force the admiral to resign in favour of a pro-German government.

But the Red Army was little more than 100km (62 miles) from Budapest. On 20 October, it captured Debrecen in eastern Hungary and attacked towards Budapest on 29 October. Soviet tanks were in Vecses and Kispest by 3 November. However, the Soviet advance was slowed by dogged German resistance as reinforcements were rushed to Hungary.

In November, the 8th SS Division was moved north to became part of the Budapest garrison. By December, the Red Army had reached the shores of Lake Balaton. By Christmas Eve, Budapest had been surrounded by 250,000 Soviet troops of the 2nd and 3rd Ukrainian Fronts. In the ensuing siege, 800,000 civilians were trapped in the city.

▶ **Schwere Panzerspähwagen 8-Rad (SdKfz 231/1)**
6.Panzer-Aufklärungs-Abteilung

In March 1944, the division's bicycle reconnaissance battalion was fully motorized
and restructured as an armoured reconnaissance battalion with five companies.
The armoured car platoon was enlarged to full company size.

Specifications

Crew: 4	Engine: Büssing-NAG 8-cylinder
Weight: 9.1 tonnes (8.3 tons)	petrol (150hp)
Length: 5.85m (19ft 2in)	Speed: 85km/h (52.8mph)
Width: 2.20m (7ft 2.5in)	Range: 300km (186 miles)
Height: 2.35m (7ft 8in)	Radio: FuG Ger 'a'
	Armament: 1 x 20mm (0.7in) cannon

Destroyed in Hungary
1945

During the fighting for Budapest, the SS units in the city were pulled back to Buda on the west bank of the Danube. Their only hope was a planned relief effort, which never came.

AFTER SEVERAL WEEKS OF BITTER fighting, the Buda pocket had been reduced to a semi-circle about 1000m (1093 yards) across. On 11 February 1945, the remnants of the division attempted a last-ditch breakout along with what was left of the *22.SS-Freiwilligen-Kavallerie-Division Maria Theresia*, and the *33.Waffen-Kavallerie-Division der SS*. Budapest fell on 12 February.

8TH SS KAVALLERIE DIVISION *FLORIAN GEYER*

▼ 8.Flak-Abteilung / 2.Batterie

Much harder-hitting and with a longer range than the 2cm (0.7in) Flak guns with which most German units had started the war, the 3.7cm (1.5in) Flak 36/37 had a maximum effective vertical range of 4800m (15,748ft) but was generally used against low-flying targets. It could also be effective against soft-skin vehicles and light armour, and was also lethal against the kind of improvised fortifications encountered in the partisan war. Initially towed by the Kfz 69 Krupp Protze, by the later years of the war these pre-war light trucks were being replaced by variants of the German Army's standard heavy car chassis, the *schwere Einheits Personenkraftwagen*.

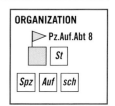

ORGANIZATION

▷ Pz.Auf.Abt 8

St

| Spz | Auf | sch |

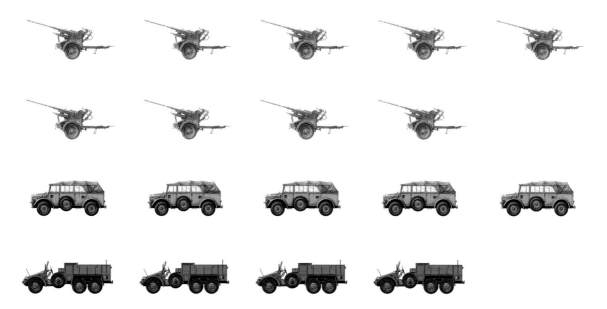

▲ Winter positions

Hungarian defence minister Marshal Karoly Beregfy visits the *Florian Geyer* Division in its defensive positions at Budapest late in 1944. By Christmas, the German garrison of the city had been cut off by the Red Army, and the 8th SS Cavalry Division was fighting for its existence.

The division was annihilated. Only 170 survivors managed to reach the German lines. The 8th SS Division's commander, *SS-Brigadeführer* Joachim Rumohr, commited suicide, while the members of the formation who got away were transferred to the newly forming 37th SS Cavalry Division. However, this unit never reached full strength.

Fegelein executed

Hermann Fegelein, the unit's original commander, did not long survive the division he had founded. Having become one of Hitler's inner circle, he had married Margarete Braun, Eva Braun's sister, on 3 June 1944. Fegelein was in the *Führerbunker* in Berlin in the last days of the *Reich*.

As Berlin fell to the Soviets, Fegelein tried to escape from the city with a mistress, who may have been an Allied spy. Captured by the *Gestapo*, he was shot for desertion on 29 April 1945.

▲ **10.5cm leichte Feldhaubitze leFH18**

8.SS-Artillerie-Regiment / I.Abteilung / 1.Batterie

Florian Geyer's artillery regiment had three battalions, each equipped with three batteries of 10.5cm (4.1in) howitzers. The division had no heavy artillery from the summer of 1944.

Specifications

Crew: 5	Muzzle Velocity: 540m/s (1770fps)
Weight: 1.95 tonnes (1.85 tons)	Range: 12,325m (13,480 yards)
Length: 3.3m (10ft)	Ammunition: High explosive or smoke
Calibre: 105mm (4.1in)	

▶ **Mittlere Lkw Opel Blitz 3.6-3600S**

8.SS Kavallerie Division Florian Geyer / Versorgungstruppe

For much of the war, the 8th Cavalry Division utilized horse-drawn transport, but by 1944 the divisional supply unit had three 120-tonne (118-ton) capacity transport companies each with 40 or more medium cargo-carrying trucks.

Specifications

Crew: 1	Engine: Opel 6-cylinder petrol
Weight: 3.29 tonnes (3 tons)	(73.5hp)
Length: 6.02m (19ft 9in)	Speed: 80km/h (50mph)
Width: 2.27m (7ft 5in)	Range: 410km (255 miles)
Height: 2.18m (7ft 2in)	Radio: None

▶ **Leichte Personenkraftwagen VW Kübel (Kfz 1)**

8.SS-Kavallerie-Division Florian Geyer / Stab

Light cars with standard military bodies were known as *Kübelwagen*, or bucket vehicles. This was not because of their shape, but because the vehicles were fitted with three or four bucket seats.

Specifications

Crew: 1	Engine: Volkswagen 998cc petrol (24hp). Later
Weight: 0.64 tonnes (0.58 tons)	Volkswagen 1131cc petrol (25hp)
Length: 3.73m (12ft 3in)	Speed: 100km/h (62mph)
Width: 1.60m (5ft 3in)	Range: 600km (375 miles)
Height: 1.35m (4ft 5in)	Radio: None

9th SS Panzer Division *Hohenstaufen*

The second major expansion of the *Waffen-SS* was planned towards the end of 1942, and early in 1943 orders were issued for the formation of new Panzergrenadier divisions.

THE SUCCESS OF HIS TROOPS in Russia prompted *Reichsführer-SS* Heinrich Himmler to expand the *Waffen-SS* still further. Four new divisions were authorized, three of them armoured. These were to become the 9.*SS-Panzer-Division Hohenstaufen*, the 10.*SS-Panzer-Division Frundsberg*, the 11.*SS Freiwilligen-Panzergrenadier-Division Nordland* and the 12.*SS-Panzer-Division Hitlerjugend*. All began forming in 1943, but none were ready to take part in the summer offensive that year.

The division that was later to be called *Hohenstaufen* was ordered to be formed in January 1943. Divisional cadres were established in Berlin Lichterfelde, and elements of the division began to be gathered later that month. The ninth division to be formed by the *Waffen-SS*, it was initially known as *SS-Panzergrenadier-Division 9*.

On 8 February 1943, the first elements of the division began to be assembled in France at the *Truppenübungsplatz* Mailly-le-Camp, east of Paris. Much of the first batch of personnel had been sent from the LSSAH Replacement Battalion in Berlin Lichterfelde. In the same month, *SS-Brigadeführer*

Commanders

Brigadeführer Willi Bittrich *February 1943 – June 1944*	Oberführer Friedrich-Wilhelm Bock *July 1944 – August 1944*
Oberführer Thomas Müller *June 1944 – July 1944*	Standartenführer Walter Harzer *August 1944 – October 1944*
Brigadeführer Sylvester Stadler *July 1944*	Brigadeführer Sylvester Stadler *October 1944 – May 1945*

und Generalmajor der Waffen-SS Wilhelm 'Willi' Bittrich arrived to take command of the division.

Conscripts

By now, the SS could no longer sustain itself on volunteers alone, and conscripts provided up to 70 per cent of two of the new divisions, the 9th and the 10th. Nevertheless, they had been given full SS-style training, and they fought at least as well as the original divisions. By accepting conscripts, the SS

▲ **BMW R75 schweres Kraftrad 750cc mit Seitenwagen**

SS-Division Hohenstaufen / 9.Stabs-Begleit-Kompanie / Kraftrad-Zug

The divisional staff of the *Hohenstaufen* Division had a mapping detachment, a military police detachment and an escort company that had a self-propelled Flak platoon and a motorcycle platoon.

Specifications

Crew: 2	Engine: BMW 750cc petrol (26hp)
Weight: 0.67 tonnes (0.61 tons)	Speed: 92km/h (57mph)
Length: 2.4m (7ft 10in)	Range: 340km (211 miles)
Width: 1.73m (5ft 8in)	Radio: None
Height: 1m (3ft 3in)	Armament: 1 x 7.92mm (0.3in) MG (if fitted)

▲ **Intense training**

The new SS divisions formed in 1943 underwent a long period of assembling and training. The 9th and 10th Divisions received additional specialist training in anti-airborne operations, which called for very fast and aggressive reaction to enemy parachute assaults.

solved at least part of its manpower problem. However, the recruits were very young, most being around 18 years of age.

The division was given the name *Hohenstaufen*, after the family that ruled the Holy Roman Empire in the twelfth and thirteenth centuries. Most of 1943 was spent in training. In addition to standard combat training, *Hohenstaufen* also received specialized instruction in countering airborne attacks, which would prove extremely useful at Arnhem a year later.

In October, the division was redesignated as a Panzer division, and a battalion of Panthers was attached. The same month IV SS Panzer Corps had been formed with SS Panzer Division *Hohenstaufen* and SS Panzergrenadier Division *Reichsfuhrer-SS*.

Early in 1944, the division was transferred to the south of France as part of II SS Panzer Corps. In March, disaster threatened in the East when the First Panzer Army was trapped in a Russian encirclement at Tarnopol. By the middle of the month, the Soviets were at the Polish border and Hitler ordered four of

Divisional History	Formed
SS-Panzergrenadier-Division 9	1943
SS-Panzergrenadier-Division Hohenstaufen	1943
SS-Panzer-Division Hohenstaufen	1943
9.SS-Panzer-Division Hohenstaufen	1943

his Panzer divisions, including the *Waffen-SS* Divisions *Hohenstaufen* and *Frundsberg*, to the Eastern Front.

Into combat

In the spring of 1944, the SS Panzer arm was a shadow of the powerful force that had spearheaded Operation *Citadel*. However, the 9th and 10th Divisions had now completed their training and went into action at Tarnopol in April 1944.

On 5 April, Fourth Panzer Army attacked the Soviets, with II SS Panzer Corps on the flank of the offensive. *Hohenstaufen* smashed through the First Soviet Tank Army. On the 9th, the division's forward tanks broke through to the German First Panzer Army, allowing it to retreat to safety.

▶ **Mittlere Schutzenpanzerfwagen I Ausf C (SdKfz 251/1)**
20.SS-Panzergrenadier-Regiment / III.Bataillon (mot)
Most of *Hohenstaufen*'s Panzergrenadiers were truck-mounted, but the 3rd Battalion of the 20th Regiment had three half-track Panzergrendier companies and a single heavy half-track Panzergrenadier company.

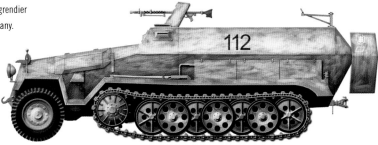

Specifications

Crew: 2 plus 12 troops	Engine: Maybach HL42TUKRM
Weight: 9.9 tonnes (9 tons)	Speed: 53km/h (33mph)
Length: 5.98m (19ft 7in)	Range: 300km (186 miles)
Width: 2.1m (6ft 11in)	Radio: FuG Spr Ger 1
Height: 1.75m (5ft 8in) or 2.16m	Armament: 1/2 x 7.62mm
(7ft) including MG shield if fitted	(0.3in) MG

▶ **Schwere Panzerspähwagen 8-Rad (SdKfz 231)**
9.SS-Panzer-Aufklärungs-Abteilung / Stab / Panzerspähwagen-Zug
The headquarters staff company of the reconnaissance battalion had an armoured car platoon equipped with three support cars with short-barrelled 7.5cm (3in) guns and 13 reconnaissance cars with 2cm (0.7in) weapons.

Specifications

Crew: 4	petrol (150hp)
Weight: 9.1 tonnes (8.3 tons)	Speed: 85km/h (52.8mph)
Length: 5.85m (19ft 2in)	Range: 300km (186 miles)
Width: 2.20m (7ft 2.5in)	Radio: FuG Ger 'a'
Height: 2.35m (7ft 8in)	Armament: 1 x 20mm (0.7in)
Engine: Büssing-NAG 8-cylinder	cannon

Normandy

JUNE–AUGUST 1944

The Allied landings in Normandy came as a surprise to the Germans, who expected the invasion to take place farther to the north, in the Pas-de-Calais.

WITHIN DAYS OF THE INVASION, *Oberkommando der Wehrmacht* (OKW) realized that this was indeed the real thing and that it was in danger of losing control of the battlefield to the enemy unless reinforcements could be brought to the front as soon as possible. To that end, the 9th SS Panzer Division *Hohenstaufen* and the 10th SS Panzer Division *Frundsberg* were immediately ordered from Poland to Normandy, but they did not arrive until almost the end of the month.

On reaching Normandy on 25 June, both *Hohenstaufen* and *Frundsberg* were fed into the line between Caen and Villers-Bocage. Their arrival was timely, coinciding as it did with Montgomery's

Operation *Epsom* (his attempt to take Caen). What initially seemed to be good Allied progress deteriorated quickly into a vicious battle for every metre of ground as the German defenders fought tenaciously to blunt the advance. The Germans counterattacked on 27 June, but their assault was stopped in its tracks by the 11th Armoured Division,

9.SS-Panzer-Division *Hohenstaufen*	Strength
Panzer strength 1944	
PzKpfw IV	46
PzKpfw V	79
StuG III	40

▶ **15cm schwere Panzerhaubitze (Sf) Hummel (SdKfz 165)**

9.SS-Artillerie-Regiment / I.Abteilung (Sf) / 1.Batterie

The 1st Battalion of *Hohenstaufen*'s artillery regiment was equipped with self-propelled guns. The 1st Battery of the battalion had six 15cm (5.9in) Hummel self-propelled howitzers.

Specifications

Crew: 6	Speed: 42km/h (26mph)
Weight: 26.5 tonnes (24 tons)	Range: 215km (133.6 miles)
Length: 7.17m (23ft 6in)	Radio: FuG Spr 1
Width: 2.97m (9ft 8in)	Armament: 1 x 150mm (5.9in) sFH
Height: 2.81m (9ft 2in)	18/1 L/30; 1 x 7.92mm (0.3in) MG
Engine: Maybach HL120TRM (265hp)	

▶ **Leichte Schutzenpanzerwagen (SdKfz 250/1)**

9.SS-Panzer-Aufklärungs-Abteilung / 1.Panzer-Aufklärungs-Kompanie / Stab

In 1944, *Hohenstaufen*'s reconnaissance battalion had one armoured car company and three companies equipped with armoured half-tracks. The 3rd Company had a staff platoon, a Panzerjäger platoon, a mortar platoon and a pioneer platoon.

Specifications

Crew: 2 plus 4 troops	Engine: Maybach HL42TRKM 6-cylinder
Weight: 5.9 tonnes (5.38 tons)	(100hp)
Length: 4.61m (15ft 1in)	Speed: 60km/h (37mph)
Width: 1.95m (6ft 5in)	Range: 300km (186 miles)
Height: 1.66m (5ft 5in)	Radio: FuG Spr Ger 'f'

which then followed through to cross the Odon River on the following day and capture the crucial Hill 112 on 29 June.

In reply, *SS-Obergruppenführer* Paul Hausser launched a major counterattack using both *Hohenstaufen* and *Frundsberg*, but the *Waffen-SS* divisions were beaten back. Fortunately for the Germans, the Allies had expected an even heavier attack and had withdrawn the 11th Armoured Division back across the Odon.

The American breakout at St Lô and Allied advances in the Caen sector threatened to trap the entire German army in a pocket around Falaise. The only possible escape lay through a narrow gap between Falaise and Argentan, and the II SS Panzer Corps – the *Hohenstaufen* and *Das Reich* Divisions – managed to get through to safety.

Hohenstaufen fought continuously and without replacements in Normandy from its arrival there in late June until its withdrawal on 21 August. Retreating northwards through France, the division provided a battalion to defend the line along the

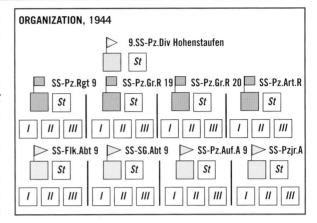

River Meuse. Moving up to Rouen, it skirted south of Brussels, crossed the Dutch border and arrived at the Veluwe area, north of Arnhem, on 7 September.

On 10 September, the remnants of the division – only 2500 men – were ordered back to Germany to be rebuilt. The men were on the point of leaving when the British airborne forces landed in the outskirts of Arnhem and near Nijmegen.

▶ **7.5cm Sturmgeschütz 40 Ausf G (SdKfz 142/1)**

9.SS-Panzer-Regiment / II.Abteilung / 8.Kompanie

The 2nd Battalion of the *Hohenstaufen*'s Panzer regiment was equipped with two companies of Panzer IVs and two companies of assault guns, which had been exchanged for tanks by June of 1944.

Specifications

Crew: 4	Engine: Maybach HL120TRM
Weight: 26.3 tonnes (23.9 tons)	Speed: 40km/h (25mph)
Length: 6.77m (22ft 2in)	Range: 155km (96.3 miles)
Width: 2.95m (9ft 8in)	Radio: FuG15 and FuG16
Height: 2.16m (7ft 0in)	

 # Arnhem, the Bulge and Budapest
SEPTEMBER 1944 – APRIL 1945

The men of *Hohenstaufen* were on the point of leaving for the *Reich* by rail on 17 September when paratroopers of the British 1st Airborne Division landed in the outskirts of Arnhem.

OPERATION *MARKET GARDEN*, a massive Allied air assault, was intended to seize a corridor of territory up to the mouths of the Rhine. It would isolate the V2 launching sites and the ports of

Antwerp, Amsterdam and Rotterdam. From there, it should have been possible to liberate northern Holland and leave the North German Plain vulnerable to an Allied offensive.

Generalfeldmarschall Walter Model ordered the understrength *Hohenstaufen* to form a battle group, *SS-Kampfgruppe Harzer*. It was ordered to make a reconnaissance in the direction of Arnhem and Nijmegen, and then to secure the Arnhem bridge and destroy the British paratroopers who had landed to the west of Arnhem at Oosterbeek.

On 20 September, *Hohenstaufen*'s *Aufklärungs-Abteilung* crossed the bridge at Arnhem, driving off the British paratroopers who had held the northern end for four days. Other elements of the division had managed to prevent the British Guards Armoured Division from driving north from Eindhoven.

Battle of the Bulge

Hohenstaufen played a major part in the Battle of the Bulge. The Ardennes offensive was launched on 16 December 1944, and *Hohenstaufen* was assigned to the II SS Panzer Corps alongside 2nd SS Panzer Division *Das Reich* and the 560th Infantry Division.

By 18 December, *Hohenstaufen* and *Das Reich* were fighting in the dense forests between Malmedy and St Vith. St Vith eventually fell to a simultaneous attack by the LXVI Corps and *Hohenstaufen* and the *Führerbegleitbrigade* attacking from the north.

However, Hitler's gamble was doomed from the beginning, and the last German offensive in the West failed. By the middle of January 1945, *Hohenstaufen* had suffered serious losses at Houffalize and had been transferred to the OKW reserve.

On 3 March, the division was moved by rail to Hungary, where the last major German offensive of the war was under way. *Hohenstaufen* suffered severe

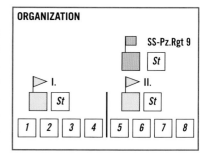

ORGANIZATION

SS-Pz.Rgt 9

▼ 9.SS-Panzer-Regiment / I.Abteilung / 1.Kompanie

After suffering heavy losses in Normandy, the 9th SS Panzer Division's 1st Panzer Battalion was reorganized with four companies, each equipped with 14 *Panzerkampfwagen* V Panther tanks. These were to be handed over to the *Frundsberg* Division in September 1944 while *Hohenstaufen*'s personnel were sent from Holland back to Germany to form the nucleus of a completely reconstructed division. After the battles at Arnhem, the reconstruction plans were reinstituted, and by December 1944 the four Panther companies had been re-equipped. More Panthers were en route at that time, intended to bring each company up to full strength.

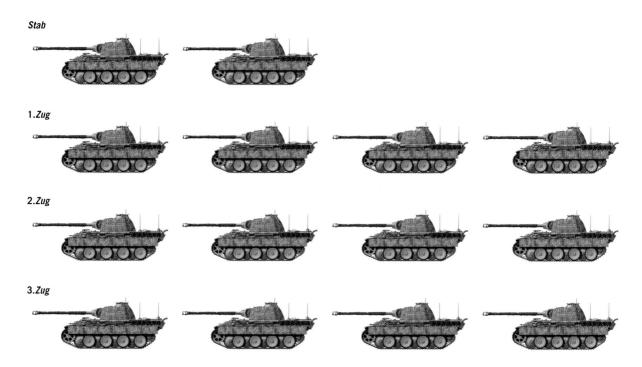

Stab

1.Zug

2.Zug

3.Zug

losses in fighting to the west of Budapest. By the middle of March, the *Hohenstaufen* Division had nearly reached the Danube, but as overwhelming Soviet superiority in numbers came into play the offensive ground to a halt. Remnants of the division were formed into two battle groups, which fought

their way back to Austria. In Vienna, the division was attached to Sixth SS Panzer Army. However, the attempt to defend Vienna failed, and on 13 April the SS abandoned the city, retreating westwards. What was left of *Hohenstaufen* continued to fight until the division surrendered to US forces at Steyr in May.

▶ Panzerkampfwagen IV Ausf H (SdKfz 161/2)

9.SS-Panzer-Regiment / II.Abteilung / 5.Kompanie

At the time of the Ardennes offensive in December 1944, *Hohenstaufen*'s 5th and 6th Panzer Companies were equipped with a total of 32 Panzer IVs.

Specifications

Crew: 5	Speed: 38km/h (23.6mph)
Weight: 27.6 tonnes (25 tons)	Range: 210km (130.5 miles)
Length: 7.02m (23ft 0in)	Radio: FuG5
Width: 2.88m (9ft 5in)	Armament: 1 x 75mm (3in) KwK
Height: 2.68m (8ft 10in)	40/43; 2 x 7.92mm (0.3in) MG
Engine: Maybach HL120TRM	(one hull-mounted, one coaxial)

▶ Panzerkampfwagen V Ausf A (SdKfz 171)

9.SS-Panzer-Regiment / I.Abteilung / Stab

The B13 on the turret of this Panther would normally indicate that it is the tank of the 2nd Battalion's ordnance officer, but in fact it belonged to the 1st Battalion.

Specifications

Crew: 5	Speed: 46km/h (28.6mph)
Weight: 50.2 tonnes	Range: 200km (124 miles)
(45.5 tons)	Radio: FuG5
Length: 8.86m (29ft 0in)	Armament: 1 x 75mm (3in)
Width: 3.4m (11ft 2in)	KwK42 L/70; 2 x 7.92mm
Height: 2.98m (9ft 10in)	(0.3in) MG (one hull-
Engine: Maybach HL230P30	mounted, one coaxial)

▶ 3.7cm Flak 43 auf Fgstl PzKpfw IV Sf (SdKfz 161/3)

9.SS-Panzer-Regiment / Stab / Flak-Zug

Issued to to the anti-aircraft platoons of Panzer regiments in Panzer divisions, the *Möbelwagen*, or moving van, was seen as a temporary defensive measure. A twin gun mounted on a Panther chassis, intended to replace this design, never entered production.

Specifications

Crew: 6	Engine: Maybach HL120TRM
Weight: 26.5 tonnes (24 tons)	Speed: 38km/h (23.6mph)
Length: 5.92m (19.4ft)	Range: 200km (124.3 miles)
Width: 2.95m (9.7ft)	Radio: FuG5 and FuG2
Height: 2.73m (9ft)	

10th SS Panzer Division *Frundsberg*

Often regarded as a twin of the 9th SS Panzer Division *Hohenstaufen*, the 10th SS Panzer Division *Frundsberg* trained and fought alongside its sister division until the end of 1944.

F ORMED AT THE SAME TIME as the 9th SS Division *Hohenstaufen*, the tenth SS division to be created served alongside its sister division for much of the war. The division's first year closely paralleled that of *Hohenstaufen*. Authorized early in 1943, the division was largely manned by conscripts, many of whom had been serving with the *Reich* Labour Service. The division spent the rest of the year assembling its constituent units and in training. It was briefly known as the *Karl der Grosse* Panzergrenadier Division. Under the orders of Army Group D, the incomplete formation was moved to various locations in southern and western France.

Named for knight

On 3 October 1943, the division was redesignated as the *SS-Panzer-Division Frundsberg*, taking its definitive title of 10.*SS-Panzer-Division Frundsberg* three weeks later. The division was named after Georg von Frundsberg, a south German knight who fought for the imperial Habsburg dynasty of Austria in the sixteenth century and who was instrumental in creating the Landsknechts, the archetypal German mercenary soldiers of the period.

At the same time, the formation of a new corps, the VII SS Panzer Corps, was ordered. *Frundsberg* was assigned to the corps along with another new formation, the 17th SS Panzergrenadier Division *Gotz von Berlichingen*. *Frundsberg* had given up part of its artillery and the motorcycle companies from its

Panzergrenadier regiments to provide a nucleus for the new division.

In March 1944, although neither formation was fully worked up, the incomplete *Frundsberg* Division was sent with the *Hohenstaufen* Division to join II *SS-Panzerkorps*. They were part of a major reinforcement of the Eastern Front, where Army Group Centre was under severe pressure as a result of advances made by the Soviet winter offensive, which had been launched at the beginning of the year.

INSIGNIA

A Germanic letter 'F', for the 10th SS Division's honour title of 'Frundsberg', was superimposed onto an oak leaf in the division's insignia.

Divisional History	Formed
SS-Panzergrenadier-Division 10	1943
SS-Panzergrenadier-Division 10 Karl der Grosse	1943
SS-Panzer-Division Frundsberg	1943
10.SS-Panzer-Division Frundsberg	1943

Commanders

Standartenführer Michael Lippert
January 1943 – February 1943

Gruppenführer Lothar Debes
February 1943 – November 1943

Gruppenführer Karl Fischer von Treuenfeld
November 1943 – April 1944

Gruppenführer Heinz Harmel
April 1944 – April 1945

Obersturmbannführer Franz Roestel
April 1945 – May 1945

▶ **Leichte Schützenpanzerwagen (SdKfz 250/10)**
10.SS-Aufklärungs-Abteilung / 3.Panzerspähwagen.Kompanie / 1.Zug

The SdKfz 250/10, armed with a 3.7cm (1.5in) Pak 35/36, was issued to platoon leaders of half-track-mounted reconnaissance platoons. The vehicle had a crew of four and carried 216 rounds of 3.7cm (1.5in) ammunition.

Specifications

Crew: 4	Engine: Maybach HL42TRKM (100hp)
Weight: 6.3 tonnes (5.67 tons)	Speed: 60km/h (37.3mph)
Length: 4.56m (14ft 11.5in)	Range: 320km (199 miles)
Width: 1.95m (6ft 5in)	Radio: FuG Spr Ger 1
Height: 1.97m (6ft 6in)	Armament: 1x 37mm (1.5in) Pak 35/36

The Soviets had pushed almost as far as the Polish border, in the process encircling the First Panzer Army around Tarnopol. Among the trapped German units were the 1st SS Panzer Division *Leibstandarte SS Adolf Hitler* and a battle group from 2nd SS Panzer Division *Das Reich*.

Even though its Panzer regiments had not yet received the Panzer V Panthers with which their first battalions were to be equipped, the division joined Army Group North Ukraine with the rest of II SS Panzer Corps. The division made its combat debut early in April, and after fighting fiercely broke through the Soviet encirclement of First Panzer Army on 6 April at Buczacz, linking up with the beleaguered *Waffen-SS* divisions the same day.

The Soviets continued to press forward, and the *Frundsberg* Division remained in the line, seeing heavy combat on the Strypa River Line and counterattacking the Red Army in the area around Tarnopol and Kovel. Fought to a standstill by the Soviet 1st Ukrainian Front, the division then spent some weeks embroiled in static defensive actions on the Bug River.

Sent to Normandy

On 6 June 1944, the Western Allies invaded Normandy. On 12 June, II SS Panzer Corps was withdrawn from the Russian Front and rushed westwards as the German High Command sought to reinforce the Normandy battle front.

▶ **10.5cm leFH18 auf PzKpfw II Wespe (SdKfz 124)**

10.SS-Panzer-Artillerie-Regiment / I. (Sf) Abteilung / 2.Batterie

Two batteries of the division's 1st (Self-Propelled) Artillery Battalion were equipped with 10.5cm (4.1in) Wespe SP field howitzers. Most were lost in Normandy, and the division was not brought up to full strength until early 1945.

Specifications	
Crew: 5	Speed: 40km/h (25mph)
Weight: 12.1 tonnes (11 tons)	Range: 220km (136.7 miles)
Length: 4.81m (15ft 10in)	Radio: FuG Spr 1
Width: 2.28m (7ft 6in)	Armament: 1 x 105mm (4.1in) LeFH 18M
Height: 2.25m (7ft 4.5in)	L/28 howitzer
Engine: Maybach HL62TR	

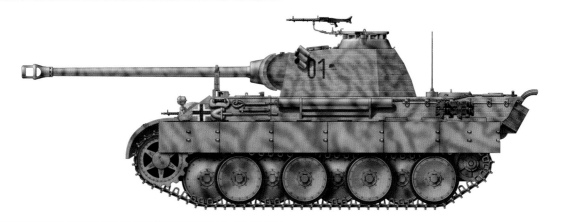

Specifications	
Crew: 5	Height: 2.98m (9ft 10in)
Weight: 50.2 tonnes	Engine: Maybach HL230P30
(45.5 tons)	Speed: 46km/h (28.6mph)
Length: 8.86m (29ft 0in)	Range: 200km (124 miles)
Width: 3.4m (11ft 2in)	Radio: FuG5

▲ **Panzerkampfwagen V Ausf A (SdKfz 171)**

10.SS-Panzer-Regiment / I.Abteilung / 1.Kompanie

Frundsberg made its combat debut early in 1944 without its PzKpfw Vs. However, by the time the division was moved across Europe in June 1944, the Panzer regiment's 1st Battalion had been equipped with four companies of Panthers.

Normandy and Arnhem
JUNE–SEPTEMBER 1944

Frundsberg was rushed across Europe with the rest of II SS Panzer Corps in only six days, the entire movement requiring the use of 67 trains to complete.

ONCE IN FRANCE, however, they were delayed by constant Allied air attacks. The 9th and 10th SS Divisions took longer to cross France than they had taken in getting to France from the Russian border. As a result, the Allies were too firmly established for an attack against the beachhead to be feasible, so the divisions were thrown into the battle for Caen.

Defending Caen, the corps immediately encountered Montgomery's *Epsom* offensive, and in a week of heavy fighting stopped the 51st Highland Division in its thrust towards the Orne River. The II *SS-Panzerkorps* suffered more than 1200 casualties; by 30 June divisional manpower was down to less than 16,000 men. The combat around Caen continued for the first three weeks in July. By 18 July, the *Frundsberg* Division had lost more than 2200 men dead or wounded. Yet, in spite of their best efforts, the British were unable to drive back the German defenders. Montgomery even used heavy bombers to blast the German positions, but the attack ground to a halt with heavy Allied losses.

The battle in Normandy ended on 21 August with the remaining divisional remnants fleeing eastwards towards the Seine. Many of the divisions were sent back to Germany for rest and refit, with the exception

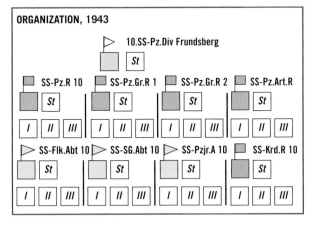

ORGANIZATION, 1943

of II *SS-Panzerkorps* under Wilhelm Bittrich. This was sent to Holland for refitting, ready to take on General Patton's forces, whom the Germans thought would launch a new offensive. However, the next confrontation would come sooner than the *Hohenstaufen* and *Frundsberg* Divisions expected – right on their very doorstep, at Arnhem.

Arnhem

On paper, two SS Panzer divisions should have been enough to annihilate the lightly armed airborne

▶ **Mittlere Schützenpanzerwagen Ausf C (SdKfz 251/9)**

21.SS-Panzergrenadier-Regiment / I.Bataillon / 1.Kompanie

In June 1944, *Frundsberg's* two Panzergrenadier regiments each had one battalion equipped with half-tracks. The first three companies of each battalion had a pair of SdKfz 251 half-tracks with short-barrelled 7.5cm (3in) KwK 37 cannon. The vehicles were attached to the company staff and were designed to provide close-range fire support to the infantry-carrying half-tracks.

Specifications

Crew: 3	Speed: 53km/h (33mph)
Weight: 9.4 tonnes (8.53 tons)	Range: 300km (186 miles)
Length: 5.98m (19ft 7in)	Radio: FuG Spr Ger 'f'
Width: 2.83m (9ft 4in)	Armament: 1 x 75mm (3in) KwK
Height: 2.07m (6ft 10in)	L/24 gun
Engine: Maybach HL42TUKRM	

forces in very short order. However, this was less than a month since a large chunk of the German Army had been annihilated in the Falaise pocket, from which the *Hohenstaufen* and *Frundsberg* Divisions had escaped by the skin of their teeth.

Vastly understrength, with their equipment replacement programme barely under way, the two SS divisions nevertheless provided a solid core on which the Germans could base their defence of the Rhine bridges.

▲ Assault guns

Although designed as an artillery piece, the *Sturmgewehr* was often used as a relatively inexpensive tank substitute in the Panzer regiments of some Panzer divisions in the last two years of the war.

The presence of these two battle-hardened units was decisive in defeating Montgomery's drive on the Rhine. Neither division acted as a unit: the *Kampfgruppen* operated independently with only the lightest of direction from Bittrich's II Panzer Corps.

▶ 7.5cm Sturmgeschütz 40 Ausf G (SdKfz 142/1)

10.SS-Panzer-Regiment / II.Abteilung / 8.Kompanie

In May 1944, the 2nd Battalion of the 10th Panzer Regiment was a mixed unit. The 5th and 6th Companies operated long-barrel Panzer IVs; the 7th and 8th Companies were equipped with assault guns.

Specifications

Crew: 4	Speed: 40km/h (25mph)
Weight: 26.3 tonnes (23.9 tons)	Range: 155km (96.3 miles)
Length: 6.77m (22ft 2in)	Radio: FuG15 and FuG16
Width: 2.95m (9ft 8in)	Armament: 1 x 75mm (3in) StuG L/48
Height: 2.16m (7ft 0in)	cannon
Engine: Maybach HL120TRM	

Defence of the Reich

JANUARY–APRIL 1945

On 18 November, the *Frundsberg* Division, now reduced to a battle group after its losses in Normandy and at Arnhem, was withdrawn to Aachen in Germany for rest and refit.

DURING DECEMBER, its strength was built up once again to around 15,500 men – about 75 per cent of establishment. In December 1944 and January 1945, it saw action around Linnich and Geilenkirchen, and Julich northeast of Aachen. In January, it was attached to Army Group *Niederrheim*, and was earmarked for use in the reserve forces for Operation *Nordwind*.

On 24 January, *Frundsberg* crossed the Moder River and captured the high ground commanding the area between Hagenau and Kaltenhaus. Despite being at near full strength after its recent refit, the division met such fierce resistance that its advance faltered, and the following day orders arrived withdrawing it from the line for immediate transfer to the Eastern Front.

Eastern Front 1945

On 10 February 1945, the division was committed to a German counteroffensive codenamed Operation *Sonnenwende* as part of III SS Panzer Corps. For the next month, it was engaged with the advancing Soviets at Stargard and Fürstenwalde, before being pulled back across the Oder into Stettin for a rest.

In mid-April, *Frundsberg* was encircled by Soviet forces near Spremberg. Despite its perilous position, Hitler ordered the division to close a gap in the

10.SS-Panzer-Regiment, Feb 1945	Strength
PzKpfw IV (long gun, side armour)	38
PzKpfw V Panther	53
FlakPanzer IV (3.7cm/1.5in)	8

German lines by immediately attacking. Heinz Harmel, the divisional commander, realized that the attack would be suicide. He decided instead to break out and head for the last major German troop concentration south of Berlin.

The breakout came at the cost of further fragmentation of the division. Some units managed to form a line of defences near Dresden. Harmel was dismissed for refusing to obey orders.

The end

Now under the control of the Fourth Panzer Army of Army Group Centre, the pitiful remnants of the division were led by *SS-Obersturmbannführer* Franz Röstel in combat against the advancing Soviets, but to little effect.

The division fell back to the Elbe near Dresden and headed south. After claiming a few Soviet T-34 tanks on 7 May, the last few Panzers of the *Frundsberg* Division were destroyed by their own crews to prevent their being captured and used against them.

The *Frundsberg* Division moved west to avoid capture by Soviet forces. Some Frundsbergers managed to reach the relative safety of US captors; the remainder of the division surrendered to the advancing Red Army at the town of Teplitz-Schönau (Teplice in the modern Czech Republic).

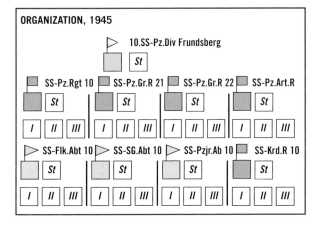

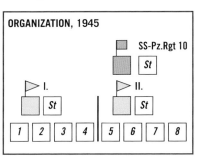

▶ Panzerkampfwagen IV Ausf G (SdKfz 161/1 or 161/2)

10.SS-Panzer-Regiment / II.Abteilung / 5.Kompanie

Before the invasion of Normandy, *Frundsberg*'s Panzer regiment was equipped with the standard Panzer inventory of the time with four companies of Panthers and four of Panzer IVs.

Specifications

Crew: 5	Speed: 40km/h (25mph)
Weight: 25.9 tonnes (23.5 tons)	Range: 210km (130.5 miles)
Length: 6.62m (21ft 8in)	Radio: FuG5
Width: 2.88m (9ft 5in)	Armament: 1 x 75mm (3in) KwK 40/43;
Height: 2.69m (8ft 10in)	2 x 7.92mm (0.3in) MG (one hull-
Engine: Maybach HL120TRM	mounted, one coaxial)

▶ Panzerkampfwagen IV Ausf H (SdKfz 161/2)

10.SS-Panzer-Regiment / I.Abteilung / 3.Kompanie

After being shattered in Normandy, the 10th Panzer Regiment was organized as a single battalion with two companies of Panthers and two companies of Panzer IVs. The 2nd Battalion was eventually rebuilt in January 1945.

Specifications

Crew: 5	Speed: 38km/h (23.6mph)
Weight: 27.6 tonnes (25 tons)	Range: 210km (130.5 miles)
Length: 7.02m (23ft 0in)	Radio: FuG5
Width: 2.88m (9ft 5in)	Armament: 1 x 75mm (3in) KwK 40/43;
Height: 2.68m (8ft 10in)	2 x 7.92mm (0.3in) MG (one hull-
Engine: Maybach HL120TRM	mounted, one coaxial)

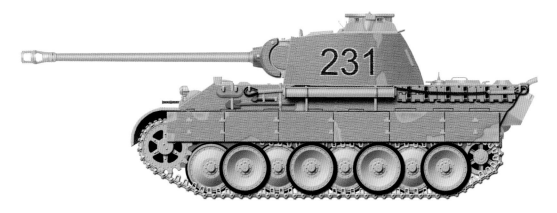

Specifications

Crew: 5	Speed: 46km/h (28.6mph)
Weight: 50.2 tonnes (45.5 tons)	Range: 200km (124 miles)
Length: 8.86m (29ft 0in)	Radio: FuG5
Width: 3.4m (11ft 2in)	Armament: 1 x 75mm (3in) KwK42 L/70; 2 x
Height: 2.98m (9ft 10in)	7.92mm (0.3in) MG (one hull-mounted,
Engine: Maybach HL230P30	one coaxial)

▲ Panzerkampfwagen V Ausf A (SdKfz 171)

10.SS-Panzer-Regiment / I.Abteilung / 2.Kompanie

In January 1945, *Frundsberg* began to receive new armour as the division was built up to full strength at Aachen. Twenty-five Panthers were delivered in the second week of that month.

11th SS Panzergrenadier Division *Nordland*

Based on the 5th SS Division *Wiking*, the *Nordland* Division was to be a Germanic formation, manned by Scandinavian and other suitably 'Nordic' volunteers.

THE 11TH SS PANZERGRENADIER Division had its origins in an OKW order to activate a new SS Panzer corps in early 1943. This new corps was to be designated III.*(Germanische) SS-Panzerkorps*, and to as great an extent as possible it was to be made up of Germanic volunteers. It was to include the 5th SS Panzergrenadier Division *Wiking*, together with a new German-Scandinavian division yet to be formed. The corps headquarters was activated on 30 March 1943, but it proved impossible to withdraw *Wiking* from the Eastern Front and the plan to field the new corps was delayed.

However, plans to create the new SS volunteer division went ahead. *Reichsführer-SS* Heinrich Himmler wanted to give the new division the name *Waräger* in reference to the Swedish Viking Varangian Guard, which saw service as the bodyguard of the Byzantine emperors in the dark ages. Hitler, more practical than his mystical SS henchman, considered the name too obscure. Deciding that the name of the veteran volunteer regiment *Nordland* deserved to be honoured, he ordered the division to be so named in July 1943.

Nordland was to differ from the prototype volunteer division *Wiking* in its make-up. Much had been made of the multi-national nature of the elite

INSIGNIA

The divisional insignia, the so-called *Sonnenrad*, or Sunwheel variant of the swastika, had been used by the Thule Society, which was an important influence on the early National Socialists.

Commanders

Brigadeführer Franz Augsberger
March 1943 – May 1943

Brigadeführer Fritz Scholz
May 1943 – July 1944

Brigadeführer Joachim Ziegler
July 1944 – April 1945

Brigadeführer Gustav Krukenberg
April 1945 – May 1945

▲ ***Nordland* reconnaissance**

An SdKfz 232 heavy armoured radio car of the 11th SS Panzergrenadier Division *Nordland* is identified by the *Sonnenrad*, or sunwheel symbol, it carries on the front hood, next to the vehicle's blacked-out headlamp.

◀ **10.5cm leichte Feldhaubitze (leFH18)**

11.SS-Artillerie-Regiment / II.Abteilung / 4.Batterie

The bulk of *Nordland*'s artillery strength was provided by the 10.5cm (4.1in) light field howitzer. A capable enough weapon, it was not all that light; in fact, it was heavier and less accurate than its Soviet equivalents.

Specifications

Crew: 5

Weight: 1.95 tonnes (1.85 tons)

Length: 3.3m (10ft)

Calibre: 105mm (4.3in)

Muzzle Velocity: 540m/s (1770fps)

Range: 12,325m (13,480 yards)

Ammunition: High explosive or smoke

Wiking Division by Nazi propaganda organs, but in truth the bulk of its strength and nearly all of its senior NCOs and officers were German. In the new division, the Germans hoped to utilize a far greater proportion of foreign volunteers, especially in the more senior ranks.

A large part of the division's manpower was provided by the remnants of the various Germanic legions, most of which were being disbanded at this time. As a result, nationalities represented in *Nordland* had the widest range to be found in any *Waffen-SS* division. By the spring of 1945, units from Denmark, Norway, Sweden, Switzerland, France, the Netherlands, Estonia, Finland, and even a handful of British volunteers, had been attached.

First action

The principle combat units were made up of veterans of the *Legion Norwegien* and the *Freikorps Danmark*. The ranks were filled out with *Volksdeutsche* and with *Reichdeutsche*. The first division commander was *SS-Brigadeführer und Generalmajor der Waffen-SS* Fritz

Divisional History	Formed
Kampfverband Waräger	Feb 1943
Germanische-Freiwilligen-Division	Feb 1943
SS-Panzergrenadier-Division 11	Apr 1943
11.SS-Freiwilligen-Panzergrenadier-Division Nordland	July 1943
11.SS-Panzergrenadier-Division Nordland	Nov 1943

Scholz, who had been commander of the *Nordland* Regiment of *Wiking*.

After completing training, *Nordland* and III. *(Germanische) SS-Panzerkorps* were posted to Croatia to gain combat experience in the war against Tito's Communist partisans. Going into action on 28 August, *Nordland* fought several vicious actions against an equally cut-throat enemy. Just before *Nordland* was reassigned, on 12 November 1943, it was upgraded to full Panzergrenadier status. Along with III.*(Germanische) SS-Panzerkorps*, *Nordland* transferred to the Eastern Front; it was fully deployed with Army Group North by 22 December 1943.

▶ **Panzerkampfwagen III Ausf E (SdKfz 141)**

SS-Panzer-Abteilung Nordland / 2.Kompanie

As formed in 1943, the *Nordland* Division was to have a Panzer battalion of four companies. However, by May 1944 in the Baltic the division was equipped with three StuG companies in place of Panzer IIIs and IVs.

Specifications	
Crew: 5	Speed: 40km/h (25mph)
Weight: 21.8 tonnes (19.8 tons)	Range: 210km (130.5 miles)
Length: 5.38m (17ft 7in)	Radio: FuG5
Width: 2.91m (9ft 5in)	Armament: 1 x 50mm (2in) gun;
Height: 2.44m (8ft)	2 x 7.92mm (0.3in) MG (one
Engine: Maybach HL120TRM	hull-mounted, one coaxial)

▶ **Sturmgeschütz III Ausf D**

SS-Sturmgeschütz-Abteilung Nordland

The short-barrelled StuG III Ausf D was still in use when the *Nordland* Division formed in 1943, but was soon replaced by long-barrelled variants.

Specifications	
Crew: 4	Speed: 40km/h (25mph)
Weight: 19.6 tonnes (17.9 tons)	Range: 160km (99.4 miles)
Length: 5.38m (17ft 8in)	Radio: FuG15 or FuG16
Width: 2.92m (9ft 7in)	Armament: 1 x 75mm (3in)
Height: 1.95m (6ft 5in)	StuK 37 L/24 gun
Engine: Maybach HL120TR (300hp)	

With Army Group North
1944

The *Nordland* Division was sent to the Eastern Front at a critical time. The initiative had been seized by the Red Army, and the new formation was almost immediately fighting for its life.

T HE DIVISION ARRIVED IN THE LENINGRAD sector to take part in the unsuccessful German attempt to fight off a massive Soviet breakout from the Oranienbaum pocket, a breakout that succeeded in relieving the 900-day siege of Leningrad. Over the next three months of continuous combat, the Germans were driven back over the Narva. In fact, so many volunteer units saw action at Narva that it became known as the 'Battle of the European SS'.

Although the Germans had been forced to retreat, the long period of combat had also exhausted the Soviets. The impetus had run out of the Red Army's advance and the battle for Narva became a battle of snipers. During this period, the battered 1st Battalions of both the *Norge* and *Danmark* Panzergrenadier Regiments were withdrawn to Germany for rest and rebuilding. They would never again be assigned to *Nordland*. In December 1944, after being brought up to strength, both battalions were assigned to the 5th SS Panzer Division *Wiking*. Early in 1945, the battalions were transferred south for the failed attempt to relieve Budapest.

Back on the Baltic Front, Soviet pressure began to increase in early June 1944, and it soon became apparent that a major Soviet thrust was in the making. Then, on 22 June, the third anniversary of Operation *Barbarossa*, the Soviets launched Operation *Bagration* against Army Group Centre. This was the long-awaited Soviet summer offensive, and it tore a 400km- (248-mile) wide gap in the German lines, annihilating the entire German army group in the process.

The Tannenberg Line

The rapid Soviet advance threatened to isolate the hundreds of thousands of German troops in the Baltic States. To avoid being cut off, the Germans began planning for the withdrawal from the Narva bridgehead to the Tannenberg Line. Through July and August, the troops of III.*(Germanische) SS-Panzerkorps* took part in some of the most vicious fighting ever seen on the Eastern Front.

The Tannenberg Line anchored on three strategic hills that protected the rear side of the town of Narva.

▲ **2cm Flak (Sf) auf Fahrgestell leichte Zugkraftwagen 1t (SdKfz 10/4)**

SS-Panzergrenadier-Division Nordland / Stab-Begleit-Kompanie

The divisional headquarters was protected from air attack by a Flak battery equipped with four self-propelled 2cm (0.7in) guns. The four batteries of the division's Flak battalion used heavier, towed weapons.

Specifications	
Crew: 7	6-cylinder (100hp)
Weight: 5.5 tonnes (5 tons)	Speed: 65km/h (40mph)
Length: 4.75m (15ft 7in)	Range: 300km (186 miles)
Width: 2.15m (7ft 1in)	Radio: None
Height: 3.20m (10ft 6in)	Armament: Twin 20mm (0.7in)
Engine: Maybach HL42TRKM	Flak 38 L/112.5

From 27 July, *Nordland* fought alongside *Sturmbrigade Langemarck* and *Kampfgruppe Strachwitz* from the *Grossdeutschland* Division to keep control of Orphanage Hill.

Despite the death of the *Nordland's* commander, *SS-Gruppenführer* Fritz Scholz, who was killed in the fighting, and the subsequent deaths of the commanders of the *Norge* and *Danmark* Regiments, the division held on to Orphanage Hill, destroying 113 tanks on 29 July.

On 14 September 1944, the German forces in Estonia were ordered to fall back into Latvia. By the morning of the 22nd, *Nordland* had taken up position 30km (18.6 miles) to the northeast of Riga, the Latvian capital. By the evening, *Nordland* had been relocated to the southeast of the city. Its arrival prevented the encirclement of the German Eighteenth Army by Soviet forces.

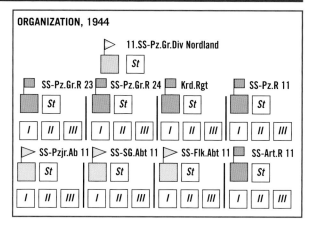

ORGANIZATION, 1944

▲ **7.5cm Panzerabwehrkanone (Pak 40)**

11.SS-Panzerjäger-Abteilung

One company of the division's Panzerjäger battalion used the powerful Pak 40; the other companies were equipped with self-propelled weapons. The heavy companies of the *Nordland's* three Panzergrenadier battalions each had three Pak 40s.

Specifications

Crew: 3	Muzzle Velocity (AP): 990m/s (3248fps)
Weight: 1.5 tonnes (1.37 tons)	Range: AP: 2000m (2190 yards), HE: 7.5km
Length: 3.7m (12ft 1.5in)	(4.66 miles)
Calibre: 75mm (3in)	Ammunition: Armour-piercing, high explosive

▶ **Leichte Panzerspähfwagen (SdKfz 222)**

11.SS-Aufklärungs-Abteilung / 1.leichte Spähpanzerwagen-Kompanie

Most of the *Nordland* Division's reconnaissance companies were motorized units, equipped with soft-skin cars and motorcycles. However, one company of the reconnaissance battalion was equipped with armoured cars.

Specifications

Crew: 3	Speed: 85km/h (52.8mph)
Weight: 5.3 tonnes (4.8 tons)	Range: 300km (186 miles)
Length: 4.8m (15ft 8in)	Radio: FuG Spr Ger 'a'
Width: 1.95m (6ft 5in)	Armament: 1 x 20mm (0.7in) KwK 30 L/55
Height: 2.00m (6ft 7in)	cannon; 1 x 7.92mm (0.3in) MG (coaxial)
Engine: Horch 3.5L or 3.8L petrol	

As the Red Army moved forward, *Nordland* slowly pulled back into the Courland pocket, fighting doggedly all the way, from where it was evacuated to Germany in early 1945. At

ORGANIZATION

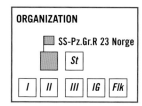

this time III.*(Germanische) SS-Panzerkorps* included *Kampfgruppen* from the 27.*SS-Freiwilligen-Grenadier-Division Langemarck*, 28.*SS-Freiwilligen-Panzergrenadier-Division Wallonien*, elements of 10.*SS-Panzer-Division Frundsberg*, and 11.*SS-Freiwilligen-Panzergrenadier-Division Nordland*; it was subordinated to the newly created 11th Panzer Army, commanded by *SS-Obergruppenführer* Steiner.

Steiner launched Operation *Sonnenwende* to destroy a Soviet salient and to relieve the troops besieged in the town of Arnswalde. However, the assault had ground to a halt by 21 February. Clearly, nothing more could be achieved against an increasingly powerful enemy without extremely high casualties, so Steiner ordered a general withdrawal back to the north bank of the Ihna.

East Prussia and Berlin

MARCH–APRIL 1945

The Soviet offensive of 1 March pushed the *Nordland* Division back to Berlin, along with the rest of the remnants of the III (Germanic) SS Panzer Corps.

I N A DESPERATE FIGHTING withdrawal, the SS Panzer Corps inflicted heavy casualties on the Soviets, but they could not stop the Red Army. By 4 March, the division was at Altdamm, the last defensive position east of the Oder itself. Over the next two weeks, *Nordland* doggedly held its position, inflicting severe casualties on the enemy but suffering equally high losses in the process. On 19 March, after the *Danmark* and *Norge* Regiments had been all but destroyed, the battered division fell back behind the Oder. It was ordered back to the Schwedt–Bad Freinwalde area to be refitted as best as could be managed at this late stage of the war.

On 16 April, *Nordland* was ordered back into the line east of Berlin. The division was still far from being at full strength, and apart from a small number of French and Spanish volunteers most of the division's reinforcements had little combat experience. Back in combat on 17 April, *Nordland* had been driven back into Berlin by the 20th. Two days later, on 22 April, the remnants of the *Nordland* Division were fighting around the Tiergarten in the centre of the city. By the end of April, any divisional organization had ceased to exist.

Last defence of Berlin

What little remained of the *Norge* and *Danmark* Regiments, with elements of the division's pioneer battalion, tried to defend the bridges across the Spree. After this futile attempt, the few survivors were pushed back into the Government District, and on 26 April they were fighting around the *Reichstag.*

At 20:00 on 30 April, the *Norge* and *Danmark* *Kampfgruppe* commander, *SS-Sturmbannführer* Ternedde, was given the news of Hitler's death. Ternedde was given orders to take the survivors and break out of the ruined city. In the event, very few of them made it to safety. Several small groups managed to reach the American forces at Charlottenburg, but many more did not, among them the 3rd (Swedish) Company of the reconnaissance battalion, who fought a desperate and ultimately useless battle to escape the surrounding Red Army.

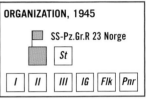

ORGANIZATION, 1945

SS-Pz.Gr.R 23 Norge

St

| I | II | III | IG | Flk | Pnr |

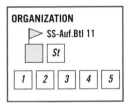

ORGANIZATION

SS-Auf.Btl 11

St

| 1 | 2 | 3 | 4 | 5 |

▶ **On the Narva Front**
A Norwegian *Oberstürmbannführer* of the *Nordland* Division still wears the cuff title of his former unit, the *Legion Norwegen.*

By 1 May, the Soviet Army had overcome the last defenders of the *Reichstag*. Organized resistance in the ruined city no longer existed. As dusk descended on 2 May, the few survivors of *Nordland* and the rest of the exhausted Berlin garrison, some 130,000, marched into Soviet captivity. The few survivors of *Nordland* who surrendered to the Soviets were never to be seen again. Those who broke out westwards and reached the Americans or the British were handed over to their respective countries and tried as traitors. Most were imprisoned for varying lengths of time; a few were executed.

When infantry vehicles carried identification numbers, they usually meant the same as they did on Panzers – in this case 1st Battalion, 1st Company, 7th vehicle of a Panzergrenadier regiment.

▶ Mittlere Schützenpanzerwagen (SdKfz 251/22)

24.SS-Panzergrenadier-Regiment Danmark / III.Bataillon / 13.Kompanie

Towards the end of 1944, the 3rd Battalion of the *Danmark* Panzergrenadier Regiment was equipped with half-tracks. The battalion's heavy company had a platoon of three 7.5cm (3in) Pak 40 anti-tank guns

Specifications

Crew: 4 or 5	Speed: 50km/h (31mph)
Weight: 8 tonnes (7.28 tons)	Range: 300km (186 miles)
Length: 5.98m (19ft 7in)	Radio: None
Width: 2.1m (6ft 11in)	Armament: 1 x 75mm (3in) PaK 40
Height: 2.25m (7ft 4.5in)	L/46 anti-tank gun; 1 x 7.92mm
Engine: Maybach HL42TUKRM	(0.3in) MG (rear-mounted)
6-cylinder petrol (100hp)	

▶ 15cm schwere Infanterie Geschütz auf Selbsfahrlafette 38(t) Ausf K Grille (SdKfz 138/1)

23.SS-Panzergrenadier-Regiment Norge / 17.Kompanie (sIG Sf)

The self-propelled infantry gun companies of the *Norge* and *Danmark* Regiments were each equipped with a battery of six Grille vehicles.

Specifications

Crew: 5	Engine: Praga EPA/2
Weight: 12.7 tonnes (11.5 tons)	Speed: 35km/h (21.7mph)
Length: 4.61m (15ft 1in)	Range: 185km (115 miles)
Width: 2.16m (7ft 0in)	Radio: FuG16
Height: 2.40m (7ft 10.5in)	Armament: 1 x 150mm (5.9in) sIG 33 gun

▶ Mittlere Schützenpanzerwagen (SdKfz 251/1)

24.SS-Panzergrenadier-Regiment Danmark / I.Bataillon / 1.Kompanie

The late-war Ausf D variant of the *mittlere Schützenpanzerwagen* had a simplified armoured body that cost less to manufacture than earlier models.

Specifications

Crew: 2 plus 12 troops	Engine: Maybach
Weight: 9.9 tonnes (9 tons)	HL42TUKRM
Length: 5.98m (19ft 7in)	Speed: 53km/h (33mph)
Width: 2.1m (6ft 11in)	Range: 300km (186 miles)
Height: 1.75m (5ft 8in) or	Radio: FuG Spr Ger 1
2.16m (7ft) including MG	Armament: 1/2 x 7.62mm
shield if fitted	(0.3in) MG

12th SS Panzer Division *Hitlerjugend*

Known as 'Hitler's Baby Division' to the Allies in Normandy, the 12th SS Division drew most of its personnel from the school-age boys of the Hitler Youth.

INSIGNIA

The *Hitlerjugend* Division honoured its close association with the *Leibstandarte* by adopting a variant of that division's 'Key' insignia.

Divisional History	Formed
SS-Panzergrenadier-Division Hitlerjugend	1943
SS-Panzer-Division Hitlerjugend	1943
12.SS-Panzer-Division Hitlerjugend	1943

Commanders

Brigadeführer Fritz Witt
June 1943 – June 1944

Brigadeführer Kurt Meyer
June 1944 – September 1944

Obersturmbannführer Hubert Meyer
September 1944 – October 1944

Brigadeführer Fritz Kraemer
October 1944 – November 1944

Brigadeführer Hugo Kraas
November 1944 – May 1945

◀ **Normandy, June 1944**

The *Hitlerjugend* Division fought with unparalleled ferocity in the battles against the British at Caen, suffering huge losses in the process.

IN A DWINDLING SUPPLY of manpower, the existence of an entire generation of ideologically pure boys, raised as Nazis, eager to fight for the Fatherland and even die for the *Führer*, could not be ignored.

The first thousand-bomber raid hit Cologne in May 1942. In that month, *Reich* Youth Leader Artur Axmann persuaded Hitler to set up pre-military training camps that all boys between the ages of 16 and 18 were obliged to attend. In turn, the SS persuaded the HJ, or *Hitlerjugend*, to reserve to them exclusively one-fifth of the product of these camps.

In this preparation for combat, especially in the camps run by the SS, German adolescents received training heavily laced with brainwashing. War was taught as a struggle of competing ideologies, culminating in victory or annihilation. The type of soldier produced under this 'fight or die' indoctrination largely explains the continuing Nazi war effort, when most outsiders and an increasing number of insiders knew the cause was lost.

During the three weeks of mandatory war training, the boys learned how to handle German infantry weapons, including pistols, machineguns, hand grenades and *Panzerfaust* anti-tank weapons.

Indoctrination

The Army high command and the SS were in constant competition for the best recruits. Both organizations assigned veterans to HJ administrative posts primarily as a means of recruitment. They regaled their wide-eyed audiences with the perils and thrills of combat. They reinforced the will to fight the 'Bolshevik hordes' and the 'Jew-backed Western powers'. These Pied Pipers did all they could to produce cannon fodder for the *Reich* war machine.

The results were impressive. Army leaders were the first to acknowledge the achievements of the HJ in preparing recruits for the battlefield. Departing from traditional methods, the *Hitlerjugend* tailored paramilitary training to the particular needs and potential of 16- and 17-year-olds. With the exception of a few coarse SS veterans, there were no hard-bitten drill sergeant types in the training camps. Most cadre members were sensitive young soldiers, most of whom had been in the *Hitlerjugend* themselves not too many years before. German youth was, in effect, training itself.

The camps also served to eliminate class distinctions. Boys from town and city, volunteer and conscript, were thrown in together. The soldiers that were turned out fought with greater professional skill, resourcefulness and independent initiative than their enemy counterparts. Between the spring of 1942 and 1945, every German volunteer and draftee filtered

through the HJ training schemes before he donned field grey or SS camouflage. But although he was better trained than his opponent, he was also more prone to embrace the barbarity of battle.

Hitler Youth Division

The natural progression to giving the HJ more military training was the formation of the 12th SS Panzer Division *Hitlerjugend*. A recruitment drive began, drawing principally on 17-year-old volunteers. However, boys of 16 and under eagerly joined. During July and August 1943, some 10,000 recruits arrived at the new division's training camp in Beverloo, Belgium.

▶ **Mittlere Funkpanzerwagen Ausf C (SdKfz 251/3)**

2.SS-Panzergrenadier-Regiment Hitlerjugend / Stab

The radio variant of the SdKfz 251 was originally equipped with frame antennae as seen here, but from 1942 these began to be replaced by less conspicuous pole antennae. However, frame-equipped vehicles were still in service in 1944.

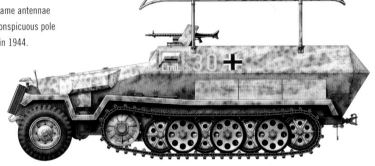

Specifications

Crew: 2 plus 12 troops	Engine: Maybach HL42TUKRM
Weight: 9.9 tonnes (9 tons)	Speed: 53km/h (33mph)
Length: 5.98m (19ft 7in)	Range: 300km (186 miles)
Width: 2.1m (6ft 11in)	Radio: FuG Spr Ger 1
Height: 1.75m (5ft 8in) or 2.16m	Armament: 1/2 x 7.62mm
(7ft) including MG shield if fitted	(0.3in) MG

Specifications

Crew: 5	Speed: 46km/h (28.6mph)
Weight: 50.2 tonnes (45.5 tons)	Range: 200km (124 miles)
Length: 8.86m (29ft 0in)	Radio: FuG5
Width: 3.4m (11ft 2in)	Armament: 1 x 75mm (3in) KwK42 L/70;
Height: 2.98m (9ft 10in)	2 x 7.92mm (0.3in) MG (one hull-mounted,
Engine: Maybach HL230P30	one coaxial)

▲ **Panzerkampfwagen V Ausf A (SdKfz 171)**

12.SS-Panzer-Regiment / I.Abteilung / 1.Kompanie

Before its losses in Normandy, the *Hitlerjugend*'s Panzer regiment was equipped with one battalion totalling 66 Panthers and one battalion with 96 Panzer IVs. After Normandy, it was reduced to a single battalion regiment.

Normandy
JUNE–JULY 1944

Nobody could question the determination of the ideologically trained teenagers who volunteered for the *Hitlerjugend* Division, but fighting spirit was no substitute for experience.

To PROVIDE THE HJ DIVISION with a cadre of experienced soldiers and officers, *Waffen-SS* veterans were drafted into the formation from the Eastern Front. Many were from the elite *Leibstandarte-SS Adolf Hitler*. The *Wehrmacht* assigned 50 officers with combat experience who had also been Hitler Youth leaders as officers for the division. The remaining shortfall of squad and section leaders was filled with Hitler Youth members who had demonstrated leadership aptitude during HJ paramilitary training.

By the spring of 1944, training was complete. The *Hitlerjugend* Panzer Division, now fully trained and equipped, conducted divisional manoeuvres observed by General Heinz Guderian and Field Marshal Gerd von Rundstedt. Both senior officers admired the enthusiasm and expressed their approval of the proficiency achieved by the young troops in such a short time.

The division was transferred to Hasselt, Belgium, in anticipation of the Allied invasion of northern France, where it subsequently fought with fanaticism

ORGANIZATION, 1943

SS-Pz.Gr.Div Hitlerjugend — St

1.SS-P.G.R HJ — St | 2.SS-P.G.R HJ — St | SS-Pz.Rgt 12 — St

I | II | III | I | II | III | I | II | III

SS-Art.Rgt 12 — St | SS-Krd.R 12 — St

I | II | III | I | II | III

SS-Auf.Abt 12 — St | SS-Pzjr.A 12 — St | SS-Wrf.A 12 — St | SS-Flk.A — St

I | II | III | I | II | III | I | II | III | I | II | III

ORGANIZATION, MAY 1944

12.SS-Pz.Div Hitlerjugend — St

SS-Pz.Gr.R 25 — St | SS-Pz.Gr.R 26 — St | SS-Pz.Art.R — St | SS-Pz.R 12 — St

I | II | III | I | II | III | I | II | III | I | II | III

SS-Flk.Abt 12 — St | SS-Nb.Abt 12 — St | SS-Pz.Auf.Ab — St | SS-Pzjr.A — St

I | II | III | I | II | III | I | II | III | I | II | III

 Panzerkampfwagen IV Ausf H (SdKfz 161/2)

12.SS-Panzer-Regiment / II.Abteilung / 5.Kompanie

The Ausf H variant of the Panzer IV differed from earlier models mainly in having thicker armour and an upgraded transmission system.

Specifications

Crew: 5	Speed: 38km/h (23.6mph)
Weight: 27.6 tonnes (25 tons)	Range: 210km (130.5 miles)
Length: 7.02m (23ft 0in)	Radio: FuG5
Width: 2.88m (9ft 5in)	Armament: 1 x 75mm (3in) KwK
Height: 2.68m (8ft 10in)	40/43; 2 x 7.92mm (0.3in) MG
Engine: Maybach HL120TRM	(one hull-mounted, one coaxial)

and bravery against the numerically superior Allies. On the morning of 6 June 1944, the Allied powers landed on the coast of Normandy. The Western Front now officially existed.

As can be imagined, great confusion existed in both the Allied and German military commands. At 14:30 on 6 June 1944, the SS Panzer Division *Hitlerjugend* was ordered to proceed to Caen. This was in close proximity to the British and Canadian landing sites of Juno and Sword beaches.

Slaughter in Normandy

As soon as the *Hitlerjugend* Division arrived in the area, they came under heavy and relentless Allied air attacks. As a result, the division did not make it to its assigned attack positions until 22:00 that night, by which time the Allies had a firm foothold on the Normandy coast.

Although the HJ troops were fanatical in their determination and tenacity to fight to the death, it did not take long for the division to suffer

horrendous casualties. In their first engagement with the Canadians, the HJ Division destroyed 28 tanks while sustaining only six casualties. Such a favourable exchange rate would not last. They fought with incredible determination, playing no small part in preventing the British from achieving their early targets in Normandy. However, the odds were against them. In just over one month of combat, the HJ Panzer Division lost more than 60 per cent of its strength, 20 per cent being killed and the remainder being either wounded or posted missing.

After the British and Canadian forces eventually captured Caen, *Hitlerjugend* was one of 24 German divisions encircled in the Falaise pocket. It was ordered to hold open the northern edge of the pocket so that the trapped divisions could escape as best they could. The remnants of the 12th SS Panzer Division escaped the encirclement, as did about 20,000 other Germans, but more than 50,000 more German troops were trapped in the Falaise pocket and surrendered to the Allies.

▸ **Flakpanzer 38(t) Ausf L (SdKfz 140)**

12.SS-Panzer-Regiment / I.Abteilung / Stab-Kompanie / Flak-Zug

In June 1944, the 12th SS Panzer Regiment had 12 self-propelled 2cm (0.7in) Flak guns mounted on the chassis of the Panzer 38(t). The single light AA gun proved relatively ineffective against fast, low-flying fighter bombers.

Specifications

Crew: 5	Engine: Praga AC 6-cylinder petrol
Weight: 9.8 tonnes (9.3 tons)	Speed: 42km/h (26mph)
Length: 4.61m (15ft 2in)	Range: 210km (130 miles)
Width: 2.13m (7ft)	Radio: None
Height: 2.25m (7ft 5in)	

▸ **2cm vierling Flakpanzer IV Wirbelwind**

12.SS-Panzer-Regiment / Stab / Flak-Zug

The *Wirbelwind* was an attempt to increase the anti-aircraft firepower of Panzer divisions. However, even with four 2cm (0.7in) cannon, it was still less effective than a single 3.7cm (1.5in) weapon, and production ceased in autumn 1944.

Specifications

Crew: 5	Engine: Maybach HL120TRM
Weight: 24.3 tonnes (22 tons)	Speed: 38km/h (23.6mph)
Length: 5.92m (19ft 4in)	Range: 200km (124 miles)
Width: 2.9m (9ft 5in)	Radio: FuG2 and FuG5
Height: 2.76m (9ft)	Armament: 4 x 2cm (1.8in) cannon

Ardennes: Wacht am Rhein
SEPTEMBER–DECEMBER 1944

After a short time to rest and refit, the division was at the front again. This time, the *Hitlerjugend* was covering the German withdrawal from France.

O N 6 SEPTEMBER, near the Franco–Belgian border, *SS-Oberführer* Kurt Meyer was captured by the Americans as the rest of the division fought with the advancing US troops trying to enter Belgium.

In November, the division was transferred to Bremen, Germany. Replacement tanks and other equipment arrived, together with additional manpower, most being former *Kriegsmarine* and *Luftwaffe* personnel. *SS-Standarten-führer* Hugo

Kraas became commander of the division, taking over from *SS-Obersturmbannführer* Hubert Meyer, and the formation was assigned to the Sixth SS Panzer Army.

On 16 December 1944, the HJ Division took an active role in the Ardennes offensive. Starting in the northern sector, the division was allocated to the right flank of the Sixth Panzer Army to provide protection as it punched forward towards Malmedy, driving deep into the thinly held Allied lines. However, stiff

▲ Panzer IV/70 (SdKfz 162/1)

12.Panzerjäger-Abteilung / 1.Kompanie

In Normandy, the *Hitlerjugend* tank-hunter battalion had two companies of the tank-destroyer variant of the Panzer IV. Fitted with a 7.5cm (3in) Pak 39 gun, the vehicles were later replaced with the Panzer IV/70 series.

Specifications

Crew: 4	Speed: 35km/h (21.7mph)
Weight: 25.8 tonnes (23.48 tons)	Range: 210km (130.5 miles)
Length: 8.50m (27ft 10.5in)	Radio: FuG5
Width: 3.17m (10ft 5in)	Armament: 1 x 75mm (3in) PaK 42 L/70 anti-
Height: 2.85m (9ft 4in)	tank gun; 1 x 7.92mm (0.3in) MG
Engine: Maybach HL120TRM (300hp)	

▶ Panzerkampfwagen VI Ausf E (SdKfz 181)

Kampfgruppe Wünsche / 101.schwere SS-Panzer-Abteilung / 1.Kompanie

The *Wünsche* battle group formed in mid-July 1944. It included units from the *Hitlerjugend* and *LSSAH* Divisions as well as the Tiger tanks of the 101st SS Heavy Panzer Battalion.

Specifications

Crew: 5	Speed: 38km/h (23.6mph)
Weight: 62.8 tonnes (57 tons)	Range: 140km (87 miles)
Length: 8.45m (27ft 8in)	Radio: FuG5
Width: 3.7m (12ft 1in)	Armament: 1 x 88mm (3.5in) KwK
Height: 2.93m (9ft 7in)	36 L/56; 2 x 7.92mm (0.3in) MG
Engine: Maybach HL210P45 (700hp)	(one hull-mounted, one coaxial)

American resistance forced the division to swing left and follow the path of the *Leibstandarte*.

By New Year's Day 1945, the HJ Division was one of the many German units forming a ring around Bastogne. But initial successes had been countered by superior Allied resources, and the German front was under heavy pressure from the flanks of the salient. In particular, the *Wehrmacht* had no answer to the overwhelming Allied air superiority, and the troops, including those of the *Hitlerjugend* Division, were eventually forced to withdraw. By 18 January, the German armies had returned to the positions they had held before the offensive had begun.

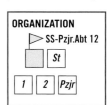

ORGANIZATION
▷ SS-Pzjr.Abt 12
St
1   2   Pzjr

▼ 25.Panzergrenadier-Regiment, III.Bataillon, 1.Kompanie

The late-war armoured infantry company was mostly equipped with variants of the SdKfz 251. These were fitted with either short or long barrel 7.5cm (3in) Pak 40s. Two of the heavy platoon vehicles carried mortars.

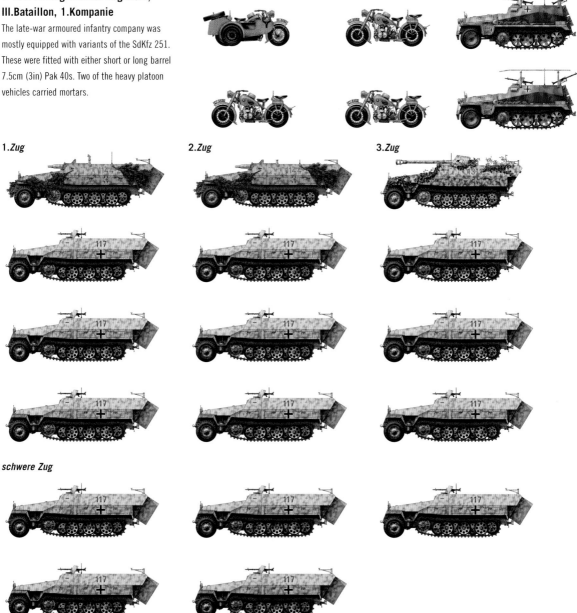

Stab

1.Zug   *2.Zug*   *3.Zug*

schwere Zug

Weapon Specifications

Crew: 7	Shell weight (HE): 9.24kg (20.34lb)
Weight: 5.1 tonnes (4.9 tons)	Muzzle Velocity (HE): 820m/s (2690fps)
Barrel length: 4.93m (16ft 2in)	Range (aerial, HE): 8000m (26,245ft)
Calibre: 88mm (3.45in)	Ammunition: Armour-piercing, high explosive

▲ **Mittlere Zugkraftwagen 8t / 8.8cm Flak 18 (SdKfz 7)**

12.SS-Flak-Abteilung (mot) / 1.Kompanie

The *Hitlerjugend* Division had more heavy Flak guns than many German Army divisions. Typically, it would deploy two batteries of six 8.8cm (3.5in) guns rather than the single battery of four guns more usually found.

 # Germany and Hungary

JANUARY–MAY 1945

The final German offensive in the West was followed by another, equally futile, offensive in the East, in which the Sixth SS Panzer Army would play a major part.

THERE WOULD BE NO TIME TO REST because on 20 January the entire Sixth Panzer Army was ordered to the East. The plan was to attack Soviet elements who had surrounded Budapest and had trapped 45,000 men of the IX.*SS-Gebirgskorps* there. Before the end of the month, the division was transferred by rail to Hungary. While the HJ Division was in transit, the IV.*SS-Panzerkorps* launched several ill-fated relief operations. Being in Army Group South, HJ was one of the first units to arrive. In early February, before the attack was launched, HJ and elements of the *Leibstandarte* attacked and successfully destroyed a Soviet bridgehead that had been established on the River Danube at Gran, the German name for Esztergom in Hungary.

Last battles

The division was next to take part in Operation *Frühlingserwachen* (Spring Awakening), the operation to retake the Hungarian oilfields. Hitler, desperate to

▶ **LeFH18/2 auf PzKpfw II (SdKfz 124)**

12.SS-Artillerie-Regiment / I.Abteilung / 1.Batterie

From the original formation of the division one battalion of the 12th Artillery Regiment was equipped with self propelled guns. Two out of three batteries operated with the Wespe 10.5cm (4.1in) howitzer.

Specifications

Crew: 5	Speed: 40km/h (25mph)
Weight: 12.1 tonnes (11 tons)	Range: 220km (136.7 miles)
Length: 4.81m (15ft 10in)	Radio: FuG Spr 1
Width: 2.28m (7ft 6in)	Armament: 1 x LeFH 18M L/28 105mm
Height: 2.25m (7ft 4.5in)	(4.1in) howitzer
Engine: Maybach HL62TR	

keep the operation a secret, had ordered that no reconnaissance of the battlefield would be allowed before the attack began.

The attack got under way on 6 March 1945 in atrocious conditions. The spring thaw meant that the German assault was confined to a few narrow roads, and after initial successes, the offensive was aborted after a Soviet counterattack threatened to encircle the German forces.

Hitler lost faith in the *Waffen-SS* and ordered that the honorary cuffbands issued to the divisions involved in the attack be returned. Outraged at the order, army commander Sepp Dietrich refused to pass it on to his men.

By the middle of March, the 12th SS Division was on the retreat heading for Austria. By 13 April, the

12.SS-Panzer-Division *Hitlerjugend*	Strength
August 1944:	
PzKpfw IV	37
PzKpfw V	41
January 1945:	
PzKpfw IV	19
PzKpfw V	36

division had reached Linz. On 8 May, the division crossed the demarcation line between the Western and Eastern Allies near the town of Enns and entered American captivity. Defiant until the end, the HJ refused to comply with the American order that its vehicles carry white flags as a token of surrender.

Specifications

Crew: 3

Weight: 9.4 tonnes (8.53 tons)

Length: 5.98m (19ft 7in)

Width: 2.83m (9ft 4in)

Height: 2.07m (6ft 10in)

Engine: Maybach HL42TUKRM

Speed: 53km/h (33mph)

Range: 300km (186 miles)

Radio: FuG Spr Ger 'f'

Armament: 1 x 75mm (3in) KwK L/24 gun

▲ Mittlere Schützenpanzerwagen (7.5cm) Ausf D (SdKfz 251/9)

25.Panzergrenadier-Regiment / III.Bataillon / 11.Kompanie

A fully armoured Panzergrenadier company typically operated with 17 or more SdKfz 251 armoured half-tracks. Two of the vehicles would be armed with short-barrelled 7.5cm (3in) KwK37 tank guns, originally fitted to Panzer IVs.

▶ Leichte Schützenpanzerwagen (SdKfz 250/9)

12.SS-Panzer-Aufklärungs-Abteilung / 2.(Spw) Aufklärungs-Kompanie

Three out of the division's four reconnaissance companies were issued with half-tracks. By 1944, the SdKfz 250 fitted with a 2cm (0.7in) turret had all but replaced the SdKfz 222 light armoured car in such units.

Specifications

Crew: 3

Weight: 6.9 tonnes (6.3 tons)

Length: 4.56m (14ft 11.5in)

Width: 1.95m (6ft 5in)

Height: 2.16m (7ft 1in)

Engine: Maybach HL42TRKM 6-cylinder (100hp)

Speed: 60km/h (37mph)

Range: 320km (199 miles)

Radio: FuG Spr Ger 'f'

Armament: 1 x 20mm (0.7in) KwK 30/38 L/55 cannon; 1 x 7.92mm (0.3in) MG (coaxial)

Chapter 7

Volunteer Divisions

The change in the nature of the *Waffen-SS*, which first became apparent with the expansion of the organisation in the first years of the war, became even more obvious with the formation of large numbers of new divisions from 1943 onwards. Many of the new formations were manned partly or entirely by foreign volunteers – a distinction which was marked by the use of *Freiwilligen,* or 'Volunteer', in the divisional titles.

◀ **SS in Normandy**
Waffen-SS divisions played a major part in the German defence of Normandy, where these men are working on a Panzer IV. For the most part, the divisions involved were Germanic formations of the 'old' SS. Elsewhere, however, the SS was opening its ranks to a wide variety of nationalities.

13th Waffen Gebirgs Division der SS *Handschar*

The formation of the 13th SS Division marked a major departure from the Nazi state's original policy of using only German or Germanic volunteers in the SS.

*R*EICHSFÜHRER-SS Heinrich Himmler was fascinated by Islam. He believed that Muslims would make excellent shock troops, since he understood their faith offered them a place in paradise if they gave their lives against an enemy. He also supported the crackpot Nazi theory that Croatians were not Slavs, but were descended from the Aryan Goths.

As a result of his beliefs, Himmler advocated the formation of a European Muslim division, which was approved by Hitler on 13 February 1943. The idea was resented by Croatian dictator Ante Pavelic, who felt that the SS was poaching on his preserves, but there was little that his government could do.

When the Independent State of Croatia proclaimed its existence on 10 April 1941, part of the

INSIGNIA The divisional symbol was the *Handschar*. This was a traditional Balkan scimitar whose name derived from the Arabic word for such weapons – *khanjar*.

territory it claimed was the former Austro-Hungarian province of Bosnia–Herzegovina. The province was a volatile ethnic and religious mix, including large numbers of Catholic Croats, Orthodox Serbs and Bosnian Muslims. It was these Muslim inhabitants of Bosnia–Herzegovina that Himmler and the *Waffen-SS* would target in their recruitment of a Croatian SS division. Grudging approval was given by the Croatian leader, Ante Pavelic, on 5 March 1943.

Muslim division forms

The division began forming on 5 March 1943, and reached its full strength of at least 20,000 men by July. Muslims already serving in the Croatian Army were keen on serving in the new division, and the

Divisional History	Formed
Kroatische SS-Freiwilligen-Division	1943
Kroatische SS-Freiwilligen-Gebirgs-Division	1943
SS-Freiwilligen Bosnien-Herzegowina Gebirgs-Division (Kroatien)	1943
13.SS-Freiwilligen-bosn.herzegow. Gebirgs-Division (Kroatien)	1943
13.Waffen-Gebirgs-Division der SS Handschar (kroatische Nr. 1)	1944

Commanders

Oberführer Herbert von Obwurzer
April 1943 – August 1943

Gruppenführer Karl-Gustav Sauberzweig
August 1943 – June 1944

Brigadeführer Desiderius Hampel
June 1944 – May 1945

▶ **Leichte Panzerspähwagen (MG) (SdKfz 221)**

SS Aufklarungs Abteilung 13

In September 1944 a number of *Handschar's* units, including its reconnaissance battalion, were detached from the division to serve as Corps troops for the II SS Cavalry Corps.

Specifications

Crew: 2	Engine: Horch 3.5L petrol (75hp)
Weight: 4 tonnes (3.61 tons)	Speed: 90km/h (56mph)
Length: 4.80m (15ft 8in)	Range: 320km (199 miles)
Width: 1.95m (6ft 5in)	Radio: None
Height: 1.70m (5ft 7in)	Armament: 1 x 7.92mm (0.3in) MG

▲ **5cm Panzerabwehrkanone (Pak 38)**

13.SS-Panzerjäger-Bataillon (mot)

For the first year of its existence, *Handschar*'s tank-hunting battalion was equipped exclusively with towed Pak 36 5cm (2in) guns. By the summer of 1944, however, these had been replaced by assault guns and 7.5cm (3in) Pak 40s.

Specifications	
Crew: 3	Muzzle Velocity (AP): 835m/s (2900fps)
Weight: 1.2 tonnes (1.13 tons)	Range: AP: 1800m (1968 yards), HE: 2.6km
Length: 3.2m (10ft 5in)	(1.6 miles)
Calibre: 50mm (2in)	Ammunition: Armour-piercing, high explosive

▲ **15cm schwere Felfhaubitze (sFH18)**

13.SS-Gebirgs-Artillerie-Regiment / IV.Abteilung / 2.Batterie

Although three of the four battalions attached to the *Handschar* Division's artillery regiment were equipped with lightweight mountain artillery, the fourth battalion operated one battery of long-range guns and two batteries of heavy howitzers.

Specifications	
Crew: 5	Muzzle Velocity: 520m/s (1706fps)
Weight: 6.3 tonnes (5.7 tons)	Range: 13km (8 miles)
Length: 4.4m (14 ft 5in)	Ammunition: High explosive or smoke
Calibre: 150mm (5.9in)	

Croats had to take measures to prevent men from deserting to serve the Germans.

Not all were Muslim volunteers, however. Several thousand *Volksdeutsche* and Catholic Croats were included, and initial Muslim enthusiasm quickly fell off, so numbers had to be made up by conscription.

Croats and Bosnians

Originally known as the *Kroatische SS-Freiwilligen-Division*, it was turned into a mountain unit and became known as the *Kroatische SS-Freiwilligen-Gebirgs-Division*. In an attempt to appease the Bosnian members of the formation, who for historical, religious and ethnic reasons did not get on with the Croats, it was renamed 13.*SS-Freiwilligen-bosn.herzogow. Gebirgs-Division (Kroatien)*, before eventually receiving its final name of 13.*Waffen-Gebirgs-Division der SS Handschar (kroatische Nr. 1)* in May of 1944. The name comes from the Croat word for a curved scimitar-like sword traditionally associated with Bosnia, the *Handzar*, which is spelled *Handschar* in German.

The division wore regular SS issue uniforms. The divisional collar patch showed an arm holding a *Handschar* over a swastika. A red and white Croatian shield was worn on the left arm, and the divisional headgear was a traditional Muslim fez. Non-Muslims wore standard SS mountain caps.

Partisan war
1944–1945

The division departed for training at Villefranche-de-Rouergue in Aveyron, in occupied France, being fully transferred by September 1943.

WHILE AT VILLEFRANCHE, it became the only SS division to mutiny, the rising being incited by Communists who had infiltrated the recruitment process. Several German officers were killed during the mutiny, though most of the troops did not take part. Fourteen soldiers were executed as mutineers.

By February 1944, after further training at Neuhammer in Germany, the division was declared operational. It was transferred back to Bosnia for active service against the partisans. Its area of operations was northeastern Bosnia and western Serbia. In a bitter irony, its operations against Bosnian and Serb partisans saw many of the division's members who came from villages and towns in the area fighting against former neighbours.

Guerrilla warfare

The division participated in several anti-partisan campaigns, including Operations *Wegweiser*, *Save*, *Osterei*, *Maibaum* and *Maiglockchen*. Some successes were achieved, and overall the *Handschar* proved itself a competent anti-guerrilla unit, as long as its men were fighting their hereditary enemies. Atrocities were committed, but atrocity was standard in the Balkans, and the *Handschar* was no worse than many other SS divisions, and less brutal than some.

In more conventional action against the Soviets, the *Handschar* Division was far less effective. With the penetration of the Red Army up to the Croatian borders in late 1944, the division was transferred to southern Hungary, and became involved in front-line fighting. Desertions plagued the division from this point on, as many of the Muslims decided to return to Bosnia to protect their homes and families. A number of the deserters switched sides and joined Tito's partisan forces.

The 9000 German personnel of the 13. *Waffen-Gebirgs-Division der SS Handschar* were deployed as an SS battle group, known as *Kampfgruppe Henke*.

▲ **Weapons inspection**

The commander of the Croatian Army inspects the weapons of a Bosnian Muslim unit. When the SS began raising similar formations, it allowed Muslim members of the divisions to retain the traditional fez as headgear.

This force fought in southern Hungary, entering combat with the Soviets near the Yugoslav border. On 7 May 1945, the remnants of the division surrendered to the British in Austria. All remaining Muslim volunteers were handed over to Tito's forces after the capitulation and most were executed at Maibor on the Drava.

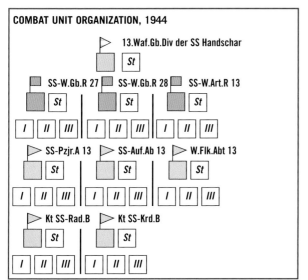

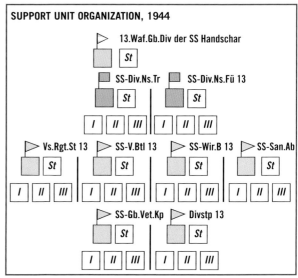

▲ 3.7cm Fliegerabwerkanonen (Flak 36/37)

13.SS-Flak-Abteilung / 2.Batterie

The 3.7cm (1.5in) Flak 36/37 was an effective low-level anti-aircraft weapon, but it was also extremely useful in engaging ground targets and improvised partisan positions in the mountainous terrain of Bosnia.

Specifications

Crew: 5	Muzzle Velocity: 820m/s (2690fps)
Weight: 1.5 tonnes (1.4 tons)	Range: 4800m (5249 yards)
Length: 3.5m (11ft)	Ammunition: High explosive or smoke
Calibre: 37mm (1.5in)	

▲ 3.7cm Panzerabwehrkanone (Pak 36)

1.SS-Freiwilligen-Gebirgsjäger-Regiment (kroat) / I.Gebirgs-Bataillon

The heavy support company in each mountain battalion had a single anti-tank platoon that was armed with three Pak 36 guns.

Specifications

Crew: 3	Muzzle Velocity: 762m/s (2500fps)
Weight: 0.43 tonnes (0.39 tons)	Range: 600m (656 yards)
Length: 1.67m (5ft 5.5in)	Ammunition: Armour-piercing
Calibre: 37mm (1.5in)	

Specifications

Crew: 1	Engine: Horch 3.5L or 3.8L V8 petrol
Weight: 1.89 tonnes (1.72 tons)	(82 or 92hp)
Length: 5.05m (16ft 7in)	Speed: 120km/h (74mph)
Width: 1.79m (5ft 10in)	Range: 400km (248 miles)
Height: 1.69m (5ft 6.5in)	Radio: None

▲ Sanitätswagen Phänomen Granit 1500A (Kfz 31)

Waffen-Gebirgs-Division der SS Handschar / 13.Krankenhraftwagen-Zug

The *Handschar* Division's medical detachment had two ambulance platoons and a stretcher-bearer company to service two medical companies.

▶ Mittlere Personenkraftwagen Mercedes 340 (Kfz 15)

Waffen-Gebirgs-Division der SS Handschar / Stab

Used as a staff and communications vehicle, the Mercedes 340 had a long wheelbase chassis that impaired its cross-country ability.

Specifications

Crew: 1	Engine: Mercedes-Benz 6-cylinder petrol
Weight: 2.4 tonnes (2.2 tons)	(90hp)
Length: 4.44m (14ft 7in)	Speed: 88km/h (55mph)
Width: 1.68m (5ft 6in)	Range: 400km (248 miles)
Height: 1.73m (5ft 8in)	Radio: Various depending on deployment

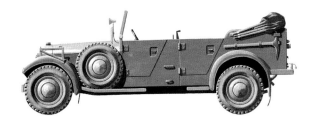

14th Waffen Grenadier Division der SS

Following the German defeats at Stalingrad and Kursk, *Reichsführer-SS* Heinrich Himmler began to reappraise the SS attitude towards the 'subhuman' Slavs of Eastern Europe.

THE 14TH WAFFEN GRENADIER DIVISION DER SS was formed in Galicia in mid-1943. The region of Galicia, covering southeastern Poland and western Ukraine, was colonized by German settlers in the fourteenth century. It had became a province of Maria-Theresa's Austro-Hungarian Empire by the 1770s, with the provincial capital at Lemberg (Lvov). Although the population was considered Germanic, or *Volksdeutsche*, by the Nazis, the main cultural influence in the region was in fact Ukrainian, as were most of the troops in the division.

What was to become the 14. *Waffen-Grenadier-Division der SS (ukrainische Nr. 1)* was authorized as the *SS-Freiwilligen-Division Galizien* in April 1943, the name being changed briefly to *SS-Schützen-Division Galizien*. The western Ukraine's historical name of Galicia was applied to the new division, possibly to avoid alerting Hitler to the fact that the SS was forming a division which included large numbers of the despised Slavs.

Training of the troops began at the *Truppenübungsplatz der SS* Heidelager in Debica in September 1943 before the division was moved to Silesia in April 1944 for further training. The recruits were mainly *Volksdeutsche* and Ukrainians from the area around Lemberg. On 22 October 1943, the division's name was changed back to *SS-Freiwilligen-Division Galizien*.

Inauspicious combat debut

The *Galizien* Division was sent to the front at Brody in the Ukraine in June 1944. Inadequately armed, poorly trained, and with troops lacking in motivation, it was no match for the powerful Soviet assault that was launched as part of the Red Army's massive summer offensive. The division was quickly encircled and smashed, with only about 3000 of its 15,000 members managing to reach the German lines and safety.

The formation was soon rebuilt as the 14. *Waffen-Grenadier-Division der SS*. After the completion of basic training at *Truppenübungsplatz* Neuhammer in Silesia, it was sent into Slovakia at the end of August

Commanders

Gruppenführer Walther Schimana *June 1943 – November 1943*	Brigadeführer Nikolaus Heilmann *July 1944 – September 1944*
Brigadeführer Fritz Freitag *November 1943 – April 1944*	Brigadeführer Fritz Freitag *September 1944 – April 1945*
Brigadeführer Sylvester Stadler *April 1944 – July 1944*	Brigadeführer Pavlo Shandruk *April 1945 – May 1945*

1944, where it was used to help suppress the Slovak National Uprising. From there, the division was deployed into northern Yugoslavia to fight partisans.

In January 1945, the division was again redesignated, now becoming known as the 14. *Waffen-Grenadier-Division der SS (ukrainische Nr. 1)*. In January 1945, it was transferred to Pressburg (now Bratislava in Slovakia), where it took part in anti-partisan operations in the *Untersteiermark* (the area which is today known as Slovenia).

In April 1945, the formation was officially transferred to the newly forming Ukrainian National Army as the 1. *Ukrainische Division der Ukrainischen National-Armee*. Although still strong numerically, the division was short of weaponry and supplies. Retreating into the Austrian Alps north of Klagenfurt, the division surrendered to the Americans between the towns of Tamsweg and Judenberg at the beginning of May.

Divisional History	Formed
SS-Freiwilligen-Division Galizien	1943
SS-Schützen-Division Galizien	1943
SS-Freiwilligen-Division Galizien	1943
14.Galizische SS-Freiwilligen-Division	1944
14.Waffen-Grenadier-Division der SS (ukrainische Nr. 1)	1945
1.Ukrainische Division der Ukrainischen National-Armee	1945

▲ 10.5cm leichte Feldhaubitze (leFH18)

SS-Artillerie-Regiment Galizische / III.Abteilung

Although poorly equipped by late-war SS standards, the Galician Division had a standard infantry division's complement of artillery, with three battalions each equipped with a dozen light field howitzers.

Specifications

Crew: 5	Muzzle Velocity: 540m/s (1770fps)
Weight: 1.95 tonnes (1.85 tons)	Range: 12,325m (13,480 yards)
Length: 3.3m (10ft)	Ammunition: High explosive or smoke
Calibre: 105mm (4.1in)	

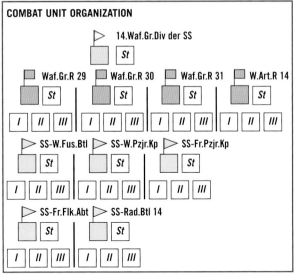

COMBAT UNIT ORGANIZATION

14.Waf.Gr.Div der SS — St

Waf.Gr.R 29 — St — I II III
Waf.Gr.R 30 — St — I II III
Waf.Gr.R 31 — St — I II III
W.Art.R 14 — St — I II III

SS-W.Fus.Btl — St — I II III
SS-W.Pzjr.Kp — St — I II III
SS-Fr.Pzjr.Kp — St

SS-Fr.Flk.Abt — St — I II III
SS-Rad.Btl 14 — St — I II III

Specifications

Crew: 1 + maintenance section
Weight: 9 tonnes (8.85 tons)
Length: 7.4m (24ft 5in)
Width: 2.5m (8ft 2in)
Height: 3m (9ft 9in)
Engine: 6-cylinder petrol (90bhp)
Speed: 45km/h (28mph)
Range: not known
Payload: printing equipment

▲ Henschel/Magirus 33 G1 (Kfz 72)

14.Waffen-Grenadier-Division der SS / Stab

Medium 6x4 van-bodied trucks were used as command posts by divisional headquarters, and were also used by mapping and printing sections.

▼ Mittlere Landkraftwagen 3t Opel Blitz 3.6 36S

14.SS-Division / Versorgungsdienst

The 14th Division's supply service had two supply companies, capable of lifting 60 tonnes (59 tons) and 90 tonnes (88 tons). A 60-tonne company was divided into four sections, each of which had five medium trucks at full strength.

Specifications

Crew: 1
Weight: 3.29 tonnes (3 tons)
Length: 6.02m (19ft 9in)
Width: 2.27m (7ft 5in)
Height: 2.18m (7ft 2in)
Engine: Opel 6-cylinder petrol (73.5hp)
Speed: 80km/h (50mph)
Range: 410km (255 miles)
Radio: None

15th Waffen Grenadier Division der SS

Early in 1943, the *Lettische SS-Freiwilligen-Legion* was formed from several SS-linked Latvian internal security units, known as *Schutzmannschaft* Battalions.

THE ORIGINS OF THE 15. *Waffen-Grenadier-Division der SS (lettische Nr. 1)* date back to 1943, when the *Lettische SS-Freiwilligen-Legion* was enlarged and upgraded to divisional status. The legion had been formed in the spring of 1943, with the raising of three infantry regiments. Along with the 2nd Latvian SS Volunteer Brigade (formerly the Latvian SS Volunteer Brigade), the Latvian Volunteer Legion served under the VI SS Volunteer Corps. In November 1943, the legion saw action at Novo-Sokolniki, northern Russia, as part of the Sixteenth Army with Army Group North.

The legion was taken out of combat in October 1943 to become the kernel of a new volunteer division, the 1st Division of the SS Latvian Legion (renamed 15. *Lettische SS-Freiwilligen-Division*). The

Commanders

Brigadeführer Peter Hansen
February 1943 – May 1943

Gruppenführer Carl Graf von Pückler-Burghauss
May 1943 – February 1944

Brigadeführer Nikolas Heilmann
February 1944 – July 1944

Brigadeführer Herbert von Obwurzer
July 1944 – January 1945

Oberführer Arthur Ax
January 1945 – February 1945

Oberführer Karl Burk
February 1945 – May 1945

division later became the 15. *Waffen-Grenadier Division der SS (lettische Nr. 1)* and was assigned to the XLIII Corps of the German Sixteenth Army.

The Soviet winter offensive that was launched at the end of December 1943 continued until February 1944. The fighting was furious, and both sides suffered heavy casualties. The 15. *Lettische SS-Freiwilligen-Division* was assigned to the VI SS Corps, where it fought alongside the 19th Latvian SS Division, which had been formed around the 2nd Latvian SS Volunteer Brigade. In March 1944, both Latvian divisions fought to control strategic points

Divisional History	Formed
Lettische SS-Freiwilligen-Division	1943
15. Lettische SS-Freiwilligen-Division	1943
15. Waffen-Grenadier-Division der SS (lettische Nr. 1)	1944

INSIGNIA

The divisional insignia of the 15th SS Division was a simple letter 'L' for Latvia, with the Roman numeral 'I' to indicate that this was the 1st Latvian Division.

▲ **15cm schwere Infanterie Geschütz (sIG33)**

32.SS-Freiwilligen-Regiment (lettische Nr. 3) / 13.Kompanie

The 13th Company of each of the three Latvian volunteer regiments in the 15th Division was an infantry gun unit. It was equipped with two heavy sIG33s in addition to six of the lighter 7.5cm (3in) *leichte Infanterie Geschütze*.

Specifications

Crew: 5

Weight: 1.75 tonnes (1.71 tons)

Length: 1.64m (64.57in)

Calibre: 150mm (5.9in)

Muzzle Velocity: 241m/s (783fps)

Range: 5504m (6000 yards)

Ammunition: High explosive or smoke

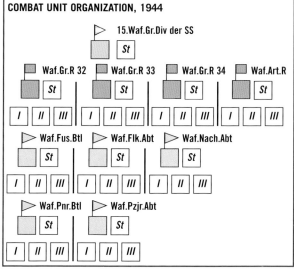

COMBAT UNIT ORGANIZATION, 1944

15.Waf.Gr.Div der SS
St

Waf.Gr.R 32 — St — I II III
Waf.Gr.R 33 — St — I II III
Waf.Gr.R 34 — St — I II III
Waf.Art.R — St — I II III

Waf.Fus.Btl — St — I II III
Waf.Flk.Abt — St — I II III
Waf.Nach.Abt — St — I II III

Waf.Pnr.Btl — St — I II III
Waf.Pzjr.Abt — St — I II III

along the Velikiye River. Although the corps faced 11 Soviet divisions, the Soviet offensive was contained at great cost.

The launch of the Soviet offensive in June 1944 saw the 15th SS Division forced back from its defensive positions on the River Sanukha. A month later, the Latvian division was fighting yet another attack, near Ostrova in Estonia. The power of the offensive meant that the Latvians could pull back only at the cost of two regiments all but wiped out.

Surviving infantrymen and the divisional artillery were transferred to the 19th SS Division while NCO and officer cadres were shipped to the *Truppenübungsplatz der SS* West Prussia. In September, conscripts from Latvia and engineers from the SS Training and Replacement Battalions at Dresden were used to reform the 15. *Waffen-Grenadier-Division der SS (lettische Nr. 1)*.

Premature action

In January 1945, although training was far from complete, the division was ordered to positions along the Oder–Vistula Canal. By end of February, the Red Army had broken through to the Baltic at Kolberg, cutting off large German forces, including the 15th SS Division. As part of *Kampfgruppe Tettau*, the division broke through the Soviet lines to reach German-held territory, its 33rd Grenadier Regiment acting as rearguard.

Survivors were sent to Neubrandenburg, north of Berlin, for refitting. As the Soviets pushed on towards the German capital, a battle group drawn from the 32nd and 33rd Regiments was dispatched towards Berlin to help in the defence of the city. On 24 April, after fighting off Soviet attacks in the south of the

▲ **Baltic SS**

A Latvian SS man fires a flare from a Walther LP signal gun. The 15th SS Division to which he belonged fought long and hard against the Soviets.

city, the *Kampfgruppe* began to withdraw westwards to surrender to the Americans. A week later, the remainder of the division also moved west from Neubrandenburg and reached the American lines near Schwerin, where it too surrendered.

▶ **Mittlere LKW Opel Blitz 3.6-6700A**

15.SS-Flak-Abteilung

Although officially a towed gun, the 2cm (0.7in) Flak 38 was small enough and light enough to be mounted on and operated from the bed of a truck, giving divisions a field-expedient self-propelled capability.

Specifications

Crew: 1	(73.5hp)
Weight: 3.29 tonnes (3 tons)	Speed: 80km/h (50mph)
Length: 6.02m (19ft 9in)	Range: 410km (255 miles)
Width: 2.27m (7ft 5in)	Radio: None
Height: 2.18m (7ft 2in)	Armament: Twin 20mm (0.7in)
Engine: Opel 6-cylinder petrol	Flak 38 cannon

16th SS Panzergrenadier Division *Reichsführer-SS*

The 16th SS Panzergrenadier Division *Reichsführer-SS* began its war service as the *Begleit-Bataillon* RFSS – Heinrich Himmler's personal escort battalion.

IN FEBRUARY 1943, a *Führerbefehl* (a personal command from Adolf Hitler) was passed that the unit be upgraded. It was expanded to an assault brigade and began building its strength at Laibach (the German name for Ljubljana, now the capital of Slovenia). The unit was redesignated as the *SS-Sturmbrigade Reichsführer-SS* and was sent to Corsica in the summer of 1943.

The brigade consisted of three *Schützen*, or rifle, companies and a machine gun company. Artillery support was provided by one infantry gun company, a Panzerjäger company and a battery of assault guns. Flak protection was provided by one heavy battery of 8.8cm (3.5in) Flak guns and a light battery of 2cm (0.7in) weapons.

The brigade was still in Corsica in early September 1943 when the new Italian Government signed an armistice with the Allies. German troops were ordered to disarm any Italian units in their area, and the *Sturmbrigade Reichsführer-SS* occupied the Corsican city of Bastia after the Italian garrison refused to hand over their weapons.

Expanded to division size

On 15 September, the *Sturmbrigade* was shipped to northern Italy. On 3 October 1943, the *Sturmbrigade Reichführer-SS* was expanded still further to divisional size, becoming the *SS-Panzergrenadier-Division Reichsführer-SS*, incorporating a number of Hungarian and Romanian *Volksdeutsche*. It also received replacements from the 3rd SS Panzer Division *Totenkopf*'s reserve organization, which also provided much of the division's officer and NCO cadres. It began working up to operational readiness in Slovenia and northern Italy, eventually moving back to near Vienna in Austria.

The division was sent into action sooner than expected. A *Kampfgruppe* was sent south in January 1944, when the Allies attempted to outflank the Gustav Line at Cassino by mounting an amphibious

INSIGNIA

The 16th SS Division's insignia was a copy of the unique lapel rank badge worn by Heinrich Himmler in his position as *Reichsführer-SS*.

Divisional History	Formed
Begleit-Bataillon Reichsführer-SS	1941
Sturmbrigade Reichsführer-SS	1943
16 SS-Panzergrenadier-Division Reichsführer-SS	1943

Commanders

Sturmbannführer Friedrich Dern
February 1941 – ? 1941

Sturmbannführer Ernst Schützeck
? 1941

Sturmbannführer Herbert Garthe
? 1941 – February 1942

Sturmbannführer Paul Massel
February 1942

Obersturmbannführer Karl Gesele
February 1942 – September 1943

Gruppenführer Max Simon
October 1943 – October 1944

Brigadeführer Otto Baum
October 1944 – May 1945

landing between Anzio and Nettuno. The rapid German reaction to the landing stalled Allied plans until May. Elements of the *Reichsführer-SS* Division were located on the coast around Pisa, attached to the XIV Panzer Corps, commanded by *General der Panzertruppen* von Senger und Etterlin.

Occupation of Hungary

The training of the rest of the division was cut short when Hungary began looking for ways to get out of the war. To prevent the government of Admiral Miklos Horthy and Miklos Kallay from negotiating a separate armistice with the Allies, German forces, including the new *Reichsführer-SS* Division, occupied the country on 19 March 1944.

Attached to the LVIII (Reserve) Panzer Corps, the division operated alongside a battalion of the 5th SS Panzer Division *Wiking* as *Kampfgruppe Simon*, after the *Reichsführer-SS*'s commander *Gruppenführer* Max

Simon. In April, the division was at Debrecen under the orders of the *Befehlshaber Ostungarn*.

In May 1944, the division returned to Italy, where it was held in reserve to counter a possible Allied landing on Elba. In June 1944, the division was assigned to LXXXV Army Corps at Grosseto, where its constituent parts were reunited.

Its first major action was around the Tuscan hilltop town of Volterra, southeast of Livorno (Leghorn). Driven off by Allied pressure, the division retreated across the Arno to Carrera, where in August 1944 it was transferred to XIV Panzer Corps of Fourteenth Army. In the heavy fighting south of Florence, the division lost 823 officers, NCOs and men.

▶ **Sturmgeschütz Ausf B (SdKfz 142)**

Sturmbrigade Reichsführer-SS / Sturmgeschütz-Batterie

Although the *Reichsführer-SS* formations spent much of their time in anti-partisan operations, they also had a conventional combat role for which they were equipped with a small unit of assault guns.

Specifications

Crew: 4	Engine: Maybach HL120TR
Weight: 21.6 tonnes (21.1 tons)	Speed: 40km/h (25mph)
Length: 5.38m (17ft 9in)	Range: 160km (99.4 miles)
Width: 2.92m (9ft 8in)	Radio: FuG15 or FuG16
Height: 1.95m (6ft 5in)	

▶ **Panzerkampfwagen IV Ausf G (SdKfz 161/1 or 161/2)**

16.SS-Panzer-Abteilung / 3.Kompanie

The Panzer battalion attached to the *Reichsführer-SS* Division had four companies of Panzer IVs when formed. However, by June 1944 it had been re-equipped with assault guns.

Specifications

Crew: 5	Speed: 40km/h (25mph)
Weight: 25.9 tonnes (23.5 tons)	Range: 210km (130.5 miles)
Length: 6.62m (21ft 8in)	Radio: FuG5
Width: 2.88m (9ft 5in)	Armament: 1 x 75mm (3in) KwK 40/43;
Height: 2.69m (8ft 10in)	2 x 7.92mm (0.3in) MG (one hull-
Engine: Maybach HL120TRM	mounted, one coaxial)

 # Italy and Hungary
1944–1945

The *Reichsführer-SS* Division was the only major SS formation to spend long periods in combat in Italy, and its record in anti-partisan operations was not a good one.

THE DIVISION'S REPUTATION dated back to the beginning of the war, when members of the *Reichsführer's Kommandostab* were accused of numerous murders in Poland. In Russia in 1943, as the *Begleit-Bataillon* RFSS, the unit is believed to have operated alongside the notorious *Dirlewanger* Brigade in massacres at Minsk. Max Simon, the division's commander from October 1943 to October

1944, had been a concentration camp guard before the war, and a Soviet military tribunal accused him of being a key player in the slaughter of 10,000 Russian civilians at Kharkov in the summer of 1943.

In Italy, the division was engaged in bitter anti-partisan battles as it took part in the fighting retreat up the peninsula, and it showed that its behaviour in Russia had been no isolated incident.

Civilian massacre

On 12 August 1944, as part of an anti-partisan sweep through the Stazzema area of Lucca, *SS-Sturmbannführer* Walter Reder of the 16th SS Division led four columns of German Army, SS and Italian SS troops towards Sant'Anna di Stazzema. They murdered civilans in Vaccareccia, Franchi and Pero before reaching Sant'Anna. There they slaughtered the population with machine guns, hand grenades and flamethrowers. Their rampage left behind 560 dead. The youngest victim was only 10 months old and the oldest was 86.

Between 29 September and 5 October 1944, soldiers of the 16th SS Panzergrenadier Division *Reichsführer-SS*, again led by Walter Reder, attacked the small town of Marzabetto as a reprisal for partisan activity in the area. Estimates of the number of victims range from 400 to as many as 2000; among the victims, 45 were less than 2 years old, 110 were under 10, and 95 under 16.

ORGANIZATION

▷ SS-Flk.Abt 16

☐ St

Flk | Flk | Flk | Flk | Sw

▶ **Panzerjäger Marder III Ausf H (SdKfz 138)**

16.SS-Panzerjäger-Abteilung / Panzerjäger-Kompanie (Sf)

The division's Panzerjäger battalion had originally been raised for the 13th SS Mountain Division *Handschar*, but was transferred to the *Reichsführer-SS* Division in September 1944.

Specifications

Crew: 4	Speed: 35km/h (22mph)
Weight: 10.8 tonnes (9.8 tons)	Range: 240km (150 miles)
Length: 5.77m (18ft 11in)	Radio: FuG Spr Ger 1
Width: 2.16m (7ft 1in)	Armament: 1 x 75mm (3in) Pak 40/3 L/46
Height: 2.51m (8ft 3in)	anti-tank gun; 1 x 7.92mm (0.3in) MG
Engine: Praga EPA 6-cylinder (140hp)	

▲ **2cm Flakvierling auf ZgKw 8t (SdKfz 7/2)**

16.SS-Panzer-Artillerie-Regiment / Stab / Flak-Batterie

Most of the self-propelled Flak guns operated by the 16th SS Division were single-barrel pieces, but the headquarters of the artillery regiment was protected by a battery of four 2cm (0.7in) Flakvierlings.

Specifications

Crew: 7	Engine: Maybach HL62TUK 6-cylinder
Weight: 1.16 tonnes (1.06 tons)	Speed: 50km/h (31mph)
Length: 6.55m (21ft 6in)	Range: 250km (156 miles)
Width: 2.40m (7ft 10.5in)	Radio: None
Height: 3.20m (10ft 6in)	Armament: Quad 20mm (0.7in) Flak 38

Battles in Hungary

In January 1945, the divison was rushed to Hungary as part of the ultimately futile effort to raise the siege of Budapest and to protect the Hungarian oilfields. Deployed as part of the LXXXIII Army Corps, it was sent to the area around Nagykanisza, where it was thrown into the fight to stop the overwhelming advance of the Red Army.

Badly mauled by the vastly more powerful Soviet forces, the remnants of the division were pushed back into the Steiermark in Austria, where they came under the orders of the I Cavalry Corps.

The division refused to surrender after Germany's capitulation at the end of the war. The divisional commander, *SS-Brigadeführer* Otto Baum, negotiated surrender terms in which it was agreed that some would surrender to the Americans at Klagenfurt and the remainder to the British at Graz. Baum made it clear that none of his men should be handed over to the Italian partisans, fearing for their perhaps

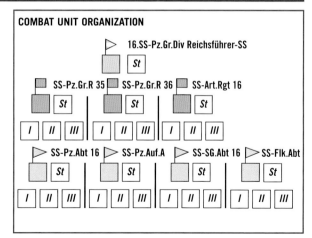

justifiable fate in such an event. Walter Reder was captured after the war. In May 1948, he was extradited to Italy and tried by a Italian military court in Bologna. In October 1951, Reder was sentenced to life imprisonment.

▼ 16.SS-Panzer-Artillerie-Regiment / 1.Bataillon

Early in the war, the organization of a typical light howitzer company in an artillery battalion attached to a motorized or Panzer division called for three batteries of four guns. In those early days of triumph, the use of three batteries allowed the guns to be used over a wider area during an advance. By 1944, however, the German forces were fighting on the defensive, and the need for more concentrated firepower saw the introduction of battalions with two six-gun batteries.

1.*Batterie*

2.*Batterie*

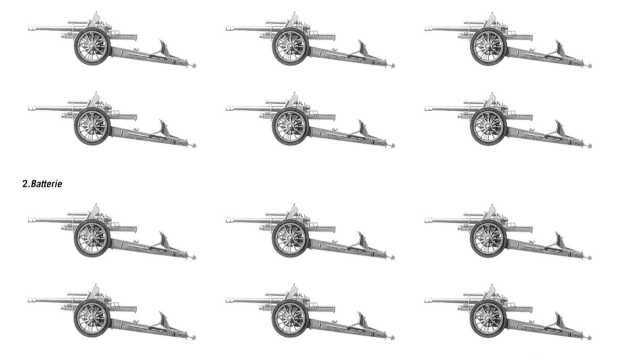

17th SS Panzergrenadier Division *Götz von Berlichingen*

The 17th SS Panzergrenadier Division was raised in the south of France in October 1943. It was given the honour title *Götz von Berlichingen*.

BERLICHINGEN (1480–1562) WAS A German mercenary who nominally served the Holy Roman Empire but who was little more than a bandit. He became a folk hero after 1773 when Goethe published a popular tragedy based on his life.

The division was one of the last SS divisions to be formed from scratch. Its personnel were mostly conscripts or were transferred from SS reserve units, with numbers being made up by a significant number of Balkan and Romanian *Volksdeutche* recruits.

By March 1944, the division had largely completed its training and was assigned to LXXX Corps. Most of its units had been fully motorized, in part by using commandeered French vehicles. The Panzer battalion was equipped with assault guns.

On 10 April 1944, the formal activation ceremony was attended by a number of Nazi, SS and military dignitaries, including *Reichsführer-SS* Heinrich Himmler, *SS-Obergruppenführer* Sepp Dietrich and General Leo Freiherr Geyr von Schweppenburg.

Commanders

SS-Gruppenführer Werner Ostendorff *October 1943 – June 1944*	SS-Standartenführer Gustav Mertsch *September 1944 – October 1944*
SS-Standartenführer Otto Binge *June 1944*	SS-Gruppenführer Werner Ostendorff *October 1944 – November 1944*
SS-Brigadeführer Otto Baum *June 1944 – July 1944*	SS-Standartenführer Hans Linger *November 1944 – January 1945*
SS-Standartenführer Otto Binge *August 1944*	Oberst Gerhard Lindner *January 1945*
SS-Oberführer Dr Eduard Deisenhofer *August 1944 – September 1944*	SS-Oberführer Fritz Klingenberg *January 1945 – March 1945*
SS-Oberführer Thomas Müller *September 1944*	SS-Oberführer Georg Bochmann *March 1945 – May 1945*

Divisional History	Formed
SS-Panzergrenadier-Division Götz von Berlichingen	1943
17.SS-Panzergrenadier-Division Götz von Berlichingen	1943

▲ **Panzerkampfwagen IV Ausf H (SdKfz 161/2)**

17.SS-Panzer-Abteilung / 2.Kompanie

When originally formed, the *Götz von Berlichingen* Division's Panzer battalion was equipped with four companies of Panzer IVs. By the time the division reached Normandy early in June 1944, these had been replaced by assault guns, which the battalion was to continue to operate for the remainder of the war.

Specifications

Crew: 5	Speed: 38km/h (23.6mph)
Weight: 27.6 tonnes (25 tons)	Range: 210km (130 miles)
Length: 7.02m (23ft 0in)	Radio: FuG5
Width: 2.88m (9ft 5in)	Armament: 1 x 75mm (3in) KwK 40/43;
Height: 2.68m (8ft 10in)	2 x 7.92mm (0.3in) MG (one hull-mounted,
Engine: Maybach HL120TRM	one coaxial)

▲ Normandy, July 1944

Two young SS soldiers man an MG 42 while awaiting an Allied attack.

▶ 2cm Flakvierling auf Zgkw 8t (SdKfz 7/1)

17.SS-Panzer-Artillerie-Regiment / Flak-Batterie

The division's Flak battalion was equipped with towed guns, but in May 1944 one self-propelled platoon with four quad 2cm (0.7in) guns was attached to the regimental staff of the division's artillery regiment.

Specifications

Crew: 5	Engine: Maybach HL120TRM
Weight: 24.3 tonnes (22 tons)	Speed: 38km/h (23.6mph)
Length: 5.9m (19ft 5in)	Range: 210km (130 miles)
Width: 2.9m (9ft 6in)	Radio: FuG2 and FuG5
Height: 2.76m (9ft)	

▶ Panzerjäger 38(t) Marder III (SdKfz 138)

17.SS Panzerjäger-Abteilung / 1.Kompanie

The division's tank-destroyer battalion had one self-propelled company with 14 tank-hunters mounting 7.5cm (3in) Pak 40s.

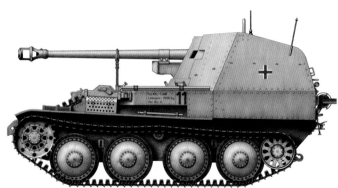

Specifications

Crew: 4	Speed: 35km/h (22mph)
Weight: 10.8 tonnes (9.8 tons)	Range: 240km (150 miles)
Length: 5.77m (19ft 11in)	Radio: FuG Spr Ger 1
Width: 2.16m (7ft 1in)	Armament: 1 x 75mm (3in) Pak 40/3 L/46
Height: 2.51m (8ft 3in)	anti-tank gun; 1 x 7.92mm (0.3in) MG
Engine: Praga EPA 6-cylinder (140hp)	

Battle for Normandy
JUNE 1944

The division was ordered to Normandy on 6 June 1944, arriving on the southern flank of the Allied beachhead on 10 June.

THE RECONNAISSANCE BATTALION engaged US airborne troops at Carentan on the night of 10/11 June. The Germans were driven back until reinforced by *SS-Panzergrenadier-Regiment 37*, the StuGs of the division's Panzer battalion and paratroopers of the 6th Fallschirmjäger Regiment.

Heavy losses
Throughout the remainder of June, the 17th SS Panzergrenadier Division fought in the St Lô sector. Heavy fighting in the bocage country saw the division suffer heavy losses, which were magnified when the formation found itself in the direct path of the US breakout from the beachhead.

COMBAT UNIT ORGANIZATION

▽ 17.SS-Pz.Gr.Div Götz von Berlichingen
St

SS-Pz.Gr.R 37   SS-Pz.Gr.R 38   SS-Art.Rgt 17
St   St   St
I II III   I II III   I II III

▷ SS-Pzjr.A 17   ▷ SS-Pz.Abt 17   ▷ SS-SG.Abt 17
St   St   St
I II III   I II III   I II III

▷ SS-Flk.Abt 17   ▷ SS-Nach.A 17   ▷ SS-Pz.Auf.Abt 17
St   St   St
I II III   I II III   I II III

▶ **Mittlere Lkw Opel Blitz Typ A / 2cm Flak 38**

17.SS-Panzergrenadier-Division / Stab-Begleit-Kompanie

The escort company attached to the divisional headquarters had a mix of weapons, including a Flak battery with four self-propelled 2cm (0.7in) Flak guns.

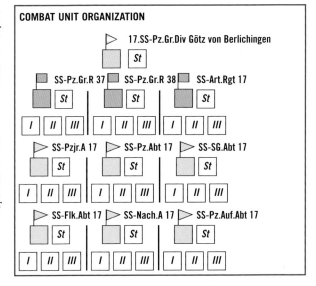

Specifications

Crew: 1	Speed: 80km/h (50mph)
Weight: 3.29 tonnes (3 tons)	Range: 410km (255 miles)
Length: 6.02m (19ft 9in)	Radio: None
Width: 2.27m (7ft 5in)	Armament: Twin or quad 20mm
Height: 2.18m (7ft 2in)	(0.7in) Flak 38 cannon
Engine: Opel 6-cylinder petrol	

▶ **Leichte Funkpanzerwagen (SdKfz 250/3)**

17.SS-Panzergrenadier-Division / Stab

Intended primarily to provide communications between Panzer and Panzergrenadier divisions and *Luftwaffe* close-support units, the SdKfz 250/3 later replaced its frame aerial with an extending pole aerial.

Specifications

Crew: 4	Engine: Maybach HL42TRKM 6-cylinder
Weight: 5.35 tonnes (4.87 tons)	Speed: 60km/h (37.3mph)
Length: 4.56m (14ft 11.5in)	Range: 320km (199 miles)
Width: 1.95m (6ft 5in)	Radio: FuG Spr Ger 1
Height: 1.66m (5ft 5in)	Armament: 1 x 7.92mm (0.3in) MG

On 6 August, the remnants of the division were attached to the *Das Reich* battle group, which was under the orders of Seventh Army's XLVII Panzerkorps. On the 7th, the *Kampfgruppe* was at Mortain and took part in the failed offensive against the US Third Army. The SS unit was split into four smaller *Kampfgruppen*. These managed to avoid being caught in the Falaise pocket, eventually retreating towards Chartres. On 28 August, the survivors were ordered to Metz, where the division was to be rebuilt.

▼ 17.SS-Panzer-Abteilung, Panzer-Kompanie, May 1944

In an ideal table of organization and equipment, Panzergrenadier divisions in 1944 usually had a single battalion of tanks divided into four companies. The tanks were generally Panzer IVs, though shortages of Panzers meant that divisions were often equipped with much cheaper assault guns instead. The *Götz von Berlichingen* Division was formed with Panzer IVs, but by the time it reached combat these had been replaced by assault guns.

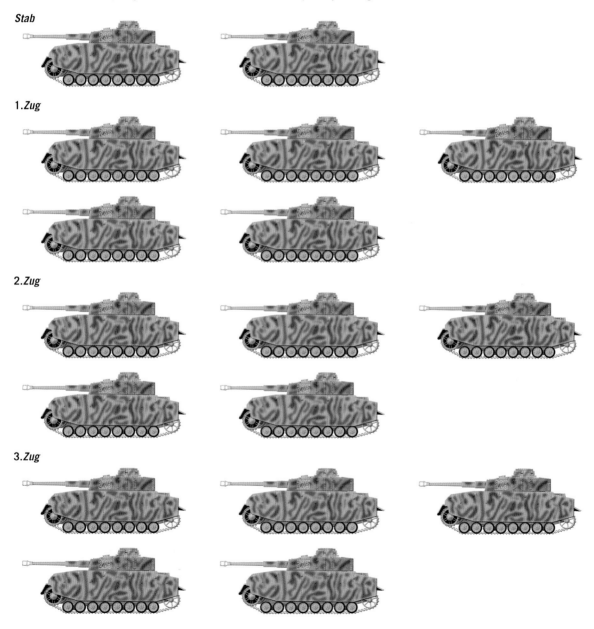

Stab

1.*Zug*

2.*Zug*

3.*Zug*

▶ **7.5cm Sturmgeschütz Ausf G (SdKfz 142/1)**

SS Panzer Abteilung 17 / 1. Kompanie

The last production series of the StuG III assault gun was the Ausf G. More than 7700 examples were produced between March 1943 and March 1945.

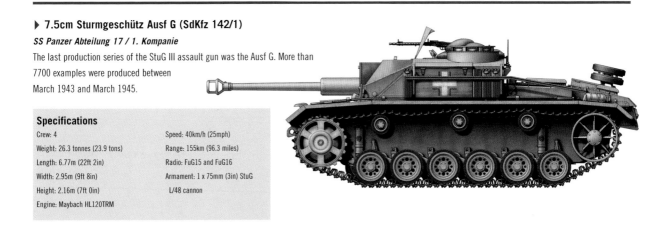

Specifications

Crew: 4	Speed: 40km/h (25mph)
Weight: 26.3 tonnes (23.9 tons)	Range: 155km (96.3 miles)
Length: 6.77m (22ft 2in)	Radio: FuG15 and FuG16
Width: 2.95m (9ft 8in)	Armament: 1 x 75mm (3in) StuG
Height: 2.16m (7ft 0in)	L/48 cannon
Engine: Maybach HL120TRM	

Metz and Lorraine
SEPTEMBER 1944 – MAY 1945

Early in September 1944, the division was reinforced when it absorbed the 49th and 51st SS Panzergrenadier Regiments, though its Panzer battalion was still understrength.

ON 8 SEPTEMBER, THE DIVISION returned to action, attacking a US bridgehead over the Moselle River held by the US 5th and 80th Infantry Divisions on 10 September. By 12 September, the rest of the division had completed refitting and had joined the attack, which was driven off. After heavy fighting, the division pulled back to the Saar and joined the defenders of Metz.

The division was pulled back to the Maginot Line in mid-November after the divisional headquarters had been destroyed in an Allied air attack. By this time, divisional strength had fallen to 4000 men and

20 armoured vehicles. Through December, the division's infantry regiments were brought up to full strength, although the ethnic German (*Volksdeutsche*) conscripts were of much lower quality than the original divisional personnel.

During this period, the division was assigned to the XIII SS Corps, under the command of *SS-Gruppenführer* Max Simon. The XIII Corps took part

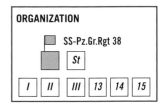

ORGANIZATION

SS-Pz.Gr.Rgt 38

St

I	II	III	13	14	15

▶ **Flakpanzer 38 (SdKfz 140)**

38.SS-Panzer-Abteilung / Flak-Batterie

In June 1944, the threat of Allied air power meant that all German formations in Normandy had increased Flak protection. The *Flakpanzer* 38 was issued to the Flak platoons of tank regiments in Panzer and Panzergrenadier divisions.

Specifications

Crew: 4	Engine: Praga AC, 6 cylinder petrol
Weight: 9.8 tonnes (9.64 tons)	engine
Length: 4.61m (15ft 2in)	Speed: 42km/h (26mph)
Width: 2.15m (7ft 0.5in)	Range: 210km (130 miles)
Height: 2.25m (7ft 4in)	Armament: 2cm (1.8in) Flak 38

in Operation *Nordwind*. This was an offensive designed to take pressure off the German offensive in the Ardennes, which had bogged down at the end of December 1944. *Götz von Berlichingen* was teamed with the 36th Volksgrenadier Division. Together the two divisions launched an attack on the US 44th and 100th Infantry Divisions at Rimling in Lorraine. Significant reinforcements had been added to the division, notably a company of Panther tanks, two companies of flamethrowing tanks and a detachment of heavy Jagdtiger tank-destroyers from *schwere Panzerjäger-Abteilung* 653.

Nordwind fails

Although the German attacks inflicted significant losses on the US Seventh Army, they could not break through the American defences. By 5 January, it was clear that Operation *Nordwind* had failed. On 10 January, the 17th SS Division's commander, *SS-Standartenführer* Hans Linger, was captured by an

American patrol. The division continued fighting elements of XV US Corps until 25 January 1945, when Operation *Nordwind* was officially brought to an end.

The division retreated to the defences of the *Westwall*, where it would continue to hold out until March 1945. On the 18th of that month, elements of Lieutenant-General Alexander Patch's US Seventh Army broke through. On 22 March, the division abandoned all its vehicles and began a retreat across the Rhine into Germany. Three days later, it was north of the Neckar River, defending the Odenwald.

By 1 April, the division had been reduced to a strength of 7000 men. It fell back to Nuremberg and continued fighting until 24 April. It retreated to Donauwörth on the Danube and the last organized engagement fought by the division was on 29 April at Moosburg. On 7 May 1945, what remained of the 17th SS Panzergrenadier Division *Götz von Berlichingen* surrendered near the Achensee.

▶ **Mittlere Pionierpanzerwagen Ausf D (SdKfz 251/7)**

17.SS-Panzer-Pionier-Abteilung / 1.Pionier-Kompanie

The combat engineer companies in the divisional pioneer battalion had light assault bridges mounted on half-tracks. There was also a bridging column which was used to build larger or more permanent bridges.

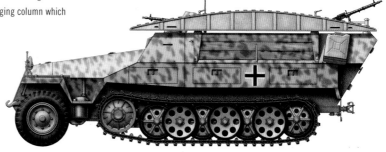

Specifications	
Crew: 7 or 8	6-cylinder (100hp)
Weight: 8.9 tonnes (8.6 tons)	Speed: 50km/h (31mph)
Length: 5.80m (19ft 0in)	Range: 300km (186 miles)
Width: 2.10m (6ft 11in)	Radio: FuG Spr Ger 1
Height: 2.70m (8ft 10in)	Armament: 1/2 x 7.62mm
Engine: Maybach HL42TUKRM	(0.3in) MG

▶ **Flakpanzer IV 2cm Vierling Wirbelwind**

SS Panzer Abteilung 17 / Stab Kompanie / Flak Zug

Issued to the Flak platoons of Panzer regiments late in the war, the Whirlwind was a conversion of old Panzer IVs in which the main turret was replaced by an open-topped quad 2cm (0.7in) mount. The 17th SS took delivery of four early in 1945.

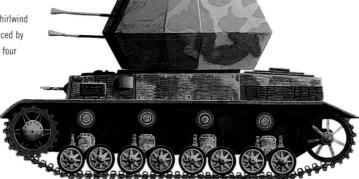

Specifications	
Crew: 5	Engine: Maybach HL120TRM
Weight: 24.3 tonnes (22 tons)	Speed: 38km/h (23.6mph)
Length: 5.9m (19ft 5in)	Range: 210km (130 miles)
Width: 2.9m (9ft 6in)	Radio: FuG2 and FuG5
Height: 2.76m (9ft)	

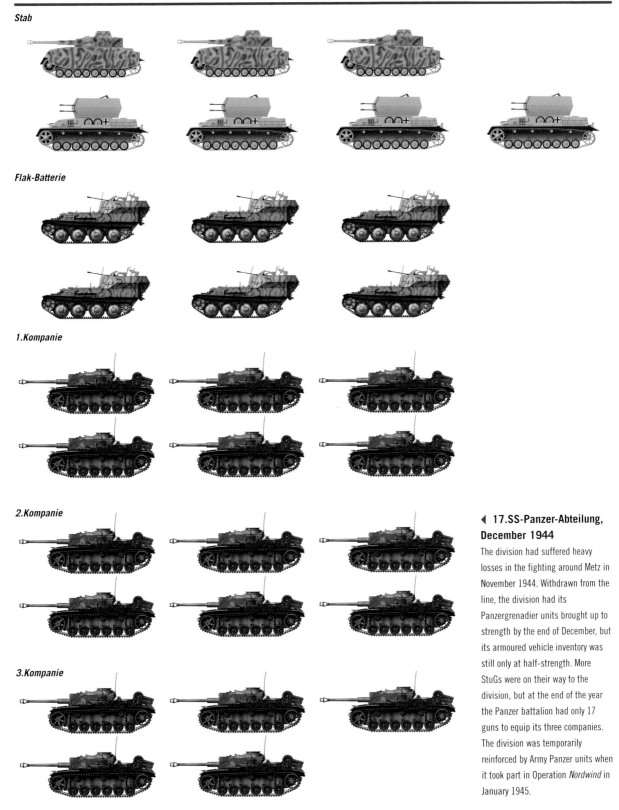

Stab

Flak-Batterie

1.Kompanie

2.Kompanie

3.Kompanie

◀ **17.SS-Panzer-Abteilung, December 1944**

The division had suffered heavy losses in the fighting around Metz in November 1944. Withdrawn from the line, the division had its Panzergrenadier units brought up to strength by the end of December, but its armoured vehicle inventory was still only at half-strength. More StuGs were on their way to the division, but at the end of the year the Panzer battalion had only 17 guns to equip its three companies. The division was temporarily reinforced by Army Panzer units when it took part in Operation *Nordwind* in January 1945.

18th SS Freiwilligen Panzergrenadier Division *Horst Wessel*

The 18th SS Division was supposed to have been a completely National Socialist formation, raised from the brown-shirted Stormtroopers of the Nazi party's *Sturmabteilung*, or SA.

IN JANUARY 1944, ADOLF HITLER ordered *Reichsführer-SS* Heinrich Himmler to raise a *Waffen-SS* division from a cadre of *Sturmabteilung* reservists. In fact, the 18th SS Freiwilligen Panzergrenadier Division *Horst Wessel* was cobbled together from 1.*SS-Infanterie-Brigade (mot)* – an SS motorized brigade created from elements of two *Totenkopf-Standarten* – together with elements from the 6.*SS-Gebirgs-Division Nord* and large numbers of Hungarian and Yugoslav *Volksdeutsche*.

Nazi 'hero'

The division was named after one of the Nazi party's heroes, portrayed in National Socialist mythology as a young Berlin Stormtrooper who was killed in a streetfight with Communists before the Nazis came to power. In fact, although Horst Wessel was indeed an SA man killed by a Communist, he was actually a street thug and pimp who was killed in a fight over

INSIGNIA

The symbol of the 18th SS Division commemorated Horst Wessel's membership of the SA by using a representation of a Stormtrooper dagger.

who would benefit from the income of Wessel's prostitute girlfriend.

As formed, each of the division's component regiments had their own pioneer companies and Flak companies. These were later merged to form divisional Flak and pioneer battalions, and a Panzerjäger battalion was attached.

The division was assembled at the Stablack training area in East Prussia. In January 1944, it was transferred to Zagreb in Croatia. From there, it was deployed to the Agram area on the Hungarian–Yugoslav border, where it went into action against Tito's partisans.

Commanders

Brigadeführer Wilhelm Trabant
January 1944 – January 1945

Gruppenführer Josef Fitzthum
January 1945

Oberführer Georg Bochmann
January 1945 – March 1945

Standartenführer Heinrich Petersen
March 1945 – May 1945

Divisional History	Formed
1.SS-Infanterie-Brigade (mot)	1941
18.SS-Panzergrenadier-Division	1944
18.SS-Freiwilligen-Panzergrenadier-Division Horst Wessel	1944

▶ **7.5cm Sturmgeschütz 40 Ausf G (SdKfz 142/1)**

18.SS-Sturmgeschütz-Abteilung / 1.Kompanie

Late-model assault guns based on the Panzer III were identifiable from their revised roof line and the Panzer-style commander's cupola equipped with all-round periscope vision blocks.

Specifications

Crew: 4

Weight: 26.3 tonnes (23.9 tons)

Length: 6.77m (22ft 2in)

Width: 2.95m (9ft 8in)

Height: 2.16m (7ft 0in)

Engine: Maybach HL120TRM

Speed: 40km/h (25mph)

Range: 155km (96.3 miles)

Radio: FuG15 and FuG16

Armament: 1 x 75mm (3in) StuG L/48 cannon

Specifications

Crew: 3	Muzzle Velocity (AP): 990m/s (3248fps)
Weight: 1.5 tonnes (1.37 tons)	Range: AP: 2000m (2190 yards), HE: 7.5km
Length: 3.7m (12ft 1.5in)	(4.66 miles)
Calibre: 75mm (3in)	Ammunition: Armour-piercing, high explosive

▲ **7.5cm Panzerabwehrkanone (Pak 40)**

SS Panzerjäger Abteilung 18 / 2. Kompanie (mot)

By the time the *Horst Wessel* Division was formed in 1944, the 7.5cm (3in) Pak 40 was the standard anti-tank gun in most German divisions. It equipped the 18th Panzerjäger Battalion and was also used by the anti-tank platoon of the divisional headquarters company.

Ukraine, Poland and Hungary
1944–1945

The division gained some combat experience in the anti-partisan war in the Balkans, but it was soon to participate in full-scale combat against the Red Army on the Eastern Front.

IN MARCH, THE DIVISION was moved into Hungary for Operation *Margarethe* alongside the 8th SS Cavalry Division *Florian Geyer*. Here the division was used as a threat to control the Hungarian Government, at that time showing signs of trying to find a way out of the war.

In July, the bulk of the division was sent, under the command of *Obersturbannführer* Ernst Schäfer, to form a *Kampfgruppe* operating under XXIV Panzerkorps in the Ukraine. The formation took under its command elements of the 8.*SS-Sturmbrigade Frankreich*, formed after the dissolution of the *Légion des Volontaires Français*.

Under intense Soviet pressure, the *Horst Wessel* battle group retreated through Podhajce and Lipica to the Dniester River, then back through Baliezne, Podrozne and Siechow. One unit was detached in August, and for the next three months it was used alongside the notorious *Dirlewanger* Brigade in the crushing of the Slovak National Uprising.

In September, the rest of the division was moved into Hungary, where it fought the advancing Soviets in the area around Jasz and Ladany. As the Soviet juggernaut pushed on towards Budapest, the division was involved in heavy fighting. It was driven aside and forced to retreat northwards, allowing the Soviets

▶ **2cm Flak 38 / leichte Zugkraftwagen 1t (SdKfz 10/5)**

39.SS-Panzergrenadier-Regiment / 16.Kompanie

The 16th Company in each of the *Horst Wessel*'s two Panzergrenadier regiments was a self-propelled Flak unit, equipped with 12 light anti-aircraft guns divided between three batteries.

Specifications

Crew: 7	(100hp)
Weight: 5.5 tonnes (5 tons)	Speed: 65km/h (40mph)
Length: 4.75m (15ft 7in)	Range: 300km (186 miles)
Width: 2.15m (7ft 1in)	Radio: None
Height: 3.20m (10ft 6in)	Armament: Twin 20mm (0.7in)
Engine: Maybach HL42TRKM 6-cylinder	Flak 38 L/112.5

to encircle the Hungarian capital. The *Florian Geyer*, *Maria Theresia* and 33rd SS (Hungarian) Cavalry Divisions were trapped in the city.

Horst Wessel was used in the attempt to break the Soviet siege of Budapest. On 1 January 1945, the Germans launched the first of three offensives intended to lift the siege. German Army troops attacked through hilly terrain north of Budapest. Simultaneously, *Waffen-SS* forces struck from the west. The Soviets replied by sending four more divisions to meet the threat, stopping the offensive less than 20km (12.5 miles) from the city. On 12 January, the German forces were forced to withdraw.

Meanwhile, the Germans launched a second offensive from Esztegom towards Budapest airport,

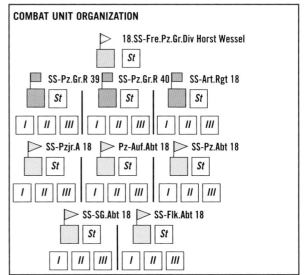

COMBAT UNIT ORGANIZATION

trying to capture it in order to allow the city to be supplied from the air. The Soviets stopped the drive before it could reach the airport.

On 17 January 1945, the last offensive was launched. German forces attacked from the south of Budapest in an attempt to encircle 10 Soviet divisions. The encirclement attempt failed.

Final days

After the failure of the Budapest offensives, the *Horst Wessel* Division was split into two *Kampfgruppen*. One was used around Karlsbrunn and Ratibor before surrendering to the Red Army at Mährisch-Ostrau.

The other *Kampfgruppe* moved to Zobten in April, where it came under the control of VIII Army Corps. There was no serious fighting in the area, and after the final German surrender small groups moved westwards to surrender to the Americans.

▲ **15cm schwere Infanterie Geschütz (sIG33)**

40.SS-Panzergrenadier-Regiment / 17.Kompanie

One company in each battalion of the Panzergrenadier regiment was equipped with light 7.5cm (3in) infantry guns; the heavy 15cm (5.9in) weapons were concentrated into a single company.

Specifications

Crew: 5	Muzzle Velocity: 241m/s (783fps)
Weight: 1.75 tonnes (1.71 tons)	Range: 5504m (6000 yards)
Length: 1.64m (64.57in)	Ammunition: High explosive or smoke
Calibre: 150mm (5.9in)	

▶ **7.5cm Pak 40 auf PzKpfw 38(t) (SdKfz 138)**

18.SS-Panzerjäger-Abteilung / 1.(Sf) Kompanie

Although it had entered service early in 1943, the first version of the self-propelled Pak 40 mounted on a Panzer 38 chassis remained operational until the end of the war.

Specifications

Crew: 4	Speed: 35km/h (22mph)
Weight: 10.8 tonnes (9.8 tons)	Range: 240km (150 miles)
Length: 5.77m (19ft 11in)	Radio: FuG Spr Ger 1
Width: 2.16m (7ft 1in)	Armament: 1 x 75mm (3in) Pak 40/3 L/46
Height: 2.51m (8ft 3in)	anti-tank gun; 1 x 7.92mm (0.3in) MG
Engine: Praga EPA 6-cylinder (140hp)	

▼ **18.SS-Panzerjäger-Abteilung, 1945**

Although the division was intended to have a tank-destroyer battalion from the time it became operational in March 1944, *Horst Wessel* did not in fact form *SS-Panzerjäger-Abteilung* 18 until February 1945. By that time, the division was retreating after German failure to relieve Budapest in January.

Stab

1.Zug

2.Zug

3.Zug

19th Waffen Grenadier Division der SS

The Germans were seen as liberators by many Latvians. Initially they had the full support of Latvian right-wing nationalists, and the SS Latvian Legion was formed in 1942.

THE 19TH WAFFEN GRENADIER DIVISION der SS was the second division of Latvian volunteers raised by the *Waffen-SS*. As in the case of its sister unit – the 15th Waffen Grenadier Division der SS – German troops formed the nucleus of the 19th SS Division, the *2.SS-Infanterie-Brigade (mot)* also providing the bulk of the NCO and officer cadre.

Divisional History	Formed
Lettische SS-Freiwilligen-Brigade	1943
2.Lettische SS-Freiwilligen-Brigade	1943
19.Lettische SS-Freiwilligen-Division	1944
19.Waffen-Grenadier-Division der SS (lettische Nr. 2)	1944

Strength was made up by the addition of a large number of Latvians who had been serving in the *SS-Schutzmannschaft* battalions.

The first large unit of the new Latvian Legion was formed at the Leningrad Front from three police battalions, later reinforced by three further battalions.

Initially known as the *Lettische SS-Freiwilligen-Brigade*, it was redesignated as *2.Lettische SS-Freiwilligen-Brigade*. It was expanded to division size, eventually becoming *19.Waffen-Grenadier-Division der SS (lettische Nr. 2)* in the summer of 1944. The division found itself in combat in June, only a month after its formation, when the Soviet summer offensive got under way. Over the next six months, it formed part of the heavily outnumbered German force in the Baltic States which managed to hold back a series of offensives by the Red Army.

The 19th SS Division fought at the long-drawn-out Battle of Narva along with many other Germanic and volunteer SS units. It was later trapped in the Courland pocket as the German forces in the Baltic States retreated from the advancing Soviet juggernaut. Little has been documented about the division's record in the last months of the war, but there are rumours that some divisional units may have mutinied at the end of 1944.

Commanders

Standartenführer Hinrich Schuldt
May 1943 – July 1943

Oberführer Fritz Freitag
August 1943

Brigadeführer Hinrich Schuldt
September 1943 – March 1944

Standartenführer Friedrich-Wilhelm Bock
March 1944 – April 1944

Gruppenführer Bruno Steckenbach
April 1944 – May 1945

COMBAT UNIT ORGANIZATION

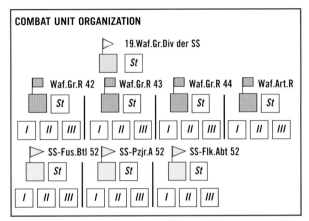

INSIGNIA

The symbol of the 19th SS Division was simply an 'L' for Latvia together with the Roman numeral 'II' to indicate that it was the second Latvian division.

▲ **2cm Fliegerabwehrkanone (Flak 38)**

52.SS-Panzerjäger-Abteilung / Flak-Kompanie

The 19th SS Division was supposed to have had its own Flak battalion, but though the 52.*Flak-Abteilung* was formed it was never incorporated into the division. The only Flak unit in the division was a company in the *Panzerjäger-Abteilung*.

▲ **Leichte Personenkraftwagen VW (Kfz 1)**

42.Waffen-Grenadier-Regiment der SS / Stab-Kompanie

Waffen Grenadier divisions, as distinct from Panzergrenadier divisions, were equipped as ordinary infantry formations. Motorization was limited to staff units and some tank-hunter and support units, including a supply troop which had two truck companies and two horse-drawn companies.

Specifications

Crew: 4

Weight: 420kg (920lb)

Length: 2.25m (7ft 5in)

Calibre: 20mm (0.7in)

Muzzle Velocity (HE): 900m/s (2953fps)

Rate of fire: 420–480rpm

Range (ceiling): HE: 2200m (7218ft)

Ammunition: High explosive

Projectile weight: 0.119kg (0.262lb)

Specifications

Crew: 1

Weight: 0.64 tonnes (0.58 tons)

Length: 3.73m (12ft 3in)

Width: 1.60m (5ft 3in)

Height: 1.35m (4ft 5in)

Engine: Volkswagen 998cc petrol (24hp). Later Volkswagen 1131cc petrol (25hp)

Speed: 100km/h (62mph)

Range: 600km (375 miles)

Radio: None

20th Waffen Grenadier Division der SS

Following the German occupation of the Baltic States, large numbers of Estonians volunteered to fight against the hated Soviets. Some were later to join the *Waffen-SS*.

T HE 20. *WAFFEN-GRENADIER-DIVISION der SS (estnische Nr. 1)* was formed from the 3. *Estnische SS-Freiwilligen-Brigade* and was directly descended from the Estonian Legion, authorized by Adolf Hitler in August 1942.

Soon after the occupation of Estonia, the Germans began to allow the formation of Estonian units, variously called security, police or defence battalions or companies. The primary purpose of these units was to provide security in German rear areas, which came to mean fighting partisans. Volunteers were plentiful, and by March 1942 there were 16 Estonian battalions and companies, with 10,000 men on active duty in Russia. Eventually more than 50 such units were to be formed, with as many as 25,000 Estonians under arms.

Their experience of Soviet oppression at first hand meant that the Baltic States were seen by the SS as potentially valuable recruiting grounds for foreign volunteer legions to take part in the 'crusade' against Communism. On 28 August 1942, the *Waffen-SS*

Commanders

Brigadeführer Franz Augsberger
October 1942 – March 1945

Brigadeführer Berthold Maack
March 1945 – May 1945

INSIGNIA

The symbol of the 20. *Waffen-Grenadier-Division der SS (estnische Nr. 1)* was a stylized letter 'E' (for Estonia) overlaid with a dagger or shortsword.

announced the intended formation of the *Estnische Freiwilligen-SS-Legion.* By the end of the year, 1280 men were under training at Debica in Poland as the 1. *Estnische SS-Freiwilligen-Grenadier-Regiment.*

Estonian grenadiers

The regiment-sized legion took some time to organize, becoming operational in the spring of 1943. Formed as a motorized infantry regiment, the legion was referred to in German orders as the 1. *Estnische SS-Freiwilligen-Grenadier-Regiment.* It quickly grew to brigade size, however. In March

▲ **10.5cm leichte Feldhaubitze (leFH18)**

20. SS-Artillerie-Regiment / I.Bataillon / 1.Batterie

The Estonian division had a four-battalion artillery regiment. Three of the battalions were equipped with towed leFH18s, while the fourth operated 15cm (5.9in) heavy field howitzers.

Specifications

Crew: 5	Muzzle Velocity: 540m/s (1770fps)
Weight: 1.95 tonnes (1.85 tons)	Range: 12,325m (13,480 yards)
Length: 3.3m (10ft)	Ammunition: High explosive or smoke
Calibre: 105mm (4.1in)	

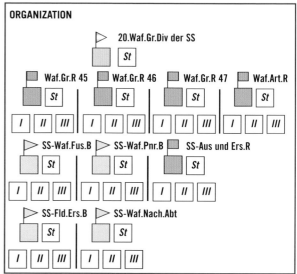

▶ **Estonian tank riders**

Detached from the *Estnische SS-Freiwilligen-Brigade* in 1943, the *Narva* Battalion was assigned to the crack *SS-Panzergrenadier-Regiment Nordland*, part of the 5th SS Panzer Division *Wiking*.

1943, one battalion was detached as the *Estnische SS-Freiwilligen-Bataillon Narva*, replacing the disbanded Finnish battalion as the third battalion of the *Nordland* regiment of the *Wiking* Division.

At the same time, continuing manpower shortages led to reinforcements being conscripted in Estonia, around 12,000 men being called into service. Some 5300 were sent to the legion battalions training at Debica, which were reinforced and organized as the 3.*SS-Freiwilligen-Brigade*. The remaining conscripts were sent to German Army units.

Estonian SS division

The 20.*Estnische SS-Freiwilligen-Division* was established in January 1944. Its component units were engaged in action at the front during the three-month campaign known as the Battle of the Narva, which meant that formation took longer than expected. In May 1944, the division was some 5000 men understrength, and its build-up was expedited under Himmler's orders. However, it did not reach combat strength until July 1944.

In September, many Estonian troops were released from German service, and the remnants of the division were evacuated from Estonia along with the rest of the German forces. The division was reconstructed at *Truppenübungsplatz* Neuhammer from October 1944. In Estonian it was known as the 20.*SS-Relvagrenadieride Diviis (Eesti Esimene)*. In February 1945, the formation was so weakened that it was now referred to as a battle group (*SS-Kampfgruppe*) rather than a division, possibly named *Kampfgruppe Augsberger* after the divisional commander. It continued fighting in Silesia and later in Czechoslovakia until the end of the war, when parts of the formation surrendered to the Western Allies while the main body of the division surrendered to the Soviets north of Prague.

Divisional History	Formed
Estnische Freiwilligen-SS-Legion	1942
Estnische SS-Freiwilligen-Brigade	1943
3.Estnische SS-Freiwilligen-Brigade	1943
20.Estnische SS-Freiwilligen-Division	1944
20.Waffen-Grenadier-Division der SS (estnische Nr. 1)	1944

▶ **Mittlere Zugkraftwagen 3t (SdKfz 11)**

20.SS-Panzerjäger-Abteilung / 1.(mot) Panzerjäger-Kompanie

The SdKfz 11 was the standard 3-tonne (2.94-ton) tractor used by the *Wehrmacht*. It towed a variety of light and medium artillery pieces, including the 7.5cm (3in) Pak 40 and the 10.5cm (4.1in) leFH18.

Specifications

Crew: 1 plus 8 troops

Weight: 7.1 tonnes (6.46 tons)

Length: 5.48m (18ft 0in)

Width: 1.82m (5ft 11.5in)

Height: 1.62m (5ft 4in)

Engine: 6-cylinder petrol (100hp)

Speed: 53km/h (32.9mph)

Range: 122km (75.8 miles)

Radio: None

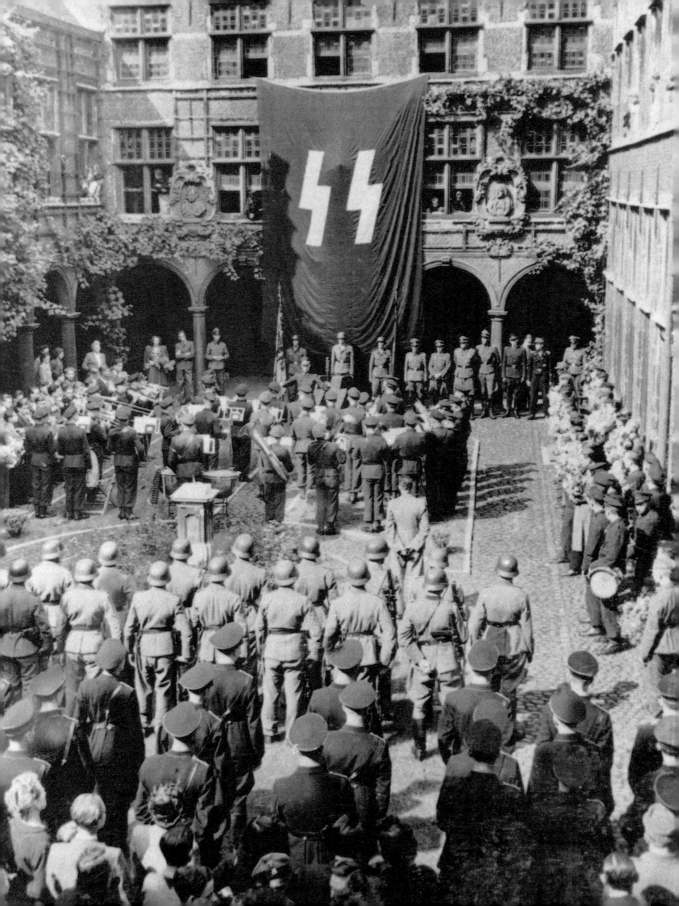

Chapter 8

Late-War Divisions

Even though the war had turned decisively
against Germany in 1943 and 1944, nothing could stop
Heinrich Himmler's ambitions for the SS. More and more
divisions were formed, but the nature of the organization had
changed. The most committed of the foreign volunteers
found a home in the *Waffen-SS*, until large parts of it were
more like a German 'Foreign Legion' than the elite of the
German race, which it had been in the earlier days
of the Third *Reich*.

◀ Belgian volunteers

SS volunteers parade in Brussels, July 1944. Even at this late stage of the war, with German forces being
pushed back both in France and on the Eastern Front, fresh volunteers were found to fill the ranks of
Himmler's rapidly expanding SS.

21st Waffen Gebirgs Division der SS *Skanderbeg*

On 17 April 1944, *Reichsführer-SS* Heinrich Himmler approved the formation of an Albanian *Waffen-SS* division. The SS Main Office envisioned an Albanian formation of 10,000 troops.

A REINFORCED BATTALION OF approximately 300 ethnic Albanians serving in the Bosnian Muslim 13th Waffen Gebirgs Division der SS *Handschar* were transferred to the newly forming division. To this Albanian core were added veteran German troops from Austria plus *Volksdeutsche* officers, NCOS and enlisted men, as well as a number of *Kriegsmarine* sailors who no longer had ships. The total strength of the Albanian *Waffen-SS* division would be 8500–9000 men.

The 21.*Waffen-Gebirgs-Division der SS Skanderbeg* did not acquire a good reputation. Intended to combat partisans, it was used in its earliest days to massacre Orthodox Serb civilians in Kosovo-Metohija. Over 10,000 Serbian families were forced to flee Kosovo. Albanian colonists and settlers from northern Albania took over their lands and homes. The goal of many members of the *Skanderbeg* Division was not to fight for the Germans; rather it was to advance Albanian nationalism by deporting and killing the non-Albanian populations of Western Macedonia, creating an ethnically pure and homogeneous region of Greater Albania, free of Serbs, Jews and Roma (Gypsies). The *Skanderbeg* Division targeted all of these groups when the formation occupied Tetovo and Skopje and other towns and cities in Western Macedonia.

Commanders
Brigadeführer Josef Fitzhum
April 1944 – May 1944

Oberführer August Schmidthuber
May 1944 – January 1945

In October 1944, the *Skanderbeg* Division occupied Skopje, the capital of Macedonia. By November 1944, the Germans were withdrawing their forces from the Aegean islands and from Greece. Called on to fight in something other than their own private war, many of the division's members deserted – so many, in fact, that the unit could not function as a division. The formation's remnants were reorganized into *Regimentgruppe 21.SS-Gebirgs-Skanderbeg*, which was concentrated at Skopje. The *Kampfgruppe Skanderbeg*, in conjunction with the 7th SS Volunteer Mountain Division *Prinz Eugen*, defended the valley of the Vardar River in Macedonia to allow *Generaloberst* Alexander Löhr's Army Group E to retreat from Greece and the Aegean. The Vardar Valley was crucial as an escape corridor.

By January 1945, remnants of the *Skanderbeg* Division had retreated to Kosovska Mitrovica in Kosovo and then to Brcko in Bosnia-Herzegovina. The *Skanderbeg* remnants would reach Austria in May 1945, when Germany surrendered following the military and political collapse of the regime.

INSIGNIA

The divisional symbol of the *Skanderbeg* Division was the double-headed eagle of Albania, mounted on the Gebirgs-style SS shield.

Divisional History	Formed
Waffen-Gebirgs-Division der SS Skanderbeg (albanische Nr. 1)	1944
21.Waffen-Gebirgs-Division der SS Skanderbeg (albanische Nr. 1)	1944

ORGANIZATION

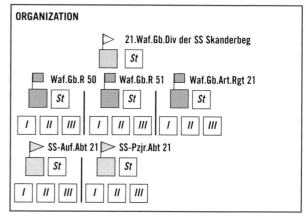

▲ **3.7cm Panzerabwehrkanone (Pak 35/36)**

21.SS-Aufklärungs-Abteilung / 1.Kompanie (mot) / Panzerjäger-Zug

Although obsolete, the 3.7cm (1.5in) Pak 35/36 was an effective weapon against partisans. With a weight of about 430kg (946lb), it was also a relatively light and handy weapon more suited to operations in mountainous terrain than were larger anti-tank guns.

Specifications

Crew: 3	Muzzle Velocity: 762m/s (2500fps)
Weight: 0.43 tonnes (0.39 tons)	Range: 600m (656 yards)
Length: 1.67m (5ft 5.5in)	Ammunition: Armour-piercing
Calibre: 37mm (1.5in)	

▲ **Mittlerer Nachrichten Kraftwagen (Kfz 15)**

21.SS-Freiwilligen-Nachrichten-Abteilung

The 21st Mountain Signals Battalion was made up of three companies – two mountain telephone companies and a mountain radio company. The Kfz 15 medium car was standard equipment in communications units, at least 30 being in the standard table of equipment of a battalion.

Specifications

Crew: 1	Engine: Skoda 3.1L petrol (80–85hp)
Weight: 2.4 tonnes (2.2 tons)	Speed: 100km/h (62mph)
Length: 4.8m (15ft 9in)	Range: 400km (250 miles)
Width: 1.80m (5ft 9in)	Radio: None
Height: 1.72m (5ft 3in)	

22nd SS Freiwilligen Kavallerie Division *Maria Theresia*

The SS formed a second cavalry division in the spring of 1944. The idea was that the new formation would serve with the *Florian Geyer* Division as part of an SS cavalry corps.

THE *MARIA THERESIA* DIVISION was formed in May 1944. Assembled at Kisber, Hungary, it was based on a nucleus provided by the 17.*SS-Kavallerie-Regiment* transferred from the 8.*SS-Kavallerie-Division Florian Geyer*.

The bulk of the strength of the division was provided by Hungarian *Volksdeutsche*, who had originally been drafted by the Hungarian Army but had been transferred to the *Waffen-SS* following an agreement between the German and Hungarian Governments.

The symbol of the division was a cornflower, adopted since it was the favourite flower of the Empress Maria Theresa (Theresia in German) of Austria, after whom the division had been named.

In September 1944, a detachment from *Maria*

Theresia, consisting of 52.*SS-Kavallerie-Regiment*, was assigned to a *Kampfgruppe* commanded by *SS-*

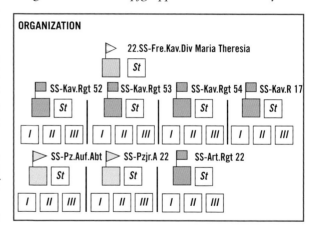

Hauptsturmführer Toni Ameiser. *Kampfgruppe* Ameiser was deployed to Romania. It was unable to reach its designated positions because of the advance of the Red Army, and after fighting alongside Hungarian troops it was encircled by the Soviets.

Break out

One section of the *Kampfgruppe*, commanded by *SS-Hauptsturmführer* Harry Vandieken, fought its way to the Harmas River, swimming across to the safety of the German-held bank. The second part of the *Kampfgruppe*, commanded by Ameiser himself, remained in the trap for a month, eventually fighting its way through to the German lines south of Budapest on 30 October.

Battle for Budapest

The rest of the *Maria Theresia* Division was still in training when it was sent to reinforce Budapest in November 1944.

When the Red Army closed a ring of iron around the Hungarian capital, the formation was destroyed along with most of the rest of the German defenders.

Commanders
Brigadeführer August Zehender
April 1944 – February 1945

Divisional History	Formed
22.SS-Freiwilligen-Kavallerie-Division Maria Theresia	1944

INSIGNIA

The divisional symbol of the *Maria Theresia* Division was the cornflower, the favourite bloom of the empress (1717–1780) after whom the division was named.

Only 170 men managed to make it through the Soviet lines to safety. The survivors, along with those parts of the Maria Theresia Division that had not been sent into Budapest, were used as the core of the newly formed 37.SS-Freiwilligen-Kavallerie-Division Lützow. What was left of the divisional Flak units was transferred to 32.SS-Freiwilligen-Grenadier-Division 30 Januar.

23rd Waffen Gebirgs Division der SS *Kama*

Approval was given for the raising of a second Croatian *Waffen-SS* division on 17 June 1944, even though the reliability of many of the personnel intended for the unit was questionable.

THE 23. *WAFFEN-GEBIRGS-DIVISION der SS Kama (kroatische Nr. 2)* was recruited from Croatian volunteers, including both *Volksdeutsche* anti-Communist Croats and Bosnian Muslims. In common with many volunteer divisions, the formation was stiffened by a German cadre of senior NCOs and officers.

Further strength was supplied by its sister formation, the 13th SS Division *Handschar*, which provided its reconnaissance battalion and a number of Croat officers and NCOs. Like the *Handschar*, the new division was named after a traditional weapon from the region – in this case, a short Turkish sword or long fighting knife known as a *kama*.

Commanders
Standartenführer Helmuth Raithel   Oberführer Gustav Lombard
July 1944 – September 1944   *September 1944*

Divisional History	Formed
23.Waffen-Gebirgs-Division der SS Kama (kroatische Nr. 2)	1944

Kama never reached anything like its planned strength. At its peak, in September 1944, it had a total of 3793 men in training to play their part in the anti-partisan war. That training was taking place at Backa in Hungary, far enough from the main areas of partisan action as to be safe from attack.

They were not safe from the Red Army, however, which by the end of September was advancing perilously close to the divisional training grounds in southern Hungary. The SS wanted the division to be ready for combat by the end of September, but as the troops still had not completed basic training this was never a realistic prospect.

Disbanded without combat

On 1 October 1944, as the Red Army advanced into Hungary, the SS decided to disband the *Kama* Division, transferring already formed units as replacements to other divisions. Most of the division's personnel were used to form the 31.*SS-Freiwilligen-Grenadier-Division.*

The Muslims of *Kama* were transferred to the *Handschar* Division. Most reported for duty, but a large minority, who had signed on primarily to fight for their homeland, deserted en route. The divisional designation '23' was assigned to the newly forming SS volunteer Panzergrenadier division being created from Dutch volunteers.

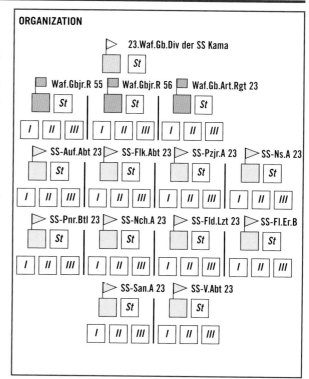

ORGANIZATION

▲ 7.5cm Panzerabwehrkanone (Pak 40)

Panzer-Aufklärungs-Abteilung 23

Although the divisional Panzerjäger battalion had become fully self-propelled over the winter of 1943/44, the Panzerjäger platoon of the reconnaissance battalion's heavy company was equipped with three towed Pak 40s.

Specifications

Crew: 3

Weight: 1.5 tonnes (1.37 tons)

Length: 3.7m (12ft 1.5in)

Calibre: 75mm (3in)

Muzzle Velocity (AP): 990m/s (3248fps)

Range: AP: 2000m (2190 yards), HE: 7.5km

(4.66 miles)

Ammunition: Armour-piercing, high explosive

▶ Leichter Einheits Pkw Stoewer 40 (Kfz 2)

SS-Gebirgs-Nachrichten-Abteilung 23

Although the division began forming with a full table of organization, few of its component units were even partially manned or equipped. The divisional communications battalion would have operated a few communications cars before the formation was abandoned.

Specifications

Crew: 1

Weight: 1.81 tonnes (1.65 tons)

Length: 3.58m (11ft 9in)

Width: 1.57m (5ft 2in)

Height: 1.78 (5ft 10in)

Engine: Stoewer AW2 or R180W petrol (50hp)

Speed: 100km/h (62mph)

Range: 500km (311 miles)

Radio: Various

23rd SS Freiwilligen Panzergrenadier Division *Nederland*

In 1943, when it was clear that the national legions within the SS would never achieve great success, Dutch Nazi leader Anton Mussert suggested that a Dutch SS division be formed.

HOWEVER, FINDING 20,000 MEN in the time scale envisaged proved to be impossible. Nevertheless, a brigade-sized formation was possible, and the *SS-Freiwilligen-Panzergrenadier-Brigade Nederland* was formed in October 1943 as part of the further expansion of the *Waffen-SS*. Some 2500 veteran legionnaires joined the brigade with an additional 3000 volunteers from the SS *Nordland* Regiment. The *23.SS-Freiwilligen-Panzergrenadier-Division Nederland (niederlandische Nr. 1)* was formed on 10 February 1945, when the *SS-Freiwilligen-Panzergrenadier-Brigade Nederland* was upgraded to divisional status.

The *Nederland* Brigade had been composed of two regiments: the *General Seyffardt* (named after the first legion commander, who had been assassinated by the Dutch resistance earlier that year) and the *De Ruyter* Regiment (named after the seventeenth-century Dutch admiral Michael de Ruyter).

The *Nederland* Brigade had been in action in the Baltic States from the end of 1943, and had shared in the retreat from Leningrad to the Narva Line and back to the Courland pocket. Along with the rest of

INSIGNIA

The 23rd SS Freiwilligen Panzergrenadier Division *Nederland* adopted a variant of the ancient runic sumbol for 'O' as its divisional symbol.

Commanders

Sturmbannführer Herbert Garthe
November 1941 – February 1942

Oberführer Otto Reich
February –March 1942

Obersturmbannführer Arved Theuermann
April–May 1942

Standartenführer Josef Fitzthum
July 19423 – May 1943

Brigadeführer Jürgen Wagner
October 1943 – May 1945

Divisional History	Formed
SS-Freiwilligen-Verband-Niederlande	1941
SS-Freiwilligen-Legion-Niederlande	1941
4.SS-Freiwilligen-Panzergrenadier-Brigade Nederland	1943
SS-Freiwilligen-Panzergrenadier-Brigade Nederland	1944
23.SS-Freiwilligen-Panzergrenadier-Division Nederland (niederlandische Nr. 1)	1945

Specifications

Crew: 3

Weight: 9.4 tonnes (8.53 tons)

Length: 5.98m (19ft 7in)

Width: 2.83m (9ft 4in)

Height: 2.07m (6ft 10in)

Engine: Maybach HL42TUKRM

Speed: 53km/h (33mph)

Range: 300km (186 miles)

Radio: FuG Spr Ger 'f'

Armament: 1 x 75mm (3in) KwK L/24 gun

▲ **Mittlerer Schützenpanzerwagen Ausf C 7.5cm (SdKfz 251/9)**

SS Frw Pzg Regt 49 / III Bataillon / 12. (schwere) Kompanie

The 49th Volunteer Panzergrenadier Regiment, known as the de Ruyter Regiment, was named after the Dutch seventeenth-century admiral Michael Adriaenszoon de Ruyter. The 3rd Battalion was equipped with half-tracks.

III SS-Korps, *Nederland* was evacuated by sea to Stettin, where the brigade was to form part of the defensive line on the Oder.

The SS had originally intended for the Dutch soldiers to be assigned to the *Nordland* Division, but after protests from the Dutch Nazi party, the *Nationaal Socialistische Beweging* (NSB), it was decided that they would form their own division. *Nederland* was given the number '23' when the *Kama* Division was disbanded.

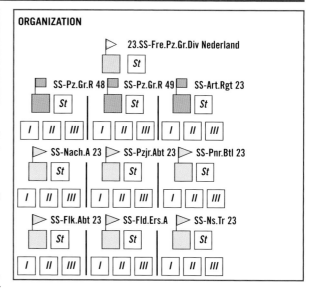

Last battles in the East

Nederland, together with the SS Divisions *Nordland*, *Wallonien* and *Langemarck*, was responsible for the defence of the Oder Front between the towns of Stettin and Neustadt.

In April 1945, Nederland was split up. The 48th Regiment General Seyffardt was destroyed near Hammerstein while fighting with the 15th SS Grenadier Division. The 13 soldiers that were captured were executed by the Soviets.

At the end of April, the 49th Regiment *De Ruyter*, which had remained on the Oder Front, was forced to withdraw to the west, around the north of Berlin.

On 3 May 1945, near the village of Parchim, the regiment destroyed an attacking Red Army tank unit, and then its members heard more tanks approaching – from the west. These proved to be Americans, and the 49th Regiment was happy to surrender to them. The *23.SS-Freiwilligen-Panzergrenadier-Division Nederland* had had little more than 1000 effective combatants when it fought its last battles on the Eastern Front.

Specifications

Crew: 6	Speed: 42km/h (26mph)
Weight: 26.5 tonnes (24 tons)	Range: 215km (133.6 miles)
Length: 7.17m (23ft 6in)	Radio: FuG Spr 1
Width: 2.97m (9ft 8in)	Armament: 1 x 150mm (5.9in) sFH 18/1 L/30;
Height: 2.81m (9ft 2in)	1 x 7.92mm (0.3in) MG
Engine: Maybach HL120TRM (265hp)	

▲ **15cm schwere Panzerhaubitze auf Geschützwagen III/IV (SdKfz 165)**

SS Artillerie Regiment 23 / I Abteilung / 1. Batterie

The 1st Battalion of the 23rd Artillery Regiment was equipped as a standard late-war self-propelled unit, with one battery equipped with 15-cm (6in) Hummels and two batteries with smaller 10.5-cm (4.2in) Wespe self-propelled guns. Each battery had six guns. The other two battalions were equipped with towed guns and howitzers.

24th Waffen Gebirgs (*Karstjäger*) Division der SS

Descended from a unit formed to fight Italian and Yugoslav partisans in the highest peaks of the Dolomites, the *Karstjäger* was a division in name only.

THE *SS-KARSTWEHR-BATAILLON* had been fighting partisans in northern Italy and the Dolomites since 1942. On 1 August 1944, it was upgraded to become 24. *Waffen-Gebirgs-(Karstjäger-) Division der SS*, though it was never more than brigade-sized. It was redesignated as the *Waffen-Gebirgs-(Karstjäger-) Brigade der SS* on 5 December 1944 but once again upgraded to division on 10 February 1945.

Originally under the control of the *Höheren SS- und Polizei-Führers Adriatisches Meer* (Higher SS- and Police- *Führer* Adriatic), it was manned mainly by Italian volunteers but also contained volunteers from Slovenia, Croatia, Serbia and the Ukraine. *Karstjäger* mainly fought partisans in Istria, with considerable success, but at the end of the war it found itself facing the Western Allies advancing through Italy. On 8 May 1945, *Karstjäger* surrendered to the British.

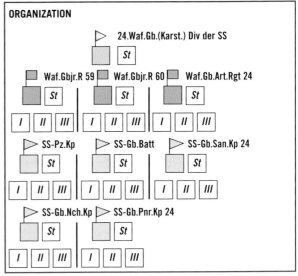

ORGANIZATION

24.Waf.Gb.(Karst.) Div der SS
St

Waf.Gbjr.R 59 — Waf.Gbjr.R 60 — Waf.Gb.Art.Rgt 24
St / St / St
I II III / I II III / I II III

SS-Pz.Kp / SS-Gb.Batt / SS-Gb.San.Kp 24
St / St / St
I II III / I II III / I II III

SS-Gb.Nch.Kp / SS-Gb.Pnr.Kp 24
St / St
I II III / I II III

Divisional History	Formed
SS-Karstwehr-Kompanie	1942
SS-Karstwehr-Bataillon	1942
24.Waffen-Gebirgs-(Karstjäger-) Division der SS	1944

Commanders

Standartenführer Dr Hans Brand
November 1942 – 1943

Sturmbannführer Josef Berschneider
1943 – August 1944)

Obersturmbannführer Karl Marx
? August 1944 – 5 December 1944

Sturmbannführer Werner Hahn
5 December 1944 – 10 February 1945

Oberführer Adolf Wagner
10 February 1945 – 8 May 1945

◀ **Mule carriers**

SS troops ford a stream in the Dolomite Mountains, early 1944. Mules were essential transport for divisions operating in the mountainous Balkans.

25th Waffen Grenadier Division der SS *Hunyadi*

The Hungarian Government originally forbade Germany from recruiting amongst its citizens, but in 1943 Hitler pressured Prime Minister Miklos Kallay to permit conscription of *Volksdeutsche*.

AFTER IT BECAME CLEAR that the Germans were on the retreat in Russia, the Regent, Admiral Horthy, and Prime Minister Kallay sought to negotiate a separate armistice for Hungary with the Western Allies. To keep Hungary (and its vital oil reserves) in the Axis fold, the Germans occupied the country on 19 March 1944.

Horthy was permitted to remain Regent, but Kallay was replaced by General Dome Sztojay, head of the Hungarian Arrow Cross fascists and fanatically pro-German. Sztojay's appointment freed the SS to recruit actively among the Hungarian population.

Hungarian SS division

Towards the end of October 1944, the SS and police commander in Hungary asked the Hungarian Government to provide the manpower for two SS divisions. The Hungarians agreed – on condition that they would fight in Hungary only, and only against the Soviets.

Himmler ordered that the 25th Waffen Grenadier Division der SS *Hunyadi* be raised. By the end of November, strength had reached 16,700 men, most being former members of the 13th *Honvéd* Light Infantry Division. It included 1000 men from *Kampfgruppe Deák*, the first Hungarian SS unit, who were used to form the 61.*SS-Grenadier-Regiment*. *Kampfgruppe Deák* had been raised from Hungarian Army and police volunteers in August 1944 and had seen action in the Banat. *Waffen-Schibataillon der SS* 25 was created from Hungarian Army mountain troops. Some divisional troops were transferred from *Waffen-SS* training schools, but the bulk of the manpower came from Hungarian recruiting depots.

Divisional History	Formed
25.SS-Freiwilligen-Grenadier-Division	1944
25.Waffen-Grenadier-Division der SS Hunyadi (ungarische Nr. 1)	1944

Commanders

Standartenführer Thomas Müller
November 1944

Gruppenführer Josef Grassy
November 1944 – 8 May 1945

INSIGNIA

The main image on the *Hunyadi* Division's symbol was the 'Arrow Cross' of the *Nyilaskeresztes Párt* – Hungary's pre-war fascist movement.

Transferred to the *Truppenübungsplatz* (training ground) at Neuhammer in Germany, the division was still far from operational when the Red Army entered Silesia. With over 22,000 men in the camp, together with many wives and families, Neuhammer was seriously overcrowded, and it was a relief when orders were given that the division should retreat to Bavaria. The 25.*Waffen-Grenadier-Division der SS Hunyadi (ungarische Nr. 1)* surrendered to the Americans after a brief firefight at Salzkammergut in Austria.

▲ **15cm schwere Infanterie Geschütz sIG33**

SS Waffen-Grenadier-Regiment 61 / Infanterie Geschütz Kompanie

Waffen-Grenadier Regiment der SS 61 was one of three such formations attached to the first Hungarian SS division. The 'Grenadier' designation was applied to standard infantry divisions and regiments in the later years of the war.

Specifications

Crew: 5

Weight: 1.75 tonnes (1.6 tons)

Length: 1.64m (64.57in)

Calibre: 150mm (5.9in)

Muzzle Velocity: 241m/s (783fps)

Range: 5504m (6000 yards)

Ammunition: High explosive or smoke

26th SS Panzer Division

The 26th SS Division was the Panzer division that wasn't. Created primarily as a propaganda and disinformation exercise, it never reached divisional strength.

SHORTLY AFTER THE NORMANDY invasion began on 6 June 1944, the *SS-Kampfgruppen* 1, 2, 3 and 4 (composed for the most part of emergency battalions from SS schools and replacement units) were mobilized. Only two of these formations were sent to the front, however. These were *SS-Kampfgruppe* 1 (later to become *SS-Panzergrenadier-Brigade* 49) and *SS-Kampfgruppe* 3 (later *SS-Panzergrenadier-Brigade* 51). Considered sister units, the two brigades would fight on the same sector of the Western Front.

SS-Panzergrenadier-Brigade 49 was a battalion stronger than its sibling, *SS-Panzergrenadier-Brigade* 51, and it lasted for a few days longer in the extremely destructive combat action. The two brigades were designated 26.*SS-Panzer-Division* and 27.*SS-Panzer-Division* respectively, for a very short time, in an attempt to mislead the Allies into thinking that they were much larger formations.

The 26th SS Panzer Division was ostensibly formed on 10 August 1944 and was disbanded on 8 September 1944 after combat in Champagne. Surviving elements of the formation, which never reached divisional strength, were absorbed by the 17th SS Panzergrenadier Division *Götz von Berlichingen*. A similar fate befell the 26th SS Division's sister formation.

Commanders

Sturmbannführer Markus Haulhaber
June 1944 – August 1944

Divisional History	Formed
SS-Kampfgruppe 1	1944
49.SS-Panzergrenadier-Brigade	1944
26.SS-Panzer-Division	1944

ORGANIZATIONS

SS-Pz.Gr.Brig 49

St

| I | II | III | Art | Flk | Pnr | Kfr |

26th Waffen Grenadier Division der SS *Hungaria*

The second SS division raised in Hungary was the 26th Waffen Grenadier Division der SS *Hungaria*. Its formation was ordered at the end of November 1944.

THE 26.*WAFFEN-GRENADIER-DIVISION der SS Hungaria (ungarische Nr. 2)*, sometimes referred to as the *Gombos* Division, was formed under the authority of the Hungarian defence minister, at the request of *Reichsführer-SS* Heinrich Himmler. *Waffen-Schibataillon der SS* 26, raised from the Hungarian Army, was ordered to join the new division. Late in December 1944, 5000 civilian

ORGANIZATION

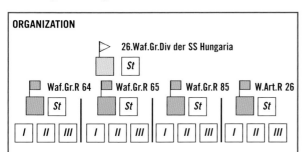

26.Waf.Gr.Div der SS Hungaria

St

Waf.Gr.R 64	Waf.Gr.R 65	Waf.Gr.R 85	W.Art.R 26
St	St	St	St
I	II	III	I	II	III	I	II	III	I	II	III

INSIGNIA

Hungaria used the same symbol as the *Hunyadi* Division, an 'Arrow Cross' surmounted by two crowns, possibly signifying the dual monarchy of Austria-Hungary.

draftees brought the strength up to 8000. By January, divisional strength was up to more than 16,000, and the formation had been moved to Siederatz in Poland for training. The formation was short of equipment and food – weapons were issued early in January, just in time to allow foraging parties to fight off attacks by Polish partisans.

Fighting retreat as training

Forced to retreat by the Soviet winter offensive (minus mortars and machine guns, which had been taken by the German Ninth Army), the partially trained division reached the Oder after suffering over 2500 casualties. Plans to refit at Neuhammer were dashed on 8 February, when the Soviets attacked the training ground. This forced the still untrained

division to make a headlong retreat towards southern Germany. The more experienced members served as a rearguard while the rest retreated westwards.

As part of XVII. *Waffen-Armee-Korps der SS (ungarisches)*, the *Hungaria* Division retreated into Austria, where it surrendered to the Western Allies at Attersee. Many of the division's surviving troops were turned over to the Soviets, and were destined for the *gulag* or the firing squad.

Commanders

Sturmbannführer Rolf Tiemann
November 1944

Oberführer Zoltan Pisky
November 1944 – January 1945

Oberführer Ladislaus Deak
January 1945

Oberführer Berthold Maack
January 1945 – March 1945

Gruppenführer Josef Grassy
March 1945 – May 1945

27th SS Panzer Division

The 27th SS Panzer Division was the name given to *SS-Panzergrenadier-Brigade* 51 in an attempt to mislead the Allies into thinking that it was a much larger formation.

THE *SS-PANZERGRENADIER-BRIGADE* 51 was formed in March 1944 as *SS-Kampfgruppe* 3. Much of its personnel came from the SS NCO school at Lauenberg, Pomerania. It was not fully activated until after the Allied landings in Normandy. On 18 June 1944, *SS-Kampfgruppe* 3 officially became *SS-Panzergrenadier-Brigade* 51 and was deployed to Denmark to relieve the 363rd Infantry Division, which was sent to Normandy.

On 4 August, the 51st SS Brigade was ordered to France. Commanded by *SS-Sturmbannführer* Walter Jöckel, the brigade's 3000 troops headed for Troyes. On 10 August 1944, the brigade assumed the title of *27.SS-Panzer-Division*, though internally it still used its old title. It was also referred to by official sources

as the *Stamm Regiment/27.SS-Panzer-Division* – that is, the 27th's 'nucleus' regiment.

Into combat

The *SS-Panzergrenadier-Brigade* 51 first saw action on 22 August at Sens, when one battalion served alongside a battalion of Army Security Regiment 199. On 23 August, Allied pressure forced them to withdraw to the Seine. Briefly cut off in Troyes by resistance attacks, the brigade headquarters ordered the other units of the formation to fight their way to the Seine independently.

The 1st battalion was all but destroyed on 25 August in a series of running battles at St Savine and Fontvannes. The brigade staff was captured by the Americans on 28 August; only the 2nd Battalion was reasonably intact.

The disintegrating brigade could do little else but retreat towards Verdun and Metz to the northeast, reaching safety with the 3rd Panzer Division near St Dizier. After the fighting in Champagne, the formation was disbanded on 9 September 1944. The brigade's surviving troops and equipment were absorbed by the *17.SS-Panzergrenadier-Division Götz von Berlichingen*.

Commanders

Sturmbannführer Walter Jöckel
June 1944 – August 1944

Divisional History	Formed
SS-Kampfgruppe 3	1944
51.SS-Panzergrenadier-Brigade	1944
27.SS-Panzer-Division	1944

27th SS Freiwilligen Grenadier Division *Langemarck*

The division was formed on 19 October 1944, when the 6.*SS-Freiwilligen-Sturmbrigade Langemarck* was upgraded to divisional status.

THE *LANGEMARCK* DIVISION, named after a village near Ypres which saw some of the bloodiest fighting in the Great War of 1914–1918, descended directly from the SS Flemish Legion, the original Flemish volunteer unit in the *Waffen-SS*.

The Flemish Legion had been less than impressive in its early actions on the Eastern Front, but experience had shown that the volunteers from Flanders could fight – and fight hard. Although the legion had been withdrawn from combat by the beginning of 1943, it was expanded to form the *Sturmbrigade Langemarck* with the addition of fresh recruits from Flanders, a Finnish battalion and several German artillery and support units. The *Sturmbrigade* was attached to the *Das Reich* Division in the Ukraine, before being sent to the Leningrad Front as part of *SS-Obergruppenführer*

Felix Steiner's III.*SS-Panzerkorps* (*Germanisches*). The *Langemarck* Brigade took part in the fighting retreat from the Baltic, and played its part in the long

INSIGNIA

The division's insignia was a triskelion, claimed by the Nazis to be an ancient Celtic symbol and so suitable for a division made up from 'Celtic' volunteers.

ORGANIZATIONS

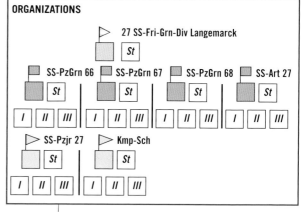

Commanders

Sturmbannführer Michael Lippert
September 1941 – April 1942

Obersturmbannführer Hans Albert von Lettow-Vorbeck *April 1942 – June 1942*

Hauptsturmführer Hallmann
June 1942

Obersturmbannführer Josef Fitzthum
June 1942 – July 1942

Obersturmbannführer Conrad Schellong
July 1942 – October 1944

Standartenführer Thomas Müller
October 1944 – May 1945)

Specifications

Crew: 4	Engine: Maybach HL120TRM
Weight: 26.3 tonnes (23.9 tons)	Speed: 40km/h (25mph)
Length: 6.77m (22ft 2in)	Range: 155km (96.3 miles)
Width: 2.95m (9ft 8in)	Radio: FuG15 and FuG16
Height: 2.16m (7ft 0in)	Armament: 1 x 75mm (3in) StuG L/48 cannon

▲ **7.5cm Sturmgeschütz Ausf G (SdKfz 142/1)**

Sturmbrigade Langemarck / Sturmgeschütz-Batterie

The *Langemarck* Brigade had a battery of assault guns attached when the formation was created around members of the disbanded Flemish Legion in the summer of 1943.

Divisional History	Formed
SS-Freiwilligen-Legion Flandern	1941
SS-Sturmbrigade Langemarck	1943
6.SS-Freiwilligen-Sturmbrigade Langemarck	1943
27.SS-Freiwilligen-Grenadier-Division Langemarck (flämische Nr. 1)	1944

▲ **Leichter Personenkraftwagen VW (Kfz 1)**

27.SS-Füsilier-Bataillon / Stab

Fusilier battalions were infantry units with reconnaissance capability, introduced mid-war when the standard infantry regiment reduced from nine battalions to six.

Specifications

Crew: 1	Engine: Volkswagen 998cc petrol (24hp). Later
Weight: 0.64 tonnes (0.58 tons)	Volkswagen 1131cc petrol (25hp)
Length: 3.73m (12ft 3in)	Speed: 100km/h (62mph)
Width: 1.60m (5ft 3in)	Range: 600km (375 miles)
Height: 1.35m (4ft 5in)	Radio: None

sequence of fierce battles on the Narva. In the autumn of 1944, the brigade was refitting on the Lüneburg Heath when it was upgraded to become *27.SS-Freiwilligen-Grenadier-Division Langemarck (flämische Nr. 1)*, though it never really approached divisional size. In February 1945, it went into action with the Eleventh Army and then with the Third Panzer Army in Pomerania. Most of the division surrendered at Mecklenburg, though a battle group that had been detached was used in the final defence of Berlin.

28th SS Panzer Division

The Soviet summer offensive in 1944 threatened to cut off large numbers of German troops in the Courland. The 28th SS Panzer Division was ordered to be established in the area.

THE SOVIET SUMMER OFFENSIVE had overwhelmed the garrisons at Mitau and Tuckum, and the division was intended to maintain a corridor to Riga in the Baltic States. It incorporated two training units based in Latvia – the SS Training and Replacement Regiment at Dondangen and the SS Panzer Personnel Training Regiment *Seelager* at Ventspils.

Two Panzergrenadier regiments (identified as the 66th and 67th but in some sources recorded as the 70th and 71st) were to be formed at the Seelager training ground, but Soviet advances meant that the area had to be abandoned. The training regiments were instead formed into *SS-Panzer-Brigade Gross*, under *SS-Sturmbannführer* Martin Gross.

The brigade took only three days to be assembled from 8 August and was organized into two infantry battalions, a mixed Panzer battalion with around 15 Panzer IIIs and IVs, which were later joined by seven Tigers, a reconnaissance battalion and an assault gun battalion. Two artillery batteries were transferred from the 19th SS Division.

The brigade went into action on 20 August as part of *Panzer-Division Strachwitz*. Over the next month,

Commanders

Obersturmbannführer Martin Gross
August 1944 – November 1944

Divisional History	Formed
37.SS-Panzergrenadier-Regiment	1943
SS-Panzer-Brigade Gross	1944
28.SS-Panzer-Division	1944

it was in constant action in Latvia and Estonia. By the middle of September, the brigade had only 300 active troops, and its vehicle strength had fallen to three Panzer IIIs, two Panzer IVs, two StuGs, one captured T-34 and four armoured half-tracks.

In November, survivors were withdrawn to Sennelager in Westphalia, where they were used to train front-line replacements.

Other units that were intended for the 28th SS Panzer Division were used to rebuild the 37th SS Panzergrenadier Regiment, and formation of the 28th SS Panzer Division was cancelled in September 1944.

28th SS Freiwilligen Grenadier Division *Wallonien*

The *SS-Freiwilligen-Grenadier-Division Wallonien* was formed when *SS-Sturmbrigade Wallonien* was upgraded to divisional status, though it never actually reached divisional size.

WALLOON (FRENCH-SPEAKING BELGIAN) troops had served as volunteers in the German Army since 1941, but many transferred to the *Waffen-SS* in 1943. The new *SS-Sturmbrigade Wallonien* fought on the Dnieper bend and was trapped in the Cherkassy pocket while serving with the 5th SS *Wiking* Division. The Walloons escaped from the pocket with 632 men of the approximately 2000 who had originally been trapped by the Red Army.

Divisional status

The 28.*SS-Freiwilligen-Grenadier-Division Wallonien* was created in October 1944, eventually as a reduced-size 'Type 45' division. In February 1945, the division was assigned to III.*SS-Panzerkorps* (*Germanisches*) in Pomerania, where it fought the Soviets until the end of the war. Some divisional units managed to retreat to Denmark; most of the rest surrendered to the Soviets in Brandenburg in May 1945.

▶ Leon Degrelle, after escaping from the Cherkassy pocket, spring 1944.

▼ **15cm schwere Infanterie Geschütz sIG33**

SS-Freiwilligen-Grenadier Regiment 69 / I Bataillon / IG. Kompanie

The 28th Division's three grenadier regiments each had a motorized infantry gun company, which was equipped with two 15cm (5.9in) heavy infantry guns and four 7.5cm (3in) light infantry guns.

Divisional History	Formed
373.Wallonisches-Infanterie-Bataillon (Heer)	1941
SS-Sturmbrigade Wallonien	1943
5.SS-Freiwilligen-Sturmbrigade Wallonien	1943
28.SS-Freiwilligen-Grenadier-Division Wallonien	1944

ORGANIZATION

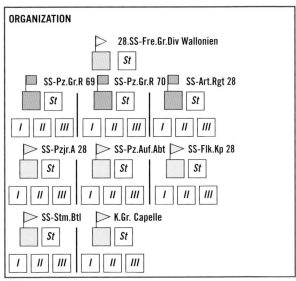

Commanders

Sturmbannführer Lucien Lippert	Standartenführer Léon Degrelle
October 1943 – February 1944	*February 1944 – April 1945*

Specifications

Crew: 5	Muzzle Velocity: 241m/s (783fps)
Weight: 1.75 tonnes (1.6 tons)	Range: 5504m (6000 yards)
Length: 1.64m (64.57in)	Ammunition: High explosive or smoke
Calibre: 150mm (5.9in)	

29th Waffen Grenadier Division der SS

The 29.*Waffen-Grenadier-Division der SS (russische Nr. 1)* **was to be formed from the Russian volunteer unit** *Waffen-Sturm-Brigade* **RONA commanded by Bronislav Kaminski.**

DESCENDED from one of the first Russian formations to fight for the Germans, it had possibly the worst reputation of any SS unit. Disbanded before its formation got under way, the number '29' was given to an Italian SS Waffen Grenadier Division (see below).

Commanders

Waffen-Brigadefuhrer der SS Bronislav Kaminski
1941 – August 1944

SS-Brigadeführer Christoph Diehm
August 1944

Divisional History	Formed
Lokot Militia	1941
Russkaya Osvoboditelnaya Narodnaya Armiya (RONA)	1942
Volksheer-Brigade Kaminski	1943
Waffen-Sturm-Brigade RONA	1944
29.Waffen-Grenadier-Division der SS (russische Nr. 1)	1944

29th Waffen Grenadier Division der SS

The 29.*Waffen-Grenadier-Division der SS (italienische Nr. 1)* **was descended from the Italian Volunteer Legion formed by Italian fascists after the fall of Mussolini.**

THE DIVISION WAS CREATED in September 1944, when the *Waffen-Grenadier-Brigade der SS (italienische Nr. 1)* was upgraded to a division. It was given the number '29' when the formation of the first Russian SS division was cancelled.

The Italian SS division never reached full divisional strength, though it came closer than many foreign SS divisions formed late in the war. It was primarily used on anti-partisan operations in northern Italy, but at the end of the war it saw some action against the British and the Americans. Some parts of the division surrendered to the Allies; members of those divisional units that surrendered to the Italian resistance were mostly executed.

Commanders

Obergruppenführer Karl Wolff
March 1944 – September 1944

Brigadeführer Pietro Mannelli
September 1944

Brigadeführer Peter Hansen
September 1944 – October 1944

Standartenführer Gustav Lombard
October 1944 – November 1944

Oberführer Constantin Heldmann
November 1944 – March? 1945

Oberführer Erwin Tzschoppe
March? 1945 – April 1945

INSIGNIA

The bundles of sticks known as fasces were symbols of the classical Roman Republic. They were adopted by the Italian fascists and gave the movement its name.

Divisional History	Formed
Italienische Freiwilligen-Legion	1943
1.Italienische Freiwilligen-Sturm-Brigade	1943
Milizia Armata	
1.Sturmbrigade Italienische Freiwilligen-Legion	1943
Waffen-Grenadier-Brigade der SS	1944
(italienische Nr. 1)	
29.Waffen-Grenadier-Division der SS (ital. Nr. 1)	1944

ORGANIZATION

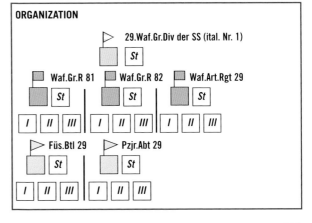

▶ **Autocarro Fiat/Spa 38R**

29.Waffen-Grenadier-Division / Versorgungsdienst

The standard 2.5-tonne (2.45-ton) truck of the Italian Army was manufactured between 1936 and 1944, and was used by German as well as Italian fascist units.

Specifications

Crew: 1	Engine: 4-cylinder petrol (43bhp)
Weight: 3.5 tonnes (3.4 tons)	Speed: 65km/h (41mph)
Length: 4.7m (15ft 5in)	Range: not known
Width: 1.94m (6ft 4in)	Payload: 1.25 tonnes (1.2 tons)
Height: 2.5m (8ft 3in)	

30th Waffen Grenadier Division der SS

The 30.*Waffen-Grenadier-Division der SS (russische Nr. 2)* was formed in August 1944 in Poland from *Schutzmannschaft-Brigade Siegling*.

THE *SIEGLING* BRIGADE had been assembled from several small Russian volunteer formations withdrawn from the front following the Soviet summer offensive. Germans provided the officer cadre; most of the rest of the division was Russian. The division transferred to France, where it immediately came under attack by the French resistance. Some divisional units avoided action, though others did engage the resistance fighters with enthusiasm. It was disbanded in December 1944; reliable Russian troops were used in *Waffen-Grenadier-Brigade der SS (weissruthenische Nr. 1)*.

Divisional History	Formed
Schutzmannschaft-Brigade Siegling	1944
30.Waffen-Grenadier-Division der SS (russische Nr. 2)	1944

Commanders

Obersturmbannführer Hans Siegling
August 1944 – December 1944

INSIGNIA

The double cross was an ancient eastern Slavic symbol used when Belarus was part of the Grand Duchy of Lithuania in the fourteenth century.

▲ **15.2cm K433/I(r) (152mm M1937 gun-howitzer)**

30.Waffen-SS-Artillerie-Regiment / I.Bataillon

The two battalions of the 30th Artillery Regiment were each equipped with three batteries of captured Soviet guns and howitzers.

Specifications

Crew: 5	Muzzle Velocity: 655m/s (2149fps)
Weight: 7.9 tonnes (7.6 tons)	Range: 17,265m (18,880 yards)
Length: 4.925m (16ft 2in)	Ammunition: High explosive or smoke
Calibre: 152mm (6in)	Projectile weight: 43.5kg (96lb)

ORGANIZATION

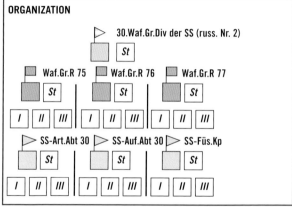

31st SS Freiwilligen Grenadier Division

Orders for the formation of the 31.*SS-Freiwilligen-Grenadier-Division* were issued in October 1944, and by the beginning of December 1944 some 11,000 recruits were in training.

MANY OF THE RECRUITS were Czech or Slovak *Volksdeutsche.* These recruits were bolstered by the attachment of parts of the disbanded 23.*Waffen-Gebirgs-Division der SS Kama* and by the addition of the *Polizei-Regiment Brixen.* The division fought briefly against the Soviets around its Hungarian training area but was soon forced to retreat into Germany, where it was intended to complete its formation at Marburg.

In January 1945, the division was converted into a reduced-strength Type 45 unit. In February, it was assigned to Army Group Centre. By the war's end, a *Kampfgruppe* was operating around Königsgrätz, where survivors surrendered to the Soviets.

INSIGNIA

Stags were popular *Wehrmacht* divisional emblems. This version is thought to have been assigned to the 31st Division but was probably never used.

Commanders

Brigadeführer Gustav Lombard
October 1944 – April 1945

Brigadeführer Wilhelm Trabandt
April 1945 – May 1945

Divisional History	Formed
Böhmen-Mähren-Division	1945
Batschka-Division	1945

32nd SS Freiwilligen Grenadier Division *30 Januar*

The 32nd SS division was formed in just five days from recruiting depots in Courland.

ALTHOUGH MADE UP of raw recruits and remnants from *Kampfgruppe Schill,* the division entered combat in April 1945. Attached to the Ninth Army, the division was defending the Seelowe Heights, east of Berlin, when it was destroyed in the Halbe 'kettle'. Survivors surrendered to the Americans on 3 May.

INSIGNIA

The ancient runic symbol for the letter 'T' symbolized the spear of Tiwaz, or Tir, the god of war in Norse mythology.

Commanders

Standartenführer Rudolf Mühlenkamp
January 1945 – February 1945

Standartenführer Joachim Richter
February 1945

Oberführer Adolf Ax
February 1945 – March 1945

Standartenführer Hans Kempin
March 1945 – May 1945

ORGANIZATION

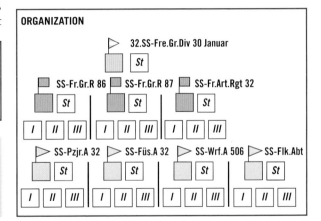

33rd Waffen Grenadier Division der SS *Charlemagne*

The 33.*Waffen-Kavallerie-Division der SS (ungarische Nr. 3)* was intended to be formed from Hungarian volunteers, mostly from the scattered remnants of Hungarian Army cavalry units.

THE FORMATION NEVER reached anything close to divisional size and was destroyed in the fighting near Budapest in January 1945. The number '33' was given to the *Charlemagne* Division.

The 33.*Waffen-Grenadier-Division der SS Charlemagne (französische Nr. 1)* was formed on 2 February 1945 when the decision was taken to expand the *Waffen-Grenadier-Brigade der SS Charlemagne (französische Nr. 1)* to full divisional status. As might be expected from the name, the *Charlemagne* Division was a largely French formation, but it also had on its strength transfers from the 18th SS Division *Horst Wessel* and volunteers from other countries. Some French sources suggest that the division had Swedish, Swiss, Laotian, Vietnamese and Japanese members.

On deployment to Pomerania on 25 February, the Frenchmen were scattered by tanks of the Soviet 1st Belorussian Front as they unloaded. They gathered into three ad hoc battle groups. One made it to the Baltic coast, eventually being shipped via Denmark to Mecklenburg. A second group ran straight into one of the main thrusts of the Soviet winter offensive, and was never seen again. The third group took heavy casualties at the railhead before making a fighting retreat westwards to the German lines.

About a third of the 1100 survivors were released from their SS vows of allegiance. The remainder were

enough to make up a single Waffen grenadier regiment. This was among the last units to enter Berlin before the Soviets completed their enclosure of the German capital. On 2 May 1945, after the general order of surrender announced by General Weidling, some 30 surviving Frenchmen went into Soviet captivity near the Potsdamer station.

Commanders

Roger Labonne (LVF) *August 1941 – March 1942*	SS-Hauptsturmführer Erich Kostenbader *August 1944*
Major Lacroix/Major Demessine *April 1942 – May 1943*	Oberst/SS-Oberführer Edgar Puaud *August 1944 – February 1945*
Edgar Puaud (LVF) *June 1943 – August 1943*	SS-Brigadeführer Gustav Krukenberg *March 1945 – April 1945*
SS-Obersturmbannführer Paul Gamory-Dubourdeau *August 1943 – July 1944*	SS-Standartenführer Walter Zimmermann *April 1945 – May 1945*

INSIGNIA

 The *Charlemagne* Division's symbol combines half of the imperial eagle of the Holy Roman Empire with the fleur-de-lys of France.

Divisional History	Formed
Légion des Volontaires Français (Heer)	1943
Französische SS-Freiwilligen-Grenadier-Regiment	1943
Französische SS-Freiwilligen-Regiment 57	1943
Französische Freiwilligen-Sturmbrigade	1944
Waffen-Grenadier-Brigade der SS Charlemagne (französische Nr. 1)	1944
33.Waffen-Grenadier-Division der SS Charlemagne (französische Nr. 1)	1945

ORGANIZATION

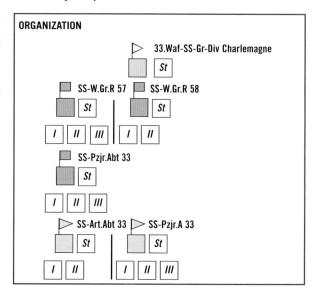

▶ **Jagdpanzer IV (SdKfz 162)**

33.Waffen-Grenadier-Division Charlemagne / Grenadier-Regiment / schwere Bataillon

In April 1944, the *Charlemagne* Division was little more than a regiment in size. The heavy battalion of the regiment had a Panzerjäger company, a Flak company and a Jagdpanzer company with a handful of vehicles.

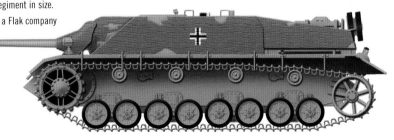

Specifications

Crew: 4	Speed: 35km/h (21.7mph)
Weight: 25.8 tonnes (23.48 tons)	Range: 210km (130.5 miles)
Length: 8.50m (27ft 10.5in)	Radio: FuG5
Width: 3.17m (10ft 5in)	Armament: 1 x 75mm (3in) PaK 42
Height: 2.85m (9ft 4in)	L/70 anti-tank gun; 1 x 7.92mm
Engine: Maybach HL120TRM (300hp)	(0.3in) MG

34th SS Freiwilligen Grenadier Division *Landstorm Nederland*

The *Landstorm Nederland* Division came into existence when the *SS-Freiwilligen-Grenadier-Brigade Landstorm Nederland* was upgraded to a division.

A DIVISION IN NAME ONLY, it was formed from the *Landstorm Nederland* unit plus Dutch Stormtroopers and other Dutch collaborationist organizations. The division saw little conventional action against Allied forces. It started life (originally as *SS-Grenadier-Regiment 1 Landwacht Niederlande*)

<table>
<tr><td colspan="2">INSIGNIA</td></tr>
<tr><td></td><td>The 'wolfshook' was used by Dutch SS members as a cap badge above the standard SS-Totenkopf and was selected as a divisional symbol for the Landstorm.</td></tr>
</table>

in March 1943 as a territorial defensive unit. The name was changed to *SS-Grenadier-Regiment 1 Landstorm Nederland* that October.

Landstorm Nederland troops fought against the Dutch resistance in northwest Holland and played a small part in the battle against British paratroopers at

Commanders

Oberführer Viktor Knapp *March 1943 – March 1944*	Standartenführer Martin Kohlroser *May 1944 – February 1945*
Obersturmbannführer Albert Doerheit *April 1944 – May 1944*	Oberführer Martin Kohlroser *February 1945 – May 1945*

▶ **Schwerer Kommandokraftwagen Horch (Kfz 21)**

SS-Freiwilligen-Grenadier-Brigade Landstorm Nederland / Stab

By the time the *Landstorm Nederland* Brigade was redesignated as a division, non-fighting elements of the formation were equipped with whatever their transport companies could lay their hands on.

Specifications

Crew: 1	Engine: Horch 6-cylinder petrol (90hp)
Weight: 2.4 tonnes (2.2 tons)	Speed: 88km/h (55mph)
Length: 4.44m (14ft 7in)	Range: 400km (250 miles)
Width: 1.68m (5ft 6in)	Radio: None usually fitted
Height: 1.73m (5ft 8in)	

Divisional History	Formed
SS-Grenadier-Regiment 1 Landwacht Niederlande	1943
SS-Grenadier-Regiment 1 Landstorm Nederland	1943
SS-Fre.Gr.Brigade Landstorm Nederland	1944
34.SS-Freiwilligen-Grenadier-Division Landstorm Nederland	1945

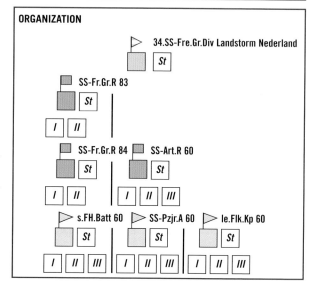

ORGANIZATION

Arnhem in September 1944. *Landstorm Nederland* troops also saw combat against Dutch soldiers, in an encounter with the 'Princess Irene Brigade', a unit of Dutch volunteers serving with the Allies.

In November 1944, the *SS-Wachbataillon Nordwest* was combined with two *Landstorm* battalions to form the *SS-Freiwilligen-Grenadier-Brigade Landstorm Nederland*. Although nominally part of the *Waffen-SS*, the *Wachbataillon* had much lower physical entry standards.

It also included a company of Ukrainian volunteers transferred from the Eastern Front. The reason for the lower physical standards was simple: *SS-Wachbataillon Nordwest* was responsible for guarding the perimeters of German concentration camps in the Netherlands.

The 3000 or so members of the *Landstorm Nederland* included fanatical Nazis who used terror to persuade the population to acquiesce in their demands. Troops from the 84th SS Volunteer

Grenadier Regiment in particular, the former prison camp guards of *SS-Wachbataillon Nordwest*, were quite happy to shoot Dutch civilians who refused to obey their commands.

The last major combat fought by *Landstorm Nederland* was against the advancing Canadians around the villages of Oosterbeek and Otterlo in March 1945. The *Landstorm Nederland* went on to fight against Dutch resistance members right up to 7 May, when the division was disarmed by the British 49th (West Riding) Infantry Division.

▲ 3.7cm Panzerabwehrkanone (Pak 35/36)
60.SS-Panzerjäger-Abteilung

The *Landstorm* Division's anti-tank battalion included the original Panzerjäger company of the *Landstorm* Brigade, which was joined by the 1st and 2nd *Nordwest* Panzerjäger Companies.

Specifications

Crew: 3	Muzzle Velocity: 762m/s (2500fps)
Weight: 0.43 tonnes (0.39 tons)	Range: 600m (656 yards)
Length: 1.67m (5ft 5.5in)	Ammunition: Armour-piercing
Calibre: 37mm (1.5in)	

▲ 3.7cm Fliegerabwehrkanone (Flak 36/37)
34.Waffen-SS-Flak-Abteilung

When the *Landstorm* Brigade was redesignated as a division, it created a Flak battalion by incorporating the personnel and equipment of the former *Clingendaal* Battery, a fixed defensive unit that had been based on the Atlantic Wall.

Specifications

Crew: 5	Muzzle Velocity: 820m/s (2690fps)
Weight: 1.5 tonnes (1.4 tons)	Range: 4800m (5250 yards)
Length: 3.5m (11ft)	Ammunition: High explosive or smoke
Calibre: 37mm (1.5in)	

35th SS und Polizei Grenadier Division

Formed in the spring of 1945, the 35th SS Division received its personnel when *Ordnungspolizei* Regiments 14, 29 and 30 were transferred from the police to the *Waffen-SS*.

THROWN INTO ACTION only partially formed in April 1945, the division was sent to the Niesse River. As part of the German Ninth Army, it was badly mauled defending Berlin during the Battle of the Seelowe Heights, and was destroyed during the Halbe breakout when the divisional hedquarters was overrun. Survivors surrendered to the Americans or the Soviets near the demarcation line of the Elbe.

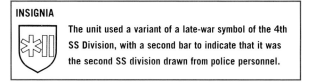

INSIGNIA

The unit used a variant of a late-war symbol of the 4th SS Division, with a second bar to indicate that it was the second SS division drawn from police personnel.

Commanders

Oberführer Johannes Wirth
February 1945 – March 1945

Standartenführer Rüdiger Pipkorn
March 1945 – May 1945

Divisional History	Formed
Polizei-Regiment z.b.V. 1	
Polizei-Regiment z.b.V. 2	
SS-Polizei-Brigade Wirth	1945
35.SS- und Polizei-Grenadier-Division	1945

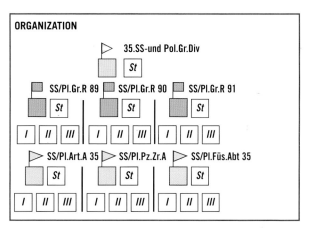

ORGANIZATION

36th Waffen Grenadier Division der SS

The 36.*Waffen-Grenadier-Division der SS* was the most notorious of *Waffen-SS* units, serving under perhaps the most sadistic of all commanders of World War II.

OSKAR DIRLEWANGER was a highly decorated veteran of World War I, but he was also a drunk and a sadist, who had been imprisoned in the 1920s for sexual assaults on children. Dirlewanger led a special punishment unit that quickly earned a reputation for barbarity. It cemented its reputation with the part it played in the brutal suppression of the Warsaw uprising in the autumn of 1944. Reclassified as a 'paper' division in February 1945, the unit was never more than the size of an understrength brigade.

INSIGNIA

Also known as the Dirlewanger emblem, the symbol of the *Dirlewanger* Brigade and Division was a pair of crossed 'potato-masher' hand grenades.

Commanders

Oberführer Dr Oskar Dirlewanger
March 1945

Brigadeführer Fritz Schmedes
May 1945

Divisional History	Formed
Wilddiebkommando Oranienburg	1940
SS-Sonderkommando Dirlewanger	1940
SS-Sonderbataillon Dirlewanger	1940
Einsatz-Bataillon Dirlewanger	1943
SS-Regiment Dirlewanger	1943
SS-Sonderregiment Dirlewanger	1943
SS-Sturmbrigade Dirlewanger	1944
36.Waffen-Grenadier-Division der SS	1945

▶ **Panzerkampfwagen T-34 747(r)**

36. Waffen-SS-Panzer-Abteilung

The *Dirlewanger* Brigade included many Russians in its number, some of whom had deserted from the Red Army with their tanks.

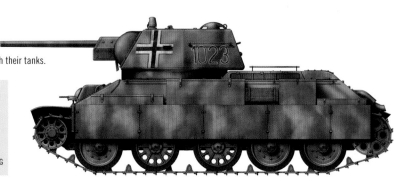

Specifications

Crew: 4	Engine: V-2-34 V12 diesel
Weight: 26 tonnes (25.5 tons)	Speed: 55km/h (34mph)
Length: 5.92m (19ft 5in)	Range: 186km (115 miles)
Width: 3m (9ft 10in)	Armament: 1 x 76.2mm (3in)
Height: 2.44m (8ft)	cannon; 2 x 7.62mm (0.3in) MG

37th SS Freiwilligen Kavallerie Division *Lützow*

The 37.*SS-Freiwilligen-Kavallerie-Division Lützow* was formed near Marchfeld on the Hungarian–Slovakian border in February 1945.

R AW MATERIAL FOR THE DIVISION came from the remnants of the *Florian Geyer* and *Maria Theresia* Divisions, both of which had been shattered in the battles around besieged Budapest. The division was to be brought up to strength as far as possible by drafts of Hungarian *Volksdeutsche*.

In March 1945, the division was far from combat-capable, not all of its units having been formed. However, a *Kampfgruppe* from *Lützow*, consisting of all veteran and battle-ready elements of the division, was sent to 6.*SS-Panzerarmee*. Commanded by *SS-Obersturmbannführer* Karl-Heinz Keitel (the son of *Wehrmacht* high command chief *Generalfeldmarschall* Wilhelm Keitel), the *Kampfgruppe* arrived on 4 April. Subordinated to I.*SS-Panzerkorps Leibstandarte Adolf Hitler*, *Kampfgruppe* Keitel

Commanders

SS-Oberführer Waldemar Fegelein	SS-Standartenführer Karl Gesele
February 1945 - March 1945	*March 1945 - May 1945*

experienced some fierce combat in the retreat through Hungary to Austria. In May 1945, a number of units were taken by the Soviets, while others moved west to surrender to the advancing Americans. Some men from the *Lützow* Division took part in a mass breakout from the Altheim prisoner of war camp on 13 May, after watching the release of regular *Wehrmacht* units while they and other SS men remained in custody.

INSIGNIA

Fitted in the cavalry/mountain-style SS shield (with a central notch at the top), the 37th Division's insignia was based on the Gothic script letter 'L' for *Lützow*.

Divisional History	Formed
37.SS-Freiwilligen-Kavallerie-Division Lützow	1945
SS-Kampfgruppe Keitel	1945

ORGANIZATION

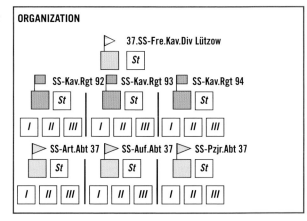

38th SS Grenadier Division
Nibelungen

Although it was designated a division, the last SS formation to be created was never more than brigade-sized, with a strength of around 6000 men.

THE DIVISION WAS FORMED around the students and staff at the *SS-Junkerschule* (Officer Training School) at Bad Tölz in Bavaria. Other troops were provided by the *Begleit-Bataillon Reichführer-SS*, the Customs Police, the 6th SS Mountain Division *Nord*, the 7th SS Mountain Division *Prinz Eugen*, a battalion-size draft from the Hitler Youth, and officers from the 30th SS Waffen Grenadier Division.

Although told to prepare for battle early in April 1945, combat units were not declared operational until 24 April. Deployed to defend the Danube Line from Vohlburg to Kelheim, the task proved too much for the understrength formation faced with heavy American pressure. By 28 April, *Nibelungen* had

withdrawn across the Danube and over the next two days continued to retreat towards Landshut.

Caught by the Americans as it crossed the Isar River, the division fought a short but fierce battle with troops of the US 14th Armored Division. By 1 May, in constant contact with two American divisions, *Nibelungen* was no longer combat-capable.

INSIGNIA

In keeping with its Wagnerian title, the *Nibelungen* Division used an ancient Germanic helmet as its divisional symbol.

Divisional History	Formed
SS-Junkerschule Bad Tölz	1945
SS-Division Junkerschule	1945
38.SS-Grenadier-Division Nibelungen	1945

Commanders

Standartenführer Hans Kempin
March 1945

Obersturmbannführer Richard Schulz-Kossens
April 1945

Brigadeführer Heinz Lammerding
April 1945

Brigadeführer Karl Reichsritter von Oberkamp
April 1945

Gruppenführer Martin Stange
April 1945 – May 1945

ORGANIZATIONS

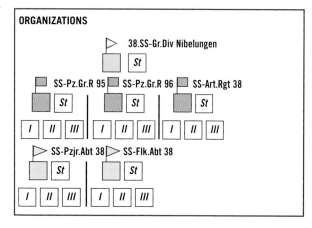

▶ **Jagdpanzer 38(t) Hetzer (SdKfz 138/2)**

38.SS-Panzerjäger-Abteilung

The division's *Panzerjäger-Abteilung* received about 10 Jagdpanzer 38s late in April 1945. It also had some 7.5cm (3in) Pak 40 towed anti-tank guns.

Specifications

Crew: 4

Weight: 14.5 tonnes (14.2 tons)

Length: 6.2m (20ft 4in)

Width: 2.93m (9ft 7in)

Height: 1.96m (6ft 5in)

Engine: Maybach HL120 petrol

Speed: 35km/h (22mph)

Range: 214km (133 miles)

Armament: 1 x 75mm (3in) Pak 39 cannon; 2 x 7.92mm (0.3in) MG

SdKfz definitions

Sonderkraftfahrzeug, abbreviated as SdKfz, means 'Special Purpose Motor Vehicle'. The term was applied to vehicles designed and built specifically for military service, rather than those adapted from non-military sources. Variants of a design were indicated by an oblique stroke and a number added to the original SdKfz designation. Major design changes were usually given a new SdKfz number.

Number	Vehicle	Description
SdKfz 2	kleines Kettenkraftrad	Motorcycle half-track tractor
SdKfz 3	Gleisketten Lkw 2t (Maultier)	2-tonne half-track lorry
SdKfz 4	schwere Gleisketten Lkw 4.5t (Maultier)	4.5-tonne half-track lorry
SdKfz 6	mittlerer Zugkraftwagen 5t	5-tonne half-track tractor
SdKfz 7	mittlerer Zugkraftwagen 8t	8-tonne half-track tractor
SdKfz 8	schwere Zugkraftwagen 12t	12-tonne half-track tractor
SdKfz 9	schwere Zugkraftwagen 18t	18-tonne half-track tractor
SdKfz 10	leichte Zugkraftwagen 1t	1-tonne half-track tractor
SdKfz 11	leichte Zugkraftwagen 3t	3-tonne half-track tractor
SdKfz 101	Panzerkampfwagen I Ausf A, B	Panzer I
SdKfz 111	Munitionsschlepper auf PzKpf I	Ammunition carrier
SdKfz 121	Panzerkampfwagen II Ausf a, A, B, C, D, E, F	Panzer II
SdKfz 122	Panzerkampfwagen II (Flamm)	Panzer II flamethrower
SdKfz 123	Panzerkampfwagen II Ausf L Luchs	Panzer II Model L Lynx
SdKfz 124	leFH 18/2 auf Fahrgestell PzKpfw II (Sf) Wespe	Self-propelled howitzer Wespe
SdKfz 131	7.5-cm Pak 40/2 auf Fahrgestell PzKpfw II (Sf)	Self-propelled anti-tank gun
SdKfz 132	7.62-cm Pak (r) auf Fahrgestell PzKpfw II (Sf)	Self-propelled anti-tank gun (Russian)
SdKfz 135	7.5-cm Pak 40/1 auf Lorraineschlepper (f) Marder I	Self-propelled anti-tank gun on Lorraine chassis
SdKfz 135/1	15-cm sFH 13 auf Lorraineschlepper (f)	Howitzer on Lorraine chassis
SdKfz 138	7.5-cm Pak 40/3 auf PzJäg 38(t)	Self-propelled anti-tank gun on Czech Pz 38 chassis
SdKfz 138/1	15-cm sIG 33 auf Geschützwagen 38(t)	Heavy infantry gun on Czech Pz 38 chassis
SdKfz 138/2	Jagdpanzer 38 Hetzer	Light tank-destroyer
SdKfz 138/2	Flammpanzer 38	Flamethrowing tank
SdKfz 138/2	Bergepanzer 38	Recovery tank
SdKfz 138/2	15-cm sIG 33/2 auf Jagdpanzer 38	Self-propelled heavy infantry gun
SdKfz 139	Panzerselbfahrlafette II für 7.62-cm Pak 36 (r) Marder III	Anti-tank gun (Russian) on Czech Pz 38 chassis
SdKfz 140	Flakpanzer 38(t) auf Selbstfahrlafette 38(t) (2-cm)	Self-propelled anti-aircraft gun
SdKfz 140/1	Aufklärungspanzer 38(t) 7.5-cm	Self-propelled heavy infantry gun on Hetzer chassis
SdKfz 141	Panzerkampfwagen III Ausf A, B, C, D, E, F, G, H	Panzer III
SdKfz 141/1	Panzerkampfwagen III Ausf J, L, M	Panzer III
SdKfz 141/2	Panzerkampfwagen III N	Panzer III
SdKfz 141/3	Panzerkampfwagen III (Flamm)	Panzer III flamethrower
SdKfz 142	gep. SF für StuG 7.5-cm Ausf A, B, C, D, E (StuG III 7.5 L/24)	Sturmgeschütz assault gun
SdKfz 142/1	gep. SF für StuG 7.5-cm 40 Ausf F, F/8, G	Sturmgeschütz assault gun
SdKfz 142/2	gep. SF für 10.5-cm StuH 42 (StuH 42)	Sturmhaubitze assault howitzer
SdKfz 143	Artillerie-Panzerbeobachtungswagen (PzBeobWg III)	Artillery observation tank
SdKfz 161	Panzerkampfwagen IV Ausf A, B, C, D, E, F	Panzer IV
SdKfz 161/1	Panzerkampfwagen IV Ausf F2, G	Panzer IV
SdKfz 161/2	Panzerkampfwagen IV Ausf H, J	Panzer IV
SdKfz 161/3	3.7-cm Flak auf Pz IV (Möbelwagen)	Anti-aircraft tank

Number	Vehicle	Description
SdKfz 162	StuG nA mit 7.5-cm Pak L/48 (Jagdpanzer IV)	Heavy tank-destroyer
SdKfz 162/1	Panzer IV/70(v) (Jagdpanzer IV lang)	Heavy tank-destroyer
SdKfz 164	8.8-cm Pak 43/1 L/71 auf Pz III und IV (Nashorn, früher Hornisse)	Self-propelled anti-tank gun
SdKfz 165	15-cm schwere Panzerhaubitze 18/1 auf Pz III/IV (Sf) (Hummel)	Self-propelled heavy field howitzer
SdKfz 166	StuH 43 L/12 auf Pz IV (Sf) Sturmpanzer (Brummbär)	Self-propelled armoured heavy infantry gun
SdKfz 167	StuG IV L/48	Heavy assault gun
SdKfz 171	Panzerkampfwagen V Ausf D, A, G Panther	Panzer V Panther
SdKfz 172	StuG für 8.8-cm StuK 43 auf Panther I – Jagdpanther	Original designation for Jagdpanther heavy tank-destroyer
SdKfz 173	8.8-cm Pak 43/3 L/71 auf Panzerjäger Panther (Jagdpanther)	Jagdpanther heavy tank-destroyer
SdKfz 179	Bergepanzerwagen Panther	Armoured recovery vehicle
SdKfz 181	Panzerkampfwagen VI Ausf E (Tiger I)	Panzer VI Tiger heavy tank
SdKfz 182	Panzerkampfwagen VI Ausf B (Tiger II, Königstiger)	Panzer VI Tiger II or King Tiger heavy tank
SdKfz 184	Pz Jäger Tiger(P) Ferdinand für 8.8-cm Pak 43/2 (Elefant)	Heavy tank-destroyer
SdKfz 185	Jagdtiger für 8.8-cm Pak 43 L/71	Heavy tank-destroyer
SdKfz 186	Jagdtiger für 12.8-cm Pak 44 L/55	Heavy tank-destroyer
SdKfz 221	leichter Panzerspähwagen (MG)	MG-armed light armoured car
SdKfz 222	leichter Panzerspähwagen (2-cm)	Cannon-armed light armoured car
SdKfz 223	leichter Panzerspähwagen (Fu)	Light armoured radio car
SdKfz 231	schwerer Panzerspähwagen 6-Rad	Heavy 6x4 armoured car
SdKfz 231	schwerer Panzerspähwagen 8-Rad	Heavy 8x8 armoured car
SdKfz 232	schwerer Panzerspähwagen 6-Rad (Fu)	Heavy 6x4 armoured radio car
SdKfz 232	schwerer Panzerspähwagen 8-Rad (Fu)	Heavy 8x8 armoured radio car
SdKfz 233	schwerer Panzerspähwagen 7.5-cm KwK 37 L/24	7.5cm (3in) heavy 8x8 armoured car
SdKfz 234/1	schwerer Panzerspähwagen (2-cm)	2cm (0.7in) heavy 8x8 armoured car
SdKfz 234/2	schwerer Panzerspähwagen Puma (5-cm) KwK39/1 L/60	5cm (2in) Puma heavy 8x8 armoured car
SdKfz 234/3	schwerer Panzerspähwagen (7.5-cm) KwK51 L/24	7.5cm (3in) heavy 8x8 armoured car
SdKfz 234/4	schwerer Panzerspähwagen (7.5-cm) Pak40 L/46	7.5cm (3in) heavy 8x8 tank-destroyer armoured car
SdKfz 247	geländegangiger gepanzerter Personenkraftwagen	Heavy armoured staff car
SdKfz 250	leichter Schützenpanzerwagen	Light armoured half-track personnel carrier
SdKfz 250/1-I	leichter Schützenpanzerwagen (Fu)	Light armoured radio half-track
SdKfz 250/2	leichter Fernsprechwagen	Light armoured telephone and wire-carrying half-track
SdKfz 250/3	leichter Funkpanzerwagen	Light armoured radio half-track
SdKfz 250/4	Luftschütz Panzerwagen (2 MG34)	Light armoured anti-aircraft half-track
SdKfz 250/5-I	leichter Beobachtungspanzerwagen	Light armoured observation half-track
SdKfz 250/5-II	leichter Aufklärungspanzerwagen	Light armoured reconnaissance half-track
SdKfz 250/6	leichter Munitionspanzerwagen Ausf A, B	Light armoured ammunition-carrier half-track
SdKfz 250/7	leichter Schützenpanzerwagen (schwerer Granatwerfer)	Light armoured mortar-carrying half-track
SdKfz 250/7	leichter Schützenpanzerwagen (Munitionsfahrzeug)	Light armoured mortar ammunition half-track
SdKfz 250/8	leichter Kanonenpanzerwagen mit 7.5-cm KwK37	Light armoured fire-support half-track
SdKfz 250/9	leichter Schützenpanzerwagen (2-cm)	Light armoured reconnaissance half-track
SdKfz 250/10	leichter Schützenpanzerwagen (3.7-cm Pak)	Light armoured platoon-leader half-track with 3.7cm (1.5in) anti-tank gun
SdKfz 250/11	leichter Schützenpanzerwagen (sPzB41)	Light armoured platoon-leader half-track with 2.8cm (1.1in) Panzerbuchse anti-tank gun
SdKfz 250/12	leichter Messtrupp-panzerwagen	Light armoured artillery calibration half-track
SdKfz 251	mittlerer Schützenpanzerwagen	Medium armoured half-track personnel carrier
SdKfz 251/1-II	mittlerer Schützenpanzerwagen (Fu)	Medium armoured radio half-track
SdKfz 251/2	mittlerer Schützenpanzerwagen (Granatwerfer)	Medium armoured mortar-carrying half-track

Number	Vehicle	Description
SdKfz 251/3	mittlerer Funkpanzerwagen	Medium armoured radio half-track
SdKfz 251/3-IV	mittlerer Funkpanzerwagen (Kommandowagen)	Medium armoured command half-track
SdKfz 251/4	mittlerer Schützenpanzerwagen mit Munition und Zubehör für leIG18	Medium armoured half-track prime-mover for 7.5cm (3in) light infantry gun
SdKfz 251/5	mittlerer Pionierpanzerwagen	Medium armoured combat engineer half-track
SdKfz 251/6	mittlerer Kommandopanzerwagen	Medium armoured command half-track
SdKfz 251/7	mittlerer Pionierpanzerwagen	Medium armoured combat engineer half-track
SdKfz 251/8	mittlerer Krankenpanzerwagen	Medium armoured ambulance half-track
SdKfz 251/9	mittlerer Schützenpanzerwagen (7.5-cm KwK 37)	Medium armoured self-propelled gun half-track
SdKfz 251/10	mittlerer Schützenpanzerwagen (3.7-cm Pak)	Medium armoured platoon-leader half-track with 3.7cm (1.5in) anti-tank gun
SdKfz 251/11	mittlerer Funksprechpanzerwagen	Medium armoured telephone cable half-track
SdKfz 251/12	mittlerer Messtrupp- und Gerätepanzerwagen	Medium armoured artillery calibration section half-track
SdKfz 251/13	mittlerer Schallaufnahmepanzerwagen	Medium armoured sound-recording half-track
SdKfz 251/14	mittlerer Schallauswertungspanzerwagen	Medium armoured sound-ranging half-track
SdKfz 251/15	mittlerer Lichtauswertepanzerwagen	Medium armoured flash-ranging half-track
SdKfz 251/16	mittlerer Flammpanzerwagen	Medium armoured flamethrower half-track
SdKfz 251/17	mittlerer Schützenpanzerwagen mit 2-cm FlaK 38	Medium armoured anti-aircraft half-track
SdKfz 251/18	mittlerer Beobachtungspanzerwagen	Medium armoured observation half-track
SdKfz 251/19	mittlerer Fernsprechbetriebspanzerwagen	Medium armoured telephone operations half-track
SdKfz 251/20	mittlerer Schützenpanzerwagen mit Infrarotscheinwerfer (Uhu)	Medium armoured infra-red projector half-track
SdKfz 251/21	mittlerer Schützenpanzerwagen mit Fla MG Drilling (1.5 oder 2-cm)	Medium armoured self-propelled triple anti-aircraft gun half-track
SdKfz 251/22	7.5-cm Pak 40 L/46 auf mittlerer Schützenpanzerwagen	Medium armoured tank-destroyer half-track
SdKfz 251/23	2-cm Hängelafette 38 auf mittlerer Schützenpanzerwagen	Medium armoured reconnaissance half-track
SdKfz 252	leichter gepanzerter Munitionskraftwagen	Light armoured munitions carrier half-track
SdKfz 253	leichter gepanzerter Beobachtungskraftwagen	Light armoured observation half-track
SdKfz 254	mittlerer gepanzerter Beobachtungskraftwagen	Medium armoured observation half-track
SdKfz 260	kleiner Panzerfunkwagen (4-Rad)	Light armoured radio car
SdKfz 261	kleiner Panzerfunkwagen (4-Rad)	Light armoured radio car
SdKfz 263	schwerer Panzerfunkwagen (6-Rad)	Heavy 6x4 armoured radio car
SdKfz 263	schwerer Panzerfunkwagen (8-Rad)	Heavy 8x8 armoured radio car
SdKfz 265	kleiner Panzerbefehlswagen (Pz I)	Light command tank (Panzer I)
SdKfz 266	Panzerbefehlswagen Ausf E, H, 5-cm KwK L/42, Ausf K	Medium command tank (Panzer III)
SdKfz 267	Panzerbefehlswagen Ausf D (Pz III)	Medium command tank (Panzer III)
SdKfz 267	Panzerbefehlswagen Panther	Command tank (Panther)
SdKfz 267	Panzerbefehlswagen Tiger I	Command tank (Tiger)
SdKfz 268	grosse Panzerbefehlswagen	Large command tank (Panzer III, Panther or Tiger)
SdKfz 280	gepanzerter Munitionsschlepper	Armoured munitions carrier
SdKfz 300	Minenräumwagen Ausf I und II	Mine-clearing vehicle
SdKfz 301	schwerer Ladungsträger Ausf A, B and C	Heavy remote-controlled demolition vehicle
SdKfz 302	leichter Ladungsträger Ausf A (Goliath)	Light remote-controlled demolition vehicle
SdKfz 303	leichter Ladungsträger Ausf B (Goliath)	Light remote-controlled demolition vehicle
SdKfz 304	mittlerer Ladungsträger (Springer)	Medium remote-controlled demolition vehicle

Index

Page numbers in *italics* refer to illustrations.